OF ISLANDS, PORTS AND SEA LANES

War and Military Culture in South Asia, 1757–1947

www.helion.co.uk/warandmilitarycultureinsouthasia

Submissions

The publishers would be pleased to receive submissions for this series. Please contact us via email (info@helion.co.uk), or in writing to Helion & Company Limited, Unit 8 Amherst Business Centre, Budbrooke Road, Warwick, CV34 5WE

Titles

No 1 *'Swords Trembling In Their Scabbards'. The Changing Status of Indian Officers in the Indian Army 1757–1947* Michael Creese (ISBN 978-1-909982-81-9)

No 2 *'Discipline, System and Style'. The Sixteenth Lancers and British Soldiering in India 1822-1846* John H. Rumsby (ISBN 978-1-909982-91-8)

No 3 *Die in Battle, Do not Despair. The Indians on Gallipoli, 1915* Peter Stanley (ISBN 978-1-910294-67-3)

No 4 *Brave as a Lion. The Life and Times of Field Marshal Hugh Gough, 1st Viscount Gough* Christopher Brice (ISBN 978-1-910294-61-1)

No 5 *Approach to Battle. Training the Indian Army during the Second World War* Alan Jeffreys (ISBN 978-1-911096-51-1)

No 6 *The Indian Army in The First World War: New Perspectives* Edited by Alan Jeffreys (ISBN 978-1-911512-78-3)

No 7 *War without Pity in the South Indian Peninsula 1798–1813: The Letter Book of Lieutenant-Colonel Valentine Blacker* Edited and with introductory notes by David Howell (ISBN 978-1-912390-86-1)

No 8 *Of Islands, Ports and Sea Lanes: Africa and the Indian Ocean in the Second World War* Ashley Jackson (ISBN 978-1-912390-74-8)

Of Islands, Ports and Sea Lanes

Africa and the Indian Ocean in the Second World War

War and Military Culture in South Asia, 1757–1947 No. 8

Ashley Jackson

Helion & Company

This book is dedicated to my wonderful wife Andrea and her equally wonderful family in Queensland and Tasmania: Mark, Sue, Allison, Paul, Chris, Johnny, Shane, Rachel, Angela, Claire, Tyson, Keely, Zach, Alex, Angus, Tullie, Charlie, George, Tayla, and Mila.

Helion & Company Limited
Unit 8 Amherst Business Centre
Budbrooke Road
Warwick
CV34 5WE
England
Tel. 01926 499 619
Fax 0121 711 4075
Email: info@helion.co.uk
Website: www.helion.co.uk
Twitter: @helionbooks
Visit our blog http://blog.helion.co.uk/

Published by Helion & Company 2018
Designed and typeset by Mach 3 Solutions Ltd (www.mach3solutions.co.uk)
Cover designed by Paul Hewitt, Battlefield Design (www.battlefield-design.co.uk)
Printed by Lightning Source Ltd, Milton Keynes, Buckinghamshire

ISBN 978-1-912390-74-8

British Library Cataloguing-in-Publication Data.
A catalogue record for this book is available from the British Library.

Contents

List of Maps

War and Military Culture in South Asia, 1757–1947
Series Editor's Preface

The aim of this academic historical series is to produce well-researched monographs on the wars and armed forces of South Asia, concentrating mainly on the East India Company and the Indian armed forces from 1757 until 1947. Books in the series will examine the military history of the period as well as social, cultural, political and economic factors, although inevitably the armies of the East India Company and the Indian Army will dominate the series. In addition, edited volumes of conference papers, memoirs and campaign histories will also be published. It is hoped this series will be of interest to both serious historians and the general military history reader.

The resurgence of interest in the history of warfare in South Asia has been very apparent in the growing historiography of the colonial period, particularly in the era of the World Wars. For example in the field of Second World War studies and the period until Partition, Daniel Marston and Tim Moreman have spearheaded this historical research with their volumes: the prize-winning *Phoenix from the Ashes: The Indian Army in the Burma Campaign* (2003), *The Indian Army and the End of the Raj* (2014) and *The Jungle, the Japanese and the Commonwealth Armies at War* (2005) respectively. These are complemented by Raymond Callahan's *Churchill and His Generals* (2007), a seminal work published in the United States that deserves better attention in the United Kingdom, and Steven Wilkinson's *Army and Nation: The Military and Indian Democracy since Independence* (2015). In addition, are the important wider studies of Christopher Bayly and Tim Harper, *Forgotten Armies: The Fall of British Asia, 1941-1945* (2004) and Ashley Jackson on *The British Empire and the Second World War* (2006). The most recent publications include *Approach to Battle: Training the Indian Army during the Second World War* (2017) published in this series, as well as Tarak Barkawi's *Soldiers of Empire: Indian and British Armies in World War II* (2017) and Raymond Callahan's *Triumph at Imphal-Kohima: How the Indian Army Finally Stopped the Japanese Juggernaut* (2017). Furthermore the Indian home front has been covered in Yasmin Khan's social history of the period entitled *The Raj at War: A People's History of India's Second World War* (2015).

The aforementioned rise in interest has been mirrored in India as eight volumes of the official histories of the Indian Armed Forces during the Second World War were reprinted in India in 2012 and another four in 2014 (they were originally published between 1954 and 1960). As Squadron Leader Rana Chhina stated at the launch of the reprints: 'As a resurgent India seeks to be a major player on the world stage, it behoves it to discard its narrow post-colonial world view to step up to reclaim the role that its armed forces played out on a global scale' during the Second World War. This resurgence is amply demonstrated by the publication of Srinath Raghavan's excellent overview *India's Wars : The Making of Modern South Asia* (2016), alongside the Kaushik Roy's *India and World II: War, Armed Forces, and Society, 1939-45* (2016) snd Anirudh Deshpande's *Hope and Despair: Mutiny, Rebellion and Death in India, 1946* (2016). However, even in this crowded arena, there is still much research and work to be published on both war and military culture in South Asia during the Second World War.

The series editors, members of the editorial advisory board and our publisher, Duncan Rogers of Helion, are all delighted to be involved in this series, most of the volumes of which are also being published in India under the Primus imprint. We hope it will be of interest in the UK, India but also globally.

Alan Jeffreys

Introduction and acknowledgements

This book is born of a longstanding fascination with the enormous extent of war-related activity that took place in colonies and outposts around the world between 1939 and 1945. For a quarter of a century now I have been enamoured of the global deployments, the humdrum tasks, and the infrastructural developments in little-known places that comprised the war experience of hundreds of thousands of men and women, occurring in theatres of conflict such as the Indian Ocean that are less trodden in histories of the Second World War. Examples of these endeavours are legion: the corvette bobbing around in the Mozambique Channel in defence of convoys; a coastal airstrip cleared in the Horn of Africa to patrol the Red Sea; civilians and servicemen and women running wireless interception stations in Mauritius and the Seychelles; a secret naval base developed in the Maldives; and thousands of tons of stone and concrete shifted by African, American, British, and Italian workers in Eritrea in order to construct new ammunition dumps for the Royal Navy. All of these activities were connected to the wider operations of war and the strategies devised in distant London and Washington, and all, in some way or another, utilized and developed land, resources, and labour in colonial and semi-colonial territories, and left their mark. These places, these sea lanes, these labours, these guns, ships, and aircraft, these people, were the defensive nuts-and-bolts of a British world system that underpinned Allied strategy.[1] All of these places and the infrastructure they contained were vital if a vast theatre spanning north-south from Egypt to Antarctica, and east-west from Kenya to Australia, was to be defended, and resources and lines of communication vital to the Allies exploited.

The book fuses aspects of imperial, colonial, and strategic history with military and naval history, impelled by a belief that Africa and the Indian Ocean region need better integration into our understanding of the war. Some are dismissive of such pursuits – peripheral goings on in peripheral theatres away from the big players and decisive actions. I have always found this a curious, even mildly shocking, perspective, an antique, one might say almost colonial, view

1 When contemplating the relationship between distant deployments and construction projects, all related to the wider operations of war and, in turn, to its grand strategies, I am minded of the familiar lines:
For want of a nail the shoe was lost.
For want of a shoe the horse was lost.
For want of a horse the rider was lost.
For want of a rider the message was lost.
For want of a message the battle was lost.
For want of a battle the kingdom was lost.
And all for the want of a horseshoe nail.

of a global conflict. While of course not trying to inflate the significance of the Indian Ocean region, or to deny the Red Army or American forces in the Pacific their war-winning laurels, it is argued here that an appreciation of the islands, ports, and sea lanes of Africa and the Indian Ocean, and the nature of the conflict here, enriches our understanding of the war and the interconnectivity of theatres and actions all around the world. Failure to understand the role of the small places and the people who lived there and who became involved in the war hinders comprehension of the broader system, and of the global logistics of war. Furthermore, neglect of the Indian Ocean region diminishes, sometimes to the point of inconsequence, a very remarkable essay in imperial warfare on the part of the British. Together with an unhealthy overemphasis on episodes such as the fall of Singapore and the sinking of the capital ships *Prince of Wales* and *Repulse,* this has contributed to an underestimation of British strategy in this region and overplayed the apparent demise of British naval power.

Some who read this book will doubtless regard it as quirky, bearing the peculiar hallmarks of the author's fixations. It is undoubtedly the case that it is born of what has developed over two decades as a clear, if haphazardly pursued, pattern of research within the broad contours of the British Empire and the Second World War, and a fascination with how the seemingly small things pertain to and are intimately linked to grand strategies and ambitious operations. How, for instance, that corvette in the the Mozambique Channel, those archipelagic base facilities, or those 'sideshow' military campaigns in places such as Iraq and Madagascar, were consciously linked to grand strategy, in particular, the defence of sea lanes without which the Empire, and indeed the Allies, could not have fought the war they did.

I have been working on aspects of the British Empire and the Second World War since 1993, and on the Indian Ocean region since 1997. Over the course of the years, I've accumulated many debts of gratitude. Some of the archival research was funded by the Defence Studies Department, King's College London, through my personal research allowance. The British Academy Small Research Grants Committee funded work in British and Sri Lankan archives in 2007. Though focused on Iran and Iraq, the AHRC-funded project 'Home Fronts of the Empire-Commonwealth', conducted with Yasmin Khan and Gajendra Singh between 2012 and 2014, supported some of the research for this book. Special thanks are due to my colleague Andrew Stewart, who with typical generosity allowed me to pillage his work and supplied valuable material drawn from a range of archives. He also read a full draft of the manuscript and saved me from some, though certainly not all, of my usual lapses into repetitiveness, chronological illiteracy, and prolix. Also, to Daniel Owen Spence of the University of the Free State who kindly sent me pre-publication drafts of two chapters of his book *Colonial Naval Culture and British Imperialism, 1922-1967* (Manchester: Manchester University Press, 2015). Fabio De Ninno of the University of Siena very generously afforded me his expertise on the wartime Italian navy and Italian naval strategy, and allowed me to see a pre-publication copy of a new article. Andrew Boyd's brilliant recent book *The Royal Navy in Eastern Waters: Linchpin of Victory, 1935-1942* (Barnsley: Seaforth, 2017) gave me confidence to develop some of the ideas in this work, and important tools with which to do so. Thanks are also due to Jonathan Hill for kindly reading a section. I would like to thank Toyin Falola for inviting me to contribute a chapter to a book on African islands, which was the point of origin for Part 1 of this book. Thanks for suggestions at various points are also due to Geraint Hughes and Chris Tripodi of King's College London, Alex Marshall of the University of Glasgow, and Camilla Schofield of the University of East Anglia. Special thanks are due to Claire Benison, Mapping

Designer, Joint Services Command and Staff College Graphic Services, Defence Academy of the United Kingdom. Duncan Rogers of Helion kindly agreed to publish this book along with its companion, *Ceylon at War 1939-1945*. Billy and Kathy Whitbread allowed me to laze by the pool at La Rocca di Rasina on the Tuscan-Umbrian border in 2009, allowing me to reacquaint myself with a project that had languished for several years while other books took centre-stage. It languished for the best part of a decade thereafter but now, here it is.

Preface

Of Islands, Ports, and Sea Lanes breathes new life into the study of the Indian Ocean as a distinct theatre of conflict during the Second World War.[1] It explains the operational and strategic importance of islands, ports, and sea lanes in this busy and indispensable theatre of martial activity. An understanding of the significance of this region, from Allied, imperial, operational, and strategic perspectives, helps bring greater unity of understanding to the British and Allied war effort in Africa, Asia, the Middle East, and the Pacific. It demonstrates how the pursuit of grand strategic objectives depended ultimately on people and infrastructure in faraway places of seemingly little consequence, and shines the spotlight on the Royal Navy's Eastern Fleet and its wartime mission to protect the sea lanes and counter enemy threats in the world's third largest ocean. This was a commitment – and, by 1945, an achievement – of greater significance than is usually acknowledged.[2] The convergence of threats in both the western and eastern Indian Ocean, and the need to continue to operate around and across the ocean and make use of its sea lanes, gave the theatre its unity and significance, one that should be more prominently marked in the historical record.

Thus the book argues for a recalibration of perspectives on British and Allied strategy regarding the Indian Ocean, which was taken more seriously by British strategic planners and decision-makers than it has been by subsequent historians. Furthermore, it argues that persistent views of Britain's war against Japan that place a strategic 'full stop' after the loss of Singapore and the capital ships *Prince of Wales* and *Repulse*, known as Force Z from their arrival at Sembawang

1 The importance of the Indian Ocean as a vital theatre of war has been a feature of my work since the publication *War and Empire in Mauritius and the Indian Ocean* (Basingstoke: Macmillan, 2001), and received extensive attention in Jackson, *The British Empire and the Second World War* (London: Continuum, 2006). It has recently received its most important treatment from the point of view of British strategy and naval history in Andrew Boyd's *The Royal Navy in Eastern Waters: Linchpin of Victory, 1935-1942* (Barnsley: Seaforth, 2017). Mention must also be made of the remarkable 'Armoured Carriers' website at http://www.armouredcarriers.com/. This slick and attractive resource focuses on the war history of Britain's fleet carriers, and has an extensive Indian Ocean section featuring expert essays, original documents, and embedded film clips. The Indian Ocean section contains the following essay-articles: 'Battle for Ceylon: HMS *Indomitable* and *Formidable*'; 'Operation Diplomat: *Illustrious* and *Saratoga*'; 'Operations Councillor to Lentil: HMS *Illustrious, Victorious, Indomitable*'; and 'Operation Meridian: The Palembang Strikes'.

2 The levels of war can be defined as tactical, operational, and strategic, though it is helpful, given the global and 'total' nature of the Second World War, to add 'grand strategic' to denote the very highest decision-making levels of national and Allied policy and strategy.

naval dockyard on 2 December 1941, need revising.[3] While these were undeniable disasters that forced Britain on to the back foot, the British coped with them in a manner aimed squarely at protecting their position in the western Indian Ocean and guarding the sea lanes that granted access to the Red Sea and Persian Gulf – possession of which was a strategic bottom line for the British war effort and of primary strategic significance to both America and the Soviet Union. Following the series of defeats culminating in the Battle of the Java Sea in February 1942 and the inconclusive but extremely dangerous Japanese raids in and around Ceylon and India in April, the British government began to implement plans to move three quarters of the Royal Navy's main units into the Indian Ocean, such was its importance to the war's grand strategy. Therefore, while there was weakness, defeat, and retreat in the Indian Ocean region, the British fought a cannier war here than is often portrayed, in terms of strategic vision and force deployment. Most importantly, the loss of Singapore and Force Z did not terminate British endeavours to defend the Empire's most important assets in the region, which were Ceylon, the Persian Gulf, and the all-important sea lanes.

British decision-makers knew that loss of control of these sea lanes, and the oil of Iran and Iraq, would have been a disaster of far higher magnitude than the loss of the South-east Asian colonies and the Singapore naval base. As Andrew Boyd convincingly argues, from as early as 1935 the British government's commitment of resources and the Royal Navy's planning for a two-hemisphere war had been remarkably realistic and ambitious. Following the loss of Force Z,

> [d]espite its numerous commitments elsewhere, and its heavy recent losses, the Royal Navy had the capacity, the resilience and determination to find considerable resources to protect this theatre. There is a discrepancy here between the established portrayal of the naval defence of Britain's empire in the East as a story of strategic illusion, weakness, and then irrelevance, and the much more positive reality of Royal Navy policy, planning and execution displayed in the official record.[4]

Even before Britain's war with Japan commenced, the government, the Chiefs of Staff, and the Admiralty understood that the security of the British Empire and its capacity to wage war revolved around far more than the Singapore naval base and the 'Singapore strategy'. It was all about protecting and leveraging the resources and strategic benefits that accrued from imperial territories and the control of a global network of sea lanes that connected them and that permitted global mobility. This crucial imperial zone stretched from the eastern Mediterranean across the Indian Ocean and Middle East to India and Australasia, and included the Atlantic's right flank

3 Sometimes in accounts of Britain's war against Japan, these losses seem to mark a strategic, rather than an operational, defeat. Thereafter, the Burma campaign rumbles on, somewhat marooned from the rest of the war, before the advances associated with the Fourteenth Army and the telling effects of American power in the Pacific lead towards victory. This book emphasizes the continuation of Britain's struggle against Japan, discernible if one focuses on the deployments and activities of British imperial forces, and the fact that a great deal of military activity was aimed at strategically important defensive tasks, not at direct offensives against enemy forces and territory. Beguiled by American strength later in war, there is a tendency to overlook British resilience, capacity to plan and recover, and British achievements in holding a region of strategic importance to all of the 'Big Three' allies.

4 Boyd, *The Royal Navy in Eastern Waters*, p. xv.

which granted access to it around the Cape of Good Hope. The eastern Mediterranean was considered essential not because of the Suez Canal, which the Admiralty expected would be closed to shipping if war came, but 'rather to protect the western boundary of the eastern core, and to shield the vital resources of the Middle East – above all, its oil'.[5]

The connectivity of the Indian Ocean and the South Atlantic had informed European expansion eastwards, a process that had pivoted on secure sea lanes and control of the Cape of Good Hope, the 'tavern of two seas'.[6] Often styled the 'Indian Ocean area' on British wartime maps, this sprawling region stretched from the South Atlantic and the great port of Freetown in Sierra Leone, around the Cape and east to the Malay Barrier, Australia, and the Dutch East Indies. It encompassed the Arabian Sea, the Bay of Bengal, the Persian Gulf, the Gulf of Oman, and the Red Sea, and abutted the Southern Ocean and the shores of Antarctica.[7] Its waters bordered or enveloped dozens of nation-states and colonial territories, from Egypt, Palestine, and the Sudan to Iran, South Africa, Thailand, and Sumatra.[8]

During the Second World War, the Indian Ocean region was a crucial theatre of operations in a global struggle, one in which the Allies might well have suffered a defeat that would have significantly altered the course of the war. The British government fully comprehended the value of the region, ranking it more important than any other part of the world save Britain itself and the North Atlantic, across which stretched the vital sea bridge connecting it to America. The Indian Ocean was the scene of intense military activity from the earliest months of conflict in late 1939 until the final surrender of Japan. This centred on the ceaseless endeavour to protect shipping by way of patrol and escort duties and also included naval duels, amphibious landings, commerce raiding, submarine warfare, land-based combat, naval gunfire in support of land operations, behind-enemy-lines deployments, and the extensive employment of air power for a range of tasks, from reconnaissance and air-sea rescue to bombing and mining attacks on enemy shipping. The nature and extent of the eventual British and Allied victory here, though very much based on battlefield decisions reached in other theatres, is seldom acknowledged, and consequently the pivotal importance of the Indian Ocean's islands, ports, and sea lanes has been obscured.

Islands, ports, and sea lanes, along with export resources vital to the war effort, gave the Indian Ocean its strategic prominence, and they were preyed upon by the vessels of all three Axis powers. Britain's position in East Africa and the Red Sea was threatened by Mussolini's

5 Ibid., p. xvii. The argument for the strategic importance of Iran and Iraq (over and above the Mediterranean and North Africa) and, conjoined with it, the Indian Ocean, has been made in Jackson *The British Empire and the Second World War* and more recently in Jackson *Persian Gulf Command: A History of the Second World War in Iran and Iraq* (London: Yale University Press, 2018).

6 See John McAleer, *Britain's Maritime Empire: Southern Africa, the South Atlantic, and the Indian Ocean, 1763-1820* (Cambridge: Cambridge University Press, 2016).

7 Depending on definition; some also have the Southern Ocean as an annex of the Indian Ocean, which makes eminent sense, because it is the same body of water.

8 Indicating how fundamentally things have changed since the major decolonizations that began in the 1940s, at the time of the war there were hardly any independent states within or bordering the Indian Ocean. Those that did exist – Egypt, Iran, Iraq, and Thailand – were subject in varying degrees to the writ of 'great powers', and would find themselves invaded during the course of the conflict, or were semi-independent dominions, such as Australia and South Africa. By contrast, today around 40 sovereign nation-states border the Indian Ocean and are contained within it, together with a significant number of remaining dependent (i. e. colonial) territories.

imperial ambitions, and French colonies loyal to the Vichy government were the cause of military operations in the western Indian Ocean. The oil resources of Iran and Iraq, which entered the Indian Ocean via the Persian Gulf for distribution around the Empire – including to American forces fighting from places such as Australia and India – were menaced by German advances in Africa and the Caucasus as well as enemy attempts to interdict the sea lanes. The rise of Japan redoubled the threat to this core source of imperial oil, as well as Britain's oilfields in Borneo and Burma.[9] Like a breaking wave, the billowing tide of Japanese expansion crashed over the colonies of the Allied powers and approached Britain's key strategic redoubts in India and Ceylon. This brought a much more serious threat than that presented by the European Axis powers to the sea lanes on which the imperial and Allied war effort depended. Moving rapidly to dominate territories stretching from India's eastern border to the southern extremities of Java, the Japanese took control of the Bay of Bengal and the waters off Malaya and Thailand, threatening to cripple British sea power in the Indian Ocean and disrupting both global and regional trade and the Allies' capacity to move men and material.

The Indian Ocean was a vital global crossroads, entered by thousands of ships each year via the Cape of Good Hope, the Sunda Strait, the Malacca Strait, and the Bab-el-Mandeb. Its wartime importance was augmented by the fact that between 1940 and 1943 the Mediterranean was fully or partially closed to merchant and military shipping. Without control of Indian Ocean sea lanes Britain would have been unable to conduct intra-imperial trade – as necessary in war as in peace – and would have been unable to access essential war-related resources or to deliver soldiers and military equipment to where they were needed. This applied not only to the British, for the Indian Ocean region was important to all of the Allied powers. Without its sea lanes, America would have struggled to assist the British in the Middle East or to help sustain Chiang Kai-Shek's China in its war against Japan. Moreover, the Soviet Union would have gone short of millions of tons of Anglo-American aid as it fought desperately to resist Hitler's armies, particularly after the virtual closure of the Arctic convoy route in 1942. Without Indian Ocean sea lanes, the vanquished Allied powers France and Holland would have had no platform from which to participate in the war against Japan as, emaciated though they were, they sought to regain possession of their lost colonies with the support of their allies, and to influence Anglo-American strategy.[10]

Conversely, had the Axis powers chosen to make a concerted and coordinated effort to sever these sea lanes, they might have dramatically altered the course of the war. They nearly achieved this when, in April 1942, the Japanese sought to annihilate the Royal Navy east of Suez, employing the same unprecedented combination of surface vessels and maritime air power

9 While the threat was mainly presented by enemy warships, it had an air dimension too. The Japanese fielded aircraft carriers and gained aerodromes in many places on the ocean's eastern rim. The Italians had air bases and air forces in the western Indian Ocean, and even mounted an audacious strike on the Persian Gulf when, in October 1940, bombers struck oil targets in Bahrein and Saudi Arabia before landing at Zula in Eritrea.

10 For South East Asia Command see Philip Ziegler (ed.), *Personal Diary of Admiral the Lord Louis Mountbatten Supreme Allied Commander, South East Asia, 1943-1946* (London: Collins, 1988). Also on South East Asia Command (though focusing on its post-war activities), see Peter Dennis, *Troubled Days of Peace: Mountbatten and South East Asia Command, 1945-46* (Manchester: Manchester University Press, 1987) and Richard McMillan, *The British Occupation of Indonesia, 1945-46: Britain, The Netherlands, and the Reoccupation of Indonesia* (London: Routledge, 2005).

that had devastated Pearl Harbor. It was arguably at this point – rather than the moment when *Prince of Wales* and *Repulse* were sunk the previous December – that Britain's naval position east of Suez reached its nadir, and the point at which the Japanese, had they chosen to exploit their advantage, might have damaged the Allied cause to the greatest extent within their grasp.[11] Throughout the war, all three Axis powers operated in the Indian Ocean, even conducting a submarine trade in raw materials and military technology. But plans to join hands across the region and deal the British and their allies a potentially war-changing blow proved harder to pursue, because of mutual suspicions and their inability to form the kind of strategic alliance that the Anglo-Americans forged, as well as the mounting pressure brought to bear against them in theatres closer to home following the Battle of Midway in June 1942.

Ports and sea lanes were so very important because of the cardinal need to move goods and people around the world. Transporting military personnel and all manner of things vital for the conduct of war and the support of human life was central to the prosecution of a conflict fought over vast distances. Conveying these people and these things – be they sacks of wheat, trade goods, barrels of oil, or crated fighter aircraft – depended upon the ability of tankers, troopships, and merchantmen to travel between ports. At these ports, vessels could embark and disembark human and material cargoes for onward distribution and dispersal, in support of wartime fighting fronts or for the sustenance of civilian populations, and they could repair and replenish for onward passage as they moved around the globe. During the war, an enormous amount of construction work was undertaken both to create new and to develop existing port infrastructure in order to increase the capacity to berth ships and expedite the unloading and onward movement of goods and people. In addition, new airstrips, ammunition magazines, gun emplacements, searchlights, wireless communication facilities, meteorological stations, and flying-boat bases proliferated across the region.

To cater in turn for their own security, ports and sea lanes depended on extensive shore establishments and military assets such as anti-aircraft guns, coastal artillery batteries, radar installations, and infantry formations. Operating from those ports, land- and sea-based combat and reconnaissance aircraft and warships patrolled and escorted convoys. It was an almighty undertaking on a global scale, as the British sought to upgrade an extant system of imperial defence in order to wage defensive and offensive war all around the world. It was this British imperial system that the Americans came to work through as they sought first to bolster the war effort of their British, Chinese, and Soviet allies, and then, upon becoming full belligerents, to develop their own system of global logistics and fashion the 'archipelago of bases' that would underwrite it and grow to become a major feature of the post-war world.[12]

All of this meant, to pluck but a single example from the innumerable instances that occurred, that in August 1944 the armoured fleet carrier *Illustrious*, serving with the Eastern Fleet, was able to travel, with a relative degree of security, from the great naval base at Trincomalee to Cape Town. She did so by way of stop offs at newly-constructed port facilities at Addu Atoll in

11 This point is elegantly argued in Angus Britts's thesis 'Neglected Skies: The Far East Demise of British Naval Superiority, 1922-42', M. Phil. Thesis (University of Sydney, 2015), subsequently published as *Neglected Skies: The Demise of British Naval Power in the Far East, 1922–42* (Annapolis, M. D.: Naval Institute Press, 2017).

12 A memorable phrase borrowed from Andrew Buchanan, *World at War: A Global History of World War Two, 1931-1953* (Chichester, West Sussex: Wiley-Blackwell, 2019).

the Maldives and Diego Garcia in the Chagos Archipelago. She also put in at Durban as she refuelled and replenished along the way, her passage watched over by a chain of air, sea, and wireless facilities. At Cape Town the 23,000 ton carrier discharged her aircraft before returning to Durban, whose shipyards then took her in hand for a major refit lasting for two months. On 1 November, she was back at Trincomalee, ready to strike Japanese targets in the eastern Indian Ocean.[13]

So, islands, ports, and sea lanes were vital to the survival of the British Empire, an integral aspect of the seapower (defined as naval strength, especially as a weapon of war) upon which its defence, and the prosecution of Allied war aims, depended. Without the ability to use these sea lanes and gain access to land-based transport and communication networks leading off from ports, campaigns could not have been sustained in distant places – and it was to distant places that the global challenge presented by the Axis powers obliged the British and their allies to deploy. According to Robert Coakley and Richard Leighton, official historians of wartime American logistics and strategy, the war produced

> a new logistics – new in that it was at once interconnected and global. Every local logistical problem was part of a global whole; none could be settled without consideration of the impact its settlement would have on other local problems, often in a widening circle of repercussions rippling clear around to the other face of the world. As the war itself was global, the logistics of each battle or campaign often had world-wide ramifications, even though the outcome of the operation itself might be purely local in its effects.[14]

Coakley and Leighton offer further characterization of the problems inherent in protecting a scattered empire during a world war, while reaching far and wide to connect battlefronts and sources of power:

> In all the imperial outposts from Hong Kong and Singapore to the West Indies, Britain and her Commonwealth associates had to maintain forces, meager in numbers but costly in shipping and material. On the seaways binding together the scattered parts of the Empire and Commonwealth, the deadly war against the submarine, long-range bomber and raider went on – a war that Britain in spring 1941 was losing.
>
> Geography forced Britain to operate on exterior lines, around the periphery of her opponents' compact land-based power.
>
> ... Britain's logistical disadvantage was not merely a matter of distance; the geographical disposition of the various parts of the Empire and Commonwealth contributed to it. The British imperial axis stretched halfway around the globe joining two centers of gravity,

13 Oliver Warner, *Admiral of the Fleet: The Life of Sir Charles Lambe* (London: Sidgwick and Jackson, 1969), pp. 122-23.

14 Richard Leighton and Robert Coakley, *Global Logistics and Strategy, 1940–43*, US Army in World War Two series (Washington, DC: The War Department, Center of Military History, US Army, 1995, first published 1955), preface, p. ix. 'Logistics' stems from the Greek 'logistikos', meaning 'skilled in calculating'. The logistical implications of a global war, from an American point of view, were captured in perceptive wartime publications such as Edgar Ansel Mowrer and Marthe Rajchman, *Global War: An Atlas of World Strategy* (London: Faber and Faber, 1942).

> the British Isles and the far eastern dominions (Australia and New Zealand). In between stood the Middle East and east Africa, draining military strength from both, their nearest support the Union of South Africa. A military liability, the whole area was essentially a link in the imperial lifeline, a valuable source of oil, and the dwelling place of peoples whose good will was vital to the Empire.[15]

Taken all together, the study of the war in the Indian Ocean region highlights the breath-taking extent of military activity required to secure victory, activity that was extensive even in non-'front line' theatres. The Indian Ocean and its islands and rim territories played host to military forces from America, the British Empire, France, Germany, Holland, Italy, and Japan. Troopships conveyed millions of men and women across the Atlantic and Indian oceans. Notable amongst these were the 'Winston Special' convoys that rounded the Cape and proceeded north through the Mozambique Channel into the Red Sea, essential for the support of the fighting fronts in the Middle East. There were then the droves of ships that crossed the Indian Ocean to deposit African, Australasian, British, Indian, and Nepalese troops in Burma, Ceylon, the Dutch East Indies, East Africa, Iraq, Malaya, and Singapore, as well as American personnel destined for service in North and East Africa, China, India, and Iran. In addition, civilian passengers, refugees, internees, and prisoners of war also took passage across the Indian Ocean, some fleeing war zones for safer places, such as those leaving Malaya and the Dutch East Indies for Australia and Ceylon, Polish refugees released from Soviet labour camps and deposited in diverse places such as India, Iran, and Tanganyika, Jewish refugees denied access to Palestine and interned instead in Mauritius, or Italian and Allied prisoners of war being moved variously by British and Japanese authorities.

Given that the imperial and Allied war effort depended on the use of sea lanes, it was only logical that Axis forces should seek to interdict them and in the process stretch their opponent's military resources as thinly as possible. One of their main means of accomplishing this was by practicing a form of sea warfare known as *guerre de course* which would have been familiar to sailors of the Napoleonic era as well as the naval strategists of Wilhelmine Germany.[16] During the course of the war scores of U-boats operated in the South Atlantic and the Indian Ocean, as did surface raiders such as the pocket battleships *Admiral Scheer* and *Graf Spee* and a range of auxiliary cruisers. Grand Admiral Carl Doenitz, head of the German navy and Hitler's eventual successor, sent U-boat packs around the Cape, and men such as Ernst Krüder skippered disguised merchant raiders, including the deadly *Atlantis*, *Kormoran*, and *Pinguin*. In the early years of war, the Italians operated submarines and surface combatants from their well-located East African ports, and the land campaign the British fought against them was intended as much to secure sea lanes vital for supporting the war effort in the Middle East as to eject an Axis power from British colonial territories.

The Japanese, meanwhile, presented a challenge of an all together different magnitude to the British Empire and its capacity to use the sea lanes to further imperial and Allied war aims. Local Japanese naval superiority led to the first major failure of British seapower since the American rebellion and the subsequent loss of the thirteen colonies, as Tokyo threw down

15 Leighton and Coakley, *Global Logistics*, p. 47.
16 For a brief overview of the First World War in the Indian Ocean region, see Ashley Jackson, 'The First World War in the Indian Ocean', in Jackson, *Distant Drums: The Role of Colonies in British Imperial Warfare* (Brighton: Sussex Academic Press, 2010).

the gauntlet to the Anglo-American powers in December 1941. The attack on Pearl Harbor, the sinking of *Prince of Wales* and *Repulse*, the loss of Singapore, Allied defeat in the Java Sea, and the Royal Navy's inability to meet head on the Japanese raids in the Indian Ocean in April 1942, ruptured Britain's long-held command of the seas east of Suez. The same Japanese battlefleet that had wasted American forces in Hawaii entered the Indian Ocean and sought to 'Pearl Harbor' the Royal Navy through attacks on Colombo and Trincomalee. The opposing forces came perilously close to a major fleet action which, had it occurred, would have been the biggest sea battle since Jutland, and one that the Royal Navy would most likely have lost. Britain was at that moment unable to compete with Japan's revolutionary brand of maritime warfare as the Rising Sun heralded a new dawn in deployed naval tactics and technology, forcing its opponents into retreat. These shocking occurrences left vital sea lanes bereft of adequate protection and caused the strategic value of Ceylon and other Indian Ocean locations, such as Durban, Mombasa, and the Maldives, to rocket.

But the episode also handed the Japanese their first lessons in the Allies' potential to resist and to contest the seas and skies with their navy's main strength, and it came to mark the limit of Japanese expansion. It also elicited a remarkably swift British redeployment of maritime forces intended to prevent the enemy from scoring the type of results – the destruction of the Eastern Fleet, the capture of Ceylon, and the severance of the sea lanes leading to the Middle East – that were Japan's only realistic hope of making operations in the Indian Ocean strategically significant to the outcome of the war.

The role of the Royal Navy and its subsidiary colonial formations is central to the study of the Indian Ocean during the war. Its Eastern Fleet operated up to 300 warships of all classes, and had under its command units from the dominions and India as well as from America, France, and Holland.[17] For much of the war it was the largest British fleet afloat, and in 1944 gave birth to the British Pacific Fleet that braved the kamikazes as part of the American armada closing in on the Japanese home islands. Though the atomic bombs and subsequent Japanese surrender removed the need for British air squadrons and army divisions to deploy to the Pacific, the British Pacific Fleet did take part in the final stages of the war after conducting a series of 'working up' carrier and battleship strikes on Japanese occupied territory in the Andaman and Nicobar Islands, Java, and Sumatra.

Land operations, from major warfighting to guerrilla activities and small coastal raids, occurred on both flanks of the Indian Ocean, as well as on Africa's northern and western shores. Air raids, bombardments, combat, invasion, and occupation – for brief moments or prolonged periods – were visited upon many Indian Ocean locations. They included the Andaman and Nicobar Islands, Australia, Burma, Ceylon, Christmas Island, the Cocos-Keeling Islands, the Comoro Islands, Eritrea, India, Iran, Iraq, Java, Kenya, Madagascar, Malaya, Réunion,

17 H. P. Willmott's tabular representation of the East Indies Fleet as at 15 August 1945 lists 324 ships of all classes serving with (or assigned to) it. The corresponding figure for the British Pacific Fleet – formed from the Eastern Fleet in November 1944 – is 370 vessels. Willmott, *Grave of a Dozen Schemes: British Naval Planning and the War Against Japan, 1943-1945* (Shrewsbury: Airlife, 1996), pp. 206-07. For a list of all the vessels assigned to the East Indies Fleet towards the end of the war, see 'The British Pacific and East Indies Fleets', 'The Forgotten Fleets of World War Two', compiled by the Royal Navy Research Archive, at http://www.royalnavyresearcharchive.org.uk/BPF-EIF/EIF_Ships.htm#.WxSyYhNViko

Singapore, Somaliland, the Sudan, and Sumatra. Combat and garrison forces were furnished by units such as the the Aden Protectorate Levies, the British Army, the Hong Kong and Ceylon Royal Garrison Artillery, the Indian Army, the King's African Rifles, the Mauritius Territorial Force, the Royal Marines, and the Royal West African Frontier Force. Hundreds of thousands of imperial servicemen and women, from every part of the British Empire, served across the Indian Ocean. Land forces also provided vital construction and engineering skills for the military installations that sprouted across the theatre, notably in places such as Addu Atoll in the Maldives, Diego Garcia in the Chagos Archipelago, and Massawa in Eritrea, along with numerous other locations on main-lands and islands.

American servicemen, often drawn from the Corps of Engineers, supported British, Chinese, and Soviet endeavours through deployments in places such as Burma, the Congo, Eritrea, the Gold Coast, India, Iran, and Liberia. So, too, did American merchant vessels and even an American aircraft carrier group, which served with the Royal Navy's Eastern Fleet in 1944. This theatre was also a stage for the activities of Allied special forces operating behind enemy lines in occupied territories such as the Dutch East Indies, Malaya, and Thailand. Special Operations Executive, the American Office of Strategic Services, the Dutch Corps Insulinde and other Allied outfits including the Calcutta Light Horse, Combined Operations Pilotage Parties, and the Inter-Services Liaison Department, conducted stand alone operations and collaborated with indigenous resistance movements such as the Malayan Anti-Japanese People's Army, as they prepared to rise against the Japanese when Allied invasion forces landed on the beaches.

Air power also played a notable part in the war in the Indian Ocean region. It witnessed extensive operations involving aircraft of the Fleet Air Arm, the Royal Air Force, the Royal Canadian Air Force, the Royal Indian Air Force, the South African Air Force, the US Army Air Force, and the 'Flying Tigers', the American airmen who flew in defence of Burma. The RAF extended its reach across the ocean, operating from land bases in all British and captured French and Italian territories be they in Africa, Aden and the Trucial States, Ceylon, Mauritius, Iraq, and India. It also operated from flying-boat anchorages and airstrips on island outposts such as the Cocos-Keeling Islands, Diego Garcia, the Maldives, and the Seychelles, crucial in closing the air gap and protecting convoys sailing from Suez and East Africa to India and the Far East. Indicating the strategic importance ascribed to the Indian Ocean region by the British government, in 1942 the RAF began the process of building up a force of 750 aircraft in India and Ceylon to meet the Japanese threat.

In a supreme contest for logistical control in order to extend and sustain one's military reach and retain or gain the capacity to move people and goods around the world, the Indian Ocean was a vital theatre. As it turned out, it was also a theatre in which the fighting had everything to do with imperial defence and imperial reconquest, and one that was considered of fundamental importance to Britain's future as a world power by Winston Churchill, the War Cabinet, and the Chiefs of Staff. This was a view shared by the region's senior commanders: General Sir Archibald Wavell, Commander-in-Chief India from summer 1941, 'firmly believed that for British India under threat of enemy attack, its imperial frontiers lay as far afield as Suez and Hong Kong, which had to be defended by Indian troops' travelling across the Indian Ocean.[18]

18 Wavell quoted in Sugata Bose, *A Hundred Horizons: The Indian Ocean in the Age of Global Empire* (Cambridge, MA: Harvard University Press, 2006), pp. 67-8.

Admiral Lord Louis Mountbatten, viewing the war from headquarters in Delhi and Kandy as Supreme Allied Commander South East Asia from 1943, considered the region 'central to the British Empire'.[19] President Franklin Roosevelt also understood the Indian Ocean's strategic importance, though his thoughts were fixed firmly on the global strategy of the emerging Anglo-American alliance rather than the imperial imperatives of Britain.[20] As he wrote to Churchill in May 1941, accepting that there might be further withdrawals from the Middle East-Mediterranean theatre, 'in the last analysis the naval control of the Indian Ocean and the Atlantic Ocean will in time win the war'.[21]

The Indian Ocean region was peripheral to the European Axis powers given their geographical locations and the direction of their central strategic war aims in terms of conquest and empire-building. It only became peripheral to the Japanese as the weight of American power began to tell ever closer to their home islands. But it was a key region if the British Empire were to survive and an increasingly complex global system of Allied military activity be preserved and utilized. Success here for the Axis, which would have involved severing sea lines of communication and disrupting or stopping the flow of oil – would have given them a significant strategic advantage. The fact that the region never received the concentrated Axis attention and requisite armed forces does not negate the fundamental nature of its importance, or invalidate the study of the preparations made to defend the region, or the extensive war-related activity that took place there.

In examining the significance of islands, ports, and sea lanes in and around Africa and the Indian Ocean, one of the tasks the book seeks to perform is to offer a 'How It Worked' guide to the British Empire's logistical and military system. It does this by explaining, in Part 1, the interconnectivity of actions and events on land, sea, and air and detailing the indispensable role of ports and sea lanes, looking at specific locations and their roles during the conflict. Part 2, meanwhile, offers a chronological narrative of the war at sea in this region, primarily from the perspective of the Royal Navy's East Indies Station – known as the Eastern Fleet for much of the war, and the East Indies Fleet from late 1944 – and how it related to land campaigns and the wider strategy of the interconnected, global phenomenon that was the Second World War.

19 Mountbatten quoted in Richard Aldrich, *The Faraway War: Personal Diaries of the Second World War in Asia and the Pacific* (London: Corgi, 2006), p. 440.

20 Though of course, while embodying American anti-colonial proclivities, the 'new world order' envisioned by Roosevelt was one in which sovereign independence would be tempered by spheres of American influence and investments of American political, military, and commercial power that could look remarkably 'imperial' in their manifestations.

21 Winston Churchill, *The Second World War*, volume 3, *The Grand Alliance* (London: Cassell, 1950), p. 208.

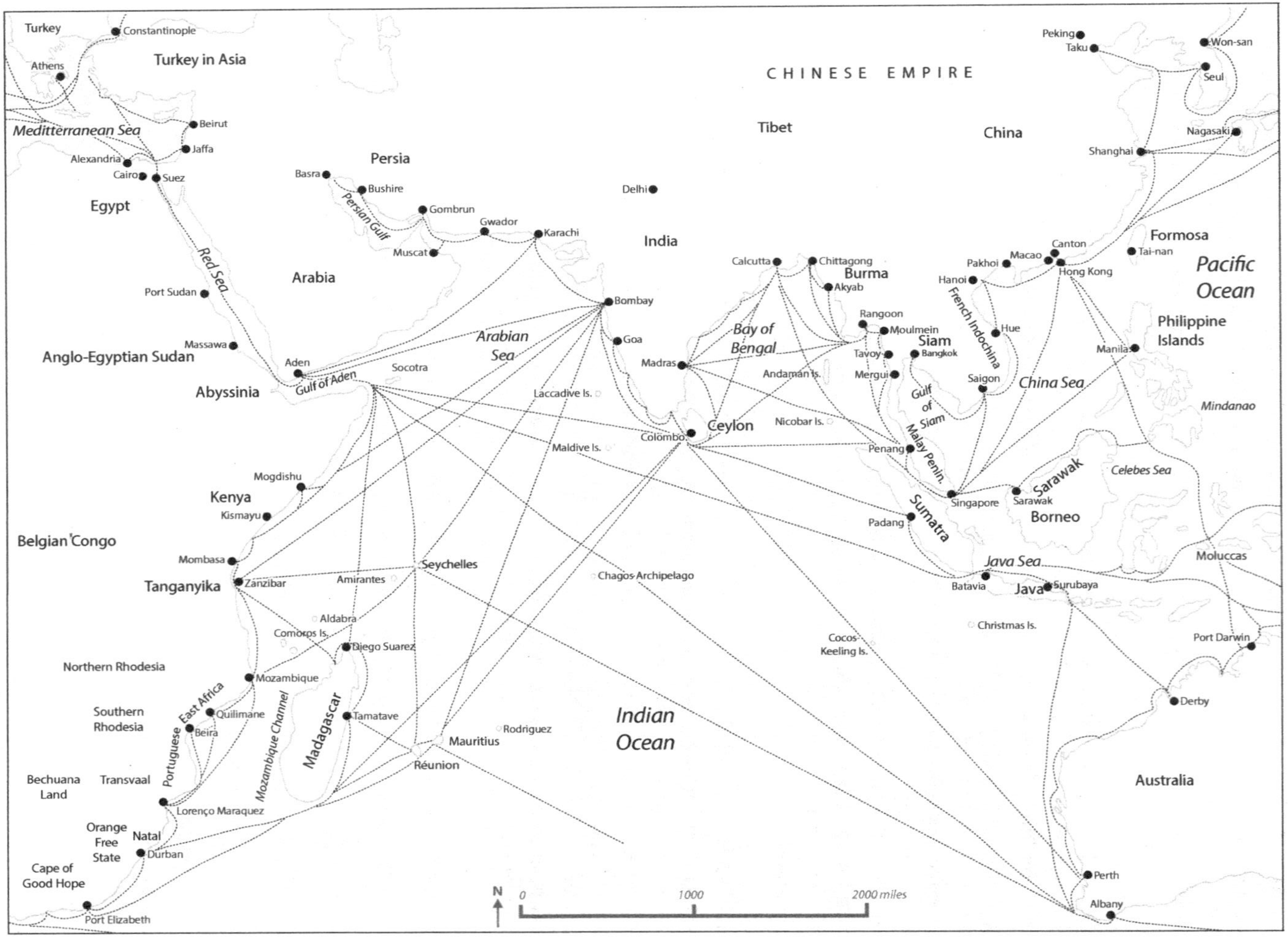

Map 1 The Indian Ocean.

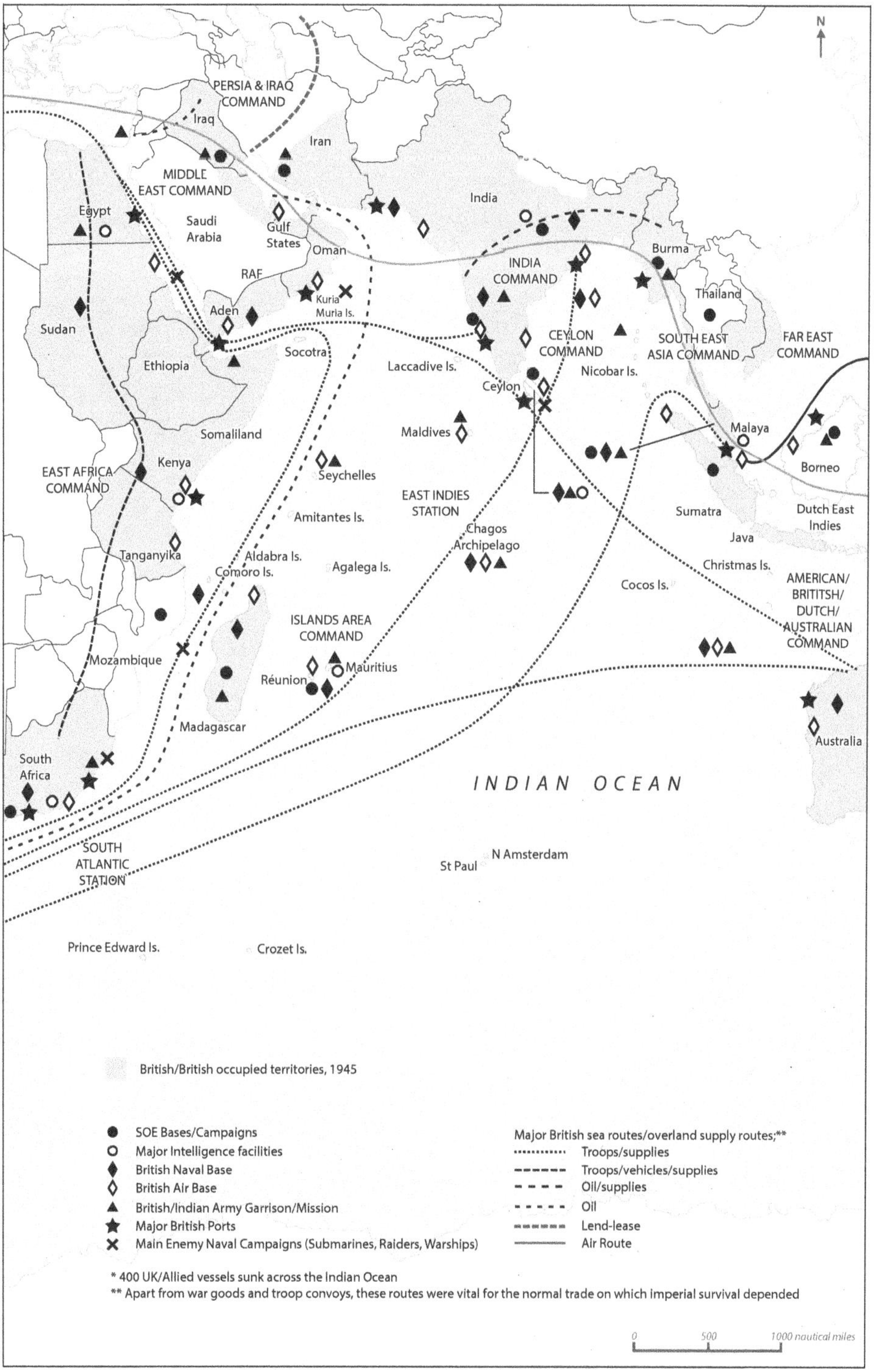

Map 2 War-time activity and bases in the Indian Ocean.

1

Islands, ports, and sea lanes in historical perspective

Chapter one offers an historical perspective on the Indian Ocean region and the significance of its islands, ports, and sea lanes. All territories of the British Empire, including the metropole, relied upon the movement of goods and people by sea for sustenance and security. The Empire's industry and commerce rested upon the extraction and shipment of raw materials from around the world and the exchange of manufactured goods and foodstuffs, and the sea lanes circumnavigating Africa and crossing the Indian Ocean, together with the network of ports that they connected, were prominent arteries in this ceaseless circulation.[1] Therefore the protection and utilization of ports and sea lanes – whether in pursuit of the routine transactions of an imperial world system or military objectives during times of war – were central to the Empire's prosperity and security.

Ports and islands had always been conquered and colonized for strategic reasons. In Britain's case, during the course of a long imperial career places such as Bermuda, Calais, Cape Town, Ceylon, Dublin, Gibraltar, Halifax, Heligoland, Hong Kong, Malta, Mauritius, Minorca, New York, the Seychelles, and Singapore had been secured for reasons of both trade and war. Indeed, though the Empire came to embody large swathes of territory on major land masses, ports and coastal enclaves were the roots from which it had grown. Though inland expansion almost always followed initial landfall – even if this sometimes took generations to manifest – when the British first alighted on a foreign shore, their gaze was usually fixed firmly out to sea, for purposes of trade and security.

Ports were prized possessions, to be utilized and defended. If they belonged to an enemy, they were to be blockaded or captured. In wartime they assumed special significance, particularly in conflicts fought at distance and over seas – which in Britain's case, meant *all* conflicts. Projecting military power beyond a nation's own shores had always depended upon capable maritime forces and their ability to use sea lanes and ports in order to deliver troops and all the paraphernalia of war to combat zones, to reinforce defensive strongholds, and to ensure that merchant vessels could continue to use those sea lanes unmolested. This was true of the Seven Years' War

1 These same sea lanes and ports were also relied upon by a host of other nation-states dependent on world trade and communication by sea. They benefited from the Pax Britannica, riding free, or at least at discounted rates, on the coattails of British maritime power. For this argument, see Lance Davis and Robert Huttenback, *Mammon and the Pursuit of Empire: The Political Economy of British Imperialism, 1860-1912* (Cambridge: Cambridge University Press, 1986).

(1765-63), the Revolutionary and Napoleonic Wars (1792-1815), and the First World War, and was just as true of the Second World War.[2]

In addition to their role as primary facilitators of global trade, ports contributed to the system of imperial defence that underpinned imperial prosperity.[3] They supported routine peacetime military activities such as the operations of the Royal Navy and army garrisons. In times of conflict, they could serve as defensive and offensive way-stations, both sally points and safe havens: patrols and other military operations could be mounted from them, and convoys mustered inside their defended harbours. They were recuperation, repair, revictualling, refuelling, and reammunitioning bases for merchantmen and warships. Forming links in a global communications chain, they also provided wireless and cable facilities, and, from the second quarter of the twentieth century, civilian and military aerodromes and flying-boat anchorages.[4] These grew both as links along imperial air routes and as bases from which to conduct 'air

2 The major difference between the two world wars was that in 1914-18 both Italy and Japan had been allies, meaning that Britain's command of the Mediterranean and the Indian Ocean had been easily maintained, and that even war with German and Ottoman forces in places such as East Africa, Iraq, and Palestine posed little threat to imperial survival. Such a threat could only have been translated into reality by defeat in Europe and the eclipse of British sea power. But in 1939-45, the situation was transformed because the Empire was assailed by Germany as well as a powerful Mediterranean nation and an even more powerful eastern one, both with sizeable and highly capable navies. It was also transformed, of course, by the early capitulation of France and the subsequent loss of French military and naval power – and ports – around the world. Projection of military force across the seas and the use ports and bases remains just as important in more recent conflicts, including the Falklands War of 1982 and the Gulf wars of the 1990s and 2000s, and key island bases, such as Ascension and Diego Garcia, remain central to American power projection around the world.

3 On imperial defence, see Greg Kennedy (ed.), *Imperial Defence: The Old World Order, 1856-1956* (London: Routledge, 2008); Kennedy and Keith Neilson (eds), *Far Flung Lines: Essays in Imperial Defence in Honour of Donald Schurman* (London: Frank Cass, 1996); Anthony Clayton, '"Deceptive Might": Imperial Defence and Security, 1900-1968', in William Roger Louis and Judith Brown (eds), *The Oxford History of the British Empire*, volume 4, *The Twentieth Century* (Oxford: Oxford University Press, 1999); David Killingray, 'Imperial Defence', in Robin Winks (ed.), *The Oxford History of the British Empire*, volume 5, *Historiography* (Oxford: Oxford University Press, 1999); Daniel Spence, *A History of the Royal Navy: Empire and Imperialism* (London: I. B. Tauris, 2016); and Ashley Jackson, 'The Commonwealth as a Strategic Alliance', in Alex May (ed.), *The Oxford History of the British Empire*, companion series, *The Commonwealth* (Oxford: Oxford University Press, forthcoming). As a recognized concept, numerous books were published on 'imperial military geography', such as Valentine Cornish's *A Geography of Imperial Defence* (London: Sifton Praed, 1922). D. H. Cole's *Imperial Military Geography* went through nearly a dozen reprints between 1925 and 1956. See Cole, *Imperial Military Geography: General Characteristics of the Empire in Relation to Defence* (London: Sifton Praed, 1933).

4 On cables, see Christina Phelps Harris, 'The Persian Gulf Submarine Telegraph of 1864', *Geographical Journal*, 135, 2 (1969); Paul Kennedy, 'Imperial Cable Communications and Strategy, 1870-1914', *Historical Review*, 86, 341 (1971); and Kenneth Inglis, 'The Imperial Connection: Telegraphic Communications between England and Australia, 1872-1902', in Frederick Madden and Wyndraeth Morris-Jones (eds), *Australia and Britain: Studies in a Changing Relationship* (London: Frank Cass, 1990). On Cable and Wireless, see Benjamin Oldcorn, 'On the Wire: The Strategic and Tactical Role of Cable and Wireless during the Second World War', Ph. D. Thesis (University of Exeter, 2013) and Lee Cable, 'Empire, Modernity and Design: Visual Culture and Cable & Wireless Corporate Identities, 1924-1955', Ph. D. Thesis (University of Exeter, 2014).

policing' and to bomb targets in neighbouring countries.[5] Airbases located on or near the coast also facilitated an air power contribution to the protection of shipping.[6] Island ports stretched the chain of imperial defence across the seas; the Seychelles, for example, were valued as a focal point for monitoring and protecting shipping passing to and from the Cape, Ceylon, and the Far East, and, to their west, traffic between the Cape and the Red Sea converged. The Seychelles were also a connecting point on the underwater cable route between Aden, Ceylon, Mauritius, and Zanzibar.

Ports were employed as forward supply and repair bases and as jumping off points for land, air, and maritime forces conducting operations in the surrounding area, and even the most remote and barren territories had their value. This was because all, if not possessed by Britain or an ally, presented an opportunity for a rival power to challenge Britain's preponderance and menace both its trade and its war-making capacity by using them as bases for commerce raiders, warships, and submarines. From the days of Hornblower to those of Mountbatten, world war was a zero-sum game of beggar thy neighbour, and islands, ports and secure sea lanes could be the difference between defeat and victory.

The British Indian Ocean world

The Indian Ocean was a cornerstone of British world power. On the eve of the war, Enoch Powell memorably described his sense of Britain's imperial presence in this region:

> In 1938 I flew from Britain to Sydney by Imperial Airways flying-boat to take up the Chair of Greek in the University, at twenty-five the youngest professor in the Empire ... Those sixteen days from Poole Harbour to Sydney were a deeply formative experience. How formative I can understand now in retrospect. I was one of the two first through-passengers on the first flying-boat to go on a scheduled flight across the Indian Ocean to Singapore, where the Qantas four-engined land planes took over for the rest of the trip through the Dutch East Indies and down via Darwin to Sydney.
>
> It was an exacting routine. Three or four times a day, the flying-boat landed on a sheet of water – lake or river or sea. Nightly the crew and passengers were transported to a neighbouring city for a few hours' rest before the ferociously early take-off next morning ... Conditions on some parts of the route were primitive. I remember a hut on the island of Timor with a table where hunks of bread and butter and glasses of lukewarm beer were

5 Meaning, specifically, the use of aircraft to quell or suppress resistance to colonial authority from indigenous communities or to bomb strategic targets belonging to great power rivals in neighbouring lands. Examples include the British airbases near Baghdad (Hinaidi and later Habbaniya), which could be used variously to suppress local unrest, support the fledgling Iraqi government, attack the fledgling Iraqi government, or strike targets in the Soviet Union or Syria.

6 The 'system' being described here is laid out in simple terms in A. J. Christopher's *The British Empire at its Zenith* (London: Croom Helm, 1988). Christopher devotes chapter 2 to a description of the nature of Britain as an imperial metropole before looking at 'linkages' (chapter 3) between Britain and its territories, focusing on sea lanes, roads, railways, postal services, and the telegraph. Chapter 4, entitled 'The Colonial Bases of Power', describes the role of naval bases, entrepôts, military outposts, and administrative capitals.

consumed under a hanging acetylene lamp. I remember it because punctually every ten minutes the tablecloth was picked up and emptied out of doors, together with the thick layer of insect life that had accumulated on it in the meantime.

The traveller of 1938 saw the world close to. It was an incomparable geography lesson – and largely a lesson in Imperial geography. Between Crete and Indonesia there was only one stop out of almost a score – it was, in fact, Bangkok – where the flying-boat touched down anywhere not under British rule or effectively under British authority. Alexandria, the Lake of Galilee, Habbaniya, Basra, Abu Dhabi, Mekran, Karachi, Jaipur, Allahabad, Calcutta, Akyab, Rangoon, Penang, Singapore – one was witnessing the ubiquity of a power on which the sun had not yet set.

I saw; I felt; I marvelled.[7]

Powell's evocative reminiscence describes an imperial geography and an imperial conceptualization of the globe that would have been familiar to millions of people at the time. Though long vanished, the seemingly powerful and enduring 'red on the map' of the British Empire was a major fixture of the world they inhabited. It was an imperial world, dotted with well-known names in 'exotic' locations. They became staging posts – caravansaries – as well as destinations for people progressing along the world's sea lanes and air routes aboard liners, merchantmen, tankers, troopships, warships, transport aircraft, and flying-boats. They were household names inked onto the maps of the world that hung in classrooms across the Empire, interlinked by trans-oceanic and trans-continental lines of communication.[8]

It wasn't only Britons who experienced the sense of *imperium* stimulated by travel and the evocations of maps and cultural products such as works of art and literature, newspapers, and school textbooks that celebrated, or at least noted, an empire on which the sun never set.[9]

7 From an article by Powell entitled 'Long Haul Back to a World Apart' that appeared in *The Telegraph* in 1988 (I can't find the exact reference and have long since lost the cutting). Camilla Schofield, author of *Enoch Powell and the Making of Postcolonial Britain* (Cambridge: Cambridge University Press, 2013), kindly offers this variation from Powell's personal papers: 'It was a living geography and imperial lesson … the extraordinary sense of the inevitability – an apparently strange word to use – of British power was very strongly borne in upon me … It seemed to me that the combination of sea power and air power which Britain still exhibited, gave to the structure of the British Empire an inherent strength which I was later to learn it didn't possess'. Churchill Archives Centre (hereafter CAC), Cambridge, The Papers of Enoch Powell, 'JEP War Memories', POLL 5.1.

8 For an introduction to the iconography of the British imperial map of the world, see Ashley Jackson, 'The Red on the Map', in Jackson, *Mad Dogs and Englishmen: A Grand Tour of the British Empire at its Height* (London: Quercus, 2009). Empire-themed maps of the world often also marked the key sea lanes and distances between major ports, some even marking coaling stations, naval bases, and details regarding the size of the Merchant Navy and the Royal Navy.

9 Cultural references to the British Empire, its visual representation and ubiquity, were extremely common. There is an abundant literature; for pioneering work, see John MacKenzie, *Imperialism and Popular Culture* (Manchester: Manchester University Press, 1986) and a phalanx of other books and chapters authored or edited by him, in the Manchester University Press 'Studies in Imperialism' series and elsewhere. For a coffee-table treatment, see Jackson, *Mad Dogs and Englishmen* and Ashley Jackson and David Tomkins, *Illustrating Empire: A Visual History of British Imperialism* (Oxford: Bodleian Library Publishing, 2011). I have recently expanded my knowledge of the realm of British Empire-themed board games (and jigsaws) thanks to Julie Anne Lambert of the Bodleian Library, who alerted me to the Bodleian's Ballam Collection of Games and Pastimes and an online games database. Usually, these games featured maps of the colonial world and the ports and sea lanes

The veteran American war correspondent Cecil Brown embarked on a journey from Egypt to Singapore in July 1941. 'Before dawn', he wrote, 'we took off [from the Nile] and flew the entire way to Bahrein Island over the Persian Gulf at ten to eleven thousand feet altitude'. The following day the flying-boat 'paralleled the Ganges' and Brown alighted at Calcutta. From here the aircraft struck out across the Bay of Bengal for Akyab Island off the Burmese coast. Then, wrote Brown, flying across South-east Asia, 'I fell asleep and the steward woke me for tea to announce we would be in Singapore in twenty minutes. For five days of flying, from Suez to Singapore, at almost every stop we had touched on water under the protection of the British flag. It was a stunning reflection on Empire'.[10]

Generations of Britons were familiar with these landmark ports of call, the essence of a maritime empire that girdled the planet. As ships sailed between east and west, they worked their way along major ocean trunk routes and the branch lines that connected them to places such as the Persian Gulf, the Bay of Bengal, and the east coast of Africa. The African coastline was studded with important ports, some frequented since the heyday of the Cape of Good Hope sea route when, before the opening of the Suez Canal, all ships sailing between east and west

connecting Britain and the territories of the Empire, or visualizations of imperial products and distant zones of colonial activity. Titles include 'A Tour Through the British Colonies and Foreign Possessions' (Betts, 1854); 'Empire Preference' (Geographia, c. 1930); 'Bricks of the Empire' (Roberts (?), c. 1930); 'The New Game of British Empire or Trading with the Colonies' (Roberts (?), c. 1925); 'Countries of Empire (Jacques, 1930); 'Aeroplane Race Round the British Empire' (Roberts (?, c. 1920); 'The Jubilee, An Interesting Game' (John Harris, 1810); 'The Exhibition Puzzle of the British Empire' (?, c. 1924); 'The British Empire, A Game for Young and Old' (?); and 'The Tar [meaning sailor] of All Weathers: A Game' (E. and M. A. Ogilvy, c. 1857).

10 Drawn from Cecil Brown's 'Flight into War' chapter in his book *Suez to Singapore* (New York: Random House, 1942), pp. 120-127. The pilot, John Alcock, was brother of the man who had made the first Atlantic crossing by air. In the same Imperial Airways flying-boat, Alcock had recently helped evacuate imperial troops from Crete, making five trips and cramming 70 soldiers in each time. From the Nile, Brown's journey proceeded thus: Sea of Galilee (time for a quick swim), across Iraq with stops at Habbaniya and Basra (vomiting 15 times on this leg), Bahrein, and Karachi in north-west India. Here there was a change of flying-boat, the journey continuing aboard *Canopus*, the original flagship aircraft of Imperial Airways. Next stop Lake Raj Samand in Rajasthan, Calcutta's Hooghly River, Akyab on the Burmese coast, and then Rangoon, the port bustling with ships bearing goods to support the Chinese war effort. It was then on to the Mekong River in Bangkok and, following his snooze, Singapore and Raffles Hotel. Brown fled before the storm; he left Singapore shortly before its fall, and did the same in various parts of the Dutch East Indies before reaching Darwin. His book, and accounts written by other travellers and often published before the war ended or shortly thereafter, offer essential eyewitness perspective on the war as it was being fought. In my recent work, and in addition to the memoirs and diaries of wartime military leaders and politicians, I have been struck by accounts published by itinerant wartime travellers including Cecil Brown and others such as Cecil Beaton, *Near East* (London: Batsford, 1943); Compton Mackenzie, *All Over the Place: Fifty Thousand Miles by Sea, Air, Road and Rail* (London: Chatto and Windus, 1948); Noel Coward, *Middle East Diary* (London: William Heinemann, 1944); Eve Curie, *Journey Among Warriors* (New York: Doubleday, Doran, and Co., 1943); Freya Stark, *Dust in the Lion's Paw: Autobiography, 1939-1946* (London: John Murray, 1961); and Alan Moorehead, *A Year of Battle* (London: Hamish Hamilton, 1943). For imperial air routes, see Gordon Pirie, *Air Empire: British Imperial Civil Aviation, 1919-1939* (Manchester: Manchester University Press, 2009); Pirie, *Cultures and Caricatures of British Imperial Aviation: Passengers, Pilots, Publicity* (Manchester: Manchester University Press, 2012); and James Hamilton-Paterson, *Empire of the Clouds: When Britain's Aircraft Ruled the World* (London: Faber and Faber, 2011).

rounded the continent's southernmost tip. Both the Atlantic Ocean and the Indian Ocean – the world's great connecting sea – were home to many of these trunk routes and branch lines and the stepping-stone ports that served them and allowed an imperial trading economy and political and military system to flourish. As well as functioning as commercial entrepôts, ports could be augmented for defensive and offensive purposes during times of war, just as vessels travelling between them could be escorted, sometimes in convoy, by the warships of the Royal Navy. Their facilities, their protection, and the ability to project force from them, were integral elements of the system of imperial defence.

The security of sea lanes and ports depended on the control of maritime gateways, and these the proficient British had acquired during the course of the nineteenth century. The Cape of Good Hope, the Malacca Strait, the Straits of Hormuz, the Bab-el-Mandeb and the Suez Canal all came under Britain's mantle, as too did important harbours in places such as Aden, Ceylon, Mauritius, Sierra Leone, and South Africa. In times of war they needed to be defended on the one hand and utilized on the other, so that the system of imperial defence could operate and war be taken to the enemy wherever his forces appeared. The system reflected the immutable verities of imperial geography and a generations-old global outlook that had entered the bloodstream of the organizations responsible for imperial foreign policy and strategy, and of those who served them.[11] This was because Britain was not just a nation state, but also a profoundly imperial one.

The Indian Ocean region had a historic unity of its own, and had for long been a global junction.[12] Its coherence, born of contacts linking communities and resources across it, had for long been a reality for indigenous traders and migrants, regional polities, and imperial powers of varying hue. Because of this, the geographical appellation 'Indian Ocean', according to Sugata Bose, had greater meaning than 'the Middle East', 'South Asia', and 'South-east Asia', which were

> relatively recent constructions that arbitrarily project certain legacies of colonial power onto the domains of knowledge in the post-colonial era. The world of the Indian Ocean, or for that matter, that of the Mediterranean, has a much greater depth of economic and cultural

11 For a treatment of this subject see Ashley Jackson, '"A Prodigy of Skill and Organization": British Imperial Networks and the Second World War', in Jackson, *Distant Drums*.

12 For a brief overview of British expansion in the Indian Ocean region, see Ashley Jackson, 'Britain in the Indian Ocean Region', *Journal of the Indian Ocean Region*, 7, 2 (2011). More specifically, see Gerald Graham, *Great Britain in the Indian Ocean: A Study in Maritime Enterprise, 1810–1857* (Oxford: Clarendon Press, 1967) and Graham, 'The Indian Ocean: From the Cape to Canton', in Graham, *The Politics of Naval Supremacy: Studies in British Maritime Ascendancy* (Cambridge: Cambridge University Press, 1965). More generally for the Indian Ocean, see Abdul Sheriff, *Dhow Cultures of the Indian Ocean: Cosmopolitanism, Commerce, and Islam* (London: Hurst, 2010); Edward Alpers, *The Indian Ocean in World History* (Oxford: Oxford University Press, 2013); Rene Barendse, *The Arabian Seas: The Indian Ocean World of the Seventeenth Century* (London: Routledge: 2001); Richard Hall, *Empires of the Monsoon: A History of the Indian Ocean and its Invaders* (London: HarperCollins, 1996); Milo Kearney, *The Indian Ocean in World History* (London: Routledge, 2004); and Michael Pearson, *The Indian Ocean* (London: Routledge, 2003). For maritime security overviews encompassing the present day, see James Russell, 'The Indian Ocean', in Daniel Moran and James Russell (eds), *Maritime Strategy and Global Order: Markets, Resources, Security* (Washington, DC: Georgetown University Press, 2016) and Robert Kaplan, *Monsoon: The Indian Ocean and the Failure of American Power* (London: Random House, 2010).

> meaning. Tied together by webs of economic and cultural relationships ... [these were arenas where] port cities formed the nodal points of exchange and interaction.[13]

In the twentieth century, the Indian Ocean retained vestiges of these historical connections, such as the dhow trade between the Swahili coast and the Persian Gulf and the ethnic composition of many of its lands. But since the days when slaves, spices, and ivory had been prised from distant continents and archipelagos and carried to Europe and the Americas under sail, the British had developed a dominant position in what came to be known as the 'British lake'.[14] British enterprise in all of its expansionist guises had spun a powerful web across the Indian Ocean, older links overlain or displaced in the process by the twin forces of colonialism and globalization. By the twentieth century, the Indian Ocean had become a British integrated region, key to the prosperity and survival of the Empire.

Centuries of imperial endeavour had led to British dominion, formal and informal, over most of the lands on the Indian Ocean's rim. In the west, the Empire encompassed Africa's Swahili coast and most of the Horn of Africa as well as Egypt, the Sudan, and South Africa. To the north lay the Aden protectorate and Muscat and Oman on the Arabian peninsula, the Trucial States of the Persian Gulf, Iraq, the enormous Anglo-Iranian Oil Company concession in southern Iran, and India. To the east, Burma, the elongated sliver of the Malay peninsula, Singapore, and Australia.[15] From these British-ruled or influenced lands some of the world's great rivers flowed into the Indian Ocean – the Limpopo and Zambezi in Africa, the Brahmaputra, Ganges, Indus, and Irrawaddy in Asia, and the Shatt al-Arab, confluence of the Euphrates and Tigris, washing into the Persian Gulf.

Framed by these lands, the broad canvas of the Indian Ocean stretched across 28 million square miles of sea spangled with islands and atolls over which the Union Flag flew. There were the Agalega and Aldabra islands, the Andaman and Nicobar Islands, the Cargados Carajos group, Ceylon, the Chagos Archipelago, Christmas Island, the Cocos-Keeling Islands, the Laccadives, the Maldives, Masirah, Mauritius, the Kuria Muria islands, Pemba, Perim, Rodrigues, Salalah, the Seychelles, Socotra, and Zanzibar. Exploration, adventure, and the search for profitable resources and new knowledge had also taken the British to the wastes of the Southern Ocean, where they laid claim to desolate places such as Heard Island and the Prince Edward Islands and a generous slice of Antarctica.[16] Stretching round the Cape into

13 Bose, *A Hundred Horizons*, p. 6.

14 Who exactly referred to it as the 'British lake' is never really explained; perhaps the occasional self-congratulatory Briton, exasperated Frenchman, or armchair strategist or historian. See Edward Alperts, 'On Becoming a "British Lake": Piracy, Slaving, and British Imperialism in the Indian Ocean during the First Half of the Nineteenth Century', in Robert Harms, Bernard Freamon, and David Blight, *Indian Ocean Slavery in the Age of Abolition* (New Haven: Yale University Press, 2013).

15 Lands on the Indian Ocean rim *not* ruled by Britain had (and were to again) come under its sway or were the scene of covert political and even military activities – especially during times of war – including the Italian possessions in the Horn of Africa, France's Indian Ocean territories in the Comoros, Madagascar, and Réunion, Portuguese East Africa, Portuguese Goa, and the Dutch East Indies.

16 For the British presence in the Antarctic, see Klaus Dodds, *Pink Ice: Britain and the South Atlantic Empire* (London: I. B. Tauris, 2002). For an important wartime mission to Antarctica, see Stephen Haddelsey, *Operation Tabarin: Britain's Secret Wartime Mission to Antarctica, 1944–1946* (Stroud, Gloucestershire: The History Press, 2014).

the Atlantic, the picture was much the same: the South Atlantic was flanked by strategically-important British territories on the African mainland, including the South African League of Nations mandate of South-West Africa, and British islands were moored throughout the ocean, from the Falklands and South Georgia north to Gough Island, Inaccessible Island, Tristan da Cunha, St Helena, and Ascension.

This summation of the very British character of the Indian Ocean area is not a retrospective boast, rather a recollection of the astonishing extent of Britain's imperial reach and responsibilities – and of its fragile dominion at the time of the Second World War. For such imperial girth had always been a double-edged sword; while dominion over palm and pine offered great reach, it meant unprecedented exposure to danger. Far-flung colonies dependent on secure sea lanes presented enemies with an array of opportunities and irresistible temptations: they could nibble away at the edges of the British world, menace distant sea lanes compelling the diversion of precious military resources to meet them, or seek to strike stunning blows against nodal points as they attempted to defeat Britain and redistribute the imperial spoils of the world.

The problem for the British in the Second World War, unlike the First World War, was that its key strategic ally, France, was knocked out within the first year of a six-year conflict. Furthermore, Italy and Japan, allies before, now presented themselves and their potent war-making potential as enemies in the Mediterranean and the Far East in 1940 and 1941 respectively, stressing the imperial system to the point of rupture. It is easy to lose sight of the fact that this was a war about empires – holding on to them, for powers like Britain and France, and gaining them, for powers like Germany, Italy, and Japan. The Indian Ocean region was a major stage in this clash for control of territory and resources.[17] As Arnold Toynbee memorably phrased it in his introduction to George Kirk's landmark study of the Middle East during the war:

> Hitler and Mussolini in 1940, like Napoleon in 1798, could dream of finding in Egypt a stepping-stone towards an invasion of India from continental Europe; and, after the intervention of Japan in the war in December 1941, the European and Asian parties to the Anti-Comintern Pact might hope to join hands across the Indian Ocean for the conquest of the territories of the British Commonwealth that hung in a giant festoon all round the shores of the Indian Ocean.[18]

The predations of great power rivals (and internal challengers) led to chronic imperial overstretch during the war, repeatedly remarked upon in the diaries and memoirs of senior British commanders and planners. There was never enough shipping to go around, and construction struggled to keep pace with sinkings. The same was true with brigades and divisions, if you wanted to meet both actual and potential threats and seek to deter as well as to combat your enemies. But stretch to meet the situation the British did, often with American help but also through their own resourcefulness and the acceptance and management of risk. Peter was

17 For a discussion of the Second World War as an imperial conflict, see Ashley Jackson, 'Empires and the Second World War', in John MacKenzie (ed.), *The Encyclopaedia of Empire* (Chichester, West Sussex: Wiley-Blackwell, 2016).

18 Arnold Toynbee, 'Introduction', in George Kirk, *The Middle East at War, 1939–1945* (London: Oxford University Press), p. 1.

habitually robbed to pay Paul, and if you needed sufficient ships for amphibious operations or sea lane protection in one theatre, then you had to denude another. Or perhaps the Americans would mount diversionary manoeuvres in the Pacific to relieve pressure in the Indian Ocean, or backfill in the North Atlantic in order to release British forces for the region. This was the complex puzzle presented by a global war in which resources were always insufficient to cover all bases at once. Admiral Sir James Somerville, commanding Britain's naval forces in the Indian Ocean for much of the war, wrote:

> Britain had dominated the area for 200 years yet by this time the Indian Ocean was a weak link in the imperial chain. It lacked an industrial base; manufactured goods had to be brought thousands of miles ... India, supposedly the jewel in the imperial crown, was in reality a gross liability. South Africa, Egypt, Iran, and Iraq were unreliable associates. Nature was distinctly unhelpful – vast distances, deserts, and jungles, the world's highest mountains, monsoons, and enervating climate, and overpopulation in many lands. There was no concrete pre-war strategy for the region. The only guiding principle was the entirely negative (and complacent) one that the region was unlikely to be threatened, cushioned as it was by substantial forces in the Middle East and Singapore.[19]

The problem, of course, was that Singapore failed. Nevertheless, and contrary to part of Somerville's assertion, the British *did* have a plan to defend the Indian Ocean region which, almost incredibly given the pressures in other parts of the world and the failure of the French alliance, they manage to execute following the destruction of *Prince of Wales* and *Repulse* and the fall of Singapore.

A war of two halves

The Second World War was a war of two halves in the Indian Ocean region.[20] From its outbreak in September 1939 until December 1941, fighting extended around the African coast and into the waters of the Indian Ocean because of the deployments and offensives of German and Italian forces in Africa and the Middle East. The pocket battleships *Admiral Scheer* and *Graf Spee* nosed their way around the Cape in order to raid towards the Arabian Sea in the early months of the war, commerce raiders operated there in 1940-41, and U-boat deployments in the Indian Ocean began in earnest in 1942, though were subsidiary to the Atlantic campaign. The Italians, meanwhile, maintained a powerful regional force of destroyers and submarines, and since the 1930s had based their strategy for territorial aggrandizement on making a nuisance of themselves in the Red Sea and beyond, and across the territories of East Africa a significant campaign was fought that lasted for eighteen months.

19 Michael Simpson (ed.), *The Somerville Papers: Selections from the Private and Official Correspondence of Admiral of the Fleet Sir James Somerville, GCB, GBE, DSO* (Aldershot: Scholar Press for the Navy Records Society, 1995), p. 354.

20 Of course, for it to have *actually* been a war of two halves, both periods would have to have been equal. It is hoped that the reader will forgive the licence taken in thus describing it, product of a football-clichéd mind.

Unobtrusively, the Americans supported the British war effort in the Indian Ocean even before they joined the conflict in December 1941 as belligerents. They sent supply ships and even deployed support troops and civilians in the Horn of Africa, as they also did in Burma, India, Iran, and West Africa. Elsewhere in the Indian Ocean, the British hunted Vichy blockade runners, and imperial forces mounted campaigns in Iran and Iraq after securing Basra as a base using troops transported across the ocean from Bombay and Karachi. In conjunction with Soviet forces they deposed Shah Reza Pahlavi of Iran, exiling him via Bombay to Mauritius and then South Africa, and soon welcomed 30,000 American troops into the British-occupied zone of Iran for the shared task of transporting military aid to the new Soviet ally. Though greedily absorbing resources that might have been deployed elsewhere, the British successfully contained the threat posed by the Germans and the Italians in the western Indian Ocean. They were able to continue using it as a transit route for all manner of military shipments that in other circumstances would have travelled between east and west via the Suez Canal before journeying across the Indian Ocean, or been delivered to the Soviet Union via the North Atlantic.

But following Japan's riotous entry into the conflict everything changed, and the war's second half was to be far less comfortable for the British in the Indian Ocean. Colonies in South Asia and South-east Asia, as well as the Far East and the Pacific, were briskly conquered by the new enemy, as were those of America, France, and Holland. The British fell back towards Africa while attempting to hang on in the Indian Ocean, reinforcing it as a matter of priority even if this meant denuding the Mediterranean of capital ships, hoping to avoid a catastrophic naval defeat and desperate to protect essential sea lanes that now lay critically exposed. As this happened, Indian Ocean sites assumed new, strategic, importance; the development of a secret naval base in the Maldives was expedited, Madagascar was seized from Vichy France lest the enemy alight there, and Ceylon became a surrogate Singapore, considered by the Chiefs of Staff and the War Cabinet to be the most important location in the Empire along with the oilfields of Iran and Iraq. One of the most alarming prospects for the British in the dark days of 1942 was that of Japan joining hands in the Indian Ocean with German forces striving to push the British out of the Middle East. The primary objectives now were to avoid defeat, retain the ability to use the sea lanes, build Allied strength, and harry the enemy when and where he presented himself – but to stay out of his way if at all possible.

This was now a global war requiring global infrastructure. The movement of military supplies and personnel demanded the utilization of extensive physical infrastructure, the development of existing facilities, and the construction of new ones. Thus was instigated a massive effort across Africa and the Indian Ocean to protect, extend, and develop the sinews of war, now essential to victory and all absolutely dependent upon the labour of indigenous people, supervised and galvanized by British and Allied service personnel and contractors. The British and their allies built facilities across the region, including brand new ports and bases – Umm Qasr in Iraq, for example, Matadi in the Congo, Monrovia in Liberia, and Addu Atoll in the Maldives – and improved existing facilities in ports such as Bombay, Bandar Shaphur in Iran, Massawa in Eritrea, Kilndini in Kenya, and Trincomalee. They constructed new repair centres, new aerodromes, new flying-boat bases, new magazines for naval ammunition, new wireless telegraphy stations, and new harbour defences. Building and developing infrastructure became a leitmotif of Allied victory, often building in the most outlandish of places, often building with the knowledge that the eventuality for which one laboured might never come to pass, but building all the same.

The battle of supply and logistics was as important as the delivery of fighting power itself, for enemies could not be engaged in the field unless soldiers and airmen could be brought into theatre with all of their weaponry, and once there sustained. The Indian Ocean was of primary strategic importance to all of the Allies. It was a thoroughfare for the millions of tons of Anglo-American aid sent to the Soviet Union via the Persian Gulf and the ports, roads, and railways of Iran. The Indian Ocean-'Persian corridor' route conveyed a greater share of aid to the Soviets than the more well-known Arctic convoy route. American aid to China also depended on Indian Ocean sea lanes, landed at ports in Burma and India before making the overland journey by way of 'The Hump' air route over the Himalayas, the Burma Road, running from Lashio to Kunming, and the Ledo Road, running from Assam to Kunming.[21] The use of Indian Ocean sea lanes also enabled the Americans to support the British – and augment their own growing presence in places such as East Africa, India, and Iran – by delivering military hardware to Egypt via the Red Sea, to Iran and Iraq via the Persian Gulf as the British built up the Tenth Army, and to Indian ports such as Bombay and Karachi. Meanwhile the vanquished Dutch and Free French could only ever hope to regain their lost colonies by virtue of Indian Ocean bases and sea lanes. Defeated in Europe, they pooled resources with the British in the Indian Ocean in order to attempt to arrest Japan's lightning advance and, later, to contribute to eventual reconquest.

Without control of ports across the region, and the sea lanes connecting them, imperial territories large and small risked being marooned, cut off from each other and from Britain and left at the mercy of the enemy. This would have caused the war effort to founder and colonies to whither on the vine, as the ships bearing food and other necessities, as well as raw materials, would have been unable to sail. Vital war-related resources extracted from Indian Ocean lands included Gulf oil, Ceylonese and Malayan rubber and tin, and Tanganyikan pyrethrum and sisal. They became especially important once traditional sources had been lost to the Japanese. The defence of sea lanes, therefore, was a strategic priority connected to imperial survival and ultimate Allied victory, reflecting the fundamental maritime verity that 'all the seas of the world are one'.[22]

Indian Ocean ports and sea lanes supported the movement of imperial and Allied troops to the Middle East, the Persian Gulf, South Asia, and the Far East; overland air routes connected West African ports to battlefronts in the Middle East and South Asia, and even the Eastern Front. The many divisions of the Indian Army that left the subcontinent to support fighting fronts and service logistical hubs in places such as Borneo, East Africa, the East Indies, Egypt, Iran, Iraq, Libya, and Malaya did so by way of troopships sailing across the Indian Ocean. The same was true of the African divisions that journeyed around the Cape from West Africa and from East African ports to Ceylon and India, and thence across the Bay of Bengal to Burma. So, too, for most of the men and material drawn from Britain's southern African empire, including the 36,000 men of the African Pioneer Corps recruited in Bechuanaland, Basutoland, and Swaziland, who travelled to the Middle East from Durban. Australian and New Zealand troops also depended on Indian Ocean sea routes as they travelled to and from the war zones.

21 Logistics were of course just as important to the enemy, and in this region the Japanese expended enormous effort building the infamous Burma-Thailand railway to facilitate the supply of their forces in Burma. It was a critical alternative supply line because the sea lanes to Rangoon through the Malacca Strait and the Andaman Sea were vulnerable to Allied attack.

22 J. H. Parry, *The Discovery of the Sea* (New York: Weidenfeld and Nicolson, 1974), p. xi.

Often, soldiers, sailors, and airmen involved in one campaign would cross the Indian Ocean to take part in another, peregrinations along the martial highways and byways criss-crossing the Indian Ocean and the land masses that framed it. The Gurkha subaltern John Masters served variously in Burma, India, Iran, and Iraq, describing the war as 'an enormous, over-shadowing, moving monster, far bigger than I had imagined it would be'.[23] The Royal Marines officer James Alan Thompson debuted in Norway but spent the rest of the war deposited on various Indian Ocean outcrops, sometimes desolate and often surreal periods of service in places such as the Chagos Archipelago, the Maldives, and the Seychelles, punctuated by time in Colombo, Trincomalee, and the rest camp at Diyatalawa in Ceylon's central highlands, the colony envisioned as the metropole of an island empire in his intense and sensual memoir.[24] Echoing Masters's sense of insignificance in the face of a global war, Thompson wrote: 'This is the journal of one wanderer, one moving maggot beneath the sun and the Southern Cross'.[25] He is worth quoting at length – an authentic voice of the Second World War in the Indian Ocean – as he describes the atolls in the southern Maldives to which his unit deployed aboard the supply ship *Clan Forbes*:

> The guarding islands burst from the clutching waves with names to be branded upon our empty tongues, lovely and evil names, the names of serpents. Gan, Willingilli, Hittadu, Maradu, Midu, Fedu, Heratera. Scene for an episode of sweat, disease and dismal dying. Sleek cocoon for the waiting typhus born of the angered rats brought to earth from the crashing jungle palms. There are no crosses, no romantic helmets resting on the soggy cross-piece. The sea, the anatomist, dissected with blunt knives our canvas covered comrades. The red equator cut across the atoll water …
>
> On Gan of the Maldives we fought the jungle and the sweeping rain for space and breath. The white tents hugged the shore, bound by the lifting glare from the brilliant coral sand. The trees dipped. Husks of coconuts bred our death. Our leather became a brown, pulpy paste. The locks rotted and fell from our mouldering baggage. The coral sand launched a cankering invasion of the human ear. No animal lived, no crop breathed, the fish swam deep. Only the coconut thrived …
>
> Tinned salmon, bully beef, tea. For months. Appetizing, nourishing, sustaining. Cold and tepid. Covered with our breeding flies. Seething and copulating on the open tin. Rags and handkerchiefs salt with sweat, the crutch cold and damp, the blistered armpits, fore-head a-rash with ceaseless itch. Prickly heat marching round the body in thickening red columns. Tinned salmon, bully beef, tea. And no mail.[26]

The high-ups also spent the war moving around the Indian Ocean region and beyond. General Sir Archibald Wavell oversaw fighting in East Africa and Iraq during his time as

23 John Masters, *The Road Past Mandalay* (London: Michael Joseph, 1961), p. 50.

24 J. Alan Thompson, *Only the Sun Remembers* (London: Andrew Dakers, 1950). He also wrote *In the East My Pleasure* (London: Andrew Dakers, 1949) and *Military Honours* (London: Fortune Books, 1946), a volume of poems.

25 Thompson, *Only the Sun Remembers*, p. 7.

26 J. Alan Thompson, *In the East My Pleasure* (London: Andrew Dakers, 1949), quoted in Alistair Currah, 'Gan – A Short History', RAF Gan Remembered, at http://www.gan.philliptsmall.me.uk/00%20-%20Articles/GanAHistory.htm

Commander-in-Chief Middle East, and then in Burma, the Dutch East Indies, and Malaya when he served as Commander-in-Chief India and, during its brief existence, Supreme Allied Commander American-British-Dutch-Australian (ABDA) Command. Air Chief Marshal Sir Robert Brooke-Popham started the war as Governor of Kenya and, after an advisory spell in South Africa, found himself on the other side of the Indian Ocean when he became Commander-in-Chief Far East, based in Singapore. Lieutenant General Henry Pownall spent much of the war in the region too, succeeding Brooke-Popham at Far East Command before serving variously as Commander-in-Chief Persia and Iraq, Chief of Staff of ABDA Command, General Officer Commanding Ceylon, and Chief of Staff to South East Asia Command. General Sir William Slim, meanwhile, progressed around the Indian Ocean rim, starting out in East Africa before migrating to Iran and Iraq before assuming the role that would make him a household name, commanding the Fourteenth Army in Burma.

As for individuals both high and low, the same was true for military formations; some spent their entire war career shuttling between destinations east of Suez, while others roamed more widely, experiencing Arctic conditions as well as jungle and desert warfare. An example of the former was the RAF's 244 Squadron, originally formed in August 1939 as a communications flight for service in Iraq, based at RAF Shaiba near Basra, from where it took part in the Anglo-Iraq war of May 1941. In spring 1942 it moved down the Gulf to RAF Sharjah in an anti-submarine role, before moving to RAF Masirah on Masirah Island in 1944, where it disbanded in May 1945. An example of the latter is the British Army's 5th Division, elements of which saw service in Madagascar, India, Iran, and Iraq, sandwiched between periods in Norway and Italy. The RAF's 11 Squadron, flying Blenheims, began the war in Singapore before being diverted to Aden to take part in the East Africa campaign, bombing targets in Eritrea and Ethiopia. It spent late 1940 and early 1941 supporting operations in the Mediterranean and the Middle East, including the Anglo-Soviet invasion of Iran. The squadron then moved to Ceylon, arriving just in time to mount an attack on the Japanese fleet as it steamed towards the island in early April 1942. It remained on high alert until January 1943, when it transferred to Calcutta in anticipation of operations in Burma. Re-equipping with Hurricanes, the squadron moved to the Arakan, where it was stationed until June 1945. It was then back to India for re-equipment with Spitfires and preparation for the attack on Malaya, to be mounted from the flight deck of the escort carrier *Trumpeter*.[27] Some American units also experienced a period of Indian Ocean itinerancy: soldiers of 835th Signal Service Battalion, for instance, saw service variously in Asmara, Bangalore, Bihar, Bombay, Cairo, Calcutta, Gura, Karachi, Lashio, New Delhi, Port Sudan, Ramgarh, and Sharjah.[28]

* * *

Though rarely afforded the status of a distinct theatre of Second World War activity, the Indian Ocean's centrality was understood by Winston Churchill and the Chiefs of Staff, commanders deployed to the region to fight the war, and American strategists and planners. Conversely,

27 Peter Dancey, *South East Asia Command* (Bromley: Galago Books, 2004), p. 2. Finally, in April 1946, it moved to Japan as part of the Commonwealth Occupation Force.

28 John Hawkins and Ward Hawkins, *History of the 835th Signal Service Battalion, 1942–1946* (World War Two Operational Documents, 1946).

though some Axis politicians, diplomats, and commanders appreciated the opportunity the Indian Ocean afforded to fracture the Allied war effort, they failed at the strategic level to grasp its significance, or were unable to get those responsible for the highest levels of war direction to do so before it was too late and the window of opportunity flung open in late 1941 began to close.

On 23 February 1942, a little over two months after entering the war, President Roosevelt addressed the American people in one of his 'fireside chat' radio broadcasts. His purpose was to explain how the war was progressing and why, regrettably, it had to be fought. Adopting a didactic as well as an avuncular tone, the president asked families across America to have ready a map of the world, so that they could locate the places he mentioned during the broadcast and perceive for themselves the logic of global supply lines and the dispersed nature of the enemy threat:

> This is a new kind of war. It is different from all other wars of the past, not only in its methods of weapons but also in its geography. It is warfare in terms of every continent, every island, every sea, every air lane in the world … The broad oceans which have been heralded in the past as our protection from attack have become endless battlefields on which we are constantly being challenged by our enemies. We must understand and face the hard fact that our job now is to fight at distances which extend all the way around the globe. We fight at these vast distances because that is where our enemies are. Until our flow of supplies gives us clear superiority we must keep on striking our enemies wherever and whenever we can meet them, even if, for a while, we have to yield ground … We must fight at these vast distances to protect our supply lines and our lines of communication with our allies – protect these lines from the enemies who are bending every ounce of their strength, striving against time, to cut them. The object of the Nazis and the Japanese is to separate the United States, Britain, China, and Russia, and to isolate them one from another, so that each will be surrounded and cut off from sources of supplies and reinforcements.[29]

The Indian Ocean was a key arena in which this 'cutting' could well take place. The following three chapters, forming Part 1 of the book, demonstrate just how these supply lines, comprised of ships, sea lanes, and the ports they connected, were utilized and developed as war came to the African and Indian Ocean regions.

29 Text reproduced on the 'American Presidency Project' website at http://www.presidency.ucsb.edu/ws/index.php?pid=16224

Part 1

The islands, ports, and sea lanes of Africa and the Indian Ocean

2

Africa's ports and sea lanes: West Africa

Part 1 provides a 'How It Worked' view of a system of imperial defence in which islands, ports, and sea lanes supported operational and strategic endeavours, a system in which colonial harbours were the must-have military shunting yards of the imperial war effort.[1] The perspectives offered in Part 1 advance scholarship relating to Africa and the Indian Ocean during the war by providing a unique overview of the extraordinary extent of military activity in these key regions. In order to make an original archival contribution, the chapters focus on a number of particular ports and islands using material drawn from numerous files stored at the British national archives. The records were variously produced by the Admiralty, Air Ministry, Colonial Office, Foreign Office, Government Code and Cipher School, and War Office. The selected locations featured here and in the following two chapters include Addu Atoll (Maldives), Bathurst (Gambia), Diego Garcia (Chagos Archipelago), Kilindini (Kenya), Pamanzi (Comoros), Tuléar (Madagascar), Massawa (Eritrea), Fernando Pó (Gulf of Guinea), and Port Sudan (Sudan). The rationale behind their selection is that other locations, such as Cape Town, Durban, Freetown, Madagascar, Mauritius, and the Seychelles, already have relatively well developed published histories regarding their wartime experience. While they are

1 The role of Africa in the war, and the islands of the Indian Ocean, is extensively covered in Ashley Jackson, *The British Empire and the Second World War*, chapter 9, 'Sub-Saharan Africa', chapter 10, 'The Indian Ocean', and chapter 11, 'The Islands of the Indian Ocean'. Extensive coverage of the military campaigns in Africa is provided in Richard Osborne, *World War Two in Colonial Africa* (Indianapolis: Riebel-Roque, 2001). A landmark study comprising numerous chapters examining aspects of Africa's wartime social, economic, industrial, cultural, and political history is Judith Byfield, Carolyn Brown, Timothy Parsons, and Ahmad Sikaingi (eds), *Africa and World War Two* (Cambridge: Cambridge University Press, 2015). For a predecessor volume, see David Killingray and Richard Rathbone (eds), *Africa and the Second World War* (Basingstoke: Macmillan, 1986). See also *Africa and the Second World War: Reports and Papers of the Symposium Organized by UNESCO at Benghazi, Libyan Arab Jamahiriya, from 10 to 13 November 1980* (Paris: UNESCO, 1985). Africa has been well served by numerous book-length single country studies on the impact of the Second World War. To take but two recent examples, Nancy Lawler, *Soldiers, Airmen, Whisperers, and Spies: The Gold Coast in World War II* (Athens, OH: Ohio University Press, 2002) and Alfred Tembo, 'The Impact of the Second World War on Northern Rhodesia (Zambia), 1939-1953, Ph. D. Thesis (University of the Free State, 2015), available at http://scholar.ufs.ac.za:8080/xmlui/bitstream/handle/11660/4561/TemboA.pdf?sequence=1&isAllowed=y

afforded some coverage here, the selected case studies have very little (if any) published record of their wartime functions.

Examining these places provides valuable new insights into just how important African and Indian Ocean islands, ports, and sea lanes were to the Allied war effort. It reveals an astonishingly intricate military and logistical system, in which activity in one area depended on facilities in another, and so on. All links in the chain were vital if the system was to work successfully in support of multiple fighting fronts in a global conflict. Apparently peripheral military activity on, say, a distant lagoon or coastal airstrip was always part of a network of military provision and was directly linked to global logistics and military operations taking place nearby or hundreds, even thousands, of miles away. For example, air patrols mounted from Gambian bases provided cover for Allied convoys travelling between the east and west, handing over to escort and patrol aircraft based in Sierra Leone and South Africa as those convoys moved around Africa's coastline. They were destined, perhaps, for the Red Sea to deliver men and material for the Western Desert, or voyaging onwards to Basra, Bombay, Rangoon, or Singapore. In the global military system developed by Britain and its allies, small cogs were crucial if the big wheels were to turn. The extensive archives charting the wartime expansion and development of places such as Bathurst, Massawa, Port Sudan, Trincomalee, and Umm Qasr offer a vivid impression of the complexity, scale, and significance of the infrastructure offered by colonial ports, vital yet seldom acknowledged in general war literature and even specialist works on logistics and military operations.[2]

In beseeching the British government not to lose sight of the importance of the war in the Southern Hemisphere, South African premier Jan Smuts sent his old friend Winston Churchill an essay entitled 'The strategical outlook'. Dated 22 June 1940, the day the French formally surrendered, it offered a prescient appreciation of the interconnectivity of wartime theatres of operations and Britain's even more numerous zones of imperial responsibility. Smuts expressed his fear that while Britain would survive the war, the price to pay would be the loss of the Empire, particularly through neglect of positions in Africa and the Indian Ocean region. 'Europe has ceased to be a war theatre on any large scale', Smuts wrote. 'Great Britain now becomes a vast fortress'. If its defence were properly conducted and sea power kept the Atlantic open, 'I do not see how she can be beaten'. The threat, Smuts believed, was that

> Great Britain may herself win through but lose her Empire and Commonwealth. While winning on the inner front [i.e. within Europe] she may be beaten on the Empire and World front. This was what happened to the French Empire in the 18th Century … The risk is that England dominated by danger at home, which she will overcome, may lose sight of the larger situation which makes her the great world power which she is, and which is so essential to the future of the world.[3]

2 Umm Qasr was developed by the British and Americans during the war. See Daniel Silverfarb, 'The British Government and the Question of Umm Qasr, 1938–1945', *Asian and African Studies*, 16, 2 (1982).

3 The National Archives (henceforth TNA), CAB 67/4/15. 'The Strategical Outlook', War Cabinet memorandum by the Secretary of State for Dominion Affairs. An exchange of telegrams between Smuts and Churchill. Smuts to Churchill, 22/6/40.

Japan, Smuts's sweeping strategic rumination continued, 'in her present blind expansionist temper may consider this the right moment to eliminate the British factor from the Far East, Hong Kong, British interests in China, French Indo-China and Burma, possibly Singapore, perhaps the Dutch East Indies'. Then there was the German menace. The 'German army threat to Africa and the Near East', he said, stemmed from the fact that

> Germany will join Italy in North Africa, conquer French Mediterranean colonies, capture Egypt and Suez and then begin to drive down Africa until if the war lasts long enough they have mastered the African continent. It will give Germany a vast tropical empire, gold and minerals in Southern Africa and a strategic position which will eventually mean world empire. If both Egypt and South Africa are lost India will also be lost and Australia and New Zealand cut off to fall within American or Japanese spheres in the future. Great Britain although saving herself at home will cease to be a world power and a beneficial force. Her essential supplies will be cut off.[4]

Smuts concluded by underlining the need to defend Africa south of the equator, even if there were losses further north and in the Mediterranean. The 'Empire was founded and reached its zenith on the Cape route not on [the] later precarious Suez route ... Southern Africa is not a side show but a vital area of the Empire'.[5] Smuts was right, because the Cape, and the ability to transit the Atlantic and Indian oceans, was in the final analysis an indispensable aspect of imperial survival.

Between 1939 and 1945 numerous African ports and islands acquired military and strategic prominence, particularly because of their proximity to key sea lanes and the access that they gave to overland (i.e. air, road, rail, and river) routes that were logistically essential for the movement of military goods and for delivering military effect to the battlefield. Sea lanes off the coast of Africa conveyed military personnel and equipment from one part of the world to another, or from one part of a moving zone of combat to another as, for example, operations moved back and forth along the coastlines of East and North Africa during the campaigns in those areas. Sea lanes around Africa were also important for the maintenance of Allied trade, which the enemy wanted to impede and if possible cause to desist (and, ultimately, acquire for itself). Africa's strategic resources needed to be utilized by belligerents while at the same time denied to enemies, continuing the longstanding colonial practice of resource extraction. Conflict in Africa was exacerbated by the fact that some of the major belligerents possessed African colonies that were a source of military competition; Italy attacked British colonies, for example, which eventually sucked in American and German forces, and the British in turn attacked and blockaded Vichy French and Italian colonies. All of these factors meant that Africa was the scene of extensive military action. Sustained fighting took place in the north and the east, and smaller, shorter military operations occurred in parts of West Africa, the Horn of Africa, and islands such as Fernando Pó and Madagascar. African ports and the facilities that developed in and around them were used as military bases and for a range of war-related tasks such as intelligence gathering, surveillance, cable and wireless

4 Ibid.
5 Ibid.

communication, and radar direction finding, and provision had to be made across British Africa to defend territory lest the invader come.

Sea lanes, commands, and bases

On all points of the compass, the African continent was enveloped by important sea lanes. They extended through the Mediterranean, around the bulge of West Africa and the Cape of Good Hope, and along Africa's eastern seaboard through the Mozambique Channel and on towards the Red Sea and the Suez Canal. Africa hosts four of the world's great maritime choke points: the Pillars of Hercules, gateway to the Mediterranean, the Cape, the Bab-el-Mandeb, and the Suez Canal. Control of the waters of the Mediterranean was heavily circumscribed by the enemy following Italy's turn to war in June 1940. This meant that the Gulf of Guinea, the Mozambique Channel, Cape Agulhas, the Cape, and the Red Sea became indispensable to a British and Allied war effort dependent upon sea transport. Ships sailing between the eastern and western hemispheres needed to work their way around the continent. Africa's eastern seaboard and its offshore islands were part of an extensive network of sea lanes and port bases stretching across the Indian Ocean to the Persian Gulf, the Bay of Bengal, Malaya, and the East Indies. The Cape and the Red Sea were key waterways, while West African ports were crucial variables in the security matrix of the Atlantic and the all-important battle to protect the convoys sailing between Britain and the Americas, as well as those sailing towards or returning from destinations east of the African continent.

Conducting military operations required ports into which men and materiel transported across the oceans from home ports of embarkation could be decanted. Andrew Stewart describes the scale and significance of Africa's coastline:

> [It] covers in excess of 16,000 miles and at the start of the Second World War there were eighty-eight harbours that were protected from wind and sea on all sides and were spacious enough and had sufficient depth to accommodate a considerable number of large, ocean-going vessels simultaneously. At this stage British control extended to thirty-seven percent of the total African coastline and within this there were a total of 32 of these 'first-class' maritime ports, a combination of undeveloped and developed natural facilities – most notably Freetown in Sierra Leone and Port Sudan in Anglo-Egyptian Sudan – and a number that had been artificially developed such as at Simon's Town in the Union of South Africa and Takoradi on the Gold Coast. Along the whole of the Indian Ocean coast from central Mozambique northward along Tanganyika and Kenya to the boundary of Italian Somaliland there were a total of 14 of these most highly sought after harbours. Not including East London and Durban, once again in the Union, there were seven others either under direct British control or within the territory of one of its Dominion partners that faced towards the Indian Ocean.[6]

6 From Andrew Stewart, '"This Temporary Strategic Withdrawal": The Eastern Fleet's Wartime African Sojourn', in Craig C. Felker and Marcus O. Jones (eds), *New Interpretations in Naval History: Selected Papers for the Sixteenth Naval History Symposium Held at the United States Naval Academy, 10–11 September 2009* (Newport: Naval War College Press, 2012).

Illustrating the continent's strategic importance, Africa was home to major British and Allied military command structures, often headquartered in port cities. Middle East Command was headquartered in the Egyptian capital Cairo (though some thought it should be moved to Alexandria). As the war spread across the Maghreb and America entered the fray, Allied Force Headquarters North Africa was established in Algiers.[7] West Africa Command was established in Accra in 1940, recruiting 200,000 soldiers and supervising the transformation of the region into one capable of supporting frontline theatres further east while defending itself against potential Vichy aggression. East Africa Command covered East Africa, the Horn of Africa, and British Central Africa, created in 1941 to relieve pressure on the overstretched Middle East Command. Headquartered in Nairobi, it in turn spawned a subsidiary command – Islands Area Command – with headquarters in Diego Suarez in Madagascar, and it took over responsibility for Madagascar, Mauritius, Réunion, Rodrigues and the Seychelles.[8] Military minutiae, one might think. But in a global war, such microsystems were connected to bigger systems of trade, logistics, and offensive and defensive operations, and they defined the manner in which the war worked at the local level.

Other African ports hosted strategic and operational level command structures and their attendant forces. Given the proximity of Italian air bases, the Royal Navy's Mediterranean Fleet and its headquarters moved to Alexandria shortly before the outbreak of war. After the Japanese raids on Ceylon in April 1942, the headquarters and main base of the Royal Navy's Eastern Fleet, responsible for guarding the sea lanes of the Indian Ocean, retreated to Kilindini Island in Mombasa in Kenya. On the outbreak of war in September 1939 the Royal Navy's Africa Command, based at Simon's Town in South Africa, was renamed South Atlantic Command, and its headquarters moved to Freetown in Sierra Leone.[9] In August 1942 a new naval command, West Africa Command, was established at Freetown in recognition of that port's growing importance as a major base for convoy assembly and escort, and the headquarters of South Atlantic Command reverted to Simon's Town. Extensive use was made of South

7 The British and Allied command structures of the Second World War have received surprisingly little scholarly attention, and histories of formations such as East Africa Command, Middle East Command, and South East Asia Command are long overdue. For Allied Forces Command North Africa, there exists a very helpful contemporary record, the 'History of Allied Force Headquarters', published in three parts by the command itself in 1945 and available online at https://archive.org/details/HistoryOfAlliedForceHeadquartersPart3December1943-July1944

8 This command was formed in September 1942 when the Indian Ocean islands were transferred from India Command and conjoined for command purposes with Madagascar. Lieutenant-General Sir William Platt, General Officer Commanding in Chief, East Africa, 'Operations of East Africa Command 12 July 1941 to 8 January 1943', *Supplement to The London Gazette*, 37655 (1946). Part five, 'Madagascar, Mauritius, Rodriquez, and Seychelles'. This report was proceeded by General Sir Archibald Wavell, Commander-in-Chief in the Middle East, 'Operations in East Africa, November 1940-July 1941', *Supplement to the London Gazette*, 37645 (1946).

9 The location of naval commands and the forces attached to them can be difficult to ascertain, particularly away from the main overseas fleets such as the Mediterranean Fleet, the Eastern Fleet, and the British Pacific Fleet. A very useful guide, embracing all Royal Navy commands during the war and the strength of the forces attached to them, is to be found in Graham Watson's 'Organization of the Royal Navy, 1939-1945', on the Royal-Navy.net website at http://www.naval-history.net/xGW-RNOrganisation1939-45.htm. For material discussed here, see the section 'Africa Command/South Atlantic Command, 1939-1942'. The Eastern Fleet, responsible for the Indian Ocean, is discussed in much greater detail later in this book.

African naval bases, harbours, and shipyards by both the Royal Navy and the South African Naval Force. Cape Town and the naval base at Simon's Town were frequent staging posts for warships, troopships, and merchantmen, the latter also acting as a base for submarines and warships operating in the South Atlantic, Indian Ocean, and Southern Ocean as Axis raiders and submarines were hunted and convoys protected.[10] Durban was an important point of call and a major repair base, as well as the springboard for the British invasion of Madagascar. The Cape route attained a status unknown since the opening of the Suez Canal because of the closure of the Mediterranean and the enemy threat to the canal. The entire British and Allied position thus depended on the Cape route, and it was heavily used; for example, the 52 separate 'Winston Special' convoys that sailed between Britain and the east via the Cape and other South African ports comprised a total of 458 troopships carrying 1,173,010 British and Allied military personnel.[11]

Imperial and Allied air power was deployed across Africa and the Indian Ocean region, including Fleet Air Arm assets flying from aircraft carriers or deployed ashore, and shore-based aircraft of the RAF, the South African Air Force, the US Army Air Force, and other air forces. RAF Coastal Command maintained a presence in West Africa for Atlantic operations, and squadrons of Catalina flying-boats were stationed in South Africa to extend the range of searches for enemy vessels. East Africa was home to an RAF group dedicated to Indian Ocean patrols and searches in conjunction with the ships of the Eastern Fleet.[12] The RAF's 246 Wing comprised three Catalina flying-boat squadrons (209, 259, and 265) which patrolled the Indian Ocean from March 1942 until the end of the war from bases in Africa and the islands of the Indian Ocean.[13] There was a major base at Kipevu in Mombasa and detached bases in Aden, Diego Suarez, Kurasini Creek (Dar-es-Salaam), Masirah, Mauritius, Oman, the Seychelles, and Tuléar (Madagascar). These flying-boats also used bases in South Africa at Congella in Durban harbour, Langebaan in the Western Cape, Lake St Lucia in Natal, and Lake Umsingazi at Richards Bay, also in Natal.[14] Not only Africa's islands, ports, and sea lanes, but even its lakes, lagoons, and coastal waters assumed operational importance during the war.

Given their importance at both strategic and operational levels, it is no surprise that military action occurred in and around Africa's ports. In September 1940 the British and Free French raided Dakar in a failed attempt to acquire the important colony of Senegal for the Allied cause, and to secure a port better located and better equipped than Freetown for the tasks of Atlantic

10 L. C. F. Turner, H. R. Gordon-Cumming, and J. E. Beltzer, *War in the Southern Oceans, 1939-1945* (Cape Town, 1961). See also Arthur Banks, *Wings of the Dawning: The Battle for the Indian Ocean, 1939-1945* (Malvern: Images, 1996).

11 Archie Munro, *The Winston Specials: Troopships via the Cape, 1940-1943* (Liskeard: Maritime Books, 2005), p. 430.

12 An RAF group would control several stations or wings, to which squadrons were attached.

13 As is the way of these things as people age, the Indian Ocean Flying-Boat Association, made up of former service men and women who worked at and flew from the RAF flying-boat bases across the region during the war, was wound up in 2012. Its website, however, remains live for the sake of the historical record, and can be found at http://www.flyingboats.org.uk/ There were 32 flying-boat bases spread across the Indian Ocean from East Africa via Aden, Ceylon and other islands and achipelagos to India, Burma, Malaya, and Singapore.

14 RAF Historical Branch, '259 Squadron', at http://www.raf.mod.uk/history/259squadron.cfm. Langebaan lagoon and Saldanha Bay were used by warships and flying-boats. See TNA, ADM 1/15278. Defence of Saldanha Bay against midget submarines and human torpedo attack.

convoy protection.[15] As the Chiefs of Staff, Britain's three most senior serving military officers, put it, seizing Dakar was 'the only complete counter to the threat of German penetration of French West Africa'.[16] On North African shores, meanwhile, Alexandria was the scene of a costly (for the British) Italian attack in December 1941 in which three human torpedoes and a submarine seriously damaged two British battleships, a destroyer, and a tanker, swinging the naval balance in the Mediterranean temporarily in favour of the Axis (and severely hindering the Admiralty's concentration of major fleet units in the Indian Ocean to try and deal with the Japanese threat). The port of Mers El Kébir in Algeria was the site of a grisly episode in which the Royal Navy reluctantly attacked a heavy concentration of the French fleet in order to prevent it from falling into German hands and to demonstrate Britain's resolve to fight on against the dictators, killing over 1,200 French mariners in the process.[17] Madagascar was invaded in May 1942 in order to prise the port of Diego Suarez from Vichy control, an operation later extended to capture the ports of Majunga and Tamatave, and enemy submarines targeted British, Allied, and neutral shipping off South Africa's major ports.

Tobruk in Libya was a pivotal port in the struggle between British and Axis forces that extended from Egypt to Tunisia, because it allowed armies to be supplied as they fought along the coastal strip where the major towns, roads, and supply lines were concentrated.[18] The surrender of its 33,000-strong imperial garrison in June 1942 stunned Churchill, the War Cabinet, and the Chiefs of Staff.[19] Benghazi, another strategically important Libyan port, changed hands between British and Axis forces no fewer than five times during the fighting that extended back and forth along the coast of the Maghreb between 1940 and 1943. The

15 See Arthur Marder, *Operation Menace: The Dakar Expedition and the Dudley North Affair* (Oxford: Oxford University Press, 1976). Dakar is the scene of an adventure for the fictional Guy Crouchback and Brigadier Ritchie-Hooke in Evelyn Waugh's *Men at Arms* (London: Chapman and Hall, 1952), part of the *Sword of Honour* trilogy (and Apthorpe dies in Freetown). Graham Greene served in Freetown during the war, a period of his life that inspired the novel *The Heart of the Matter* (London: William Heinemann, 1948). John Harris's *A Funny Place to Hold a War* (London: Hutchinson, 1984) is another novel set in wartime Sierra Leone, as the British attempt to deal with Nazi saboteurs intent on disrupting Allied sea lanes.

16 TNA, CAB 66/28/1, Appreciation of the Military Situation in West Africa, War Cabinet report by the Chiefs of Staff, 21/8/42.

17 See Warren Tute, *The Deadly Stroke* (New York: Coward, McGann, and Geoghegan, 1973), published in Britain by Pan in 1976, recently republished by Pen and Sword, 2007. Also, Raymond Dannreuther, *Somerville's Force H: The Royal Navy's Gibraltar-Based Fleet, June 1940-March 1942* (London: Aurum Press, 2005).

18 There are numerous books (not to mention films) on Tobruk, its significance, and the sieges. See Robert Lyman, *The Longest Siege: Tobruk – The Battle that Saved North Africa* (London: Macmillan, 2009).

19 Text of the speech at the *Bulletin of International News*, 19, 14 (11 July 1942), at https://www.jstor.org/stable/25643275?seq=1#page_scan_tab_contents. Churchill was at the White House with President Roosevelt in his study when the news came in. 'Presently a telegram was put into the President's hands. He passed it to me without a word. It said "Tobruk has surrendered, with twenty-five thousand men take prisoner". This was so surprising that I could not believe it ... This was one of the heaviest blows I can recall during the war'. In particular, along with the surrender of 85,000 men at Singapore six months earlier, it was the reputation of British arms, as well as the 'grievous' military effects, that so staggered him. 'I did not attempt to hide from the President the shock I had received. It was a bitter moment. Defeat is one thing; disgrace is another'. Winston Churchill, *The Second World War*, volume 4, *The Hinge of Fate* (London: Cassell, 1951), pp. 343-44.

Anglo-American invasion of Algeria and Morocco in November 1942 heralded the arrival of over 100,000 Allied troops at Algiers, Casablanca, Oran, and Safi. This invasion initiated the final phase of the fighting in Africa, Axis forces eventually being overwhelmed. They surrendered in May 1943 following the capture of the port cities of Bizerte and Tunis. In the Horn of Africa, the British placed a land and sea cordon around the French port of Djibouti, from where Vichy sympathizers had provided information on Allied convoys transiting the Red Sea. It is clear that African ports and coastal waters featured prominently during the war, and what follows is a more focused investigation of precisely what this meant, beginning in West Africa.

Bathurst, Freetown, Takoradi, and Fernando Pó

Seldom do War Cabinet minutes or the memoirs of politicians and senior officers involved with strategic planning fail to mention West Africa, particularly in the first three years of the war. In the same breath as they discussed challenges in the Middle East and the Empire's precarious position in the Far East, they would also mention West Africa, so important was it to the security of the Atlantic, communications with the east, and the global movement of trade goods and military resources. Given this, the possibility of enemy attempts to seize West Africa or sabotage Britain's position there presented Whitehall with one of the innumerable strategic headaches brought on by a global war. In May 1941 Major General Sir John Kennedy, Director of Military Operations at the War Office, was visited by General Sir George Giffard, Commander-in-Chief West Africa. 'We had to consider', wrote Kennedy, 'the possibility that the war might move down into his parish, if the Germans occupied French North Africa'.[20] In his 'Notes on the next phase of the war', composed that same month, Kennedy wrote: 'In West Africa we should have far stronger defences at Freetown, and we should have sufficient forces on the spot to be able to advance to the line of the Senegal River, which is the best line on which to hold German penetration from the north'.[21]

A War Cabinet report by the Chiefs of Staff entitled 'Appreciation of the military situation in West Africa' sketched the region's importance:

> West Africa owes its strategic significance principally to its geographical position relative to the Central Atlantic 'waistline' through which pass shipping routes to West and South Africa, South America, the Middle East, India and Australia, as well as those between

20 John Kennedy, *The Business of War: The War Narrative of Major-General Sir John Kennedy, GCMG, KCVO,KBE, CB, MC* (London: Hutchinson, 1957), p. 119.

21 Ibid., p. 131. In a letter to General Sir Claude Auchinleck quoted by Kennedy, General Sir John Dill, Chief of the Imperial General Staff, wrote: 'You know, too, what the essentials are in our great picture – to hold England, retain a position in the Middle East, maintain a firm hold in Malaya and keep open our sea communications, which last-named involves such things as continuing to be able to use West Africa'. Ibid., p. 136. In his 'Strategy in the Middle East' note prepared for Dill in June 1941, Kennedy wrote that maintaining such forces as Britain had in the Middle East 'constitutes a drain on our resources which we can ill afford in the face of the threat to the British Isles and to ill-defended key points, in particular, West Africa and Malaya'. Ibid., p. 137.

> Germany and Japan. Freetown is of particular importance as a bunkering and convoy assembly port half-way between the United Kingdom and the Cape.[22]

Britain's ability to control the sea lanes of the Central Atlantic depended, the report continued, upon 'retention for our own use of the Naval base at Freetown, together with subsidiary fuelling bases at Bathurst and Pointe Noire, and their associated air bases', and the 'denial of similar facilities to the enemy in this area (*e. g.*, at Dakar)'. There were at the time two British and one American air route across West Africa, 'essential to the air reinforcement of Middle East and India', a significant example of ports acting as points of access for overland supply routes stretching across thousands of miles.

> While we are unable to use Malta as a staging point, and so long as our forward aerodromes lie east of El Alamein, Bathurst will remain a key point in our medium bomber route to the Middle East and India. Without it we would be unable to deliver these aircraft from the United Kingdom and their conveyance by sea is impractical.[23]

The German submarine threat was significant, but limited by distance from bases and the existence of more attractive targets elsewhere.

Available defence forces at the time the report was written in August 1942 included seven West African infantry brigades, one-and-a-half Hurricane squadrons divided between Freetown, Kaduna, and Takoradi, two flying-boat squadrons, and a Hudson squadron. There were also some Free French and Belgian assets, and an American fighter squadron 'manned by negro personnel' was due in Liberia. In addition, 'there are always about forty-five fighters and fourteen bombers operationally serviceable at Takoradi or along the air route which could be diverted for defence purposes'.[24] At sea, the navy's West Africa Command, just established shortly before the report was written, could call on the eight destroyers of the 18th Destroyer Flotilla, two sloops, and 23 corvettes.[25]

A report compiled by American naval intelligence in November 1942 summed up the problem faced by the Allies in the West Africa region: 'The West Coast of AFRICA is handicapped by a lack of harbour and port facilities. With the exception of the natural harbors of FREETOWN, SIERRA LEONE, LAGOS and PORT HARCOURT, NIGERIA, and the artificial harbor at TAKORADI, GOLD COAST, there are practically no facilities for unloading cargoes'.[26] Freetown, therefore, became a vital port.[27] The British had started preparing the city for war in

22 TNA, CAB 66/28/1, Appreciation of the Military Situation in West Africa. The report also noted Britain's economic interest in West Africa's valuable resources.

23 Ibid.

24 Ibid.

25 Watson, 'Organization of the Royal Navy'.

26 National Archives and Records Administration (hereafter NARA), Washington. RG165, Box 2892, US War Department (Sierra Leone – Regional Files, 1942-1944). Intelligence Report of the Navy Department, from US Naval Observer at Freetown, 9 November 1942 'Sierra Leone – Wharves and Jetties of Freetown Harbor'.

27 Wartime Freetown has been the subject of several studies. See Andrew Stewart, 'The Second World and the "Quiet Colony" of Sierra Leone', in Ashley Jackson, Yasmin Khan, and Gajendra Singh (eds), *An Imperial World at War: Aspects of the British Empire's War Experience, 1939-1945*

1938 and in the following year began a 'comprehensive militarization'. The origin or destination port for no fewer than 32 convoy routes, it was a peacetime backwater transformed by war into a major hub.[28] It was 'central to Allied strategy for several years, primarily as a convoy station', and was one of the most important bunkering sites in the Atlantic region.[29] As the American report explained:

> FREETOWN in normal times is no more than a small trading post and fuelling station. However, it is now very active as all convoys going around AFRICA stop here for fuel. There are several convoys in port at one time. The harbour is used for assembling convoys for north and south routing ... Approximately seventy-five to 150 freighters and several tankers are standing in the harbour at all times.[30]

Capable of accommodating up to 250 ocean-going vessels, Freetown now came into its own. 'During the peak period, up to 200 cargo and military vessels might be moored in Freetown's wide, well-protected harbour: Hundreds of convoys formed there, mostly Europe-bound, and many thousands of soldiers and sailors passed through the port'.[31] A June 1940 report considered the German threat to the region and the ramifications of French collapse in Europe. 'In the last event it is essential that the port of Freetown should be secured at all costs as a naval fuelling base', stated the directive given to General Giffard when he became Commander-in-Chief West Africa.[32] On a single day in 1941, 50 vessels steamed into its harbour. Throughout 1942, the importance of West Africa grew further, the region described in a Dominions Office telegram as a 'vital link in communications' and 'a source of essential supplies'.[33]

A wartime map of Freetown supplied to the American military by their British allies captured the scale of port facilities required for the operation of essential maritime activity.[34] World war necessitated the maintenance of a network of overseas bases, and this in turn necessitated the infrastructure and the forces with which to utilize and defend them. The map labelled key geographical features in and around Freetown, their names betraying the European colonization of this particular space: Cape Sierra Leone, Cockerill Bay, Bunce River, Bullom Shore, Destruction Bay, White Man's Bay, Pirate Bay, Aberdeen, and Kru Bay. It detailed the port's extensive facilities: the government headquarters, port war signal station, Cable and Wireless office, wireless telegraphy mast, boom defence jetty, man of war hulk, quarantine anchorage,

(London: Routledge, 2016); A. M. Howard 'Freetown and World War Two: Strategic Militarization, Accommodation, and Resistance', in Byfield et al, *Africa and World War Two*; and Gilbert Sekgoma, 'The Second World War and the Sierra Leone Economy: Labour Employment and Utilization', in Killingray and Rathbone (eds) *Africa and the Second World War*.

28 The following link details the 32 convoy routes to and from Freetown and gives their two or three letter code names. See http://www.convoyweb.org.uk/os33/freetn_conv.htm. (Accessed March 12, 2015).

29 A. Howard, 'Freetown and World War Two', p. 185.

30 NARA RG165, Box 2892. Intelligence Report of the Navy Department.

31 A. Howard, 'Freetown and World War Two', p. 183.

32 TNA, CAB 121/189. West Africa Command, Report on 'Defence of British Interests in West Africa', Joint Planning Sub-Committee, Chiefs of Staff, 22 June 1940. Annex: Directive to Lieutenant-General G. J. Giffard.

33 Ibid., Dominions Office to High Commissioner South Africa, 2/6/42.

34 NARA RG165, Box 2892. Intelligence Report of the Navy Department.

and emergency landing ground.[35] Torpedo nets guarded the harbour entrance and a channel running 20 miles out to sea was regularly searched by minesweepers.

The American intelligence report listed the location and capacity of all of Freetown's wharves and jetties. It noted, for example, that at the boom defence jetty at King Tom peninsula a new steel jetty was being constructed that would extend at a right-angle 100 feet from the shore and 300 feet in a north-easterly direction. Here it would be possible to berth a minelaying ship. The three jetties extending from Government Wharf were handling about 600 tons of supplies a day. Improvements were made to the main wharf and new facilities developed at Cline Town. In early 1944 there were 7,000 labourers engaged in building a new naval base at Kissy. There was a radar station at Cape Sierra Leone, a runway under construction at Makeni and a landing field at Port Loko, defended by an infantry battalion. Waterloo aerodrome 15 miles north of Freetown was defended by two Vickers machine-guns, two eighteen-pounders, two 3.7-inch anti-aircraft guns, four Bofors, and an infantry company. There were additional landing fields at Bo, Daru, Hastings, and Wellington, and a seaplane base in the harbour. Heavy gun emplacements were built at Cockerill Point, Aberdeen Hill and elsewhere.

Stocks of fuel in Freetown were replenished from Lagos, where Shell held 3-4,000 tons of each grade of fuel. Bunker oil and diesel oil were available in large quantities, brought in by tankers from Venezuela and the West Indies. There were always several oil tankers in port and when the American intelligence report was compiled in November 1942, there were 80,000 tons of oil ashore in tanks.[36] Water was in short supply, leading to the introduction of rationing and a large water gathering and delivery project. Ships in harbour were supplied from Charlotte Falls and to a limited extent from the City of Freetown's water supply. HMS *Invella* was a stationary Royal Navy water supply ship with a capacity of 2,200 tons. At Kissy East there were two 1,000 ton oil tanks used for water (one hopes they were thoroughly cleaned!) drawn from Charlotte Falls, while at Kissy Oil Jetty there were two 500 ton open water tanks. The Sierra Leone Coaling Company operated two water boats which watered ships at anchor in the harbour.

Extensive infrastructure and the concentration of supplies, clearly, was crucial to using such bases during wartime, and in turn this usage had implications for social and economic relations. Sustaining forces required food, causing competition for resources with local consumers, and concomitant inflation. The American report summarized the supply situation in Freetown, concluding that banana, papaya, pineapple, limes, oranges and sweet potatoes were available locally in fair quantity, though 'Irish' potatoes were unobtainable and meat scarce. In terms of human resources, the picture painted by the American observer was not encouraging:

> The natives are reported to be the least honest and reliable of all the tribes of WEST AFRICA. They are inclined to be insolent and troublesome … For the most part, labourers for unloading cargoes are inexperienced, uneducated, South African 'Blacks' who are slow and inefficient. However, some stevedores are 'Kru' men mostly from LIBERIA – tall, husky natives – who have spent most of their lives on the ocean and are efficient.[37]

35 Ibid. There was also a map of Pepel Island, seven miles off Freetown at the mouth of the Sierra Leone River, from where iron ore was exported.
36 NARA RG165, Box 2892. Intelligence Report of the Navy Committee.
37 Ibid.

These unfair, poorly informed, and biased opinions were based on ignorance and racial prejudice, and coloured by exceptional wartime conditions, which squeezed African communities while simultaneously allowing in-demand local labour to flex its muscles. The British also expressed concerns about the slow speed of dock work, a problem exacerbated by the rapid growth of traffic in and around Freetown and one common in docks around the world as the vicissitudes of war dramatically increased the cargoes that needed to be handled. The 'appalling congestion' afflicting Government Quay, for instance, was noted.[38] Plenty of ostensible 'solutions' were proffered by British service personnel; an officer from the repair ship *Vindictive* reported that there was 'insufficient white supervision' of African labour. If 'the coloured labour were forced to work', he opined, 'there would be a subsequent speed-up of 100%'.[39]

British military authorities in Freetown also recorded problems in the port, focusing on those relating to African labour, crime, and general challenges faced as traffic through the port and the numbers it accommodated expanded dramatically. The Commander-in-Chief of the Royal Navy's South Atlantic Station, Rear Admiral Algernon Willis, described Freetown and its environs as 'a foul place for sailors', lacking in amenities.[40] Steps were, however, being taken; in December 1941 the 4th Sea Lord was sending out seven buses to ferry sailors on leave to Lumley Beach, and two Seaman's Institutes had opened. There were other problems, too, such as those documented in a file entitled the 'Question of gangsterism and lawlessness in Freetown', containing reports on topics like 'Molestation and robbery of service personnel by Africans'.[41] There were many reported incidents of robbery, both on the streets and in private homes. At pains to emphasize that all servicemen understood that it was imperative not to strike a 'native' (thereby augmenting the desired impression of restraint on the part of military personnel), it was suggested that off-duty servicemen should be armed, and the local colonial police force was accused of inefficiency. Some officers advocated flogging to discourage robbery.

There were certain thieving hotspots, such as the environs of the Lion and Palm Tree Club and on Lumley Beach, from where bathers' clothes were regularly stolen and organized street robbery occurred. There were also incidents of gang fights between Africans and British servicemen. The Commander, Sierra Leone Area, told the governor that there had been 133 reported cases of larceny from British military personnel between April and July 1943, and there was also thieving in billets, camps, and residences. 'Burglary', it was reported, was 'a flourishing industry in Freetown and takes bungalows and messes of Service people in its unhampered stride'. As well as crime targeted at individuals and their homes and property, there was a problem with theft from government and military stores, including 'wholesale robberies' from Government Wharf and 'pilferage of Army and other service stores in transit' on a 'huge scale'.[42] British military authorities had to contend with other debilitating challenges, not least the prevalence of very high sick rates due to malaria, a disease that could not be overcome until proper

38 TNA, CAB 121/189, West Africa Command, Naval Intelligence Division Report 165, 16/4/42.
39 Ibid.
40 CAC, Papers of Admiral Sir Algernon U. Willis, WLLS 5/4. Willis to 2nd Sea Lord, 19/12/41.
41 TNA, CO 267/683/17. Report by the Staff Officer (Intelligence), Freetown, on increased lawlessness in Freetown: Molestation and robbery of service personnel by Africans, May 1943.
42 Ibid.

anti-malaria discipline was adopted and medical resources – such as a malaria laboratory which arrived in Freetown with a consignment of anti-aircraft guns – had been applied.[43]

American forces in West Africa

From 1942, America joined Britain in moving military resources across West Africa and building military installations. The population of Freetown continued to rise, the number of Europeans in Sierra Leone growing from about 400 to nearly 7,000. The war brought employment opportunities but also inflation, rationing, and strikes as well as racial, ethnic, and class tensions, illustrating the manifold ramifications of Allied build-ups in colonial and semi-colonial territories around the world. The threat of Axis attack was real early in the war and the population was subjected to precautionary air raid drills and black outs, as well as movement restrictions. First aid stations were opened, and sirens, drums, and bells were employed to alert people during practice raids, which included mock attacks from aircraft. One such rehearsal occurred as early as May 1940 and involved the aircraft carrier *Hermes*, then stationed in Freetown. With the Commander-in-Chief South Atlantic on board as an observer, as the ship left port the Swordfish of 814 Squadron Fleet Air Arm flew dummy raids to test the harbour defences, losing an aircraft and three crewmen due to a crash.[44]

American servicemen deployed to various West African locations, not least through wartime expansion in Liberia but also through the deployment of large numbers of troops to Accra and Takoradi in the Gold Coast. Takoradi was an important link in an Allied supply chain connecting the Americas and Britain to the Middle East and South Asia via a South Atlantic stop-off on Ascension island and a series of aerodrome and airstrips spanning the African continent.[45] This enormous supply network funnelled thousands of military aircraft from Britain and

43 See Andrew Stewart, 'Malaria: Sierra Leone's Other War', Defence-in-Depth blog post, 2015, available at https://defenceindepth.co/2015/04/27/malaria-sierra-leones-other-war/

44 Neil McCort, *HMS* Hermes *1923 and 1959* (Cheltenham, Gloucestershire: Fan Publications, 2001), p. 40. Chapter 4, 'Tragedy in the East June 1938-April 1942'. The first ever purpose-built aircraft carrier, she had spent much of the 1920s and 1930s on the China Station. At the start of the war she had been laid up in the Reserve Fleet following her participation in the Coronation Review of 1937, and few expected her ever to see active service again. Yet many of the 120 ships of the Reserve Fleet were called up when war began. *Hermes* sailed from Devonport, recommissioned under Captain F. E. P. Hutton, flew on the twelve Swordfish of 814 Squadron, and proceeded to West Africa, where she took part in operations around Dakar and Freetown. During the Dakar raid her aircraft took part in an operation at dawn on 8 May 1940 to torpedo the French battleship *Richelieu*, damaging her propellers and temporarily disabling her. The ship's motor boat also attacked the battleship. See chapter 4, '*Richelieu* and Corfu Incidents', in Rex Morgan, *The* Hermes *Adventure* (Manly, NSW: Runciman Press, 1985). After the Dakar raid she deployed to St Helena to join the search for the German pocket battleship *Admiral Scheer* and then led a convoy to Simon's Town, where she docked for repairs, and soon joined the East Indies Station.

45 See Deborah Wing Ray, 'The Takoradi Route: Roosevelt's Prewar Venture beyond the Western Hemisphere', *Journal of American History* 62, 2 (1975). See also F. Kenneth Hare, 'The Takoradi-Khartoum Air Route', *Climatic Change* 1, 2 (1977), written by Hare in 1943 for official purposes; Erik Benson, 'Suspicious Allies: Wartime Aviation Developments and the Anglo-American International Airline Rivalry, 1939-1945', *History and Technology: An International Journal* 17, 1 (2000); Yomi Akenyeye, 'The Air Factor in West Africa's Colonial Defence, 1920-1945: A Neglected Theme',

America via Brazil and Ascension to Takoradi, for onward conveyance across the belt of Africa to the Sudan and Egypt, to then either be used by Allied forces fighting in North Africa and the Middle East, or by Allied forces fighting in the China-Burma-India theatre. Many of these aircraft, which numbered nearly 10,000 in total, arrived at Takoradi by ship, packed in crates. They were then assembled at the airbase in a facility run by the RAF and used by the US Army Air Force, before beginning their journey along the Trans-African Ferry Route. The main 'air reinforcement route' as the British termed it ran from Bathurst to Khartoum, the 'relief route' from Takoradi to Khartoum. There was then a US Army Air Corps reinforcement route from Pointe Noire in French Equatorial Africa to Mombasa via the Congo. A projected further stage was to run via Mogadishu to Aden thence to Karachi and Khartoum.[46] Takoradi airbase was also home to the Wellington bombers of 26 Squadron South African Air Force, deployed on anti-submarine patrol and convoy protection duties.

Elsewhere on the West African coast, the Gambia, a sliver of territory either side of the eponymous river, had been a British colony since the eighteenth century. Its capital, Bathurst, was located on St Mary's Island and housed a subsidiary fuelling base employed by forces policing the Central Atlantic sea routes. The station had opened in December 1940 with the arrival of a flying-boat control unit, and it became an advanced operational base for Sunderland flying-boats of 95 Squadron RAF when they were working away from their home base at Freetown, 400 miles south. The Bathurst station was also used by British Overseas Airways Corporation flying-boats on the run between Britain and Lagos. Also based at Bathurst were military aircraft deployed on anti-submarine and convoy protection patrols. These forces included the eight Sunderlands of RAF Coastal Command's 204 Squadron, based there from July 1941 until the end of the war. A new RAF landing strip was established at Jeswang, located on the mainland opposite St Mary's Island.[47] In 1943 this new airbase became home to 200 Squadron RAF, its Hudson and Liberator aircraft dedicated to anti-submarine patrols and convoy escort. There was an additional airstrip at Yundum and a flying-boat base at Half Die Marine.[48] The Gambia's air bases also provided a stop-off point on the medium bomber air route to the Middle East and India from Europe and the Americas. Up to 100 American aircraft a month were handled here as they flew to the Middle East via Brazil and Bathurst.

The Americans had examined the possibility of opening a defended airbase in the Gambia as a staging post on the air route to the Middle East in the summer of 1941. The fact that the subsequent survey was conducted by President Franklin Roosevelt's son made noteworthy what would otherwise have been routine, setting British officialdom atwitter. London was keen to ensure that colonial and military authorities on the ground were as accommodating as possible, as this particular American visitor's report would likely command attention back in Washington. Prime Minister Winston Churchill set the tone, believing that an American base in the Gambia

Itinerario: International Journal on the History of European Expansion and Global Interaction 25, 1 (2001); William Stanley, 'The Trans-South Atlantic Air Link in World War Two', *GeoJournal* 33, 4 (1994); and Thomas Culbert, 'South Atlantic/Trans-Africa Air Route', in Walter Boyne (ed.), *Air Warfare: An International Encyclopaedia* (Santa Barbara: ABC-CLIO, 2002).

46 TNA, CAB 66/28/1, Appreciation of the Military Situation in West Africa, Appendix E, map of air routes.

47 TNA, AIR 2/4494, Overseas: Dominions and colonies: Bathurst, Gambia: Development for use by Beaufort squadron.

48 TNA, AIR 20/5474, Report of RAF Station Bathurst, August 1941.

would be yet another tie binding that country to the British war effort.[49] In a telegram to the president, Churchill said that he welcomed the proposal and envisaged extending the same kind of arrangement as that which had seen the lease of bases in the British West Indies in exchange for 50 old destroyers to help protect convoys in the Atlantic.[50]

But despite the keen interest of the prime minister, the visit did not go well, and there was concern lest the unfavourable impressions gained by Captain Elliott Roosevelt during his visit should unduly influence the thinking of the president and his administration. Officials in Whitehall lamented the condition of the 'old and somewhat squalid coast settlements' that Captain Roosevelt had visited. As a Colonial Office minute put it:

> It is a serious misfortune to us that the development of the air route to the East since the fall of France has brought into the limelight three of our most unattractive colonial towns. Lagos, Freetown, and Bathurst were never designed for the shop window: and the war has not improved their appearance. Accra, which relatively is a model of amenity and enlightenment, is unfortunately off the air route.[51]

The episode sparked a mixture of alarm and exasperation at the Colonial Office, and officials worried about the possible 'political motive behind American criticism'. Simultaneously, they fortified themselves with calls to 'advance to the attack' in the light of such criticism and devise propaganda to counter common American 'misperceptions' about British colonialism. This echoed wider thinking in Colonial Office and government circles as London sought to deal with incipient American anti-colonialism through argument and propaganda.[52]

Lord Swinton, Britain's Cabinet-ranking Resident Minister in West Africa, expressed concerns about rising American influence in the region later that same year, 1942. He was particularly perturbed by the apparent subordination of British to American interests in French West Africa, and the potential effects on the African population.[53] The Secretary of State for the

49 TNA, CO 968/46/1, Proposed American Airbase at Bathurst: Visit to the UK of Captain Roosevelt. See also CO 968/4/8, Bathurst aerodrome and CO 554/127/9, Naval defence of West Africa: Storage of ammunition at Bathurst. See also ADM 1/20706, Admiralty and Air Ministry oil installations Bathurst and AIR 29/449, Air-Sea Rescue Unit, Bathurst. Elliott Roosevelt was at the time charged with identifying potential airbases

50 TNA, PREM 3/502/1, US base at Bathurst.

51 Ibid., minute, 16/7/42.

52 This subject is covered in William Roger Louis' seminal work *Imperialism at Bay: The United States and the Decolonization of the British Empire, 1941-1945* (New York: Oxford University Press, 1978). See also Suke Wolton, *Lord Hailey, the Colonial Office and the Politics of Race and Empire in the Second World War: The Loss of White Prestige* (London: Macmillan, 2000) and J. M. Lee and Martin Petter, *Colonial Office, War, and Development Policy: Organization and the Planning of a Metropolitan Initiative, 1939-1945* (London: Maurice Temple Smith/The Institute of Commonwealth Studies, 1982). A memorandum by the Secretary of State for the Colonies following correspondence with Lord Swinton, Resident Minister West Africa, was circulated at Churchill's request. Swinton was concerned about rising American influence in West Africa, perturbed by the apparent subordination of British to American interests in French West Africa, and the potential effects on the Africans of British West Africa. (TNA, CAB 66/32/31, American Influence in West Africa, War Cabinet memorandum, 22/12/42).

53 TNA, CAB 66/32/31, American Influence in West Africa.

Colonies, Oliver Stanley, wrote a memorandum on the subject containing his correspondence with Swinton, which was circulated at Churchill's request. The government discerned the need to assert British interests in the strategic and economic fields; 'the vast territories of French West Africa, over 1,800,000 square miles in extent, sprawl across vital sea and air routes and among their varied tropical products are commodities such oilseeds and rubber which are most valuable to the Allies'.[54] Swinton was concerned that American business interests 'may be seeking a predominant role', mentioning as examples Pan-American Airways and the Socony Vacuum Company, an oil company and forerunner of Mobil. He felt, in Stanley's words,

> that the African people in our Colonies are affected by the fact that the British are playing second fiddle to the Americans in negotiating with the neighbouring French territories. This impression on the African mind is reinforced by the high-handed behaviour of irresponsible Americans in British West African Colonies. The result, as Lord Swinton says, is a crop of rumours that the British are quitting West Africa and the Americans taking their place.[55]

Concerns regarding American impressions of Britain's West African colonies, and Britain's colonial record in general, were well-founded. Roosevelt junior and senior later met in the Gambia during the president's trip overseas for the Casablanca conference (January 1943), and the poor impressions gained by the latter caused him to badger Churchill about conditions in the Empire and inspired his thinking about a future 'United Nations' organization, antithetical to British colonial interests.[56]

One of the major consequences of the great increase in traffic and facilities at these key ports was that Africans had to vacate requisitioned or compulsorily-purchased land. For example, in the Gambian case, accommodation and land was required for a flying-boat squadron and two squadrons of general reconnaissance aircraft and the hundreds of RAF personnel that came with them, as well as 10,000 tons of aviation fuel to be stored in both the Gambia and Sierra Leone. In negotiations between the Colonial Office and the Air Ministry regarding the RAF's acquisition of real estate in and around Bathurst, consideration had to be given to the cost of 'evacuating the people and clearing the site'.[57] The governor of the Gambia wrote of the 'imperative need for alleviating the over-crowding in and around Bathurst by the resettlement of persons evicted from land required for the Flying Boat Base in a model village to be situated in the Province of Kombo St Mary'.[58] The Air Ministry in turn agreed 'to accept the capital cost of the re-settlement of persons evicted form the land required for the flying boat base'. While these official correspondences give no insight into what this meant for Africans, it was clearly a significant issue, compounded by population increases and overcrowding caused by wartime employment opportunities and the rising cost of living. This was an experience common to millions of people across the world during the war.

54 Ibid.
55 Ibid.
56 See Donald Wright, 'That Hell-Hole of Yours', *American Heritage*, 46, 6 (1995), at https://www.americanheritage.com/content/%E2%80%9C-hell-hole-yours%E2%80%9D
57 TNA, CO 968/46/1. US airbase at Bathurst. Air Ministry to Colonial Office, 30/12/41.
58 Ibid., 21/11/41.

For their part, the Germans understood just how important West African sea lanes were for the British and Allied war effort, and deployed submarines there. This led to worrying losses of merchant vessels, and plans were developed to counter the threat. In one episode, the Admiralty believed that German U-boats were refuelling at bases in Equatorial Africa, a region largely under the control of pliable Vichy and neutral Spanish colonial administrations. The Spanish-controlled island of Fernando Pó was of particular interest to British intelligence because of its location close to key Atlantic shipping lanes. Considerable effort was invested in establishing a network of spies and intelligence gatherers, revolving around a pair of British agents. Special Operations Executive (SOE) monitored Spanish, Portuguese, and Vichy territories in this region 'in order to detect and disrupt any activity threatening British possessions and in preventing the smuggling of diamonds from West Africa to the Axis powers (Operation Malpas)'.[59] A covert inspection of Fernando Pó was undertaken in order to infiltrate British agents and to increase knowledge of the island, especially the east coast and Concepcion areas which, the British authorities conceded, were 'completely unknown to us'. A detailed report of the island was prepared, containing geographical and topographical information and comprehensive Photostat plans of the north coast defences. A network of 'carefully chosen and specially trained natives' were 'to be infiltered and contracted on to those plantations in areas of military and strategical interest'.[60] In pursuit of this and to provide a cover for an extra British agent, a labour treaty was concluded between the Nigerian government and the authorities responsible for administering Spain's Gulf of Guinea territories.

SOE was ordered to gather intelligence, and in August 1941 *Maid Honor*, a Brixham trawler crewed by commando-trained personnel, set sail for Sierra Leone. *Maid Honor* spent a few months combing the mangrove swamps of the French West African coast searching for facilities used by the enemy. The SOE station in Nigeria identified Fernando Pó, lying 20 miles out in the Gulf of Guinea, as an area of particular interest. The Spanish colonial government had provided a neutral haven for three Axis ships that had lain at anchor there for more than a year. They were the 8,000 ton Italian merchantman *Duchessa d'Aosta* with a cargo valued at £355,000, and the German tug *Likomba* and barge *Bibundi*. Mindful of the delicacy of the situation and the need to avoid an obvious breach of Spanish neutrality, the Foreign Office reluctantly agreed that SOE should attempt to hijack the vessels. The British Vice-Consul at Santa Isabel, working for SOE, facilitated reconnaissance visits and blackmailed the governor.[61]

The assault party assembled at Lagos. The plan was to enter the port on a moonless night, disable the wireless, blow the mooring chains, and tow the vessels out to sea. Loaded with ammunition and weapons, the Nigerian government tugs *Nuneaton* and *Vulcan* left Lagos in

59 TNA, HS 3/77, Final report Fernando Po and Spanish Guinea. The HS 3 series contains material relating to SOE operations in East and West Africa.

60 Ibid.

61 This vignette is taken from James Owen, *Commando: Winning World War II Behind Enemy Lines* (London: Abacus, 2013), chapter 5, 'Postmaster'. See also Brian Lett, *Ian Fleming and SOE's Operation Postmaster: The Untold Top Secret Story* (Barnsley: Pen and Sword, 2012). Fernando Pó files at TNA include: FO 371/26922, Situation in Fernando Pó; HS 3/77, Final Report on Fernando Po and Spanish Guinea; FO 371/26908, Nigerian labour in Fernando Pó; FO 371/39661, Labour conditions and Axis activity; WO 173/1286, Operation P (Scorpion) later Gracechurch attack on Santa Isabel and occupation of island; and HS 3/86, Operation Postmaster removal of Italian merchant ship and 2 German vessels from harbour and Santa Isabel.

the dead of night. Just before midnight on 14 January 1942 they were 200 yards off the harbour of Santa Isabel. At midnight, on cue, the lights of Fernando Pó vanished; SOE had bribed the wife of the power station's chief electrician with a diamond bracelet. To further aid the raiders in their task, the crew of the three Axis ships had been invited to an event at the casino organized by the British consul. The scene was set for the raiders to plant explosive charges on the vessels' cables. *Duchessa* was detached from her moorings and towed off by *Vulcan*, while *Nuneaton* towed *Bibundi* and *Likomba* away from the port. All three vessels were successfully returned to Lagos, where the raiders were welcomed by the governor himself on the landing stage, whisky and soda in hand. Congratulatory cables from Foreign Secretary Anthony Eden and Prime Minister Churchill followed, and the SOE agent on Fernando Pó escaped to the Cameroons by canoe. *Duchessa* was recommissioned as the *Empire Yukon* and joined the Ministry of War Transport's fleet.

The United States had deep historical ties with Liberia, located between Sierra Leone and the Ivory Coast, and Africa's solitary independent state when war broke out. The Liberian government declared neutrality, infuriating the British, who undertook numerous measures to block Liberian-German trade and contact, violating Liberia's neutrality in the process.[62] A British agent also stole the German ambassador's codes. Liberia's strategic location and natural resources inflated its wartime significance and brought major American involvement and investment. Its rubber was in great demand following the loss of eastern sources to the Japanese, the industry supervised by the Firestone Corporation, and the construction of new infrastructure, including a major dam, was taken in hand.[63] Liberia also became a base for American forces patrolling the sea lanes of the South Atlantic, and an important stop-off on the air ferry route taking military aircraft from America and Britain to North Africa and the China-Burma-India theatre. Liberia's new airbases meant that it could play an important role in ferrying aircraft to such war zones, of particular significance as America built up its presence during the North African campaign against Rommel. The Americans were granted permission by the Liberian government to construct a base on the Farmington River close to Harbel, which lay about 15 miles up river from the Atlantic. A new flying-boat base for anti-U-boat patrols was built at Fisherman's Lake in Great Cape Mount. All of this military activity brought American soldiers and civilians flooding into Liberia. In July 1942, African-American soldiers arrived to commence the construction of air bases, barracks, warehouses, and stores, and there were around 5,000 GIs in country by the end of the year. Construction and related activity also brought employment for thousands of local men and women.

The wartime build up of American forces and the increased importance of Liberia's natural resources led to large scale infrastructural development.[64] Pan American was given permission to operate a new airfield. Built by the American government and connected to the capital Monrovia by a newly-built road, it would become the country's major airport, Roberts Field

62 Harrison Akingbade, 'US-Liberian Relations during World War II', *Phylon*, 46, 1 (1985).

63 William Clarence-Smith, 'Africa's Battle for Rubber in the Second World War', in Byfield et al, *Africa and World War II*. See also 'Firestone in Liberia', and 'World War II and the US Scramble for Rubber', in Stephen Harp, *A World History of Rubber: Empire, Industry, and the Everyday* (Chichester, West Sussex: Wiley-Blackwell, 2016).

64 See 'Defending the Lands of Their Ancestors: The African American Military Experience in Africa during World War II', in Byfield et al, *Africa and World War II*.

(now Roberts International Airport). It was often used by the Takoradi-based aircraft of 26 Squadron South African Air Force. There was also an agreement between the two governments permitting the Americans to establish a naval station and build a new port, which would revert to Liberian ownership at the end of the war. Though it was not completed before the war's end, it became the country's major port, the Freeport of Monrovia.

An illuminating example of the importance of links between African resources and the West – and the facilitative role played by African ports – is provided by the case of Congolese uranium. In order to expedite the export of uranium from the Shinkolobwe mine in Katanga province – the world's largest deposit – soldiers of the US Army's Corps of Engineers arrived to reopen the disused facility. To expedite the export of this precious material, essential for the progress of the Manhattan Project, they developed new aerodromes and built an improved facility at Matadi, the main sea port located nearly one hundred miles inland from the River Congo's mouth. The large stockpile of uranium already dispatched by sea to New York in September 1940 by the director of the Union Minière du Haut Katanga could then be supplemented by thousands of tons mined here and sold to the US Army. An extensive and highly secretive project involving the Office of Strategic Services was launched to ensure that Congo uranium was not smuggled to Germany.[65]

Further off the West African coast, Churchill planned to occupy the Canary Islands should the Germans take Gibraltar or Spain join the war on Germany's side. As he wrote to the First Sea Lord, if Britain had to quit Gibraltar it 'must immediately take control of the Canaries' which would serve as a good base for control of the western entrance to the Mediterranean.[66] The Chiefs of Staff thought that with the occupation of the Canaries 'we could severely restrict, but not entirely prevent, the building up of Axis forces in French West Africa'.[67] Madeira, ruled by neutral Portugal, received and accommodated 2,000 Gibraltarian evacuees when the British removed the civilian population in order to fully militarize the territory, and because of the threat of Axis occupation.[68] The Allies also prevailed on the Portuguese to allow them to develop military facilities in the Azores, which they occupied in October 1943.[69]

65 See Jonathan Helmreich, *United States Relations with Belgium and the Congo, 1940–1960* (Newark: University of Delaware Press, 1998) and Susan Williams, *Spies in the Congo: The Race for the Ore that Built the Atomic Bomb* (London: Hurst, 2016).

66 CAC, Papers of Admiral Sir Ralph Bevan Edwards Papers, REDW 2/13, Churchill to First Sea Lord, 17/6/40.

67 TNA, CAB 66/28/1, Appreciation of the Military Situation in West Africa.

68 For an important recent study, see Nicholas Rankin, *Defending the Rock: How Gibraltar Defeated Hitler* (London: Faber and Faber, 2017) and also T. J. Finlayson, *The Fortress Came First: The Story of the Civilian Population of Gibraltar during the Second World War* (Gibraltar: Gibraltar Books, 1991).

69 Kennedy noted on 13 October that 'the occupation of the Azores was announced yesterday and seems to have gone off quietly'. Kennedy, *The Business of War*, p. 306. Andrew Stewart kindly offers the following references for this operation and its genesis: Donald Stevens, 'Franklin D. Roosevelt and the Azores Dilemma, 1941', *Historian*, 54, 4 (1992) and Norman Herz, *Operation Alacrity: The Azores and the War in the Atlantic* (Annapolis MD: Naval Institute Press, 2004). The Churchillian view can be traced through Martin Gilbert, *Finest Hour: Winston S. Churchill, 1939–1941* (London: Heinemann, 1984). As part of what was referred to as the 'Atlantic Islands Project', the projected Operation Accordion anticipated a move against the Azores on or after 23/5/41 (TNA, ADM 202/349, Dill to OC 1st and 2nd Marine Brigades, 25/7/40). Churchill saw it as a combined

As the chapter has revealed, West African ports and sea lanes, and those of North Africa too, were intimately involved in the operations of war and vital to their various outcomes. The same was also true of the ports and sea lanes on the eastern side of the continent, as the following chapter will show.

operations' opportunity and tried to persuade Roosevelt to support it, though he opposed the plan. Eventually, however, it went ahead in 1943 as Operation Alacrity.

3

Africa's ports and sea lanes: East Africa

Having considered some key West African examples, chapter three examines some of East Africa's most important ports and sea lanes. The British determined that all ports along the East African coast were to be defended because even if one were captured, Japanese forces could land and then attempt to capture other ports from the landward side. Once hostilities against Japan had begun, the British envisaged an estimated scale of enemy attack involving 150-200 aircraft operating from three or four aircraft carriers supported by a bombardment from fourteen-inch gun battleships, along with attacks by torpedo and mine laying craft. Accompanying this would be a land force of approximately one brigade equipped to seize and hold a base or smash and burn its facilities.[1] In the light of this, detailed notes were prepared on all of East Africa's strategic coastal points. Yet with the prevailing scarcity of resources it was acknowledged that not all 600 miles of East African coast controlled by the British could be defended. As a result it was decided that coastal and anti-aircraft guns would be sent to Berbera and Zanzibar, some equipment would go to Tanga, but Mogadishu and Kismayu, captured from the Italians during the East Africa campaign, would have to be left undefended. In all of the planning, Kilindini in Mombasa was held to be 'undoubtedly the primary port' for it would be impossible without it 'to maintain a force of any size' or conduct 'a defensive campaign of any magnitude'.[2]

The ports of British and Italian East Africa were central to the campaign fought there between June 1940 and November 1941. This was because of the strategic value of the sea lanes that lay off the coast and Britain's need to use them in order to augment and supply forces fighting on land here and in North Africa, while denying the enemy the opportunity to do the same. The garrison defending British Somaliland was evacuated by sea from Berbera in August 1940, along with civilian members of the colonial administration. All together, the Royal Navy took 7,000 people off the dockside as the Italians closed in. Shortly after the evacuation, Freya Stark, a British information officer, met a dejected Major General Alfred Godwin-Austen, who had commanded British forces in Somaliland. He told her wistfully that he was 'the first to lose a bit of the Empire'.[3] He was not to be the last, but in this instance revenge was relatively swift in

1 TNA, WO 106/5213, based on Admiralty to Commander-in-Chief East Indies, 14/3/42, 1442A; Admiralty to C-in-C East Indies, 2/4/42, 2016A.
2 Ibid.
3 Stark, *Dust in the Lion's Paw*, p. 50.

coming because when the East Africa campaign swung in Britain's favour, Berbera and British Somaliland were recaptured the following March.

Massawa

Possession of Massawa (Eritrea), headquarters of the Italian East Africa command, would better secure the sea route to the Middle East and help the British neuter Italian maritime activity in the western Indian Ocean. At a meeting of the British War Cabinet on 31 March 1941, Churchill decreed that steps be taken to ensure that the Italians did not scuttle the 25 merchant ships reported to be in the harbour. As a result, the Duke of Aosta, commanding Italian forces, was told that if they did so, the British would 'consider ourselves free of any obligation to feed the Italians in Eritrea or Abyssinia or to remove them from those countries'.[4] In effect, the British threatened simply to leave the Italians in captured colonies to fend for themselves. Plans were made to counter the Italian threat in the Red Sea and to protect Port Sudan, aimed particularly at destroying the Italian warships based at Massawa. The Commander-in-Chief of the East Indies Station maintained a Red Sea Force for this purpose, and the Senior Naval Officer Red Sea had at his disposal a striking force based at Port Sudan, another at Suez, and ships patrolling the Bab-el-Mandeb, the narrow strait between Djibouti and Yemen separating the Red Sea from the Gulf of Aden.[5]

The combined plan for Operation Abaft aimed at seizing Massawa indicates why the port was so valued. Its capture would have very considerable results and might well 'break the enemy's will to resist in ITALIAN EAST AFRICA'.[6] From the naval point of view, it would free East Indies Station warships for other duties, 'dispose of remaining Italian warships in the RED SEA', 'considerably reduce time of passage of shipping from UK and elsewhere', and 'avoid present necessity in certain cases for transshipment at Bombay and Aden'.[7] Its capture would also release army units for operations elsewhere, and remove the requirement for the RAF to patrol the Red Sea from airbases in Aden and Port Sudan.

Massawa was naturally well defended by the many islands and shoals lying off the mouth of the harbour. Not only did they present obstacles to seaborne invaders, they contained military and surveillance assets. Islands such as Difnein, Dohul, Hamil, Harat, Isratu, Mersa Deresa, and Taclai housed listening posts and coastal defence and anti-aircraft guns. The British assailed this major Italian port by air, land, and sea. Naval attacks were aimed at demoralizing the enemy, destroying men and material, and preventing Italian forces from being resupplied, especially with petrol. As an example, on 13 February 1941 Operation Composition saw 14 Fairey Albacores fly off the aircraft carrier *Formidable* to attack shipping in and around the harbour. The *Monacalieri* was sunk and probable hits scored on other vessels, despite stiff resistance from Italian aircraft and anti-aircraft guns, causing the loss of two British aircraft. An operation

4 TNA, CAB 65/18/12, War Cabinet 38 (41) minutes.
5 TNA, ADM 223/516, Projected Attack on Suez and Port Sudan, Commander-in-Chief East Indies, 31/4/41. For the Suez Canal during the war, see D. A. Farnie, *East and West of Suez: The Suez Canal in History, 1854-1956* (Oxford: Clarendon Press, 1956).
6 TNA, WO 169/915, War diary G Plans GHQ MEF, January 1941.
7 Ibid.

the following day saw the coastal batteries at Kismayu and Muanga bombarded by East Indies Station warships at a range of 2,300 yards in support of advancing imperial troops. They also bombarded the coast road north of the Juba River and Massawa's mainland gun batteries, the offshore islands, and the town itself. On 20 February, as *Formidable* passed Perim island en route to Suez, seven of her aircraft launched a dawn dive bomb attack on the port.[8] The results of these and similar attacks were considered favourable by the British. The Senior Naval Officer Kilindini signalled the Director of Naval Intelligence in London that Kismayu had been 'evacuated in 2 panic repeat panic stages'. He contended that the 'inevitable conclusion' to be drawn from these attacks was that the enemy was 'terrified of sea and air bombardment especially of aircraft carriers'. It was suggested that a 'similar display of naval force prior to military investment of Massawa and Mogadiscio may accomplish same results'.[9]

Britain's stranglehold on East Africa's coastal waters meant that eventually the Italians were defeated in this region by maritime power as well as the activities of imperial troops on land. Clearing the Italians out secured the entirety of the East African coast for Britain and its allies. Strategically, this was very important. Not only did it bring greater security for convoys and merchantmen using the busy sea lanes along the African coast and across the Indian Ocean, it also meant that American merchant vessels were now able to help supply British imperial forces fighting out of Egypt. This was because according to the terms of the American Neutrality Acts the Red Sea could now be classified as a neutral zone, and therefore a permissible route for American merchant vessels to sail. As will be seen, it was also the beginning of a remarkable essay in Allied cooperation, as British and American forces moved into the ex-Italian colony of Eritrea to develop a new military complex aimed at supporting the war effort in the Western Desert.

The Allies in Eritrea: Massawa naval base

British imperial forces captured Massawa on 8 April 1941, its surrender yielding 10,000 prisoners of war. As the British entered the surrendered town, a dejected Rear Admiral Mario Bonetti, Massawa Fortress Commander, was discovered in a deck-chair on the harbour front. He had attempted to break his sword across his knee, but had only succeeded in buckling it. He then threw it into the water, from where it was recovered to become a trophy for the British land commander, Lieutenant General Sir William Platt.[10]

Massawa and its environs was now to become an Allied base supporting a range of military activities, aimed primarily at aiding the fighting in the Western Desert. It was in an ideal location because it was close enough to Alexandria, home base of the Mediterranean Fleet, to give direct naval support, yet far enough away so as to be safe from enemy attack, by land, sea, or air. Like the navy, the air force also saw in Eritrea's conquest an opportunity to develop an

8 TNA, ADM 223/681, Operation Composition – attacks on Massawa, Eritrea: Operation Canvas – occupation of Kismayu, Somalia. Also in February, *Formidable*'s Fleet Air Arm aircraft bombarded Mogadishu and laid magnetic mines in the harbour.

9 Ibid. 22/2/41.

10 Andrew Stewart, *The First Victory: The Second World War and the East Africa Campaign* (London: Yale University Press, 2016), p. 187.

important new base to support the Desert Air Force. Massawa also became a regional hub for the movement of troops and supplies and a centre for repairing British aircraft and ships. Other Allied facilities sprouted in Eritrea too, including an American radio relay station at Asmara. As in West Africa, where American forces arrived to help develop the trans-continental air route discussed in the previous chapter, here was another 'non combat' role that they could perform in support of Britain.[11]

To understand America's presence in Eritrea, it is useful to consider the nature of its growing contribution to the British war effort. While isolationists had urged President Roosevelt to resist the temptation of entanglement in Europe's war, interventionists argued that America was simply too involved in world affairs to remain on the periphery of a war with global ramifications. Though Roosevelt reasserted his country's neutrality and embargoed the shipment of war material to belligerents, this position was soon modified as it proved so damaging to British defence, especially after the fall of France; there was a reasonable chance, for example, of the Royal Navy losing control of the Atlantic. Spurred by a sense of America's own vulnerability, Congress responded with the Selective Service Training and Service Act, multi-billion dollar war appropriations, and authorization of the greatest naval expansion programme in history.[12] The subsequent appearance of American military and civilian personnel in many parts of the British Empire was aimed at performing specific tasks in order to bolster Britain's fighting capacity. From the middle of 1941, specialist American soldiers – port workers, railway men, salvage experts, air traffickers – arrived in places such as the Gold Coast, India, and Iran. All of this, for a variety of reasons, was also to lead to an impressive build up of American personnel in Eritrea.[13]

Shortly before Pearl Harbor, Colonel (later Major General) Russell Maxwell established the headquarters of the US North African Military Mission in Cairo. Its purpose was to work alongside the British Army and maintain and repair British military vehicles and equipment and to assemble equipment and vehicles arriving in theatre under the auspices of the Lend-Lease scheme, Maxwell also serving as regional Lend-Lease coordinator.[14] Eritrea was to become a

11 The extent of American support for the British war effort before America became a belligerent is seldom grasped in its entirety. Studying aspects of the British Empire's wartime history, one often encounters American service personnel, as well as economic and political influence, in British colonial territories. There was significant American activity in the Atlantic, including the Destroyers-for-Bases deal which presaged the arrival of Americans in Newfoundland and British Caribbean islands; American service personnel arrived in British West Africa to help man the overland air route to the Middle East and beyond; American forces fighting in the Burma campaign, such as the airmen of the American Volunteer Group; American forces taking over the defence of Iceland from the British; the growth of America's footprint in India, for reasons associated with supporting China, and significant involvement in the China-Burma-India theatre; the growth of Persian Gulf Command and its 30,000 troops in Iran, under Britain's wing; and America's presence in North Africa and the Mediterranean.

12 See John Rasmuson, *A History of Kagnew Station and American Forces in Eritrea* (US Army Garrison Kagnew Station, 1973), available on the Kagnew Station website in PDF form at http://www.kagnewstation.com/history/book/index.html, chapter 2 'Lend-Lease and Project 19', p. 20.

13 This section has benefited enormously from Rasmuson, *A History of Kagnew Station* and Dave Engstrom, 'Kagnew Station: The Earliest Days' (2012), available in PDF form at http://www.kagnewstation.com/earlydays/engstrom/TheEarliestDays.pdf.

14 Foreign Relations of the United States, Memorandum by Counsellor of Legation in Egypt, 10/1/45. The mission expanded when America entered the war, and in June 1942 was renamed US Army

focal point 'in an effort to blanket the Middle East with airfields, ordnance depots and support bases' to help the British fight the enemy.[15] The immediate concern was Rommel in the Western Desert and Britain's precarious position in the Mediterranean. What, materially, could America do to help? It could relieve British personnel of vital repair and maintenance tasks necessary to keep fighters in the air and cargo ships at sea transporting military equipment to the frontline soldiers.

The military mission expanded on America's entry into the war, and in June 1942 was renamed US Army Forces in the Middle East, reflecting the involvement of American personnel not just in North Africa but also in East Africa and the Persian Gulf. In order to be able to use Massawa to support forces fighting the Axis in North Africa and the Mediterranean, the considerable destruction caused by the recent military operations – especially Italian scorched earth measures – had to be cleared up and made safe. Mine clearance was the initial task, and on 15 April the Royal Indian Navy ship *Hindustan* began the process of clearing the harbour, attention then turning to the outlying islands. Once this was done, American and British salvage experts got to work to render the port usable. This was where Edward Ellsberg of the US Navy came in, along with soldiers of the US Army's Corps of Engineers. He was tasked with clearing the harbour, raising the sunken floating dock and the merchant vessels that the Italians had scuttled, heedless of Churchill's admonition. The merchant vessels had been sunk across the harbour's entrance in a well-planned and systematic scorched earth retreat, which also included smashing up the naval installations ashore and dumping equipment into the harbour, measures carried out on Bonetti's orders. Though Bonetti's defence of Massawa had been ineffective – even the large steamer he'd scuttled to block the harbour entrance had drifted in the water, allowing ingress and egress of vessels – he'd certainly done a huge amount of damage.[16] As Ellsberg put it, the port contained 'the greatest mass of wrecks in the world (not excluding Pearl Harbor)'.[17] Much of the salvage and repair work was undertaken by American personnel working under the President's Scheme of Technical Assistance to British Forces, and the regional umbrella of Maxwell's North African Military Mission. The fruits of Massawa's capture, and of the wider victory of which it was a part, soon became manifest. Only three days after Massawa's surrender, President Roosevelt announced that both the Red Sea and the Gulf of Aden were no longer considered combat zones, and were therefore open to American shipping.

Having received his orders, Ellsberg had hurried east, crossing the Atlantic to West Africa and then travelling across the continent on the Takoradi air route, manned by, among others, the aircraft and pilots of Pan American. He alighted in Cairo to confer with Maxwell, his theatre superior. With the British entrenched in Tobruk and the Mediterranean Fleet taking a battering, Maxwell exhorted Ellsberg to get to Eritrea as soon as possible. An immediate problem as he set about his work was a lack of resources, both human and material. On arrival in Massawa, he found that Maxwell's deputy was fully occupied trying to turn it into a massive

Forces in the Middle East, reflecting the involvement of American personnel not just in North Africa but also in East Africa and the Persian Gulf.

15 Rasmuson, *A History of Kagnew Station*, p. 21.

16 Ibid.

17 Edward Ellsberg, *Under the Red Sea Sun* (New York: Dodd, Mead, and Company, 1946), last line chapter 1. For a biography, see John Alden, *Salvage Man* (Annapolis, MD: Naval Institute Press, 1997). He later unblocked the sabotaged North African port of Oran.

war support complex and could only offer him Italian prisoners of war and local labourers. Stateside, there was a severe scarcity of divers, salvage gear, and salvage craft. Most were at Pearl Harbor, though Ellsberg did manage to ferret out four divers working in Hollywood film studios.

Ellsberg's predecessor, a British salvage officer killed when his boat hit a mine near Dahlak, part of the archipelago of islands off the harbour, had concluded that salvaging the two dry docks sunk in the North Harbour was impossible. This meant that an Italian-built floating steel dry dock, belonging to the Iranian government and towed by the British from Bandar Shahpur to Massawa, was a real boon. With its 6,000 ton capacity, it was anchored in North Harbour and soon began servicing Royal Navy warships. The US Naval Repair Base was up and running by 8 May 1942, five weeks after Ellsberg's arrival. The first order of business was the freighter fleet serving the Eighth Army. The top speed of many of its vessels had been effectively halved due to leaks caused by near misses from enemy bombs, as well as the natural accretion of barnacles and grass on the hulls. As well as slowing the delivery of vital military equipment to the fighting front in the Western Desert, this meant that the ability of the ships to manoeuvre to avoid bombs was circumscribed. Ellsberg scheduled one ship for overhaul every three days, employing 200 Eritreans to scrape the ships' bottoms in dry dock and paint the hulls. An impressive 80 vessels were repaired in the first 120 days of operations.

Ellsberg then divided his team to continue this work and raise the two scuttled Italian docks, which would significantly increase Massawa's capacity. The Italians had acknowledged their value by blowing seven 20 foot holes on the floor of each dock as they retreated. Ellsberg's unit also turned its attention to raising the scuttled ships that were obstructing the port, the salvaged vessels being added to the Allies' merchant fleets. The large ex-German freighter *Liebenfels* was renamed *General Russell Maxwell* by Ellsberg, and the raised freighter *Frauenfels* yielded a valuable cargo of 1,400 tons of ore. By the time of the Allies' Torch landings in North Africa in November, Ellsberg's team had salvaged six ships, an enormous floating crane, and both of the Italian dry docks, and had repaired over 100 British vessels. For his work here Ellsberg was later promoted to captain by presidential order and awarded the Legion of Merit. On 24 November, he was ordered to take his salvaging talents to the newly-won ports of North Africa, where he was appointed Principal Salvage Officer.[18]

Massawa's harbour was fully restored by the time Ellsberg left Eritrea. Three cruisers had 'docked and repaired there under his direction at a time when it was impossible to deal with them elsewhere in the Near East owing to enemy activity'.[19] It is worth dwelling on the significance of this, because it demonstrates the value of African (and other colonial) bases and the infrastructure that they contained: if warships could not have been repaired and refitted in Massawa – or Bombay, Colombo, Durban, or Simon's Town – then they would have had to have been returned to Britain's over-subscribed, bomb-threatened shipyards, or sent to America. Simply put, fighting a global war depended upon colonial facilities and the labour of those who lived nearby or migrated to find work, along with Allied service personnel and Italian prisoners of war.

18 Ellsberg was later associated with the Mulberry harbours and D-Day landings, and, though an American national, was awarded the Order of the British Empire by King George VI.
19 TNA, ADM 1/14232, Captain E. Ellsberg USNR recommendation for an award, minute 9/3/43.

In order to accomplish their task, the Americans also had to develop the infrastructure necessary to accommodate the labour force: one could not simply bring in thousands of people to operate a base if there was nowhere for them to live in and none of the infrastructure necessary to support life, and perhaps even make it pleasant.[20] Therefore, major construction work was undertaken at Asmara and Ghinda, where commodious living quarters were erected. These projects illustrate an important feature of the way that the war was fought: the need to prepare for what looked likely to happen, even in the knowledge that it might not. Thus by the time these major accommodation projects had been completed, the war had moved on, and they were not required for their intended use because Massawa's transient strategic importance ended as the Allied position in the North Africa-Mediterranean region improved.

British units were also involved in Massawa's operations, and their activity provides further evidence of how the logistical sinews of a global conflict were configured and the range of activity occurring in this hub region. The restored port functioned as both an important repair facility and a regional transit junction. August 1941, for example, found No. 4 Detachment Docks Group Royal Engineers labouring in stifling heat and sandstorms as they loaded and unloaded supply ships. This work was interrupted when, on 7 August, a 'huge fire' developed at the ordnance sheds at Campe di Marti, spreading to and destroying the 'native quarters'. Ammunition stores went up 'in great profusion' throughout the day, the conflagration taking five days to subside.[21] Military administrators from another department based in Massawa, the Port Transit Depot, organized stores and provisioned service personnel passing through the port. On 14 December 1941, for example, it dispensed supplies to Movement Control sufficient to provision 500 British soldiers with rations for a four day sea voyage and ten days on land, and 600 tons of flour destined for Aden arrived from Middle East Command. The port housed facilities such as military bakeries and butcheries needed to feed thousands of service personnel and labourers, as well as a military hospital.[22] A Field Supply Depot unit was responsible for loading and unloading ships in port and repairing them.[23] Up to 1,000 tons a day of coal, supplies, and ammunition were being discharged, much of it American.[24] Massawa's storehouses extended to 30,000 square feet, and 1,500 workmen were employed there.[25]

Massawa was required by the Admiralty as a repair and maintenance base for light cruisers, destroyers, and small craft, an assembly depot for RAF and FAA aircraft, and as an armament storage depot.[26] This was particularly important in the year after its capture. The commanders-in-chief of both the Royal Navy's Mediterranean and Eastern fleets wanted it developed as a central ammunition reserve, and lobbied for its facilities to be extended to a capacity of 20,000 tons. Massawa was considered 'most desirable' because it was far removed from areas

20 This was the way that the Americans worked in Iran, too, when they established Persian Gulf Command in 1942. See A. Jackson, *Persian Gulf Command.*
21 TNA, WO 169/2654, War diary Detachment No. 4 Docks Group Royal Engineers, Massawa.
22 TNA, WO169/2691, British Troops Sudan and Eritrea: Royal Indian Army Service Corps: Port Transit Depot Massawa. See also WO 177/1084, Massawa Military Hospital.
23 TNA, WO 169/4440, Sub-areas: 95 Sub-area Massawa: Field Supply Depot Massawa.
24 TNA, WO 169/4464, Movement and transport Massawa. See also ADM 116/4690. Naval repair base: Massawa: Development and operation.
25 TNA, ADM 116/5802, History of the Naval Store Department 1939-45, Appendix II, Africa Volume I Massawa, Kilindini, Durban, Port Elizabeth, Simonstown.
26 TNA, ADM 1/12205, US Salvage Unit for Massawa.

exposed to enemy attack, beyond the reach of Rommel's Afrika Korps and the Luftwaffe in the Western Desert, and far away from the focal point of Japanese activity on the other side of the Indian Ocean.[27] It was remote from places such as Alexandria and Lake Timsah, where the Mediterranean Fleet's main ammunition stores were located, and from the Eastern Fleet's exposed ammunition dumps in Ceylon.

The Eastern Fleet was particularly keen on the expansion of ammunition storage facilities at Massawa. The extant, Italian-built depot at Embatcalla was capable of holding 4,600 tons, and the hulk *Danubian* arrived and could hold 2,000 more.[28] Responding to the demand, the Americans operating the port developed new semi-underground magazines at Embatcalla, and ammunition trains began to run between Massawa docks and this central magazine facility. About 2,000 feet below Embatcalla, a new depot storing 5,000 tons was built at Ghinda.[29] The Eastern Fleet came increasingly to depend on African facilities as those in South Asia and South-east Asia were either lost to the enemy or at serious risk of enemy attack. The hulk *Corsica* was sent to Durban and could hold 1,000 tons of shells and cartridges, and the port's facilities were extended to handle and store armaments to the tune of 10,000 tons, as were facilities at Port Elizabeth. Temporary storage for 5,000 tons was also arranged in a disused magazine at Umbogintwini (eZimbokodweni), located on the coast about twelve miles south of Durban.[30] The extent of African facilities employed by the Allies in the Second World War was staggering.

Gura air base and Asmara relay station

In addition to the Massawa naval repair facility, Eritrea was home to a camp dedicated to repairing and reconditioning RAF aircraft, taken over from the British by thousands of Americans and their Italian prisoner of war labourers. 'Project 19' was the name of the classified American base, which also housed facilities for tank and motor vehicle repair and reconditioning. Its main job was to receive British aircraft damaged in combat, crash-landed, or simply clapped out from use. They were brought to Massawa by sea and transported overland to Gura, where they were repaired for return to the Western Desert under their own power. As America was still neutral at the time the base was establishment it was staffed by civilians, initially 2,000 American employees of the construction company Johnson, Drake, and Piper, along with an equal number of hired or conscripted Italians and Eritreans. In October 1941 Douglas Aircraft Company was selected to operate a British air depot as contractor for the Air Corps under the aegis of Maxwell's US North African Military Mission.

Prospective employees in America were enticed with promises of well-equippzed shops, high salaries, recreational facilities, and a contract that ensured employment in non-combat zones only. In December 1941, 120 engineers recruited to staff the Gura base assembled in New York.

27 TNA, ADM 1/13253, Eastern and Mediterranean Fleets reserves of ammunition.
28 TNA, ADM 1/13253, Massawa, Eritrea: Development of ammunition depot to serve Eastern and Mediterranean fleets. Minute 24/4/42.
29 TNA, WO 169/2970, East Africa: Lines of communication: HQ Sub-Area Massawa. War diary, November 1941.
30 TNA, ADM 1/13253, Massawa, Eritrea: Development of ammunition depot to serve Eastern and Mediterranean fleets, 15/5/42.

> Douglas also marshalled an impressive housekeeping staff: 20 American doctors, including neuro-surgeons and a psychiatrist, 24 nurses, two chaplains, three dentists, two lens grinders, seven chefs, 20 cooks and bakers, eight barbers, two shoemakers, five dry cleaners, three tailors, ten laundrymen and a bevy of welfare personnel which included athletic directors. There is little doubt as to the ebullience of those engineers upon learning the extent to which Douglas had gone to create what one wartime journalist called 'an African Shangri-La'.[31]

Each one of the original recruits was screened by the FBI, but still not told of their destination. Nevertheless, Lord Haw Haw made a radio broadcast on the folly of America's Eritrean venture, assuring listeners that the American vessels would be sunk en route. He was partly right; two of the original 22-strong convoy were sunk by U-boats off Cuba, and half of the specialized equipment lost en route.[32]

Given all of the promises, Gura turned out to be a great disappointment to the recruits. Instead of swimming pools and air conditioned billets, they found remnants of an Italian base which had been decimated by RAF bombs during the East Africa campaign, and crate upon crate of P-40s 'riddled with bullet holes and spattered with dried blood', British aircraft that had been in combat in the Western Desert and Mediterranean.[33] The water wells were contaminated with dead bodies, and hyenas and baboons roamed through the deserted buildings. Cleaning up was the first, unpleasant task, Italian POWs employed to detect and clear mines under the direction of South African sappers. While they were waiting for Gura to become operational, an advance Project 19 team was sent to Benghazi and Tobruk to start repairing British aircraft and vehicles. The fact that this was very much a war zone, whatever their contracts specified, was underlined by the death of eight of these men.

Gura's facilities were quickly developed, new buildings including four mess halls, a chapel, and the Gura Ice Cream Bar, which became famous throughout the Middle East (men were allowed two ice cream sodas a day and two quarts of beer a week). The base also boasted its own newspapers and a nine-hole golf course with the following rules:

> Balls may be lifted from bomb craters and trenches without penalty.
> Do not touch bombs or craters, notify authorities.
> In case of air raid the trenches are located in back of 5th and 7th greens.
> Out of bounds to right of 1st, 5th and 9th holes.
> If baboon steals ball drop another ball no nearer hole—no penalty.
> If ball hits an animal play ball as it lies.[34]

Gura was also the site of the first American hospital in Eritrea, a 250-bed facility established by Douglas. In November 1942, 21st Station Hospital, with 500 beds, was the first complete US Army unit to arrive; it disembarked at Massawa and then established itself at Mai Habar, between Asmara and Gura, where it took over hospital buildings formerly used by the British

31 Rasmuson, *A History of Kagnew Station*, p. 22.
32 Ibid., p. 19. In early 1942 men from the Hamilton Standard Propeller Corporation of East Hartford, Connecticut, arrived as part of the project team.
33 Ibid., p. 23.
34 Ibid.

and Italian armies. A second US Army hospital, the 104th Station Hospital, arrived in January 1943 and set up a 100-bed facility in Massawa. But battlefield decisions elsewhere meant that all of these facilities soon became surplus to requirements.

Eritrea was also an important way-station on the air ferrying and transport network. Responsibility for delivering American aircraft to overseas theatres had been invested in a new agency, the Air Corps Ferrying Command, in May 1941. Among the command's overseas air routes was the one across the South Atlantic, via Brazil, to West Africa and other parts of Africa, the Middle East, India, and China. Military pilots would not deliver all of these aircraft, instead the American government employing private companies and civilian pilots. The first such operations began over the South Atlantic in June 1941, carried out by a subsidiary of Pan American Airways. Juan Trippe, founder of Pan Am, had met with Churchill in London, and the prime minister asked for his help in moving aircraft from West Africa to British forces in North Africa. By June 1942, Asmara was on the map of the Army Air Forces' principal foreign transport and ferrying routes, linked to Khartoum and Aden.

Finally, another distinct American military facility in Eritrea was opened by the US Army's Signal Corps. Kagnew Station was a communications facility established when it became apparent that a fixed radio station was required in Africa. As American forces spread around the world in support of their allies, a global communications network had to be extended. The radio beam connecting the Karachi facility run by 835th Signal Battalion to Washington passed over the North Pole, meaning that communication with the capital was only possible for a few hours a day.[35] A relay station was required, and this was developed at Asmara. A station here would allow traffic from Karachi to be relayed to Accra in the Gold Coast, then on to Washington. To establish the installation, Team 7 was assigned to Asmara in June. Using three Italian steel towers as antennae, the facility was established on the site of an Italian station called Radio Marino, located on a hill overlooking the city and known as Asmara Barracks. The 850th Signal Station arrived to run the facility, comprising over 300 men, their task to handle messages between Washington and American forces in the China-Burma-India theatre, including highly classified tasks associated with the heavy load of secret intelligence traffic.

By the spring of 1943 American activity in Eritrea had diminished to the point where there was no need for all this capacity. The 21st Station Hospital moved to the Persian Gulf and 104th Station Hospital handed over its facilities in Massawa to the Royal Navy and moved its personnel to Gura to share the Douglas Aircraft hospital there. This then closed in November when Gura shut down, and the 104th transferred to Asmara. When Axis forces in Africa finally surrendered in May 1943, Project 19's purpose evaporated; 3,000 Americans left, and 2,000 Eritreans and Italian POWs were dismissed. An American consulate to Eritrea, opened in July 1942, closed its doors in June the following year. The war had moved on, Eritrea's strategic significance had dwindled, and little record was to remain of the frenetic activity that had occurred there.[36]

35 Hawkins and Hawkins, *History of the 835th Signal Service Battalion*.

36 Eritrea also functioned as a temporary bolt hole; when Axis forces threatened Cairo during Rommel's summer offensive of 1942, many non-combat units were evacuated here, including the US Army's 525th Heavy Maintenance Company (Tank).

Port Sudan

Nearly 400 nautical miles north of Massawa along the vital East African sea line of communication lay Port Sudan in the Anglo-Egyptian condominium of the Sudan. It was a notable strategic point, linked by rail to Khartoum, and another important hub for regional military operations and the transit of material and personnel. Significant work was undertaken to improve Port Sudan's coastal defences, such as installing anti-aircraft guns, and to enhance its capacity to vet ships entering the harbour. Boom defences were installed and mine-swept entrance and exit channels instituted.[37] Even these precautions, however, were not proof against all threats. On the eve of Italy's declaration of war, 9 June 1940, the merchant ship *Umbria* was on her way to Massawa with supplies for Italian forces in Eritrea, including 360,000 aircraft bombs. The East Indies Station sloop *Grimsby* obliged her to anchor at Wingate Reef off Port Sudan, and a party from the cruiser *Leander* boarded to inspect the cargo. During this lengthy process, *Umbria*'s captain heard the news that Italy had entered the war, and made the decision to scuttle the ship rather than have it fall into British hands. Subsequently, British engineers concluded that the *Umbria* was too dangerous to salvage.

Port Sudan became an important centre for air operations, including attacks on Italian targets on land and at sea, surveillance and reconnaissance sorties, and operations to help the ships of the East Indies Station perform their convoy protection duties. In May 1940 a section from 112 Squadron RAF was ordered to Summit Airfield south of Port Sudan to form 'K' Flight, tasked with the port's defence and the conduct of operations in the Red Sea. Flying Gloster Gladiators, it also helped defend Egypt from Italian aircraft. 114 Squadron was also based at Port Sudan, and its Wellesley bombers launched attacks on Italian fuel storage and other facilities at Massawa. Later, 114 Squadron upgraded to Blenheim bombers and attacked Keren in Eritrea in support of advancing ground forces. In March 1941 the aircraft carrier *Eagle* disembarked two squadrons of FAA Swordfish torpedo-bombers (813 and 824 squadrons, both of which had taken part in the famous raid on the Italian naval base at Taranto the previous November). While based in Port Sudan, these aircraft flew convoy escort and reconnaissance missions over the Suez Canal and the Red Sea and attacked Italian destroyers in Massawa, sinking two of them. In anticipation of their arrival, the RAF assembled drums of fuel and stacks of 200-pound bombs.

The extensive archives on the development of places such as Massawa and Port Sudan offer a vivid impression of the complexity, scale, and significance of the infrastructure offered by African ports, and their wartime expansion. One War Office file contains 20 plans of Port Sudan, showing its extensive facilities.[38] Surveyed initially by the Royal Navy in 1904 and further developed by the Sudan Government and the navy in the 1920s, the maps 'Port Sudan' and 'Approaches to Port Sudan' depict the port and town and the location of a twelve-pounder battery installed in 1940. It shows a shaded arc indicating the radial reach of the port's Defence Electric Lights (manned by the Royal Engineers) and the nearby guns, their range extending 16,500 yards out to sea. The map also depicts the examination anchorage just inside Wingate Reef, where vessels visiting the port were inspected before being allowed to enter. Another plan,

37 TNA, WO 201/310, Port Sudan: Coast and anti-aircraft defensive role and layout, November 1939-April 1944. See also WO 201/315, Sudan: Reports on protective works on oil installations at Port Sudan and Massawa and FO 371/24632/430, Admiralty oil fuel depot at Port Sudan.

38 TNA, WO 78/4848, Port Sudan: Plans.

dating from December 1939, shows the port's coast defences, which included anti-aircraft gun installations. A series of detailed plans illustrate the scale of construction required to install a magazine for the storage of 550 shells and cartridges for the two six-inch coastal gun emplacements, a range finder, and an engine room, testifying to the extensive and intricate work required in order to secure and utilize such facilities.

The war diary of the Movement Control section at Port Sudan details the comings and goings of this extremely busy, strategically-located port. It captures the logistical complexity of military operations as troops and supplies were shunted hither and thither as the rhythm of war dictated.[39] Numerous ships arrived each day from ports such as Aden, Berbera, Bombay, and Massawa. Movement Control had to arrange for the arrival and unloading of these ships and the disembarkation and accommodation of troops and their onward passage. The port was serviced by Indian soldiers and workers of the Royal Indian Army Service Corps, who were used for unloading and stevedoring, assisted by 'local hired labour'. After military units had been disembarked, Movement Control then had to cater for their temporary accommodation, rationing, water, latrine and ablution facilities, medical inspections, and air raid shelter arrangements.

The war diaries for 1941 detail the tons of supplies and large numbers of troops being dealt with by Movement Control at the port's Base Transit Supply Depot. British and Indian army formations arrived regularly, and there were the less frequent visits of Free French forces and units such as the Sudan Defence Force's band and the 883 African and 21 British officers and non-commissioned officers of the 3rd Ethiopian Battalion. With the East Africa campaign in full spate there were also large numbers of prisoners of war being handled as they were shipped off to internment in South Africa and elsewhere in the Empire. All of this meant troop trains. The thousands of troops transiting through Port Sudan were moved on along the railway lines to places such as Atbara, Derudeb, Haiya, Kassala, Khartoum, and Suez. This was all part of the remarkable endeavour to move military resources over vast distances. The railhead at Haiya was the point at which the roads and railways from Atbara and Kassala met and continued towards the intriguing port of Suakin.[40] The distances involved were great: the running time from Port Sudan to Haiya was seven hours, Atbara by rail was 14.5 hours, and Kassala was 21 hours. From Kassala some of the troops went on for another two hours to Tessenei (Teseney) in Eritrea during the campaign against the Italians.

Large amounts of rolling stock were required for military purposes: to transport a company of 365 men, for example, nine fourth class carriages were required, along with an anti-aircraft truck, a brakevan, and a driver's coach. As well as moving troops, it was all about moving military supplies. Port Sudan was capable of handling (in 1941) up to 3,000 tons of supplies per day. In May alone, the movement control authorities handled 1,500 wagons of military stores. In the same month the shipment of cased vehicles from America and Canada to the Middle East increased greatly, arrivals at Port Sudan and Port Suez rising to 9,000 by July.[41] Space in

39 TNA, WO 169/2595. British Troops Sudan and Eritrea Headquarters: Movement Control Port Sudan. War diary of detached movement control group Port Sudan, 23/8 to 23/9/40.

40 TNA, WO 169/4463, Sudan Headquarters: Movement Control Port Sudan. See also WO 169/2616, British Troops Sudan and Eritrea: Line of Communication Port Sudan Area. See also AIR 29/8, RAF Embarkation Office: Port Sudan.

41 TNA, WO 193/520, Port capacity for vehicles at Suez and Port Sudan, 14/5/41, D of ST to PSTO Egypt.

the port area was at a premium; when storage was required for the surplus baggage of the 5th Indian Infantry Division, for example, a warehouse belonging to Barclays Bank was earmarked for the purpose.

It was not only the great ports of the East African coast that were employed by the Allies: the utterly obscure RAF Bendar Alula was located on the northern shores of Italian Somaliland, a simple runway strip on the edge of the Red Sea serviced by about 100 RAF personnel and a number of local labourers.[42] The unit's record book reveals Bendar Alula to have been a busy transit point connecting various destinations in Africa and providing a stop-off for aircraft crossing the Red Sea to Aden. On such tiny cogs turned the wheels of a complex global logistics system.

Kilindini, Mombasa

While Massawa and Port Sudan attained strategic significance early in the war for purposes of troop and supply movement generated by the proximity of fighting in East and North Africa, Mombasa came to the fore because of the threat posed by Japan in the Indian Ocean region. Kilindini Harbour ('kilindini' meaning 'deep' in Swahili) was located between the mainland and the west coast of Mombasa Island where the harbour facilities were centred. Before war broke out, it had been developed to such a point that it could provide a measure of protection for convoys and escorts along with the maintenance of an examination service to inspect visiting ships before they entered harbour, a port war signal station, and a small number of minesweeping and other patrol vessels.

Kilndini was not just a dockyard and repair facility for the Royal Navy but a convoy assembly and commercial port with an oil fuel depot, ammunition storage facilities, a cable and wireless station, and an aerodrome at Port Reitz. Six-inch coastal guns had been installed and trenches dug in case of Italian air raids. In the town, bomb and splinter barricades had been constructed, an air raid precaution system organized, and a partial black-out was in force.[43] Despite all of this, Kilindini was relatively undeveloped as a fleet base, and 'had an awkward entrance and was rather cramped when the whole fleet was there, but it was safe and ideally situated for the fleet's main role – convoy protection'. The success enjoyed by the Japanese in the early months of 1942 gave Kilindini new significance because the Royal Navy's Eastern Fleet was forced to leave Ceylon following the Japanese raids on the island that April. Retreating to the Swahili coast, the fleet was to remain stationed in East Africa until autumn 1943. This called for an upgrade, and extensive work was undertaken to fit the port out as a major fleet base. From now

42 TNA, AIR 29/146, RAF Operations Record Book, RAF Unit Bender Alula.

43 This is drawn from Andrew Stewart's chapter '"This Temporary Strategic Withdrawal"', in which he employs Eric Jolley, 'An Account of the Development of Kilindini at Mombasa in East Africa as a Naval Base for Eastern Fleet', Mombasa, 8/10/42, TNA, ADM1/13010. Jolley was the Eastern Fleet's Accountant Officer and he compiled this detailed report running to more than 30 pages and including maps and pictures. Undertaken at the explicit direction of the base's Commander-in-Chief, Eric Jolley's report sought 'to provide a historical record of the early steps in the development of the Fleet Base' and also 'to act as a guide for the development of a large Naval Base at a place with the minimum of facilities, should a similar requirement arise in future' (Ibid., minute by Admiral, 28/9/43).

on Mombasa was to be one of the most important British ports east of Suez, and it bustled with naval activity ashore and afloat. As one sailor commented on 22 May 1942, '[I had] never seen so many warships in one port before'.[44]

Kilindini now needed to accommodate a large fleet comprising all classes of warships. This meant speedy infrastructural development, including the construction of new defences, berths for ships, and accommodation, and brought an influx of people, centred on the 15,000-plus sailors of the Eastern Fleet. All of this took place in an already crowded environment, bringing attendant cultural, social, and economic change. Given official British agreement that Kilindini was East Africa's most important port, with the neighbouring island of Zanzibar earmarked as an overflow, it was decided that it would receive the greatest resource.

Visiting Kilndini in May 1942, the month after his fleet headquarters and its staff had transferred there, Admiral Somerville recorded that much preliminary work had been accomplished by his second in command, Vice Admiral Algernon Willis, former Commander-in-Chief South Atlantic and now deputy commander-in-chief Eastern Fleet, and the Flag Officer East Africa and Zanzibar, Rear Admiral A. D. Read. This included berthing arrangements for warships, but as of yet the base staff was only adequate for the administration and functioning of a minor base and convoy assembly port, not a major fleet base. There were currently only two six-inch guns and two twelve-pounders, and so Somerville ordered the monitor *Erebus*, with its big fifteen-inch guns, to sail from Trincomalee in order to augment Kilindini's static coastal defences.[45] *Kirriemoor* completed the laying of an anti-submarine boom to protect the entrance to the port, and *Manchester City* and *Jay* were expected at Kilindini by the end of May to lay a controlled minefield. Later, the cable ship *Recorder* relaid the existing cable from Kilindini to Fort Jesus and tested and repaired the cables from Mombasa to Zanzibar, Zanzibar to Dar-es-Salaam, and Zanzibar to Durban. Wireless telegraphy on shore was still rudimentary, and most of the communications work was being undertaken by the warships. The submarine depot ship *Adamant* was to take over all communications, progress on land hampered by a serious shortage of telephones and wire. Somerville also noted that recreation facilities were poor, and ordered a special committee to be formed to address this. An additional canteen was needed, as well as reading rooms, more playing fields, and possibly an open air cinema.[46] Admiral Willis wrote to the governor's wife, Lady Moore, saying that he had visited the children's holiday camp she had told him about and thought it would be 'an admirable place for a Sailors Rest Camp'.[47]

44 BBC 'World War Two People's War' oral history archive, William Smith, 'Serving on HMS *Anthony* during Operation Ironclad', A8187762.

45 A monitor was a class of vessel relatively small in size and lightly armoured but heavily gunned – basically a floating gun battery. The First World War era *Erebus* was deployed to various Indian Ocean locations to beef up defences while new shore-based batteries were under construction. On the subject of old warships, the battleship *Centurion*, built in 1911, also briefly served with the Eastern Fleet. Both vessels were to have a role in the Normandy landings, *Erebus* as a gun platform, *Centurion* scuttled as a breakwater off Omaha beach.

46 'Admiralty War Diaries of World War II' transcribed by Don Kindell, at http://www.naval-history.net/xDKWD-EF1940-41.htm, Reports of proceedings, 10 May to 5 June 1942.

47 CAC, Willis Papers, 5/5, letter, 24/4/42.

Contemporary aerial photographs give an excellent sense of Kilindini's facilities and layout, and the island's relationship to the mainland.[48] They show Port Mombasa, Old Town, Port Tudor, and the causeway to the mainland on the north of the island. On the southern side, defensive batteries guard the channel leading to the 'entrance to deep-water ports'. They show the island's 'European residential area', the lighthouse, and Mombasa Golf Course along the shoreline. The naval base is prominent, along with oil storage areas, the British Overseas Airways Corporation's shore station and depot, anti-aircraft gun emplacements, the wireless station, oil jetty, docks, deep-water wharves, and another golf course. Behind the naval base lies the Kenya and Uganda Railways yard and the railway track leading over the causeway to the mainland. Pictured on the mainland opposite the Kilindini naval base is Port Reitz and a spit of land where the RAF had its base and a slipway for flying-boats.

The Eastern Fleet's arrival in Africa brought extensive development to Kilindini and its environs, including new forts, bunkers, gun emplacements, tunnels, and command towers.[49] By 1943 there was 130,000 square feet of workshop space, and facilities approximating to one-and-a-half times those that had been available at Simon's Town on the outbreak of war. Quarters for 500 female naval personnel were prepared, women who would primarily be employed in handling signal communications, and at English Point a 'Naval Pool Camp' capable of accommodating 1,500 service personnel under canvas was readied.[50] Far East Combined Bureau, the main Bletchley Park code-breaking facility for the east of Suez region, moved to Mombasa in 1942, evacuated from Ceylon because of the Japanese threat. The code-breakers took over Allidina Visram Boys' High School in the Mzizima district of Kilindini Island, renaming it HMS *Allidina*, the Indian girls' school was requisitioned for the headquarters of the commander-in-chief and his deputy, hotels were taken over, and the commander-in-chief's personal staff moved into Government House.[51] Somerville ordered the evacuation of all non-essential civilians from Kilindini Island, an order countermanded by the Colonial Office.

With provision needed on shore for 1,500 headquarters and administrative personnel, requisitioning accommodation until such time as new quarters could be constructed and forcibly evacuating the island's civilian population was an understandable plan. In late April 1942 Lieutenant General Platt, Commander-in-Chief East Africa, informed London that in light of the reports of what had happened in Singapore he and Vice Admiral Willis had 'agreed that

48 To view the photograph, see Ashley Jackson, 'Of Sea Lanes, Strategy, and Logistics', at http://defenceindepth.co/2014/10/09/of-sea-lanes-strategy-and-logistics-africas-ports-and-islands-during-the-second-world-war/.

49 For extensive research on and photographs showing the defences and installations built to defend and service Kilindini and Mombasa, see the websites of Richard Walding (Griffith University, Brisbane): 'Mombasa Forts: Kilindini and Mombasa Harbours in World War Two' at http://indicatorloops.com/mombasa_forts.htm and 'Indicator Loops: Royal Navy Harbour Defences, Kilindini Island, Mombasa' at http://indicatorloops.com/mombasa.htm. There was discussion with the Americans about deploying an American construction battalion to help out. TNA, ADM 1/2984, Rear Admiral C. Stuart, Flag Officer East Africa and Zamzibar, to Admiralty, 22/10/42.

50 TNA, ADM 1/12977, Kilindini, meeting, Admiralty, Review of Bases Commitments in West Africa, South Atlantic, and Indian Ocean, 17/3/43.

51 Hugh Denham, 'Bedford-Bletchley-Kilindini-Colombo' in F. H. Hinsley and Alan Stripp (eds), *Codebreakers: The Inside Story of Bletchley Park* (Oxford: Oxford University Press, 1993) and Michael Smith, *The Emperor's Codes: Bletchley Park and the Breaking of Japan's Secret Ciphers* (London: Bantam, 2000).

certain categories of useless mouths should be compulsorily removed from Mombasa Island and mainland immediately adjacent now while there is yet time'.[52] The order had Winston Churchill's personal approval but was eventually cancelled in mid-June as the threat subsided.[53] The circumstances in which the Eastern Fleet turned to Kilindini as its base constituted an emergency, and there was a scramble for manpower to provide adequate defence for the base. With a little under two battalions of troops available to mount a defence the intention was to do the maximum possible to improve local conditions and Platt hoped that the War Office would exert full pressure to see to it that their plans were not frustrated.[54] Aside from garrison troops the British commander needed specialist gunners and he asked that one heavy and light battery be sent out immediately, these men to be given simple Swahili text books and the instruction that they should read them on the voyage out.[55] Meanwhile he asked permission for West African troops who were held up in Mombasa due to a lack of shipping to be used to man small boats and local port defences. Other troops would be posted at scattered points to act as coast watchers.[56]

Andrew Stewart writes that

> The main body of Somerville's administrative staff left Colombo on board *HMS Alaunia* on 24 April 1942 and arrived at Kilindini nine days later, a total of 229 people which included 43 officers and a number of women and children. The latter caused special difficulties as their equivalents not employed on essential war work had been evacuated from Mombasa and some local residents were aggrieved that the new arrivals were allowed to stay. Tensions were not improved when the naval officers and these 'non-essential' civilians were billeted in three hotels which had been retained exclusively for their use; this relatively small number of additional personnel placed a premium on all other accommodation and created a gulf not just with the local populace but with the previously incumbent naval staff. This was the position when on 7 May the Commander-in-Chief with a large proportion of the Eastern Fleet carrying about 15,000 officers and men arrived. For the most senior officers, including the Admiral, there was an even more opulent residence as they were given permission by the Governor of Kenya to use Government House. Hence the decision to drastically increase the building programme at the base to try and provide sufficient accommodation available and office space for the huge numbers who had arrived.[57]

Kilindini would remain the Eastern Fleet's headquarters until it returned to Ceylon in September 1943 when the Japanese threat had sufficiently abated.

52 TNA, WO 106/5213, GOC-in-C East Africa to War Office, No.19203, 22/4/42. Thanks to Andrew Stewart for the material in these two paragraphs.
53 TNA, ADM 1/12982, Admiralty to Deputy C-in-C Eastern Fleet, 11/6/42.
54 TNA, ADM 1/12977, GOC-in-C East Africa to War Office, No.19203, 22/4/42.
55 Ibid., GOC-in-C East Africa to War Office, No.08966, 4/3/42; his intention was that within six months 40 percent of these troops would be trained Africans and he also allowed for the possibility of using European women in a number of associated roles.
56 Ibid., GOC East Africa, No.10352, 11/3/42; GOC-in-C East Africa, No.09565, 7/3/42
57 Stewart, 'This Temporary Strategic Withdrawal', p. 90.

Durban, Tanganyika, and Zanzibar

A few further East African examples are also worthy of consideration to demonstrate the range and nature of the war's impact here. Churchill and Smuts were alive to the fact that with the closure of the Mediterranean, South Africa's ports were more important than ever before. There was a huge increase in traffic and, as their strategic importance grew, so their defences were augmented. Loops of electric cable were installed at Cape Town and the entrance to Durban's harbour, along with depth-charge throwers. More defences were on order, and by September 1942 the protection of South Africa's ports from aerial attack had been enhanced, ten anti-aircraft guns and Bofors having risen to 104 3.7-inch and 104 forty-millimetre guns as well as 60 searchlights, variously installed at Saldanha Bay, Table Bay, Simon's Bay, Port Elizabeth, East London, and Durban. There was a commensurate increase in the dominion's maritime patrol capabilities, provided by the growth of the South African Air Force as well as the deployment of RAF squadrons.

Les Pivnic was a schoolboy living with his mother in a residential hotel on Durban's Esplanade while his father, a sergeant-pharmacist in the South African Medical Corps, had left the port to go 'up north' to the Middle East. Pivnic attended Addington School on South Beach near the harbour. 'My classmates and I were acutely aware of the War, because we had air-raid practice once a day, every day', as well as the frequent appearance of troopships and all classes of Royal Navy warships.[58] Given all of this activity, the slogan 'zip your lips about ships' was taken very seriously. There were plenty of other tell-tale signs of war, too. The Bluff overlooking the harbour bristled with heavy-calibre gun batteries. For practice, a South African Railways and Harbours tug would tow a target off-shore between Umhlanga to the north and Umbongintwini to the harbour's south. Flying-boats took off on patrol from the Maydon Channel, and spares for repairing them were stored in a warehouse opposite Addington School. Durban also instituted a black-out and the Durban Corporation even stopped running trolley buses to Marine Parade and South Beach to avoid arcing trolley poles at junctions in the wires being seen out to sea. Buildings facing the sea had to install heavy curtains and cars had cowls fitted to their headlights.

Among other things observed by Pivnic and his classmates were unusual arrivals and departures. Drab grey troopships were a regular feature in the harbour, and, less frequently, hospital ships, painted white with a green band running the length of the hull and red crosses at bow and stern. These vessels often bore wounded and sick servicemen who would be moved for treatment to military hospitals such as the one at Oribi near Pietermaritzburg, while tuberculosis patients were taken by rail to the Baragwanath Hospital near Johannesburg. Pivnic also remembers the

58 For Durban during the war see Les Pivnic, 'Durban Harbour, 1942-1945: The War-Time Memories of a Schoolboy during the Second World War', *Military History Journal*, 16, 3 (2014). For a 'mutiny' aboard a British troopship at Durban, see Gerry Rubin, *Durban 1942: A British Troopship Revolt* (London: Hambledon, 1992), and the testimony of Sergeant G. H. Jackson, 'Mutiny in Durban: The Full Story', deposited with the wonderful but unfortunately now defunct (but still accessible) BBC 'World War Two People's War' oral history archive, item number A4145320. See also Ralph Callebert *On Durban's Docks: Zulu Workers, Rural Households, Global Labor* (Rochester, NY: University of Rochester Press, 2017).

export of thousands of mules needed for the campaign in Burma, many dying aboard sunken ships.

Tanganyika, like Ceylon, Kenya, and other colonial territories in the Indian Ocean region, was an important source of food and raw materials, to such an extent that labour conscription was reluctantly sanctioned. The loss of the American Philippines and the Dutch East Indies saw demand for its produce increase dramatically, following an initial downturn in trade on the outbreak of war when links with Germany, the territory's former colonial ruler, were severed. Now, the demand for sisal was limitless, as was thst for cotton, tobacco, rubber, and pyrethrum. Thousands of men were also recruited for the military, and the war had all manner of disruptive effects on the home front, including serious food shortages and urbanization.[59]

Tanganyika provides an example of a situation experienced in several British territories: the presence of German nationals and Nazi sympathizers and activists.[60] Captured by the British in the First World War and now administered by the Colonial Office as a League of Nations mandate, it had a well-known Nazi element, and German refiltration of Tanganyika had commenced soon after the First World War as a policy of 'peaceful penetration' was pursued.[61] When Rear Admiral Heinz-Eduard Menche visited Tanga in the 1930s, 200 Nazis in uniform met him.[62] The territory boasted its own Hitler Youth branch, the Swastika was publicly flaunted, there was drilling and military practice, and Nazi pamphlets and books from Germany were widely circulated. A network of subversive cells was established with a comprehensive organization, led by Landesgruppenleiter (territorial leader) Dr Ernst Troost. The contingency plan, in the event of Italy entering the war at the same time as Germany, was for this trained organization to create diversions in conjunction with an Italian campaign in East Africa. The groups in Kilimanjaro and Tanga provinces, for instance, had orders to mount guerrilla activities to disrupt British lines of communication.[63]

There were more German than British nationals working in the private sector, particularly the sisal, tea, and coffee farming communities, and it was decided to detain all adult males. On the outbreak of war 3,000 Germans were duly rounded up, and those identified as Nazis were sent to camps in South Africa, some being temporarily interned on Honeymoon Island off Dar-es-Salaam. Those Germans remaining in Tanganyika were permitted family visits and exercised daily, marched under King's African Rifles escort through the streets of Dar-es-Salaam to the beaches. While most were sent to South Africa for internment, some considered too ill or unfit for active service were repatriated. At various points throughout the conflict, Tanganyika was host to thousands of Italian prisoners of war, 13,000 Polish refugees removed from the Soviet

59 Greater detail is provided in Jackson, *The British Empire and the Second World War*.

60 In varying degrees, the British encountered this problem in a range of colonial and semi-colonial territories during the war, including Iran, Iraq, Portuguese East Africa, Portuguese Goa, and South Africa, while in Djibouti and Mauritius Vichy French supporters presented a security challenge.

61 Much of this section is based on Michael Macoun's memoir, *Wrong Place, Right Time: Policing the End of Empire* (London: The Radcliffe Press, 1996). The book has a chapter on the war years, and three interesting appendices: 'German Political Organizations in Tanganyika, 1925-39'; 'Prewar Nazi Penetration of East Africa and its Potential Threat, 1939-40'; and 'The Todd Mission: Madagascar, 1941-2'.

62 Ibid., p. 118.

63 Ibid., p. 130.

Union via Karachi and Tehran, approximately 500 Greek refugees from the Dodecanese, and German Jewish refugees from Cyprus.[64]

Michael Macoun, Director of Intelligence and Security in the Tanganyika police, was posted to Combined Services Security Bureau in Nairobi, which covered MI5 and MI6 and processed all security intelligence and counter-intelligence activities relating to East Africa, including shipping intelligence, enemy agents, detention and interrogation centres. This was important work, for East Africa remained of strategic importance to the British throughout the war, and Tanganyika was a base for the South African Air Force, working on anti-submarine patrols as far south as the Mozambique Channel. Also, for RAF Catalinas on long-range reconnaissance flights via Mauritius into the southern Indian Ocean. Along Tanganyika's coast, survivors from sunken ships sometimes washed up on beaches, often in 'boatloads of half starved and dehydrated merchant seamen'.[65] Macoun recalls a 19-year old sailor who had spent two weeks at sea on a floating spar after being sunk near the Maldives before being picked up by a dhow off Tanganyika. Macoun had the immense pleasure of being able to tell the his parents in Liverpool that their son was alive.

Off Africa's eastern coast, the dearth of merchant shipping and severance of commercial links with enemy territories created serious food shortages in Zanzibar. The island relied on food imports, and was one of the many territories in the region that had depended on rice from Burma.[66] The need to bring new land under cultivation in order to produce more food contributed to soil erosion, which in turn led to the silting up of the Chake Chake creek on Pemba and the encroachment of mangroves into the creek's channel, making it impassable. The colonial government and the Zanzibar Naval Volunteer Force made plans for the defence of the wireless station at Chake Chake, and carefully monitored the arrival of immigrants.

For decades the colonial government had tried to replace dhows with modern steamers, though the chronic lack of such vessels in wartime allowed the dhows to claw back some of the lost ground. Though dhows had dominated private shipping between Pemba and Zanzibar, the carriage of the valuable clove exports had been reserved for steamers, as was the carriage of government supplies. War-time conditions led to a renaissance of the dhow trade as more steamers were requisitioned by the Royal Navy, including the Zanzibar government steamer *Al-Hathera*, taken up for minesweeping duties. The government had no choice but to turn to dhows and they were kept so busy that demand exceeded their capacity to carry, and vessels from Arabia sailed south to take advantage of the employment bonanza brought about by war. War-time food regulations and shortages created a black market, and many dhows illegally shipped Mozambiquan sugar to Arabia. Clove-exporting firms bought new dhows to cope with the demand, encouraged by the belief that these traditional sail vessels were less likely to attract the attention of enemy submarines. By 1944 nearly a quarter of Zanzibar's exports were being carried by dhow, representing over half a million pounds-worth of trade. Other islands in the Indian Ocean, as the next chapter will show, were even more deeply affected by wartime demands.

64 Ibid., 'The War Years', pp. 17-26.
65 Ibid., p. 21.
66 Erik Gilbert, *Dhows and the Colonial Economy of Zanzibar, 1860-1970* (Oxford: James Currey, 2004).

4

The role of Indian Ocean islands

Sir Arthur Grimble dubbed his memoir of colonial service in the British Empire 'A pattern of islands'.[1] Sent to the Gilbert and Ellice Islands as a colonial civil servant after the First World War, the title reflected British suzerainty over an array of Pacific territories. A similar situation pertained in the Indian Ocean, where British colonial officers administered islands and atolls scattered across millions of square miles. By the outbreak of the Second World War Grimble was one of them, having been appointed governor of the Seychelles in 1936. Away from Earth's major land masses the British Empire was an island empire, with extensive holdings in the Indian Ocean as well as the Atlantic, the Caribbean, the Mediterranean, and the Pacific. Though the acquisition of these scattered islands had occurred incrementally and for various reasons, strategic logic underlay the process. As was described in chapter one, islands offered ideal locations from which to protect sea lanes, prosecute local military operations, and replenish vessels on long hauls across the ocean. For those very reasons, they needed to be denied to potential foes. Ergo, they had to be defended, leading to the construction of aerodromes and fortifications to guard against seaward and landward attack, the raising of local forces, the deployment of anti-submarine vessels, and the maintenance of imperial garrisons. Underpinning their defence, and its ultimate guarantor, lay the supremacy of the Royal Navy at sea.

The strategic logic of the eighteenth and nineteenth centuries still pertained at the time of the Second World War. Merchant ships needed way-stations to allow safe passage as they progressed around the world, and the warships protecting them required bases from which to conduct their patrols and reconnaissances. The advent of air power and submarine and wireless communications had rendered them even more important, both to the British and their enemies. The islands and atolls of the Indian Ocean region assumed greater significance than might otherwise have been the case because of the threat to global sea lanes presented by German submarines and raiders, the closure of the Mediterranean, and the extraordinary rise of Japan. This brought operational and strategic importance to locations that would not otherwise have experienced the levels of militarization that occurred, as the British and their allies developed a global logistical network essential to the conduct of a war dependent on maritime reach.

Continuing in the same vein as chapters two and three, this chapter offers insights into the utility of a selection of ports and islands in the Indian Ocean region, including Diego Garcia in

1 Arthur Grimble, *A Pattern of Islands* (London: John Murray, 1952).

the Chagos Archipelago, Addu Atoll in the Maldives, and Tuléar in southern Madagascar. It also offers a summary of the wartime role and significance of the better-known case studies of Mauritius and the Seychelles. Later chapters address the wartime significance of the Comoro Islands and Madagascar, while Ceylon, the most strategically important location in the Indian Ocean region following the fall of Singapore, is also discussed in Part 2 and in a separate volume.[2]

Axis forces sought to interdict Allied vessels sailing between Europe and the east in both the Atlantic and Indian oceans. Of especial importance was the route running along the East African coast as ships sailed around the Cape and proceeded through the Mozambique Channel and the Red Sea to the battlefronts of the Western Desert and the wider Middle East via places such as Massawa, Port Sudan, and Suez. Japanese submarines reconnoitred islands and operated off the East African coast, as did the surface raiders and submarines of all three major Axis powers. One British response was to mount operations to wrest the Comoro Islands, Réunion, and Madagascar from their Vichy rulers in order to prevent Axis bases being developed there. Britain had already had its fingers burned in this respect. In September 1940 it had failed in an attempt to decouple Dakar in French West Africa from its Vichy masters; in Syria, Axis forces had been permitted to use local bases to funnel military aid and Luftwaffe aircraft to support the Iraqi coup of May 1941; and in December 1941, Vichy bases in French Indo-China were used by Japanese aircraft to sink *Prince of Wales* and *Repulse*. Better, therefore, to be safe than sorry. Securing occupied France's collection of Indian Ocean islands, large and small, would help protect the sea lanes along the African coast and those stretching across the Indian Ocean. In addition to this, Britain already possessed an array of islands that could be used to protect shipping and act as jumping off points for military operations, warships and flying-boats as they refuelled and ammunitioned during fleet manouevres and in preparation for operations in surrounding areas.

Mauritius and the Seychelles

Established British colonial possessions in the Indian Ocean had an important role to play in the war, as bases and as contributors and consumers of military resources. The British used the Mauritian and Seychelles island groups for a range of military purposes, as a deeply penetrative global war brought 'home front' experiences to distant outposts. With war came the need for defensive preparations, the construction of military infrastructure, and the recruitment of local civilian and military labour. The scattered Seychelles were difficult to supply, given their remoteness, and in anticipation of war the colonial government had advanced money at low interest rates to traders in order that they might build food reserves. Once the conflict had begun, in a bid to develop local production and relieve unemployment arising from the depression in the copra and guano markets caused by wartime shipping shortages, the government arranged to employ 500 workers on Crown Land to produce food. In line with people across the British Empire, Seychellois contributed to war charities and funds such as the 'Win the War' fund, the 'Spitfire Fund', and the Red Cross.

2 Ashley Jackson, *Ceylon at War, 1939-1945* (Solihull: Helion, 2018).

The Seychelles were located on important trade routes and acted as a refuelling depot for merchantmen and warships, a staging post for aircraft travelling to the Far East, and an operational base for squadrons serving under Air Headquarters East Africa. RAF Seychelles, stood up at Port Victoria in June 1943, formed part of a chain of flying-boat bases stretching from East Africa to Ceylon known as Allied Surveillance Net East. Flying below Japanese radar cover, for two years RAF flying-boats provided the only available intelligence regarding Japanese movements in the Indian Ocean.

In May 1942 the Royal Marines of the Marines Base Depot Organization (MNBDO) arrived in the Seychelles aboard *Clan Forbes*, a 'literal transportation to another world' following enervating months spent working on infrastructure projects in the Maldives.[3] Their task was to mount gun batteries on a Mahé headland and at a strategic site on St Anne's Island, 'to create a token semi-effective defence for the anchorage which was occasionally used by units of the Eastern Fleet as a watering, fuelling and provision base'.[4] One of the tasks for this Royal Marines pioneer unit, commanded by Lieutenant-Colonel W. B. F. Lukis, was to build a road 'over most difficult country from the beach to the new gun sites at St Anne's', wrote Admiral Somerville when he visited in June 1942. To boost the anti-submarine defences of Port Victoria and protect the several tankers now routinely kept there and the ships that called in to refuel, he ordered a pair of anti-submarine trawlers to be despatched from Ceylon. James Thompson, one of the marines, enjoyed his time on 'the enchanted islands', riding giant tortoises, having one of his numerous love affairs, and soaking up the hospitality of the locals at the French Club in Port Victoria. Soon,

> [t]he long, grey guns protruded from the wild, hill vegetation and the usual fascinating rumours riddled the ship. We were going tomorrow, staying forever, were bound for Mauritius, wanted in Madagascar, even the Antarctic; Arctic clothing and equipment suitable for operations in Kerguelen or the Macdonald and Heard Islands had been dispatched from Colombo. And the daydream; we were going home.[5]

Two companies of Seychellois military pioneers and artisans, totalling nearly 1,000 men, were sent to the Middle East, where they joined tens of thousands of other colonial recruits as part of the British Army's Royal Pioneer Corps, forming a vitally important rear echelon military labour force supporting the fighting formations of the Eighth Army.[6] All together over 1,500 Seychellois served in the forces. Given the strategic significance of the Seychelles, garrison forces arrived, commanded by HQ Troops Seychelles which by December 1942 was responsible for the 27th Coastal Battery Hong Kong and Singapore Royal Artillery (manning the six-inch guns at

3 Thompson, *Only the Sun Remembers*, p. 101, chapter 6, 'The Lotus Time'.
4 Ibid.
5 Ibid., p. 128.
6 Athalie Ducrotoy, *Air Raid Sirens and Fire Buckets: Wartime Seychelles, 1939–1945* (Kent: Rawlings Publications, 1997). Elizabeth Watkins, *Cypher Officer* (Brighton: Pen Press, 2008) recounts the experience of working in the Seychelles on intelligence gathering work. The role of this large Royal Pioneer Corps colonial force is detailed in Ashley Jackson, *Botswana 1939–1945: An African Country at War* (Oxford: Clarendon Press, 1999), and Jackson, 'Supplying War: The High Commission Territories' Military Logistical Contribution in the Second World War', *Journal of Military History* 66 (2002).

Port Victoria), the 3rd Indian Garrison Company, and the Diego Garcia Garrison Company. Also under command was the locally-raised Seychelles Defence Force which consisted of a transport unit, a Royal Engineers unit, a rifle and machine gun unit, and a coast-watching unit. The value of the Seychelles increased when the cable line through the Mediterranean was cut, meaning that it was the only British territory with a cable and wireless station able to contact South Africa and thence India and Australasia. This was located on Mahé Island, camouflaged and protected by splinter proof barricades and a company of imperial troops.

Mauritius was affected by the war in numerous ways. Over 5,000 men were dispatched to the Middle East, also as part of the Royal Pioneer Corps, over 1,000 Mauritian women served in the same theatre as part of the Auxiliary Territorial Service, and 2,500 men were recruited into the Mauritius Defence Force, a 'home guard' formation. A small volunteer air force was employed to man seaplane tenders used to service anchored flying-boats. In addition, the locally-raised professional military force known as the Mauritius Territorial Force expanded to two battalions. Renamed the Mauritius Regiment in 1943, the 1st Battalion was sent overseas to form part of the garrison around the naval base at Diego Suarez in Madagascar, and for much of the war a King's African Rifles battalion garrisoned Mauritius alongside the local volunteer defence force for fear of an enemy raid.

Air raid precaution and military ambulance services were established, the Fire Service was overhauled and air raid shelters prepared. There was also a Coastal Defence Force which patrolled the gaps in the reef surrounding Mauritius in thirty-foot motor vessels. Over 8,000 men were conscripted into the Civil Labour Corps, as the colonial government arrogated the powers necessary to control the allocation of labour for war purposes. Mauritian forces were also used to garrison the island's Indian Ocean dependencies, guarding, for example, the cable and wireless station on Rodrigues, and providing forces to defend the naval base on Diego Garcia.

When Japan entered the war and Singapore was lost, a Japanese attack or invasion of Mauritius became a realistic prospect.[7] Flying-boat bases were developed and an aerodrome constructed, and the Admiralty maintained fuel and ammunition stockpiles for the use of Eastern Fleet warships as they broke their journey or arrived to operate from Mauritius. Conflict heralded new communication facilities and networks: never having been visited by an aircraft until 1939, just three years later Mauritius boasted numerous RAF and Fleet Air Arm facilities, including the RAF flying-boat base at Tombeau Bay and Royal Naval Air Station at Plaisance constructed by the Civil Labour Corps, and by 1944 a regular air service linked it with Madagascar and South Africa. The island was also part of the navy's wireless network across the Indian Ocean. There was a wireless station at Rose Belle, and meteorological facilities, including those of an observatory. Considerable defensive work was required to prepare the island to withstand an enemy attack, including the installation of anti-aircraft guns, torpedo booms in the main ports, and minefields in the approaches.

As well as acting as a base for military operations in the region, notably naval and air operations to sink German supply ships and submarines, Mauritius was a gathering point for warships blockading Vichy territory and attempting to intercept blockade-runners travelling between

7 See Jackson, *War and Empire*, chapter 2, 'Defence of Empire and the Sea Lanes: The Royal Navy and the British Indian Ocean World', and chapter 6, 'The Secret War: Censorship, Radio Propaganda, and Code-Breaking'. Also Jackson, 'The Mutiny of the 1st Battalion The Mauritius Regiment, Madagascar, 1943', *Journey of the Society for Army Historical Research* 80 (2002).

Indo-China, Madagascar and Europe. Operation Kedgeree in August 1941 and Operation Bellringer in November 1941, for example, were directed against Vichy convoys and made use of Mauritian facilities. From Mauritius, Bellringer targeted ships sailing from French Indo-China to Tamatave, Madagascar, bound for France and escorted by the sloop *D'Iberville*.[8] It involved the cruisers *Colombo* and *Devonshire* and the armed merchant cruisers *Carnarvon Castle* and *Carthage*, supported by South African minesweeping whalers. On 3 November all five merchant vessels in the convoy were captured by the British force east of the Cape and taken to East London and Port Elizabeth, with valuable cargoes including graphite and a large amount of rice. In response, the Vichy government ordered two submarines on passage to attack British shipping, resulting in the sinking of the Norwegian vessel *Thode Fagelund* on 17 November, 60 miles east of East London. She was en route from Chittagong and Madras to South Africa and Britain with a cargo of scrap metal, jute, and tea.[9]

Mauritius was also a base for covert operations against neighbouring Vichy territories. SOE broadcast propaganda from a secret wireless station in a sugar-cane field, and mounted operations in Madagascar and Réunion. In the case of Réunion, SOE agents were inserted from Mauritius to reconnoitre and develop an informer network, and military operations were conducted along with the Free French destroyer *Leopard* in November 1942 in order to persuade the island's staunch Vichy governor and his garrison to surrender. Somerville recorded that:

> LEOPARD, acting under the orders of the French National Committee, was diverted whilst on passage from the Cape to Australia to Reunion Island to rally inhabitants to the Fighting French Cause. After refuelling at Port Louis, Mauritius, she proceeded to St Denis, where it was intended to land Marines to capture the Island. The landing took place on the 28th November, but the Governor retired to the mountains with a force of 400 men. After occupying the northern portion of the Island, LEOPARD was faced with the problems of dealing with these local defence forces and asked for British assistance. This, however, was unnecessary when, on the morning of the 30th, the Island authorities accepted the Fighting French terms.[10]

The British cruiser *Hawkins* had been diverted to Diego Suarez to be available to transfer troops from Madagascar to Réunion should this be necessary. Illustrating the deleterious ramifications of war, *Leopard*'s commanding officer, reported that the 'population of Reunion are [sic] in danger of starvation. No clothing is available in shops and in parts of the island the French White population are practically naked'. There was an immediate need for rice, flour, salt, cooking fats, cattle, and clothing.[11]

8 See TNA, ADM 223/530, Operation Bellringer: Interception of Vichy French Convoy in South Atlantic.

9 See http://codenames.info/operation/bellringer/ and for the fate of the Norwegian ship, https://www.warsailors.com/singleships/thodefagelund.html. Both Bellringer and Kedgeree were part of the overall naval programme aimed at blockading Vichy territories, codenamed Operation Ration. See http://codenames.info/operation/ration/

10 'Admiralty War Diaries of World War II', War diary, November 1942.

11 TNA, WO 193/888, Mayotte Islands: Pamanze and Reunion: telegrams on occupation, organisation and rebuilding on the islands. The operation to topple Réunion was mounted from Mauritius. In May the following year *Leopard* ran aground off the port of Tobruk and was declared a total loss.

Given the threat of Japanese attack, SOE maintained 'stay-behind' teams in Mauritius intended to harry Japanese occupiers and supply British forces with intelligence, and plans were made for a scorched earth retreat, destroying key infrastructure, should the Japanese threaten to overrun the island. A cable and wireless interception centre was established on the island and came to employ over 300 people under Sir Edward Twining, providing a valuable addition to the work of Far East Combined Bureau in Colombo (and later Kilindini), the region's main Bletchley Park outstation engaged in the work of intercepting Japanese military and diplomatic codes and those of the region's Vichy regimes. Initially the work was centred on the cable traffic that passed through Mauritius (neighbouring French territories relied on British cables), though increasingly it came to play a role in intercepting and deciphering French and Japanese diplomatic, commercial, and military wireless traffic.

Tuléar, Madagascar

While the invasion of Madagascar is examined in chapter nine, here the little-known occupation of the port of Tuléar and its subsequent employment as a military base is described. As a case study it highlights the sheer scale of resources required to sustain a global defence system, and the need to develop and man extensive military facilities, even in remote places, 'just in case'. Captain A. G. S. Forrest, a member of the light cruiser *Birmingham*'s Royal Marines detachment, wrote a narrative of the operation to take Tuléar, sited on Madagascar's south-west coast on the Mozambique Channel. The assault took place between 26 and 29 September 1942, nearly six months after the British had successfully taken Diego Suarez harbour on the giant island's northern tip, part of the Stream-Line-Jane sequence of operations devised to conquer the rest of the island. The assault on Tuléar (Operation Rose) was intended, Forrest wrote, 'to secure the peaceful capitulation of the town by an ostentatious display of overwhelming force', and was mounted by *Birmingham*'s complement of 84 marines together with two companies of the Pretoria Rifles, covered by the ship's 12 six-inch guns.[12] Along with some destroyers, the cruiser's Walrus seaplane and the transport vessel *Empire Pride* provided additional support for the landings.

Designated Force M, the ships appeared off the port in the early morning. The operation began with a wireless signal demanding the town's surrender, and as the seaplane circled the town dropping leaflets, the troops went ashore. Soon, a white flag was spotted, the Vichy governor wisely deciding to avoid unnecessary bloodshed. The marines were met by local Malagache who were described as 'deferential' and 'conspicuous by their ragged attire and somewhat dejected demeanour', as well as a 'little white man' who proclaimed himself British and offered to act as a translator.[13] His sole request, 'pathetically enough, was for a loaf of bread which he said he had not seen since Christmas last … [The] appalling lack of everyday necessities was very noticeable'.

Free French flags appeared in the streets, and the police force was drawn up ready to surrender. 'Greetings and gratitude unfortunately took the shape of bottles of a particularly noxious and potent rum, of which there seemed an unending supply. Eventually quite large patrols had to

12 TNA, ADM 202/425, Operation ROSE Tuléar Madagascar.
13 Ibid.

be maintained to check this form of generosity'. All key points were occupied without incident, and no significant casualties were inflicted or sustained. Before departing the following day, *Birmingham*'s band gave a concert in the square, concluding the performance with *La Marseillaise*. The capture of Tuléar and Fort Dauphin deprived Vichy forces of control of the last ports available to them in Madagascar.[14] So ended what appears to have been a textbook operation as the British closed in on the Vichy governor and concluded the conquest of Madagascar.[15]

Once the port was taken, it was a question of garrisoning it. The war diary of the Tuléar Garrison, stationed in and around the town for the remainder of the war, offers an insight into the activity of this little-known military outpost, illustrating the investment in resources demanded by a global conflict.[16] In 1944 the garrison comprised two companies of troops (drawn from the King's African Rifles and then the Northern Rhodesia Regiment), RAF personnel servicing the airbase and flying-boat anchorage, and an East African coastal battery unit. Stationed nearby was a battalion of French African pioneer labourers, supplemented by prisoners of war, working on the petrol dump or quarrying. This meant that even in this backwater around 2,000 military personnel were required so that the base could fulfil its operational role. Tuléar boasted a jetty and a petrol dump, a detention centre, and an airstrip. Catalinas, Hudsons, and Lysanders called at the airbase or were stationed there on detachment for operational purposes, particularly patrol of the sea lanes, and RAF Hurricanes conducted meteorological flights. The port was visited by destroyers and motor torpedo boats; frigates and minelayers called in to refuel on their way from Durban to Majunga; and a regular air service linked Tuléar to Diego Suarez over 1,200 miles north at the other end of the island.[17]

Life in an outpost far away from the front line presented challenges for the troops and their commanding officers. Morale was a constant concern, sapped by a cloying sense of distance from the 'real' action and of the pointlessness of daily endeavours. To try and guard against plummeting spirits, there was a great deal of sport, that ubiquitous occupier of off-duty military personnel. There were inter-unit cricket and football matches, the army taking on the air force, for example, and 'British' Africans played 'French' Africans. A tour of duty in Tuléar presented an opportunity for sustained troop training, and routinely one of the garrison's African companies would devote itself to training exercises while the other performed garrison duties. Entertainments were provided by the French community, local festivals, and the occasional visit by entertainers such as the Royal Artillery concert party and the 'Hullo Africa' Entertainments National Service Association (ENSA) concert party which arrived by flying-boat from Pamanzi in July 1945. There were other recreational pursuits, too, and successive garrison commanders lamented the high incidence of venereal disease – the 'prevalent crime of breaking barracks', as it was put, 'caused by prostitutes living within a few yards of the Camp'.[18]

14 'Admiralty War Diaries of World War II', 'Operation Stream Line Jane September 1942', taken from 'The War at Sea', volume 3, 'January to December 1942', Historical Section, Tactical and Staff Duties Division, Naval Staff, Admiralty, 1945.
15 TNA, ADM 202/425, Operation ROSE Tuléar Madagascar.
16 TNA, WO 169/18297, East Africa: Command areas and sub areas: Tuléar Garrison, war diary, 1944.
17 TNA, WO 169/21766, HQ Troops Tuléar.
18 TNA, WO 169/18297, Commanding Officer Troops Tuléar Garrison, Report for September 1944 to HQ Islands Sub Area, East Africa Command. See WO 169/14173, Tuléar independent garrison company for another year's Tuléar war diary.

The secret fleet base: Port T in the Maldives

Perhaps the most remarkable of these scattered Indian Ocean bases grew on the Maldives atoll of Addu. The Maldives had been frequently charted since the nineteenth century, and their potential strategic value recognized. The British benefited from having such possessions in their imperial locker, along with an accompanying wealth of hydrographical and topographical knowledge. Addu, the most southerly of the Maldives atolls, had the added attraction of being so remote as to be immune from land-based air power.

Pre-war plans had earmarked it as a potential refuelling base for major warships progressing eastwards in the event of the 'Singapore strategy' being activated and, more generally, to support an anticipated need to deploy and sustain powerful naval forces in the Indian Ocean.[19] Stepping-stone facilities were important because battleships could not transit the Suez Canal fully laden with fuel.[20] In the light of this, oiling and supply bases were to be developed at Kamaran Bay in the Red Sea (Base M), Addu (Base T), and Nancowry in the Nicobar Islands (Base W).

By the end of 1939 the Admiralty had begun to withdraw ships from the China Station for European and Home waters and for convoy protection duties in the Indian Ocean. That December the Air Ministry decided to examine the possibility of laying down stocks of fuel on various Indian Ocean islands to enable flying-boats from Trincomalee to move at short notice to the Seychelles, Mauritius and the Cape. From these locations they could provide air cover for the Admiralty's convoy protection programme. In early 1940 the first flying-boat mooring and refuelling facilities were established at Malé, capital of the Maldives, and emergency stores for the Far East began to be stockpiled. Even before the Air Ministry established its depot at Malé, the Admiralty had been considering how best to counter the threat to Allied shipping in the Indian Ocean if Japan entered the war, and planning was afoot to build up a powerful Eastern Fleet if the eventuality arose.[21] If the main regional ports were blockaded, a safe haven would be needed between South Africa and the Far East, well away from mainland Africa and India and capable of being defended. With this in mind, Lieutenant-Colonel Lukis was put in command of a reconnaissance party consisting of FAA, Royal Artillery, Royal Engineers, and Royal Navy personnel. The party sailed from Ceylon in the strictest secrecy aboard the cruiser *Glasgow* and, landing on the island of Hitaddu in Addu Atoll, were met by the Sultan's nephew, Abdullah Afif Didi.

With the possibility of Japan entering the war the Admiralty decided in 1941 to develop Addu on an all together larger scale, developing it as a fleet base to shelter and provision the Eastern Fleet should Ceylon fall to the enemy. Known as Port T, the base was developed in absolute secrecy. Described by Thompson as 'the empty fort in the sea desert', it became a link in the convoy route across the Indian Ocean as well as a fleet anchorage and airbase.[22] What the

19 See W. David McIntyre, *The Rise and Fall of the Singapore Naval Base, 1919–1942* (London: Macmillan, 1979).

20 See Andrew Field, *Royal Navy Strategy in the Far East, 1919–1939: Preparing for the War Against Japan* (London: Frank Cass, 2004).

21 This section relies on the excellent study by Peter Doling, *From Port T to RAF Gan: An Illustrated History of the British Military Bases at Addu Atoll in the Maldive Islands, 1941–1976* (Bognor Regis, West Sussex: Woodfield Publishing, 2003).

22 Thompson, *Only the Sun Remembers*, p. 153.

navy wanted was a defended fleet anchorage that could be used if Singapore was lost and British forces had to fall back across the ocean. From the air force point of view, the Maldives could be developed for the use of land-based aircraft as well as flying-boats to police a vital sea lane that was growing in importance. Shipping putting into Ceylon was increasing dramatically as the war progressed; by March 1941 Colombo alone was dealing with well over 200 ships per month, and the need for improved air cover in the Indian Ocean was becoming urgent. Given these compelling reasons it was decided in London that large-scale defences should be constructed on Addu in order for it to be fully utilized as a naval and air base.

Two MNBDO units were duly transferred from the Mediterranean, known as Force 'Piledriver' and Force 'Shortcut', together amounting to over a thousand men. The formations left the Mediterranean aboard two transport ships on 20 September 1941, escorted to Addu Atoll by the cruiser *Cornwall*. James Thompson was aboard one of the transports, the *Clan Forbes*. Leaving Suez, the ship turned east from the Red Sea, 'five hundreds cursing, wondering humans on a gasping freighter'.[23] Eleven days east of Suez,

> on a hot, dull afternoon, the silence pressing upon a flat, dull sea, I saw the dark, rounded mushroom silhouettes of the islands sharply outlined against the heat-white skyline. Under an oppressive, leaden sky we approached the horizon mounds; green hedgehogs asleep in the sea. A hush of voices, serried rows of silent, curious faces. This was the guarded secret, here is the code name, the cypher. This is Port 'T'. The white foam circle and the deep, white thunder of waves as they broke upon the coral barrier surrounding the atoll.
>
> The lagoon extended to the middle horizon, completely enclosed by a circular chain of islands, a wonderful anchorage ringed by the dangerous, impassable coral reef.
>
> In a continent of water, on that deserted Equator, the hidden atoll, the secret of the Maldives. The unknown kingdom.
>
> Few ordinary, fortunate humans have either knowledge or vague idea of the existence or position of the Maldives, the Kingdom of the Twelve Hundred Islands, or know of Male, the inaccessible capital of the Sultan's feudal island empire.[24]

Permission was sought from the Sultan (some time after the work had actually commenced) for this additional construction, and was granted. There was plenty to be done. The lagoons had to be properly surveyed if they were to harbour the various classes of warships it was intended would be able to use Addu's facilities, and the cruiser *Mauritius* spent time conducting harbour trials. Gun emplacements had to be constructed to defend the base from the air and the sea, and link roads cleared. The gun batteries then had to be connected by telephone and submarine cable. Underwater defences had to be installed, along with controlled minefields and booms and indicator loops at the entrance of the main lagoon.

Reporting to Whitehall on the situation in the Indian Ocean, General Wavell, Commander-in-Chief India, wrote that 'when Japan entered the war, and especially after the loss of Singapore, the Navy felt the need of additional bases in the Indian Ocean'.[25] This imperative was driven

23 Ibid., p. 73.
24 Ibid., pp. 74-5.
25 Wavell, 'Operations in Eastern Theatre'. All wartime despatches are available on *The Gazette*'s website at https://www.thegazette.co.uk/awards-and-accreditation/content/100325

primarily by Admiral Somerville, commander of the Eastern Fleet from March 1942. Bases were selected in the Maldives, Diego Garcia in the Chagos Archipelago, the Seychelles, and Mauritius (as well as other locations).

All of the new construction, and the presence of hundreds of European troops, created a strange new world for the islanders. At first, Matador lorries (or 'artillery tractors' as they were properly known) driven up the beaches caused villagers to flee. Palm trees were torn down, land built over, local labour enlisted, and cigarettes and beer – religious taboos – entered the islands' exchange networks:

> To the Maldivian workers, before they were tired to uselessness and evasion, a rounded cigarette tin of rice or a small quota of cigarettes were as the payments of all the gracious gods. But it was not long before their stimulated craving for cigarettes and our carelessness, bred envy and common theft; the latter a crime virtually unknown, the first bitter fruit of civilisation. Discovered theft brought swift, stern punishment upon the itinerant visits of 'Big Fat' to neighbouring Hittadu; and punishment brought sorrow and distress to one more smiling house in Gan village. So war came home to the nameless village on the desolate Equator; the iron ripples on the pool extending to the hidden shore.[26]

Trade, fishing, and cultivation were disrupted by, among other things, islanders having to work for the military whenever required and by the presence of a growing number of troops. For the immigrant soldiers themselves, the working conditions were extremely trying because of the climate, the remote location, the poor mail service from Britain via India and Ceylon, and the ever-present fear that the Japanese would learn about Port T and deem it a worthwhile target. This was not to mention the nature of the work which included stevedoring, digging, and seemingly endless construction work. Conditions placed such a strain on the medical staff that the hospital ship *Vita* was sent out for a month. Among other medical complaints, wrote Wavell, scrub typhus and malaria caused a very high sick rate among the garrison and labour units working on the airfield and defences.[27] While Addu had excellent credentials as a base, 'a convoy anchorage, a place to fall back on should Ceylon fall and move forward from when the time came to retake Singapore, should the Japanese take it', there was only 'one opposing factor in the fine concept; the grey factor of disease'. Thompson suffered along with many others: 'Fevers both known and strange, our proud discovery of the new typhus; the suppurating, incurable

26 Thompson, *Only the Sun Remembers*, p. 79.

27 Wavell, 'Operations in Eastern Theatre'. Later in the war the Supreme Allied Commander South East Asia, Admiral Lord Louis Mountbatten, visited the hospital on the atoll and met the staff of No. 1 Typhus Research Team, 'which I had been instrumental in getting started'. The entymologist showed him the scrub typhus, which he had succeeded in isolating. A bite from one of the tiny mites caused the disease, which had proven fatal in about 15 per cent of cases, Indians being more likely to succumb than Europeans. Ziegler (ed.), *Personal Diary of Admiral the Lord Louis Mountbatten*, p. 152. 'Following their arrival in October 1941 on Gan Island, Addu Atoll, the Royal Marines suffered an outbreak of 42 cases. In 1942, the British had another 582 cases, 382 in 1943, 92 in 1944, and none in 1945'. Michael Lewis, Abdul Azeez Yousuf, Kriangkrai Lerdthusnee, Ahmed Razee, Kirkvitch Chandranoi, and James Jones, 'Scrub Typhus Reemergence in the Maldives', *Emerging Infectious Diseases*, 9, 12 (2003).

ulcers, gnawing through flesh to the white bone'.[28] Thompson's condition became so bad that he was sent to Colombo, 'barely able to walk, each leg movement a separate, blister chafing pain, the soft, red sores issuing down my body from the armpit arsenals. I suffered dreams of cold Arctic winds, soothing, chilled fresh water, winter stiff linen sheets in an English bed'.[29]

Despite the ravages of diseases, in less than two months the MNBDO units and their hired labourers had cleared sites, filled in swamps, built roads, installed and tested coastal artillery and generally established a tented military garrison. The atoll had been converted into a defended base with the Gan Channel – the harbour's main entrance – screened by a minefield controlled from a hut on the island of Wilingili. Submerged indicator loops spanned the channel so that any metallic object that passed over them would be detected and indicated on a screen. The naval personnel who monitored this screen could then detonate the channel mines if the approaching vessel was deemed hostile.

Indian troops were sent to replace the MNBDO force as soon as the initial stages of construction work had been completed in late December 1941. The Admiralty was informed that Port T was now an operational defended port, and it was decided to increase Port T's role to that of a main fleet base, with maximum facilities for the maintenance of an entire fleet (the main lagoon was wide and deep enough to accommodate even the largest class of warships). The main Addu Atoll shore station was named HMS *Haitan* after Port T's base ship and each shore station was linked by telephone.

By early 1942 all of the basics were in place at Addu Atoll, including store ships, tankers, hospital ships, harbour defences, communications, and searchlights. The Ceylon raids in April caused the Admiralty to temporarily scale down the work at Port T so as not to attract enemy attention and offer, in the event of a successful attack, ready-made facilities. The lull did not last long, and in June the Admiralty and the Commander-in-Chief Eastern Fleet agreed to restart the development work. In that month Somerville visited the island of Gan and the site of the new aerodrome that would be needed to enable Addu to accommodate carrier aircraft.[30] The airbase site was in a 'natural clearing a mile long and 800 yards wide in the middle of a coconut plantation. With excavators it will take 1,000 Indians about two months to clear and level the space'.[31] Work on the Gan aerodrome and its three runways necessitated the evacuation of all the villagers, a further example of the disruption brought to people hardly touched by the Western world until the war. Thompson wrote:

28 Thompson, *Only the Sun Remembers*, p. 76. 'Oddly harsh to my tongue', he wrote, 'are the wild names I once used in my everyday speech, the names of those intriguing and beautiful, deadly and detestable islands. Gan, Fedu, Maradu, Hittadu, Midu, Heratera, the horrible Willingilli. As foreign as the names of the moon mountains or the suburbs of a mythical sunken city', p. 76. Again, giving a powerful sense of the sheer *difference* of these islands from anything previously encountered, Thompson wrote: 'To the sensitive or the imaginative a visit to the isle of Willingilli came as a blow out of the darkness on to the base of the skull', ibid., p. 89.

29 Ibid., p. 167. 'In that climate the ulcers were incurable. They required months of treatment in the Ceylon hills, only to re-emerge on the return to the islands', ibid., p. 82.

30 The RAF took over this facility after the war, and RAF Gan remained operational until 1969.

31 'Admiralty War Diaries of World War II', Report of proceedings of Eastern Fleet, 5 June 1942 to 1 July 1942.

> These dark, jungle-shuttered native villages were scrupulously neat and orderly, each dim dwelling surrounded by a square, grass fence. I remember the intimate, quietly forbidding silence and the loneliness of the deserted homes when the Gan villages were ultimately evacuated and the heartless bull-dozers swept the little hut homes along the ground. I avoided the puzzled, disbelieving eyes of the uprooted natives, together on the beach like worried sheep, waiting for flat-bottomed iron craft to take them from their lifelong island homes.[32]

Admiral Arbuthnot, Commander-in-Chief East Indies, placed on record his thanks to the Sultan for all of his help in the transformation of his kingdom for the benefit of the Royal Navy and RAF. Even the request to evacuate the population from Gan, he reported, had been 'acceded to without demur'.[33] All of the heavy clearance work having been accomplished, the Royal Marine Engineers 'Q' Company arrived on the armed merchant cruiser *Chitral* on 19 August to lay the Gan aerodrome runways, a force consisting of 720 men providing expertise in every aspect of engineering and construction. By the end of the year the garrison stood at over 4,000 men.

Despite its strategic importance, Port T stirred mixed emotions among those who visited. In November 1943 Admiral Lord Mountbatten, Supreme Allied Commander South East Asia, flew from Ratmalana RAF base in Ceylon in an American B-25 Mitchell bomber to what he called 'the great naval and air base at Addu Atoll'. 'Air Command', he wrote with his habitual grandness, 'was so nervous about my safety that they had got the Eastern Fleet to send a destroyer out halfway to pick us up if we fell into the ditch and were sending a Sunderland [flying-boat] to escort us'.[34] When he reached the atoll, Mountbatten liked what he saw.

> I had never seen an atoll in my life, and had only heard them described. No description can give one an adequate idea of the amazing beauty of these atolls, particularly when one sees them from the air. The various shades of blue and green, according to the depth of the coral, are indescribably lovely. In the places where there is any land, it sticks out above the coral, beginning as a bright fringe of glistening white sand which merges into glamorous palm groves.[35]

Mountbatten's, however, was a minority view. Other officers and ratings thought Addu a hell-hole. On 3 April 1942, with the Japanese fleet at large in the Bay of Bengal, Somerville wrote in a letter to his wife: 'Now I'm off to one of my ruddy atolls which I understand is quite the last word in beastliness'. The visit confirmed Somerville's suspicions, and he described Addu as 'an abomination of heat and desolation'.[36] The following day, as the Eastern Fleet gathered at Addu, Commodore Ralph Edwards, Somerville's Chief of Staff, wrote: 'It is, I think, the most

32 Thompson, *Only the Sun Remembers*, p. 76.

33 'Admiralty War Diaries of World War II', War Despatch, Vice Admiral Arbuthnot, 18/6/42.

34 Ziegler (ed.), *Personal Diary of Admiral the Lord Louis Mountbatten*, p. 152. As it turned out, Air Command's concerns for his safety were well-founded, for after taking off from the Gan aerodrome for the return journey the B-25 'nearly crashed into the sea at 200 miles an hour when the rudder jammed'. The Sunderland was recalled to collect the Supreme Allied Commander, and while he waited he swam a quarter of a mile out to sea. Ibid., p. 153.

35 Ibid.

36 Simpson (ed.), *The Somerville Papers*, to wife, 3/4/42, p. 399.

horrible place I have ever visited'.[37] Ordnance Artificer Pearson of *Warspite* agreed, describing it as a dreadful, desolate, barren place. Some called it 'Scapa with palm trees'.[38]

But even if they didn't relish being there, naval officers appreciated Port T's raison d'être. In December 1941 Lieutenant Commander T. J. Cain made a brief call with his destroyer *Electra*, breaking the journey between Cape Town and Colombo. She was escorting the battleship *Prince of Wales* on her voyage to Singapore. 'And then, in the morning', wrote Cain, 'we came to our secret refuelling base – a blue lagoon encircled by silver sand and screened by green palm trees, but with its present purpose betrayed by the smoke from the lurking oiler which was visible up to twenty miles away'.[39] The following April, with the Royal Navy on the back foot and a powerful Japanese fleet at large, Augustus Agar, captain of the heavy cruiser *Dorsetshire*, considered it a 'blessing' born of 'commendable foresight', a 'secret naval base where the Fleet could shelter, receive oil, stores, ammunition, and be free from submarine attack'.[40] Soon after, Agar entered Port T again, this time aboard *Paladin*. The destroyer had rescued him after his ship had been sunk by Japanese aircraft, and Agar described the scene: 'Imagine a large blue lagoon in the middle of the Indian Ocean, surrounded by small hummocks of coral sands and clusters of coconut trees. This was our secret base, unknown to the Japanese. At anchor were the usual collections of oilers, store ships, and Fleet auxiliaries'.[41]

The Maldives facilities remained a work in progress into the following year. Throughout the islands, camouflage and deception measures protected the new facilities, searchlights and observation towers, for example, being made to look like 'native' structures, and tents being hidden among the palm trees. On 8 February 1943 the cruiser *Gambia*'s Walrus seaplane became the first aircraft ever to land on one of the runways at the now-completed Gan aerodrome. The following day a convoy containing thousands of Australian troops en route from Aden to Fremantle on board the liners *Aquitania*, *Ile de France*, *Nieue Amsterdam*, *Queen of Bermuda* and *Queen Mary*, together with their Eastern Fleet escorts, broke their journey at Port T. Whenever vessels approached the port it became an established precaution to dispatch a Sea Otter from Gan for submarine detection.

By July 1943 ground clearance programmes were virtually complete, a fighter control office was operational, navigation beacons had been erected on Maruda and Gan, and the searchlight and anti-aircraft gun emplacements completed on Wilingili. A chain overseas low tower (radar) had been erected by December, standing 180 feet high and manned by ratings from the Royal New Zealand Navy. The 7,000-ton tanker *British Loyalty* arrived in October and was anchored in the lagoon as a storage hulk and refuelling station for Allied vessels calling in. She had been sunk by a Japanese submarine at Diego Suarez in May 1942, though subsequently raised from the shallows. On 9 March 1944 the unfortunate ship was sunk again, on this occasion torpedoed at anchor by the German submarine *U-183*, which managed to aim and fire through the Gan Channel that gave access to the main lagoon. Several thousands gallons of crude oil

37 CAC, Edwards Papers, REDW 2/7, diary, 4/4/42.

38 Ian Ballantyne, Warspite, *From Jutland Hero to Cold War Warrior* (Barnsley: Pen and Sword, 2001), p. 155.

39 T. J. Cain, *HMS* Electra (London: Futura, 1976), p. 157.

40 Augustus Agar, *Footprints in the Sea* (London: Evans Brothers, 1961), p. 177.

41 Ibid., p. 189.

escaped from the ship and spread over the water and the shore. The British righted the vessel and continued to use it as a hulk, before scuttling it in position shortly after the war.[42]

Military activity continued to disrupt the life of the islanders. Traffic congestion became acute because so many vehicles had been brought to the islands, requiring the issuance of licences and the employment of motorcycle police for traffic control duties. New wells were bored in order to relieve the base of its dependence on fresh water shipped from Ceylon. 'For many months', Thompson wrote, 'all water was transported from Ceylon; our solid rations were appallingly insufficient in content and quantity. I existed selfishly, together with two companions, on whisky and two stolen and buried crates of tinned peaches. *Sauve qui peut*.'[43]

Food shortages affected both islanders and troops, for whom rationing was introduced. The islanders suffered because general stores in India and Ceylon, and the effects of the loss of rice supplies from Burma, dramatically increased the price of imported food. Rice, a staple, was not grown anywhere in the Maldives. The government authorities responsible for the islands handed full authority for introducing and controlling rationing and the distribution of food to the military. Control was exercised by headquarters staff in Ceylon, with distribution by ships and flying-boats. In an effort to become more self-sufficient, troops were allocated to farm duties and several hundred goats, chickens and rabbits imported from Ceylon, a worthy though unsuccessful scheme. At the same time, some of the islanders were better off than those in other parts of the Maldives, because their diets were supplemented by the military.

To provide relief for the troops, sports pitches were laid and the 'Empire Cinema' opened its doors. A copy of the *Haitan Bulletin* from 1 August 1942 reveals a busy programme of activities. Fifteen teams were entered in the seven-a-side football league, and the MNBDO team had recently been walloped 6-1 by the Seamen. Angling 'off the blunt end' of the base ship, *Haitan*, was popular; the men were 'expecting a new supply of fish hooks from Colombo shortly', and were reminded that ham bones and lemonade bottles did not make for good bait. A cricket pitch had been laid out between the two football pitches, an athletics and tug-of-war meet was in the offing, and tombola was proving popular. The final question of the *Haitan Bulletin*'s quiz was: 'Do you want to say Adieu to Addu?'.[44]

As was common in the case of military bases rapidly built up in case of a certain eventuality, when the anticipated assault failed to materialize and the danger passed, their significance faded. From mid-1943 it was very unlikely that Port T would be needed as a major fleet hideout or a main servicing base, yet the Maldives retained significant operational importance. It functioned as a link in the imperial chain between Africa and the Far East, valued for its refuelling and servicing facilities in sheltered waters. It also formed a link in the chain of bases servicing the sea lanes of the Indian Ocean, the base ship *Haitan* continuing to act as the communications centre for all signals traffic with the outside world, maintaining a constant radio link with Colombo and transmitting messages for visiting ships which where thus able to adhere to radio silence. It also kept a continuous listening watch for distress signals, and London shipping messages were received each day and retransmitted.

42 For a wreck dive video, see https://www.youtube.com/watch?v=NFLmr7NPoKc

43 Thompson, *Only the Sun Remembers*, p. 77.

44 See the scanned copy on the Royal Navy Research Network Forum at http://www.royalnavyresearcharchive.org.uk/SMF/index.php?topic=662.0

In early 1944 it was decided that Addu Atoll had served its purpose as a major naval base and become obsolescent. Port T's function was therefore redefined as an occasional fleet base and a temporary base for flying-boats. Its value as a communications link remained though, and with the departure of *Haitan*, Plan 'R' was implemented. This was a multi-site shore-based naval communications station with wireless transmitters and towers housing the chain overseas low equipment, the transponder radar unit and the RDF equipment (other Indian Ocean islands like Mauritius were also part of the chain). On 1 February 1944 the base was commissioned as a Royal Naval Air Station shore establishment named HMS *Maraga*.[45] There were plans for the construction of ten wireless transmitter and receiver towers of between 80 and 110 feet. The transponder radar unit and chain overseas low installations did not function for long, however, as there was no longer a need for an air raid intelligence service across the Indian Ocean now that the Axis threat had receded.

Despite Addu Atoll's diminished status, in July 1944 there were still 1,349 Indian and a hundred British troops on station, together with a 400-bed Indian general hospital. Slowly, parts of the base were dismantled or decommissioned. Four of the eight Bofors anti-aircraft guns and the coastal defence searchlights were removed. Nine of the gun emplacements on Gan and Wilingili, comprising one four-inch and eight twelve-pounders, were declared redundant and the guns dispatched to the Far East. Six-inch batteries on Midu and Hitaddu were abandoned but not removed. As the military slowly withdrew, leaving things behind them, the indigenous village communities made use of everything that was left – cordage, corrugated iron, forty-gallon drums, non-ferrous metals, reparable tools and discarded tentage all found welcome homes. In March 1945 HMS *Maraga* closed, and the Addu Atoll facilities were once again designated as a refuelling facility and RAF observation centre. Though the air force was to remain for a further quarter of a century, the Admiralty classed the base as non-operational from October 1945. Over £180,000 and years of hard labour had been invested in the island during the preceding five years, and thousands of imperial servicemen had passed through or been stationed in the middle of the Indian Ocean.

Diego Garcia, Chagos Archipelago

Coming under the jurisdiction of the British colony of Mauritius, the Chagos Archipelago comprised 55 islands. These included Diego Garcia, the Six Islands, the Three Brothers, the Salomons, Legour Island, and the 22 smaller islands of Peros Banhos. As with the Maldives, the archipelago's potential utility as a military base and a stop-off for shipping had long been known, and the British had considered a trans-Indian Ocean air route to improve communications with the Far East before the outbreak of war. Captain P. G. Taylor had piloted a flying-boat from Australia to Mombasa to survey a possible route, taking aerial photographs of

45 See 'RNAS Addu Atoll' on the 'Fleet Air Arm Bases, 1939 to the Present Day' website, at http://www.royalnavyresearcharchive.org.uk/FAA-Bases/Addu_Atoll.htm#.WtH6KhNViko. See also 'Now it Can Be Told! How Royal Navy Hacked a Base from Jungle', *War Illustrated*, 9, 214 (1945), at http://www.thewarillustrated.info/214/now-it-can-be-told-how-royal-marines-hacked-a-base-from-jungle.asp

potential stop-off points along the way, including Diego Garcia.[46] In 1939 the cruiser *Liverpool* visited as she toured Britain's Indian Ocean realm showing the flag and testing defences.[47]

Of course, the fact that any military operations were taking place in this faraway location is the striking thing, illustrating the astonishing reach of a global conflict and the variegated business of an empire at war. The Chagos Archipelago's importance arose from the need to protect Allied shipping and to stage ships and flying-boats across vast distances There was proven enemy activity in the area: the Axis had a rendezvous point, Viechen (Violet), at 14 degrees south by 73 degrees east, several hundred miles south of Diego Garcia, and in late 1940 the raider *Atlantis* and the accompanying vessel *Speybank* met up with the Vichy ship *Lot* and the Japanese *Africa Maru* in the general vicinity of Chagos.[48] On 17 May 1941 the British achieved a good radio fix on the German raider *Kormoran* only 200 miles from the island. The nearest ships were *Cornwall* and *Glasgow* in distant Mauritius, which were sent in pursuit, but by the time they arrived the raider had slipped away.[49] During a naval operation in September 1941 to intercept a Vichy French convoy en route from Indo-China to Madagascar, the Royal Navy searched the archipelago and reconnaissance aircraft scoured its islands. *Hermes*, *Enterprise*, and *Mauritius* were all involved along with *Hawkins*, detached from escorting convoy WS10B, while two Catalina flying-boats used Diego Garcia as a base from which to fly missions in support of the operation.[50]

One of those destined for Diego Garcia was James Thompson, who arrived aboard *Clan Forbes* in October 1941 after his unit had completed its work in the Maldives. Thompson found Diego Garcia oppressive, primitive, and uncomfortable, far worse than the Maldives. Under the twin strains of distance and war, ill-fed troops and workers struggled to build the military facilities. Particularly debilitating was the lack of contact with the outside world; a pre-Christmas letter from his wife arrived in late March 1942 ('a Christmas which I had nearly forgotten, on the other side of the earth'). 'I was never so near the sun', Thompson wrote:

> so near the soul of the elemental, so fearful or so overwhelmed; East or West along the Equator Line, degrees North or South, the sun burned nearer to the earth in Chagos … [I]n flat projection, on a line with Java and Southern Sumatra. But utterly lost in the great water wastes … A thousand sea miles to passionate Mauritius; far home and civilisation for the sun-soured exiles immolated in Diego Garcia, the end of Chagos, an end of the world … Trapped, imprisoned by thousands of miles of ocean to every point on the polished brass compass, by-passed by ship trail and sky path; feebly fastened to life by the haphazard supply ship coming from Mauritius, once, twice, three times each long year. Until the temporary installation of a RAF wireless station at East Point, completely devoid of contact

46 This section has benefited enormously from Steven Forsberg, 'Island at the Edge of Everywhere: A History of Diego Garcia', M. A. Thesis, Sam Houston State University (2005), reproduced at http://www.zianet.com/tedmorris/dg/realhistory-2.html. See Chapter 11, 'The Third Ocean in the Second World War', p. 30. Also, see Nigel Wenban-Smith and Marina Carter, *Chagos, A History: Exploration, Exploitation, Expulsion* (Chagos Conservation Trust, 2016).

47 The cruiser's work is described in Jackson, *War and Empire.*

48 August Karl Muggenthaler, *German Raiders of World War Two* (Englewood Cliffs, NJ : Prentice Hall Inc., 1977), p. 98.

49 Ibid., p. 169.

50 TNA, ADM 223/523, 'Operation RATION/SNIP', 1941.

> with the distant world; at one time unaware of the world's new war [meaning the entry of Japan into the conflict].[51]

The troops and labourers were at the distant end of a long and tenuous supply chain. The island did not produce enough fruit and vegetables for the new population and many of the troops began to suffer maladies of malnutrition such as scurvy and even beriberi. Though far from combat zones, the work could be dangerous. A young sergeant died a 'lingering death' after falling overboard and striking his head on an adjacent landing craft. Another accident occurred while one of the old six-inch guns was being lifted off the *Clan Forbes*. The winch teeth slipped, causing the barrel to drop eight feet and the winch handle to spin off. It hit a man square in the forehead. He survived, albeit with a 'terrible dented scar on his brow'.[52] Thompson also wrote of the Mauritian soldiers deposited on the island to man the naval guns they were installing:

> the anchorage had to be given the surface defence of two old six-inch guns, ultimately manned by a wretched, ill-disciplined, spiritless battery raised in Mauritius, transported to Diego Garcia, and literally flung ashore without semblance of tentage, equipment, proper rations and devoid of the knowledge or will to provide in any way for their own future existence.[53]

The island did, however, have one redeeming feature in Thompson's view:

> Diego Garcia is the fisherman's paradise; the incredible Valhalla where all lies come true, where two exaggerating arms cannot span the fish caught; where there is neither doubt nor hope but only the certainty of catching fish until his arm is tired or the line snaps. Until there is no longer room to move in the boat, until there are sufficient fish to feed a ship full of hungry men. Fishing in paradise, in the kind waters of greedy and ignorant fish; dream fish, fish weighing ten, twenty, fifty, one hundred pounds. The one sport of Chagos; in which to indulge our small excitement until the sun burned our bodies and the revolting stench of the dead sharks became unbearable.[54]

As the British contemplated war with Japan in summer 1941, writes Steven Fosberg, the role envisioned for Diego Garcia was that of a cruiser fuelling base with some gun and boom defences.[55] At the same time, the Royal Navy's Director of Plans made a slightly more pessimistic assessment. If Singapore became unusable as a fleet base due to Japanese air attack, the British would be unable to prevent enemy surface forces entering the Indian Ocean. With Singapore out of the picture, the British might have to fall back on a line running from Durban to Mauritius to Diego Garcia to the Nicobar Islands. This would protect the vital sea lanes in the

51 Thompson, *Only the Sun Remembers*, pp. 151-52.
52 Ibid., p. 166.
53 Ibid., p. 161.
54 Quoted in Steven Fosberg, '*Only the Sun Remembers*: J. Alan Thompson and Diego Garcia', at http://www.zianet.com/tedmorris/dg/realhistory-2.html
55 TNA, ADM 1/ 26876, Naval fuelling anchorages in the Indian Ocean and Far East, 19/6/41.

north-west Indian Ocean. The report noted further that Port T in the Maldives was centrally located behind this line and therefore a logical choice as the main fleet base.[56]

Given all of these plans, the Admiralty needed more information on the archipelago as extant studies were deficient. The Royal Indian Navy sloop *Clive* was duly dispatched to conduct a hydrographic survey. It was eventually decided that Diego Garcia was indeed suitable for aircraft carriers and cruisers, but ships with deeper drafts (battleships and very large merchant vessels) could not use the anchorage.[57] In October 1941, following a reconnaissance by the Indian Army, the Commander-in-Chief East Indies commented on the development of the Diego Garcia base. A shore battery was to be sited near Eclipse Point, its guns covering the main channel into the lagoon. In addition, there would be a battery observation post, a port war signal station and a wireless telegraphy station.[58]

Moves to develop military facilities in the archipelago had begun in earnest as early as January 1941. The MNBDO force was sent from Addu to Diego Garcia, escorted by *Glasgow*. At the same time, the steamer *Zambezia* was sent to Diego Garcia from Mauritius with supplies. Plans were made for an Indian infantry company to garrison the island, along with the Mauritian troops, while artillerymen from Hong Kong and Singapore Royal Artillery regiments manned the coastal defence batteries.[59] When Japan entered the conflict, Diego Garcia's potential significance was realized. A War Cabinet sub-committee approved two plans. The less ambitious, Plan A, was to be started immediately and foresaw three major roles for Diego Garcia – as a fuelling and minor operational base, an advanced flying-boat base, and an aerodrome.[60]

The more ambitious plans for the island were never fulfilled. Resources were limited, and the situation in the Indian Ocean slowly improved, the potential nightmare presented by Japan's intrusion in late 1941 and early 1942 never fully materializing, American victory at Midway in mid 1942 helping ensure that the Japanese were unlikely to mount a serious offensive east of the Malacca Strait (events covered in Part 2). In addition to a small garrison, refuelling and replenishing facilities, and some meteorological and communications infrastructure, the main military investment was the establishment of Advanced Flying Boat Base No. 29, which supported Catalina flying-boats on reconnaissance missions and antisubmarine warfare patrols. The two six-inch Vickers guns were installed in December 1941 at Kerry Point, known today as Cannon Point, where they remain as reminders of the war along with the concrete bunkers and ammunition boxes of the fort. Put in place by the MNBDO and manned initially by Royal Marines, the first relief was a Mauritian battery in January 1942, followed by the 12th Indian Coast Battery of the Indian Army in September. It was not until October that construction of the shelters and magazines began.[61] Diego Garcia was occasionally used by Eastern Fleet warships and more frequently by flying-boats. There were normally at most three flying-boats present at any time and, though small in number, these aircraft played an important role in the surveillance of the

56 Ibid., Director of Plans, register LD02445/41, 11/7/41.
57 Ibid., Survey of Diego Garcia, 12/8/41 and 16/8/41.
58 TNA, ADM 1/ 26876, Commander-in-Chief East Indies, 11/10/41 and ADM 1/ 26876, from the Admiralty, 24/10/41.
59 Jackson, *War and Empire*, p. 44.
60 TNA, ADM 1/ 26876, Defence Place for Diego Garcia, War Cabinet Ad Hoc Subcommittee on Indian Ocean Defence, 15/2/42.
61 TNA, WO 192/36A, Eclipse Point Garrison Kerry Point Battery Fort Record Book.

central Indian Ocean. While they did not sink any submarines, their presence complicated enemy operations and they also conducted the less glamorous task of reporting on general shipping. Air operations were centred in the lagoon adjacent to the East Point plantation.

On 16 September 1944, RAF Pilot Officer James Park of 240 Squadron RAF took off from Madras bound for Diego Garcia aboard a Catalina flying-boat named 'Katie' after the squadron letter 'K'.[62] Here she was to be based along with other flying-boats to search for a Japanese submarine reported to be heading towards Madagascar. The aircraft flew more than eight hours to Kelai in the Maldives where it was to refuel. This proved impossible, however, because the bowser had sunk in a storm. Katie therefore flew on to Diego Garcia, a trip of over ten hours. She landed just in time, the engines cutting out as the aircraft ran up to the mooring buoy. Since another aircraft took precedence for refuelling, Park went to bed with Katie bobbing lightly on the water with a crewman on board. But an unusually strong storm soon blew up and tore the Catalina from its mooring. Normally the crewman aboard would have started the engines and taxied to keep the aircraft from blowing ashore, but Katie was light because she had none of her usual 1,450 gallons of fuel on board. Consequently, she bobbed around like a cork. The crewman fired Verey pistol shells to alert those ashore, but the craft ran aground and was severely damaged by a palm tree, which took off the aileron and a portion of the wing, rendering her unflyable. And there she stayed.

As with all such military infrastructure developed the length and breadth of the Empire, there were significant consequences for the local people. The British had no plans to utilize the indigenous plantation workers of the Chagos Archipelago for military labour purposes. One report, redolent of the prejudiced attitudes of the times and reflecting the troubled pattern of labour relations, stated that the 450 or so 'natives' were used to 'easy living' and 'will be of no use whatsoever'.[63] Another said that 'people less likely to be able to do work of any kind can scarcely be imagined'.[64] The British government arranged to compensate the Diego Garcia company for any loss of plantation revenues caused by the military build up. Though most of the inhabitants did not need to be relocated, the presence of the military distorted the economy. The managers felt the workers would be 'spoilt' by the occupation, as they would find it easier to catch and sell fish or do odd labour for the troops rather than harvest coconuts. An additional symptom was rapid inflation as the inhabitants sold food to hungry troops that were suffering from a substandard diet.[65]

Cocos-Keeling Islands

The Cocos-Keeling Islands were formed from coral atolls located 1,040 miles south south-west of Singapore. Despite their proximity to Java and the presence of a cable and wireless station on Direction Island, the Japanese had not taken them, though they regularly reconnoitred them.

62 Ted Morris, 'The Story of "Katie", Jim Park's PBY Catalina', at http://www.zianet.com/tedmorris/dg/pby.html. PBY stands for 'Patrol', 'Bomber', and the manufacturer's identification, 'Y' for Consolidated.
63 TNA, WO 106/3719, Engineer appreciation.
64 Ibid., Report of the siting, description, construction, and requirements of Flying Strips at Diego Garcia.
65 TNA, WO 106/3719.

Guarded by a small imperial force, the station relayed traffic throughout the war save for an interruption in March 1942 when the Japanese shelled the islands. To lessen enemy attention, the flying-boat anchorage was not used, and the location was removed from maps. The garrison was provided by the Ceylon Garrison Artillery, though there was a mutiny in May 1942.[66] Three of the soldiers were executed, the only capital sentences for mutiny issued to British forces during the war. The ringleader was motivated by nationalism and the desire for racial equality, and wanted to turn the island over to the Japanese. They were replaced by a platoon of the King's African Rifles, manning six-inch guns covering the main anchorage at Horsburgh Island.

Corporal Fred Roles served with 357 Wireless Unit in Ceylon, part of the 'Y' Service listening in on enemy transmissions. In early 1944 he was sent to Direction Island to work alongside civilians running the cable and wireless station and Royal Navy wireless operators. His unit installed new antennae, employing local boys to climb coconut trees to conceal them, all part of the attempt to deceive Japanese reconnaissance flights into believing the site was uninhabited (the islands' population lived on Home Island). Intercepted traffic was reported to Colombo. There were also Australian meteorologists on the island, and Catalinas flew over most nights travelling from Ceylon to Perth. Direction Island was bombed on one occasion, and in August 1944 Royal Marines arrived with anti-aircraft guns.

The Cocos-Keeling Islands were about to take on an important war role as the site of a Forward Strategic Air Base intended to support the reconquest of South-east Asia and the Dutch East Indies.[67] Bases to the south were required for heavy bomber squadrons supporting the advance of the Fourteenth Army in Burma and attacking Japanese targets, such as shipping, airfields, command posts, and ammunition dumps. An airbase in the Cocos-Keeling Islands could act as a valuable stop-off and photo reconnaissance base, and be used by bombers and mine-laying aircraft attacking targets in Japanese-held territories. Soon a force of 6,500 service personnel was stationed there, mainly from the RAF. Two all-weather runways were cleared and laid on West Island, comprising 2,000 yard pierced steel planking. Specially-recruited RAF elephants were employed to haul aircraft around, and to retrieve them when they skidded off the artificial runways into the mud.

The first aircraft to arrive, in April 1945, were the Spitfires of 136 Squadron, unpacked and assembled from crates delivered by sea. As the islands were considered vulnerable to Japanese air attack, the unit's mission was to provide air defence for the Liberator bombers, the first of which arrived in May. Two Liberator squadrons, 99 and 356, were also stationed here, intended for use in the reoccupation of Malaya and Singapore. As the pathfinder for the Liberator deployment, the navigation officer of 231 Group had flown from India to the Cocos-Keelings, fuelling at Kankesanteria in Ceylon en route. Along with the fighters and bombers, Mosquitos flying from the islands conducted photo reconnaissance missions over Malaya and Sumatra. Coastal aircraft for anti-shipping operations also arrived, including elements of 321 Squadron of the Dutch air force from China Bay in Ceylon, and elements from 160 and 203 squadrons RAF.[68]

John Behague and his 99 Squadron Liberators were posted from India, sleeping rough in tents on West Island and enduring the usual tropical hazards of falling coconuts, land crabs,

66 See Noel Crusz, *The Cocos Islands Mutiny* (Freemantle: Freemantle Arts Centre Press, 2000).
67 See J. E. H. Fail, 'Forward Strategic Air Base Cocos Island', at http://www.rquirk.com/cocos/cocosart.htm
68 Ibid.

and giant centipedes. Behague spent his days on wireless duties or Sten gun training and his evenings producing the forces newssheet, *Atoll*, using news pirated from Reuters.[69] 99 Squadron had previously been deployed bombing Japanese targets during the Imphal operations. Now operating from the Cocos-Keelings, long flights of up to 16 hours were undertaken, with particular attention being paid to the Burma-Thailand railway, a vital Japanese supply line.[70] Targets including aerodromes were also hit in Java and Sumatra.

As the war moved towards its climax, Cocos-Keeling based Liberators made supply drop runs to Malaya in support of the anticipated British landings. 99 and 356 squadron assets were placed at the disposal of Force 136 (SOE's regional appellation) units operating behind enemy lines in Malaya and Thailand. Cocos-Keeling-based aircraft took part in Operation Zipper, the invasion of Malaya, on 28 August. Following Japan's surrender, helping relieve Allied prisoners of war throughout South East Asia Command took priority. The Cocos-Keeling aircraft therefore began work on Operation Birdcage, the supply of relief to Allied prisoners of war and internees in Malaya, losing a 99 Squadron Liberator when it crashed while dropping food and medical supplies to Palembang in Sumatra on 1 September.

In the war's dying months, therefore, as in the first days of the conflict with Japan, the islands of the Indian Ocean continued to provide bases essential for Britain's ability to prosecute military operations. Having examined the role of islands, ports, and sea lanes in Africa and the Indian Ocean in Part 1, Part 2 now turns to a chronological account of the war in the Indian Ocean region, beginning with the threat posed by Germany and Italy.

69 For Behague see https://andywibble.wordpress.com/2013/03/25/memoirs-from-john-behague-wwii/#more-566. Also the photographs at https://andywibble.wordpress.com/

70 Dancey, *South East Asia Command*, p. 9.

Part 2

From Africa to Malaya: The Indian Ocean's war

5

The German and Italian challenge and sea lane protection

Part 2 turns towards the war at sea in the Indian Ocean region, charting the rhythm of conflict as enemy challenges developed in various locations and in a variety of forms, and British forces did their best to meet to them. It explains the interconnectivity of operations on land around the Indian Ocean's rim and the defence of its sea lanes by air and maritime forces, as hundreds of merchant vessels and troopships went about their business. To begin with, chapter 5 chronicles the threat posed by Germany and Italy before Japan entered the war, and the Royal Navy's attempts to counter it and to continue to use the Indian Ocean as a great connecting sea while supporting military operations on land. While not an exhaustive narrative it offers representative examples of the types of convoys and patrols conducted by British surface vessels and submarines as part of the routine business of war, and their engagements with the enemy. It also explains the maritime activities associated with the East Africa campaign as the British and Italian empires clashed in Abyssinia, Kenya, Somaliland, and the Sudan, and the deployment of German commerce raiders and warships.

In what was an imperial conflict on a variety of levels, the Germans and the Italians wanted colonies and control of sea lanes here and elsewhere. Both powers needed to contest Britain's dominant position in the Indian Ocean in order to disrupt its economic and military system and stretch its resources, thereby degrading its capacity to wage war. From a British point of view, therefore, the challenge was to manage the allocation of overstretched resources in order to police a vast oceanic estate against an enemy that could appear almost anywhere. This had to be done while juggling the requirements of other theatres of actual or potential combat operations and the need to maintain intra-imperial trade and communications.

The combined presence of enemy surface raiders and submarines obliged Britain to conduct a coordinated campaign in the Indian Ocean and the South Atlantic so that ships carrying troops and supplies to key locations such as Australia, Egypt, India, Iran, Iraq, Singapore, and the Soviet Union could move safely across perilous seas. This required the dispersal of naval and air forces and the utilization of military bases, airstrips, and ports in colonies territories, amounting to a vast disbursement of civilian and military effort. It was characterized by humdrum but absolutely essential tasks involving long hours closed up in patrol aircraft skimming the ocean waves searching for a periscope or a lifebelt, days of sea time aboard destroyers or cruisers escorting a line of grey troopships or searching for a reported raider, weeks of building barracks, magazines, and all manner of infrastructure, and endless months manning coastal defence batteries. All of this in the knowledge that what one searched for might never be found, what one built might never be required, and what one aimed at might never appear.

As we have seen, Axis forces threatened key shipping lanes and choke points such as the Cape of Good Hope, the Mozambique Channel, and the Red Sea. Once more, the corsairs returned to the Indian Ocean, and for the British the challenges of maritime security, familiar to admirals such as Curtis Barnett and George Pocock in the eighteenth century, arose again. The Germans knew that if they won the war a new overseas empire would be one of the fruits of victory. Experience had taught them that a successful strategy had to embrace lands and oceans far away from Europe and the waters of the Atlantic and the North Sea, even if they hoped that the decisive action would take place there. The Germans fully comprehended the importance of ports and islands for projecting power and contesting sea lanes. Hitler hoped that Spain might cede one of the Canary Islands to Germany, for example, along with the right to establish bases in places such as Agadir and Mogador in Morocco.[1] In June 1940 Rear Admiral Kurt Fricke outlined a plan for annexations overseas and the development of new client states, and the potential benefits of cooperation with the Japanese in the Indian Ocean region were well understood in German and Italian naval and political circles.[2] Admiral Rolf Carls, commander of Naval Group Command North, wrote in the same summer that Germany would need to establish many naval bases in the Atlantic and Indian oceans and dominate the choke points granting access to them. In spring 1941 Hitler sketched broad but vague plans for Operation Orient, a joint approach to German and Japanese strategy that envisaged the seizure of strategic locations such as Ceylon and Madagascar, and even the invasion of India.[3] Linking with the Japanese would ideally occur after German victories in the Soviet Union had secured the oil resources of Iran and Iraq and advanced the Third Reich towards the Persian Gulf and the Indian Ocean.[4]

The Germans approached leaders of South Africa's anti-British National Party to discuss the prospect of the dominion declaring itself neutral thereby damaging Britain's war-making capacity, and sought to support the activities of the 300,000-400,000-strong anti-British Ossewabrandwag organization which, naturally, objected to the war. Home-grown Nazi sympathizers and their nationalist political organizations were defining features of the wartime political scene and circumscribed the manner in which pro-British politicians such as Smuts could support the imperial war effort.[5] German nationals here and in the ex-German colony of Tanganyika organized along Nazi lines and required surveillance and in many cases internment.

1 Unsigned memorandum, 17/9/40. Indicating Germany's imperial ambitions, the Foreign Minister said at this meeting that 'Germany, Italy, and Spain as a family of three would have to direct the destinies of Europe and Africa jointly. What they had jointly won in Europe and Africa, however, they would also have to defend jointly if necessary'.

2 Quoted in M. Kearney, *The Indian Ocean in World History*.

3 See Peter Tsouras, 'Operation Orient: Joint Axis Strategy', in Kenneth Macksey (ed.), *The Hitler Options: Alternative Decisions of World War Two* (Mechanicsburg, PA: Greenhill, 1995).

4 For Hitler's thinking, and influences on his thinking, with regard to operations in the Indian Ocean region, see Horst Boog et al (eds), *Germany and the Second World War*, volume 6, *The Global War* (Oxford: Clarendon Press, 2001), pp. 124-128.

5 See Albrecht Hagemann, 'Very Special Relations: The "Third Reich" and the Union of South Africa, 1933-1939', *South African Historical Journal*, 27 (1992); Christoph Marx, *Oxwagon Sentinel: Radical Afrikaner Nationalism and the History of the Ossewabrandwag* (London: Lit Verlag, 2011); Marx, 'The Ossewabrandwag as a Mass Movement, 1939-1941', *Journal of Southern African Studies*, 20, 2 (1994).

There were fifth columns and spy networks, founded upon cultural, political, and economic ties, in numerous Indian Ocean locations, including Egypt, Goa, India, Iran, Iraq, and Portuguese East Africa, as well as in South Africa and Tanganyika.[6] Their aim was to disrupt the imperial war effort and force Britain to commit valuable resources to distant theatres where its vital interests, such as oil and lines of communication, were located and where, regardless of resources or strategic significance, it bore the fundamental defensive responsibility associated with imperial possession: the British Empire was a global entity, and it was Britain's duty – no one else's – to protect it.[7] Everywhere in the world the Germans determined to attack British interests when opportunity arose, even as Hitler focused his attention on European conquests both east and west of Berlin. The fact that ultimately they failed does not diminish the significance of these actions and initiatives, part of a multi-faceted global war as it presented itself to people looking forward into an unknown future.

Axis spy networks in the Indian Ocean region could, among other things, monitor the movement of British naval assets and convoys. During the autumn of 1941 the Japanese consul in Cape Town reported weekly to Tokyo with details of the comings and goings of British vessels. The agents of Umberto Campini, Italian consul in Portuguese East Africa targeted Allied sailors, using alcohol, gambling, and prostitutes to elicit information. Lourenco Marques was a notorious haunt of Axis spies and a hotbed of activities aimed at disrupting Allied sea lanes. Kim Philby, part of the Secret Intelligence Service's Section V sub-section responsible for counter-espionage and counter-intelligence in Portugal's African territories, wrote that Campini's work constituted 'a serious menace'.[8] When the Japanese consulate in South Africa was shut down, they too began to make use of the Italian intelligence network in Portuguese East Africa.

Italy had more direct imperial ambitions in Africa, the Mediterranean, the Middle East and the Indian Ocean region than Germany, as demonstrated by its conquest of Abyssinia in the mid-1930s. Mussolini dreamed of a new Roman Empire and bitterly regretted Britain's position of strength in Italy's 'natural' sphere of influence. This was represented by its mastery of the eastern Mediterranean, its fortified presence in Malta, its casual occupation of Cyprus, its military encampment in Egypt, its stewardship of the prized Suez Canal, and its position in the lands around the Red Sea and the Horn of Africa. These places, Mussolini believed, should by rights form part of Italy's domain, and it galled him to see his country set about by the Union

6 See Helmut Stoecker, *German Imperialism in Africa: From the Beginnings Until the Second World War* (London: Hurst, 1986) and Patrick Bernhard, 'Hitler's Africa in the East: Italian Colonialism as a Model for German Planning in Eastern Europe', *Journal of Contemporary History*, 5, 1 (2016).

7 These German links with the wider world, and attempts to woo it, were underpinned by sophisticated propaganda, most notably associated with radio broadcasts. See Jeffrey Herf, *Nazi Propaganda for the Arab World* (New Haven: Yale University Press, 2010); Ashley Jackson, 'Axis Broadcasts Relating to India, Australia, Iran, and Iraq', at https://www.iwm.org.uk/sites/default/files/images/gallery/Axis%20Broadcasts%20relating%20to%20Australia%2C%20India%2C%20Iran%20and%20Iraq%20-%20Ashley%20Jackson%20.pdf; Diya Gupta, 'Propaganda Wars: India as a Contested Site between Rival Imperialist Powers', at https://www.iwm.org.uk/sites/default/files/bbc_monitoring_paper_for_website.pdf; and Louis Allday, 'German Propaganda in Sharjah', at http://blogs.bl.uk/untoldlives/2013/07/german-propaganda-in-sharjah.html.

8 E. D. R. Harrison, 'On Secret Service for the Duce: Umberto Campini in Portuguese East Africa, 1941-43', *English Historical Review*, cxxii, 499 (2007), p. 1318. For Nazi networks elsewhere in the region, see Benjamin Zachariah, 'Nazi Hunting and Intelligence Gathering in India on the Eve of the Second World War', in Jackson, Khan, and Singh (eds), *An Imperial World at War*.

Flag and the warships and Bombay bowlers of the British.[9] He maintained powerful forces in the Red Sea-Horn of Africa region, so much so that as soon as Italy declared war in June 1940, the Admiralty ordered ships bound between Bombay and Suez to form into convoy.

Operations in the western Indian Ocean had been included in Italian naval plans since the end of the 1920s.[10] Until the mid-1930s, Italy's strategy for naval operations had been conceived with France in mind as the principal enemy. Eritrea and Italian Somaliland were to accommodate a force structured around long-range submarines and auxiliary cruisers designed to harass French communications in the western Indian Ocean. The strategic logic behind this was to force the French admiralty to divert naval forces there, removing valuable units from the Mediterranean. Essentially the deployment of naval forces in the Indian Ocean was diversionary, and this approach was maintained when Italian planning in the second half of the 1930s began to target Britain as the potential enemy. Both Mussolini and the Italian navy believed 'that Britain's worldwide naval position was overstretched as a consequence of the rise of three formidable opponents' in the shape of Germany, Italy, and Japan.[11]

Indicating Italy's ambitions in the wider Indian Ocean, in 1936 the policy and planning division of the navy had supported a proposal to acquire Silhouette, the third largest island in the British-ruled Seychelles, and had produced descriptions of its geographical characteristics including an assessment of its potential as a naval base.[12] According to naval historian Fabio De Ninno, this was an extension 'of former projects for a clandestine supply base to be prepared in the Comoro Islands. The objective was to use that base to resupply submarines attacking British and French shipping in the Mozambique Channel and offshore of Mombasa'.[13]

Italian preparation for war against Britain from 1935 onward reinforced the necessity of developing a naval force capable of operating in the Indian Ocean, and early plans called for an 'escape fleet' with aircraft carriers.[14] Its purpose would be the closure of the Bab-el-Mandeb Strait, thereby neutering Aden while conducting raids against British sea lanes in the western Indian Ocean from Kismayu, mainly using submarines.[15] Bases were expanded and plans devel-

9 'Bombay bowler' was a nickname for the pith helmet or solar topi, that signature headgear of the British Empire. Though often used generically, in actual fact the Bombay bowler was one particular variant of a hat that had several different civil and military guises. For those interested, see the website MilitarySunHelmets.com at http://www.militarysunhelmets.com/2014/the-bombay-bowler. The nickname 'Bombay bloomers' was coined for the baggy shorts that became another iconic item of apparel in the overseas' Briton's wardrobe. The 'Bombay fornicator', meanwhile, was a type of long-seated wicker and wood armchair found throughout India and the eastern Empire, which featured extendable arms so that one could recline and put one's feet up.

10 Fabio De Ninno, 'The Italian Navy and Japan: The Indian Ocean, Failed Cooperation, and Tripartite Relations, 1935-1943', *War in History* (forthcoming, 2018), p. 3 proof. Thanks to Fabio for allowing me to see a pre-publication draft of this article, and for the enormous amount of help he has given me in this area. The following section relies on his work and his advice.

11 De Ninno, 'The Italian Navy and Japan', *War in History*, p. 1 proof.

12 See Appendix 1, 'Isola de Silhouette: Proposta di Acquisito', 14/4/36, in Patrizio Rapalino and Giuseppe Schivardi, *Odissea di un Sommergibilista: Dal Mar Rosso al Mediterraneo, 1940-1943* (Milan: Mursia, 2008), pp. 215-218.

13 Personal correspondence, March 2018.

14 Discussed in Robert Mallett, *The Italian Navy and Fascist Expansionism, 1935-1940* (London: Frank Cass, 1988).

15 See De Ninno, *I Sommergibili del Fascismo: Politica Navale, Strategia e Uomini tra le Due Guerre Mondiali* (Milan: Unicopli, 2014), title translated as 'The submarines of fascism: Naval politics,

oped to dispatch a force of two or three cruisers and ten submarines to the area, their objective to gain control of the Bab-el-Mandeb and attack shipping.[16] Objectives in the Red Sea for this force would be the destruction of the enemy naval presence, commerce raiding, and the neutralisation of Aden, with the support of the Italian air force, as well as the seizure or at least the closure of the Bab-el-Mandeb.

Italian attempts to establish cooperation with the Japanese in the Indian Ocean were important.[17] By 1937, 'Italian plans for seizing the Suez Canal were based on the assumption that the Japanese Navy would pin down large Royal Navy forces in the Far East'.[18] Despite the challenges facing Italian strategists and the struggle to finance Mussolini's ambitions, the 1939-40 naval programme proposed the construction of three new cruisers,[19] eight destroyers, 12 torpedo boats, six coastal submarines for operations in the Red Sea, as well as six 'oceanic' submarines for operations in the Indian Ocean. But ambitions for East Africa and the wider Indian Ocean were not fully realized, the cruiser programme, for example, being cancelled after the start of the war in Europe due to a lack of raw materials.[20] Italian difficulties in the Mediterranean were to force the navy to reduce its ambitions and its commitments in this theatre, as were early defeats, though Rome continued until the end to place hope in Japanese prowess to help restore the situation.

Convoys, escorts, troopships, and trade

Protecting a global maritime empire presented the British with unique challenges. Some idea of the extent of the Royal Navy's commerce-protection responsibilities, writes Dudley Pope, 'is given by the fact that in 1939 more than 3,000 foreign-going merchant ships were registered in Britain, and more than 1,000 coasters. An average of 2,500 ships flying the Red Ensign were at sea on any one day in positions ranging from the east coast of England to the far ends of the Pacific'.[21] The British government fully appreciated the country's, and the Empire's, inescapable

strategy and men between the two world wars', pp. 213-214 for the plans regarding attacks on Anglo-French shipping in the Southern Indian ocean; De Ninno, 'I Piani della Regia Marina per l'Oceano Indiano, 1922-1934', in Virgilio Ilari and Mariano Gabriele (eds), *Naval History: The SISM (Società Italiana di Storia Militare/Italian Society for Military History) Remembers Alberto Santoni (1936-2016)* (Rome: SISM, 2014), pp. 541-562 for the naval plans during the period 1925-1934 against the French. By 1938 plans to occupy Aden were also being discussed. See also John Gooch, *Mussolini and His Generals: The Armed Forces and Fascist Foreign Policy, 1922-1940* (Cambridge: Cambridge University Press, 2007).

16 This is well covered in the official history volume. See P. F. Lupinacci, *Le Operazioni in Africa Orientale*, volume 10, *La Marina Italiana nella Seconda Guerra Mondiale* (Rome: Ufficio Storico della Marina Militaire (the Italian navy's historical department), 1961).

17 See Valdo Ferretti, *Il Giappone el la Politica Estera Italiana,* (Japan and Italian foreign policy) *1935-1941* (Milan: Giuffrè, 1995).

18 De Ninno, 'The Italian Navy and Japan', p. 4 proof.

19 The Costanzo Ciano class. See Maurizio Brescia, *Mussolini's Navy: A Reference Guide to the Regia Marina, 1940-1945* (Barnsley: Seaforth Publishing, 2012).

20 See Giorgio Giorgerini, *Da Matapan al Golfo Persico: La Marina Militaire Italiano dal Fascismo alla Repubblica* (Milan: Mondadori, 1989), p. 379.

21 Dudley Pope, *The Battle of the River Plate* (London: The Ramage Company, 1974), p. 16.

dependence upon seaborne trade. Figures summarizing the shipping and supply situation were circulated to ministers with frequent regularity. During the course of the single week 20 to 27 June 1940, for example, they learned that imports to Britain by convoy had amounted to 959,498 tons. Nineteen tankers had transported 219,646 tons of oil, and mineral imports amounting to 255,037 tons had also arrived. Imports of cereal amounted to 196,576 tons and other foodstuffs to 56,284 tons, including 10,300 tons of sugar and 20,883 tons of refrigerated and canned meat. In that one week, 882 ships had been escorted in convoy and the total since hostilities commenced stood at 26,355.[22] In moving these goods around the world, the sea lanes of the Indian Ocean were indispensable. To take but one sea lane as an example, in October 1940 the ships of the East Indies Station escorted 127 merchant vessels and troopships travelling north to the Red Sea, and 106 travelling in the opposite direction.[23]

The same, naturally, was true of military personnel and material, and in the first year of the war 274,402 imperial servicemen moved through the waters of the East Indies Station, stretching from the Cape to Australia.[24] By March 1941, the number had risen to 643,198.[25] The first dedicated troop convoy had sailed around the Cape in June 1940, inaugurating the phenomenon that was to be the 'Winston Special' convoys which funnelled forces through the Indian Ocean to the North African theatre and points east given the Mediterranean's impassability. These crucial 'WS' convoys sailed on average thereafter once a month for the next three years, carrying troops destined principally for Egypt, India, and the Far East. The transit of troops to and from Australasia and India was also vital: between August and December 1940 alone, 50,000 troops sailed from Australasia and India, and 77,000 crossed the Indian Ocean from Britain. By the end of the war, a staggering 6,000,000 service personnel had transited through South Africa's ports.

The 'Winston Special' convoy system was made feasible because 'British shipping companies owned and operated half of the world's passenger vessels'.[26] Because of the war and the imperative need to transport service personnel, ultimately over 200 ocean-going passenger ships were adapted to serve as troopships with a carrying capacity of over 400,000 personnel at any one time. Troop convoys sailed across the Indian Ocean to strengthen overseas garrisons. Typical of them was convoy WS10, which sailed from Greenock in Scotland on 2 August 1941, comprising 19 ships including *Andes*, *Britannic*, *Highland Monarch*, *Indian Prince*, *Nigerstroom* (Dutch), *Orcades*, and *Windsor Castle.* Three of the ships carried explosives, and the convoy's 13 troopships accommodated 25,903 service personnel. The convoy put in at some of the Empire's most important ports as it journeyed eastwards, calling at Freetown, Cape Town, and Durban. In South Africa the convoy dispersed, some ships heading for Suez and some for Bombay, with stop-offs at Mombasa, Aden, Suez, and Colombo along the way.[27] Mounting such convoys was

22 TNA, CAB 66/9/7. War Cabinet, Weekly Résumé of the Naval, Military, and Air Situation from 12 Noon June 20th to 12 Noon June 27th, 1940. See C. B. A. Behrens, *Merchant Shipping and the Demands of War* (London: HMSO, 1955) for wartime shipping.
23 Naval Historical Board (NHB), Eastern Fleet war diary, volume 10.
24 Ibid.
25 Ibid., volume 9.
26 Munro, *The Winston Specials*, p. x.
27 See 'Convoy Web: The Website for Merchant Ships during World War Two'. For convoy WS10, see http://www.convoyweb.org.uk/ws/index.html?ws10.php?convoy=10_1~wsmain

an enormous organizational undertaking. 'Each convoy was elaborately planned, assembled, and dispatched and proceeded throughout as a military operation rather than as a trade convoy'.[28]

Merchant and passenger lines both famous and obscure had their ships requisitioned by the Admiralty and converted into armed merchant cruisers or troopships.[29] They included the Aberdeen and Commonwealth Line, the Alfred Holt Line, the Anchor Line, the Blue Funnel Line, the British India Line, the Cunard-White Star Line, Elder Dempster, Ellermans, Furness-Withy, the Orient Line, the Pacific Steam Navigation Company, Peninsular and Oriental, and the Union Castle Line. Among their number were the world's largest luxury liners, known as 'the Monsters', converted for use as troopships and responsible for ferrying millions of Allied servicemen and women. Four – *Aquitania* (44,000 tons), *Mauretania* (35,000 tons), *Queen Elizabeth* (83,000 tons), and *Queen Mary* (81,000 tons) – were from the British Cunard-White Star fleet and the largest ships in world. The other two were the French ship *Ile de France* (43,000 tons), requisitioned by the British in 1940, and the Dutch ship *Nieuw Amsterdam* (36,000 tons).[30]

As the historian of the 'Winston Special' convoys writes,

> From the worldwide trade routes came the passenger ships that now formed the bulk of the British trooping fleet. Augmented by others charted or requisitioned from the conquered nations of Europe, these great liners, together with their officers and crews, and given safe escort by the Royal Navy, represented the means by which Britain was able to implement a successful maritime strategy by carrying her military might around the Cape of Good Hope to face her enemies afresh in the Middle East and Far East, a feat scarcely comprehensible to those who actually accomplished it.[31]

The 52 separate 'Winston Special' convoys that sailed between 1940 and 1943 featured 458 troopships carrying 1,173,010 British and Allied personnel.[32] James Alan Thompson was one of them, his Royal Marines unit joining a convoy of 'weary, sea-battered ships … journeying around a continent to war' in March 1941.[33] Like so many others travelling this route, he had the opportunity to disembark at stops along the way and so to hail the 'great white city of the Cape' and the 'splendid curve' around Durban's 'beautiful bay', 'alive with surf thunder', and to enjoy their hospitality.[34]

28 Munro, *The Winston Specials*, p. xii.
29 The Cunard White Star Line's *Queen Mary*, now permanently moored in Los Angeles, is one of the very few remaining in existence. She alone carried a jaw-dropping 1,243,538 service personnel over the course of the war.
30 On 15 September 1941 *Queen Elizabeth* and *Queen Mary* arrived in Ceylon, and *Cornwall* escorted them to the Middle East. 'As we sped across the Indian Ocean it was fascinating during the daytime just watching these two supermonsters. Graceful despite their huge size, seemingly imperturbable and the embodiment of such immense power'. Ken Dimbleby, *Turns of Fate: The Drama of HMS* Cornwall (London: William Kimber, 1984).
31 Munro, *The Winston Specials*, p. 16. Fittingly, the last WS convoy to sail carried the 81st West African Division to India for service in Burma.
32 Ibid., p. 430.
33 Thompson, *Only the Sun Remembers*, p. 32.
34 Ibid. It was then on to Cairo and thence to Palestine, its ports full of men and ships involved in the Cretan expedition.

A year later, Alan Shaw, a lieutenant in the Royal Engineers, also experienced a typical convoy journey east. On 17 March 1942 he embarked at Halifax railway station in West Yorkshire for an undisclosed destination which turned out to be Liverpool. Here, '[d]imly visible in driving sleet, a line of grey troopships lay in the River Mersey'.[35] Conveyed from shore to ship by motor launch, losing a man when he fell between boat and ladder, Shaw stepped aboard the *Nieuw Holland*, an 11,000 ton Dutch liner under British management. Designed to carry 370 passengers and crew on the Java-Australia route, she now accommodated 2,000 troops. In addition to Shaw's Royal Engineers draft, destined for India, there were troops of the 5th British Division and the 29th Independent Brigade Group, destined for the invasion of Madagascar and the reinforcement of India given the worrying threat now posed by the all-conquering Japanese.

> Sometime after dark the convoy slipped its moorings and headed out into the Irish Sea, zigzagging in unison for protection ... A day or so later we sailed up the Clyde estuary into the great anchorage known as the 'Tail of the Bank'. Here we merged with one of the biggest convoys ever assembled. Ships of all shapes, size, and description lay at anchor.[36]

This enormous floating collection of men and metal left the Clyde on 23 March.

> Like all troopships, *Nieuw Holland* had a military Commandant, an elderly lieutenant-colonel 'dug out' of retirement for the duration, supported by an Adjutant, Regimental Sergeant Major, and various NCOs. Their job was to prevent the voyage from becoming a pleasure cruise by continuously creating employment for everyone on board. Perhaps it only seemed like that. We had to be kept fit enough to be of use when we landed in India two months later. There were deck games, physical training sessions, Urdu lessons for those destined to join the Indian Army, and, for the officers, a roster of Orderly Officer duties stretching some way into the future. These involved attendance on the ship's captain and the Commandant during daily inspections of every person and nook and cranny in the ship, inspection of food and hygiene in the troop decks. Sunday church services included the choir recruited and rehearsed during the week. Evenings were occupied by chess or bridge, or by a sing-song around the piano in the Officers' Lounge. The tradition of self entertainment still lingered on and many were quite musically talented. As the weather improved and the temperature steadily increased large canvas ventilating tubes were rigged from the masts and ducted through open hatchways into the troop decks below.[37]

The convoy sailed passed the Mull of Kintyre and west into the Atlantic, the ships zigzagging in unison at a siren blast from the convoy commodore's ship. After stopping at Freetown,

> our giant convoy resumed its passage for a further two weeks to the Cape of Good Hope. There it split in to two, one half going to Durban. To our delight our half sailed into Cape

35 BBC 'World War Two People's War' oral history archive, Alan Shaw, 'Marching on to Laffan's Plain', chapter 4, A3209500. The convoy Shaw describes was the one carrying the forces that would mount the invasion of Madagascar in May 1942.

36 Ibid.

37 Ibid.

> Town harbour. As our ship tied up in the brilliant afternoon sun, an army staff car arrived on the quayside and decanted an embarkation staff officer. The driver also emerged, an extremely attractive girl in military uniform, who evoked a deafening barrage of wolf whistles and unbelieving cries of, 'Look! A woman!'. The entire compliment rushed to the port side to see this vision and *Nieuw Holland* took on an alarming list shorewards. A memorable programme of hospitality was organized in Cape Town. Vivid memories remain of being taken with several shipboard friends to the Kelvingrove [Kelvin Grove] Country Club, to the Rotunda Ballroom, and to the private houses of residents who were members of the Hospitality Committee, established to host the many thousands of servicemen and women who passed through South African ports. We were taken up Table Mountain by cable car and visited many historic places.[38]

After a memorable period of rest and recreation in South Africa, an experience common to hundreds of thousands of servicemen as they moved between Europe and the east and back again, the troop-laden liner set sail for the long haul across the Indian Ocean. Over 4,000 nautical miles from the Cape to Bombay, which *Nieuw Holland* entered 'through a flat calm in the final miles, through small groups of picturesque fishing boats'.[39]

Unsurprisingly, despite possessing the world's largest navy Britain lacked sufficient escort vessels to give armed cover to all the Empire's convoys and the many ships routed independently. It was a tricky balancing act, because while smaller warships, such as destroyers, were ideal for protecting convoys against submarines, they were in great demand because capital ships – battleships and aircraft carriers – could not operate without destroyer screens. The workhorses of sea lane patrol – cruisers – were also stretched by the demands of a global conflict, and there were never enough corvettes – dedicated escort and anti-submarine vessels – to go around.[40] The lack of adequate escorts led to innovation and improvisation, as the hulls of merchant ships were converted for offensive and defensive purposes. Some large merchantmen became Armed Merchant Cruisers, fitted with guns and accompanied by Royal Navy personnel to operate them. Many were given guns and gun crews, becoming known as 'Defensively Equipped Merchant Ships'. Other ships had a catapult added to the superstructure so that they could carry seaplanes (Catapult Armed Merchant Ships); converting decks from the hull also produced escort carriers, a special breed of small aircraft carrier capable of embarking a squadron or two of Albacores, Fulmars, Seafires, or Swordfish.

Smaller vessels were pressed in to service too. Trawlers and whalers, from Britain and Empire countries such as South Africa, were converted for escort and minesweeping duties. Australian shipyards built corvettes for both its own forces and the Royal Navy. The largest contribution came from American shipyards and vessels of all shapes and sizes slid down the slipway with unprecedented speed to join the Royal Navy under the Lend-Lease programme, including 150

38 Ibid.
39 Ibid.
40 Agar, captain of *Dorsetshire*, described the Colony class cruisers as having been 'designed to protect our commerce on the trade routes'. Agar, *Footprints in the Sea*, p. 163. Pope writes that the Admiralty had always maintained that the minimum number of cruisers necessary to meet British commitments was 70, but that only 58 were on the strength, some of them of inferior quality due to lack of endurance. Pope, *The Battle of the River Plate*, p. 16.

or so wooden-hulled 'BYMS' motor minesweepers, some of which served in the Indian Ocean, and the escort carriers that were to become a feature of the Royal Navy's presence in the region.[41]

Ships were requisitioned wherever they could be found and put to good use after hasty conversions kitted them out as patrol, escort, or mine countermeasure vessels. *Kedah*, for example, was requisitioned by the Royal Navy from the Straits Steamship Company. As a passenger liner, she had been a feature on the Singapore to Penang 'tropical express' run. The navy changed her superstructure, added new masts, and installed a pair of four-inch naval guns, a three-inch anti-aircraft gun, and depth charge launchers, converting her into an 'armed auxiliary vessel'. Colonial naval forces were also very important in supporting the Royal Navy. The Ceylon Royal Naval Reserve, the Royal Indian Navy, and the South African Naval Service expanded rapidly and worked hand in hand with the Royal Navy across the Indian Ocean, as did local naval forces in Kenya and Tanganyika.[42] The role of these colonial forces in wartime was to expand and to perform as many essential local duties around their home ports and coastal waters as they possibly could, thus releasing Royal Navy units for service further afield.

To meet wartime challenges, the Admiralty shuffled its pack, transferring vessels from one imperial fleet to another as threats arose and were met. The Royal Navy's China Station, for instance, though quite a substantial force in 1939, soon began transferring ships to other commands, particularly the Indian Ocean and Mediterranean fleets.[43] Japanese operations in China together with London's desire to avoid provoking Tokyo meant that the China Station became increasingly moribund. It became virtually an Indian Ocean force, a fact recognized when Admiral Sir Percy Noble, Commander-in-Chief China on the outbreak of war, moved

41 BYMS stood for 'British Yard Minesweeper', the vessels having derived from the American 'Yard' class. See Kenneth Poolman, *Escort Carriers of World War Two* (London: Weidenfeld, 1989) and David Wragg, *The Escort Carrier of the Second World War: Combustible, Vulnerable, Expendable* (Barnsley: Pen and Sword, 2015). Poolman also has titles on Armed Merchant Cruisers, escort carriers, and catapult-arms vessels. Like with so many aspects of naval history, the internet offers an embarrassment of riches. See, for example, 'Royal Navy Escort Carriers', at http://www.royalnavyresearcharchive.org.uk/ESCORT/#.WsOLjBNViko

42 See the recently-published 'long' official history of South Africa's naval forces, H. R. Gordon-Cumming, *Official History of the South African Naval Forces during the Second World War, 1939-1945* (Simon's Town: Naval Heritage Trust South Africa, 2008) and D. Collins, *The Royal Indian Navy, 1939-1945*, part of the *Official History of the Indian Armed Forces in the Second World War* (Bombay: Orient Longmans/Combined Inter Service Historical Section India and Pakistan, 1964), available online at http://tothosewhoserved.org/ind/indnavy/. Of particular interest are chapters 4 and 5 on operations in the Red Sea and Persian Gulf. For the Royal Indian Navy also see the memoir of its commander from 1943, Rear Admiral John Godfrey, former Chief of Naval Intelligence at the Admiralty. Godfrey, 'The Naval Memoirs of Admiral J. H. Godfrey', volume 6, '1943-1946', copy held in the Library of the Joint Services Command and Staff College, Defence Academy of the United Kingdom. On colonial naval forces, see Daniel Owen Spence, *Colonial Naval Culture and British Imperialism, 1922-1967* (Manchester: Manchester University Press, 2015), part 2, 'East Africa' and part 3, 'South-east Asia'.

43 For the China Station, see Martin Brice, *The Royal Navy and the Sino-Japanese Incident, 1937-1941* (London: Ian Allan, 1973). At the outbreak of war the Fleet comprised the carrier *Eagle*, the four vessels of the 5th Cruiser Squadron, the nine vessels of the 21st Destroyer Flotilla, and the 16 vessels of the 4th Submarine Flotilla. For local defence there were the four destroyers of the Local Defence Flotilla, the Yangtse Flotilla of 15 gunboats, the West River Flotilla of four gunboats, and the nine minesweepers of the 2nd Minesweeping Flotilla. See 'China Station, 1939-1942', in Watson, 'Organization of the Royal Navy'.

his flag to Singapore.[44] From here the resources of both the China Station and the East Indies Station combined to patrol the trade routes of the Indian Ocean and offer protection to convoys. The cruisers *Emerald* and *Enterprise* of the East Indies Station, for instance, together with China Station cruisers *Danae*, *Dauntless* and *Durban*, spent the early months of the war searching for raiders and enemy blockade runners. The carrier *Eagle*, meanwhile, along with the cruisers *Cornwall* and *Dorsetshire*, formed a raider hunting group in the Bay of Bengal, known as Force I, as the Admiralty discerned the need to deploy effective modern units in the Aden-Singapore-Simonstown triangle on the outbreak of war.[45]

The China Station's famous 'Insect' class river gunboats, for so long a symbol of the Royal Navy in China's coastal and inland waters, were moved westwards. The days of British pre-eminence in Shanghai and the Yangtze Delta were drawing to a close as the Japanese war in China intensified. With virtually no riverine trade to protect anymore due to the disruption caused by the Sino-Japanese war, and given the fact that the gunboats were a source of irritation to the Japanese, it was decided to usher them west. At Singapore they could be converted into minelayers, minesweepers or anti-submarine vessels, and could then find profitable employment as part of the East Indies Station or Mediterranean Fleet.[46] *Tarantula*, for example, wound up in Trincomalee after leaving Hong Kong and then Singapore as the British were harried west by the Japanese. Here 'this quite unseaworthy and very ancient river ship' was used as office accommodation and became the base ship for the Ceylon Escort Force and flagship of the Commander-in-Chief East Indies.[47] Her sister ship, *Cockchafer*, spent much of the war working in the Persian Gulf and supporting ground forces in Burma, while three other members of the twelve-strong 'Insect' class served as part of the Mediterranean Fleet's inshore squadron. Useful even in decline, HMS *Gnat*'s six-inch guns were installed for coastal defence at Port Victoria in the Seychelles after she had been torpedoed in the Mediterranean and beached off Alexandria.[48]

Submarines and early German forays in the Indian Ocean

Submarines from the China Station were also transferred to Alexandria, Colombo, and Singapore, and the British were to deploy dozens in the Indian Ocean region over the course of the war. On its outbreak, British submarines east of Suez had a specific role. The China Squadron's 4th Submarine Flotilla, based in Hong Kong and comprising 13 submarines and two minelaying submarines, was intended to hold a seaborne attack on Malaya if war with Japan broke out. It was to act as an underwater tripwire that would give the guns of Singapore, and the powerful fleet that would, it was hoped, operate from its new naval base, time to mobilize. But with war against Germany looming in 1939, Britain's submarine force east of Suez had more immediate priorities. That August eight of the 4th Submarine Flotilla's vessels were transferred

44 Noble was succeeded by Vice Admiral Geoffrey Layton in September 1940.

45 NHB, Eastern Fleet War Diary. This was part of the effort to track down the *Graf Spee*.

46 HMS *Aphis*, *Cicala*, *Cockchafer*, *Cricket*, *Dragonfly*, *Gnat*, *Grasshopper*, *Ladybird*, *Moth*, *Scarab*, *Scorpion*, and *Tarantula*.

47 Simpson (ed.), *The Somerville Papers*, p. 484. She was ignominiously sunk off Trincomalee a year after the war finished as gunnery practice for a pair of destroyers.

48 NHB, Eastern Fleet War Diary.

to Singapore, from where they patrolled the Malacca Strait, the Sunda Strait, and the waters off Sabang in northern Sumatra.

The movement of submarines reflected the War Cabinet and Chiefs of Staff's need to allocate resources across multiple theatres. In late October four more submarines were detached from the China Station to join the East Indies Station, forming the 8th Submarine Flotilla based at Colombo. They were serviced by the depot ship *Lucia*, previously the *Spreewald*, which had been captured from the Germans in the West Indies in September 1914 and converted into a submarine depot ship. This was an essential item on a fleet's inventory, and in 1939 she was brought out of retirement at Bombay, re-commissioned, and sent to Ceylon to sustain the newly-formed flotilla. Depot ships were important assets, containing extensive workshops and machine rooms, a foundry, a periscope repair room, a bakery, and a cold store for food. There were six and ten ton cranes on the deck, eight 4.5-inch guns, and a ship's company of over 1,100 officers and ratings. A depot ship was

> a valuable floating city of workshops, stores, and technical knowledge ... Depot ships are designed for changing base quickly according to the strategic needs of the moment. At a few days notice they can achieve a removal which a shore base would need months to complete ... A floating factory, with torpedo and engineering workshops, crew accommodation, stores, 'attack teacher' training, operations rooms [the Submarine Attack Teacher contained model ships and a rotating 'submarine' with a short periscope and was used to simulate attacks].[49]

In early November 1939 two special patrols were instituted for these Ceylon-based submarines: one 'short' to the Chagos Archipelago and the Maldives, the other 'long' to the Seychelles and back and taking two months to complete. These patrols searched the seas and the profusion of small islands scattered across the Indian Ocean for enemy vessels. This was necessary work, because the ocean offered so many locations where enemy raiders, submarines, and their supply ships could rest, conduct essential repairs, and take on board fresh supplies of food, fuel, and ammunition.

Extensive patrols instituted to hunt for German vessels were lonely, tedious, and uncomfortable affairs, 70-odd men living in cramped conditions with precious few contacts with the enemy to boost morale. On 19 December 1939, over a month after leaving her home base in Ceylon to take part in the hunt for the pocket battleship *Graf Spee* (see later), the Commander-in-Chief East Indies ordered *Olympus* from Madagascar to Prince Edward Island, 1,200 miles south-east of South Africa. This followed reports of an unidentified signal emanating from what was believed to be an enemy unit, and *Olympus* was the nearest British vessel and so was sent to investigate. The signal came from the German raider *Pinguin*, which had left for the Prince Edward and Crozet islands after rendezvousing with her fellow raider *Atlantis* south-east of Madagascar.

So *Olympus*, kitted out for tropical patrol, headed for the chill seas of the Roaring Forties and a clutch of uninhabited volcanic islands, with no warm clothing aboard and inadequate charts.

49 Edward Young, *One of Our Submarines* (London: Rupert Hart-Davis, 1952), p. 107 and 160. Material in square brackets is from Brian Lavery, *Churchill's Navy: The Ships, Men, and Organization, 1939–1945* (London: Conway, 2006), p. 213.

Mountainous seas were made more perilous by the presence of icebergs, identified by sonar, and the failure of one of the engines.

> In sight of the bleak towering cliffs which rose to 6,500 feet in the centre of the Isle de la Possession [in the Crozet islands], with gigantic waves breaking at their base, the second engine failed. By heroic efforts the Engine room staff got one engine to start again and the submarine clawed its way back from the inhospitable shore, which obviously provided no shelter for any ship, enemy or otherwise.[50]

Having checked both island groups for signs of the mystery enemy vessel, Commander King left the area and set course for Durban, the crew celebrating a dreary Christmas 1939 at sea. Approaching the port, German-built aircraft of the South African Air Force conducted dummy attacks on *Olympus*, rather alarming the crew. After repairs at Durban, *Olympus* crossed the Indian Ocean, arriving back at her home base of Colombo on 22 January 1940 having covered 12,000 miles during the course of a single patrol.[51]

These submarines were also used as convoy escorts for merchantmen and troopships moving between the Empire's ports. In early 1940, for example, *Olympus* and *Orpheus* were sent from Ceylon to cover the passage of the convoy taking the first Australian and New Zealand troops to the Middle East. Starting near the Chagos Archipelago 'they worked up through the islands towards the track of the convoy. Finally on the night of 1-2 February, they had the satisfaction of remaining unseen whilst they watched the twelve large liners packed with troops pass safely through the Nine Degree Channel'.[52] Despite the important work performed by submarines in the Indian Ocean in the first year of the war, the situation in the Mediterranean meant that their number dwindled, as one theatre took priority over another in the constant struggle to match resources against threats. The 8th Submarine Flotilla left Ceylon in March 1940, and by the following month there were no British submarines in the Indian Ocean at all. This remained the case nearly 20 months later in December 1941when Japan entered the war.

Another early war task for the Royal Navy in the Indian Ocean was the blockade of Vichy French territories and the interception of French convoys and blockade runners. The blockade was 'imposed above all upon French North Africa [Djibouti] and the Indian Ocean territories of Madagascar, Réunion, and French Somaliland'.[53] From 1941 Madagascar depended on American trade to provide essential imports, though this trade diminished as President Roosevelt was wary of breaching the British blockade. According to Martin Thomas, this was the most effective blockades against Vichy: 'By 1942 the economic hardships it produced were biting hard among the French planter community and Madagascar's town populations. By the time of the invasion [May 1942], Madagascar's export trade was only 22 per cent of its pre-war

50 Brian Wilson, *A Submariners' War in the Indian Ocean, 1939-1945* (Stroud, Gloucestershire: Tempus, 2000), p. 23. This book is complemented by Lawrence Paterson, *Hitler's Grey Wolves: U-Boats in the Indian Ocean* (Barnsley: Pen and Sword, 2016).
51 Commander King was awarded the OBE for this patrol.
52 Wilson, *A Submariners' War*, p. 24.
53 Martin Thomas, *The French Empire at War, 1940-1945* (Manchester: Manchester University Press, 1998), 71.

level'.[54] There were several interception missions, such as Operation Snip which in September 1941 sought unsuccessfully to capture or destroy a Vichy convoy crossing the Indian Ocean from Indo-China to Madagascar. It involved the carrier *Hermes*, the cruiser *Hawkins* detached from escorting convoy WS10B for the purpose, and the cruisers *Enterprise* and *Mauritius*. Two Catalina flying-boats from Diego Garcia were also involved, and searches were made around the Chagos Archipelago, the Saya de Malha bank, and the Cargados Carajos Group.

German surface raiders

The sea lanes of the Indian Ocean attracted enemy commerce raiders from the earliest months of war. In November 1939 Captain Hans Langsdorff rounded the Cape in the heavy cruiser ('pocket battleship' to the British) *Graf Spee*.[55] His intention was 'to carry on the trade war south of Madagascar and create alarm there and draw off the British forces'.[56] He soon expanded his plan and decided to hunt up the Mozambique Channel and, if that did not prove fruitful, to attack South African coastal traffic and launch an air strike on Durban. The British knew the German warship was at large, and drew forces from East Indies Station bases as far away as Ceylon in order to hunt her down. The venerable battleship *Ramillies* (with midshipman Prince Philip of Greece aboard) was diverted from Indian Ocean escort duties to join the search. Detached to Aden, she joined the battleship *Malaya* and the carrier *Glorious*, loaned from the Mediterranean Fleet and entering the Indian Ocean through the Suez Canal. Dubbed Force J, this powerful ensemble searched fruitlessly for the *Graf Spee* towards the northern end of the Mozambique Channel.

Other vessels joined the hunt. Commander King's *Olympus* had just left Colombo for the 'long patrol' to the Seychelles when she was diverted to the area as news came through that *Graf Spee* had sunk the British tanker *Africa Shell* on 16 November 160 miles north-east of Lourenco Marques. A newly-launched ship of 706 tons, *Africa Shell* had been sighted by *Graf Spee* on the northern approach to Delagoa Bay. The crew were allowed to get away on boats, the master was taken prisoner, and the ship was sunk.[57] Other submarines also joined the search for *Graf Spee*; even in the distant Lombok Strait between the islands of Bali and Lombok on the far side of the Indian Ocean, subsurface patrols were intensified. The response of the Admiralty and Naval Headquarters Colombo was sufficiently robust that *Graf Spee* quit the Indian Ocean after a month. But though pickings were slim, efforts taken to thwart her were considerable,

54 Ibid., 142.

55 See Siegfried Breyer, *Pocket Battleship* Admiral Graf Spee (West Chester, PA: Schiffer, 1989) and Richard Woodman, *The Battle of the River Plate: A Grand Delusion* (Pen and Sword, 2008). Also, Theodore Krancke, *Pocket Battleship: The Story of the* Admiral Scheer (London: Norton, 1958).

56 Pope, *The Battle of the River Plate*, p. 60.

57 This was all caught on camera. For fascinating photographs of *Africa Shell* taken from *Graf Spee* as she closed her, boarded her, and finally sunk her, see http://www.maritimequest.com/freighters/02_pages/a/africa_shell_1938_page_1.htm. The ship's master, Captain Patrick Dove, was treated well by Captain Langsdorff while aboard *Graf Spee* and released in Uruguay. He played himself as the story was recounted in the 1940 British documentary-film *For Freedom*, directed by Maurice Elvey. The sinking of *Africa Shell* also forms part of the opening sequence in the 1956 film *Battle of the River Plate*, and Dove is a prominent figure aboard the *Graf Spee* thereafter.

illustrating the strain on resources that the appearance of even a single enemy vessel could cause. Beginning her journey back around the Cape on 16 November, Langsdorff had achieved his objective of diverting the British hunting groups. With her departure from the Indian Ocean, East Indies Station ships resumed their normal duties.[58]

Entering the South Atlantic, the German heavy cruiser sunk the Blue Star Line's *Doric Star* on 2 December 500 miles off the coast of South-West Africa. This merchantman had been heading to Britain from New Zealand via Sydney and the Cape with a cargo of frozen meat, dairy produce, and wool. Her distress signal was picked up by Commodore Henry Harwood, who was hunting the German raider, and he now correctly anticipated her next move. *Graf Spee* crossed the Atlantic and fought the Battle of the River Plate on 13 December 1939 against Harwood's cruiser squadron, resulting in the scuttling of the ship near Montevideo, and Langsdorff's suicide.[59]

The ability of a single powerful raider to disperse enemy resources was demonstrated by the fact that the Royal Navy and its French ally had had to form so many hunting groups to search for the *Graf Spee*. At the time she sank the *Clement* on 30 September, her first victim, the hunting groups looked like this:

> Force F, *Berwick*, *York*, North America and West Indies.
> Force G, *Cumberland*, *Exeter*, east coast of South America.
> Force H, *Sussex*, *Shropshire*, Cape of Good Hope.
> Force I, *Cornwall*, *Dorsetshire*, *Eagle*, Ceylon.
> Force K, *Ark Royal*, *Renown*, six-inch cruiser joining, Pernambuco-Freetown.
> Force L, *Dunkerque*, *Bearn*, three six-inch cruisers, Brest.
> Force M, two eight-inch cruisers, Dakar.
> Force N, *Hermes*, *Strasbourg*, West Indies.[60]

This was an enormous diversion of Allied naval power:

> The effect of forming the eight groups was immense and world-wide – Force F consisted of ships diverted from Halifax, Nova Scotia; Force H from the Mediterranean; Force I from China and Force K from the Home Fleet. But that was not all – in addition to the hunting groups, the battleships *Resolution* and *Revenge* and cruisers *Enterprise* and *Emerald* were to sail to Halifax to escort homeward-bound convoys, and were followed later by *Repulse*,

58 *Olympus* was ordered to the French base of Diego Suarez in Madagascar to refuel and take on supplies of fresh food. The French harbour was inhospitable because of the heat, the flies, the lack of shore facilities, and dockyard inefficiency. Matters were not helped, recalled Lieutenant Lennox Napier, by the attitude of the French commandant. 'His view was that life for French soldiers in the Maginot line was extremely disagreeable and it was, therefore, the duty of French forces elsewhere to lead an equally miserable existence – and this also applied to any ally who visited the French base'. Wilson, *A Submariners' War*, p. 22.

59 For a recent reprint of a 1956 classic, see Gordon Landsborough, *The Battle of the River Plate: The First Naval Battle of the Second World War* (Barnsley: Frontline Books, 2016). 1956 also saw the release of the Technicolour film *The Battle of the River Plate* starring Anthony Quayle and Peter Finch.

60 Pope, *The Battle of the River Plate*, p. 48.

> *Furious*, and *Warspite*, while a battleship and aircraft carrier were sent through the Suez Canal to form a ninth hunting group in the Indian Ocean.[61]

Other major German units made commerce raiding sorties in the Indian Ocean. The heavy cruiser *Admiral Scheer*, *Graf Spee*'s sister, operated successfully off Madagascar and in the northern Indian Ocean in February 1941, where the merchantman *Canadian Cruiser* was among her victims. The search for *Admiral Scheer* once again witnessed the employment of East Indies Station assets, coordinated from a central headquarters. The British rushed to deploy forces to find and sink the vessel, entailing close cooperation between warships and the maritime patrol aircraft of the RAF. One of the units involved was 230 Squadron, flying Sunderlands, which in late 1940 had been in the process of transferring from Seletar in Singapore to the Middle East. En route it was ordered to halt and survey Koggala lake near Galle in Ceylon as a potential flying-boat base. While in the process of doing so, the squadron received orders to remain in Ceylon and join the effort to keep *Admiral Scheer* away from the massive convoy then crossing the Indian Ocean taking thousands of Australian and New Zealand troops to the Middle East.

Numerous East Indies Station units mustered to join the hunt. The cruiser *Enterprise* was at Brava in Italian Somaliland, the cruiser *Ceres* at Mogadishu, the cruiser *Emerald* was accompanying convoy WS5BX bound for Suez, and the cruiser *Hawkins* was escorting convoy WS5B steaming towards the Persian Gulf. Also nearby was the cruiser *Glasgow*, and all were rallied to help in the search. The carrier *Hermes* and cruiser *Shropshire* had been making attacks on Kismayu and Mogadishu when, on 22 February, they were also ordered to join the hunt. She sailed with the cruiser *Capetown* and joined the Royal Australian Navy heavy cruisers *Australia* and *Canberra* and the other ships. But although an aircraft launched from *Glasgow* sighted *Admiral Scheer* on 22 February, she escaped the closing net and left the Indian Ocean unharmed, to the Royal Navy's intense frustration.[62] It was a classic raider foray on the part of the German vessel, tying down precious resources in a costly wild goose chase while all the time posing a real and immediate danger to British and Allied shipping.

While enemy vessels could appear anywhere in the Indian Ocean, there were favoured hunting grounds determined by their proximity to busy ports and sea lanes and, of course, their proximity to Axis-held ports. Thus the Red Sea and Gulf of Aden were the scene of significant actions, because of the high value convoys that sailed these waters, and the existence up until April 1941 of several Italian ports in the region. Also important was the Persian Gulf, which was the British Empire's main source of oil, some of which was delivered by a network of overland pipes to British installations in Palestine, and some of which left Abadan and its enormous refinery in tankers, entering the Indian Ocean via the Straits of Hormuz and the Gulf of Oman. The Mozambique Channel, dense with convoys, was another key area for British shipping, and the naval base at Diego Suarez in Madagascar, in which the French had invested heavily before war broke out, was a prize coveted by the enemy.

61 Ibid.

62 'The aircraft was carrying out a special search as the result of two raider distress reports on successive days in the Seychelles-Madagascar area'. 'Admiralty War Diaries of World War 2', East Indies Station War Diaries, April-May 1941, War Despatch, 7/3/41. All references to these war diaries and the 'reports on proceedings' come from this source unless otherwise stated.

There were other hotspots, too, and enemy naval intelligence officers monitored British fleet traffic through ports such as Cape Town, Durban, East London, and Port Elizabeth.[63] The waters around the Cape became a hunting ground for enemy submarines and mine-layers, and the Royal Navy's South Atlantic Command based in Freetown, the East Indies Station, the RAF, and the South African Naval Service and South African Air Force, had to develop methods to defend Allied shipping at this nodal point on the global communications map.[64] On the other side of the Indian Ocean, an Axis spy network existed in Portuguese Goa. It gathered information concerning British ships leaving Indian ports, which was relayed to U-boats surfacing at night in the Indian Ocean in order to receive their transmissions (see chapter 11).

The threat posed by enemy raiders and submarines meant that measures were taken across the Indian Ocean region to protect important British installations. As an example, a slew of official files recorded the initiatives to provide a measure of security for ports and oil installations along the Gulf's eastern coastline. 'Defence of Qatar' laid out the British Political Agent Bahrein's scheme for arming the staff of Petroleum Concessions Limited and other key personnel, and there were similar measures for the defence of oil fields and refineries in Bahrein.[65] There were also secret plans for the defence and emergency demolition of oil refineries and fields operated by the Bahrein Petroleum Company and those operated by the California-Arabian Standard Oil Company in Saudi Arabia.[66] Plans were made for the deployment of a company of Indian troops to defend Bahrain, which could be moved at short notice to Bushire in Iran by Imperial Airways seaplanes or sloop if necessary.[67] There was also a plan for the evacuation of Bushire if there was a German-sponsored coup in Iran, and plans for the evacuation of British, British Indian, American, and other personnel from the region.[68]

The war against Italy

Italian East Africa covered part of Somaliland, Eritrea, and Abyssinia and the Italian navy had several bases in the region. As has been discussed, chief among them was Massawa, a port which Mussolini hoped to develop into a naval base capable of dominating the Red Sea-Suez area.

63 For SOE operations in East Africa and the Indian Ocean region, see E. D. R. Harrison, 'British Subversion in French East Africa, 1941-42: SOE's Todd Mission', *English Historical Review* 114, 456 (1999) and Harrison, 'On Secret Service for the Duce'. Malcolm Muggeridge was a British agent operating in Portuguese East Africa; see the second volume of his autobiography *Chronicles of Wasted Time: The Infernal Grove* (London: Morrow, 1974); John Bright-Holmes (ed.), *Like it Was: The Diaries of Malcolm Muggeridge* (London: HarperCollins, 1981); and Richard Ingrams, *Malcolm Muggeridge: The Biography* (London: HarperCollins, 1996).

64 See Turner et al, *War in the Southern Oceans.*

65 British Library (BL), IOR/R/15/2/728, file 28/35, Defence of Qatar. Thanks to Andrew Stewart for telling me of these papers. See IOR/R/15/2/864, File 38/31, C. L. Qatar Concession for petroleum work in Qatar during the war. BL, IOR/R/15/2/661, file 28/1KI, Defence of Oil Field and Refinery.

66 BL, IOR/R/15/2/662, file 28/1KII, Defence of Oil Field and Refinery.

67 BL, IOR/R/15/2/690, file 28/8, War: Evacuation of Bushire. Includes British Resident in Tehran Sir Reader Bullard's 23/5/40 message to all British consuls in Iran recommending the burning of 'unostentatiously secret papers' and preparation of plans to burn cyphers and confidential papers.

68 BL, IOR/R/15/2/672, file, 28/1S, Evacuation of Personnel and Families from BAPCO and CASOC'. See also IOR/R/15/2/660, file 28/1J, Sabotage to Oil Wells.

Italian destroyers and submarines presented the British with a challenge in the western Indian Ocean from June 1940 when Mussolini declared war. Sea lanes running along East Africa's coast were strategically vital; supplies for Middle East Command and the Western Desert Force, which became the Eighth Army in September 1941, sailed around the Cape, through the Mozambique Channel, and into the Red Sea for delivery to ports in Egypt and the Sudan.

Because of economic difficulties, and despite the fact that most of the logistical infrastructure was completed in Massawa, at the moment of the Italian declaration of war, only eight submarines were in Africa. In March 1940, the Italian naval staff had ordered Rear Admiral Carlo Balsamo, commander of naval forces in Italian Africa, to send all units out of their bases to take advantage of the surprise effect at the moment Rome declared war, placing them close to Port Sudan, Djibouti, Aden, Berbera, and Muscat. Due to the fear of rapid attrition, however, Balsamo decided to operate with only four units. Their objective was to endure as long as possible and pin down enemy forces, but they soon fell victim to the poor technological adaptation to the tropical climate of the Italian submarine fleet. The same was true for the surface units that were in Africa in June 1940; seven destroyers, two torpedo boats, five antisubmarine motorboats, and a handful of auxiliary units. Their main objective was to attack enemy shipping in the Red Sea, but due to the lack of suitable enemy traffic – one assumes, suitably *unguarded* traffic, the British having instituted a convoy system – they scored little success.[69]

A major campaign was fought in East Africa to neutralize the Italian threat, supported by the ships of the East Indies Station and air power provided by its aircraft carriers and RAF squadrons in Aden, Kenya, and the Sudan.[70] Britain prioritized the destruction of Italian naval assets and the capture of the Italian ports in order to secure the sea lanes and seal enemy land forces off from seaborne assistance. Before Italy's entry into the conflict the chief functions of the East Indies Station, wrote its commander-in-chief, Vice Admiral Ralph Leatham, had been 'the protection of trade and escort and cover of troop convoys and individual troopships'.[71] Tension with Italy meant that in the spring months of 1940 the East Indies Station's better ships were transferred to the Mediterranean, and a Red Sea Force was instituted under the command of Rear Admiral Arthur Murray.[72] 'The actual outbreak of war with Italy', Leatham wrote, 'came as a relief for all officers and men, who welcomed the prospect of action after the enforced passivity that had obtained hitherto on the East Indies Station'.

When Italy declared war on 10 June 1940, the submarines *Galileo Galilei* and *Evangalista Toricelli* were patrolling off Djibouti, where the *Galilei* sank the Norwegian tanker *James Stove*. British naval and air activity forced the submarines to abandon their patrol and take evasive

69 Details of these operations can be found in 'Le Operazioni in Africa Orientale', in G. Giorgerini, *Uomini sul Fondo: Storio del Sommergibilismo Italiano dalle Origini a Oggi* (Milan: Mondadori, 2002).

70 For the most up to date scholarship on this topic, see Stewart, *The First Victory*. For a a detailed and chronological account of the role of air power in this campaign, as well as the campaigns in Iran, Iraq, and Madagascar, see Christopher Shores, *Dust Clouds in the Middle East: The Air War for East Africa, Iraq, Syria, Iran, and Madagascar, 1940-1942* (London: Grub Street, 1996). Chapter 9 is entitled 'Securing the Indian Ocean'.

71 East Indies Station War Diaries, April-May 1941, Leatham's War Despatch covering the period, dated 15/10/40.

72 Ibid. The Mediterranean Fleet was given overall responsibility for the Red Sea. Because of the overlap of the responsibilities of the commanders-in-chief East Indies and Mediterranean, the C-in-C East Indies had a liaison officer attached to GHQ Middle East.

measures. Captain Nardi's *Galilei* successfully evaded British forces in the Perim Strait, intent on making for Massawa, and on 18 June *Kandahar* and *Shoreham* were dispatched to search for her.[73] *Shoreham* spotted the submarine and a chase ensued, *Galilei* soon being pursued by five vessels. The Commander-in-Chief East Indies had concentrated the destroyers *Kandahar*, *Khartoum*, and *Kingston* along with *Shoreham* and the anti-submarine trawler *Moonstone*. Gloster Gladiators of the RAF's 94 Squadron from RAF Sheikh Othman in Aden were joined by Blenheims and Vickers Vincents of 8 Squadron from RAF Khormaksar, also in Aden, in order to assist the surface units. The Blenheims attacked the submarine, though their bombs fell wide. Captain Nardi decided to dive, though Flying Officer Haywood of 94 Squadron machine-gunned the submarine as it did so. A Vincent arrived over the target and dropped depth charges at the spot where she had submerged, nearly blowing itself up in the process as it released its bombs while perilously close to the surface. Later, Captain Nardi resurfaced and sent a Morse message which allowed *Kandahar* to get a good location bearing. With *Kandahar* observed approaching, the submarine dived once more.

Christopher Havergal was on board *Kandahar*, which along with the other destroyers had been deployed to the Red Sea 'for convoy defence, support of military operations and interception of Italian warships and submarines'.[74] Having detected *Galilei*'s radio transmissions, she proceeded to depth charge and the armed trawler *Moonstone*, commanded by Boatswain William Moorman, was ordered into the attack. On 20 June *Moonstone* obtained a contact at 5,000 yards and attacked with depth charges. The magazine *War Illustrated* reported the action: 'Emboldened by having sunk the Norwegian tanker *James Stove* on 16 June, the Italian captain fired torpedoes and surfaced to engage his boat's puny tormentor with gunfire; but he had not reckoned with the anger and determination of the boatswain, who commanded *Moonstone* and had earlier picked up the Norwegian survivors'.[75]

The Italian submarine mounted two modern 3.9-inch guns against the trawler's single old four-inch, but faced a determined opponent.

> 'The Italian tracer flashes made it easy to pinpoint the target', said Moorman. 'My twin Lewis guns poured a withering fire into the enemy. Spare hands manned rifles and formed a sniping party keeping slow and deliberate fire, using the gunwale as breastworks. After a hit with my fourth round of four-inch the range closed rapidly. The submarine appeared to stop. The enemy rushed on deck and hauled down their colour and those who had any clothing of a white nature waved it frantically'.[76]

73 In addition to the titles mentioned earlier in this chapter's footnotes, for the Italian navy in the Red Sea see James Sadkovich, *The Italian Navy in World War Two* (Westport, CT: Greenwood Press, 1994).

74 *Kandahar* war diary. See Geoffrey Mason, 'Service Histories of Royal Navy Warships in World War', available at http://www.naval-history.net/xGM-aContents.htm. This is an amazing resource containing the wartime service history of over 1,000 Royal Navy and Dominion vessels. See also Christopher Havergal's testimony at Marine History Information Exchange Group. See also 'Commander Christopher Havergal', obituary, *The Times*, 11/9/05.

75 See 'His Majesty's Ships – HMS *Moonstone*', *The War Illustrated*, 10, 241 (1946), at http://www.thewarillustrated.info/241/his-majestys-ships-hms-moonstone.asp. Due to the wonders of the internet and the endeavours of keen and clever people, the whole sweep of *The War Illustrated* magazine is becoming searchable online. See http://www.thewarillustrated.info/default.asp.

76 Banks, *Wings of the Dawning*, p. 27.

Rounds from *Moonstone*'s well-aimed four-inch gun had killed everyone in the conning tower and hulled the submarine. As *Kandahar* approached, '*Moonstone* was circling her prey like a puppy with a bone too big to chew'. Havergal and his engineers boarded *Galilei* and captured valuable documents. The submarine was then towed under the White Ensign into Aden, Havergal insisting that his stokers have the honour of lining the casing. Havergal had done the job of securing the vessel so well that *Galilei* was later commissioned as the British submarine *X2*. 'Mr William Moorman, Boatswain, RN, in command of the *Moonstone*, opened fire simultaneously with the submarine, but with better aim. Her captain killed, the *Galilea* surrendered, and was brought proudly into Aden with the White Ensign flying over the Italian colours. This was the first enemy submarine captured in the War'.[77]

The recovery of *Galilei*'s codebooks and charts by Havergal's boarding party led directly to the hunt for another Italian submarine in the Red Sea, *Evangelista Torricelli*, which was engaged on 23 June near the island of Perim. At point blank range she faced the far superior fire of the four British warships. As the captain, Salvatore Pelosi, recounted, though outmatched the fight went on for over half an hour, concluding at 400 yards when the weight and intensity of the British fire forced him to give the order to abandon ship. The engagement had not been a one-sided affair: not only had *Evangelista Torricelli* hit *Shoreham*, which had to put into Aden for repairs, but the damaged inflicted on *Khartoum* led to an ammunition explosion five hours later, causing her to be declared a total loss. Eventually the Italian submarine was sunk. In recognition of the gallantry of his crew, Pelosi was treated as the guest of honour at a dinner given by the Senior Naval Officer in Aden that evening.

On the same day, 23 June 1940, the submarine *Luigi Galvani*, captained by Renato Spano, sank the Royal Indian Navy patrol craft *Pathan*.[78] *Falmouth* and the destroyer *Kimberley* had been dispatched to search for her following information found aboard *Galilei*. On 24 June *Falmouth* approached to within 600 yards, opening fire with her four-inch main armament when her challenge went unanswered. After receiving a direct hit the submarine began to dive and *Falmouth* turned to ram, though struck only a superficial blow. The sloop then dropped three depth charges, which blew the *Luigi* to the surface again, at which point the crew emerged on deck waving a white flag, and she began to sink.

By the end of the month in which Italy had entered the war, June 1940, its submarine force in the Red Sea had been greatly reduced. But a decision on land would take many more months to come, and require the ceaseless endeavour of the warships of the East Indies Station and the RAF working in support of the army. Though things seemed to be going Britain's way at sea, the land campaign was proving more difficult. On 26 June 1940 the police detachment at Buramo on the border of British and Italian Somaliland withdrew intact after an attack by enemy tanks and tribesmen, the same day *Kingston* attacked an Italian submarine with guns and depth charges in the southern Red Sea.[79] On 19 August 1940 the navy evacuated nearly 6,000 troops and 1,000 civilians from British Somaliland, whisking them across the Red Sea to safety in Aden, as British Somaliland became the first British colony to capitulate to Axis forces.

77 'His Majesty's Ships – HMS *Moonstone*'.

78 There is some confusion over the loss of this ship. Vice Admiral Leatham writes that he learned of her loss off Bombay owing to an explosion, 'but the definite cause of this has not been established'. East Indies Station War Diaries, April-May 1941, War Despatch, 15/10/40.

79 TNA, CAB 66/9/7, War Cabinet Weekly Résumé (No. 43), Chiefs of Staff Committee, 28/6/40.

Kandahar was one of the East Indies Station ships 'nominated' (the term used in ships' war diaries) to support the evacuation. She was deployed along with the cruisers *Caledon*, *Carlisle*, *Ceres*, *Hobart*, *Kimberley*, and the sloops *Auckland* and *Paramatta*. Three armed merchant cruisers and a hospital ship also took part in the operation.[80]

The Horn of Africa-Red Sea area remained dangerous for merchant vessels. On 6 September 1940, East Indies Station cruiser *Leander* was escorting convoy BN4 through the Red Sea towards Suez. The 19 ships forming the convoy had originated in Bombay and Karachi. 'As the convoy passed the port of Aden five ships had detached their cargoes of troops and, strangely, camels to reinforce the garrison. At the same time another eighteen ships had joined the convoy, taking more troops, fuel, and necessities to the army in Egypt'.[81] *Leander*'s presence was required because of the threat posed by the Italian destroyers and remaining submarines at Massawa. During the afternoon the Greek tanker *Atlas* dropped astern of the convoy, and Captain Carlo Tucci attacked with torpedoes from the submarine *Guglielmotti*. *Atlas* sank, though the destroyer *Kimberley* rescued thirty survivors.

The following month convoy BN7 was attacked by Italian destroyers based at Massawa. The convoy's East Indies Station escort, which included *Leander* and *Kimberley*, drove the Italian destroyer *Francesco Nullo* ashore with gunfire on 21 October, where she was destroyed the following day by RAF Blenheim bombers in a classic demonstration of joint air-maritime cooperation. Other Italian destroyers were flushed out by land operations during the campaign and sunk. Another key role for East Indies Station warships was blockading Italian ports. For example, as Vice Admiral Leatham told the Admiralty: 'For some time I ... had been concerned about the evidence that the Italians were obtaining supplies through the ports of Kismayu and Mogadiscio – allegedly from Japanese sources'.[82] Therefore, his ships mounted a constant patrol off the coast to prevent resupply from the Indian Ocean. But it was clear that material was still getting through to the Italians, so in November and December Leatham ordered a fresh round of targeted bombardments of military objectives at these and other ports involving *Colombo*, *Dorsetshire*, *Leander*, and *Southampton*.

The carrier *Hermes* had among other tasks formed part of a force blockading Kismayu while it was besieged by South African land forces, preventing reinforcements reaching the beleaguered Italians, sea power combining with air and land power to doom the defenders of this corner of Mussolini's evanescent empire. On 12 February, she located Italian vessels in the approaches to Mogadishu harbour and bombed them. A boarding party captured the merchant vessel *Leonardo da Vinci*, and sent her to Mombasa flying the White Ensign. *Hermes* was then dispatched to patrol the shipping lanes between Mombasa and Ceylon.

Having completed a routine refit at Bombay, February found *Kandahar* off Italian Somaliland as part of Force T, operating against enemy forces in Mogadishu and its environs, and there followed a brief stop at Mombasa for some rest and recreation for the crew. Back at sea, on 21 February she escorted the troopships *Empress of Australia*, *Empress of Japan*, *Ormonde*, and *Windsor Castle* from the military convoy WS5B for passage to Mombasa after detaching from the main body of ships, a precaution taken because *Admiral Scheer* had been reported in the

80 Mason, 'Service Histories of Royal Navy Warships in World War'.
81 Quote untraced.
82 'Admiralty War Diaries of World War 2', East Indies Station War Diaries, October 1940-March 1941, Leatham's War Despatch covering the period, dated 7/3/41.

area.[83] In March 1941 she took part in the recapture of British Somaliland from the Italians, forming Force D with the cruisers *Caledon* and *Glasgow*, the destroyer *Kingston*, and Armed Boarding Vessels *Chakdina* and *Chantala*.[84] The force landed Indian troops from Aden at Mersa Kuba for the reoccupation of Berbera on 16 March (Operation Appearance). An 'effective naval bombardment practically cleared the town of Italian troops', wrote Leatham, 'so that the landing met with negligible resistance'.[85] In an operation heavily dependent on access to ports, the 'recovery of Berbera', the admiral noted, 'provided British Forces operating in Italian East Africa with a strategically better base for supplies'.[86]

With the British closing in on Massawa, Axis ships attempted to break out. The sloop *Eritrea* and auxiliary cruiser *Ramb II* made it to Japan, the German merchantman *Wartenfels* to Madagascar, and the auxiliary cruiser *Ramb I* was sunk by *Leander* as she attempted to escape.[87] *Oder* was caught, and on 30 March *Khartoum* intercepted the German freighter *Bertram Rickmers*, attempting passage from Massawa, and the ship scuttled itself. Massawa soon fell to imperial land forces, three brigades of primarily Indian troops attacking the port's perimeter on 8 April, supported by *Formidable*'s aircraft and other East Indies Station assets from the seaward side.[88]

As the East Africa campaign came to something of a crescendo in spring 1941 and the capture of Massawa drew nigh, the four Italian submarines remaining in East African ports (*Archimede*, *Ferraris*, *Guglielmotti*, and *Perla*) attempted to escape. Operation Supply was mounted using Mauritius as a base, and *City of Manchester*, *Leander*, and *Canberra* set out to find the submarines which, it was feared, might make a 'death or glory' attack on British bases or convoys in the Red Sea. The Italian submarines successfully evaded their hunters, however, and arrived in Bordeaux after the long journey around the Cape and through the Atlantic. Other Italian vessels sought to run the Royal Navy's gauntlet; three cargo ships attempted to break out from Massawa and reach Rio de Janeiro, two successfully evading British patrols in Assab Bay, Eritrea, and completing the journey.

Three large Italian destroyers (*Leone*, *Pantera* and *Tigre*) made a bid to attack Suez through narrow, enemy-infested waters. The Luftwaffe had agreed to help by bombing the Canal at the same time, though this operation was subsequently cancelled. The destroyers set off regardless on 31 March but one promptly grounded itself on the islets off Massawa and was so severely damaged that it was sunk by gunfire from its two sister ships, which, as daylight was approaching, then returned to port. There they joined three smaller destroyers (*Battisti*, *Manin*, and *Sauro*) which were about to make an attack on Port Sudan. The British assembled forces to deal with this threat. *Eagle* was directed to Port Sudan, where she deposited ashore the Swordfish of 813 and 824 squadrons Fleet Air Arm (which had taken part in the highly successful raid on the Italian battlefleet at Taranto the previous November). The RAF had provided drums of fuel and stacks of 200-pound bombs for their use. The Italian destroyers departed Massawa for the attack

83 See Mason, 'Service Histories of Royal Navy Warships in World War'.

84 These were passenger-cargo vessels taken over by the Admiralty and kitted out for military purposes. *Chakdina* was torpedoed and sunk by Italian aircraft between Tobruk and Alexandria in December 1941, and *Chantala* mined and lost off Tobruk in the same month.

85 East Indies Station War Diaries, March-July 1941, Leatham's War Despatch covering the period, dated 16/7/41.

86 Ibid.

87 *Eritrea* was later captured by the British and put to work by the Royal Navy around Trincomalee.

88 For an account of the battle, see Stewart, *The First Victory*, pp. 184-87.

on 2 April, knowing that success was almost impossible. British air reconnaissance removed the element of surprise and the following day, just 30 miles from Port Sudan, a sustained air attack developed from the Swordfish, led by Captain C. Keighley-Peach. *Pantera* and *Tigre* were able to make it to the Arabian coast where they beached off Jeddah and were promptly shelled by *Kandahar. Manin* and *Sauro* continued to fight until both were sunk by *Eagle*'s Swordfish. Even when Massawa was captured, the Italian navy did not give up the fight, scuttling cargo vessels in the harbour and destroying port installations (see chapter three). A motor torpedo boat successfully targeted *Capetown*, which had to be towed to Port Sudan for a year-long repair.[89]

Axis activity in the eastern Mediterranean and North Africa in spring 1941 had 'brought home the necessity of arming merchant vessels using the Red Sea and Persian Gulf against enemy air attacks'. A 'scheme to effect this to the fullest extent' possible had been instituted, wrote Leatham. The enemy threat here also meant that the British needed the use of alternative ports for the purposes of loading and unloading troops and military hardware. Leatham continued: 'The increased menace from the air by bombs or mines to the safe arrival at Suez of the large and valuable transports included in troop convoys, has necessitated also the selection of alternative anchorages where, if circumstances indicate the desirability of doing so, disembarkation will be effected instead of Suez'.[90]

While all of this was going on, the navy still had its routine duties to perform, and fighting flared up in other parts of the Indian Ocean region too. In May 1941 anti-British and nationalist officers and politicians had seized power in Iraq following a coup the previous month.[91] Soon, Iraqi forces were attacking British forces stationed in the country. Indian forces were building up in Basra, dispatched across the Indian Ocean under East Indies Station protection from Karachi. The Commander-in-Chief East Indies temporarily transferred himself and his headquarters to the Gulf, flying his flag aboard *Leander*, arriving at Basra on 19 April and then transferring his flag to *Seabelle* at the Outer Bar of the Shatt al Arab.[92] Until almost the last moment, it was unclear as to whether the landing of additional British troops would be opposed. During the conflict that ensued, East Indies Station ships 'formed an integral part of the defences' of Basra, including the Australian sloop *Yarra*, berthed near the British consulate with its guns trained in order to dissuade demonstrators.[93] A landing party from *Emerald* seized Fao, while other East Indies Station assets conducted a waterborne expedition to Kut and assured the safe

89 'Admiralty War Diaries of World War 2', East Indies Station War Diaries, March-July 1941, Leatham's War Despatch. Paragraph 7 deals with this episode.

90 Ibid., paragraph 16.

91 For a recent treatment, see Jackson, *Persian Gulf Command*. This also explains the concerns of Commodore Cosmo Graham, Senior Naval Officer Persian Gulf under Leatham, regarding the security of the Shatt al-Arab.

92 East Indies Station War Diaries, March-July 1941, Leatham's War Despatch. Leatham remained here for four days and held conferences with the General Officer Commanding British Troops and the Senior Naval Officer Persian Gulf, Graham. Returning to Colombo aboard *Leander*, he stopped at Bahrein, where Leatham met its ruler and inspected the naval establishment. 'Off Muscat I carried out a "flag showing" demonstration having previously informed the Political Agent'. While this was going on, and indicating the geographical extent of this command's responsibilities, Leatham's Chief of Staff represented him at a conference in Singapore in April to discuss the Far East. *Seabelle* was one of the many ships requisitioned on the outbreak of war, serving with the Royal Indian Navy as an armed yacht patrol vessel.

93 J. E. Macdonnell, *Valiant Occasions* (London: Constable, 1962), p. 111.

passage of troopships arriving from India. *Hermes* aided troops fighting to relieve the RAF base at Habbaniya and those attacking Baghdad along the line of the Euphrates from Basra. For five consecutive days her aircraft undertook daily bombing missions.[94] With the end of her Gulf deployment, in June 1941 *Hermes*, in company with *Emerald*, patrolled between Ceylon and the Seychelles, spending October with the battlecruiser *Repulse*. The end of the year saw her refitting in South Africa, concluding her part in the war against Germany and Italy. Her contribution to the fight against Japan was to be far less successful.

British operations against the Italian navy, even less heralded than those against opposing ground forces in East Africa, sped the demise of the Italian Empire in Africa. Italy's naval record in the Indian Ocean was underwhelming, reflecting a preoccupation with the Mediterranean and poor strategic awareness. The Italians, like the Germans, should have given greater weight to the Indian Ocean and what could have been achieved there by resolute action. If the Red Sea, like the Mediterranean, had been closed to Allied shipping, Britain's forces in Egypt and the Western Desert would have faced slow strangulation. Furthermore, if Axis forces could have prevented British victory in the Red Sea and sustained their military operations there, the American government would have been unable to declare it a 'non combat' zone, thereby preventing them from aiding the British war effort in the region.

Possessed of one of the world's strongest submarine forces and operating over a hundred submarines in the Mediterranean, Italy spared scant resources for the Red Sea region. The shortcomings of Italian naval strategy are highlighted by the number of British convoys that continued to ply the Red Sea, even as Italy laid down its challenge to Britain in East and North Africa and Mussolini opened his bid for a new Roman Empire. Four large British convoys sailed in each direction up and down the Red Sea in August 1940, five more in September, and another seven in October, totalling 86 ships sailing northbound, and 72 sailing southbound. The overriding problem for the Italians was that the war in the Mediterranean drained the navy of resources – supporting, for example, the convoys crossing to North Africa. As the war wore on, Rome looked to Japan to take the lead in the Indian Ocean, even hoping to regain the lost colonies. Tokyo, however, looked in turn with derision on Italian naval capabilities and performance. The most important Italian defeat, from Japan's perspective, was 'the fall of the last Italian naval base on the Red Sea in June 1941, which left the possibility of future co-operations in the Indian Ocean dependent on Japanese logistical support'.[95] Though British victories against the Italians in the Indian Ocean region went largely unremarked, they expunged a dangerous threat to British supremacy and afforded Britain the right to continue to use the western Indian Ocean as a thoroughfare for traffic vital to imperial survival and the pursuit of Allied war aims. As for Germany, of more significance than the transient raids of *Admiral Scheer* and *Graf Spee* were the operations of a peculiar class of dedicated commerce raiders, as the following chapter will show.

94 Leatham added in his report, written before the conclusion of hostilities in Iraq, that the arrival of German aircraft into theatre in support of the 'rebel' Iraqi government 'brought the problem of protecting the vulnerable Shatt el Arab from enemy mining urgently to the fore'. Because of the importance of Iranian and Iraqi oil, this was one of the most strategically important locations in the British world system.

95 De Ninno, 'The Italian Navy and Japan', p. 7 proof.

6

Pinguin and the German commerce raiders

Unlike 1914, Germany did not enter the Second World War with a navy capable of bringing the Royal Navy to action in pursuit of a decisive engagement; there was to be no Jutland-style encounter that might break British sea power and pave the way for an invasion of the British Isles. Germany's powerful fleet of battleships and cruisers – the nucleus of a future High Seas Fleet, though one not yet ready in 1939 – was to be used instead to pin down British units by its very presence, and to maraud on the high seas disrupting the sea lanes upon which the Empire depended for survival. In attempting to bring Britain to its knees, Germany had a lethal weapon to hand in the shape of its growing submarine fleet, the most successful arm of its navy in the preceding war. This was to be the principal German means of taking the fight to the four corners of the globe, and the U-boats were joined in this pursuit by a small fleet of dedicated commerce raiders, along with commerce raiding warships such as the *Graf Spee*. Together, they executed a strategy of *guerre de course*, an approach to naval warfare that was a product of Germany's geographical position and its history. Chapter 6 furthers the representation of the war at sea in the Indian Ocean developed in the previous chapter, focusing on German activities and, in particular, the voyage of the raider *Pinguin* and the operations of the British cruiser *Cornwall* that was sent to find her.

As in the First World War, commerce raiding was central to the approach of a continental, land-based power as it harassed the far-flung interests of a maritime empire. The navy's commander-in-chief, Erich Raeder, was an expert on cruiser warfare, and understood how a weaker navy could disperse its opponents strength and create diversions by adopting commerce raiding tactics. Obliging the British and their allies to sail more ships in convoy brought more damage to their economies, and for every ship sunk by a German raider in the course of a matter of hours, scores of others might be re-routed or retained in harbour, causing disruption that could last for weeks.[1] Presenting the British with a more prolonged challenge in the Indian Ocean than the sorties of dedicated German warships such as *Graf Spee*, commerce raiders, such as *Komet*, *Kormoran*, *Orion*, *Pinguin*, and *Thor* were well-armed merchantmen converted specially for the purpose.[2] To support their global operations, the Germans retained agents in

1 Stephen Robinson, *False Flags: Disguised German Raiders of World War Two* (Wolombi, NSW: Exisle, 2016), p. 14.
2 See Charles Gibson, *Death of a Phantom Raider: The Gamble that Triumphed and Failed, Atlantic, 1942-43* (London: Robert Hale, 1987); H. J. Brennecke, *Ghost Cruiser HK33* (London: William

neutral ports, a small fleet of supply tankers – the largest and fastest in the world – and a network of secret mid-ocean rendezvous points, such as 'Tulip', 900 miles south-east of Madagascar, 'Siberia', in the central Indian Ocean, 'Violet', north-east of Mauritius, and 'Andalusia', 200 miles north-west of Tristan da Cunha in the Atlantic.

The commerce raiders functioned by menacing busy ports or by luring merchantmen towards them on the high seas through various ruses. They masqueraded as Allied or neutral merchant vessels, altering their appearance through the erection of false superstructure, repainting, and mimicking the signals of other ships. When within range of an unsuspecting ship, fake superstructure would be torn aside to reveal heavy guns, from which flames would spout if the unfortunate freighter failed to comply with the raider's wishes, or if the 'RRR' 'raider warning' signal continued to be broadcast in the hope that a British warship or flying-boat might be able to get to the scene in time to effect a rescue.[3] Dispatched to all of the world's oceans, the raiders achieved their strategic purpose by forcing Britain to commit more and more resources to convoy protection and the hunt for an elusive enemy, creating conditions of resource-to-task overstretch. As Augustus Agar wrote, the purpose of the surface raiders 'was to launch sporadic and widely separated attacks, designed to cause *diversions and delays* to our shipping and force the British Fleet to spread themselves farther afield. Destruction of British ships was *only secondary*'.[4]

Unlike British ships, these lone raiders did not depend upon colonial ports and naval bases for succour, because history had decreed that by 1939 Germany no longer had colonies of its own. Ships' crews could not relax in friendly ports and visit brothels, taverns, and colonial hill stations, as could their British counterparts; their vessels could not be dry docked in Bombay, Durban, or Singapore, as could British and Allied ships by virtue of Britain's domain in the Indian Ocean region and the facilities it yielded. Given this situation, access to secure Italian colonial bases would prove very useful. During joint German-Italian naval meetings in June 1939, Raeder had 'emphasized that having Italian bases in East Africa would allow the possible deployment of commerce raiders from the Indian Ocean up to the coasts of Japan'.[5] Unfortunately, by the time German raiders deployed to the Indian Ocean, those Italian bases were either heavily patrolled by the Royal Navy, or had been captured.

Bereft of bases, these feral hunters depended on furtive rendezvous' with supply vessels, consorting in isolated seas far away from shipping lanes and the prying eyes of British reconnaissance aircraft and warships. They depended on clandestine visits to remote coves in order to careen their hulls or overhaul their engines, and on their mid-ocean rendezvous points. They also depended on their prey, from which all manner of foodstuffs, luxury goods, and fuel supplies could be plundered. If possible, captured ships were sent back to Germany, where additions to the merchant fleet were always welcome, or themselves transformed into raiders and minelayers. They were pirates of the modern age, sailing under false colours, tricking victims with their assumed appearance and false radio signals, commissioned to raise havoc and win prizes.

Kimber, 1955); and for more recent treatments, see Robinson, *False Flags*, Bernard Edwards, *Beware Raiders! German Surface Raiders in the Second World War* (Barnsley: Leo Cooper, 2001), and James Duffy, *Hitler's Secret Pirate Fleet: The Deadliest Ships of World War Two* (Westport, CT: Praeger, 2001).

3 These signal codes replaced the 'SOS' call: 'QQQ' for 'armed cruiser wishes to stop me', 'RRR' for 'warship raider', 'SSS' for 'submarine', 'AAA' for 'aircraft'.

4 Agar, *Footprints in the Sea*, p. 165. Emphasis in original.

5 De Ninno, 'The Italian Navy and Japan', p. 6 proof.

The Germans deployed ten raiders, or auxiliary cruisers as they were sometimes known, seven dispatched from European waters in 1940 alone. They sunk an average of 15 ships each, but their real value lay in the sheer disruption they caused. Compared to the mighty German battleships *Bismarck* and *Tirpitz*, and indeed the pocket battleships, they were incomparably more cost effective and more likely to sink enemy merchantmen. In order to counter the threat they posed in the Indian Ocean, the Commander-in-Chief East Indies formed hunting groups assigned to different areas. For example, as we have seen, at one point or another *Cornwall*, *Dorsetshire*, and *Eagle* were designated Force I, the cruisers *Shropshire* and *Sussex* Force H, and the battle-cruiser *Renown* and the carrier *Ark Royal* Force K. Despite tying down such force packages in often fruitless, but always necessary, patrol work, German ships were seldom found and their strategy enjoyed considerable success. British luck was thin, not surprising given the needle in a haystack nature of hunting an enemy that could be anywhere in an ocean that from Cape Town to Singapore spanned 5,200 nautical miles. To make matters worse, the enemy might not even be in the Indian Ocean at all, having slipped around the Cape in order to operate in the Atlantic for a spell, or having exited through the Sunda Strait to poach in the Pacific.

One of the ships most heavily involved in the struggle against the commerce raiders was the cruiser *Cornwall*, which had spent many years on the China Station before the war. A Kent, or County, class cruiser of 10,000 tons displacement completed at Devonport Dockyards in 1926, she was a typical example of the modern British cruiser, showing sleek lines and at 630 feet in length only 30 feet shorter than two rugby pitches. Although conforming to the limitations laid down by the 1922 Washington Naval Treaty, County class cruisers packed a powerful punch, with four turrets of two eight-inch guns each which fired 256-pound shells.

As soon as Neville Chamberlain's ultimatum to the German government expired on 3 September 1939, orders were received to round up German merchant ships. For *Cornwall* and her colleagues this entailed long periods patrolling at sea, stopping and inspecting all intercepted ships, including Allied and neutral vessels because of the German practice of sailing under the colours of other nations. It was tedious, yet essential, work. Soon *Cornwall* was transferred from the China Station to the East Indies Station and sailed for Singapore en route to Colombo, wearing the flag of Rear Admiral Commanding 5th Cruiser Squadron. At her new home she took over the task of providing protection to troop and merchant convoys in the Bay of Bengal.[6] Cruisers were essential as they were specifically designed for maritime policing, and were gunned heavily enough to deal with anything afloat bar battleships.

The Commander-in-Chief East Indies, Vice Admiral Leatham, extended his fleet's searches to the Andaman and Nicobar Islands, and westwards to the Laccadives, the Maldives, the Seychelles, the Amirantes, and the Chagos Archipelago. On these lonely patrols *Cornwall* often operated alongside the carrier *Eagle*. Among the quarry that they hunted in these early months were the *Graf Spee* and *Lützow*. Transferring commands, as was standard practice, and in November 1940 *Cornwall* sailed to Simon's Town to join South Atlantic Command. She was soon returned to the East Indies Station, and between 6 January and 12 February 1941 escorted 13,000 New Zealand troops from Wellington to Suez in company with the battleship *Ramillies*, and between 15 April and 7 May escorted Australians from Melbourne to Suez. In July she visited Liverpool, and then two months later took part in Operation Menace, the British attack

6 NHB, 'Summary of service'.

on the Free French port of Dakar in West Africa. In company with Royal Indian Navy's *Delhi* she intercepted the French cruiser *Primaguet* and the oiler *Leniger.*

For their part, the Germans initiated the deployment of commerce raiders soon after war begun. On 11 November 1939 Ernst Krüder was chosen to command an auxiliary cruiser, *HK* (*Hilfskreuzer* – 'auxiliary cruiser') *33*, launched in 1936 and requisitioned by the German navy. In the final month of peace, as the Hansa Line merchantman *Kandelfels* she had crossed the Indian Ocean to Germany via the Suez Canal carrying a cargo of jute, oil cakes, oil nuts, ground nuts, rubber, quinine, molybdenum, wolfram, and a variety of piece goods from India. While unloading at Antwerp, the ship was ordered to Hamburg; German troops had crossed the border into Poland, and war had begun. At Hamburg, most of the crew, including the captain, were paid off. The ship was soon under the orders of the Germany navy, and swarming with naval officers and ratings. They did not yet know what was intended for the ship, such was the level of secrecy. While it lay in dock, set about by mechanics, welders, and all manner of dockyard journeymen, the sailors speculated and spread rumours as to the meaning of it all. When it was learned that she was to be an auxiliary cruiser, the men were delighted. 'Two words that meant something, two words with an aura of legendary heroism and adventure on the high seas', a class of warship that the Germans had used to good effect in the First World War, and which had entered the country's maritime lore.[7] This was not a view of raider warfare shared by the British; Agar described German raider warfare as 'a loathsome and horrible form of sea-warfare contrary to all the traditions of humanity among seamen'.[8] It was an approach in direct contrast to the British employment of armed merchant cruisers, which operated openly as warships, flying the White Ensign at all times.

After many weeks of secret and frenetic preparation, *HK 33* left for gunnery trials in the Baltic, and in May 1940 practiced camouflaging and de-camouflaging and took on board a seaplane. On 15 June, fully worked-up, *HK 33* was sent out to hunt on the high seas, the fifth of her breed dispatched by the Reich. The ex-*Kandelfels* had become a formidable weapon of war, fitted with six six-inch guns, a smaller gun camouflaged in her bows for firing warning shots across the bows of recalcitrant foes, and many machine-guns. At various points along the upper deck were dispersed a number of light anti-aircraft guns, invisible to prying eyes. Four torpedo tubes and 400 mines in the lower hold completed her armament. All these weapons were hidden so that they could not be detected from the sea, 'but when the moment came for action and international law demanded that the war flag should run up the mast, then, whether a moment before the ship had been masquerading as a harmless Latvian freighter or a peaceful Australian going about her proper vocations', the screens could be dropped in a matter of seconds and the guns unmuzzled.[9]

Pinguin, as *HK33* was named by her new captain because of his intention to hunt in Antarctic waters, was a special ship, kitted out and administered in a way calculated to make long and lonely spells at sea as tolerable as possible. Even the most remote islands of the Indian Ocean were out of bounds because they were British-controlled, and most likely sported a garrison of colonial troops and a battery of coastal defence guns. To help overcome this, Captain Krüder introduced innovations such as on board leave and special recreational facilities for men off duty.

7 Brennecke, *Ghost Cruiser HK33*, p. 27.
8 Agar, *Footprints in the Sea*, p. 165.
9 Brennecke, *Ghost Cruiser HK33*, p. 33.

A room was converted for leave purposes, comfortably equipped with pictures on the walls, easy chairs, and other amenities. At any time, barring emergencies, eight members of crew were on a week's leave. In another part of the ship a cinema was improvised in order to screen the ship's collection of 60 full-length films. It was an impressive auditorium filled with seats carpentered from old boxes and upholstered with woollen blankets, rising in tiers. During intervals cigarettes and chocolates were sold by canteen ratings bearing trays suspended from their necks. Livestock such as pigs was kept alive on board to provide fresh meat and new supplies were procured from captured ships by boarding parties, porcine prisoners of war destined for the galley.

A week after leaving German waters on her maiden cruise, *Pinguin* encountered a British submarine near a Norwegian fjord. Refusing to heave to when ordered to do so, *Pinguin* was lucky to avoid being hit by a spread of torpedoes. This was an unnerving though predictable experience for any German ship attempting to run the British naval blockade and reach open waters, in this case via the Denmark Strait. Shortly after entering the Atlantic, *Pinguin* began to practice her new profession as she steamed towards her designated hunting ground in the Indian Ocean, sinking the *Domingo de Larrinaga* close to Freetown. This new threat led the British to temporarily halt all shipping movements in the Central and South Atlantic, resulting in the loss of thousands of tons of cargo space to critical supply lines as ships were forced to lie idle in various ports. After enduring the Roaring Forties *Pinguin* rounded the Cape on19 August 1940 and entered the Indian Ocean.

Arriving in her designated zone of operations she headed towards Madagascar and began to quarter the sea in the hope of coming across enemy ships, using her Arado sea plane to hunt further afield. The Norwegian tanker *Filefjell* was tricked into believing that she was the British cruiser *Cumberland*, and lured to her capture, gifting the Germans 10,000 tons of petrol, five hundred tons of fuel oil, and the ship's papers. While the tanker was still being dealt with,

> the look-out spotted two faint lights to starboard, the one ruby red, the other poisonous green, undoubtedly the partly blacked out navigation lights of a fairly big ship. It was midnight and the moon was rising. From the bridge of the *Pinguin* they could make out the shadowy shape of the new ship, and Krüder ordered his crew to action stations.[10]

After opening fire, the tanker soon stopped resisting and made to abandon ship. When this had been done, torpedoes were fired and the 7,000 ton *British Commander* was sent to the bottom. Thus *Pinguin* announced herself in the Indian Ocean, often choosing to attack at night, beneath a sky spangled with unfamiliar stars, brighter and more beautiful than those of the northern hemisphere, with the magnificent Southern Cross as the show-piece.

Despite her advantage when closing merchant vessels, *Pinguin* was still the hunted, for the Indian Ocean was a British lake, and the cruisers, destroyers, submarines, sloops, and flying-boats of the East Indies Station and the RAF, dispersed from East Africa to Malaya, knew that she was there and were intent upon her destruction. Aiding them in their attempts to pin *Pinguin* down, and to join the dots in naval headquarters and ships' plotting rooms, were the reports of sightings sent by vessels in different parts of the Indian Ocean, along with the signals sent out by merchantmen in close contact with, or under attack from, *Pinguin* or one of

10 Ibid., p. 87-88.

her sister ships. When *Pinguin* attacked the *British Commander*, for example, the tanker's wireless operator continued tapping out distress signals until the very last moment. 'RRR', 'LAT 29.37S LONG 45.50E. STOPPED BY SUSPICIOUS VESSEL'. This alerted British naval bases across the Indian Ocean, as well as the warships that they controlled. 'The ether was in fact now alive with signals flashing back and forth between station and station, ship and shore'.[11]

Soon after this attack, *Pinguin* met a 12,000 ton tanker which turned away and sent out urgent messages. It wasn't long before the raider's wireless telegraphy officer reported that 'the Royal Navy's nearby Mauritius station had answered. Then Durban and Port Elizabeth came in. Then the ether, previously so silent, was full of W/T signals. Some hours later the *Pinguin*'s wireless picked up the quick rhythm of a warship's messages'. Further assisting the British in their attempts to run the raiders to ground, the Royal Navy kept psychological profiles of every senior officer in the German navy. Captain Rögge, for example, was described as 'Cautious and efficient. He will fight if cornered and may have become overbold owing to his run of success. Reported to be determined to beat the *Wolf*'s record of 420 days at sea, made in the last war'.[12] These were used by British captains to try and guess a ship's likely movements as they digested the Weekly Intelligence Reports and contemplated their charts. As Agar wrote, all of the German raiders were 'known to us by name, silhouette, and other details'.[13] As an Admiralty 'Raider Supplement' to the Weekly Intelligence Reports noted, in the Indian Ocean and the Pacific the Germans 'appear to be very well informed about British and Allied shipping movements. There appears to be no doubt that they have agents in Empire and neutral ports'.[14]

Despite mounting British activity, Krüder elected to stay put in the Indian Ocean and to head for shipping lanes around Madagascar, rather than to flee. Nearly three months after leaving home, on 12 September 1940, camouflaged as a Dutchman, *Pinguin* came across the British freighter *Benavon*, almost running into her before the British ship realized its peril. She was bound for London carrying rubber, jute, and hemp from Manila and Singapore. Krüder ran up the war flag and cleared for action as the crew of *Benavon* could be seen preparing their gun and it wasn't long before they brought it to bear. The British vessel scored a hit near number five hatch, a little above *Pinguin*'s mine compartment. The shell was deflected and ended up in the stokers' locker. Petty Officer Streil found the smouldering shell, picked it up, and threw it out through the hole whence it had come. Despite this accurate strike from the British gunners, *Pinguin*'s shells made short work of *Benavon*, knocking off her mast and funnel, destroying her gun, and causing the ready ammunition to explode. The freighter was boarded, survivors rescued, and the wounded treated. *Benavon*, according to her captain, had repeatedly been warned of the presence of German raiders in the vicinity. *Pinguin*'s next victim was the Norwegian ship *Nordvard*, on her way from Australia to South Africa. After capturing her crew, *Pinguin* was uncomfortably full with 150 captives on board in addition to a crew of 420. It was therefore decided to transfer prisoners to the *Nordvard* for transit back to Germany along with her valuable cargo of 7,500 tons of wheat.

11 Edwards, *Beware Raiders!*, p. 53.
12 TNA, ADM 223/150, Weekly Intelligence Reports 56-68, 'Raider Supplement' to 'Weekly Intelligence Report 64, 30/5/41, p. 8. Thanks to Andrew Stewart for a copy of this document.
13 Agar, *Footprints in the Sea*, p. 165.
14 TNA, ADM 223/150, Weekly Intelligence Reports 56-68, 'Raider Supplement'.

Pinguin remained on an easterly course, which would take her to Christmas Island and the Sunda Strait, hunting on the main shipping routes from India to South Australia. Krüder now began planning his ship's career as a minelayer, studying special charts of Australian and New Zealand ports and their environs. *Pinguin* stopped the 8,900 ton Norwegian motor-tanker *Storstad*, carrying 14,000 tons of diesel oil from Miri in British Borneo to Melbourne. After taking on board 2,000 tons of oil, Krüder revealed to his crew his ingenious plan to use *Storstad* as a proxy minelayer. The two ships moved to a point off North West Cape, away from the main shipping routes, so that the chief engineer and his team could begin *Storstad*'s conversion to a minelayer, named *Passat* by her new masters.[15] Krüder was now able to mine the sea lanes to Australia and New Zealand, and the waters around all the big ports in South Australia, using two vessels. On 13 October the crew of *Pinguin* celebrated news from Berlin that Krüder had been awarded the Iron Cross First Class and that 50 Second Class Iron Crosses were available for distribution among the crew. Things were going well for the German raider.

After brief celebrations, it was back to the serious business of interdicting British, Allied, and neutral shipping. In order to make best use of its mines, *Passat* approached the Australian coast close enough to be able to see the lights on shore at night as they crossed the Bass Strait separating the Australian mainland from Tasmania. This busy sea lane was *Passat*'s first target area, the main route for all vessels approaching Sydney, the ports of New Zealand and the other eastern islands from the south, or leaving them on a south-westerly course. The approaches to Melbourne and Port Phillip were the second objectives. In the Bass Strait *Passat* passed many British ships and Australian fishing boats, none of them dreaming that the old tanker was an enemy minelayer. After laying a chain of mines, *Passat* headed on for Melbourne. As she passed Wilson's Promontory, the Australian mainland's southernmost tip, a signal from the shore asked, 'What ship? What ship?'. *Passat* replied as the *Storstad*, which was cleared for Melbourne anyway, and was allowed to pass. The entrance into Melbourne's Port Phillip Bay was duly mined, and then *Passat* proceeded along the Australian coast, laying mines around Adelaide.

Pinguin meanwhile was operating in the Tasman Sea between Australia and New Zealand. She laid mines off Newcastle and Sydney, less than four miles from the shore, and was swept by the searchlights of Port Jackson even as she was depositing her deadly cargo. Her next objective was the southernmost tip of Tasmania, where she laid mines in the approaches to Hobart. *Pinguin* then set course for Spencer Gulf west of Adelaide. The minefield laid by the two German ships extended from Cape Catastrophe on the west of Spencer Gulf to West Cape on the Yorke Peninsula, and across Investigator Strait and Backstairs Passage, the two shipping lanes leading to Adelaide.

The Germans soon had the gratification of learning that their labours had not been in vain. On 8 November 1940 *Pinguin*'s wireless officer began deciphering messages from British vessels that had struck mines, the first an SOS sent by a stricken ship after an unexplained underwater explosion off Promontory Point. This was the British merchantman *Cambridge*, which had indeed fallen foul of one of *Pinguin*'s mines. The following day the *City of Rayville* hit a mine in the Bass Strait as she began a journey from Melbourne to New York, becoming the first American ship sunk as a result of belligerent action, and bringing the neutral country's first war

15 Robinson, *False Flags*, chapter 8, 'The Australian Minefields'.

casualties. On 23 November Australian wireless stations warned shipping against transiting the zone between Sydney and Newcastle; on 6 December the area south of the entrance to Newcastle was also declared dangerous; and on 7 December the Spencer Gulf was closed to all shipping. Then came SOS signals from the approaches to Hobart. Thus *Pinguin* continued her work of disrupting the sea lanes of the British Empire, a Pimpernel sought here and there, but stubbornly elusive and deadly at the same time.

After their successful Australasian tour, *Pinguin* and *Passat* staged a rendezvous. *Passat*'s mine room was turned into a banqueting hall. Signal flags decorated the bulkheads, and the whole crew celebrated their success, feasting on mountains of potatoes and allowed two bottles of beer per man. Krüder now laid an innovative plan before the German naval command in Berlin, calculated to extend *Pinguin*'s utility as a raider. It involved employing *Passat* as a 'second eye', capitalizing on her harmless appearance in order to use her for long-range reconnaissance 50-150 miles distant from *Pinguin*. There was no precedent in the history of naval warfare for a tanker becoming an auxiliary cruiser, and it was confidently predicted that an encounter with *Passat* would not arouse suspicion aboard an enemy warship or merchantman.

Following their celebration the two vessels went about their business, travelling across the Indian Ocean on the Australia-Durban route on a parallel course about 40 miles apart. On 17 November *Pinguin* caught the British freighter *Nowshera*, carrying 4,000 tons of zinc, 3,000 tons of wheat, and 2,000 tons of wool from Adelaide to Durban. She was crewed by 25 Britons and 120 'Lascars', and captained by Dudley Crowther. Captured sheep were taken aboard to add to *Pinguin*'s floating menagerie, sea-grass being employed as fodder. The crew were able to enjoy a bounty of smoked meats, drinks, and Australian Christmas parcels. Two days later *Pinguin* captured the 10,000 ton refrigerator ship *Maimoa* carrying 1,500 tons of Australian butter, 16,000,000 eggs, 5,000 tons of frozen meat, and 1,500 tons of grain. Unfortunately for the German sailors, Krüder could not tarry long enough to take off her cargo or send her to Germany as a prize, and so she was sunk.

Even in the midst of such success, *Pinguin* remained in mortal danger. Before being silenced, *Maimoa*'s wireless had broadcast descriptions of the enemy vessel's size, structure, and silhouette, which could be used by those at East Indies Station headquarters who were painstakingly constructing a plot of the raider's movements. Nevertheless, for the time being *Pinguin*'s luck held, and the sinkings continued. *Port Brisbane*, an 8,700 ton refrigerator ship, was sent to the bottom two days after *Maimoa* (refrigerator ships were much more highly prized than freighters of equal tonnage). *Port Wellington*, another ship spotted in daylight by the 'second eye' *Passat*, was sunk by the light of a new moon, causing a tremendous conflagration just two days after *Port Brisbane* had been dispatched. From this ship, *Pinguin* acquired 70 women to add to the growing collection of prisoners aboard.

Krüder next steered for the western Indian Ocean where he had arranged a rendezvous with Captain Rögge and the raider *Atlantis*. On 1 December 1940 a coded message was transmitted to Berlin, informing naval high command of *Pinguin*'s tally so far. 'Have sunk 79,000 gross register tons to date', said Krüder. 'Mining successes still uncertain. Am detaching prize *Storstad* on course with orders to make for point Andalusia in Atlantic'.[16] *Storstad* took 405

16 Ibid., p. 118.

captives from *Pinguin*, leaving over 200 still on board. At the meeting point 'Andalusia' in the Atlantic, *Storstad* took on more prisoners from the pocket battleship *Admiral Scheer*. The raiders fuelled from *Storstad*, which then made for the French Atlantic coast. A week later, back in the Indian Ocean, *Pinguin* and *Atlantis* met 1,000 miles south-east of Madagascar. The crew donned white service uniforms and swapped stories and banter for two days. Krüder then set course for the Crozet Islands and Prince Edward Island deep in the wastes of the Southern Ocean near Antarctica.

While *Pinguin* was spending Christmas Day 1940 in freezing conditions in the polar seas, watching out for icebergs, 2,000 miles due north *Cornwall* was sailing through the Mozambique Channel. She had left Aden on 19 December, en route to the popular naval base at Simon's Town, where she was due to spend two months being refitted. For his next daring move, Krüder planned the capture of the entire Norwegian whaling fleet. Captain Rögge had handed over valuable documents during the rendezvous with *Atlantis*, including charts found on board the Norwegian tanker *Teddy*, a former supply ship for the whalers. *Pinguin* also made use of intercepted wireless conversations, and Krüder transferred every scrap of information to his charts. *Pinguin* began this new enterprise by capturing the factory ships, *Ole Wegger* and *Polglimt*. Then, without firing a shot, the raider captured 40,000 tons of shipping in a day by tricking the whaler captains into reporting to the factory ships, now in German hands.[17]

While the factory ships were dealing with the dozens of whales killed by the fleet, Krüder came up with a new ruse. He sailed at full speed and sent a long coded message home, which took three-quarters of an hour to transmit. While *Pinguin* returned to her original point, her wireless operators picked up messages that told of a British battleship, aircraft carrier, and various other units putting to sea from Simon's Town and the Falklands to search for the German vessel. Now Krüder and his new charges set off, the 11 whalers following his ship with the factory ships at the rear. *Admiral Scheer* had left prize crews at the 'Andalusia' rendezvous point, so that *Pinguin* could send the whalers home. When the raider arrived it met the refrigerator ship *Duquesa*, captured before Christmas by *Admiral Scheer* and employed as a static supply ship, the fuel on board used to keep the refrigerators running. Such were the ingenious piratical arrangements of a nation bereft of colonies but determined to operate across the oceans of the world with skill and economy.

On 25 February 1941 *Pinguin* again met *Atlantis*, and on that same day *Cornwall* began sea trials after her refit at Simon's Town, soon proceeding to sea and intercepting the Vichy French vessel *Ville de Majunga* 450 miles west of Cape Town with 600 troops on board.[18] At the same time, the pocket battleship *Admiral Scheer* swept around the Cape and into the Indian Ocean, capturing a merchantman and sinking three others north of Madagascar, two of which managed to make 'RRR' 'warship raider' signals, one adding, 'Battle-cruiser chasing'. With the German ship sighted by an aircraft from *Glasgow*, it decided to leave the Indian Ocean immediately, passing Cape Town on 2 March.

By this point so many merchant ships had been captured that there was a surfeit of eggs, partially solved when the enterprising chief quartermaster made a potent Advokaat, using a litre of pure alcohol, 150 egg yolks, and a tin of Australian condensed milk as his measurements.

17 Ibid., chapter 15, 'The Raiders in the Antarctic'.
18 An armed guard was placed on board and the ship was taken to Simon's Town.

While *Pinguin* rested at 'Andalusia', the German freighter *Alstertor* arrived bearing eagerly-awaited mail sacks. The two ships then moved to the Kerguelen Islands, uninhabited French possessions deep in the Indian Ocean, where they could transfer supplies undisturbed. Both vessels then sailed round Kerguelen and made for the entrance to Port Couvreux on the northern side. This was a storm-swept and inhospitable place, made slightly more bearable by the profusion of rabbits. *Pinguin* took on board stores from *Alstertor*, including a new seaplane. The ship's hull was scrubbed clean of barnacles and other underwater flora and fauna. As the barren island did not afford the facilities of a dry dock, to accomplish this *Pinguin* had to be careened from one side to the other by trimming and cargo shifting. Work was also undertaken to give her a new disguise, that of the Norwegian freighter *Tamerlane*. A rabbiting expedition was organized by the crew on the last day of their stay, and by the afternoon enormous quantities had been brought on board, and the cook prepared a banquet.

As *Pinguin* set sail for another hunting expedition, her captain knew that the Royal Navy was becoming more active.[19] The capture of Italian Somaliland and British successes against the Italian navy meant that more ships were available for anti-raider activities. But *Pinguin* still had a job to do, and more British and Allied ships meant more prey. Soon she fell in with the supply tanker *Ole Jacob* and moved towards the Maldives in order to try her luck along the shipping routes between Ceylon, Madagascar, and Durban. But pickings were lean, her seaplane making 35 flights without spotting a single target. So Krüder switched his attention to the Bombay-Mombasa route and the Mozambique Channel.

Meanwhile convoy work continued to occupy *Cornwall* as the spring of 1941 unfolded. Working mostly in the Indian Ocean since the start of the war, she had undertaken many abortive patrols between Durban, Aden, and Ceylon, often as a result of raider reports from merchantmen. A scheduled stay and some rest and recreation in Durban was eagerly awaited by the crew. The ship's company was therefore dismayed to hear the tannoy announce that 'the ship is now proceeding on service to the South Atlantic to search for a German raider'. This was in March 1941, and *Cornwall* was sent to St Helena. Crossing the equator, she sighted a convoy of 32 ships with the cruisers *Birmingham* and *Phoebe* in attendance. *Cornwall* joined this convoy as senior escorting ship as it rounded the Cape and headed for the Mozambique Channel. The thousands of troops on board the troopships were bound for the Western Desert, along with military supplies that included railway engines and trucks, motor torpedo boats, tanks, and armoured cars. After leaving the convoy at Durban on 1 April *Cornwall*, in company with the cruiser *Phoebe*, left to escort another merchant armada, this one bound for Aden. *Cornwall* steamed up and down the lines of the convoy while her Royal Marines band, its music boosted by specially rigged loudspeakers, provided a programme of light music to relieve the monotony of the long voyage and raise the spirits of the crews and the troops in the ships.[20] It was on this journey that *Cornwall*'s Captain, P. C. W. Manwaring, heard reports of a raider to the east. This was *Pinguin*, sailing on a parallel northerly course.

Cornwall deposited her convoy at Aden on 17 April, and four days later left for Mombasa in company with the carrier *Eagle*. The voyage was broken by exercises in which the carrier's aircraft made dummy dive-bombing and torpedo attacks, presaging *Cornwall*'s doom further

19 See Robinson, *False Flags*, chapter 18, 'Tanker Hunt in the Arabian Sea'.
20 Dimbleby, *Turns of Fate*, p.66.

east a year later. As the British warships were travelling south, *Pinguin* was passing them on a northerly course, close to the route from India to the Mozambique Channel. She was working in tandem with a captured merchantman, the *Adjutant*, which on 25 April came across the *Empire Light*. Making no 'QQQ' signal, *Empire Light*'s peril was unknown to *Cornwall* and *Eagle* as they prepared to dock at a misty Mombasa on the morning of 26 April. As Ken Dimbleby remembers, 'by the time we sailed up the river-like harbour the mist had cleared and a hot sun shone on the beautiful, green country'.[21] Here the crew enjoyed some relaxation and some ale in the canteens and bars. It was a brief stay, however, and *Cornwall* soon departed, setting course for the Seychelles, Manwaring telling his men that there was a distinct possibility of an encounter with an enemy raider.

On 28 April *Clan Buchanan*, carrying military stores to India, was sunk by *Pinguin*. A feeble signal was sent before shells knocked out the radio cabin. Among the debris the Germans discovered valuable documents, including two bags of secret mail, the War Diary of the East Indies Station cruiser *Hawkins*, and coding keys for British warships. On 7 May and now hunting tankers leaving the Persian Gulf, the *British Emperor* was attacked. Krüder hoped to capture her intact in order to use her as a minelayer. But the tanker's captain refused to stop when bid. Though her cargo was soon ablaze, sending sheets of flame shooting into the skies on a misty day, *British Emperor*'s wireless operators kept signalling the appearance of the vessel attacking them as well as their position. The British vessel was able to foil attempts to silence her wireless because the equipment had been removed from the wireless telegraphy cabin and hidden. In desperation, Krüder ordered his boarding party to leave the ship, which he then proceeded frantically to shell in order to silence her. He was even compelled to use torpedoes to dispatch the burning wreck, though the first torpedo fired began to describe a circle, promting desperate evasive action on *Pinguin*'s part. By this time the wireless was alive with messages because of the heroics of *British Emperor*'s wireless operator.

The signalling had been clear and long enough to allow British forces, including *Cornwall*, to fix the position of the action. Eight degrees north, 55 degrees east, and only 400 miles south of Socotra. Dangerous waters for British, Allied, and neutral merchant vessels, but dangerous waters for German raiders, too. As *Cornwall*'s Summary of Service recorded, 'on 7 May, as the direct result of a distress message from the tanker BRITISH EMPEROR, CORNWALL was ordered to search for a German raider'.[22] Before this order was received from the Commander-in-Chief East Indies, Manwaring slewed his ship around, increased speed to 26 knots, and raced northwards. Fleet headquarters ordered the cruisers *Glasgow* and *Leander* to join the hunt, and air patrols from Socotra were arranged. *Cornwall* was instructed to cover an area north of the gap between the Seychelles and the Chagos Archipelago, and she used both of her Walrus seaplanes to extend the hunt. Nothing was sighted, though one of the aircraft flew within 40 miles of *Pinguin* before having to return to ship.

At 3:30 am on 8 May 1941 *Cornwall* was sighted against the setting moon by the men of *Pinguin*'s watch. That day, as *Cornwall*'s crew were closed up at dawn action stations, 'there was an undercurrent of excitement, though the sun rose and bathed the calm tropical sea in its light, with no ship in sight'.[23] The Walrus seaplanes were flown off at 6:30 am, and just after

21 Ibid., p. 68.
22 NHB, 'Summary of service'.
23 Dimbleby, *Turns of Fate*, p. 74.

7am one of them spotted a ship steaming south-west at speed about 65 miles from *Cornwall*. At first, the British aircrew were not suspicious; *Pinguin* looked exactly like a Norwegian tanker, which was the disguise she had adopted whilst resting at Kerguelen, and there was no reason to doubt her. As was later recalled, the 'only thing that struck us as odd was that there were so few people on deck. And the captain of our cruiser was struck by the same thing when he studied our pictures. Normally when flying low over merchantmen, crew pile on deck to have a look at us'.[24] The British airmen were also surprised to see no coloured sailors on board. *Cornwall* did not receive this sighting report until the aircraft returned, however, and could not begin the pursuit immediately because she had to wait for the second Walrus. It was not until 8:25 am, therefore, that the cruiser was able to turn nearly 180 degrees to get on a westerly course to try and overhaul the mystery vessel.

On board *Pinguin* the aircraft had been spotted, and the roundels of the Fleet Air Arm discerned. Tension mounted as the crew awaited events. Binoculars were glued to eyes on the bridge, and slowly the funnels and bridge structure of a British cruiser hoved into view as *Cornwall* raced to overtake the raider. Dimbleby was awakened by loud and excited voices and water splashing along the deck as *Cornwall* crashed through the swells at 28 knots. Slowly *Pinguin* was overtaken, its masts becoming visible above the horizon, then the funnel, and finally the whole ship. At this stage action stations was sounded and Dimbleby donned his steel helmet and went to his position as look-out on the air defence platform. Krüder likewise ordered his men to action stations, though on board *Cornwall* Manwaring was still uncertain as to the true identity of the ship he was inspecting. *Pinguin* was using a British wireless transmitter in order to confound the British ship and, attempting to further confuse the picture, broadcast the 'RRR' 'warship raider' signal pretending to be the Norwegian *Tamerlane*. 'CORNWALL eventually came within range and challenged her'.[25]

A boarding party was piped to muster on deck and signals flashed to the raider to stop, which were ignored. *Cornwall* fired an eight-inch shell as a warning shot, then another when the first was also ignored. Manwaring's opposite number had decided to fight it out. For the German vessel, this was a very dangerous, but not necessarily fatal, decision. Krüder's ship was powerful and, as the raider *Kormoran* was to show in its fight to the death with *Sydney* in the eastern Indian Ocean later that year, a raider could account for a cruiser. Furthermore, Krüder was conscious of the honour of his service, and was a brave man. Perhaps a memory of Jutland flickered across his mind as he put his peaked cap on, together with his uniform jacket, and gave the order, 'Unmask battery! War flag up! Open fire!'.[26]

From *Cornwall* this activity was clearly visible. The raider turned very deliberately to port and then suddenly, at 5:14 pm, there were four flashes and four puffs of dirty brown smoke as the German ship fired a broadside at *Cornwall*, which was only 10,500 yards away. Two torpedoes were also launched. A Walrus seaplane spotted their path, allowing *Cornwall* to take evasive action. A *Cornwall* signalman had been repeatedly flashing in Morse to the raider the signal 'OL-K', which meant 'Heave to or I will open fire'. In the middle of repeating the signal when *Pinguin* opened fire, he omitted the 'L', and simply signalled 'OK'.[27] As *Pinguin* entered

24 Brennecke, *Ghost Cruiser HK33*, p. 179.
25 NHB, 'Summary of service'.
26 Brennecke, *Ghost Cruiser HK33*, p. 181.
27 Dimbleby, *Turns of Fate*, p. 77.

this death match, she sent her final wireless message to Berlin: 'After sinking 136,550 gross register tons and obtaining excellent mine results am now engaged with British heavy cruiser *Cornwall*'.[28]

Cornwall's large battle ensign had been hoisted and the fight was on. 'The roar of guns shattered the peace of a tropical day in the soft light of afternoon just north of the equator. Shells straddled the cruiser and splashed into the sea nearby, sending up surprisingly high columns of water. Broadsides from *Cornwall*'s guns jarred the ship with their strong recoil'. But the contest was disturbing at first. 'Whereas the raider was firing rapid, accurate salvoes, our more powerful turrets were aiming a long way off the target'.[29] *Cornwall* was in trouble. 'One of the first German shells had hit the cruiser on the starboard side, blasting a hole large enough for a car to drive through and upsetting our gunnery control'. 'What the hell's going on?', the Captain asked the Chief Yeoman of Signals standing nearby, and then repeated the question to the Gunnery Officer via the voice-pipe. The German shell had put the forward steering-gear out of action, and so the cruiser had to rely on hand-steering.

> All this happened within minutes, though in the heat of battle it felt very much longer. Four minutes after *Pinguin* opened fire, our gunnery control was back to normal and the eight guns in the four turrets were straddling the enemy ship with their eight-inch shells. It was comforting to feel the thud in the cruiser every time a salvo was fired.[30]

Cornwall had altered course to open the range, which was to the advantage of her heavier guns. The two ships continued to trade blows, *Pinguin* firing a total of 200 projectiles during the engagement, *Cornwall* firing 136 shells from her eight-inch and four-inch armament.

The range between the two ships increased, and with the cruiser's gunnery now on target, Krüder knew that it was the end for *Pinguin*. He gave his last order – to release the prisoners held on board and to abandon ship. Before this order could be carried out, however, a salvo of four shells crashed into the raider at 5:26 pm. The most devastating hit was scored on a hold containing 130 mines that *Pinguin* had planned to lay off Karachi. As Dimbleby recalls,

> it was an unforgettable sight. On the air defence platform we heard a sudden cheer and jumped up in time to have a grandstand view of the end of *Pinguin*. The raider disintegrated in a terrific explosion. Most of the ship, from the bridge to the stern, just disappeared and a huge cloud of smoke shot up to a height of about 2,000 feet.[31]

All that remained to mark the spot where 579 people including 238 prisoners had died in the raider's explosive end were dark patches of oil, debris, and some survivors. A few seconds after the sinking, one of *Pinguin*'s last shots splashed into the sea short of *Cornwall*. The engagement had lasted for twelve minutes.

28 Brennecke, *Ghost Cruiser HK33*, p. 183. In addition to this total *Pinguin* sent 52,000 tons to Germany with prize crews. Her mining operations sunk an estimated 50-60,000 tons. *Pinguin* had sunk or captured 32 ships.

29 K. Dimbleby, *Turns of Fate*, p. 77.

30 Ibid., p. 77-78.

31 Ibid., p. 79.

By the end of 1941 two more German raiders had been destroyed in the Indian Ocean, both by imperial cruisers. *Kormoran* had operated for many months, though with little success.[32] In June 1941 she entered the Bay of Bengal to mine the approaches to Madras, and the Commander-in-Chief East Indies took steps to catch her. On 1 July Force T (*Hermes* and *Enterprise*) left Trincomalee to search between Ceylon and Sumatra, and *Australia* was sent to search around the Kerguelen and Crozet Islands. Force T visited the Seychelles, again finding no trace. The failure of these ships to find *Kormoran* was to lead to one of the Royal Australian Navy's worst war-time disasters when on 19 November *Kormoran* engaged *Sydney* 200 miles off the coast of western Australia. Luring the more heavily gunned cruiser close before opening fire, *Kormoran* was eventually abandoned and scuttled, 315 crew members reaching safety in Australia. *Sydney*, however, was lost with all hands.

Atlantis, the former Hansa Line ship *Goldenfels*, sank 16 vessels in the Indian Ocean between April 1940 and 11 November 1941. Her most famous victim was *Automedon*, a 7,500-ton Blue Funnel liner attacked on 11 November 1940, 250 miles north-west of Sumatra. Bound for Penang, she was closed by *Atlantis*, which was flying a Dutch ensign with some of the crew visible on deck disguised as women. Captain Rögge's ship crippled the unsuspecting *Automedon* with broadsides from its 5.9-inch guns fired at point blank range. *Automedon* was carrying crated aircraft, cars, spare parts, alcohol, and tobacco bound from Britain for Penang, Singapore, Hong Kong, and Shanghai. She was also carrying top secret documents, which the crew did not have time to destroy, and so the German boarding party reaped a rich reward. They found maritime codebooks, shipping route charts, and the courier mail for British Headquarters Singapore, including a secret War Cabinet and Chiefs of Staff report on the whole Far East situation destined for the Commander-in-Chief Far East, Air Chief Marshal Brooke-Popham. Rögge decided that the documents needed to reach Berlin without delay. *Ole Jacob*, a Norwegian ship taken by *Atlantis* the previous day as it travelled from Singapore bound for Suez, was dispatched to Japan with the papers, which reached Germany on 30 December. In Japan the *Ole Jacob*'s 10,000 tons of aviation fuel was exchanged for 11,000 tons of diesel fuel and an aircraft. The captured papers shaped the Japanese decision to go to war given their revelations about the weakness of Britain's position in the East, of which the Japanese had not been aware. In recognition of the value of his haul, Rögge was later presented with a samurai sword by the Japanese Emperor.[33]

As well as the pocket battleships and commerce raiders, over the course of the war 'nearly fifty U-boats were assigned to penetrate the Indian Ocean, as far north as the Arabian Sea'.[34] Nevertheless, their initial deployment was an abject failure. This occurred in 1941 when the 2nd U-Boat Flotilla based at Lorient began operating a class of submarine 'capable of ranging 13,450 miles and patrolling distant targets'. In October, after pressure from on high, the U-boat commander-in-chief, Grand Admiral Dönitz, directed four of these vessels towards the Indian Ocean.[35] Led by Nicolai Clausen's *U129*, joined by *U124*, *U68*, and *UA*, on 21 October they headed for the Cape.

32 For *Kormoran*'s Indian Ocean sortie, see Robinson, *False Flags*, chapter 19, 'A New Operational Area'.
33 See Eiji Seki, *Mrs Ferguson's Tea-Set, Japan, and the Second World War: The Global Consequences Following Germany's Sinking of the SS* Automedon *in 1940* (Folkestone, Kent: Global Oriental, 2007).
34 Paterson, *Hitler's Grey Wolves*, p. 11.
35 Ibid., p. 39.

> West Africa, particularly the vital Allied central Atlantic stopover port of Freetown, had long been under fire and the opportunity for a fresh onslaught against an unprepared enemy attracted [Dönitz's] attention. *Abwehr* operatives within South Africa had reported upwards of 200 ships passing through Cape Town in recent months and as many as 50 moored within the harbour and its approaches at any given time.[36]

Unfortunately for this U-boat group, Enigma intelligence alerted the British to the activities of the raider *Atlantis* and the supply ship *Python*, from which the submarines were to refuel. *Devonshire* sank *Atlantis* 500 miles south of St Helena while refuelling *U126*. Then on 1 December *Dorsetshire* caught *Python* in the act of refuelling *U68* and *UA*, and sank her too.[37] In the light of this disastrous start, the plans for the submarine campaign off Cape Town were abandoned.

German commerce raiders sank nearly a millions tons of Allied and neutral shipping as well as capturing scores of vessels for the Reich. Their sorties demonstrated the potential for much more ambitious Axis surface campaigns against Allied shipping, ports, and sea lanes, but also the effectiveness of the Royal Navy's response to their deployment. As the raiders' brief period of success came to a close in late 1941, the British and their allies were about to face a far sterner challenge from the east.

36 Ibid.
37 Agar describes the action in *Footprints in the Sea*, pp. 167-69.

7

The consequences of Japanese aggression

Chapter 7 describes the opening of the 'second half' of the British Empire's war in the Indian Ocean region heralded by Japan's egregious entry into the conflict in December 1941. This endangered Britain's position east of Suez in ways that the Germans and Italians had proved incapable of achieving in the first half of the war. From an Indian Ocean perspective, the chapter considers the consequences of the Japanese attack on Pearl Harbor and the loss of Force Z – the Royal Navy capital ships sent as a deterrent against Japan.[1] These calamities led inexorably to the loss of Malaya and the naval base at Singapore, supposed to shield all British territories east of Suez. The subsequent loss of control of the sea, signalled by the defeat of a combined Allied fleet at the Battle of the Java Sea in February 1942, doomed Burma and the Dutch East Indies, leaving land forces to fend for themselves and air squadrons to do what they could before their bases were overrun. The innovative new American-British-Dutch-Australian (ABDA) Command established to rally remaining Allied forces folded within six weeks, its men killed or captured in the East Indies or lost at sea, a lucky few escaping to Australia and Ceylon. Soon after, and signifying the perilous weakening of British sea power, the Royal Navy was given a salutary lesson by the Imperial Japanese Navy when it attacked Ceylon and India in April, sinking merchantmen and warships and forcing the British into a cascading strategic retreat towards African shores.

The stunning reverses of December 1941-April 1942 obliged Britain and the defenders of the Indian Ocean, particularly the ships and shore stations of the East Indies Station, on to the back foot, and raised the spectre of German and Japanese forces meeting somewhere in the region as the one pushed from the west and the other from the east. But although in apparent full retreat, Britain did what it could to stem the tide, rapidly developing Ceylon as a surrogate Singapore and focusing on the security of the sea lanes across the Indian Ocean that had now become even more vital to the imperial and Allied war effort. A strategic recalibration was required, duly enunciated by the Admiralty in December 1941 and endorsed by the Chiefs of Staff in February as the Allied position crumbled. It was a strategy formulated before the outbreak of war, envisaging a major build up of naval power in the Indian Ocean. At its heart was the Eastern Fleet – a major new concentration of warship, forming alongside those of the East Indies Station – and the Indian Army, and whatever land and air reinforcements could be rushed east from Britain

1 The ships were formally designated Force Z after their arrival at Singapore's Sembawang naval base on 2 December.

and the Middle East.[2] The emphasis placed on the loss of Force Z – supposed to be the spearhead of the new Eastern Fleet – and the surrender of Singapore that has dominated narratives of Britain's war against Japan should not obscure the remarkable reinforcement of the Indian Ocean that ensued, as the British government redeployed the Royal Navy in order to defend the strategic 'bottom line' – the sea lanes of the Indian Ocean.

The loss of Force Z

Much has been made of Churchill's determination to send a deterrent force to Singapore, influenced by the manner in which the German battleship *Tirpitz* successfully occupied a large tranche of the Royal Navy's Home Fleet simply by virtue of her presence in European waters.[3] British capital ships operating from Singapore or 'disappearing' into the region's endless archipelagos could, it was reasoned, similarly tie down and deter Japanese forces in the event of hostilities. In August 1941 the prime minister told Admiral Sir Dudley Pound, the First Sea Lord, that it should soon become possible to 'place a deterrent force in the Indian Ocean'.[4] Encapsulating a more cautious approach, so the standard narrative goes, Pound thought that while a powerful force, most likely built around the 'R' for 'Revenge' class battleships, could be sent to Singapore, it should retire to Trincomalee if war with Japan broke out. The idea of building up the East Indies Station as a trade protection force based on Ceylon was a key element of Admiralty thinking should war come in the east, involving three modern or modernized battleships, an aircraft carrier or two, and the 'R' class battleships.[5] Nevertheless, even before the war the limitations of these old battleships, which were slow, inadequately armoured, and of limited endurance, were widely acknowledged in naval circles. Churchill had dubbed them 'floating coffins', 'unsafe to face any modern vessel or air attack'.[6] The prime minister reacted strongly against the idea of placing such ships where they could neither fight the Japanese nor provide an effective deterrent.[7]

Apparently the Admiralty, including Acting Vice Admiral Sir Tom Phillips, then serving as Vice Chief of the Naval Staff, dissented from the proposal to send *Prince of Wales* to Singapore. 'Such was the background', wrote Stephen Roskill, 'to the shocking disaster which was to destroy British prestige throughout the East and, in the long run, must surely have contributed

2 The loss of Force Z by no means terminated Britain as a naval power east of Suez, though one might be forgiven for thinking so given the manner in which the opening period of Britain's war against Japan is often represented. At the time of the loss, there were still scores of warships in theatre carrying out important work – and the British commitment to ABDA Command, most of it lost during the Battle of the Java Sea, did not represent the main strength of the Eastern Fleet which, wisely, was kept away from the doomed defence of the East Indies.

3 Stephen Roskill, *Churchill and the Admirals* (Barnsley: Pen and Sword, 2004), p. 198.

4 Ibid., p. 197.

5 H. P. Willmott, *Empires in the Balance: Japanese and Allied Pacific Strategies to April 1942* (Annapolis, MD: Naval Institute Press, 1982), p. 127. Willmott's work offers a splendid bridge between two usually separated theatres, connecting the Indian Ocean to the Pacific.

6 Arthur Marder, *Old Friends, New Enemies: The Royal Navy and the Imperial Japanese Navy*, 2 volumes (Oxford: Oxford University Press, 1981 and 1990). Volume 2, p. 222.

7 Roskill, *Churchill and the Admirals*, p. 201.

to our loss of empire'.[8] As late as September 1941 Vice Admiral Layton, Commander-in-Chief China Station, believed that the 'main fleet to Singapore' strategy would go ahead, and that a fleet of approximately six battleships, a battlecruiser, a carrier, 13 cruisers, 34 destroyers, and ten submarines would be formed.[9]

Directly countering the key elements of this narrative – Churchill bamboozling a reluctant Admiralty into sending an insufficient force to Singapore – Andrew Boyd's recent account inverts the equation. In fact, he argues, the prime minister did not urge an offensive strategy on an Admiralty intent on a more cautious build up in the Indian Ocean. 'This interpretation ignores unambiguous Admiralty and Cabinet Office records demonstrating that the naval staff shifted in September that year from their previous cautious strategy in the Indian Ocean to the concept of a forward offensive strategy based on Singapore and, potentially, Manila'.[10] Force Z was supposed to be a part, albeit a rather egregiously deployed part, of a general build up already planned. Two 'R' class battleships were due at Singapore before the end of 1941 to join *Prince of Wales* and *Repulse*; *Revenge* was already in the Indian Ocean; *Royal Sovereign* sailed east as escort to convoy WS12 on 10 November (reaching Durban on 17 December); and *Ramillies* and *Resolution* departed for the Indian Ocean in January.

Though the 'Singapore strategy' was part of a far more credible and informed plan to protect the eastern Empire than is often acknowledged, there is no doubt that unrealistic political and public expectations, in Britain and across the world, attached to it.[11] It was hailed as a grand security catch-all, depicted in newspapers and newsreel films, as well as in diplomatic and military circles, as the solution to the challenges of imperial defence and the conundrums caused by the machinations of foes in Europe and the Mediterranean as well as in the Far East.[12] Singapore was no secret base; in fact, part of its potency appeared to derive from everyone knowing about its fortress-like impregnability and the intention to operate a powerful battle

8 Ibid. See Roskill's *The War at Sea, 1939-1945*, 3 volumes (London: HMSO, 1954-61) for the discussions on this in the Chiefs of Staff and Defence Committee.

9 For Layton, see Jonathan Parkinson, *The China Station, Royal Navy: As Seen Through the Careers of the Commanders-in-Chief, 1864-1941* (Kibworth Beauchamp, Leicestershire: Matador, 2018). He ceased to be C-in-C China Station on 8 December 1941 when the position lapsed and Tom Phillips took over as C-in-C Eastern Fleet.

10 Boyd, *The Royal Navy in Eastern Waters*, p. xvi.

11 The Singapore strategy and the Malayan campaign are the subject of regular publications; like the defence of Malta, the battles of Kohima and Imphal, and the see-saw struggle in the Western Desert, Singapore is an erogenous zone for historians and publishers alike. Recent contributions to what Blackburn and Hack term the 'never-ending post-mortem' include: Kevin Blackburn and Karl Hack, *Did Singapore Have to Fall? Churchill and the Impregnable Fortress* (London: Routledge, 2003); Colin Smith, *Singapore Burning* (London: Penguin, 2006); and Peter Thompson's *The Battle for Singapore: The True Story of the Greatest Catastrophe of World War II* (London: Portrait, 2006). (A poor title because whichever way you look at it, the fall of Singapore was not the war's greatest catastrophe, either in terms of strategic significance or human tragedy.) See also A. Marder, *Old Friends, New Enemies* and Field, *Royal Navy Strategy*. Brian Farrell describes the literature on Singapore as ranging from 'the useless to the enduring'; see his *The Defence and Fall of Singapore, 1940-1942* (Stroud, Gloucestershire: Tempus, 2005), republished by Monsoon, Singapore, in 2015, and his edited collection *Churchill and the Lion City: Shaping Modern Singapore* (Singapore: National University of Singapore Press, 2013).

12 See 'Alert in the East', a Ministry of Information film from 1938, available at https://www.youtube.com/watch?v=AqoCNsFFq7k

squadron from it if ever the Empire were threatened. To dependents in the British Empire and those supposedly protected by Britain's system of imperial defence, including Australia, New Zealand and smaller allied powers such as the Dutch, it was designed to give assurance, a symbol of Britain's intent to do what was necessary, come what may.

The development of the Singapore base had been hampered by hefty domestic and strategic brakes in the 1920s and 1930s, growing in a stop start manner as wrangles over money and strategy ensured that less than optimal solutions were adopted. More importantly, the requisite numbers of warships to protect the Empire against all comers were never likely to be built in an era of naval disarmament and economic depression. A mooted 'Empire Pacific Fleet' failed to materialize, the evolution of the Fleet Air Arm lagged behind its Japanese competitor, and the self-perpetuating 'ten year rule', enunciated in 1919 and renewed each year until finally abandoned in 1932, anticipated that Britain would *not* be involved in a great war for the next decade, and so didn't need to prepare to fight one. Nevertheless, Admiralty planning for a possible war against Japan in the 1930s was more ambitious and realistic than the emblematic failure of Singapore and Force Z would have us believe.

Despite these limitations and the impact of wartime events preceding the dispatch of *Prince of Wales* and *Repulse*, the idea of 'the main fleet to Singapore' had become engraved on British minds, along with visions of the fortress's alleged prowess. Too many British people, including senior officers and politicians, came to believe their own propaganda, bolstered, no doubt, by both the myth and the reality of Britain's long-standing maritime preeminence. Making things much worse was the fact that, when the time came to activate the strategy, the circumstances of war had already created a worst case scenario, and the deployment therefore occurred in a sub-optimal fashion. Events in the summer of 1940 made all the difference. In particular, the fall of France and loss of French naval support meant that Britain could not send core elements of the Mediterranean Fleet east, and that now, in Singapore's neighbourhood, a pliant Vichy administration in Indo-China was obliged to grant Japan base rights. Furthermore, Italy had joined the war on Germany's side, requiring the British to maintain large forces in and around the middle sea. Also, from June 1941, some of the aircraft that might otherwise have gone to Far East Command were instead being sent to aid the Soviet war effort. Finally, the British had recently suffered significant losses of battleships; the British had entered the war in 1939 with 14 battleships and three battlecruisers, but by early 1942 had lost three battleships and two battlecruisers sunk and two battleships were out of action having been badly damaged during the Italian frogmen attack on Alexandria harbour in December 1941. The battleship *Duke of York* had entered commission in November 1941, though the battleships *Anson* and *Howe* would not commission until April and August 1942 respectively. Down to 10 battleships and a single battlecruiser at this moment, British naval resources were stretched as never before.

This situation was compounded by the fact that, even if the British could have assembled an optimal force at Singapore, the revolutionary form of maritime air power that the Japanese now practiced, underpinned by requisite doctrine, training, and equipment, was for the moment beyond the capacity of the Royal Navy to match in this theatre. But this fact was not yet grasped, and so faith in 'fortress Singapore' and the dispatch of capital ships to operate from it remained a grand if vaguely articulated concept, in which reposed the security of the British Empire east of Suez. As a backstop, there was also the hope that America, and its formidable if latent power, would balance the scales in this region. At the time, this must all have appeared both reasonable and practical; only what happened, and its refraction through hindsight, has given the whole episodic sequence of events stretching from Pearl Harbor onwards its air of tragic inevitability, and cast the main protagonists as variously blind, stupid, and villainous.

Everyone seemed to know about the dispatch to eastern waters of the powerful new battleship *Prince of Wales* and the battlecruiser *Repulse*, and to trust in the efficacy of their deployment. Along with their destroyer escorts and an aircraft carrier they were to be a visible reassurance that the Singapore strategy was working, warning Japan and showing imperial subjects and allies alike that Britain meant business. The Admiralty wanted Tokyo to know that the ships were on their way, and the Director of Naval Intelligence learned from intercepts on 22 November that the Japanese consul-general in Cape Town had reported *Prince of Wales*'s visit and that Malaya was her destination. The now Acting Admiral Sir Tom Phillips and his ship had already called in at Freetown, where he conferred with Vice Admiral Algernon Willis, the Commander-in-Chief South Atlantic. Following the visit, Willis wrote to the First Sea Lord: 'It was a great pleasure to have Tom Phillips through last week and I much enjoyed having a yarn with him ... It's a fine strategical move – if I may say so – sending a strong force out there. From my little knowledge of our little yellow friends it's the one thing that will scare them'.[13] But like so many others, events were to prove that Willis had no useful knowledge on the subject at all. Nevertheless, similar views wildly underestimating the Japanese threat were commonly held, even by those on the spot. On 13 November, two days after Willis had penned his missive, General Wavell wrote to Air Marshal Brooke-Popham at Singapore, saying:

> I am left with the impression that you ought easily be able to deal with any Japanese attack on Malaya provided that you get the necessary air reinforcements when required. Personally, I should be most doubtful if the Japs ever tried to make an attack on Malaya, and I'm sure they will get it in the neck if they do.[14]

Lieutenant General Sir Henry Pownall, arriving to take over Far East Command from Brooke-Popham in December, agreed that aircraft were the crucial variable in defending Malaya. But the desired number of first-class modern fighters was never sent.

As *Prince of Wales* progressed eastwards, all along the line people were proud and impressed by the spectacle of the enormous vessel and the message, the strategy, the hope, that she embodied. James Thompson, the young Royal Marines officer, was stationed on Addu Atoll at the time. He warrants quoting at length, for the splendour of his prose, the remoteness of his station, and a rare glimpse of *Prince of Wales* as she journeyed east to meet her fate:

> Under the sun, a veiled, wistful memory of a grey, proud ship and a small, kind Admiral. The man who found the time to say a few words; who, on a darkening evening sailed his two great ships over the Addu bar, his flag brave in the headwind as the *Prince of Wales* turned East to Singapore.
>
> At the beginning of December, 1941, we looked out across the water to where the two battleships lay anchored in the lagoon. With a certain pride: for they had come to the

13 CAC, Willis Papers, 2 WLLS5/4, 11/11/41.
14 Brian Bond (ed.), *Chief of Staff: The Diaries of Lieutenant-General Sir Henry Pownall*, volume 2, *1940-1944* (London: Leo Cooper, 1974), p. xii.

> anchorage we had created from coral and jungle. Tattered, dirty, bedraggled regiments; sick, ill-fed; the pristine paint and glitter worn from the soldiers long taken from their box.
>
> We were proud, grateful, our simplified emotions stirred as the Aldis lamps flashing from the grey signal bridges, despatched their invitations to the frankly hopeful marines.
>
> That evening, every available officer and marine on the atoll islands enjoyed the generous hospitality of the two battleships; found delight in a good hot meal, a cinema show, the different faces from the lost world, the news and rumours. I remember the laughter and the jokes in the smoke-laden wardroom, the small glasses that were never empty.
>
> In the crowd and the noise a respectful travelling wave of silence for the small, quietly-spoken Admiral, his heavy gold braid epaulettes glinting through the haze. Sir Tom Philips [sic]; Admiral Tom Thumb, the little Admiral came to the party to meet and welcome and encourage the straggling companies mouldering on Addu.
>
> On the evening of the following day H. M. S. *Prince of Wales* and *Repulse* sailed East into the fiery sunset. Many a rough heart wished them Godspeed and remembered the small Admiral who lead [sic] the line.[15]

On 28 November *Prince of Wales* and her destroyers arrived at Colombo, where they met *Repulse*. As Boyd argues, the situation with regard to Japan was now darkening. There was evidence of a Japanese build up, and at this moment the Admiralty had the opportunity to halt the ships in Ceylon, from where they could act as a deterrent just as effectively as from Singapore. But having created a new Eastern Fleet and given it a commander, a momentum had been created that was now hard to check. On the subject of the fleet's deterrent role, it is instructive to note that it failed to have the intended effect. The Japanese believed that the British had a force in the Indian Ocean based around six battleships and two carriers. Not only was this a significantly stronger force than the British, at that juncture, actually had in the Indian Ocean, it was one that the Japanese felt that they could manage. At 8pm on 29 November, the capital ships left Ceylon in company with the destroyers *Electra*, *Encounter*, *Express*, and *Jupiter*.

And, so, onwards to Singapore. Phillips completed the last leg of the journey east by air, flying from Colombo on 29 November 1941, arriving three days ahead of his capital ships. There he hoisted his flag as Commander-in-Chief Eastern Fleet – the new designation for *Prince of Wales*, *Repulse*, and their destroyer escort – at 8am on 3 December. Vice Admiral Layton remained in temporary command of the shore establishments and the China Station until, on 8 December, the latter ceased to exist and its ships merged into the Eastern Fleet to operate alongside those of the East Indies Station, which retained its own commander-in-chief, responsible for Ceylon's shore establishments and, confusingly, the ships that were not part of the Eastern Fleet.[16] In this post, Vice Admiral Leatham had been replaced by Vice Admiral Sir Geoffrey Arbuthnot

15 Thompson, *Only the Sun Remembers*, pp. 91-92. According to *Prince of Wales*'s war diary, she arrived at Addu Atoll at 5:45pm on 26 November with the destroyers *Electra* and *Express* (not *Repulse*, as Thompson seems to think). They departed at 8:40am the following morning. See http://www.naval-history.net/xGM-Chrono-01BB-Prince%20of%20Wales.htm. *Repulse*'s summary of service shows her leaving Mombasa on 15 November and arriving Colombo on 22 November, and does not record a stop at Addu.

16 It is clear from the war diaries that in this period, the C-in-C Eastern Fleet had to ask the C-in-C East Indies to sail ships to take part in his operations, permission that might be denied.

in April 1941.[17] Layton, meanwhile, prepared to sail home to assume the post of Commander-in-Chief Portsmouth. Handing over to the junior and inexperienced Phillips must have been hard for this experienced sailor, though he had known since May that if a battleship force was despatched east, Phillips would command it.

On 7 December Japanese forces attacked American bases in Hawaii. 'Dawn action stations', wrote Ken Dimbleby, recalling *Cornwall*'s entry into the Mozambique Channel on 8 December, sailing south for Durban. 'It was a typically muggy morning in the tropics',

> humid even before the sun had risen, especially down below on the mess decks with all portholes closed because the warship had to be blacked out … The call to dawn action stations was an essential precaution every day when the warship was at sea. In the darkness one did not know if an enemy ship was nearby. Everyone closed up about twenty minutes before dawn so that the ship was in a state of readiness to go into action immediately, and stayed closed up until full light after sunrise … *Cornwall* was not even equipped with radar, so it was even more essential to have dawn action stations because the ship depended entirely on human eyesight, even for gunnery.[18]

Having stood the middle watch between midnight and 0400 hours, Dimbleby was not particularly alert that morning, though heard snatches of excited conversation – references to 'Pearl Harbor', 'Yankee battleships', and 'dirty Japs'.[19] The day that President Roosevelt said would 'live in infamy' had been and gone. Over 2,400 Americans lay dead in Hawaii, and the global balance of naval power had shifted dramatically as eight battleships were sunk or damaged and nearly 200 aircraft destroyed. Japanese forces were even now attacking British possessions from Hong Kong to Malaya, along with the colonial territories of the other Western powers.

On 10 December, hunting for reported Japanese transports heading for Malaya, *Prince of Wales* and *Repulse* were sunk in the Gulf of Siam, attacked by Japanese bombers based in French Indo-China, the first battleships ever to succumb to aircraft.[20] Phillips had been commander of the Eastern Fleet for barely a week when he went to the bottom with his flagship, the pride of the Royal Navy. Three hundred and twenty-four sailors died alongside him, and a further 513 were lost from *Repulse*. Layton was on board the troopship *Dominion Monarch* due to leave Singapore in half an hour when he heard the news, coming ashore immediately to take command and

17 Boyd points out that the temporary division of command between Layton and Phillips was unhelpful – Layton, for instance, retaining control of the intelligence outfit Far East Combined Bureau – and that the handover left much to be desired. Boyd, *The Royal Navy in Eastern Waters*, p. 326.

18 Dimbleby, *Turns of Fate*, p. 13.

19 Ibid.

20 See Blackburn and Hack, *Did Singapore Have to Fall?*; Ian Cowman, 'Defence of the Malay Barrier? The Place of the Philippines in Admiralty Naval War Planning, 1925-1941', *War in History*, 3 (1996); Cowman, *Dominion or Decline? Anglo-American Naval Relations in the Pacific, 1937–41* (Oxford: Berg, 1996); Roskill, *Churchill and the Admirals*; Richard Hough, *The Hunting of Force Z: The Sinking of the* Prince of Wales *and the* Repulse (London: Phoenix, 1999); and Greg Kennedy (ed.), *British Naval Strategy East of Suez, 1900–2000: Influences and Actions* (London: Routledge, 2004). See also V. H. Rothwell, *War Aims in the Second World War: The War Aims of the Key Belligerents, 1939–1945* (Edinburgh: Edinburgh University Press, 2005).

quickly confirmed as Phillips's successor.[21] The news of the lightning Japanese attacks and the destruction of the two ships in particular sent shock waves around the world. Captain Malcolm Kennedy was a codebreaker at Bletchley Park in Buckinghamshire. On that day 'something like a gasp of dismay went round the dining room at B. P. when the 1pm news opened with the announcement that *Prince of Wales* and *Repulse* had been sunk'.[22]

Commodore Ralph Edwards, en route to Singapore to join the *Prince of Wales*'s crew, arrived at Malta at 6:30am on 8 December. 'When we landed we were told that Japan had attacked Pearl Harbor, Guam, and Hong Kong ... I wonder where the Far East Fleet is today and when I shall find my to the *Prince of Wales*', he wrote in his diary.[23] The following day, proceeding along the familiar air route connecting Britain to its eastern empire, he was in Cairo. After checking in at the Continental Hotel ('a foul place') he visited GHQ Middle East, where he discussed Indian Ocean lines of communication with fellow naval officers. After dining at the famous Shepheard's Hotel that evening, he learned that German and Italian sources were reporting that *Prince of Wales* and *Repulse* had been sunk. 'I was feeling a bit shaken and sad', he wrote, and the news was confirmed that afternoon. 'What an awful blow I don't feel quite able to take it in. It upsets the whole balance of naval power in the world'.[24] Leaving Cairo, it was the long haul across Palestine and Iraq, stopping at RAF Habbaniya and Basra, 'which hums with activity'. Here he met the Senior Naval Officer Persian Gulf, Commodore Cosmo Graham, and worried about what the future held, both for him and the British war effort, now that *Prince of Wales* was no more.[25]

Also reacting to the news, Algernon Willis at Freetown, who like so many had been overconfident regarding the navy's ability to teach 'our little yellow friends' a thing or two, was aghast. As he wrote to Vice Admiral Sir William Whitworth, the Second Sea Lord: 'I'm afraid the war in the Far East is going to strain the old Empire to the limit. It's devastating about the *Prince of Wales*, *Repulse*, and little Tom – awful. The little yellow devils seem to have some powerful bombs'.[26] Few people forgot the moment when they heard the news of the Japanese attacks. It was shattering enough to people in Britain, never mind those stationed in the eastern territories of the Empire. Reginald Carter was working for the Indian Civil Service in Rangoon: 'So the war has come to the east at last. A good deal of talking, and not so much work, is done in the offices. The Army say there is no likelihood of Burma being invaded by land but there may be air

21 John Winton, *Sink the* Haguro! *The Last Destroyer Action of the Second World War* (London: Seeley, Service, & Co., 1979), pp. 7-8.

22 Quoted in Aldrich, *The Faraway War*, p. 132.

23 CAC, Edwards Papers, REDW2/7, Diary extracts November 1941-May 1942.

24 Ibid. Edwards's progress east was typical in terms of the stop offs along the way, and, given his rank, the type of meetings he had on the journey. During the stop-over in Malta he met Vice Admiral Bernard Rawlings and had a chat on the quay at the seaplane base RAF Kalafrana with Sir Phillip Mitchell and Brigadier Daniel Sandford, both typical of the figures cutting around the Empire's war zones (Mitchell, former Governor of Uganda, had been employed to coordinate the war effort of the East African colonies and was now employed by Middle East Command to help administer conquered Italian African colonies. In July 1942, he was appointed Governor of Fiji. Sandford was an important intelligence officer and organizer of guerrilla resistance during the East Africa campaign, with a special interest in Ethiopia). For Mitchell, see Richard Frost, *Enigmatic Proconsul: Sir Philip Mitchell and the Twilight of Empire* (London: Radcliffe Press, 1992).

25 CAC, Edwards Papers, diary, 12/12/41.

26 CAC, Willis Papers, 2 WLLS5/4, 19/12/41.

raids. I collect some coolies to dig air raid trenches in our garden at Windermere Park'.[27] Mollie Panter-Downes, an American journalist, recorded the reaction in Singapore:

> The satisfaction over the arrival at Singapore of the *Prince of Wales* with her consorts was still so recent that her loss seemed at first almost incredible. It was as if some enormously powerful and valuable watchdog which had been going to keep burglars away from the house had been shot while exercising in the front yard. The big battleship's disappearance made the landscape look so menacing that British spirits, which always react better to disaster than to triumph, promptly rose to a new high pitch of belligerence.[28]

On the other side of the Indian Ocean aboard *Cornwall*, Dimbleby wrote:

> So the balloon had gone up ... Standing on the air defence platform (ADP) I instinctively looked towards the east. The rising sun, red in the early morning summer haze, was just peeping over the horizon, sending crimson streaks across the calm, blue water of the Mozambique Channel. What was normally a lovely sight seemed to be a sinister setting for the news that Japan had entered the war ... I remembered my wife's foreboding that *Cornwall* was doomed if Japan came into the war.[29]

James Thompson, who had beheld *Prince of Wales* at Addu Atoll, was now, less than two weeks later, on leave 'high in the beautiful Ceylon hills'. On this particular day, he was out drinking with fellow Royal Marines' officers. Haggling over a taxi fare, he casually asked a passing British Army sergeant for the latest news. 'With the typical Service pleasure in dispensing gloom and disaster he quickly offered the ridiculous rumour: "Haven't you heard, Sir? *Prince of Wales* and *Repulse* – both sunk. Sunk off Malaya by Jap bombers". Jeeringly, incredulously deriding we voiced our raucous disbelief, and without further word or serious thought bundled ourselves into the dilapidated car'.[30] The marines carried on about their business, which later in the day involved drinking a large amount at the Bandarawela Hotel, leaving its bar 'alcoholically humorous, our laughter loud, gin confident, pleased and content at the prospect of our extended leave in the civilised amenities of Diyatalawa'.[31] Next stop was the 'open, dimly-lit terrace-veranda of a small native hotel' in search of beer; 'Beer for the leathernecks, for the officers of the proudest Corps', decreed the Ceylonese waiter, earning four 'inane, surprised and delighted smiles'.[32]

Now, smashing-glasses drunk, it was time to go home.

> We returned to Diyatalawa for dinner. With a feeble attempt at restraint, assuming a false decorum, we entered the Mess. I immediately slipped on the polished tiles, falling noisily

27 Quoted in Aldrich, *The Faraway War*, p. 141
28 Ibid.
29 Dimbleby, *Turns of Fate*, pp. 14-15.
30 Thompson, *Only the Sun Remembers*, p. 92.
31 Diyatalawa was a large British military rest camp.
32 Thompson, *Only the Sun Remembers*, p. 92.

> against the wall, unable to repress a laugh; my shoes seemed inordinately loud on the hard floor. We sat down to the fruit-laden table; the Colonel already dining.
>
> And then we heard the truth of the disaster East of Malaya.
>
> The party was over; the lights were out; the façade of gaiety cracked.
>
> We ate slowly, without appetite; in silence; an intimate, strangely personal sorrow flowering in my heart. I saw again the great dark ships sailing out of Addu, their guns in grim silhouette. I heard again the voice of the small, kindly Admiral, whose flag no longer commanded the sea winds.
>
> We did not speak; we made no mention of our thoughts; but how dark the night behind the hills as a gentle storm of sadness broke in our troubled hearts.[33]

The British Empire now braced itself for its sternest challenge. The conflict was now truly global, and Britain's position in the Indian Ocean, dogged for two years by the depredations of the Germans and Italians, was about to face the ferocity of Japan, bent on conquest and imperial gain and possessed, at that moment, of a devastating combination of advanced naval capabilities and maritime tactics. Michael Simpson, editor of Admiral Somerville's papers, offers an incisive overview of the situation that now pertained:

> There was no concrete pre-war strategy for the region. The only guiding principle was the entirely negative (and complacent) one that the region was unlikely to be threatened, cushioned as it was by substantial forces in the Middle East and at Singapore. However, by late 1941 there was a dawning realisation that the area could not be protected against a determined and co-ordinated Axis attack. The imperial bluff was about to be called, overstretch was about to lead to overbalancing. Between December 1941 and June 1942, the Axis threat was at its most dire and came simultaneously from three directions. The German thrust into the Crimea might very easily turn south to the Gulf oilfields, while Rommel might seize the Suez Canal; in the east, the Japanese rampaged northwards from Singapore, through Burma, to the gates of India. Should the Axis succeed in co-ordinating their strategy, there was little to prevent their overwhelming and rapid triumph.[34]

Back in London, the Chiefs of Staff, the War Cabinet, and the services ministries tried to work out what to do. On 14 December Major General John Kennedy, Director of Military Operations at the War Office, sent the Chief of the Imperial General Staff, General Sir Alan Brooke, a 'Note on the situation':

> The problem before us now is to decide how far we can strengthen our position in the Indian Ocean and the Far East without weakening ourselves unduly at home and in the Middle East. It would be right to strengthen the Navy in the Indian Ocean, not only because the Americans can take a greater share of the Naval commitment in the Atlantic, but because, without a strong fleet in the Indian Ocean and apart from the difficulty of

33 Ibid., p. 93.

34 Simpson (ed.), *The Somerville Papers*, p. 354-5. While this last point is generally true, it should not obscure the existence of imperial forces still stationed east of Suez and either fighting the Japanese or preparing to defend the region against them.

> maintaining our convoys east of the Cape, we may lose our position, not only in the China Sea, but in the oceans around our Indian and African Empires, not to mention Australia and New Zealand. How far we can reinforce Malaya and Burma and the East Indies is a matter which will require the closest consideration and nicest calculation but it is certain that we must do something for Burma, and it is certain that we must do something for Ceylon as a naval base.[35]

Already, Kennedy continued, certain measures had been taken to meet the situation.

> The 18th Division, which was already approaching the Red Sea, has been diverted to India. The 50th Division which was destined for Iraq has been handed back to the Middle East. The 17th Indian Division which was about to embark for Iraq from India is to be retained in India and may possibly be used in Burma. In addition, a number of anti-aircraft and anti-tank units and some squadrons of fighters have been diverted to India. A MNBDO is being sent from the Middle East to Ceylon.[36]

At the Admiralty, the response to Force Z's destruction was rapid and realistic, based on pre-war plans to build up strong forces in the Indian Ocean, a process already in train. With only the carrier *Hermes* and the 'R' class battleships in or nearing the Indian Ocean, serious reinforcements were needed immediately. The First Sea Lord had already – before 10 December – consulted Admiral Sir Andrew Cunningham, Commander-in-Chief Mediterranean, about transferring all of his capital ships to the Indian Ocean.[37] A paper entitled 'Future British naval strategy' was prepared for the Chiefs of Staff on 14 December, emphasizing the cardinal need to control the sea lanes of the Indian Ocean. It was immediately endorsed by the Chiefs of Staff and Churchill, all agreeing that the defence of the Indian Ocean had overriding priority. Up to nine battleships and three fleet carriers were available for the Eastern Fleet, which would operate from Addu Atoll and Trincomalee.

Meanwhile, and despite the enormous sense of loss, almost bereavement, stimulated by the destruction of Force Z, the routine business of war had to go on; for the men and women of the Royal Navy, there was no choice except 'business as usual'. *Cornwall* was resting at Colombo, her crew playing cricket against that of *Exeter*. Soon she was sailing halfway to Australia to take over the escort of the super-liners *Queen Elizabeth* and *Queen Mary* from the cruiser *Canberra*, bringing the ships, laden with thousands of Australian troops, fast to Trincomalee. Christmas 1941 was spent in Aden though on Boxing Day *Cornwall* sailed south of the equator to take over a convoy, WS12ZB, from the battleship *Royal Sovereign*, which she accompanied to Bombay. On land, meanwhile, the Japanese pushed the British imperial troops defending Malaya all the way down the peninsula, until they withdrew across the Johore Strait onto Singapore Island, which fell on 15 February 1942.

Scheduled reinforcements for the Eastern Fleet continued to arrive, a task given new moment and urgency by the naval defeat in the Gulf of Siam. *Royal Sovereign*, commanded by Algernon Willis, former Commander-in-Chief South Atlantic and now commanding the 3rd Battle

35 Kennedy, *The Business of War*, chapter 20, 'Pearl Harbor and the Far East 1941', p. 188.
36 Ibid.
37 Boyd, *The Royal Navy in Eastern Waters*, p. 341.

Squadron and Deputy Commander-in-Chief Eastern Fleet, arrived. He had learning of his appointment in a personal signal from the Admiralty on the night the BBC announced the fall of Singapore.[38] *Royal Sovereign* had sailed from Durban to Mombasa at Christmas, soon embarking on a trip to the Seychelles, Zanzibar, and the Maldives before steaming on to Trincomalee where her fifteen-inch guns were exercised off the coast. For the crew these long voyages required special efforts to combat boredom and maintain morale, through constant work, sporting activity, and a range of high and low brow cultural events, from hymn-singing broadcast over the tannoy to variety shows such as the ubiquitous *On Board Tonight*. Conditions were famously bad aboard the 'R' class battleships in the Indian Ocean, as they were designed for service in cold northern climates. As Lieutenant Colonel C. L. Price of the Royal Marines remembered, this meant that tropical showers occasioned a mad dash of men rushing naked to the upper deck with a cake of soap.

American-British-Dutch-Australian (ABDA) Command and the Battle of the Java

In the wake of Japan's entry into the war and its rapid and successful expansion, the Allies formed a new joint command structure. ABDA Command was to be the Allies last hurrah in South-east Asia and the East Indies. Fighting desperate rear-guard actions, and having suffered grievous defeats, the remnants of Allied military power regrouped as best they could and prepared to fight it out, the circumstances in which they did so entirely unforeseen. Thousands of miles away in Washington, over Christmas and New Year 1941-42, Churchill was staying at the White House with President Roosevelt, conducting a round of meetings, as were their chiefs of staff. This would come to be known as the Arcadia conference and it forged the historic Anglo-American alliance in the days following Japan's opening attacks. It was at this summit that the idea was hatched to create the first of the war's joint Allied command structures.[39]

The British and the Dutch already had a military alliance in place, and the British and the Americans had had discussions about joint action in the event of war with Japan. So this was a bringing together, at a moment of crisis, of pre-existing themes, now with the imprimatur of the most powerful political and military leaders in Britain and America, spurred on by a Japanese boot at their backs. On 27 December Churchill telegraphed deputy prime minister Clement Attlee to say that

> last night [after a showing of the film *The Maltese Falcon*] the President urged upon me to appoint a single officer to command the Army, Navy, and Air Force of Great Britain, USA, and Dutch … You will be as much astonished as I was to learn that the man the President has in mind is General Wavell.[40]

The idea had come from General George Marshall, the US Army's Chief of Staff, and reflected the fact that most of the forces and territories in the region were British and Commonwealth

38 CAC, Willis Papers, 5/5.
39 David Bercuson and Holger Herwig, *One Christmas in Washington: Churchill and Roosevelt Forge the Grand Alliance* (London: Weidenfeld and Nicolson, 2005), p. 157.
40 Ibid., p. 175.

as well as Dutch. Roosevelt had wanted an American, preferably General Douglas MacArthur, partly because he thought a non-Briton would be more popular with the Australians than a Briton. The British were not keen on having their own man in command, rightly sensing a military disaster in the offing and believed that in its wake the American public might readily blame Britain if one of its own had been at the helm.[41]

The British Chiefs of Staff had major reservations about both the appointment of Wavell and the whole joint Allied command concept. But although last minute alterations to the command structure in this stricken theatre was like rearranging the deckchairs on the *Titanic*, the new joint Allied structure was an early milestone in Anglo-American military planning at the strategic level. Later supreme commanders, such as General Dwight Eisenhower and Admiral Lord Mountbatten, were to benefit from the experience gained during this early experiment.

> Stimson as well as Marshall knew, of course, that unity of command for ABDA was almost meaningless in terms of the immediate conduct of the war. The Japanese were running rampant throughout South-east Asia and there was little prospect that Wavell could put a stop to them. But they understood that the principle involved had to be implemented somewhere for the first time.[42]

The appointment led on to hard negotiations between the British and the Americans about the nature of the 'joint body' that would issue Wavell with his orders, a hugely important step in forging an effective trans-Atlantic alliance, and what emerged came to be known as the Combined Chiefs of Staff Committee.

Wavell was duly installed as Supreme Allied Commander ABDA on 4 January 1942, following a telegram from Churchill alerting him to the decision of the combined chiefs to form a command to coordinate the actions of Allied forces still fighting in the South-West Pacific, the East Indies, and South-east Asia. Already serving as Commander-in-Chief India and having just taken over responsibility for Burma, the British general now had a new challenge.[43] It 'was a complete surprise … to come back from a day's pig-sticking in the Kadir to find a telegram from the Prime Minister telling him to take over command'.[44] Wavell left Delhi on 5 January, spending the night in Madras before flying on to Colombo and then to Singapore, 'where he was starkly confronted with the weakness of the British position'.[45] He realized that he was involved in a race against time. After a flying visit to Kuala Lumpur to see the fatigued and shocked troops facing the Japanese advance he returned to Singapore, a supreme commander having to issue orders all the way down to brigade level as the situation went from bad to worse. On 10 January he flew to Batavia and the scratch ABDA Command held its first meetings in the Hotel

41 The CIGS described the scheme as 'wild and half baked'. But the plain fact, writes Adrian Fort, 'was that the Americans had become the paymasters of the British Empire, and were beginning to take the paramount position in what had finally become a world war'. Adrian Fort, *Archibald Wavell: The Life and Times of an Imperial Servant* (London: Jonathan Cape, 2009), p. 260.

42 Bercuson and Herwig, *One Christmas in Washington*, p. 197.

43 Though Wavell and the governor of Burma did not want Burma transferred to ABDA Command, it having so recently transferred from Britain's Far East Command to its India Command, the Americans insisted on it, with their focus on the Burma Road and supplying Chiang Kai-Shek.

44 Fort, *Archibald Wavell*, p. 260.

45 Ibid., p. 262.

des Indes. On 18 January the headquarters was established at the Grand Hotel, Lembang, near Bandoeng in the western interior of Java.

By the time ABDA had been established, 'the military situation in the Command area was beyond salvation'.[46] Lieutenant General Pownall, Wavell's new Chief of Staff in the headquarters, wrote that it was overwhelmed by the 'practical problems of improvising an international headquarters in a primitive part of the world and virtually under the nose of a dominant enemy'.[47] Wavell was under no illusions regarding the magnitude of the task, saying when he took up the command that 'I've heard of holding the baby but this is twins'.[48] He believed that attacks on enemy shipping and airbases by aircraft and submarines should be the primary objectives, and that to secure a line of naval and air bases running Darwin-Timor-Java-Southern Sumatra-Singapore represented the limits of the possible for the Allies. Tellingly, he did not think that airbases in Northern Sumatra could be held with the enemy already in possession of the Malayan port of Penang.

The American and British Chiefs of Staff were able to give Wavell little encouragement, replying to his assessment with the bad new that they weren't able to say what resources would be at his disposal. Unsurprisingly, the British commander's heterogeneous force was unable to stop the Japanese landing in the Dutch East Indies. As in the case of Malaya, if there had been better air cover it might have been a different story and Japanese landing craft spilling troops along the beaches might have been made to pay a heavy price. But what was sent was far too little, far too late.[49] The European Axis powers watched on with glee and admiration. In a strategic assessment of 19 January the Italian naval high command, sensing an opportunity to hitch Italy's flagging fortunes to Japan's coattails, argued that:

> [If the Japanese occupy Singapore] the Indian Ocean, where Great Britain has dominated in recent months in carrying reinforcements to Egypt and the Middle East, will once again be an area threatened … by the Axis forces … The advantages of an energetic offensive in the Indian Ocean for all the Axis powers are evident: It will allow the Japanese to block precious supplies of fuel from the Arabian Gulf to the Australian and New Zealand dominions, and will allow the Axis powers to impede the supply of weapons and material directed to the operational theatres of the Middle East, which are strongholds of British power in the Mediterranean.[50]

The day before, the Axis powers had agreed to the division of the Indian Ocean region into two zones of operations at the 70th meridian east, off India's west coast. Looking back, it seems like

46 David Thomas, *Battle of the Java Sea* (London: André Deutsch, 1968), p. 110. See also 'Battle of the Java Sea, 27 February 1942', *Supplement to the London Gazette*, 38346 (London: HMSO, 1948).

47 B. Bond (ed.), *Chief of Staff*, p. xiii.

48 Quoted in Alan Warren, *Burma 1942: The Road from Rangoon to Mandalay* (London: Continuum, 2011), p. 49.

49 For an account of the air war, see Christopher Shores and Brian Cull with Yasuho Izawa, *Bloody Shambles: The First Comprehensive Account of Air Operations Over South-East Asia, December 1941-April 1942* (London: Grub Street, 1992). For the Dutch East Indies during the war, see Peter Post (ed.), *The Encyclopaedia of Indonesia in the Pacific War* (Leiden: Brill, 2009).

50 De Ninno, 'The Italian Navy and Japan', p. 14 proof.

as good a point as any in the war for the Axis to have been drawing lines on maps and repartitioning the world.

Following what the Japanese called the 'Hawaiian operation' – the 7 December attack on Pearl Harbor – Vice Admiral Chuichi Nagumo's First Air Fleet regrouped. Japanese forces had also attacked the Philippines, Malaya, Hong Kong, and Wake Island, Borneo, the Celebes, Sumatra, Java, Timor, and New Guinea. On the island of Ambon, a mixed garrison of Australian and Dutch troops and Royal Australian Air Force and Dutch aircraft failed to stem the tide. Following this successful attack in late January-early February, Nagumo refuelled at Staring Bay in the Celebes before entering the Timor Sea.

With Singapore a lost cause, on 5 January Vice Admiral Layton, the Eastern Fleet's interim commander, had decided to move his headquarters to Colombo after a temporary period in Batavia, in order to better organize convoys and the protection of sea lanes in the Indian Ocean.[51] He arrived in Colombo aboard *Emerald* on 21 January, and on 27 January was informed by the Admiralty that a new man, Somerville, was being sent out to take over the Eastern Fleet.[52]

Still, reinforcements continued to arrive. The carrier *Indomitable* had offloaded her aircraft at Port Sudan and collected 50 Hurricanes destined for Singapore. Accompanied by three Eastern Fleet destroyers, she sailed for the East Indies, where Hurricanes of 232 and 258 squadrons were flown off to Batavia on 27 January. This took place near Christmas Island, the aircraft intended to fly on to Singapore via Batavia and Palembang, but instead squandered fighting from Sumatra. After delivering the aircraft, the carrier, screened by its destroyers, wheeled away and headed for Trincomalee on 2 February. *Indomitable* was lucky to still be afloat, for she had been the carrier nominated for Force Z. But the previous November, about to sail for Trincomalee to join Phillips's capital ships, she had run aground while working up in the West Indies.[53] Repaired in Norfolk, Virginia, the following month she took passage to join the Eastern Fleet.

The problem for ABDA was that by the time it was formed, the Japanese were well into their conquest spree – and were simply better at fighting than their opponents and had already collected some key strategic aces. These included Borneo, important because of its natural resources, especially the oil wells. 'Its attraction was enhanced by its position on the sea route between Singapore and Japan. Seizing British North Borneo, Brunei, and Sarawak would also help Japan develop its attack on the Dutch East Indies'.[54] Elsewhere, the defeat at Slim River in January stymied the defence of the Malayan interior, and there was now no realistic chance of retaining the peninsula or even delaying the Japanese for an appreciable amount of time. This all meant that Singapore was bound to be besieged, and it surrendered on 15 February. The next target for Nagumo's carriers and battleships was the Australian port of Darwin. Here the Allies were again caught off guard as Captain Takagashe Egusu's dive bombers swept in on 19

51 Heralded by his much-criticized, 'I'm all right Jack', signal to the fleet: 'With your heads held high and your hearts beating proudly, I leave the defence of Singapore in your strong and capable hands. I am off to Colombo to collect a new fleet'.

52 'Admiralty War Diaries of World War II', The diary of Admiral Layton, November 1941-March 1942.

53 *Indomitable* 'Record of War Service' at http://www.naval-history.net/xGM-Chrono-04CV-Indomitable.htm

54 Willmott, *Empires in the Balance*, p. 158.

February. They destroyed 24 aircraft on the ground, sank ten ships and damaged 13 more. By 21 February, Nagumo's task force was back at Staring Bay.

Upon his arrival, Layton found Ceylon 'virtually defenceless'. On 7 February, it being 'obvious that the Malaya-Netherlands East Indies barrier, on which it really depended for its defence against the enemy, was about to collapse, I represented to the Admiralty its deficiencies'. This was very important; though the fighting was taking place in Malaya and the East Indies, the British government well understood that the whole strategic position, ultimately, was going to depend on the security of the Indian Ocean's sea lanes, and for that Ceylon was a strategic must-have. Layton's arrival, and his immediate concern for Ceylon's security, chimed with London's appreciation of the situation. This was that Ceylon was indispensable and all now needed to be done to bolster both the Eastern Fleet and the island's defences. 'The first essential', wrote Layton, 'was clearly a strong fighter force at Colombo and Trincomalee, and adequate RDF [radio direction finding – radar] at these places to give warning of attack'.[55] From this point on, Layton became intimately involved with preparations to ready Ceylon for attack, and he was soon appointed Commander-in-Chief Ceylon, tasked with turning the island into a fortress in short order. This was an innovative new position born of the bitter experience of unpreparedness and civil-military discord that prevailed in Malaya and Singapore and so hampered their defence. In Ceylon's case, Layton, an aggressive military figure, was put in charge of everything, with authority over the governor and the State Council, and told by Churchill to do what ever he thought necessary with London's full authority behind him.

Singapore's surrender and the relocation of Eastern Fleet headquarters to Colombo thrust the island and its ports into the strategic limelight, now the only major British naval base between the Cape of Good Hope and Australia. *Cornwall* had just returned to Colombo from Rangoon on 24 February 1942, flying a yellow flag because there was smallpox on board. Coming alongside, her crew were barracked by Australian soldiers lining the decks of the troopships, breaking their journey from the Middle East back home to defend Australia. 'Where were you at Singapore? Why are you in port?', they asked, with good-natured humour. As *Cornwall* left the harbour there was an engine failure, and so she had to moor again. 'What's up, scared?', enquired the Australians. *Cornwall* then had the pleasant duty of escorting the Australians back to their homeland. This was a particularly dangerous time to be sailing in the waters of the eastern Indian Ocean, and great risks were run. The dispatch of this convoy, carrying the 7th Australian Division, coincided with the Japanese rampage south of Java, and was escorted by *Royal Sovereign*, *Cornwall*, and five escorts.[56]

On 26 February an invasion force under Admiral Sokichi arrived in the Java Sea, comprising nearly 100 troop transports protected by four cruisers and 14 destroyers. To meet this force the Allies gathered their remaining ships, which met the Japanese under the Dutch Rear Admiral Karel Doorman. With no capital ships left in the Java Sea the defence of the Malay Barrier and the Dutch East Indies, and the maintenance of the Allied lines of communication, rested upon a hastily-assembled fleet of ill-assorted British, Australian, American, and Dutch cruisers and destroyers of mixed vintage. At the ensuing Battle of the Java Sea (26-28 February), this uncoordinated collection of ships – barely stronger than a cruiser squadron supported by a couple of

55 'Admiralty War Diaries of World War II', The diary of Admiral Layton.

56 Willmott, *The Barrier and the Javelin: Japanese and Allied Pacific Strategies, February to June 1942* (Maryland, MD: Naval Institute Press, 1983), p. 162.

flotillas of destroyer – faced a superior Japanese force, more cohesive, confident, and better led.[57] The Allied warships put up a spirited fight against the odds, losing all but four vessels, which managed to escape to Australia or Ceylon, along with some aircraft, with Doorman killed when *Haguro* sank the *De Ruyter*.[58] ABDA Command was severely handicapped by the Allies' weakness at sea following the destruction of their major naval assets, as well as by inadequate air power.[59] It was further hampered by the fact that Wavell's composite multinational forces were fighting a desperate campaign that none of them were prepared for, such had been the belief that Japan would not go to war, the faith in the combined deterrent effect of Anglo-American naval power, and the underestimation of Japanese fighting power and intent.

Lieutenant General Pownall, waiting to be evacuated from Lembang with Japanese invasion imminent, summarized the situation:

> There's no doubt that we've underestimated the Jap. He is far more efficient, a far better fighter than we ever thought. We thought (I among them) that when they got up against something other than the Chinese they would begin to quail … But suppose we'd made a better shot and had got the Jap at his true worth, would it have made any real difference? I very much doubt it. Our policy was to avoid a war with Japan as long as we could (or to make America cause it, if it was to happen) and we gambled on that policy succeeding (or if it didn't succeed America bearing the brunt). With all our other commitments I don't believe that, however highly we rated the Japs as fighters, we would have been caused thereby to improve the condition of our Services in the Far East. We just hoped it wouldn't happen. And it did. The surprise attack by the Japs on Honolulu has had the short term result of neutralizing US offensive power. On the long term it has made America an implacable

57 Thomas, *The Battle of the Java Sea*, p. 18.

58 The historian Peter Boer cautions that too often the loss of the Dutch East Indies is ascribed to the defeat of the Allied Combined Striking Force (the Allies joint naval formation) in the Battle of the Java Sea. But the campaign also involved four major land and air battles over the possession of Java which was lost in only eight days following the Japanese landings on the night of 28 February – 1 March 1942. There was then an Allied counter-air campaign (18 to 27 February), the objective of which was to win time for the reinforcement of Java by destroying stocks of fuel captured by Japanese forces at Palambang and destroying as many Japanese aircraft as possible by bombing conquered air bases. The campaign won the Allies only two days. Then the Battle of the Java Sea took place (27 February), followed by the Battle for Kalidjati (28 February-3 March), contesting control of the strategically vital Allied air base there. Finally there was the Battle for the Tjiater Pass in the mountains north of Bandoeng (5 to 7 March). The loss of this battle 'gave the Japanese access to the city of Bandoeng where all the major military and civilian headquarters were and which housed thousands of refugees from other parts of the Indies and Singapore. It made capitulation unavoidable and all Allied troops surrendered on 8 March 1942'. See also Boer, *The Loss of Java: The Final Battles for the Possession of Java Fought by Allied Air, Naval and Land Forces in the Period of 18 February to 7 March 1942* (Singapore: National University of Singapore Press, 2011) and Jack Ford, 'The Forlorn Ally: The Netherlands East Indies in 1942', *War and Society*, 11, 1 (1993).

59 See Donald Kehn, *In the Highest Degree Tragic: The Sacrifice of the US Asiatic Fleet in the East Indies during World War II* (Lincoln, NE: Potomac Books, 2017), chapter 4, 'Birth of a Nasty, Brutish, and Short Life: ABDA is Formed'. Also see chapters 9, 'Arcadia, ABDA, Anzac, and the Dutch', 10, 'The Breaking of the Dutch, 11 January-21 February 1942', and 11, 'The End in the Indies', in Willmott, *Empires in the Balance.*

> enemy who will now never forget or forgive. In the end Japan will be made to pay for it dearly.[60]

Pownall's assessment was to prove correct, but that was of no help to him or his boss at that moment because the Japanese had taken the Malayan peninsula and were swarming across the Dutch East Indies.

ABDA Command was dissolved on 25 February and Wavell left for Ceylon, believing that Java was doomed. This left the Governor-General of the Dutch East Indies to fight on. The British had been more concerned with their ability to reinforce Malaya, not defend the East Indies. Once Singapore had fallen, their attention migrated to Burma, Ceylon, and India, and the defence of the all-important Indian Ocean sea lanes. This was inevitable; the East Indies were Dutch, not British, and the East Indies and even South-east Asia were, ultimately, discretionary – whereas Ceylon and the Indian Ocean's sea lanes were not. The defeat in the Java Sea continued the tale of woe begun with the attacks on Pearl Harbor and *Prince of Wales* and *Repulse*. It resulted 'in the destruction and dispersal of the entire Allied fleet assembled to oppose the Imperial Japanese Navy' – though not, it is seldom noted, British naval resources performing essential tasks elsewhere in the Indian Ocean.[61] The Allies had sacrificed a fleet in the Java Sea in the hope of buying time because they did not know what else to do and because they could not countenance simply 'running away'. Nagumo's fleet took part in mopping up operations around Java, which included a raid on Tjilatjap on 3 March, in which 180 aircraft accounted for 20 more Allied vessels. On 7 March Java finally fell to the Japanese, the same day that Burma Army evacuated Rangoon, and within two days the whole of the Dutch East Indies had been taken. On the same day, Operation X saw the battleships *Haruna* and *Kongo* bombard Christmas Island in order to destroy its commercial installations. Attracted by the phosphate deposits and the possibility of creating an airbase, the island was marked for possible occupation.[62]

Defending Ceylon and the sea lanes and attempting to attack the Japanese should they appear were not the only burdens placed upon the Eastern Fleet at this critical juncture. As Commodore Edwards recorded: 'Wavell signalled to suggest we should try and engage enemy forces attacking the Arakan. As we have no air support whatsoever, this is obviously out of the question'. Wavell also 'wants help to defend Rangoon, where he's sending all available forces'.[63] Vice Admiral Arbuthnot sent Commodore Cosmo Graham, former Senior Naval Officer Persian Gulf, to Burma as Commodore Burma Coast. But there was little that could be done, and it was a 'story of retreat before an enemy superior in numbers and weapons and vastly superior in air power', Arbuthnot wrote. 'The almost total lack of support that the Navy had been able to render throughout the Burma campaign has been a matter of deep concern to me'.[64]

The Eastern Fleet did what it could to support the beleaguered Burma Army, but all it could really do was help in the retreat and evacuation. *Dorsetshire*, for example, was sent twice to

60 Bond (ed.), *Chief of Staff*, p. 92.
61 Thomas, *The Battle of the Java Sea*, p. 15.
62 Paul Dull, *A Battle History of the Imperial Japanese Navy, 1941-1945* (Cambridge: Patrick Stevens, 1978), The island was bombarded again at the end of March, and a task force and captured the British garrison. The Japanese left on 3 April, the island deemed unsuitable as an airbase.
63 CAC, Edwards Papers, REDW 2/8,
64 'Admiralty War Diaries of World War II', War despatch, Vice Admiral Arbuthnot.

Burma, on the first occasion transporting a hundred Royal Marines to man river launches and harass the Japanese and help with the evacuation of troops and civilians, on the second occasion escorting the last convoy to leave Rangoon.[65] The beleaguered port fell on 8 March 1942, 'the Japs entering the shell of a burning town' that the British had just evacuated. Meanwhile, the work of convoy escort carried on apace. Layton communicated the manifold difficulties facing Ceylon and the Eastern Fleet to the Admiralty, not least the fact that convoys packed with tens of thousands of troops were being escorted by weak naval forces, risking a major maritime disaster. The Admiralty's reply was full of sympathy, but the simple fact was that it had to manage global demands on its resources, and even though the Eastern Fleet was being reinforced, it took time for ships to arrive on station.

With Malaya and the Dutch East Indies gone and Burma on its way, the enemy now controlled the Bay of Bengal and all the territories on its eastern seaboard. The Imperial Japanese Navy could now do as it pleased in South-east Asia and the East Indies, and the Indian Ocean lay at its mercy. 'To Japan the glittering prizes of war must have seemed tantalizingly close at hand and ridiculously simple to attain'.[66] But British plans to reinforce the Indian Ocean were in hand, and the Japanese had – though it was not known at the time – only a short window of opportunity. The defences of Ceylon were building, too; the Dutch commander-in-chief, Vice Admiral Helfrich, arrived in Colombo on 3 March and established his headquarters, bringing remaining Dutch warships and placing them under British command; Layton officially became Commander-in-Chief Ceylon on 6 March with the acting rank of admiral; the following day *Indomitable*, diverted from Java, flew off another batch of Hurricanes for Ceylon's aerodromes; and on that day, Wavell told Layton that by 20 March, the 16th Infantry Brigade (part of the British 70th Division), the 21st East African Infantry Brigade, and the 16th and 17th infantry brigades of the 5th Australian Imperial Force Division would have arrived in Ceylon to join the 34th Indian Division.[67] On 10 March, with the ABDA job having disappeared, Lieutenant General Pownall became General Officer Commanding Troops Ceylon.[68]

Britain's new strategy east of Suez

The British Empire's eastern ramparts had been breached, and this set the context for the next phase of Britain's war against Japan. In the opening phase, the British had been 'forced to respond to events beyond their control and to fight where they were rather than where they would'.[69] For most of the month preceding the Allied capitulation in the Dutch East Indies, the War Cabinet had known that the game was up, the writing well and truly on the wall once

65 Agar, *Footprints in the Sea*, p. 172.
66 Thomas, *The Battle of the Java Sea*, p. 17.
67 Admiral Helfrich left for Ceylon on 1 March, where he and remaining Dutch naval assets were placed under British command. On 9 March Admiral Furstner, acting Minister of War for the Dutch government in exile in London, visited Major General Kennedy at the War Office. He asked that 'Dutch troops evacuated from the East Indies should be concentrated in Ceylon, and used to reinforce our garrison there until they could be sent back to the Dutch Colonies to take part in guerrilla warfare. I arranged to have this done'. Kennedy, *The Business of War*, p. 210
68 'Admiralty War Diaries of World War II', The diary of Admiral Layton.
69 Willmott, *Grave of a Dozen Schemes*, p. 6.

Singapore fell. Shortly before ABDA's pale flame guttered out the Chiefs of Staff outlined a new strategy for the British Empire east of Suez, in many ways a reversion to pre-war plans to build up a major naval force in the Indian Ocean. In this new strategic environment, the island of Ceylon and other Indian Ocean bases, along with the Eastern Fleet, were to be of paramount importance.

On 21 February 1942 the War Cabinet considered a report from the Chiefs of Staff entitled 'Far East appreciation'. First of all, it acknowledged that the Dutch East Indies could not be held. While they would not be abandoned, they would not be reinforced: 'If we attempted to reinforce Java our forces would be destroyed piecemeal leaving us without resources to provide for the minimum security of our essential main bases. Thus, our sound policy strategically is to withhold major reinforcements from Java and to concentrate on holding Burma, Ceylon, India, Australia and New Zealand'.[70] Regarding 'Japanese intentions', the Chiefs offered a bleak assessment:

> Japan is pressing her offensive with the greatest vigour in order to take full advantage of her present superiority. Her immediate objectives appear to be to complete her conquest of the Philippines, Sumatra, and Java, and to exploit her invasion of Burma, which would threaten China's ability to continue fighting. She may also assault Port Darwin and Ceylon.
>
> Japan must realise that the defeat of Germany would very seriously prejudice her chances of ultimate victory. Her strategy therefore is likely to be biased towards helping Germany insofar as that is compatible with her own requirements.
>
> Once Japan has effectively breached the Malayan Barrier, she has a clear run into the Indian Ocean where we are dangerously weak in all respects. By an attack on Ceylon and India, Japan could raise overwhelming internal security problems in India and induce instability in Indian forces in all theatres of war. By the occupation of Ceylon, Japan would prevent us from reinforcing Burma and achieve a position suitable for building up a serious threat to our Indian Ocean communications. This would go far towards meeting both Japanese requirements, would help the offensive against Burma and provide relief to Germany by threatening India and the Middle East.[71]

In the light of this assessment, the Chiefs concluded that:

> Our immediate objective is to stabilise the situation so as to ensure the security of bases and points vital to our prosecution of the war in the Middle East and Far East and to our eventual return to the offensive against Japan.
>
> The basis of our general strategy lies in the safety of our sea communications for which secure naval and air bases are essential. We must therefore make certain of our main bases i.e. Burma, India, Ceylon, Australia, and New Zealand.[72]

70 TNA, CAB 66/22/24, War Cabinet, 'Far East Appreciation', Report by the Chiefs of Staff (Brooke, Portal, and Pound), 21/2/42.
71 Ibid.
72 Ibid.

Addressing the naval situation, the Chiefs wrote: 'For the defence of Indian Ocean sea communications, we are building up our Eastern fleet. At present there is no secure base in the Indian Ocean. Thus we must: (a) Secure Ceylon. (b) Develop Addu Atoll. (c) Develop additional bases for reconnaissance and striking forces'.[73] The loss of Ceylon 'would imperil the whole British war effort in the Middle and Far East, owing to its position in relation to our sea communications'.[74]

Sea lanes were the be all and end all in the region because of the need to keep the Empire together and connect imperial and Allied theatres of war with their sources of supply, and the British also needed to be able to continue to find the ships to sail on them. Writing of the shipping situation, the Chiefs stated that it was 'very grave', and that

> unless ways and means of increasing our shipping resources and of using these resources to the greater advantage of our war effort can be discovered, we shall be unable to move the forces overseas demanded by our strategic requirements …
>
> To move overseas from England the land and air forces necessary to replace the formations in the Middle East and give additional strength in the Far East, we must exploit our shipping resources to the utmost and if necessary incur a temporary reduction in our import programme.[75]

In the light of their findings, the Chiefs recommended a line of policy that was to define British strategy in the Indian Ocean theatre. That policy was 'to provide for the safety of our sea communications by building up our Eastern fleet and by securing the bases necessary to use it:'

> a) to withhold major reinforcements from Java but defend the island with the available forces with the utmost resolution:
> b) to provide reinforcements as quickly as possible to secure essential points vital to the continuance of the struggle against Japan, namely Burma, Ceylon, Australia and India:
> c) to accept risks in the Middle East to stabilise the Far East:
> d) to exploit our shipping resources to the utmost in the interests of our strategy.

The British government understood that maritime power would have to be reconstructed in the Indian Ocean, with Ceylon as the main base of a fleet kept 'in being' and building for future offensive operations and, one day, a forceful return to Far Eastern waters. Meanwhile, in the here and now, there were vital convoys crossing the sea lanes of the Indian Ocean that needed protection if the Empire was to survive.

73 Ibid.
74 Ibid.
75 Ibid.

After ABDA : The rise of Ceylon and Admiral Layton's intent

Commanders on the ground waited as the government formulated its approach. Whitehall and Washington, wrote Agar, were 'working out the new strategical moves to put things right, and at least give us a fairly level balance at sea in the Indian Ocean, from which we could keep our convoys going to India and Ceylon'.[76] The British government would build the naval forces in the Indian Ocean, augment the defensive capabilities of India and Ceylon, and complete the secret fleet base in the Maldives which was to be the emergency fall-back position should Ceylon fail too. The modernized battleship *Warspite* had been nominated for service with the Eastern Fleet in December and was on her way following a refit in America, and together with the four 'R' class battleships and two fleet carriers had became the nucleus of the fleet.

For many imperial and Allied service personnel and civilians, Ceylon was a last chance saloon, a rallying point for those whom the tide of Japanese expansion threatened to maroon in conquered territories, condemning them to death or incarceration (which, for so many, amounted to the same thing).[77] Many made it to Ceylon before the fall of Singapore. The naval base, for example, upon which the security of Britain's eastern empire had for so long rested, was quietly abandoned in the last days of January, 'Rear Admiral Ernest "Jackie" Spooner, the Naval Commander-in-Chief, ordering the entire European naval and civilian dockyard staff to quit the base and fall back on Singapore City, from where they were shipped off to Ceylon'.[78] Throughout February and March, civilians and service personnel, including Wavell and his ABDA Chief of Staff, Pownall, arrived piecemeal in Colombo having escaped from Java, Malaya, Singapore, and Sumatra.

Agar was one of those involved in ferrying refugees to Ceylon. His ship, *Dorsetshire*, had been sent to Singapore shortly before it fell, tasked with evacuating as much of the garrison possible, and had also escorted the last convoy from Rangoon. The 'last refugee convoy to leave, led by *Manchester City*, consisted of all types of craft' and was escorted safely to Ceylon, 'which was rapidly becoming a refugee centre'.[79] 'Colombo was so overcrowded that we now worked from Trincomalee', he wrote. Layton had already told the Admiralty about the 'appalling congestion' in Colombo harbour, and was loathe to further occupy it with warships.[80] The harbour was packed with storeships, fleet auxiliaries, ammunition ships, and oilers, all ex-Singapore:

> Colombo might well have been called 'Refugee Harbour', which indeed it was. The conglomeration of ships of all shapes and sizes was beyond belief, from large liners used as

76 Agar, *Footprints in the Sea*, pp. 171-2.
77 This theme receives a full chapter treatment in Jackson, *Ceylon at War*.
78 Peter Thompson, *The Battle for Singapore: The True Story of the Greatest Catastrophe of World War Two* (London: Portrait, 2006), p. 9.
79 Agar, *Footprints in the Sea*, p. 171.
80 BL, Layton Papers, 74800, Appreciation of Situation in the Indian Ocean, Commander-in-Chief Eastern Fleet, February 1942. This was sent in reply to the 1st Sea Lord's request for an appreciation of the situation sent on 16 February. On the same day Major General Kennedy gave his boss, General Alan Brooke, a note for the Chiefs of Staff entitled 'New Situation in the Far East'. Kennedy, *The Business of War*, p. 200.

troops transports to small Dutch coasting vessels which had escaped from the Java Seas. The target thus presented can well be imagined, while anti-aircraft defences were negligible.[81]

Given the new strategic situation, Layton as interim Commander-in-Chief Eastern Fleet had a range of immediate concerns. Oil supply accounted for much of the Indian Ocean's importance, a factor of which he was well aware. By the end of February 1942 Britain had sent 49 tankers, more than 12 per cent of its total tonnage working on the oil supply programmes in the west, when Japan entered the war in December 1941.[82] There was a call for more tankers in the Indian Ocean as imperial defeats mounted and as large oil supplies and stocks were lost with the surrender of Singapore, Borneo, Burma, and the Dutch East Indies. As Layton told Pound, the enemy could attack reinforcements being taken to the Dutch East Indies as well as oil supplies emerging from the Persian Gulf in order to cross the Indian Ocean to various destinations, demonstrating the geographically-dispersed responsibilities faced by the men charged with organizing the defence of the Indian Ocean region. 'With Netherlands East Indies oil supplies denied to us the importance of the Persian Gulf line cannot be exaggerated', he wrote.[83] Burmese oil, carried in small tankers across the Bay of Bengal, had supplied much of India's needs, but now supplies had to come from Iran in ocean tankers sailing from Abadan to Karachi and Bombay. Trade in the Indian Ocean began to assume a new wartime pattern, and commodities as well as troopships and ships carrying military goods needed the protection of convoys and British naval and air forces.

One of the biggest problems Layton faced as he sought to meet these threats was his 'very weak' anti-submarine capability. For the whole of the Indian Ocean and the protection of its vital sea lanes he had for anti-submarine work, at this critical juncture, only six sloops, five corvettes, two Australian minesweepers, three trawlers, six Royal Indian Navy auxiliaries, and a yacht. His intention, given the breadth of his responsibilities and the limits of his anti-submarine forces, was to concentrate anti-submarine work in the Bay of Bengal. Layton was also preparing to face attacks from enemy surface ships, particularly as recent Japanese victories had yielded them first class naval bases on the Indian Ocean rim, chief among them Penang and Singapore. Given the situation, the admiral intended to use all his other resources to escort convoys. In doing this, however, some of his major units, including the battleships, were hampered by inadequate anti-submarine vessels as well as the lack of endurance of the 'R' class battleships. Therefore, he planned to focus these units in the 'Western Area' of the Indian Ocean – west of Addu Atoll – where the most important sea lanes of all were located (those going into the Red Sea and the Persian Gulf). He would operate in the Eastern Area with his cruisers, less the old County class vessels. It was a plan, but Layton couldn't help but think how desperate it all was. As he wrote in his 'Appreciation' for the First Sea Lord: 'The risks, of course, are appalling when it is appreciated that convoys containing 20,000 men and their equipment will be passing through waters directly threatened by considerable enemy forces working in conjunction with

81 Agar, *Footprints in the Sea*, p. 174.
82 D. J. Payton-Smith, *Oil: A Study of Wartime Policy and Administration* (London: HMSO, 1971).
83 BL, Layton Papers, 74800, Most secret: The situation February to April 1942: Appreciation of the situation in the Indian Ocean.

carrier air reconnaissance. It appears to me that by comparison a convoy on the Atlantic routes is in blissful security'.[84]

Pound's reply, befitting an exchange between senior officers, was conversational, the head of the Royal Navy making suggestions rather than meting out orders. He wrote of the heavy global burden afflicting the British government in allocating resources, but thoroughly understood Layton's predicament. 'As we see it the most dangerous thing the enemy can do is to take Ceylon from us, as this would undermine our whole naval position in the East'. The best that Pound could do to help Layton at present was to send six cruisers, a destroyer, some corvettes, four Catalina flying-boats, and some submarines. The First Sea Lord continued, speaking on behalf of the Admiralty and the Chiefs of Staff:

> We rate the chance of the Japanese 'Pearl Harbouring' [sic] very high. As the security of Ceylon is of vital importance we suggest your two best RDF [radio direction finding] fitted R Class battleships *Royal Sovereign*, temporarily *Ramillies* and finally *Resolution* should leave the convoy routes and be stationed in Ceylon whence they could operate to repel any landing under fighter umbrella as soon as you have sufficient fighters.[85]

Layton dissented, believing that to position the battleships thus would be to present the Japanese with tempting, vulnerable targets. Pound's reply demonstrated the room granted the man on the spot to make the final judgement – as well as the extraordinarily high price that the British government was prepared to play in order to hold Ceylon. Pound said that the decision was Layton's, but that the loss of the battleships was considered acceptable if it would appreciably interfere with a Japanese invasion 'in view of the vital repercussions should the enemy obtain possession of Ceylon'. This meant that the War Cabinet was prepared to write off a sizeable proportion of Britain's remaining battleship strength in order to protect Ceylon, an extraordinary fact. In making up his mind on this matter, Layton had had a meeting with his deputy, Vice Admiral Willis. He was also of the opinion that before the Japanese attempted to take Ceylon they would want to reduce the Eastern Fleet by attrition, and that keeping 'R' class battleships in Ceylon's harbours would provide a good opportunity for them to accomplish this aim. 'The whole future of our cause must depend on the battlefleet and to risk it without air support in that area would be to court a disaster similar to 10 December 1941'.[86] When he had some submarines he intended to establish patrols north of the Malacca Strait for early warning and offensive purposes. He would need the whole fleet together if it was to give a good account of itself against an expedition escorted by heavy Japanese units.

The threat to Ceylon and India moved a step closer when the Japanese invaded the Andaman and Nicobar Islands in the Bay of Bengal and proceeded to station thousands of troops there. Until 1938 the islands had been used as a penal colony for political prisoners. They normally contained a garrison of 300 Sikh militiamen with 20-plus British officers, but in January 1942 a Gurkha detachment of 4/12 Frontier Force Regiment of the 16th Indian Infantry Brigade had arrived to augment the defences. Following the fall of Rangoon on 8 March, however, the British recognized that Port Blair was impossible to defend, and two days later the Gurkhas

84 Ibid.
85 Ibid.
86 BL, Layton Papers, 74800, Appreciation of Situation in the Indian Ocean.

were withdrawn to the Arakan. The Government of India knew that the islands could not be defended, so had decided to abandon them, a move opposed by Layton and the Admiralty, for it would afford the Japanese an excellent forward base in the Bay of Bengal. The garrison and families of European and Indian officers and employees had been evacuated to Calcutta aboard *Maharaja* and *Alagna* in January. More were taken off by *Norilla*, which sailed fully loaded from Chatham Jetty on 13 March. She intended to return for one last trip, but as she was about to leave Calcutta to collect the last evacuees from Port Blair, news of Japanese landings was received. Before the British withdrew, leaving the islanders to their fate, a party was flown to Nancowry in the Nicobar Islands charged with the demolition of installations and supplies, as well as the evacuation of civilian and military personnel. Fuel stocks were torched, bombs dumped into the sea, and huts smashed and burned.

The Japanese swiftly occupied both sets of islands, attracted by their strategic position in the Bay of Bengal, close to important shipping routes and the coasts of India and Burma. On the day of the invasion, 23 March, Malaya Force ushered nine troopships towards the islands. Commanded by Vice Admiral Jisaburo Ozawa, Malaya Force – properly, the Second Expeditionary Fleet – consisted of the light aircraft carrier *Ryujo*, six cruisers, seven destroyers, six minesweepers, and a minelayer. When the Japanese landed, the Sikh troops did not resist and were interned, many later joining the Indian National Army, while the British militia officers were sent to Singapore. A Japanese fighter squadron in southern Burma was allocated to protect the islands (where a new airfield was constructed), 18 flying-boats were sent to take advantage of the location as a reconnaissance base, and a garrison of over 5,000 troops was installed. 'This island group was of immense importance to the Japanese because its occupation allowed them to secure a shield to Malaya, Singapore, and western and northern Sumatra. By taking the islands the Japanese denied the British what might have proved an idea base from which to mount operations against their western conquests'.[87]

Even at this nadir in their fortunes, the Allies retained a limited capacity to strike back when the opportunity arose. Soon after the Japanese occupied the Andaman and Nicobar Islands, a Hudson reconnaissance aircraft from Akyab spotted nine Japanese flying-boats moored in Port Blair harbour. RAF strikes followed, and all of the aircraft were destroyed at their moorings, a significant blow for Japan's aerial reconnaissance capabilities in the Bay of Bengal. On the night of 2 April 1942 an attack by American Flying Fortresses on Port Blair was reported to have left a cruiser on fire and a troopship and two other vessels damaged. Nevertheless, such opportunities to strike back at this stage of the war were extremely rare. Retreat was the order of the day, and the enemy was to remain in these particular islands – and all of the other conquered territories of Britain's eastern empire – for the remainder of the war.

The situation facing the British Empire in March-April 1942 demonstrated just how the war's major theatres – either fighting fronts or logistical hubs – were interlinked. As Major General Kennedy observed, the situation in Europe and the possibility of the Japanese getting into Indian Ocean and shooting up British convoys around the Cape made it all the more important to grip all of North Africa's shore so that the Middle East could be supplied directly through the Mediterranean.[88] Furthermore, their were the strategic problems associated with the German

87 Willmott, *Empires in the Balance*, p. 441.
88 Kennedy, *The Business of War*, p. 184.

advances in the Soviet Union. If 'the Russians are defeated', Kennedy continued, 'there is a poor prospect of holding the Middle East. We may then be reduced to defending the key points only. These are a) the oil supplies in the Persian Gulf, and b) Ceylon and such part of India as is necessary to security of Ceylon', vital because of its role in defending the Indian Ocean's sea lanes.[89]

89 Ibid., p. 220.

8

The reinforcement of the Indian Ocean

Into the turbid waters of defeat and uncertainty stepped Admiral Sir James Somerville, dispatched to the Indian Ocean as Commander-in-Chief Eastern fleet to preserve Britain's fragile position and keep the sea lanes open and fight the Japanese. The war against Japan, and indeed the war in all its global dimensions, had entered a critical phase. Chapters eight and nine chronicle the sequence of events in the Indian Ocean during the crucial months of March and April 1942. They explain the role of Somerville's fleet in this new and unexpected strategic landscape, the challenges he encountered as he strove to grip the situation and enact the new strategy approved by the War Cabinet, and the drama of the Japanese raids into the waters off Ceylon and India.

No stranger to eastern waters, James Fownes Somerville had served as Commander-in-Chief East Indies from July 1938 until early 1939.[1] At that point he had been invalided home with tuberculosis, knighted, and placed on the retired list. But the outbreak of war dramatically extended his active service career, as it did for many senior officers in all the belligerent nations. Such an experienced man simply could not be left on the shelf. First he commanded Force H in the Mediterranean, playing a key role in the destruction of the *Bismarck*, directing the harrowing attack on the French fleet at Oran, and fighting convoys to Malta. His achievements impressed Churchill, who wrote that he 'acquitted himself so well in command of the famous Force H at Gibraltar' that he 'was selected to command in succession to the ill-fated Tom Phillips'.[2] For much of his time in eastern waters, where he was to remain until late 1944, Somerville's was to be the most awkward and frustrating of naval tasks – that of keeping a fleet 'in being', exerting its influence by virtue of its existence rather than its offensive actions, and ensuring that the essential but unglamorous work of sea lane protection continued.

1 For Somerville, see The Papers of Admiral of the Fleet Sir James Fownes Somerville, Churchill Archives Centre, Cambridge; Simpson (ed.), *The Somerville Papers*, Part II, 'The Eastern Fleet, January 1942-August 1944', pp. 349-585; Donald Macintyre, *Fighting Admiral: The Life and Battles of Admiral of the Fleet Sir James Somerville, GCB, GBE, DSO* (London: Evans, 1961); and 'Dash and Daring: Admiral Sir James Somerville RN', in David Wragg, *Fighting Admirals of World War Two* (Barnsley: Pen and Sword, 2009).

2 Winston Churchill, *The Second World War*, volume 4, p. 153, in chapter 10, 'Ceylon and the Bay of Bengal'.

At the moment Somerville took over, the Eastern Fleet was being hunted by an Imperial Japanese Navy force of much greater power and efficiency, and submarine sinkings of Allied merchantmen in the Indian Ocean were at an all-time high.[3] His opponent was flush with victory and still going strong. For their part, the Allies desperately needed to regroup and hold the line while striving to anticipate Japan's next move. Whitehall and its regional commanders agreed that the enemy advance had far from peaked, and that India, Ceylon, and the Eastern Fleet were obvious targets. There was growing impetus for a forward Japanese strategy west of Singapore, spurred on by the signing of the Axis Tripartite Pact on 19 January and invigorated by battlefield success. 'The idea of the three nations [Germany, Italy, and Japan] joining hands across the globe was one loudly championed by the tightly controlled Japanese press at this time, and it was one that commanded strong support from the many admirers of Nazi Germany in the imperial armed forces'.[4] The British government made moves to reinforce Ceylon as best it could, sending imperial divisions, squadrons of modern fighters, and reconnaissance aircraft, while local civil and military authorities oversaw frenetic defensive preparations. At sea, Admiral Somerville was expected to try and work miracles with the Eastern Fleet, coordinating his efforts with Wavell's India Command as reinforcements mustered.

Somerville's journey east and arrival in Ceylon

Somerville sailed to Ceylon in one of the many armoured convoys that left British shores during the course of the war. Leaving the Clyde in February, this particular one contained, among other vessels, a number of warships that were to form part of the Eastern Fleet.[5] He travelled aboard the carrier *Formidable*, passing the voyage in the company of Lieutenant Colonel Peter Fleming. Brother of the naval intelligence officer and future novelist Ian, Fleming was on his way to the Deception Section in Delhi, and the pair 'delighted in each other's witty company'.[6] The journey afforded ample time for Somerville to cogitate on the strategic and operational situation in the Indian Ocean, and to correspond with the First Sea Lord as, together, they sought to define the fleet's role and thrash out likely courses of Japanese action. It was clear, wrote Somerville, that he would have to 'stand on the defensive until he had wielded his heterogeneous command into a fleet approaching Force H's legendary efficiency'.[7] As the carrier

3 Willmott, *Grave of a Dozen Schemes*, p. 157. The twin peaks of losses in the Indian Ocean throughout the war occurred in March (65 ships destroyed) and April (31 ships) 1942.

4 Willmott, *The Barrier and the Javelin*, pp. 41-42.

5 This was convoy WS16. In its original form, destined first for Freetown, it comprises 21 merchant vessels escorted by a battleship, two carriers, a cruiser, and eight destroyers. See Arnold Hague, 'Route to the East – the WS (Winston Special) Convoys', at http://www.naval-history.net/xAH-WSConvoys05-1942A.htm

6 Fleming had been appointed as head of the deception staff of India Command by Wavell as he attempted to replicate the arrangements he had established while Commander-in-Chief Middle East. The staff later expanded into 'D' Division of Mountbatten's South East Asia Command. See Michael Howard, *Strategic Deception in the Second World War: British Intelligence Operations Against the German High Command* (London: Norton, 1995), p. xii and p. 25. Originally published in 1990 as volume 5 of the the official HMSO series *British Intelligence in the Second World War.*

7 Simpson (ed.), *The Somerville Papers*, p. 353.

progressed eastwards, Somerville 'continued to ponder in secret the enormity of the task facing him, while maintaining his customary light-hearted and resolute air in public'.[8] He worried about the attitude of those around him. Five days out, and exasperated by his pilots and ships' shortcomings during exercises, he wrote to his wife: 'I'm beginning to be seriously disturbed by the lack of skill and lack of pep in this party here. They are all quite complacent and think they are the cat's whiskers and in my opinion they are quite bum'.[9]

Training and combined exercises were to be a leitmotif of Somerville's time in command east of Suez. During the voyage he practiced what he preached, beginning a comprehensive training programme, exercising the Eastern Fleet ships sailing with him as they journeyed from Biscay to the Cape. He was deeply concerned about the lack of experience and the skill level of his crews, especially that of the pilots, several of whom were lost during exercises, and had insisted on officers with recent experience for higher positions. The journey was broken at Cape Town, where Somerville met his second in command, Vice Admiral Willis. He also took the opportunity to confer with Jan Smuts, whom Somerville described as 'a great little man' who 'feels strongly we must not throw away EF [Eastern Fleet]'.[10] The two men agreed that the biggest disaster that could befall the Empire would be for the Japanese to capture Ceylon and destroy the fleet.

The previous December, Somerville had viewed the dispatch of Force Z with foreboding, believing that it was a political rather than a specifically military move. Compounding his concern, he was aghast when he learned that none of its senior officers had seagoing experience in the present war – particularly, experience of the kind of air attacks on ships that had accounted for *Prince of Wales* and *Repulse*, and that were soon to be faced in the Indian Ocean. As Somerville wrote to Cunningham, Commander-in-Chief Mediterranean: 'Why the hell didn't they send *someone* out there who has been through the mill and knows his stuff?'.[11] In terms of his conception of the Eastern Fleet's role, in the light of the disasters that had befallen British and Allied seapower, Somerville was convinced that its focus should be on Indian Ocean sea lane security. In this he concurred with Layton, as well as the Chiefs of Staff: 'Both imperial geography and enemy pressures decreed that it should be an Indian Ocean fleet. That vast sea was a crucial strategic area for the British Empire, especially as convoys could not then pass through the Mediterranean; in early 1942, all men and material for the defence of Egypt had to be sent through the Indian Ocean'.[12]

Discretion was wisely considered the better part of valour as a gung-ho approach would court disaster for his inexperienced and composite fleet. As Somerville wrote to his wife during the voyage: 'On thinking matters over it seems to me that the idea of trying to wrest back from the Japs what we've lost by means of a large sea-borne expedition is wrong. It's like trying to stamp

8 Macintyre, *Fighting Admiral*, p. 180.

9 Simpson (ed.), *The Somerville Papers*, letter to wife, 23/2/42, p. 386. In particular, Somerville felt that his ships were not very good at fleet work. This was not surprising, because many of them, including the 'R' class battleships, had spent most of the war to date operating alone or as part of small, transient, force packages as they escorted convoys or hunted raiders, rather than experiencing large, coordinated, fleet actions.

10 Ibid., pocket diary, 10/3/42, p. 392.

11 Roskill, *Churchill and the Admirals*, p. 200. See also Somerville to Pound 12/2/42, Simpson (ed.), *The Somerville Papers*, p. 383.

12 Ibid., p. 354.

rather feebly on a man's feet instead of kicking him in the fork'.[13] The stakes were high; as the Admiralty informed Somerville, though future Japanese intentions remained obscure, 'Attacks on Ceylon relative to Pearl Harbor type or full scale invasion considered possible'.[14] They added that the 'worse thing the Japanese could do would be to take Ceylon from us, as this would undermine our whole naval position in the East ... We rate the chance of the Japanese "Pearl Harbouring" very high and hope you will take all possible precautions'.[15]

At the same time, in a telegram to Wavell copied to Somerville, the Chiefs of Staff outlined the purpose envisaged for the reconstituted, post-Tom Phillips, Eastern Fleet:

> [The f]unction of this Fleet will be to maintain control of the sea communications of the Indian Ocean. Both the Middle East and India depend on these. Such control would at the best be precarious if Japan obtained and we were denied bases in Ceylon ...
>
> Nevertheless so long as our fleet remains in being, Japanese would have to provide permanent cover to the lines of communication of any direct sea borne attack on the coast of India or Ceylon with her fleet. They are unlikely to accept such a commitment particularly if pressure is applied by the US Pacific Fleet as it recovers from Pearl Harbor.
>
> Therefore policy of our Fleet will be to act as a Fleet in being, avoiding unnecessary risks, crippling losses, and attrition. While it does so we agree that the most likely courses of action for the Japanese are coast-wise movement via Burma and raids of the Pearl Harbor type on Ceylon. It is to prevent risks of loss to the Fleet by the latter that strong Fighter Forces in Ceylon are necessary even at the expense of NE India about whose need we fully agree with you.
>
> We fully realise that the defence of Ceylon is essentially an air and naval problem. Land forces now there are intended as a deterrent to attempts at occupation by the Japanese until air forces in Ceylon and naval forces in the Indian Ocean are built up.[16]

A debate developed between Somerville and the Admiralty concerning the defence of Ceylon. The Admiralty suggested that Somerville should keep two 'R' class battleships in Colombo, where their powerful armaments might deter the Japanese, the same suggestion that had been made to Layton. Somerville and his senior staff completely disagreed. They believed that keeping the Eastern Fleet in being was the single-most important strategic requirement: Ceylon could be lost, but the fleet could not. Therefore, basing two of the fleet's most powerful units in Ceylon might tempt the Japanese to seek to destroy them, severely weakening the fleet. As Somerville told the Admiralty on 14 March 1942, 'the whole of our cause in the Indian Ocean must depend on the Eastern Fleet being kept in being. The crippling of this fleet would of course make the loss of Ceylon almost a certainty, but far more important it would open our vital supply lines both oil and to the Middle East to any enemy raiding force'. Somerville's will was allowed to prevail.[17]

13 Ibid., 17/3/42, p. 385.
14 Ibid., p. 388.
15 CAC, Edwards Papers, REDW 2/8.
16 Simpson (ed.), *The Somerville Papers*, 19/3/42, p. 395.
17 Ibid. Captain Agar summarized the situation thus: 'possession of Ceylon with a powerful fleet would bring the Japs to the threshold of India ... Critical position in the Indian Ocean, and the vital

Like Layton, Somerville was a colourful character. *Cornwall*'s Ken Dimbleby, recently-promoted sub-lieutenant, recalled an encounter with the admiral aboard his flagship at Durban. It was a very hot day, and Somerville 'detested tropical heat and humidity'. He 'was sitting behind his desk and looked flushed by the heat. He had discarded the tunic of his white uniform, and all he wore above the waist was a vest and a pair of braces. He got up, greeted me jovially, then waved to a chair and said: "Anchor your arse!"'.[18] Acting Squadron Leader John Barraclough (later, Vice Chief of the Defence Staff and Commandant of the Royal College of Defence Studies) was another young man who had a chance encounter with Somerville and recorded his impressions. Commanding 209 Squadron based in East Africa, he was helping establish an RAF flying-boat anchorage at Saldhana Bay in South Africa, alongside an old whaling station at Langebaan on the edge of the bay. Suffering from a 'poisoned foot', Barraclough was on the beach when he was told that an admiral's pinnace was heading for the jetty. In a limping trot he managed to reach it in time to welcome not one, but two, admirals:

> These proved to be Admiral Jimmy Somerville, Commander-in-Chief Eastern Fleet, and Admiral Danckwerts ... The former was witty, sharp and a 'lot of fun'; the latter more severe and not a little stuffy. They came up to the Panoramic [Hotel] and sat down in the rush chairs. Then, while being plied with drinks ... they proceeded to get down to developing their naval strategy for the Atlantic and Indian Oceans.[19]

Somerville's sharp-wittedness was noted by Mountbatten. Describing a dinner he held later in the war at his headquarters in Kandy, he wrote:

> I must say to have Somerville together with Noël Coward was most amusing. They both have the gift of quick repartee and are used to being the centre of interest. They crossed tongues the whole evening, Somerville's opening thrust being quite unexpected. Noël announced that he had been out to [Air Marshal Sir] Guy Garrod's bungalow to say goodbye when Somerville staggered him with: 'That must have been a relief to Guy anyway'. Noël was not quite certain he had heard correctly until a second and ruder crack came from James, whereupon Noël replied: 'Take care; you are dicing with death! I shall write a song about you'. From then on we never had a dull moment for the rest of the evening.[20]

Nevertheless, according to Roskill, Somerville's staff 'sometimes found his peculiar brand of bawdy humour, and his repartee heavily larded with obscenities, tedious and overdone'.[21] But

necessity of maintaining our convoys to India via Bombay, and the Middle East via Aden. A defeat would uncover these routes and lay open the way, not only for an invasion of India (where there were no defences worth considering), but also cut us off from the Middle East'. (Agar, *Footprints in the Sea*, pp. 176-77).

18 Dimbleby, *Turns of Fate*, p. 147.

19 Barraclough quoted in Banks, *Wings of the Dawning*, pp. 80-1. Acting Vice Admiral Victor Danckwerts became deputy commander-in-chief of the Eastern Fleet in May 1942.

20 Ziegler, *Personal Diary of Admiral the Lord Louis Mountbatten*, p. 110.

21 Roskill, *Churchill and the Admirals*, p. 270.

others liked him more than Roskill, John Winton writing that he had 'a somewhat Rabelaisian sense of humour and the common touch'.[22]

Arriving in Colombo on 24 March aboard one of his carrier's aircraft, Somerville took up his command just as Japan was about to unleash its battleships and carriers in an attempt to 'Pearl Harbor' his fleet. He was faced with the most challenging sea command in Britain's long history east of Suez, and arrived in the nick of time. From the perspective of Commodore Edwards, things began to look up as soon as he arrived. Last encountered at Basra in the previous chapter, Edwards had received orders regarding his new appointment during his stop over at the Iraqi port. With *Prince of Wales* gone, the Admiralty had decided to send him to Colombo for temporary duties with the Commander-in-Chief East Indies, Vice Admiral Arbuthnot. 'What an anti-climax!', Edwards wrote, selfishly but understandably as he digested the news, still numbed by Force Z's destruction. 'Deputy Chief of Staff of the new Eastern Fleet was a job – this though – Lord knows what it means ... It is difficult that Sir Tom has gone and how many others ... I feel desolated and hate life'.[23]

Now, three months later, Edwards was given a job commensurate with that originally intended for him – Chief of Staff to the Commander-in-Chief Eastern Fleet, aboard the fleet flagship *Warspite*, just arrived in Ceylon on 22 March.[24] He met Somerville at Ratnapura aerodrome when the new Commander-in-Chief landed and immediately took him to a meeting of the Ceylon State Council, where Layton was presiding in his role as Commander-in-Chief Ceylon.[25] Somerville thoroughly approved of Layton's appointment to this new position. To Pound he wrote: 'From what I saw of the soldiers and the Governor, I'm convinced that they want a good driving hand on them all the time'.[26] The fiery and salty Layton certainly provided

22 Winton, *Sink the* Haguro!, p. 10.

23 CAC, Edwards Papers, REDW 2/7, diary entry, 12/12/41. Flying on from Basra, Edwards had stopped off at Bahrein and a couple of other ports on the way to Karachi, Bombay, and then Hyderabad. 'I'm still worrying about my job', he wrote. 'Why don't they send me to Singapore?'. (ibid., 14/1/41) The view 'all seems bad. We seem incapable of stemming the enemy's advance'.

24 Later he operated from HMS *Tana* at Kilndini in Mombasa and then HMS *Lanka* in Colombo, spending the rest of the war in this theatre. For *Warspite* in the Indian Ocean, where she arrived in mid-March 1942, see Ballantyne, Warspite, chapter entitled 'Player in a New Theatre'.

25 Like Layton and Somerville, Edwards shared the view that the C-in-C East Indies (distinct from Layton as Commander-in-Chief Ceylon, and Somerville as Commander-in-Chief Eastern Fleet), was unfit for purpose. 'Geoffrey Arbuthnot becomes more and more impossible. He can only see the black side of the picture and is full of moans and grievances', Edwards wrote in his diary on 26 March (CAC, Edwards Papers, REDW 2/7). His impression of Arbuthnot clearly had not changed since when he had arrived in Ceylon on 15 December: 'The muddle here is appalling' he wrote, only three days into the job, 'and old Arbuthnot and his people just don't understand'. (ibid.) *Dorsetshire*'s captain Agar disagreed with this assessment, and wrote that Arbuthnot was 'level-headed, calm, and solid, he was just the man we needed at a critical time like this, when events were moving so quickly and our defences and bases crumbling all around us. "Buthie", like Admiral Layton, was under no illusions as to our new perils'. Agar, *Footprints in the Sea*, p. 296. Another who defends him is A. A. Loveridge, a naval paymaster on his staff: 'Arbuthnot was a very great man', and praises his role in the capture of Abadan and Khoramshah during the Anglo-Soviet invasion of Iran (August 1941), in which he took responsibility for the order to attack the Iranian fleet on sight. Liddell Hart Military Archives, King's College London, Correspondence of Sir Arthur Bryant, 1919-1984, Bryant, F7-15/2, Loveridge to Arthur Bryant, November 1957. Thanks to Andrew Stewart for this material.

26 Simpson (ed.), *The Somerville Papers*, to Pound, 11/3/42, p. 394.

that, and this meant that Somerville had one less thing to worry about, though he did what he could to support Layton's efforts, endorsing, for example, Rear Admiral Palliser's plan 'to annex everything in Trincomalee required to build and run a port on a warlike footing'.[27] But what he really needed to do was focus all of his attention on the Japanese fleet, and having Layton taking care of Ceylon was a relief. 'I think it's a good plan', he wrote to his wife, 'as I certainly cannot tackle the defence of Ceylon and the Fleet'.[28]

Within hours of his arrival in Colombo, Somerville and Layton were in urgent discussions about the defence of the island and the Eastern Fleet's prospects. Two days later, wrote Agar, 'Somerville, called a conference of his Captains [at which] he unfolded his plans and made his intentions clear to us'.[29] On the same day, 26 March, *Cornwall* arrived back in Colombo from escort duties that had taken her to Australia. The harbour was crammed with ships, including *Formidable*. 'We had hardly finished making fast the buoys', wrote Dimbleby, when news got around that Somerville was to be Commander-in-Chief. 'The effect of this information was exhilarating. In fact, the atmosphere among naval personnel became quite electric. After all the news of depressing defeats at the hands of the Japanese, it was a tonic to have in command of the fleet a man who had distinguished himself as the daring Flag Officer commanding Force H in the Western Mediterranean'.[30] *Cornwall*'s sister ship, *Dorsetshire*, was also involved in the toings and froings from Ceylon at this time. Agar recalled

> Colombo was so overcrowded that we now worked from Trincomalee ... *Hermes* turned up from Cape Town whilst we were there, as well as two R. Class battleships ... There was also in harbour a number of storeships, fleet auxiliaries, ammunition ships, oilers, all ex-Singapore, and I knew Admiral Somerville would want them. I found myself the Senior Officer afloat.[31]

There was an anti-submarine boom protecting Trincomalee, and Agar countermanded the order forbidding bathing in the harbour for fear of sharks, sailors now encouraged to bathe and play water polo. 'The result was that quite a number of the men became good swimmers (how thankful I was later to have made this rule)'.[32] Swimming and floating, it transpired, were to stand crewmen in good stead. *Dorsetshire*'s bottom was cleaned, new anti-aircraft guns were fitted, a new radar set installed, and a boiler and engine refit undertaken. Everyone was 'on alert', but the fleet was going about its normal business of patrolling, fetching and carrying. On 27 March, Naval Headquarters Colombo received reports of Japanese movements in the vicinity of the Andaman Islands.

27 CAC, REDW 2/7, Diary extracts November 1941-May 1942, 27/3/42. Rear Admiral Arthur Palliser was serving as Fortress Commander Trincomalee, his previous two jobs having disappeared with unseemly speed: he had been Phillips's Chief of Staff Eastern Fleet, and then ABDA Command's deputy naval commander. He went on to represent the Royal Indian Navy in New Delhi before becoming 4th Sea Lord in 1944.
28 Simpson (ed.), *The Somerville Diaries*, to wife, 8/3/42.
29 Agar, *Footprints in the Sea*, p. 175.
30 Dimbleby, *Turns of Fate*, p. 145.
31 Agar, *Footprints in the Sea*, p. 172.
32 Ibid., p. 173. See also chapter 8, 'Exit *Vampire* – Fighting', in Macdonnell, *Valiant Occasions*.

Somerville formally assumed command of the Eastern Fleet at 8am on 28 March: 'and now my troubles begin', he confided to his diary.[33] He was right. This was what Churchill referred to as 'the most dangerous' moment of the war, a well-known assertion that some have poo-pooed. But such criticisms miss the point; in reading memoirs, diaries, and histories of the war, many are the moments when it is claimed that the war hung in the balance, many are the strategic locations or combat operations on which, it is claimed, rested success or failure. Of course, with them all, one cannot say for certain what would have happened if a different course of action had been followed, a different result obtained, and different things occurred thereafter. The point of emphasizing this particular 'moment' is to acknowledge that loss of control of Indian Ocean sea lanes could have had a catastrophic effect on the British Empire's war effort, and, consequently, the Allied war effort. As has been acknowledged by some specialists, but rarely in general histories of the war, while the conflict could not be won in the Indian Ocean, it might possibly have been lost there, and herein lies the significance of the operations that took place in this theatre in the early months of 1942.

The trials of getting used to a new command were dwarfed by Somerville's immediate task – facing the flower of the Imperial Japanese Navy with a scratch collection of ships, some of them suffering from the indignities of age, unused to operating as a fleet, with inadequate air power on land and at sea. This is why Somerville placed such great emphasis on training, sending, for example, the 'R' class battleships to Addu Atoll along with a carrier in order to train in comparative safety. Every opportunity was taken to train; he tested his carriers offensive and defensive capabilities, while simultaneously testing those of Ceylon's defenders, whenever the fleet approached the island by means of large-scale dummy attacks from fleet to shore and shore to fleet. When at sea, carrier aircraft would 'attack' battleships, and the fleet war diaries and reports of proceedings, describing the day-to-day activities of all its ships and shore bases, are replete with descriptions of training activities from the moment Somerville assumed command.

While Japanese intentions were unclear, most senior officers, Somerville wrote, 'expected attacks against Ceylon and our sea lanes'.[34] As has been described, Somerville and Willis rejected Admiralty suggestions that Ceylon should be defended principally by naval forces, echoing Layton's objection to using battleships as static gun emplacements. Somerville

> proposed to keep his fleet 'in being', avoid attrition, defend the sea lanes and train it thoroughly so that when substantial reinforcements of modern ships and aircraft became available he could use it offensively as a fast carrier strike force, a form of naval warfare to which he was already giving some thought and which was well suited to that vast ocean.[35]

Somerville believed that the proper way to defend Ceylon was through shore-based air assets, not warships. But though the British government was putting in motion a massive air reinforcement of the region, at this moment there were precious few aircraft with which to do the job – 60-odd Hurricanes by March, a squadron of Blenheim bombers, some flying-boats, as well as squadrons of outdated Fulmars, Swordfish, and Vildebeestes. There were about 100 FAA aircraft of all types available for the carriers, though modern machines were thin on the ground.

33 Simpson (ed.), *The Somerville Papers*, 28/3/42, p. 396.
34 Ibid., p. 356.
35 Ibid.

As Somerville wrote in his diary, 'air cover [is] quite inadequate to dispute this Command', and in a communication to the Admiralty he lamented the FAA's 'arrested development'.[36] Other nations', he noted acerbically, had devoted themselves to 'providing aircraft fit for sailors to fly in'. He was convinced that the overall quality of the FAA and its aircraft needed 'new doctrine and handling', and that the British needed to 'learn from the Americans'.[37] From the Japanese, too, he might have added.

Of course, few people yet understood the true nature of the situation, even the highest level commanders and politicians. Many sailors and armchair pundits felt an understandable apprehension given Japanese victories to date, but one mixed with a large measure of frustration and bellicosity. This was the case for the thousands of men and women operating the Eastern Fleet's ships and shore bases, most of whom were simply unaware of the factors that prevented the large and powerful Eastern Fleet from dealing a sharp and decisive blow to the enemy. Thomas Russell was at Trincomalee aboard *Ramillies*. Upon hearing of the Battle of the Java Sea, he and his mates had 'wondered why we were not sailing eastwards to teach these little yellow bastards a lesson … [it] looked like we could tackle anything with our battleships, cruisers, and destroyer screens'.[38] But the crew had yet to experience the effects of the maritime airpower that the Japanese could deploy.

The scheduled build up of British naval forces in the Indian Ocean would not reach its peak until around the middle of the year. When he arrived in late March, Somerville had, in terms of major vessels, five battleships, two fleet carriers (*Indomitable* and *Formidable*), the light carrier *Hermes*, seven cruisers, 16 destroyers and seven submarines (two of the cruisers and two of the submarines were Dutch). Four of Somerville's five battleships were of First World War vintage: the 'R' class, slow and lacking armoured decking.[39] Designed for short-range work in Home Waters, these ships consequently required regular stops when operating over the much greater distances of the Indian Ocean. *Warspite* was actually pre-First World War, though had been extensively modernized. Coupled with the inadequacies of British airpower at that moment, it was not a fleet that one would choose to put into the front line. 'I also hear a lot of blah about how everything depends on our maintaining control of the Indian Ocean', wrote Somerville to his wife. 'That's poor bloody me and I wonder how the devil it's to be accomplished. My old battle-boats are in various states of disrepair and there's not a ship at present that approaches what I should call a proper standard of fighting efficiency'.[40] Nevertheless, Somerville had to work with what was to hand, and needed to inspire his sailors. 'So this is the Eastern Fleet', he signalled when his ships first assembled at sea. 'Well never mind, there's many a good tune played on an old fiddle'.[41]

Somerville assumed personal command of Force A, the 'fast division' and the fleet's main striking force, which comprised *Warspite*, *Formidable* and *Indomitable*, *Cornwall* and *Dorsetshire*, the light cruisers *Emerald* and *Enterprise*, and the destroyers *Napier*, *Nestor*, *Paladin*, *Panther*, *Foxhound*, and *Hotspur*. Willis commanded Force B, the 'slower division', comprising the

36 CAC, Edwards Papers, REDW 2/9, Somerville to Admiralty, not dated.
37 Ibid.
38 BBC 'World War Two People's War' oral history archive, Thomas Russell, A7358844.
39 The opposing Japanese battleships were old too, but extensively modernized.
40 Simpson (ed.), *The Somerville Papers*, p. 394, 14/3/42.
41 Winton, *Sink the* Haguro*!*, p. 10.

'R' class battleships *Ramillies*, *Revenge*, *Resolution*, and *Royal Sovereign*, *Hermes*, the cruisers *Caledon*, *Dragon*, and *Jacob Van Heemskerck*, and the destroyers *Arrow*, *Decoy*, *Fortune*, *Griffin*, *Isaac Sweers*, *Norman*, *Scout*, and *Vampire*.

Somerville's Indian Ocean bases and the view from India Command

We momentarily leave the Eastern Fleet in the final days of March 1942 bracing itself for a Japanese attack, to consider the fleet's base infrastructure in the Indian Ocean, and the view from Wavell's India Command. The Chiefs of Staff report of 16 February had acknowledged the importance of providing the Eastern Fleet with suitable bases from which it could variously repair, replenish, hide, and support operations. Somerville's difficulties in terms of the fleet's capabilities were exacerbated by the fact that he had no strongly defended bases from which to operate, particularly ones capable of housing the entire fleet. That had been Singapore's job, and the British, understandably, had not built a reserve naval 'fortress'. Ceylon was the new Singapore but it was just as vulnerable to the scale of attack the enemy had directed against Pearl Harbor and the many other targets that they had assaulted with impunity, and was an obvious 'next target'. The point was that at this moment, nowhere was safe. Of course, some of Somerville's bases offered a degree of protection; Ceylon's defences were being beefed up day by day, and with foresight the Admiralty had begun, in 1941, to prepare Addu Atoll as a secret fleet base should the navy be forced to fall back from Singapore (see chapter 4). Now, the programme needed to be expanded and expedited as a matter of urgency.

By virtue of Britain's longstanding presence across the region, the Royal Navy enjoyed the benefits of naval and military facilities throughout the Indian Ocean. There were major harbours and naval facilities at Bombay, Colombo, Durban, Mombasa, and Trincomalee, the new fleet base being developed at Port T, and smaller facilities at Diego Garcia in the Chagos Archipelago, Port Victoria in the Seychelles, Grand Bay in Mauritius, and Aden. Of course, facilities in Africa and the Gulf, while essential for convoy defence work in the western Indian Ocean, were of no use for a fleet expecting at this particular juncture to operate against powerful Japanese forces in the eastern region. Colombo was over 2,700 nautical miles from Mombasa.

The Eastern Fleet's headquarters were at the shore base HMS *Lanka* in Colombo, while the main home for its warships was Trincomalee harbour and its shore base HMS *Highflyer*. At China Bay and in many other locations, facilities for the Fleet Air Arm and the aircraft of the RAF were maintained. There were seven Eastern Fleet shore bases and depot ships in India, and about a dozen elsewhere in the region. These included HMS *Euphrates* (Persian Gulf), HMS *Haitan* (Addu Atoll), HMS *Ironclad* (Madagascar), HMS *Jufair* (Bahrein), HMS *Maraga* (Addu Atoll), HMS *Oman* (Kuwait), HMS *Sambur* (Mauritius), HMS *Sangdragon* (Seychelles), HMS *Sheba* (Aden), and HMS *Tana* (Kilindini), and a range of facilities in South Africa.[42]

42 See Ben Warlow, *Shore Establishments of the Royal Navy Being a List of the Static Ships and Establishments of the Royal Navy* (Liskeard: Maritime Books, 1992). For a list of shore establishments, naval hospitals, naval air stations and the vast array of warships, submarines, boats, and landing craft under command of the Eastern Fleet later in the war, see 'East Indies Fleet', part of 'The British Pacific and East Indies Fleets: Forgotten Fleets of the Second World War' website of the Royal

The Eastern Fleet's work across the ocean required the infrastructural support of these bases, protected by anti-aircraft guns, torpedo booms, mined harbour approaches, port war signals organizations to identify and inspect incoming vessels, and the guns with which to fire upon them if they were unfriendly. These bases could be used for shelter, for repair, and for provisioning ships and crews, as well as the prepositioning of resources for operations in surrounding areas, and were vital for the operation of ships such as the 'R' class battleships with their short, three-day, seagoing endurance.[43] A network of radio receivers and transmitters was also extended across the ocean to connect British and Allied vessels and to detect the transmissions of hostile ships. Also scattered across the Indian Ocean, the RAF and FAA operated airbases for fighters, bombers, meteorological aircraft, and long-range reconnaissance flying-boats.[44]

Churchill was critical of Somerville's strategic proposals at this time, and his requests for additional resources. He castigated Somerville's plan to develop bases in various islands and scatter aircraft and anti-aircraft defences among them. The admiral, in his words, was 'asking for everything and giving the least possible'.[45] Though the prime minister had a point about trying to defend island bases strewn across the vastness of the Indian Ocean, the trouble was that because Somerville did not possess a fleet train of supply ships that would enable him to stay at sea for long periods, he had no alternative but to use shore bases to solve logistical problem – and so, obviously, it was necessary to defend them. Furthermore, at the time he took command, having bases that would allow him to fox the Japanese, and safely shelter his ships, was a paramount consideration.

Somerville felt keenly the inadequacies of his bases and his fleet given the imminence of the Japanese threat.

> I feel perhaps it is not fully appreciated at home the enormity of the task of creating bases for and administering this and the future Eastern Fleet.

Navy Research Archive, at http://www.royalnavyresearcharchive.org.uk/BPF-EIF/EIF_Ships.htm#.Ww6KuBNViko. For the shore establishments of the Royal Indian Navy, see 'Shore Establishments of the Royal Indian Navy during the War', in Collins, *The Royal Indian Navy*, appendix 4, at https://www.ibiblio.org/hyperwar/UN/India/RIN/RIN-A4.html

43 Somerville was both amazed and dismayed when he discovered that the three-day endurance was not because of lack of fuel storage, but of water storage; the ships could carry no more than three days supply of the fresh water needed for the functioning of their hydraulics systems.

44 The muted note sounded in the historical record – sometimes – for Indian Ocean forces and military activity stands in stark contrast to the vociferous focus on Britain's war against the Japanese in the 'Burma campaign' (much more effectively construed under the American nomenclature of the 'China-Burma-India theatre'), Malaya/Singapore, and, much less frequently, the Pacific war through a focus on the British Pacific Fleet. As well as numerous books on the 'forgotten army' in the 'forgotten war' – David Smurthwaite (ed.), *The Forgotten War: The British Army in the Far East, 1941-1945* (London: National Army Museum, 1992); James Fenton, *The Forgotten Army: A Burma Soldier's Story in Letters, Photographs, and Sketches* (Stroud: Fonthill Media, 2012). There is also a book on the 'forgotten air force' (Henry Probert, *The Forgotten Air Force: The Royal Air Force in the War against Japan, 1941–45* (London: Brassey's, 1995)) and the 'forgotten fleet' which almost always refers to the British Pacific Fleet, *not* the Eastern Fleet, and has received a lot of scholarly attention (John Winton, *The Forgotten Fleet* (London: Michael Joseph, 1969 and a range of recent books and articles by the likes of Hobbs, Robb-Webb, Sarantakes, and Smith – see notes in chapter 11)).

45 Roskill, *Churchill and the Admirals*, p. 205.

> In the Home and Mediterranean Stations, particularly the former with the Admiralty close at hand, each command and each main base has more amenities and staffs than all the harbours and bases in the Indian Ocean put together. Furthermore, these have been built up over a period of time and I suggest are now out of proportion to the forces they have to operate and administer. To be frank I feel that whilst my brother Commanders in Chief are riding comfortably in their Rolls Royce, I am pushing a broken down Ford with a flat tyre.[46]

Like Somerville's Eastern Fleet, the Indian Ocean region's major land forces, drawn overwhelmingly from the Indian Army, confronted a dire situation in the early months of 1942, having watched with incredulity as the Empire's defences were swept aside in Malaya, command of the sea lost, and Burma invaded. A good barometer of the situation was offered in a review document entitled 'India's war effort', prepared by India Command and the Government of India and presented to the War Cabinet in London by the Secretary of State for India, Leo Amery. The situation at this juncture was likened to that which had faced Britain in the aftermath of the evacuations from Dunkirk in the summer of 1940: 'well-trained troops were scarce and equipment scarcer still'. In the air things were equally as bad 'owing to demands of an even higher priority elsewhere' on the still limited resources of the RAF. 'The situation on Japan's entry into the war', the report stated:

> was that the Army in India had an overall strength of 600,000 British and Indian troops, and 300,000 Indian Army soldiers were serving overseas at that time, including two divisions in the Middle East, three in Iraq, two in Malaya, two infantry brigade groups in Burma, and large numbers of Line of Communication and Base units for the maintenance of these formations and the protection of lines of communication ... India's overseas forces were in fact at this time larger than those of any other country in the British Empire.[47]

In facing the threat of possible attacks and with the Indian Army going through a process of rapid expansion, the troops were not fully trained or properly equipped. This was an acute problem; 'not one of the divisions in India, with the exception of the 17th Indian Division, had more than a training scale of any weapons except rifles'. Artillery was in short supply, as were anti-tank weapons, wireless and signals equipment, and even basics such as steel helmets. That notwithstanding, the desperate situation following the the fall of Singapore meant that India needed to do more to provide for regional security. By March, it had despatched two more infantry brigades to Burma, which arrived shortly before the fall of Rangoon on 7 March, and the 34th Indian Division, minus a brigade group, had been sent to Ceylon as the island's defences were prioritized. Things were moving in the right direction, but time was of the essence; anti-aircraft guns and reinforcements of anti-aircraft regiments were beginning to arrive from

46 'Admiralty War Diaries of World War II', reports of proceedings, 10 May to 5 June 1942.
47 TNA, CAB 66/34/39, 'India's War Effort', War Cabinet memorandum by the Secretary of State for India, 1/3/43. Wavell writes that in March one British and six Indian divisions were all that was available for the defence of Ceylon and India, excluding forces on the North-West Frontier and those devoted to internal security. Wavell 'Operations in Eastern Theatre', p. 4663.

Britain, and the ground defences were taking shape. The question was whether they would be sufficient if Japan attacked.

In the air, for the defence of eastern India there were only two squadrons equipped with obsolete Audaxes. While reinforcements of fighters and bombers 'in considerable numbers were on their way', the fact what that 'our operational strength could not be materially increased before the middle of April'.[48] To meet the Japanese threat on land, the North-West Frontier was denuded of all reserves and a force was concentrated in eastern India, the Eastern Army comprising the 4th Indian Corps, responsible for the defence of Assam (less than two brigades and the remnants of the 'tired and disorganised' Burma Army as it passed into India), and the 15th Indian Corps, responsible for the defence of Bengal and the Arakan coast (14th and 26th Indian divisions, both incomplete, and the Calcutta garrison). In March the 70th British Division, less a brigade in Ceylon, was dispatched to Ranchi to meet a seaborne expedition on the Orissa coast and to form a reserve for the defence of Assam and Bengal.[49] When Rangoon fell in March, Wavell wrote, it was obvious that the whole of Burma might be occupied by the Japanese and that India itself and Ceylon lay under imminent threat of invasion. Reinforcements were on their way, though this took time, and the 5th British Division didn't arrive until May, the 2nd British Division in the following month.

India's situation remained troubling and Wavell felt that Ceylon was getting too much attention from the Chiefs of Staff. The Calcutta area 'was still practically defenceless', he wrote.[50] By the end of March Ceylon had three fighter squadrons equipped with Hurricanes and defences were further strengthened by the arrival of an East African brigade, two Australian brigades, and the third brigade of the 70th British Division, meaning that the island was defended by more than two full divisions. Reviewing the situation, Wavell wrote that the 'only portion of my command which had any scale of air protection at all was Ceylon'.[51]

On 7 March 1942 Wavell cabled the Chiefs of Staff with a short appreciation. He 'considered at this time that an undue proportion of our inadequate land and air resources in the East was being allocated to the defence of Ceylon'. He was particularly concerned that the brigade from the 70th Division had been deployed there. 'Ceylon already had two Indian Brigades and two brigades of local troops; two Australian brigades were being lent to its defence and an East African brigade was on its way'.[52]

> My view was that if we lost command of the sea and air around Ceylon an additional brigade would be of no avail to secure the naval bases at Trincomalee and Colombo, which the Japanese could destroy without landing, in the same manner as at Pearl Harbour [sic] or Manila: whereas a complete British division in North-East India would have been a most valuable reserve and would have done something to restore shaken public morale.[53]

48 Ibid., p. 4664.
49 Ibid., p. 4663.
50 Wavell wrote that Calcutta at that moment had less than 150 heavy and light anti-aircraft guns against an estimated total requirement of some 1,500. Ibid., p. 4663.
51 Wavell 'Operations in Eastern Theatre', p. 4664.
52 Ibid.
53 Ibid., pp. 4663-64.

The War Cabinet, however, ruled 'that the defence of the naval bases in Ceylon must have priority, and confirmed the diversion thither of the 16th Brigade of the 70th Division'. Three fighter squadrons allotted to the defence of the island had been equipped with the Hurricanes recently flown in and as well as some obsolete units there was a squadron of Blenheim bombers and seven or eight Catalina flying-boats, essential reconnaissance 'eyes' given their extraordinary range and endurance.

London sympathized with Wavell, but did not agree with him. Major General Kennedy at the War Office recounts the exchanges with Wavell at this moment:

> Wavell in a series of strong and well-reasoned telegrams, advocated the reinforcement of India. In particular, he was woefully short of aircraft; he had only about a sixth of the number he needed. His whole position might collapse if we did not defend Calcutta, which was at the moment practically naked; the Japanese were concentrating in Burma, and presumably preparing to descend on Bengal and Assam; Alexander was hard pressed in Burma, and without supply routes; our fleet cold not operate in the Bay of Bengal for lack of fighter cover; the Japs had occupied the Andamans, from which we had evacuated our minute garrison; Ceylon, not our main fleet base, was not strongly enough held, but Wavell advised we should accept risk there. With this last we could not agree.[54]

At the time that this correspondence was taking place, the War Office and Chiefs of Staff were also receiving missives from General Auchinleck about the weakness of his position in the Middle East. It was a global balancing act at a desperate moment, and Ceylon was assessed to be more important than Libya, and risk had to be accepted in north-east India.[55]

With the benefit of hindsight, and while acknowledging the (entirely warranted) clamant calls of commanders for more and better resources, what we have here in terms of the defence of Ceylon and parts of India is an impressive reinforcement of land, sea, and air forces given general war circumstances (such as the situation in the Middle East), distance, and the completely unexpected course that the war in the east had taken in the three short months since Japan entered the conflict. The Chiefs of Staff and the War Cabinet understood the nature of the predicament that the Empire found itself in at this moment. Brooke realized that Britain's global war effort was gravely endangered by Japanese expansion, particularly if Japan struck west and the Germans pushed through Egypt to the Suez Canal and the oilfields beyond, or successfully approached them through the Caucasus. As he noted, 'we were at that time literally hanging by our eye-lids! Australia and India were threatened by the Japanese, we had temporarily lost control of the Indian Ocean, the Germans were threatening Persia and our oil, Auchinleck was in precarious straits in the desert, and the submarine sinkings were heavy'.[56]

54 Kennedy, *The Business of War*, pp. 216-17.
55 Boyd, *The Royal Navy in Eastern Waters*, p. 361.
56 Alex Danchev and Daniel Todman (eds), *War Diaries, 1939-1945: Field Marshal Lord Alanbrooke* (London: Weidenfeld and Nicolson, 2001), addendum to diary entry, 14/4/42, p. 248.

German and Japanese thinking

The Indian Ocean was a peripheral theatre for the European Axis powers, given the respective geographical location of their homelands and the thrust of their main strategic war aims in terms of conquest and empire-building.[57] It was more important to the Japanese, if only because they needed to build a defensive perimeter here to protect the western flank of their new empire. For the British it was a crucial region if the Empire were to survive and an increasingly ambitious and complicated system of Allied military activity be preserved – and therefore it was a crucial arena for the Axis powers if they were to defeat the Allies and realize their own vaunting dreams. The fact that Axis plans for world domination never received the concentrated attention commensurate with their realization does not negate the fundamental nature of their importance.

Despite their shared objectives, Germany and Japan's alliance was compromised by the Nazis sense of racial superiority, and Japan's febrile suspicions regarding German intentions. Nevertheless, cooperation was evident and improved as the war progressed. The Tripartite Pact of 27 September 1940 had seen the export of scarce raw materials from Japan to Germany increase, thought it did not initially lead to a breakthrough in either military or economic cooperation.[58] On 23 February 1941 the Reich foreign minister had requested a Japanese attack on Singapore, appreciating how such actions in the east could seriously hamper British operations against German forces in the Mediterranean and Middle East. On 15 December 1941 Baron Oshima Hiroshi, Japanese ambassador to Berlin, delivered a draft proposal to foreign minister Joachim von Ribbentrop which considered the Indian Ocean as the nucleus of Axis combat cooperation.[59] Hitler 'responded positively to Oshima's grand strategy, mentioning plans for the advance of German troops into Iraq and Iran via the Caucasus in spring 1942, and in that way threatening India'.[60]

What transported the east-west Axis alliance to new levels of expectation was the success of Japanese conquests in early 1942. It made Hitler sit up and take notice, Germany warming to Japan as it realized that it now possessed a treasure trove of crucial raw materials. This delighted the German leader, even more so as the closure of the trans-Siberian route following the invasion of the Soviet Union meant that Germany needed raw materials more than ever before, and new routes by which to obtain them. On 18 January 1942 the Chief of the High Command of

57 Without getting drawn too deeply into counterfactual imponderables, it might be speculated that this was true only up to a point. For if the Axis were to win the type of war that their aggression – and the Allied response to it – had created, they were ultimately going to have to break the Allies' ability to move men, military material, and important resources by sea, here in the Indian Ocean as well as elsewhere, also to extract the important resources which, after all, they had gone to war to obtain. A supreme irony of Japan's war is that once it had gained the resource-rich empire it craved, it was unable to utilize it because its capacity to safely transport material by sea was limited to start with and, once the Allies' were up and running, increasingly degraded.

58 See Rotem Kowner, 'When Economics, Strategy, and Racial Ideology Meet: Inter-Axis Connections in the Wartime Indian Ocean', *Journal of Global History*, 12 (2017).

59 Quoted in ibid., referencing 'Draft of a military agreement among Japan, Germany, and Italy, 11 December 1941', in John Chapman (ed.), *The Price of Admiralty: The War Diary of the German Naval Attaché in Japan, 1939-1943*, 4 volumes (Ripe, East Sussex: Saltire Press, 1989), volume 4, pp. 921-23.

60 Ibid.

the Wehrmacht, together with Italian and Japanese representatives, signed a document entitled 'Military arrangements among Germany, Italy, and Japan'. Offensive operations in the Indian Ocean were Germany's major interest in Japan's war effort, a point repeatedly made to Tokyo by Baron Oshima. He was widely respected among the German leadership, taking its cue from Hitler himself who was a surprisingly close confidant of the Japanese ambassador. From Oshima's signals traffic to Tokyo the Americans learned of Operation Orient, the proposed German-Japanese strategic link in India, and duly passed this information to the British. German strategists and diplomats urged the Japanese to act as far west as possible, seeking to distract the British from the Middle East and interdict the sea lanes that nourished British and Soviet fighting formations and disbursed oil to the Empire and the Allied military formations fighting from its territories.

The German naval staff grasped the significance of a strategic link between Germany and Japan via the Middle East and the Indian Ocean. Vice Admiral Kurt Fricke, chief of staff of the naval high command, 'explicitly supported Axis cooperation in the Indian Ocean. In a study of 12 February 1942, his office urged that the Suez Canal be seized and German forces push on to Basra and Aden and join hands with the Japanese. There was a unique historical opportunity which had to be grasped without delay'.[61] Also in February, Raeder told Hitler that Japan planned to protect its Burma front by capturing Ceylon and thereby gain control of the sea in the region,

> and she also plans to gain control of the sea in that area by means of superior naval forces ... With Rangoon, Sumatra, and Java gone, the last oil-wells between the Persian Gulf and the American continent will be lost. Oil supplies for Australia and New Zealand will have to come from either the Persian Gulf or from America. Once Japanese battleships, aircraft-carriers, and submarines, and the Japanese naval air force are based on Ceylon, Britain will be forced to resort to heavily escorted convoys if she desires to maintain communications with India and the Near East.[62]

In March Raeder wrote to Hitler saying that 'the Japanese have recognized the great strategic importance of Madagascar for naval warfare ... they are planning to establish bases there in addition to Ceylon, in order to cripple sea traffic in the Indian Ocean and the Arabian Sea'.[63] The U-boat supremo Dönitz endorsed this view and was confident that British overstretch made the vastness of the Indian Ocean a profitable haunt for U-boats. In April, Vice Admiral Nomura, Japanese naval attaché in Berlin, and Vice Admiral Fricke, discussed the commitment of Japanese forces to the western Indian Ocean. Although Fricke had nothing of substance to offer, he spurred Nomura, telling him that 'the establishment of a direct link between Germany and Japan would decide the war'.[64]

Hitler regarded 'the vast distance between Germany and Japan as a strategic asset, enabling the two powers to stretch their opponents' forces to the utmost'.[65] Japanese planners initially

61 Harrison, 'On Secret Service for the Duce', p. 1319.
62 Raeder quoted in Churchill, *The Second World War*, volume 4, p. 122.
63 Wilson, *A Submariners' War*, p. 57. Dated 12/3/42.
64 Harrison, 'On Secret Service', p. 1320.
65 Ibid.

thought that their forays into the Indian Ocean would be met by a German advance through the Middle East. When this did not happen, the Imperial Japanese Navy decided to seize control of the ocean.[66] While the Germans might deploy U-boat packs in the region, they were clearly focused on the war against the Soviet Union, and confidently, almost insouciantly, expected advances towards the Persian Gulf and Indian Ocean to form a natural 'next stage' of the war once the Soviets had been defeated and the British ejected from Egypt and the eastern Mediterranean.

But the Japanese were looking much more closely at the Indian Ocean region given their proximity to it and the fact that, by March 1942, they had become a very significant Indian Ocean power courtesy of their conquest of its eastern seaboard. The opening of the war against Japan 'in effect marked the point of transition from what was largely a continental war, fought with characteristics of mass, to one that primarily embraced naval and maritime dimensions'.[67] Access to ports and sea lanes became more important than ever before. Having failed to sink a single American carrier at Pearl Harbor, the Japanese decided that they needed to finish the job and also pursue other lines of offensive action, such as exploiting the opportunities that the course of the war so far had created in the Indian Ocean. Four possible courses of action were on the table in early 1942: an assault on Australia; operations in the south-west Pacific to cut American lines of communication between Australia and Hawaii; operations in the central Pacific towards Johnston and Midway islands; and an offensive in the Indian Ocean with the possibility of linking hands with the Germans and Italians. 'This alliance was itself one of the factors that provided the rationale for this option: the collapse of the British position in Malaya, and the anticipation of the early fall of Singapore, offered an extra reason and the opportunity for such an offensive'.[68] But the Imperial Japanese Army's refusal to countenance the Australian or Indian Ocean options put paid to them, as the army baulked at the ideal of sustaining large forces in Australia or west of the Malay Barrier. Nevertheless, the Indian Ocean option was not entirely discounted.

> Planning was sufficiently advanced by the first week of February for representatives of both services' staffs to be invited to [Admiral Isoroku] Yamamoto's flagship for three days of discussions and war games [including plans for the invasion of Ceylon] that began on 20 February, two days after the German naval attaché in Tokyo reported to Berlin that the Japanese had made inquiries about a joint German-Japanese move to secure Madagascar.[69]

On 17 February, the Germans furnished their allies with all the information they possessed regarding potential landing sites in Ceylon. The attractiveness of the Indian Ocean at this moment, Willmott writes, was down to four factors: the fall of Malaya and Singapore, the fact that a considerable portion of Japan's naval strength was in the south, the possibility of rounding off victories in South-east Asia and the East Indies, and the prospect of operating in conjunction with the Germans.

66 Ibid.
67 H. P. Willmott, *The War with Japan: The Period of Balance, May 1942-October 1943* (Willmington, DE: Scholarly Resources, 2002), p. xiii.
68 Ibid., p. 10.
69 Ibid., p. 11.

> In the course of Japanese staff discussions one more consideration emerged. With the Combined Fleet planners thinking in terms of using two divisions to secure Ceylon and to take an outpost in the Chagos Archipelago, the possibility of shattering British prestige and authority in India and throughout the Indian Ocean seemed a likely outcome of a Japanese offensive.[70]

But by the first week of March this option had been consigned to the waste-paper basket along with the Australia option.[71] There was one caveat: as early as December 1941 the navy had considered a single raid into the Indian Ocean following the conquest of South-east Asia. 'When the idea of a major endeavour in the Indian Ocean died, this earlier idea was revived with a provisional timetable set for the first week of April'.[72] And so, the Japanese prepared for a three-pronged raid into the Indian Ocean.

Strongly influencing Japanese thinking at this moment was something that all senior commanders agreed upon – the need for continued offensive action. They were aware that the British were pulling out all the stops to reinforce the Indian Ocean following the fall of Singapore and the Dutch East Indies. Despite 'the extremely grave situation in the Atlantic and the Mediterranean at this time, the British had managed to undertake a massive reinforcement of their forces' in the Indian Ocean.[73] This, Willmott writes, 'could only bode ill for the Japanese in the long term. Therefore, within the Japanese naval hierarchy, many favoured an offensive operation against the British in the Indian Ocean at the earliest possible opportunity'.[74]

By late March Japanese forces seemed poised to move against India from Burma, while across the subcontinent popular opposition to British rule in the form of the 'Quit India' movement intensified. In London, the combined threat of invasion and internal revolt suddenly made the loss of India seem a real possibility. It was recognized by Churchill and the War Cabinet as a crisis requiring immediate action, hence the emergency transfer of military resources eastwards, and the mission led by Sir Stafford Cripps to try and persuade Gandhi and the Indian National Congress to back the war effort. Swathes of British territory east of Suez had been lost in a mere four months, and after the fall of Rangoon a sense of impending crisis gripped British officials in India. Hundreds of thousands of soldiers and civilians fled from Burma towards India, and Indian morale, in the eyes of the British, visibly wilted. Wavell informed London

70 Ibid. Willmott also considers the genesis of Operation C, the Indian Ocean raid, in *The Barrier and the Javelin*, pp. 46-54.

71 See Bob Wurth, *1942: Australia's Greatest Peril* (Sydney: Pan, 2010).

72 Willmott, *The War with Japan*, p. 11. See also John Bradley and Jack Dice, *The Second World War: Asia and the Pacific* (New York: Square One Publishers/Department of History, U. S. Military Academy West Point, 2002).

73 Willmott, *Empires in the Balance*, p. 440.

74 Ibid. In discussing the ins and outs of Japanese strategic thinking and decision making at this moment, from a 'what might have been' perspective, Willmott argues that a major offensive in the Indian Ocean aimed at securing the mouth of the Persian Gulf would have served them much better than a brief sortie which would not enable Japan to impose its will on the enemy, and targeted against a British fleet strong on paper but with hardly any offensive value – and one that could decline to give battle. 'It is ironic that, while overall the Japanese can be criticized for waging war with too few resources over too great an area, in the case of the Indian Ocean operation the reverse was true. In this operation the Japanese were attempting too little with too much: it would have been better to make either an all-out effort or none at all'. Ibid., p. 441.

that he anticipated an assault on northeast India and 'large scale Japanese landings in Madras following victory in Burma. Such was the magnitude of the rout that the British commander was already planning to form a last-ditch 'bastion' around Calcutta. Wavell's naval counterpart, Somerville, had a similar view. Hoping for the best and trying to hold on was the only thing to do. As Burma was being evacuated, Major General Kennedy, observing proceedings from the War Office, said that 'if we could save Ceylon and India, or at least part of India, we would still be able to restore the situation in time'.[75]

It wasn't just British military planners who worried about the situation. Inhabitants of territories across the Indian Ocean were familiar with tales of Japanese atrocities from the Sino-Japanese war, fuelled by propaganda demonizing a rather easily demonized enemy.[76] For instance, panic gripped the inhabitants of the island of Rodrigues, 350 miles east of Mauritius, when, on 3 March, the cable link across the Indian Ocean was temporarily broken: 'At Oyster Bay was heard a humming that was the sound of people praying aloud, even those who had never prayed before, that they would be saved from the Japanese. Rosaries were cut into pieces and shared with neighbours'.[77] The break in imperial communications had been caused by a Japanese attack on the cable and wireless station on the Cocos-Keeling Islands, a tiny speck of British territory over a thousand miles south-southwest of Singapore. The Japanese were coming.

75 Kennedy, *The Business of War*, p. 204.

76 One of the many striking propaganda posters produced in Ceylon, for example, showed a civilian being held by a monstrous, giant, Japanese person, the legend reading: 'In the grip of Japanese co-prosperity'. Image reproduced in Ashley Jackson, '"Defend Lanka Your Home": War on the Home Front in Ceylon, 1939-1945', *War in History*, 16, 2 (2009).

77 Jackson, *War and Empire*.

9

The Japanese raids in the Indian Ocean

In April 1942 Admiral Nagumo sought to reprise the greatest day in his country's military history when he attempted to 'Pearl Harbor' the Royal Navy with a battleship and carrier raid on Ceylon. At the same time, a second Japanese force shot up merchant shipping around India and bombarded Indian ports. The desired result – the destruction of British seapower east of Suez – would leave the Indian Ocean wide open to the Japanese and establish the western defensive perimeter of their new empire.[1] With the British maritime threat eliminated, the Imperial Japanese Navy would then be able to concentrate its full force against the US Navy in the South Pacific, having secured the sea lanes connecting the westernmost territories of the nascent Greater East Asian Co-Prosperity Sphere. This would guarantee untrammelled resupply of Japanese troops based as far away as Burma and the Andamans, and provide access to the cornucopia of raw materials that were the major fruits of victory, not least, the region's oil, rubber, and tin. The raid would also teach the population of Ceylon and India a graphic lesson regarding the proximity of Japanese power – then romping through Burma towards India's eastern provinces – and the commensurate weakness of their colonial masters.

Under Admiral Nagumo's command were the carriers of the First Air Fleet, *Akagi*, *Hiryu*, *Shokaku*, *Soryu*, and *Zuikaku*, carrying around 350 modern fighters and bombers. They were protected by four fast battleships, the *Haruna*, *Hiei*, *Kongo*, and *Kirishima*, three cruisers, and 11 destroyers. This awesome force – by some margin the most powerful concentration of warships afloat – left Staring Bay on 26 March 1942, entering the Indian Ocean undetected on 2-3 April.[2] At the same time, and having secured the Andaman and Nicobar Islands the previous week, the Japanese took Mergui and Phuket and sailed an Imperial Japanese Army division from Singapore to Rangoon in 50-odd transports, confirming their newfound mastery of the eastern Indian Ocean.

1 Dull, *A Battle History*, p. 104.
2 See 'Waltzing Matilda: The Early Carrier War', chapter 5 in J. Bradley and J. Dice, *The Second World War: Asia and the Pacific*. For the Imperial Japanese Navy see Dull, *A Battle History*, chapter 7, 'Raids in the Indian Ocean'. The Christmas Island raid was Operation X. Also see Stephen Howarth, *Morning Glory: The Imperial Japanese Navy* (London: Arrow Books) and Marder, *Old Friends, New Enemies*.

The raids had two purposes:

> [To] foment trouble in India at a time when Anglo-Indian political relations were particularly delicate: and to secure the supply lines through the Straits of Malacca and the Bay of Bengal to Rangoon. Admiral Kondon, the Commander-in-Chief of the *Second Fleet* and the naval commander of southern operations, directed the huge operation, which sent Vice Admiral Jisaburo Ozawa's *Malaya Force* into the Bay of Bengal to raid shipping and bomb India, a pack of submarines to the west coast of India to destroy merchantmen, and Admiral Nagumo's *First Air Fleet* to Ceylon to neutralize the British naval forces in the area – the major threat to the line of communications to Rangoon.[3]

Opposing the Japanese, Somerville could call upon a large fleet built around carriers and battleships. It was an impressive force, but one deficient in areas such as training and organic air power. Furthermore, in both Ceylon and India the British lacked the scale of land-based air power that would have improved their chances of attacking the Japanese fleet at sea, if it came within range and, crucially, if they could find it.

The challenges of locating the enemy dictated the nature of the response, an equation that worked both ways. The sooner the British could locate the enemy and discover its size and composition, the more time they would have to decide and to act. In order to do this, the British depended on radar in Ceylon and aboard warships (though this was not very long-range) and the reconnaissance patrols of long-range flying-boats. An advantage that the British did possess was access to intelligence derived from Bletchley Park and that broken locally by its Far East Combined Bureau (FECB) outstation. The British war effort in the Indian Ocean, no less than in Europe and the Middle East, was greatly aided by the sophistication of Allied code-breaking techniques. On 28 March, wrote Commodore Edwards from Colombo, intelligence 'leads us to believe that the Japanese intend a carrier bourne attack on this place'.[4] FECB cryptanalysts had intercepted a Japanese signal. They 'were working one sultry afternoon in Colombo on a message that described plans for a massive attack somewhere. Then they spelt out the name of the place that was to be clobbered – KO-RO-N-BO; an electric shock ran through the up-to-then relaxed office'.[5]

Somerville and his senior commanders and staff spent the following day in conference discussing the immediate threat to Ceylon and the Eastern Fleet.[6] Their belief was that an attack would occur on the morning of 31 March. It was likely to be a tip and run raid, but the prospect of full scale landings could not be discounted, and attacks on the sea lanes were considered likely too. It was assessed that the Japanese would most likely seek to destroy the port facilities and their defences, destabilize India, cut air supplies to China, and make preliminary

3 Bradley and Dice, *The Second World War*, pp. 99-100.

4 CAC, Edwards Papers, REDW 2/7.

5 Desmond Ball, *Signals Intelligence (Sigint) in South Asia: India, Pakistan, Sri Lanka (Ceylon)* (Canberra: Strategic and Defence Studies Centre, 1996).

6 At that moment, the fleet was dispersed thus: at Colombo, *Formidable*, *Dorsetshire*, *Cornwall*, *Enterprise*, *Dragon*, *Caledon*, *Paladin*, *Panther*, *Nestor*, *Hotspur*, and *Express*. At Trincomalee, *Warspite*, *Emerald*, *Hermes*, *Heemskerk* (Dutch), and *Vampire*. At Addu Atoll, *Resolution*, *Ramillies*, *Royal Sovereign*, *Indomitable*, *Napier*, *Norman*, *Nizam*, *Fortune*, *Foxhound*, *Griffin*, *Decoy*, and *Isaac Sweers* (Dutch).

moves to coordinate operations with Germany.[7] And, of course, seek to neutralize the Eastern Fleet's main strength.

With his submarines probing ahead for the British fleet, and others off Ceylon's ports providing weather forecasts, Nagumo steamed towards his target with the First Air Fleet's carriers and the 3rd Battle Division's battleships and escorting cruisers and destroyers. Wanting to avoid being caught in harbour with inadequate air cover, Somerville decided to depart with all sea-going units as soon as possible. He believed that his best chance of damaging the Japanese fleet was through a night-time air attack. For this Agar wrote, Somerville 'had a flotilla of our most modern destroyers (*Jarvis* class) and the torpedo aircraft from the *Indomitable* and *Formidable* ... In addition he had the fast cruisers, *Emerald* and *Enterprise*, whose combined torpedo armament of thirty-two torpedoes and high speed was the equivalent of at least of another destroyer flotilla'.[8]

Somerville's plan was to:

> concentrate the Battlefleet, carriers, and all available cruisers and destroyers and to rendezvous on the evening of the 31st March in a position from which the fast division (Force A, consisting of *Warspite*, *Indomitable*, *Formidable*, *Cornwall*, *Emerald*, *Enterprise* and 6 destroyers) could intercept the enemy during the night of 31st March/1st April and deliver a night air attack. The remainder (Force B) to form a separate force and to manoeuvre so as to be approximately 20 miles to the westward of Force A. If Force A intercepted a superior force, I intended to withdraw towards Force B.[9]

This is interesting, because while one usually only encounters references to the 'R' class battleships (both at the time and subsequently) in terms of their shortcomings, they were nevertheless integral to Somerville's tactics; if he got into trouble with Force A, he intended to make a dash towards the 32 fifteen-inch guns of the four 'Rs', and see what the Japanese made of that.

Keeping out of reconnaissance range by day and launching an air attack at night, 'when his fleet's weakness would be veiled and British superiority in gun power could be brought into play', was Somerville's only realistic chance of hitting the enemy.[10] He simply could

7 Simpson (ed.), *The Somerville Papers*, referencing Marder, volume 2, pp. 81-94.

8 Agar, *Footprints in the Sea*, p. 176. Like so many people at the time, and rather astonishingly, Somerville laboured under some preposterous suppositions about the proficiency of Japanese people in the dark. 'I'm told the Japs are afraid of the dark', he wrote to his wife from Freetown on 1 March, 'so I must try and specialise in night attacks'. Simpson (ed.), *The Somerville Papers*, p. 388.

9 'Admiralty War Diaries of World War II', reports of proceedings, 29 March to 13 April 1942. Boyd, *The Royal Navy in Eastern Waters* offers the latest blow-by-blow account of the manoeuvres at sea between 4 and 9 April, a remarkable reconstruction. Other naval historians have also attempted this, notably Marder and Willmott. They scrutinize Somerville's tactics noting, for example, that he significantly underestimated the size of the Japanese fleet, as well as examining the equivocal Japanese performance.

10 Willmott, *Empires in the Balance*, p. 444. 'Somerville encountered criticism for taking unacceptable risks in maneuvering his fleet in the enemy's vicinity. In light of the Japanese superiority in ships, aircraft, and battle technique, such criticism would appear well justified'. Vice Admiral Willis thought he had run risks in the face of Japanese air superiority and wrote that 'I'm sure Geoffrey Layton realized Somerville was overreaching himself'. CAC, Willis Papers, 5/5. Dull suggests that the idea was to get in range at night so as to launch an air attack at daybreak. Dull, *A Battle History*, p. 104.

not risk a full frontal attack that might lead to the loss of all or most of his capital ships. As Agar put it, because he could not allow the Indian Ocean sea lanes to be left unprotected, 'the risk of *seeking* battle was one which he simply couldn't accept'.[11] Accounting for his decision-making to the Admiralty, Somerville wrote that 'first and foremost, the total defence of the Indian Ocean and its vital lines of communication depend on the existence of the Eastern Fleet'.[12] His thinking was endorsed by Their Lordships at the Admiralty back in London, and the First Sea Lord signalled Somerville at this moment strongly advising him not to allow his fleet to become engaged with anything except inferior forces until reinforcements arrived.[13]

'Crocks can't play centre court tennis and that's the answer', was Somerville's frustrated response to those back in Britain who, he knew, would be asking what he was doing with his sizeable fleet while the Japanese were on the rampage. First amongst them was Winston Churchill, who thought the Eastern Fleet 'idle'.[14] Everyone was on tenterhooks. Agar cancelled *Dorsetshire*'s refit 'and brought the ship to short notice. Boilers and engines had to be put together again'.[15] Somerville planned to assemble his fleet at a point 80 miles off Dondra Head, Ceylon's southernmost tip, and steam so as to be in a position to attack the enemy carriers.[16] He led Force A out aboard *Warspite* on 30 March, expecting to rendezvous with Willis and Force B at 4pm the following day. The entire fleet rendezvoused as planned, and 'shaped a course to the northward'.[17] The search now began, the British fleet hunting for the Japanese as they, in turn, steamed north expecting to find their enemy dozing in Colombo.

The coming together of the Eastern Fleet south of Ceylon was 'a memorable occasion':

> especially for those of us who had never sailed in a fleet. The tropical sea was calm and rich blue, creased white by the bow waves and wakes of the warships. On the horizon appeared small black dots. They became bigger ... more black dots ... gradually they all took shape ... battleships, aircraft carriers, cruisers, and destroyers. Signals were flashed from the flagship. The forces merged and manoeuvred into position. Cruisers wheeled while destroyers, the terriers of the seas, sped to take up their stations. The battleships formed up in line ahead with the flagship, *Warspite*, a stately leader of the fleet. It was an imposing inspiring sight,

11 Agar, *Footprints in the Sea*, pp. 176-77.
12 'Admiralty War Diaries of World War II', reports of proceedings, 29 March to 13 April 1942.
13 Agar, *Footprints in the Sea*, p. 177.
14 Simpson (ed.), *The Somerville Papers*, p. 399, to wife, 4/4/42. Like other theatre commanders during the course of the war, Somerville felt the impatient prime minister's breath on his neck, having to fight a constant rearguard to try and convince him that the Eastern Fleet was not being used offensively did *not* mean that it was not doing any good. Churchill's characteristic impatience, and his inability to understand, or willingness to forget while in mid-harangue, that not every soldier or warship could be shooting at the enemy every day, also meant that Somerville had to fend off unreasonable requests to employ his ships elsewhere. The First Sea Lord Sir Dudley Pound provided important top cover on this front, deflecting some of the more unreasonable verbal broadsides. This was the case, for example, in April 1942 – the month of greatest peril in the Indian Ocean – when Churchill hatched a plan to have the Eastern Fleet pass through the Suez Canal in order to protect a convoy sailing to Malta and entice the Italian navy into a major fleet action.
15 Agar, *Footprints in the Sea*, pp. 175-76.
16 Ibid., p. 176.
17 'Admiralty War Diaries of World War II', reports of proceedings, 29 March to 13 April 1942.

> a fleet of five battleships, three aircraft carriers, seven cruisers, and fourteen destroyers – twenty-nine warships, the biggest fleet assembled in the Indian Ocean.[18]

From aboard *Hermes*, R. Bell wrote that 'As I scanned the view, I suddenly saw the object of our "rendezvous", and I shall never forget the sight which my eyes beheld: a great number of fighting ships such as I had never seen before'.[19] As Admiral Somerville wrote to his wife, 'the fleet I now have is much bigger than anything anyone has had to handle before during this war'.[20]

Confidence was high. Thomas Russell aboard the Force B battleship *Ramillies* recalled rain squalls

> heavy and warm and as good as any shower bath. Those that could, stood on the upper deck and with a cake of soap availed themselves of this heaven sent unrationed shower bath … 'What would your fucking party think if she saw you with a little chopper like that?', someone shouted amid the howls of mirth as pot bellies glistened among skinny limbs. We were like school kids. With lookouts extra alert, the rain cleared and blistering sun returned.
>
> What we did know as the signals came in was a possibility of a major fleet action and we knew it would be no picnic. I didn't relish the prospect of being a prisoner of war of the Japs, we had already heard of the atrocities they had perpetrated on prisoners and civilians alike, so if we did go into action against them I hoped that rather than having to be made a prisoner in the event of our sinking, I would already be dead. It may seem defeatist to think that way, but on the other hand it is an added incentive to fight to the end if your foe is capable of such acts.
>
> Looking at the ponderous but majestic battleships ploughing through the blue seas, their foam-whitened wakes, and seeing the great fo'castle dipping with an occasional flurry of foam as the bows broke into the waves which had now risen on a freshening breeze, it was hard to imagine anything could stand against us. The carrier's planes flying off occasionally as she turned away into the wind with her close destroyer escort, added an extra sense of power to the fleet. Signal lamps would flicker between the ships, sometimes pennants would be run up, each ship coordinating and communicating with each other. The day passed, though at that time we on the lower deck did not know how near we had been to a major fleet battle.[21]

Yet despite the impressive size and strength of this armada, in the words of one of its senior commanders, it was 'difficult to believe that any British force has been less drilled and well equipped to meet an enemy'.[22]

On 1 April British aircraft attacked an enemy submarine 150 miles south east of Koggala.[23] But there were no reports of the enemy fleet on that day, so Somerville turned Force A back

18 Dimbleby, *Turns of Fate*, p. 150.
19 Morgan, *The* Hermes *Adventure*, p. 129.
20 Simpson (ed.), *The Somerville Papers*, to wife, ???, p. ??
21 BBC 'World War Two People's War' oral history archive, Thomas Russell.
22 CAC, REDW 2/7, diary, 31/3/42.
23 BL, Layton Papers, 74802, Report on GR [general reconnaissance] and Striking Force Operations, 28 March-9 April 1942, Air Vice Marshal Air Officer Commanding 222 Group Ceylon.

towards the south-east and rejoined Force B, proceeding to exercise the fleet all day. There were heavy squalls on the 2 April and a Catalina spotted a submarine near the British fleet, though its depth charges failed to go off when it went in to attack.[24] This day also brought no news of the Japanese fleet. The following day, 3 April, was very hot and fine, but still the enemy fleet remained undiscovered, though it was reported that the enemy had landed at Akyab, 'so Calcutta is now threatened'.[25] Somerville detached *Fortune* to collect survivors from the torpedoed merchantman *Glensheil*, sunk 300 miles east of the Maldives en route from Colombo to Fremantle. Then, to the mixed frustration and relief of the thousands of British and imperial sailors holed up at action stations on the warships of this great assembly, the operation was called off. There was no sign of the Japanese. 'At this time', Somerville wrote, 'I felt convinced that something must have occurred to delay the Japanese attack or alternatively that their objective had been inaccurately appreciated'.[26]

A false alarm, possibly. Perhaps the intelligence had been wrong. Whatever the reason, the fleet dispersed, some, like the 'R' class battleships, already at the end of their endurance. Most of the ships sailed for Addu Atoll to replenish and refuel, while other left to take up convoy duties or resume scheduled repairs. Having failed to locate Nagumo's force after three days of searching, Somerville had had little choice. There was nothing to indicate an imminent attack, and the chances of detection by Japanese submarines were increasing. *Hermes* and *Vampire* entered Trincomalee harbour and began to prepare for participation in the forthcoming invasion of Madagascar, the carrier scheduled to have her boilers cleaned. *Cornwall* sailed for Colombo as escort to Australian troop convoy SU4, *Dorsetshire* in order to resume her refit, which included new anti-aircraft guns. It was decided to allow normal shipping movements in the Indian Ocean to resume.

Dispersing the fleet suggested that Somerville believed the code-breakers had got it wrong. An associated problem was that no one appreciated the great range of the Japanese aircraft, so it was thought that the fleet transporting them would have to approach very close to Ceylon in order to launch an effective attack. As Agar wrote, the 'range and performance of the Japanese naval aircraft' had 'escaped the notice of everyone'.[27] As the British fleet approached Addu Atoll, anti-submarine sweeps were conducted, Force A arriving at 12:00pm on 4 April, Force B at 3pm. The base was alive with action, as ships refuelled and charts were studied and motor boats took flag officers and captains from the various ships to *Warspite* for a conference with Somerville.

The saviour of Ceylon

Ceylon's flying-boats 'gave us the most wonderful service by flying patrols 500 miles out as far as the Nicobars'.[28] There were only eight on station at the time, five British, one Dutch, and

24 Based on Edwards's diary entries, CAC, Edwards Papers, REDW 2/7.
25 Ibid., diary, 3/4/42.
26 'Admiralty War Diaries of World War II', reports of proceedings, 29 March to 13 April 1942.
27 Agar, *Footprints in the Sea*, p. 180.
28 Ibid., p. 175.

two Canadian.[29] 413 Squadron Royal Canadian Air Force had begun arriving on 31 March (its 331-strong ground crew following on in May), its aircraft arriving by way of a series of hops across the Empire, calling at Gibraltar, Cairo, and Abukir. Arriving on 2 April, the squadron commander, Leonard Birchall, didn't even have time to unpack his kit before being called in to action.[30] Flight Lieutenant Rae Thomas and his Catalina had been 'first to reach Koggala where the base had been established among coconut plantations. The lake was full of obstructions and was surrounded by marshes and tall palms. Only a short clear stretch existed for landings and take-offs'.[31]

While his crew spent 3 April unloading the aircraft, Birchall checked out the RAF station at Lake Koggala as well as the accommodation for the officers at a Galle hotel and for the crew at a commandeered girls' school called Richmond Hill. But there was no time to settle in. Given the Eastern Fleet's abortive search for Nagumo's fleet, Catalinas were needed in the air at all times to keep a look out. Birchall recounted that

> we arrived just around noon and I was taken into the operations room where we were briefed, interrogated, and the crew were sent to the rest house. The next day we went back to the aircraft and started to unload our supplies. It was at this time that I was informed that they suspected the Japanese might be somewhere in the vicinity of Ceylon ... They asked if I would take off first thing in the morning before dawn.[32]

In this manner Birchall and his crew, on 'a wonderful day, nice and clear', were dispatched to make their single, but telling, contribution to the war against Japan. On the morning of 4 April they 'were taken to the jetty on the lake to prepare for a 24 hour flight. Because there had been no time to practice night landings on Lake Koggala's hazardous take-off area, the Catalina would have to stay aloft all night in order to land by daylight.[33]

> Everything was going along merrily. We had just finished a little snack and were getting ready to go home – this was four o'clock in the afternoon – when somewhere out in the horizon we suddenly saw some specks which appeared as if they were a convoy. We had had no notification of convoys in that area, so we immediately went in that direction to investigate. As we got in the area where the convoy could be identified we ran into the outer screen of the Japanese fleet.

Birchall's aircraft had been spotted, and the ships below were swift to attack, desperate to bring the interloper down before it could reveal their position.

29 Banks, *Wings of the Dawning*, p. 48. Somerville wrote that there were seven, which meant that only three could be on patrol at any one time.

30 For Birchall, see Rob Stuart, 'Leonard Birchall and the Japanese Raid on Colombo', *Canadian Military Journal* (Winter 2006-2007); Sanji Gunasekara, 'Target Ceylon, 1942', *Travel Sri Lanka* (September 2008); and M. Tomlinson, *The Most Dangerous Moment*.

31 A. Banks, *Wings of the Dawning*, p. 49.

32 Leonard Birchall, 'The Japanese Ceylon Attack and Afterwards', in *The Empire Club of Canada Speeches, 1945-1946* (Toronto: The Empire Club Foundation, 1946).

33 For images of the base, see the 1944 RAF film 'Ceylon Flying Boat Base', Imperial War Museum, ABY 61.

> As they attacked us we identified the ships and immediately started out on our first signing point. This had to constitute the position, course, and speed, the actual composition of the forces, and also we gave our position. The normal procedure was that we repeated this three times. We got through twice, and half way through the third time, when an explosive shell came in and knocked the wireless set out and also laid the wireless operator *hors de combat* at that time. In the meantime, about forty Zeroes were buzzing around us. The first casualty was our port gunner who had his leg practically knocked off at that time. It was necessary to put him inside the aircraft on the crew bunks. The engineer then got into that position and the fight was on. We got as low as we could to stop attacks from underneath us, but they started coming in from the top and the next thing we knew they had punctured the gas tank and the gasoline was on fire and flowing down inside the aircraft. We managed to get that out. At the same time we were blazing away with all we had in the vicinity of the attackers and the machine started to break up.
>
> When we were in that particular situation the fire broke out and this time we eventually went down and landed on the water. The machine sank instantly. We got everybody out that we could. The only person we couldn't get was the poor lad on the bunk. He went down with the machine. The remainder of us were left swimming as hard as we could away from the burning gasoline. While we were getting away we tried to form a group. At that particular time we noticed the Japanese aircraft starting to come after us. We were by ourselves and we didn't think anything was going to happen. The next minute they opened with guns and for the next twenty minutes we had to keep repeatedly diving under the water in order to evade the Japanese. When we had finished two more lads were gone and there was only six left.[34]

Following this terrifying ordeal, Birchall and the remaining crew were picked up by a destroyer, interrogated and beaten, and confined for two days in a paint locker so small that the men had to take turns standing. The Japanese were very anxious to know if the British crew had managed to transmit a message to Colombo, which they denied, a lie exposed when the delayed response, asking the now-defunct Catalina to repeat its signals, was heard aboard the Japanese fleet.[35]

The Eastern Fleet sails to battle

Arriving back at Colombo after the excitement of the fleet mobilization had been an anticlimax for *Cornwall*'s crew. Things appeared to return to normality. Liberty boats took off-duty men ashore, the daily chores associated with life on board were carried out, and minor repairs

34 Leonard Birchall, 'The Japanese Ceylon Attack', *The Empire Club of Canada Addresses* (Toronto, 18/10/45), at <https://speeches.empireclub.org/60830/data?n=3>.

35 Beginning their lengthy stint as prisoners of war in Japan, the crew were displayed to angry crowds in Yokohama; the Doolittle raids had taken place on the previous day. In the POW camp they mixed with survivors from the Battle of the Java Sea, including men from *Exeter* and USS *Houston*. There were others who had been captured on Guam and Wake islands, and the Dutch East Indies. On moving camp they encountered more allies, this time British and Canadian troops captured upon the fall of Hong Kong. They were then transferred to Tokyo, where they remained, no longer interrogated on a daily basis but forced to work, for the rest of the war.

and adjustments were made. But the stand down did not last long. All leave was soon cancelled, and the general recall went around Colombo's hotel lounges and bars, bazaars, clubs, and places of entertainment. 'All naval personnel return to your ships'. Ken Dimbleby missed out on a hoped-for glass of beer ashore, while many of his crew mates enjoyed their last.

Agar was in Colombo on that Saturday afternoon, 4 April, when an 'urgent message summoned me again to the Operations Room'. Arbuthnot, Commander-in-Chief East Indies, had received Birchall's report of a large force of enemy carriers accompanied by battleships and cruisers steering west from the Malacca Strait. 'It was Nagumo's force, and the attack on Colombo was obviously on'.[36] *Cornwall* and *Dorsetshire*'s captains, Manwaring and Agar, conferred with Arbuthnot and Victor Danckwerts, deputy Commander-in-Chief Eastern Fleet. They were given orders to sail south as soon as possible that night and rejoin the Eastern Fleet.

Away to the west at Addu Atoll, news of Birchall's sighting came through at 4:30pm during the conference aboard *Warspite*. It was clear that the original impression concerning Japanese intentions had in fact been correct. Somerville was furious that he had not trusted the intelligence and had allowed the fleet to disperse; 'damn and *blast*', he wrote to his wife, 'it looks as if I've been had because a Catalina has just reported a large enemy force 350 SE miles of Ceylon – evidently the party I've been waiting for and here I am miles away and unable to strike'.[37] But he still thought that he had a chance of getting his fleet into a position from which his torpedo-bombers could deliver an attack, and this was the course of action decided upon.

The fleet put to sea as soon as it completed refuelling, Force A sailing at 12:15am on 5 April, Force B at 7am. Somerville ordered 'the heavies' – the heavy cruisers *Cornwall* and *Dorsetshire*, to rejoin the main fleet as soon as possible, leaving the selection of a rendezvous point to the Operational Headquarters in Colombo. Willis, commanding Force B, wrote: 'So we filled up and put to sea again. Commander-in-Chief with *Warspite* and the two aircraft carriers, and me lumbering along behind with the Rs. I get 18 and a half knots out of them as a squadron, creaking at every joint'.[38] Meanwhile British submarines patrolled to the south-east of Ceylon hoping to give early warning of a Japanese attack. Easter Sunday, 5 April, was very hot. Steaming east at 19 knots, at 8:30am Somerville heard that Colombo had given the red warning and reported that it was being bombed by Japanese aircraft.[39] At 10:30am, Colombo reported at least two battleships and destroyers 250 miles north of the Eastern Fleet's position, steaming south-east.

As well as ordering Eastern Fleet warships to leave Ceylon's harbours, the safety of dozens of British and Allied merchant vessels, waiting to be unloaded or to collect cargoes from the ports of Ceylon and India, also required attention. Arbuthnot decided to order all ships in Colombo to disperse, as tightly-packed in harbour they would have little chance against air attack.[40] Scores of vessels left Colombo, as Arbuthnot's 'herculean efforts with a team of British tugs

36 Agar, *Footprints in the Sea*, p. 179.

37 Simpson (ed.), *The Somerville Papers*, to wife from Addu Atoll, 4/4/42, p. 399.

38 CAC, Willis Papers, 5/5, letter, 10/4/42.

39 CAC, Edwards Papers, REDW 2/7, diary, 5/4/42.

40 The air raids themselves on Colombo and Trincomalee are given a detailed treatment in Jackson, *Ceylon at War*, while this chapter focuses on the action at sea. See Robert Stuart, 'Air Raid Colombo, 5 April 1942: The Fully Expected Surprise Attack', *Royal Canadian Air Force Journal*, 3, 4 (2014). Stuart, the undisputed expert on the subject of the raids, has also written a forensic appraisal of the Trincomalee attack.

and pilots, managed to get all this motley array of shipping clear of the port'.[41] A. A. Loveridge writes that 'there has been a hundred and forty merchant ships in Colombo harbour, so crowded that a single bomb could have been diastrous'. During the week

> Arbuthnot had soothed the nerves of the multi-racial and very jittery ship-masters with a series of cocktail parties. Meanwhile, he set himself to guess the intensions of the Japanese Admiral; I have a vivid memory of him pacing up and down his office, a short, square, grey an with his hands behind his back and a cigarette dropping ash onto the black tie he insisted on wearing with his tropical shirt. As a result, he gave the order on Saturday morning that by 0800 Easter Sunday all ships that could steam were to be forty miles north or south of Colombo.[42]

Despite Arbuthnot's order to clear the harbour, there were still some merchantmen, Fleet Auxiliaries, and warships alongside when 91 Japanese bombers accompanied by 36 fighters appeared and were met by the RAF in a 'brief but intense dogfight'.[43] Six torpedo-bearing Swordfish, on their way from Colombo to Trincomalee, blundered into the fight and were promptly shot down. The Japanese lost a fighter and six dive bombers, the British, in addition to the Fulmars, around 15 Hurricanes. The raid on Colombo damaged installations, half the attacking force targeting infrastructure – learning from the omission at Pearl Harbor – the other half going for the ships, hitting the destroyer *Tenedos*, the Armed Merchant Cruiser *Hector*, and the submarine depot ship *Lucia* as she prepared to load torpedoes onto the submarine *Trusty* moored alongside. But losses were really rather light, and Nagumo's aircraft had failed in their main mission, because they had not found the Eastern Fleet.

But the Japanese pilots had not yet finished. After leaving the skies above Ceylon they returned to the carriers and refuelled. Given that the main task of the Japanese fleet was to destroy their opponent, a reconnaissance report from an aircraft launched by the cruiser *Tone* – regarding a sighting of British warships – was followed up with alacrity. Fifty-three bombers and 35 fighters took off to search south of Ceylon. *Tone*'s aircraft had in fact spotted *Cornwall* and *Dorsetshire*, and accurately reported their position. What followed was a textbook demonstration in the use of air power at sea. *Dorsetshire* was going fast towards the fleet rendezvous and 'the protective umbrella of the carriers'. At 11:30am 'we sighted a dot bobbing up and down the horizon, every minute or so'. It was 'a Jap "shadower"'.[44] The two cruisers were 90 miles from the main body of the British fleet. It was just after noon, and off duty crew were having their Easter Sunday dinner. Then the Japanese aircraft arrived.

41 Agar, *Footprints in the Sea*, p. 175.

42 Liddell Hart Military Archives, Bryant, F7-15/2, Loveridge to Arthur Bryant, November 1957. In this letter, Loveridge, a Royal Navy paymaster, takes issue with references to the Japanese raids in Bryant's book *The Turn of the Tide*, specifically, page 351. Loveridge is quick to Arbuthnot's defence, stating that not only did he do good service during the abortive defence of Rangoon when he dispatched Force Viper, 100 Royal Marines formed from MNBDO men recovering from scrub typhus (see earlier references to James Alan Thompson). 'The way in which he out-thought the Japanese at Easter 1942 was only what we who served him would have expected'.

43 Dull, *A Battle History*, p. 108.

44 Agar, *Footprints in the Sea*, p. 181.

> They came diving at us out of the sun in waves of three. The first made straight for the *Cornwall* scoring a hit aft in that ship within seconds of being sighted. The next three came straight for us. We could see the bombs falling, black and shiny, blunt-nosed 1000-pounders … There followed afterwards, in quick succession, a series of thuds and heavy thumps as further bombs exploded in the engine and boiler rooms … The ship kept on turning to starboard with the steering gear jammed, and I could see little from the bridge through the inferno of smoke and fire. The few guns we had left were firing intermittently but most were out of action after the first two bombs hit. There followed a frightful explosion as a bomb reached one of our magazines.[45]

Cornwall's summary of service dryly recorded that 'the cruisers were steaming at 27½ knots on 5 April when an enemy aircraft was sighted by CORNWALL. At 1.30pm 50 dive bombers attacked down sun and CORNWALL, without any air cover, was repeatedly hit within a few minutes and heeled over and sank in position 1° 55' N: 77° 56' E.[46] It was the same story for *Dorsetshire*, and only eight minutes elapsed between the first attack and the cruiser slipping beneath the waves.[47] Japanese airman took a dramatic picture of both ships on fire, their wakes describing desperate evasive manoeuvres.[48] 'In terms of technique, these sinkings have been recognized generally as among the most professional operations carried out by carrier aircraft during the whole war'.[49] From aboard *Warspite*, Edwards 'saw a column of smoke' in the cruisers' bearing about the time that aircraft were noticed on the radar. At 4:30pm reports were received of an enemy formation including carriers 120 miles north.[50] The Eastern Fleet attempted to get contact with this force, but failed. If the Japanese aircraft had been ordered to carry on and search in the direction in which the cruisers had been heading, they would have discovered the Eastern Fleet. Fortunately, they did not.

Somerville sent *Enterprise*, *Paladin*, and *Panther* to pick up survivors, assisted by air searches and a fighter escort. 'We left Colombo with 800 men', wrote Agar; 'when the ship sank there must have been well over 500 in the water. Of these we could not have lost more than sixteen'.[51] *Cornwall* lost ten officers and 180 ratings. In total, 424 men died but over 1,122 survivors were rescued by the three ships and taken to Addu Atoll. After the war, Somerville offered a private view on his thinking at this juncture. In a letter to his former deputy Ralph Edwards he said: 'I felt we must go back and pick up the cruiser boys but once we'd got clear my only idea was to "eff" off out of it as soon as possible. Nelson just turned in his grave but otherwise took no notice'.[52]

45 Ibid., p. 182.
46 NHB, 'Summary of service'. Dimbleby's account of *Cornwall*'s final fight appears in chapter 5, 'Japanese Easter Eggs', in *Turns of Fate*.
47 Ibid., pp. 182-84, for Agar's description of the action.
48 See 'HMS *Dorsetshire* and HMS *Cornwall* Sunk', at http://ww2today.com/5th-april-1942-hms-dorsetshire-and-hms-cornwall-sunk
49 Willmott, *Empires in the Balance*, p. 444. But Willmott does point out the fact that, had the aircraft extended their search in the direction in which *Cornwall* and *Dorestshire* were travelling, which was *away* from the Japanese at high speed, they might have made contacted with Somerville's main force.
50 CAC, Edwards Papers, REDW 2/7, diary, 5/4/42.
51 Agar, *Footprints in the Sea*, p. 188.
52 CAC, Edwards Papers, REDW 2/17, Somerville to Edwards, 21/9/45. Writing from his home, the beautiful mansion of Dinder, Wells, Somerset, where he died in 1949.

Despite these successes, the Japanese hadn't had it all their own way. Back in London General Brooke wrote: 'At any rate the air action over Ceylon was successful yesterday and we downed 27 Japs!', an encouraging, but over-inflated, figure.[53] But there was no denying the sense of enfeeblement that the attack accentuated. As Brooke also recorded, he arrived for his daily meeting with the Chiefs of Staff on the morning of 6 April and 'discovered that most of the Japanese fleet appears to be in the Indian Ocean with our Eastern Fleet retiring westwards. Up to the present no sign of transports [meaning an invasion force]. I don't like the situation much as we are very weak in the Indian Ocean'. The following day, he added: 'I suppose this Empire has never been in such a precarious position throughout its history! I do not like the look of things. And yet a miracle saved us at Dunkirk and we may pull through this time. But I wish I could see more daylight as to how we are to keep going through 1942!'.[54] In a signal to the Admiralty on this fateful day, Layton said that the Eastern Fleet 'faces immediate annihilation'.[55] Though there were contacts reported with submarines and reconnaissance aircraft, 'somehow or other due to the Commander-in-Chief's decision to move Eastward, we dodged them all'.[56] The following day at 4:28am two enemy submarines were located south of the fleet, possibly an enemy patrol covering Addu Atoll. Somerville decided to get out of the area, and the Admiralty signalled to suggest that the 'R' class battleships retire to the safety of the Kilindini naval base in Mombasa. It had been a close run thing, and Somerville had nearly risked it all. But at one point, though he didn't know it, he had been 'superbly placed for a night attack' which might have sent the Japanese limping home.[57]

The cruise of of Vice Admiral Ozawa's Malaya Force

In conjunction with Nagumo's raid on Colombo, Ozawa's Malaya Force, centred around the light carrier *Ryujo*, attacked shipping and shore targets in India. Assisted by flying-boats operating from the Andamans, Ozawa sortied from Mergui in Burma on 1 April and manoeuvred between the Andaman and Nicobar Islands from 2 to 4 April in order to match Nagumo's schedule, before dividing into three forces and launching simultaneous attacks on shipping, the majority occurring on 6 April. The Northern Force found ships to sink, despite attempts by the British to halt east coast convoys. It patrolled the northern Indian coast for 200 miles, south from Calcutta. The Central Force scoured the coast from Vizagapatam north, attacking shipping, while the Southern Force worked the area off Cocanada.

Ozawa's ships, Somerville lamented, 'have been roaring up the Bay of Bengal and sinking merchant ships right and left, and I can do nothing'.[58] In just one sequence on 6 April, the Japanese fleet intercepted an unescorted British convoy and sank 11 ships in under two hours. In total, Ozawa's brief foray destroyed 23 merchant ships (112,000 tons) and bombarded

53 Alanbooke, *War Diaries, 1939-1945*, diary, 6/4/42, p. 245.
54 Ibid.
55 Ibid., diary, 6/4/42.
56 CAC, Edwards Papers, REDW 2/7, diary, 6/4/42.
57 Boyd, *The Royal Navy in Eastern Waters*, p. 378.
58 Simpson (ed.), *The Somerville Papers*, to wife, 6/4/42, p. 401.

Cocanada and Vizagapatam.[59] His force wrought havoc among the unescorted and unprotected merchantmen which had scattered south from Calcutta and other eastern ports to avoid being attacked in harbour. In addition, the five-strong submarine force torpedoed a further five British ships off the west coast of India (32,000 tons), and shipping along both of the subcontinent's coastlines was brought to a standstill. Shore bombardment from the Japanese ships together with the destruction of so many merchantmen within sight of land, depositing corpses and survivors on the beaches, caused much alarm.

John Simpson was in the Bay of Bengal aboard the Norwegian tanker *Elsa* when Malaya Force struck.[60]

> It was dawn. I woke up to the noises of shellfire. I looked out towards the horizon and saw guns flashing on a Japanese cruiser. I actually saw holes appearing in the decks, as the shells were arriving quite accurately … The Second Mate was organizing lowering of the lifeboat. It all happened so quickly. The main concern was to get off this explosive vessel. Fortunately we were not carrying aviation spirit on that occasion – the ship had been condemned in Abadan for carrying aviation fuel, and they loaded power kerosene, six thousand tons, and we had discharged some at Colombo, and some at Madras. The rest was for Calcutta, but we never got there.
>
> When the attack was over the Japanese ships steamed past us with all the ratings lined up on the deck as if they were on review. We all thought they would machine-gun us for sure, the Norwegians thought that, and everybody started holding the gunwale of the boat, watching for the machine-gun fire, because you can see the shots landing before the bullets get to you, and dive into the water.[61]

'But nothing happened', Simpson continued with enviable understatement, 'which I thought was very good'. They sailed overnight and sighted land, coming ashore in Orissa.[62]

When the bombs fell on Cocanda and Vizagapatam – the first to fall on Indian soil – alarm among the local population became panic. This spread to Madras, where an exodus began after an air raid warning on 7 April. The governor advised people to leave if they could, and the Government Secretariat withdrew inland. The Indian Army's Southern Command ordered the 19th Division to concentrate to defend the city, and the civil and military authorities began to immobilize the port and dislocate the railways. Having been driven ignominiously from South-east Asia and fleeing from Burma, the foundations of the Raj were shaking. With Colombo

59 Dull, *A Battle History*, pp. 110-11.

60 *Elsa* was an Indian Ocean veteran: 'We had made several trips from Australia to Sumatra and Singapore, evacuating stocks of aviation fuel from Singapore to the Dutch East Indies ahead of the advancing Japanese. On the last of these voyages the Japanese got to Singapore first, so we diverted to Sumatra. We loaded at Palembang in Sumatra and headed for Batavia, Java. We were in a convoy of six Norwegian tankers. Three were sunk and two others were hit by Japanese bombs. We were the slowest ship, but we were the ones who got through to Batavia unscathed. After unloading the fuel, we set sail for the Persian Gulf via Sunda Strait, arriving at Abadan'.

61 See 'M/T *Elsa*' at https://www.warsailors.com/singleships/elsa.html

62 They were then sent to Calcutta, where they remained for about three weeks as the port was closed due to enemy action before travelling on to Bombay. Here they joined the *Dominion Monarch* bound for Sydney, arriving off Sydney Head to find it also was now under attack from Japanese submarines.

still wreathed in smoke, Indian soil violated, and sinkings occurring with disturbing frequency, Somerville's frustration was monumental. 'I can do nothing ... This is the biggest problem I've ever had to face and I look back with longing to what now appears to be the carefree days I had in Force H' in the Mediterranean.[63]

The Eastern Fleet's redeployment

After Somerville had 'effed off' out of Nagumo's way, Force A and B headed for Addu. Here they docked on 8 April after conducting 'very heavy' air searches of the base first in case the Japanese had discovered it and deployed submarines to lie in wait. Somerville and his senior advisers 'racked our brains as to where to go next'.[64] Ceylon, by Admiralty instruction, was out of the question, and so the Eastern Fleet's home bases were no longer available, temporarily at least. Bombay was too small for the whole fleet, Addu too dangerous because it was still insufficiently protected. The Admiralty had suggested Mombasa as an alternative. In the end, a pocket atlas was produced, and the fleet's top brass decided on the mouth of the Persian Gulf as a temporary measure. But when it was discovered that it had a summer temperature of 100 degrees, Mombasa became the only possibility. We 'were not at all clear whether we could fit the fleet in that small harbour', wrote Edwards, and it proved to be 'the devil of a squeeze'.[65] So now Willis's 'Slow Division', Force B, retreated to Kenya to focus on convoy protection, sailing at 2am on 9 April, while Somerville and the 'Fast Division', Force A, would loiter for the time being around India and Ceylon in case of another Japanese sortie. Vice Admiral Willis wrote:

> Well the outcome of it all is that the Admiralty suggested and James [Somerville] felt obliged to concur that a temporary withdrawal westward was necessary until reinforcements arrive particularly more and better aircraft... So here we are naval strategy dominated once AGAIN by the air or as usual the lack of it... The defenceless Addu is threatened by carrier borne air attack, so I've been sent with 3rd BS [Battle Squadron] some destroyers and 2 of the old 6 inch cruisers to Mombasa – there being no other place bar Aden that can take a battleship – and am on my way there now. James is on his way to Bombay to see Wavell, and then I think intends to 'rove' with the carriers hoping for more and better aircraft.[66]

Somerville intended to cruise off the Maldives in anticipation of another Japanese strike on Ceylon. He told the Admiralty that unless the Eastern Fleet was reinforced, there 'is really nothing to stop the Japanese establishing themselves in East India and eventually Ceylon'.[67] At sea aboard his flagship, he dispatched a stark appreciation of affairs in the light of the Colombo raid and the naval losses sustained at sea.

63 Somerville
64 Ibid., 7/4/42.
65 Ibid.
66 CAC, Willis Papers, 5/5, letter to Cunningham, 10/4/42.
67 CAC, Edwards Papers, REDW 2/7, 8/4/42.

> Enemy has complete command of Bay of Bengal and can, at his selected moment, obtain local command of the waters S and SW of Ceylon. Our present naval forces and land-based forces are quite inadequate to dispute this command. The Battlefleet is slow, out-gunned and of short endurance. Its available carrier-borne air protection would be of little use against repeated air attack on the scale used against the 8" cruisers [*Cornwall* and *Dorsetshire*]. There is little security against air or surface attacks at our naval bases in Ceylon and none at Addu.[68]

He also reported the dispatch of Force B to East Africa 'where they can protect Middle East and Persian Gulf communications and do some collective training. They are only a liability in this area at present'. Somerville had witnessed for himself the awesome power of Japanese carrier-borne aviation. Force A would continue operating in the Indian Ocean using Colombo, Addu, Bombay, the Seychelles, Mauritius and occasionally East African ports as fuelling bases, with Bombay and Durban employed as maintenance bases. Its object would be

> to deter enemy from attacking our communications in Indian Ocean with light forces and make it necessary for him to employ substantial forces for this purpose ... Operations of Force A in Colombo-Addu area will be attended by some risks. This, I consider, must be accepted, but by constantly changing fuelling bases it should be difficult for the enemy to locate this force.[69]

The time and effort expended in creating a network of scattered maritime bases across the Indian Ocean region now proved a worthwhile investment. It was also fortunate that, in the shape of Bombay, Durban, and Mombasa, Britain enjoyed possession of some established bases. It was to the Indian port that Somerville now turned, and four hours after Force B had left for Kilindini, at 6am on 9 April Somerville led Force A towards Bombay. Soon after, *Paladin* closed *Warspite* and a group of staff officers were transferred to the destroyer. They were to go to Colombo to inform the deputy commander of Somerville's decisions, and to tell him to make arrangements to transfer the Eastern Fleet's administrative staff and secretariat to Kilindini. The retreat was on, and this meant, among other things, that the Eastern Fleet was not around to disrupt Nagumo when he launched a second raid on Ceylon.

The raid on Trincomalee and destruction of *Hermes*

On the afternoon of 8 April a 240 Squadron Catalina resighted Nagumo's fleet 400 miles east of Ceylon, and Trincomalee was cleared of shipping. Early the following morning, at 7:16am, a fading report was received from a 413 Squadron Catalina reporting a large enemy force about 200 miles from Trincomalee. The aircraft was shot down and the crew killed by Zeros from *Hiryu*. The RAF's official report records that the attacking aircraft were seen on radar plots

68 Simpson (ed.), *The Somerville Papers*, to Admiralty from aboard *Warspite*, 8/4/42, p. 403.
69 Ibid.

at 5:20am, and that China Bay was bombed at 7:25am by 50-plus bombers and fighters.[70] The codebreakers were on it too, and FECB at HMS *Anderson* 'was able to provide intelligence on the size, composition, movement, and attack plans of the Japanese task force, but it could not make up for the disparity in capabilities'.[71]

Approximately 130 Japanese aircraft struck the port the following day based around 91 Kate bombers. Met by anti-aircraft fire and the guns of the monitor *Erebus*, and Hurricanes of 261 Squadron, they destroying ships, buildings, and an oil tank, the latter apparently destroyed in kamikaze fashion and burning for days after. Fortunately, their pattern bombing narrowly missed the naval ammunition stores. 'A section of three Hurricanes on Dawn Patrol vectored to meet the raiders', and again a dogfight developed in which the British came off worse, having fewer and less capable aircraft, while the bombers concentrated on their targets. Somerville received the red warning from Trincomalee, indicating that it was being attacked.

The raid damaged *Erebus* and partially sank the ship *Sagaing*, which had arrived from Britain as recently as 4 April carrying Hurricanes, mines, and thousands of depth charges and lashings of beer and whisky. It now was the turn of a small force of British ships cleared from the port the previous day and that was in position about 10 miles off the coast. 'On the morning of 9 April, the Colombo [intelligence] station intercepted a signal from a Japanese reconnaissance floatplane informing Nagumo that it had sighted the *Hermes* and its companions'.[72] Though Trincomalee harbour was bristling with anti-aircraft guns and defences which included live torpedoes tied to buoys intended to disrupt an enemy landing, the view was taken that the ships were safer at sea given the likely strength of any Japanese attack. *Hermes* therefore sailed, without her compliment of Swordfish, which had been disembarked at the China Bay air station and were to be kept ashore to act as a striking force.

Stan Curtis was aboard *Hermes*.

> The dawn came up that morning as it only can over the Indian Ocean, the sky filled with red and gold streaks. During the morning watch our Captain spoke to us over the Tannoy system, he read out a signal he had received from the C-in-C, to the effect that the Japanese had sighted us and we could expect to be attacked at any time, but that fighter aircraft were being sent for our protection, 'Now, repeat now'. We waited and waited but no aircraft put in an appearance, only Japanese. At 10.30 am we had the report, 'Enemy aircraft in sight' and immediately our AA opened up. *Hermes* was a sitting duck, our anti-aircraft defence was inadequate against the number of dive bombers that attacked us, there were eighty-five of them. Zero dive bombers each carrying a 250-pound bomb that was delay fused, they went through our flight deck (we had no armour plating) exploding below decks.

70 BL, Layton Papers, 74802, Air Staff Commander-in-Chief Ceylon, 'Japanese Attack on Trincomalee' and 'Enemy Air Raid on China Bay 9 April 1942', 24/7/42.

71 Ball, *Signals Intelligence*, p. 75.

72 Ibid. The British carrier, last encountered in the western region of the Indian Ocean supporting operations in Africa and the Persian Gulf, had been called upon to operate in the eastern Indian Ocean following Japan's entry into the expanding conflict. When ABDA Command was dissolved on 25 February, ANZAC Command was formed under Vice Admiral H. F. Leary of the United States Navy, comprising the survivors of the Battle of the Java Sea. *Hermes* was sent to reinforce him along with her escort *Vampire*, leaving off patrol duties from Trincomalee.

The planes dived out of the sun and apart from a few near misses every bomb was on target, they went through our flight deck like sticking your finger through tissue paper causing absolute destruction below decks. One of the first casualties was our forward lift, it received a direct hit, was blown ten feet in the air to land upside down on the flight deck eventually sliding into the sea, all personnel in that area were instantly killed. Wave after wave of these aircraft came at us. Our Captain was doing his best to dodge the bombs by using the speed of the ship. We were moving flat out at about 20-25 knots shuttering from stem to stern, not only from the speed, but from the continual pounding we were getting from those little 'Sons of Nippon' up in the air. Where oh where was our fighter cover, we never did get any [the squadron ordered to the ship's defence failed to receive the message in time; eight Fulmars of 806 Squadron were ordered to provide cover. They arrived in time to meet the enemy but not to stop the ships being sunk.]

The AA gun crews did a magnificent job ... The planes at the end of their dive flew along the flight deck to drop their bombs and because the guns could not be fired at a low angle, all the 5.5's, mine included, had orders to elevate to the maximum so that as the ship slewed from side to side to fire at will hoping that the shrapnel from the shells would cause some damage to the never ending stream of bombers that were hurtling down out of the sun to tear the guts out of my ship that had been my home for the past three years.

Suddenly there was an almighty explosion that seemed to lift us out the water, the after magazine had gone up, then another, this time above us on the starboard side. From that moment onwards we had no further communication with the bridge which had received a direct hit, as a result of that our Captain and all the bridge personnel were killed. Only about fifteen minutes had passed since the start of the action and the ship was already listing to port, fires were raging in the hangar, she was on fire from stem to stern, just aft of my gun position was the galley, that received a direct hit also, minutes later we had a near miss alongside our gun, talk about a tidal wave coming aboard, our crew were flung yards, tossed like corks on a pond ... We were lucky; our gun was the only one that did not get hit.

At this stage *Hermes* had a very heavy list to port and it was obvious that she was about to sink. As the sea was now only feet below our gun deck I gave the order, 'Over the side lads, every man for himself, good luck to you all'. Abandon ship had previously been given by word of mouth, the lads went over the side and I followed, hitting the water at 1100 hours, this is the time my wristwatch stopped.

As she was sinking the Japs were still dropping bombs on her and machine gunning the lads in the water. In the water I swam away from the ship as fast as I could, the ship still had way on and I wanted to get clear of the screws and also because bombs were still exploding close to the ship, the force of the explosion would rupture your stomach, quite a few of the lads were lost in this way after surviving Dante's inferno aboard, so it was head down and away.[73]

73 BBC 'World War Two People's War' oral history archive, Stan Curtis, 'The Sinking of HMS *Hermes*', A4667826. Rex Morgan's extraordinary *The* Hermes *Adventure* contains a superb collection of interviews with *Hermes* survivors and others associated with the ship – including Japanese pilots – as well as contemporary letters. It also features the story of a 1982 wreck dive involving Charles Morgan and the Sri Lankan navy. The text is at least matched by the unique collection of photographs, many taken by Morgan's father, Sub Lieutenant Charles Morgan, an official navy photographer, who served

The attack on *Hermes* was witnessed by men at action stations aboard *Vampire*. One moment, the carrier seemed fine, the next it had been penetrated by bombs and was exploding, 'converted into a cratered mess of smoke and flame and bent-up sticks, like a rumpled crow's nest'.[74] The Japanese lost four or five aircraft in the attack, but the British aircraft ordered from Ratmalana arrived after the carrier had slipped beneath the waves. According to Loveridge, this was because the telephone line from Colombo to Ratmalana had been destroyed in the Colombo raid, and so the message had to be sent by dispatch rider.[75] Within sight of Ceylon's shoreline throughout the entire engagement, the venerable carrier had been steaming at over 25 knots as she tried to avoid the bombs. According to the FECB intelligence summary 'Air Attacks on HM Ships *Hermes* and *Vampire*, 9 April 1942', the attack commenced at 10:35am. Sixty to 70 enemy aircraft 'relentlessly and fearlessly' attacked in 'vics', standard V-shape formations. *Hermes* was sunk by 10:55am, hit by at least 40 bombs, dramatic aerial photographs taken by Japanese airmen showing her almost driving down into the sea, her funnel still steaming. Moving at full speed and preparing to fight for her life, *Vampire* was the next target.[76] She was down by 11:05am, broken in two, her ensign the last thing to submerge. Half an hour's brisk and deadly work, the attack was similar to that which had been visited upon the heavy cruisers four days earlier.[77] The corvette *Hollyhock* was 30 miles south-south east of Batticaloa, escorting the Royal Fleet Auxiliary tanker *Athelstane*, and they were seen and sunk too. So too was the tanker *British Sergeant*, dispatched off Elephant Point.[78] Captain Onslow, 18 officers, and 288 members of *Hermes*'s crew lost their lives, along with nine from *Vampire* and 53 from *Hollyhock*. The hospital ship *Vita* later arrived on the scene, and 590 survivors were collected and taken to Colombo.

Alfred Pieres, the *Daily Mail* Special Correspondent in Colombo, interviewed survivors and reported the conversation in his article 'Bombs Set *Hermes* on Fire'.[79] Two sub-lieutenants

> described to me today the sinking of their ship by Japanese bombers off the east coast of Ceylon on Thursday morning. The officers, one a Londoner and the other from Essex, are now in the naval hospital at Colombo. They told me that the battle lasted some time and the *Hermes* was all the time in sight of land. As soon as action stations were sounded three planes were seen on the starboard beam. The ships AA guns and pom-poms opened up, but the Jap planes flew threw the barrage, unloosed a stick of bombs, then dive-bombed and machine-gunned the ship.
>
> Their bombs exhausted, they made off, and then the attack really developed. Wave after wave of planes in formation of six and three came over. 'Their bombing was pretty deadly', one of the lieutenants told me. 'Good enough, at any rate, to score several hits. We caught

aboard the ship and took the historic photographs of *Hermes* last moments afloat, putting the film in his shorts pocket before jumping off the flight deck into the Indian Ocean. See chapters 5 to 11, 'Tropical Patrols', 'Attack on Ceylon', 'The Last Night of *Hermes*', 'The Sinking', 'Abandon Ship', 'Hours in the Ocean', and 'On the Hospital Ship'.

74 Macdonnell, *Valiant Occasions*, p. 105.

75 Bryant, F7-15/2, Loveridge to Arthur Bryant, November 1957.

76 Macdonnell describes *Vampire* as *Hermes*'s 'crash-destroyer', part of her function being to rescue ditched pilots. See Chapter 8, 'Exit *Vampire* – Fighting', in Macdonnell, *Valiant Occasions*.

77 BL, Layton Papers, 74802, 'Air Attacks on HM Ships *Hermes* and *Vampire*, 9 April 1942'.

78 At the start of the month *Hollyhock* had been minelaying in the Palk Strait.

79 BBC 'World War Two People's War' oral history archive, Judie James, U2300517.

> fire and started blazing furiously. The one thing we expected, however, did not materialize. There were no torpedoes. Some of the raiders came in low despite our AA fire. They paid for their audacity. We reckon that at least four can never have reached their bases. We saw them being smacked good and hearty, and three staggering away. One came hurtling down into the sea.[80]

Other members of the carrier's crew recovering in Ceylon's military hospitals and hotels adopted a more vindictive view of proceedings. Joan Gottelier, working at Naval Headquarters Colombo, remembers visiting survivors in hospital. The refrain 'Bloody butcher Layton' was a common one, referring to the decision to send *Hermes* to sea without her aircraft.[81] She was the first carrier ever sunk by the aircraft of another carrier, just as *Prince of Wales* and *Repulse* had gained the distinction of being the first battleships sunk from the air.

The loss of *Hermes* troubled many people. The fact that she was dispatched from Trincomalee without her aircraft raised eyebrows, as did the order that she should remain close to the island. Reflecting on the loss, Agar wrote that she was ordered to sail and hug the coastline 'though how an aircraft carrier can disappear from view against the background of a low coastline has never been explained'. Back in Britain Henry Walker's daughter remembers

> sitting having my breakfast, listening to the 0800 news bulletin with my mother when the BBC news reader announced that news was just coming in that the *Hermes* was under heavy attack ten miles off the coast of Ceylon, but that more news would follow. I remember that morning so well, it was an awful time for my dear mother and my two brothers, but I went to work with a heavy heart and tears, but with the words of my brave mother ringing in my ears: 'Now don't you worry you know your dad's a great swimmer and ten miles is nothing to him, he will be safe I'm sure … It was about eight weeks before we heard from the War Office that my dad had been officially reported as missing presumed drowned at sea.[82]

The Japanese success against the ships of the Royal Navy dismayed the sailors of the Eastern Fleet, already frustrated by their apparent inability to strike the enemy, viewed by many as upstarts. Sailors aboard *Ramillies* had been 'staggered' to learn of the loss of *Cornwall* and *Dorsetshire*, and when they learned that *Hermes* and *Vampire* had also succumbed to 'fierce air attack', came to the conclusion that 'things were not sounding so good'. Yet 'morale didn't sink too much, men had died who some of my mates knew and I think the main feeling was one of revenge'.[83]

Somerville vented his anger in a letter to his wife in which he described the destruction of *Hermes*.

80 Ibid.

81 Joan Gottelier interview with the author, 1999. It had in fact been Arbuthnot's decision to sail the warships from Trincomalee, and Layton was highly critical of his decision.

82 BBC 'World War Two People's War' oral history archive, Henry Walker, 'HMS *Victory* and HMS *Hermes*', A7464297.

83 BBC 'World War Two People's War' oral history archive, Thomas Russell, chapter 19, 'Approach of the Storm'.

> We are having a hell of a time and no mistake – everything going against us at present and here I am quite unable to do anything to strike back. The situation is damned serious. If we only had a fraction of the hundreds of bomber that go from the UK to Germany every night out here it would alter the whole picture … The people at home don't seem to take any notice of the appreciations one sends them and it really looks as though we might lose India for the sake of a handful of aircraft and one or two decent ships.[84]

Other senior commanders made exactly the same point. Wavell wrote that it 'gave us pause when we saw 1000 bomber raid on Germany, as we manage with only a score of light bombers to meet the Japanese'.[85] Willis, Somerville's second in command, wrote to Cunningham in the Mediterranean: 'If only some of the hundreds of bombers who fly over Germany (and often fail to do anything because of the weather) had been torpedo aircraft and dive-bombers the old Empire would be in a better condition than it is now'.[86]

When the British had used their aircraft against the Japanese fleet, the results were indifferent. On the day of the Trincomalee raid, Blenheims from 11 Squadron attacked the Japanese fleet, concentrating on the carriers, particularly Nagumo's flagship, *Akagi*. They were ordered up at 7:40am, just as the attack on the port was broken off by the Japanese fighters and bombers. Eleven took off half an hour later, two having to turn back. It was over a two hour flight to the Japanese fleet, and the bombers took the Japanese by surprise. But it didn't take long for the Zeros to get airborne, which accounted for three of the Blenheims for the loss of one of their own. The remaining five RAF aircraft then set out for the return journey, though were unfortunate to counter enemy Vals and Zeros returning from the attack on *Hermes*. Another Blenheim was shot down and crashed on a beach, in return for another Zero. Five of the original nine Blenheims made it home to the airbase at Colombo racecourse, all badly battle damaged and unserviceable. Though their attack had been unsuccessful, they had come very close to hitting some of the carriers having penetrated the fleet's airspace, a fact that should have given the increasingly confident Japanese pause for thought.

Willis was not impressed by the general air situation:

> Some Blenheims – which is all the Air Staff with their usual strategic foresight, have managed to put there for attacking sea targets – attacked the carriers. Half were shot down but they claim some near misses … So here we are – Naval Strategy dominated once AGAIN by the air or as usual the lack of it … And still the RAF haven't got a Dive Bomber or Torpedo aircraft that's any good.[87]

He continued: 'Out of it all emerges that the Japanese Fleet Air Arm is much superior to us in numbers, carrier for carrier, speed range and performance and therefore we're in a pretty fair mess'.[88] Regarding the decision to retire to Mombasa, he wrote: 'This temporary strategical withdrawal – for it can be called no less – is depressing but very necessary til we can be rein-

84 Somerville.
85 Quote untraced.
86 Roskill, *Churchill and the Admirals*, p. 206.
87 CAC, Willis Papers, 5/5, letter, 10/4/42.
88 Ibid.

forced, particularly the Fleet Air Arm. Of course this concedes control of the Bay of Bengal to enemy and uncovers Ceylon and increases the threat to India. But as things are there seems no alternative'.[89]

* * *

In the space of five days two modern cruisers, an aircraft carrier, two destroyers, a corvette, a monitor, an armed merchant cruiser, a submarine depot ship, and 23 merchant vessels had been sunk or damaged, and at least 40 aircraft destroyed. Nearly a thousand servicemen had perished, the majority from the cruisers and the carrier. Civilians in coastal areas of of Ceylon and India had been panicked and the evacuation of white civilians to South Africa and elsewhere was given new impetus. Installations had been damaged, and at least a hundred civilians killed by shrapnel and falling masonry. Thousands of port workers fled, many never returning. The other major effect of the raid was economic loss caused by sea lane disruption. Malaya Force's cruise along the Indian coast paralyzed shipping using Calcutta and other ports, and the raids on Ceylon led to the highest war-risk rates yet quoted for shipping goods to New York, Calcutta, Madras, and Colombo.

On the plus side, by accident as much as design, and the fact of not being able to give battle, Somerville had saved his fleet carriers and battleships, and the wisdom of investing in the construction of a main fleet anchorage at Addu Atoll was revealed. Layton's assessment was that the raids showed the Japanese that they need not worry about the British on the western flanks of their new empire. But though their losses had been relatively small, they had not achieved the hoped-for strategic victory, which could only have been delivered if they had succeeded in sinking or crippling the capital units of the Eastern Fleet. The pilots who attacked Ceylon were surprised on three accounts: first, the harbours had not contained the Eastern Fleet, to be decimated like the Americans at Pearl Harbor; secondly, the bombers had encountered accurate and heavy fire from anti-aircraft guns; and, finally, they had come under fire from modern fighters for the first time in their brief history of conquest. The first noticeable loss of Japanese aircraft in the face of modern fighters manned by experienced pilots had dented the spell of invincibility which they had enjoyed over the last four months. For the first time the Japanese had run up against 'substantial and organized opposition in the air over their objectives and, significantly, the Japanese carriers had themselves been bombed [and were] ... very lucky to escape unscathed'.[90] Though the balance of losses were in favour of the Japanese, the results obtained were poor – five fleet carriers and about 300 bomber missions accounting for just nine warships. 'In addition, the Japanese air losses were heavy in terms of the forces available and they were large in relation to the losses incurred by the Japanese up to that time. The fact that over Colombo the Japanese encountered opposition from Hurricanes and Fulmars suggested harder going in the future'.[91]

89 CAC, Willis Papers, 5/5, Willis to Vice Admiral H. R. Moore, Vice Chief of the Naval Staff.
90 Ibid., p. 446.
91 Ibid. If Marder's figures are accurate, and the Japanese did lose thirty-three aircraft, this represents nearly 10 per cent of the aircraft aboard the carriers, a significant proportion. A. Marder, *Old Friends, New Enemies*, volume 2, pp. 134-36. Willmott claims the Japanese lost 29, the British 37. *Empires in the Balance*, p. 445. Boyd has the figure as 18 destroyed and 'about' 31 damaged. *The Royal Navy in*

After disasters against the Japanese elsewhere, the British could be forgiven for seeing this as something of a success, not unlike the sentiments elicited by the Dunkirk evacuations. But they weren't so foolish. While there might have been a silver lining or two, commanders on the ground and their masters back in London could see the dark clouds clearly enough. Angus Britts argues that the events of 4-9 April represented the 'operational level culmination of a two-decade process which resulted in the Royal Navy possessing an insufficiently-developed fleet-support air arm which was no match for the Imperial Japanese Navy's modern aerial armada'.[92] As such it was unable to deal with the 'rapid evolution in operational method' that the Japanese had mastered.[93] Nagumo's fleet embodied the 'greatest quantum leap in naval warfare since steam power supplanted the days of sail'.[94] It was this brief period in April 1942, Britts claims, that represented Britain's naval eclipse in eastern waters, not the destruction of Force Z the previous December, for all of the latter's 'mythical prominence'.[95] Command at sea had come to reside in 'an effective partnership between a fleet and an air force' and it was the Japanese, not the British, who had perfected this.[96] None of the Royal Navy's previous opponents over four centuries 'had exercised anything approaching the relative degree of tactical and material dominance which the Imperial Japanese Navy here enjoyed over its former mentor'.[97]

As Somerville reported to the Admiralty, he recognized that he could 'only create diversions and false scents, since I am now the poor fox'.[98] The Japanese effectively now had a free hit, and the British could do no more than keep on with the manifold tasks associated with convoy protection while preparing as much as they could and hoping for the best. Fortunately the bluff was never called, as the Japanese failed to mount any further major operations in the Indian Ocean. And, it was not all gloom. Even at this moment of apparent Japanese invincibility, the Royal Navy and its allies were probing the perimeters of the new Japanese Empire and, most importantly of all, the sea lanes of the western Indian Ocean remained open and Ceylon unconquered. Willmott writes that superficially the Japanese foray was indeed a rampage; the British were overwhelmed and humiliated. But, as was so often the case in this initial phase of the war, the reality of the situation was rather different, and there were certain lessons from the raid that the Japanese would have been well advised to consider carefully'.[99]

Back in London, Churchill registered the fright of this near encounter in the Indian Ocean, writing after the war that 'we had narrowly escaped a disastrous fleet action'.[100] At the time he used the episode to add weight to Britain's strategic objective of getting the Americans to take

Eastern Waters, p. 384. Churchill had the figure at 21 destroyed at Colombo (and 19 British), and 15 at Trincomalee (and 11 British). *Hinge of Fate*, p. 158. Rob Stuart's latest researches moderate these scores downwards, and it would appear that taking both raids together the Japanese lost 12 aircraft destroyed with about 20 damaged.

92 Britts, 'Neglected Skies', p. 6. See his coverage of the Indian Ocean raids in chapter 6, 'Supremacy Surrendered: The Indian Ocean, 4-9 April 1942'.

93 Ibid., p. 11.

94 Ibid., p. 19.

95 Ibid.., p. 13.

96 Ibid., p. 146.

97 Ibid., p. 240.

98 Somerville

99 Willmott, *Empires in the Balance*, p. 442.

100 Churchill, *The Second World War*, volume 4, p. 158.

action to relieve pressure on British forces here – for a defined, temporary period while the British marshalled their resources. As he wrote to Roosevelt on 15 April:

> Until we are able to fight a fleet action there is no reason why the Japanese should not become the dominating factor in the Western Indian Ocean. This would result in the collapse of our whole position in the Middle East; not only because of the interruption of our convoys to the Middle East and India, but also because of the interruption to the oil supplies from Abadan, without which we cannot maintain our position either at sea or on land in the Indian Ocean area. Supplies to Russia via the Persian Gulf would also be cut. With so much of the weight of Japan thrown upon us we have more than we can bear.[101]

Referring to this letter, Somerville told his wife that Churchill had sent the president 'a pretty good stinker pointing out our situation and asking him to reinforce me and do something but I don't flatter myself it will have any effect'.[102]

Wavell, always the first to admit when he might have been mistaken and the judgement of others sounder than his own, wrote:

> It was, as it turned out, fortunate that such defence as was available was mainly in Ceylon, since a Japanese naval raid into Indian waters took place ... Our defending fighters inflicted considerable losses on the enemy aircraft, which did little damage on land but they suffered some losses themselves and the Blenheim squadron, which was sent to attack the Japanese aircraft-carriers, was practically destroyed without accomplishing anything. Had the attack been renewed it would have been difficult to meet ...
>
> This was India's most dangerous hour; our Eastern Fleet was powerless to protect Ceylon or Eastern India; our air strength was negligible; and it was becoming increasingly obvious that our small tired force in Burma was unlikely to be able to hold the enemy, while the absence of communications between Assam and Upper Burma made it impossible to reinforce it.[103]

In the days between the raid on Colombo and the raid on Trincomalee, Kennedy dictated two notes, one on 6 April, the other the following day. They revealed the strategic significance of the Indian Ocean theatre and the interconnectedness of all the theatres of war at this moment. The first was titled 'The relative importance of the Middle East and India'. It reasoned that the Syria-Persia front was essential, and that Britain could not permit the affairs of the Western Desert to dominate strategic thinking:

> From the purely military point of view, the retention of Iraq and Persia is perhaps more important to us than the retention of Egypt. This is so because the holding of these two countries is necessary for the protection of the oil at the head of the Persian Gulf. Without this oil we should be unable to carry on the war in the Indian Ocean.

101 Ibid., pp. 161-62. Churchill also reported to Roosevelt on the situation here on 7 April. Ibid., p. 160.
102 Simpson (ed.), *The Somerville Papers*, p. 414, 22/4/42.
103 Wavell, 'Operations in Eastern Theatre', p. 4664.

> Ceylon: Ceylon is the only base, except Madagascar, from which we can operate a fleet in the Indian Ocean. If Ceylon were lost, and the Japanese were able to establish a fleet and air force there, it would be impossible to defend India. We should not be able to put essential supplies or reinforcements into India. Moreover, it is doubtful whether we could draw supplies of oil from the Persian Gulf if the Japanese were established in Ceylon.
>
> India: If the Japanese were established in India – even on the coast alone – it is doubtful whether we could hold Ceylon. If we held Ceylon, and had lost part of India, it might be possible to maintain our position in the Indian Ocean, but it would be difficult. It is very doubtful whether we could hold the remainder of India if we lost the Calcutta area – the effect on the people, added to the loss of the chief industrial area from which the fighting forces an be supplied, might well cause a complete collapse.
>
> The whole structure is to a great extent interdependent. Without Cyrenaica, we may not be able to hold Malta, although there is a chance that we might. Without Malta, we may not be able to reinforce the Middle East and Far East with aircraft. Without destroying Rommel, we may not be able to free forces to meet a threat from Turkey and the Caucasus. By destroying him, we may get caught, unrecovered, by an attack from the north. If the Russians are not defeated, there is a good prospect of holding the Middle East. If they are defeated, there is a poor prospect of doing so. We may then be reduced to defending the key points only. These are (a) the oil supplies in the Persian Gulf, and (b) Ceylon and such part of India as is necessary to ensure the security of Ceylon. These two are again interdependent. It is probably impossible to hold one without the other.
>
> The threat to all these areas cannot arise simultaneously. The threat to India and Ceylon appears to be the more imminent. Therefore our immediate efforts should be to make them secure. Even now we may be too late. If this is accepted, the Cyrenaican offensive must be postponed, for air forces, essential to it, will have to be sent to India at once.[104]

Kennedy's 'Additional note on the situation' stated that:

> In the Indian Ocean our naval position is fundamentally unsound: our fleet is inferior to the Japanese fleet. At this moment Somerville is seeking to evade them somewhere west of Ceylon. He cannot use his base at Ceylon so long as the Japanese fleet is operating within a few hundred miles of it ... Sooner or later, our Indian Ocean fleet is bound to be sunk unless something can be done to reduce the strength of the Japanese fleet operating there. The only possibility of bringing this about is to drive the Americans to a more active naval policy in the Pacific or, alternatively, to take over the Atlantic, and allow us to reinforce the Indian Ocean.
>
> The Air Force is the other big problem in the Indian Ocean. Wavell estimates that some 70 squadrons are required for India, and about a dozen for Ceylon. He has now about a dozen in India. Ceylon is operating about as many aircraft as it can maintain, but casualties are bound to be heavy. It therefore appears that, while there is some chance of building Ceylon up to its proper air strength, there is no chance whatever of building up India. And Ceylon can only be built up quickly at the expense of the Middle East.

104 Kennedy, *The Business of War*, pp. 219-20.

> I do not see how we can prevent the Japanese getting into India. If they do, it will be a very big commitment for them, and they must be fought hard, and as much of India retained as may be possible. Whether we can hold Ceylon with the Japanese in partial occupation of India is a doubtful matter, but we must try.

Kennedy ended by writing that 'It may turn out to be a lucky stroke that we sent off the IRONCLAD force in good time'.[105] This was a convoy containing a significant body of troops and military vehicles and equipment that, on the day of the Trincomalee raid, departed Freetown bound for the Indian Ocean under the protection of the Royal Navy's Gibraltar-based Force H. It was intended to reinforce India and Ceylon – and use the forces so dispatched to invade Vichy Madagascar on the way. All together, it was a reassuring example of Britain's continued ability to summon resources and deploy them. Kennedy's thinking was that as the Japanese were at that moment rampaging in the Indian Ocean, these reinforcements might represent a stitch in time. Furthermore if Ceylon were lost, Madagascar would become a very important base for a reduced British defence of the sea lanes of the western Indian Ocean.

Willis summarized the situation facing the British in the aftermath of the raids, and the approach that Somerville, his immediate superior, had decided to adopt:

> It appears that for some time our main fleet must be prepared to practice strategical evasion with the object of preventing the enemy knowing precisely where it is for any length of time. He will then find it difficult to plan raids on the fleet in harbour and on our lines of communication; and if he tries he may give us a chance of cutting off a raiding force. We shall need to develop ruses and deceptions to fox the enemy as to the whereabouts of our forces and as to their strength. At present we want to make him think that we are stronger than we are – later we may be able to deceive him in the other direction.[106]

105 Ibid., p. 221.
106 CAC, Willis Papers, 5/5, 'Appreciation of Policy and Strategy in the Eastern Theatre', 8/3/42.

10

Holding the ring: 1942

As previous chapters have shown, the events of March and April 1942 forced a strategic withdrawal in the Indian Ocean. As Burma Army beat its ragged retreat to Manipur, the Eastern Fleet removed its headquarters to distant Mombasa. This completed an eastward migration of British naval resources that had begun with the withdrawal of warships, personnel, base infrastructure, and intelligence-gathering facilities from Hong Kong to Singapore, then from Singapore to Ceylon and now, finally, from Ceylon to Kenya. Though Colombo and Trincomalee remained in use, with Japan in the ascendant discretion was considered the better part of valour. Major General Kennedy wrote that

> We are faced, in a more acute form than ever before, with the problem of trying to do too much with too little. The dispersion, forced upon us, is worse than ever before ... We are in urgent need of some relief in the Indian Ocean, which can only be provided by a more active policy on the part of America.[1]

The overriding imperative now was to keep the Eastern Fleet out of harms way, enabling it to concentrate its main strength on guarding the Indian Ocean sea lanes while also presenting a deterrent should the Japanese decide to mount further raids or expand their new-found territorial portfolio beyond the Bay of Bengal. It was a game of bluff in which, as Somerville put it, he had 'to lie low in one sense but be pretty active in another – keep the old tarts [the unmodernized 'R' class battleships] out of the picture and roar about with the others' (the modernized *Warspite* and fleet carriers). As his Chief of Staff, Ralph Edwards, put it on the day of the Trincomalee raid, outclassed, the Eastern Fleet's job was to remain in being 'whilst doing everything possible to suggest that there was still a considerable British force in these waters'.[2] Nevertheless, the reinforcement programme for the Eastern Fleet was underway, which would enable it to fulfil its task and – should the Japanese reappear – meet them on a more level playing field. In the wake of Force Z's destruction and April's costly brush with the Imperial Japanese Navy, the Eastern Fleet was bloodied but unbowed, and not the spent force that is sometimes portrayed in accounts of the British war east of Suez.

1 Kennedy, *The Business of War*, p. 220.
2 CAC, Edwards Papers, REDW 2/7, 9/4/42.

Addressing the House of Commons on 23 April and reviewing the course of the war with Japan thus far, the prime minister offered a lengthy and detailed overview. He described the fall of Singapore, the loss of the Dutch East Indies, and the actions off Ceylon a fortnight before, and speculated as to what the Japanese might do next. He articulated the frankly exasperating situation that now pertained, in which the Japanese had 'a move either way'.[3] Nevertheless, as Churchill conceded, the war in the Indian Ocean region was 'the lesser war – for such I must regard this fearful struggle against the Japanese'.[4] But while the war against the Japanese in the eastern Indian Ocean might have been considered the 'lesser war', the defence of the sea lanes of the Indian Ocean was acknowledged by London, as we have seen, to be a primary task, to the extent that the Admiralty was prepared to denude the Mediterranean of capital ships in order to boost the Eastern Fleet.[5]

Referring to the efforts currently underway to reinforce the region, and the vital role of sea lanes, Churchill said:

> we have actually moved from this country or from the Middle East across the sea against Japan more than 300,000 men, and we have over 100,000 on salt water at the present time. All these great convoys have hitherto been carried through the perils of mines and U-boat attacks without appreciable loss of any kind since the beginning of the war. I regard this as a prodigy of skill and organization on the part of all those responsible for it.[6]

Stirring though these achievements were, the situation in the Indian Ocean was desperate, and many in London were convinced that the Japanese planned to exploit their advantageous position. One of the papers placed before the Chiefs of Staff stated that 'if the Eastern Fleet is defeated *and* we lose Ceylon, the threat to our sea communications is so serious as to likely lead to a stoppage of military supplies to the Middle East and India'. In simple terms, writes Willmott, the planners were warning that the war would be lost if the Japanese repeated their sortie into the Indian Ocean, overwhelmed the inferior British fleet and occupied Ceylon, 'the strategic keystone of the Indian Ocean'.[7]

In the aftermath of the raids, the Eastern Fleet's Force B concentrated on convoy protection in the western Indian Ocean, whilst Force A roamed more widely, because British interests in the eastern Indian Ocean, such as the build up of forces in India, could not simply be abandoned. Somerville, who spent as much time at sea as possible, understood that greater Axis cooperation and resolve in the region could cripple Britain's position. It is clear from letters to his wife that 'the experiences of 5 to 9 April 1942 shook him more than any other in his flag career'.[8] Nevertheless, as each week passed the Eastern Fleet's chances of successfully achieving its tasks increased, while the window of opportunity that had opened for the Japanese began,

3 Charles Eade (ed.), *Secret Session Speeches by the Right Honourable Winston S. Churchill* (London: Cassell, 1946), p. 47. 'The Fall of Singapore: A Speech to the House of Commons, 23 April 1942', p. 61.
4 Ibid., p. 65.
5 Ibid., pp. 46-75.
6 Ibid., p. 66.
7 Willmott, *The Barrier and the Javelin*, p. 334.
8 Simpson (ed.), *The Somerville Papers*, p. 361.

imperceptibly at first, to close. There was little to stop the Japanese exploiting their advantage, and they would have been well advised to finish the job while they had the chance, destroy the Eastern Fleet, and take possession of the British Empire's ocean crossroads. This certainly appeared to be a likely and logical course of action to policy-makers in London and commanders on the ground trying to second guess their formidable new opponent. On 12 April Edwards wrote that he had heard the prime minister on the BBC talking about the loss of *Hermes* and the two cruisers. 'The news in every part of the world appears to be bad at the moment', he wrote. 'If the Axis are really fighting a war in cooperation with each other, surely the Japanese must come this way rather than continue their thrust towards Australia?'.[9]

Bombay and beyond

Having left Ceylon behind the day before the strike on Trincomalee, Force A's arrival at Bombay on 13 April was very good for morale. The governor of Bombay, Sir Roger Lumley, broadcast reassuring messages to the public, and Somerville and Wavell claimed that the Japanese were far too stretched and now embroiled in the Pacific. Other messages promised that with the Fast Division the British possessed a force with which to strike when the opportunity was suitable. Propaganda was important, as the raids had had a bad effect in India. But the reality was that the Eastern Fleet's vanguard arrived at Bombay with its tail clenched between its legs.[10]

On arrival Somerville went to Government House with his senior staff to meet Wavell and Air Marshal Richard Peirse, Air Officer Commanding in Chief India, General Brodie Haig, commander of the Southern Army, and Lumley. In conference during 13-14 April, Somerville and Wavell, Britain's principal military actors in this vast region, laid their cards on the table. The admiral confirmed that he could neither defend Ceylon or southern India, nor protect shipping in the Bay of Bengal. He also said that practically the whole Eastern Fleet would at some point in the near future be engaged in operations against Madagascar and therefore unavailable in Indian waters.[11] Contrary to this, Somerville reported to the Admiralty, Wavell had assumed that the fleet was capable of dealing with the enemy seaborne threat against south India or Ceylon and had therefore disposed the majority of his available forces, i.e. four division, in north-east India, 'retaining only 1 division, and that partially trained and equipped, for South India'.[12] Explaining the situation, Somerville told Wavell about the strength of the fleet and his planned short term dispositions: 'My intentions are to remain at sea as much as possible and

9 CAC, Edwards Papers, REDW 2/7, 12/4/42.

10 Britts (over)dramatizes this moment: Somerville 'now issued one of the most crucial orders in British naval history. Having spent the better part of the previous nine days conducting a fruitless search for a hostile force in waters to the south of Ceylon, Somerville's Eastern Fleet proceeded to vacate its advanced base at Addu Atoll and withdraw to Bombay. This decision, which had been readily endorsed by the Admiralty later the same afternoon, undoubtedly spared numerous British warships and saved thousands of lives. Yet at the same instant it also marked the finality of British naval superiority. Three hundred years of tradition and reputation were no defence against an opponent whose principal means of waging war at sea was virtually unchallengeable'. Britts, 'Neglected Skies', p. 196.

11 Wavell, 'Operations in Eastern Theatre', p. 4664.

12 'Admiralty War Diaries of World War II', reports of proceedings, 13 April to 1 May 1942.

use unfrequented anchorages in order to make the Japanese uncertain of my movements. It is hoped thereby to deter them from attempting any interference with our Middle East and Indian communications, except with a heavy fleet concentration'.[13]

Force A remained in Bombay for seven days. Liberty ships took hundreds of sailors for a break ashore, hospitality was provided at services and town hall canteens organized by a hospitality committee, and at the Prisoners of War Missions to Seamen canteen. Lord and Lady Lumley also offered entertainment at Government House. On 16 April, at Lumley's request, the carriers put on a display of fighters and Albacores over Bombay. On 19 April Wavell joined Somerville aboard his flagship for the journey to Colombo, the whole of Force A setting sail. Somerville noted in his pocket diary that day: 'So far as I can work out, coast clear but Japs have told Germans they intend to attack in W Indian Ocean. Shall be glad when my reinforcements arrive'.[14] The news was that Churchill had promised to send the battleships *Nelson* and *Rodney*. The four-day sea voyage provided a really important opportunity for the two men to get the measure of each other and sort out their strategy. Somerville wrote that:

> It's given me a good chance to have a really good talk to him and for him to see how the fleet does its stuff at sea and how the air works. We have floods of messages from Winston telling us what a lot of aircraft and ships we have, or are going to have, and how vital it is for this, that and the other to be done. WC's arithmetic must be his weak point because his figures never correspond to ours. So far as I can judge the Japs don't meditate another strike at Ceylon just yet so with luck I ought to get in and away without running into a superior force.[15]

Force A arrived in Colombo on 23 April. As in Bombay, Somerville and Wavell now entered further conferences, this time with the local commanders responsible for the island's defence. They agreed on the following changes: that Somerville's Chief of Staff, Edwards, would become Deputy Commander Eastern Fleet in charge of fleet headquarters, now being moved to Kilindini, and that the position of Commander-in-Chief East Indies would lapse, replaced by a Flag Officer Ceylon.

> Other meetings were also held between my staff and that of Commander in Chief, East Indies, to decide a number of administration problems which had arisen consequent on Colombo being no longer suitable as a main base for the Eastern Fleet. Time did not permit of all these matters being so fully considered as I could have wished. No doubt Their Lordships will fully appreciate the difficulties which have arisen as the result of the new situation created in the Indian Ocean where we are forced to temporarily abandon Ceylon as a fleet base and rely on undefended ports in East Africa and in the islands in the West Indian Ocean, none of which have proper administrative staffs. A considerable amount of administration now undertaken by Commander in Chief, East Indies will of necessity,

13 Simpson (ed.), *The Somerville Papers*, to Wavell, 21/4/42, p. 412.
14 Simpson (ed.), *The Somerville Papers*, pocket diary, 19/4/42, p. 411.
15 Ibid., letter to wife, 22/4/42, pp. 413-14.

> have to be transferred to Kilindini and the building up of a new organization will be a lengthy process and result in inevitable delays.[16]

Things were moving quickly. By nightfall on 23 April Force A had been refueled and was off again. 'I intended', wrote Somerville, 'to sail Force A and ALAUNIA (with Eastern Fleet secretariat and administrative and Special Intelligence Staffs aboard) for Kilindini before daylight, but owning to very heavy rain, low visibility, and congested berthing arrangements, it was necessary to postpone departure until 0700'.[17]

Also on 23 April, Wavell received an appreciation from the Chiefs of Staff saying that if the 'Japanese press boldly westwards without pause for consolidation and are not deterred by offensive activities or threats by Eastern Fleet or American fleet, nor by rapid reinforcement of our air forces in N. E. India, our Indian Empire is in grave danger'.[18] 'May and June seemed likely to be the critical months', wrote Wavell, so he was naturally disturbed to learn that the Eastern Fleet was likely to be diminished for Malta convoy work. Furthermore, that two brigades of the 5th British Division, on the way to reinforce India, were being diverted for the proposed invasion of Madagascar, along with 'an East African brigade [which] I had been led to expect for Ceylon'. Added to this, the Australian government 'was demanding the return to Australia of the two brigades in Ceylon'.[19] As was the way with these things, Peter was being robbed to pay Paul. 'I protested with some vigour', wrote Wavell, who must have been struggling to contain himself, 'but the Minister of Defence [i.e. Churchill], who had to look at the whole picture, decided that the attempt to relieve Malta must be made; that Madagascar should be occupied to secure the sea route to the Middle East and India; and that it was necessary for political reasons to release the Australian brigades' (which in fact remained in Ceylon until August).[20]

On 30 April, Somerville and Force A arrived at the Seychelles, en route for Kilindini. Here they left *Indomitable*, *Paladin*, and *Panther*, due to take part in the imminent invasion of Madagascar. On 2 May the remaining Force A ships left the Seychelles, *Formidable*'s aircraft conducting a search of the Saya de Malha bank and Nazareth bank looking for Japanese forces that might be attempting to capture Diego Suarez in Madagascar themselves. On 4 May Force B refuelled in the Seychelles too, and joined Force A for exercises at sea, the whole fleet entering Kilindini harbour together on 10 May.[21]

Somerville continued to put his energy into preparing his fleet for action against the Japanese while making all possible dispositions to protect trade and military convoys sailing across the Indian Ocean and building up the defences available at its scattered bases. One of his priorities was to turn the naval bases of Ceylon into fortresses which if necessary could defend themselves using air and land forces, and from which the Eastern Fleet could operate in an optimal manner. This was a challenge, and as he wrote to Admiral Sir Dudley North soon after the raids, the

16 'Admiralty War Diaries of World War II', reports of proceedings, 13 April to 1 May 1942.
17 Ibid.
18 Wavell, 'Operations in Eastern Theatre', p. 4665.
19 Ibid.
20 'Events', Wavell wrote, 'proved his judgement correct'. Ibid, p. 4665. Wavell had the enviable habit of formally acknowledging instances in which his judgement had been wrong and that of others right. He did the same in reviewing the pressure placed on him as Commander-in-Chief Middle East to furnish troops to put down Rashid Ali's rebellion in Iraq in spring 1941.
21 'Admiralty War Diaries of World War II', reports of proceedings, 2 May to 10 May 1942.

'problem of starting a Scapa from nothing is terrific. It irks me to know that all the other ships [meaning stations] have lots of facilities & no boats whereas my case is just the reverse'.[22] The scale of work involved was enormous, Trincomalee alone being made ready to properly accommodate – as opposed to simply anchor – a fleet of ten capital ships, ten cruisers, 24 destroyers, three depot ships, ten submarines, and 16 fleet minesweepers.

As Somerville's strategy for the defence of the sea lanes depended on ships being able to put in at disparate ports in order to extend their range, other bases were being developed and afforded greater protection too. In an appreciation of the base infrastructure for the First Sea Lord, for example, he wrote that the Seychelles were 'so important as a fuelling base that I feel it is essential to afford it some degree of protection'.[23] He also decided that Salalah in Oman was required 'to deal with the possibility of Ceylon falling into enemy hands and as base to deal with enemy raiding forces in Arabian Sea'.[24] This was another indicator of the extent of the retreat that had been forced upon him, and of the continuing efforts to protect key shipping lanes. Somerville's natural desire to take the offensive was constantly thwarted by the fact that the demands of other theatres often saw his reinforcements transferred away. As he wrote to Admiral North, '[e]very time I try & get things going with my Fleet something intervenes'.[25] This was to become a depressingly familiar refrain over the course of the next two and a half years. But despite pressing needs elsewhere and the string of defeats and withdrawals to date, Britain and its allies were doing their best to shore things up, to deal with the consequences of Japanese attacks, and to develop forces and bases that would first of all be able to hold the line and then, one day, to support offensive operations. Furthermore, what the British did manage to concentrate in the Indian Ocean was sufficient to present a credible deterrent to the Japanese and, as is the way with seapower, even when units were transferred elsewhere – to the Mediterranean, say – they could always be brought back if an emergency arose. Risks were being run, but in a multi-theatre conflict, the management of risk was the name of the game. A crucial variable in the minds of Churchill and his advisers was the (accurate) estimation that Japan's front line carrier air capabilities were weakening and unlikely to be sustained, and that its reliance on Dutch East Indies oil was going to be a problem given its tanker strength and weak anti-submarine resources.

In some key areas, modern reinforcements were arriving. One of them was carrier aircraft for the FAA. On 15 May the First Lord of the Admiralty, A. V. Alexander, told Churchill that the Eastern Fleet presently had 31 Sea Hurricanes and 43 Martlets. A further 29 Martlets were en route from America due to arrive at Mombasa before the month was out. Thirty-six more were scheduled to arrive by 7 July, then 21 in each of three succeeding months and 33 more by 7 November.[26] It was also in this period that the Eastern Fleet's submarine capabilities began to grow, eventually to become an important offensive arm. On 11 April Layton had said that 'The security of Ceylon as an advanced base will increase considerably if an adequate force of submarines can be provided with which to take the offensive in the Malacca Straits and the Western

22 Simpson (ed.), *The Somerville Papers*, 27/5/42, p. 421.
23 Ibid., to Pound, 29/6/42, pp. 427.
24 Ibid., to Admiralty, 9/5/42, p. 419.
25 Ibid., 27/5/42, p. 421.
26 Simpson (ed.), *The Somerville Papers*, Alexander to Churchill, p. 419.

Approaches to them'.[27] The depot ship *Lucia* had arrived at Colombo from Bombay in March, as had the submarines *Trusty* and *Truant* and seven Dutch boats. *Wuchang*, which had escaped Singapore and the East Indies, was taken over as a submarine crew accommodation ship. In July the Admiralty ordered the Mediterranean Fleet to release seven boats to the Eastern Fleet (*Severn*, *Tally-Ho*, *Templar*, *Tactician*, *Trespasser*, *Taurus*, *Surf*, and *Simon*) and later in the year another depot ship, *Adamant*, arrived at Colombo from Kilindini.

The invasion of Madagascar

Amid the general gloom of 1942, the British Empire's *annus horribilis*, a ray of light appeared in the form of the invasion of Madagascar. Though invariably dubbed a 'sideshow', along with the campaigns in Iran, Iraq, and Syria, it was in fact an action taken with grand strategy firmly in mind, evincing a well-developed grasp of the requirements of the various theatres of war on the part of the British government. Capturing the island was intended to ensure Britain's ability to use the all-important Cape-Mozambique Channel-Red Sea sea lane at this moment of greatest Allied weakness, which, given the situation, was cause enough. It might also prove to be an essential asset should the British position further east crumble, which it would do if the Japanese established themselves in Ceylon. East and west and west and east, the verities of global logistics, dependent on ports and sea lanes, ensured that all things were interrelated, and the Indian Ocean remained a critical enabler of operations elsewhere.

Geography and the proximity of key sea lanes dictated Madagascar's importance. The world's fourth largest island, it had for some time been a source of anxiety to the War Cabinet because of the possibility of enemy occupation, either by force or at the invitation of its Vichy governor.[28] On 1 December 1941 the Chiefs of Staff had reported that in the event of Japan going to war, Vichy was likely to grant the Germans and the Japanese 'use of Madagascar to forward their strategic purpose'.[29] Acting on this advice, when war with Japan commenced a week later, the War Cabinet decided to prepare a force to occupy Diego Suarez, and on 23 December Major General Robert Sturges, who had commanded British forces during the occupation of Iceland, was told that he would lead the land forces. Frustratingly, the plan for what was originally to be known as Operation Bonus was put in abeynance in mid-January in favour of reinforcing

27 Ian Trenowden, *Operations Most Secret: SOE, The Malayan Theatre* (London: William Kimber, 1978), pp. 54-5.

28 For the invasion of Madagascar see Rear Admiral E. N. Syfret, Flag Officer Commanding Force 'F', 'The Capture of Diego Suarez', *Supplement to the London Gazette*, 38225 (1948), despatch submitted to the Lords Commissioners of the Admiralty, 16/6/42. See also Martin Thomas, *The French Empire at War*, Thomas, 'Imperial Backwater or Strategic Outpost? The British Takeover of Vichy Madagascar, 1942', *Historical Journal* 39 (1996); Tim Benbow, 'The British Invasion of Madagascar: Operation Ironclad, May 1942', in T. A. Lovering (ed.), *Amphibious Assault: Manoeuvre from the Sea – Amphibious Operations from the Last Century* (London: Ministry of Defence, 2005); and Benbow, "'Menace' to 'Ironclad': The British Operations against Dakar (1940) and Madagascar (1942)," *Journal of Military History* 75, 3 (2011).

29 Christopher Buckley, *Five Ventures: Iraq-Syria-Persia-Madagascar-Dodecanese* (London: HMSO, 1977), p. 167.

India and supporting a renewed campaign in North Africa.[30] Nevertheless a sizeable combined arms rehearsal took place in February, and on 14 March Sturges was told that the plan had been revived, the same day that Grand Admiral Raeder informed Hitler that the Japanese were eyeing Madagascar once they had occupied Ceylon. Clearly, the British needed to try and get there first, and things began to happen quickly. As Sturges recorded in his official report, he met the commander of the 5th Division, from which he was to borrow a lot of troops, on 17 March; he was interviewed by the Chiefs of Staff regarding his plans on 18 March; and on the following day, he met Churchill. On 21 March he embarked on *Winchester Castle*, which sailed for African shores two days later.[31]

The Madagascar venture demonstrated the challenges associated with force generation, amphibious operations, and strategic prioritization. It was possible because forces were being sent to reinforce the Indian Ocean region – such as the 5th British Division and the carrier *Illustrious* – and showed British capacity to respond to the Japanese challenge. Whether or not the operation got the final nod depended on a range of factors, especially the availability of shipping and requisite ground forces. The passage of a troop convoy destined for Ceylon and India provided the opportunity. Brigadier Francis Festing's 29th Independent Brigade became the nucleus of the force for Madagascar, No. 5 Commando and other units placed under the brigade's command, including a special service squadron of tanks, a Royal Artillery battery, and an anti-aircraft troop. Two brigades of the 5th Division (13th and 17th), destined for India, was also allocated to Festing's force. Festing was appointed Military Assault Commander of Force 121, as the land component was named, under Sturges as Military Commander and Rear Admiral Neville Syfret, commander of the Royal Navy's Gibraltar-based Force H, as Combined Commander. Illustrating the pressure on resources, the 5th Division was urgently needed in India for the defence of Assam and Bengal as Alexander's fighting retreat from Burma drew to a close and India Command sought to slam the door shut along India's border. Things were finally set in motion when, in late March, the troop convoy left Britain, bound for Freetown.

Madagascar was a prime strategic target because of its ports. In Diego Suarez, at the island's northern tip, it boasted a fine natural harbour, capable of safely accommodating any fleet afloat and there were also good harbours at Majunga and Tamatave. Japanese submarine offensives in the Mozambique Channel had recently commenced, and German maritime forces were still active in the region. Smuts remained particularly concerned by the possibility of a Japanese strike against the East African coast which would threaten British territories, disrupt the sea lanes to the Middle East and Far East, and deepen the prospect of the Japanese linking hands with Axis forces further north. Consequently he urged a pre-emptive strike, telling Churchill that Madagascar was 'the key to the safety of the Indian Ocean'.[32] For obvious reasons the South African appreciated the island's strategic value, and realized that nearby Durban might become a principal fleet base for the Royal Navy should Japan come to dominate the Bay of Bengal and the Eastern Fleet's retreat to East Africa last longer than was hoped. The instincts of both leaders told them that resolute action was required. Experiencing a similar strategic impulse, Berlin strongly encouraged Tokyo to seize the island. Pierre Laval, French prime minister from

30 Churchill, *The Second World War*, volume 4, Appendix B, 'List of Code-Names', p. 748.

31 Warren Tute, *The Reluctant Enemies: The Story of the Last War between Britain and France, 1940–1942* (London: William Collins, 1989), p. 203.

32 Thomas, *The French Empire*, 143.

18 April, 'demanded 'a Japanese occupation so that any move made by the English or the de Gaullists might be forestalled'.[33]

In what was to be an innovative joint operation, the land force sent out from Britain was accompanied by a powerful naval force, including battleships and carriers, supported by air units based in South Africa. Most of the warship belonged to Force H, designated Force F for the Madagascar operation. The warships of Force H nominated for the operation accompanied the transport fleet to Freetown, arriving on 6 April and departing for South Africa three days later. Alan Shaw writes that

> At Freetown the men had to remain on board for a full five days whilst powerful naval units assembled – prevented from sailing because of U-boat activity, though this was not the real reason, which was to allow Rear Admiral Neville Syfret, naval commander for the forthcoming invasion of Madagascar, to have his first meeting with his combined operations force to plan the final details of the operation. The *Winchester Castle* was the assault headquarters and *Malaya* the flagship, until the convoy reached Cape Town when *Malaya* was ordered back to the Mediterranean [on 18 April, after she reached Cape Town] and was replaced by *Ramillies* from the Eastern Fleet.[34]

Secrecy was paramount, 'the main participating ships being issued with charts of Burmese waters, during the voyage to South Africa, to disguise their true destination'.[35] The story was put about that the force was destined for operations in the Bay of Bengal aimed at recovering Rangoon. The first ships arrived at Cape Town on 19 April, where the commanders conferred with Smuts. As in other parts of the world, the British benefited from possession of established bases, where the locals were friendly and the infrastructure well-established. In this case, Durban functioned as the invasion fleet's launch pad, and supporting operations were mounted from Eastern Fleet bases at Diego Garcia, Mauritius, Mombasa, and the Seychelles.

The fleet that massed in Durban totalled 46 ships, 86 aircraft, 14,000 soldiers, and 340 vehicles and guns. There were three troopships, five assault ships (including a relatively new innovation, the Landing Ship Tanks *Bachaquero*), six stores and motor transport ships, one hospital ship, an oiler, and two Royal Fleet Auxiliaries. The remainder of the invasion force comprised the warships charged with protecting these vessels and providing air and naval gunfire support for the troops. Alongside ships from Force H, significant units were loaned from the Eastern Fleet. The combined force included the Eastern Fleet battleship *Ramillies* which replaced *Malaya* as flagship, the aircraft carriers *Illustrious* (sailing to join the Eastern Fleet as part of the reinforcement programme, giving Somerville a third fleet carrier) and *Indomitable* embarking 42 fighters and 44 torpedo-strike-reconnaissance aircraft, the cruisers *Devonshire* and *Hermione*, 11 destroyers, six corvettes, and six minesweepers.[36] Additional air power was provided by the South African Air Force, which contributed a wing of 37 aircraft, including Glen Maryland and

33 Buckley, *Five Ventures*, p. 174.

34 BBC 'World War Two People's War' oral history archive, Alan Shaw.

35 John Winser, *British Invasion Fleets: The Mediterranean and Beyond, 1942-1945* (Gravesend: The World Ship Society, 2002), p. 7.

36 Winser claims that the minelayer *Manxman* carried £100,000 in bullion 'for use in effecting French cooperation'. Ibid., p. 46.

Bristol Beaufort bombers.[37] Some of these had been gathering photographic data on Madagascar for some time, and during the course of the campaign they flew over 400 sorties.[38]

While at Durban and with a final decision on the operation still pending, the invasion force made final preparations, the equipment of 17th Brigade, for instance, being tactically restowed, fitness training intensified, and landing craft tested. Sturges moved to the flagship, *Ramillies*, and the combined headquarters of the Assault Force prepared aboard *Keren*. As these preparations were made, Whitehall continued to cogitate: Churchill was all for going ahead while Brooke was of the opinion that the Japanese would not make a move to occupy the island. The CIGS expressed concern that a British attack might in fact persuade the Vichy government to give German forces the run of important bases elsewhere, including Dakar and Bizerta, and the use of French warships; it might also lead to the retaliatory bombing of Gibraltar.

Brooke's concerns were clearly those of the War Office. Kennedy wrote that Madagascar 'had been arranged for one reason and one reason alone: to secure our sea communications round the Cape of Good Hope'.[39] When the expedition had sailed from Britain, the DMO continued, 'the view of the Naval Staff was that it might be necessary to establish a base at Diego Suarez; but they changed their minds more than once while the force was on its way. On 21 April, they stated that Kilindini, Ceylon and Zanzibar would suffice for the control of the Indian Ocean'.[40] Kennedy's opinion was that the case for occupation looked weak unless Ceylon was lost, and the Naval Staff also pointed out that the Japanese could operate in the region from the East Indies and therefore did not need Madagascar as a base.

Given all of this, on 24 April Churchill called the Chiefs of Staff to deliberate on the pros and cons of Ironclad. Time was pressing. Kennedy was against it, for fear of the French being difficult in North Africa, Gibraltar being bombed, and because of the equivocal view of the Naval Staff. Instead, he thought the troops should be sent direct to India where reinforcements were badly needed. But the operation gathered momentum as the invasion fleet sailed south. When it departed, it had been agreed that even though it was on its way, it was not committed. But Churchill showed a tendency to assume that it was, influenced perhaps, Kennedy wrote, by the fact that he had told Roosevelt and Smuts that the operation was on.[41] On 27 April the Defence Committee agreed to postpone a decision until the last possible moment – which would be 3 May – and on the following day Brooke and Kennedy discussed the operation again. Brooke was inclined not to fight against the operation, and his fellow Chiefs, Pound and Portal, were apparently now in favour.[42]

37 See Andre Wessels, 'South Africa and the War against Japan, 1941-1945', *Military History Journal*, 10, 3 (1996).

38 J. A. Clayton, 'The South African Air Force in the Madagascar Campaign 1942', *Military History Journal*, 9, 2 (1992).

39 Kennedy, *The Business of War*, p. 214.

40 Ibid.

41 Looking back on Ironclad, Kennedy wrote: 'A project planned for one purpose sometimes turns out to have its greatest value for another. When, for instance, the Prime Minister insisted on mounting an expedition against Madagascar, in the face of much Service advice, the Service advisers were glad in the end to have been overborne, because of the effect of the expedition's arrival in the Indian Ocean on the relative strengths of the British and Japanese fleets'. Kennedy, *The Business of War*, p. xii.

42 Kennedy, *The Business of War*, p. 215.

Meanwhile, for months prior to the invasion, a clandestine sabotage and reconnaissance outfit had been operating in Madagascar, controlled by SOE. Michael Macoun, the policeman in Tanganyika, was involved in developing a back up and supply base at Dar-es-Salaam, and charted the schooner *Lindi* as part of the preparations.[43] He recalls a schooner carrying Free French supporters escaping from Diego Suarez and making it to Dar-es-Salaam. Some were soldiers, and they brought with them detailed plans of the Diego Suarez defences. While discussions were in motion in Whitehall, SOE was busy running agents from its base in Mauritius. A Franco-Mauritian agent, Percy Meyer, and his wife regularly relayed intelligence by wireless, and in February had even made an attempt to bribe the commander of the Diego Suarez fortress area to give up his post. Secret wireless stations in Mauritius, manned by Franco-Mauritians who supported the British and Free French cause, broadcast pro-Allied propaganda and entertainment shows from a clearing in a sugar cane field.[44] SOE's main mission in the region was based in Cape Town and commanded by Lieutenant Colonel J. E. S. Todd.[45] Under the cover of the Imperial Movement Control Intelligence Section and with an office at naval headquarters in Durban, its principal target was Madagascar. Despite attempts to sway the French authorities, they remained stubbornly loyal to Vichy. Léon Cayla, who had been governor until April 1941, had attempted to ingratiate himself with his superiors in Paris by applying Vichy edicts with particular vigour, even incarcerating those among the colonial administration in Tananarive likely to support the Free French cause. His successor, Armand Annet, continued to stick to the Vichy cause.

Time was passing, and duty called elsewhere for the the assembled ships and men. As the scheduled date for D-day approached, the invasion fleet divided in two. A slow convoy, Convoy Y, left Durban bound for Madagascar on 25 April, comprising six fully-laden cargo ships, a fleet oiler, the landing ship *Bacaquero* with its bow-opening doors, and *Derwentdale*, converted to transport landing craft.[46] It was escorted by the cruiser *Devonshire*, three destroyers, six corvettes, and six minesweepers. The faster Convoy Z carried the troops, departing Durban on 28 April. It comprised the sister ships *Karanja* and *Keren*, formerly of the British India line, the Union Castle Line's *Winchester Castle*, and the Polish-flagged *Sobieski* carried 56 landing craft with which to get the men ashore.[47] Other personnel travelled in three larger ships, Canadian Pacific's *Duchess of Atholl*, the Cunard White Star line's *Franconia*, and the Orient line's *Oronsay*. Convoy Z was escorted by *Ramillies* and *Illustrious*, the cruiser *Hermione*, and six destroyers. 'So on we sailed', wrote Thomas Russell aboard *Ramillies*,

> the harsh clatter of the Oerlikon cannons as close range weapons were tested, then the steady hammer beats sounding hard and solid of the eight-barrelled pom poms as they pumped a hail of shells into the sky exploding in a flock of small black smoke bursts and

43 Macoun, *Wrong Place, Right Time*, appendix C, 'The Todd Mission: Madagascar, 1941-2', pp. 134-6.

44 See Jackson, *War and Empire*. Meyer is also featured in Marcus Binney, *Secret War Heroes: The Men of Special Operations Executive* (London: Hodder and Stoughton, 2005), chapter 7, 'Percy Meyer and the Liberation of Madagascar'.

45 See E. D. R. Harrison, 'British Subversion in French East Africa: SOE's Todd Mission, 1941-1942, *English Historical Review*, 114, 456 (1999).

46 Winser, *British Invasion Fleets*, p. 7.

47 Ibid.

> the sound of small popping noises in the air. Turrets were tested, training up and down and starboard to port, the great guns looked eager for the battle we half hoped would come. All the training was pitched to that end and we were ready. 'Shit or bust', as we used to say.[48]

While making their preparations, the British were being observed by Axis intelligence agents, specifically those belonging to Umberto Campini's network in Lourenco Marques.[49] On 1 May Trompke informed Berlin that the Italians had learned that two big troopships, ten submarines, five minesweepers, five torpedo boats, and an aircraft carrier were ready for action against Madagascar. Churchill was receiving decrypts of Campini's intelligence reports, and said in a speech that 'while the troops were on the sea I must tell you I felt a shiver every time I saw the word "Madagascar" in the newspapers'.[50] The Axis powers didn't bother to pass information onto the Vichy authorities, however, so the invasion came as a complete surprise to Madagascar's defenders.

On 3 May Kennedy attended the Chiefs of Staff meeting on behalf of Brooke. Churchill asked that the scope for reducing the scale of the invasion be examined so as to meet Wavell's request to get the whole 5th Division to India. They agreed that this was sound, and this decision ensured that the Madagascar operation would be limited to the capture of Diego Suarez, not the entire island.[51] On the same day, the assault convoy assembled off Madagascar and was strengthened by the arrival of the Eastern Fleet carrier *Indomitable* and her destroyer escorts, and on the 4 May, Admiral Syfret received the final go-ahead from London.[52]

Though Madagascar lay squarely on Somerville's patch, his fleet was not to play the starring role. Reflecting prevailing strategic priorities, the main naval strength was provided by Force H because the Eastern Fleet's convoy protection duties were regarded as too critical for it to be tasked with the Madagascar operation. Furthermore, its Fast Division needed to be ready to meet another sortie from the Imperial Japanese Navy. Instead, it loaned vessels to Syfret's force (*Indomitable*, *Ramillies*, and others) and placed its mass between Madagascar and the direction of any possible Japanese interference from the east. The Eastern Fleet ships detailed for this mission assembled in the Seychelles and, as the convoys left Durban, moved to their allotted positions 130-220 miles east of Madagascar. The units involved in this screening operation were the battleships *Resolution* and *Warspite* and the carrier *Formidable*, together with their escort of five cruisers and seven destroyers.[53] The warships were supported by RAF Catalina patrols from Diego Garcia.

Going in, the major problem presented by an attack on Madagascar was the fact that Diego Suarez bay and the Antsirane naval base and airfield lay behind formidable defences. The only channel through which the bay could be approached was just three-quarters of a mile wide, and heavily defended from the Orangea Pass. Intelligence assessments in February had declared

48 BBC 'World War Two People's War' oral history archive, Thomas Russell, Chapter 19, 'Approach of the Storm', A7359737.
49 Harrison, 'On Secret Service for the Duce'. See also Christopher Vasey, *Nazi Intelligence Operations in Non-Occupied Territories: Espionage Efforts in the United States, South America, and Southern Africa* (Jefferson, NC: McFarland, 2016).
50 Harrison, 'On Secret Service for the Duce', pp. 1327-28.
51 Kennedy, *The Business of War*, p. 215.
52 Winser, *British Invasion Fleets*, p. 8.
53 Ibid.

Diego Suarez impregnable from the seaward, all approaches commanded by high ground and well-sited guns. The only hope of taking the position came from the fact that Diego Suarez was on a narrow isthmus. If a force could be landed on the west coast, it might be able to advance overland into the defenders rear. In addition, a night attack on the base, which the French considered impossible because of navigational difficulties, might provide a second means of advantage.

And so the British launched their attack on the French colony. 'At dusk 4 May', wrote Sturges, 'the complete convoy, which now consisted of the slow and the fast elements, formed up in its assault formation and I observed with some relief that, when darkness fell, we did not appear to have been discovered by enemy air reconnaissance or surface vessels'.[54] The approach to the beaches through narrow channels 'bristling with mines' was 'a stunning feat of navigation'. SOE marked the passage with lights to help the lead destroyers mark the channel with buoys. Minesweepers then led the force in. By 2am on 5 May, the assault ships were at anchor off the beaches and the landing ships were on their way. 5 Commando went ashore at Red Beach in Courrier Bay, and 29 Brigade at White Beach, Green Beach, and Blue Beach, before advancing inland to Antsirane. The first landings went according to plan, and complete surprise was achieved by 5 Commando. 29 Brigade also landed successfully, SOE at the last minute discovering 12 machine-guns defending Blue Beach, which were cleared by troops from White Beach. Half an hour after the assault, aircraft from the carriers attacked the airfield and shipping in harbour, sinking a submarine and an armed merchant cruiser, destroying hangars, and briskly winning air superiority for the invaders.

By 6:30am all of the beaches had been taken, 2,300 troops were ashore, and *Bachaquero* had landed 54 vehicles together with 25-pounder artillery pieces. As the operation continued, the cruiser *Hermione* conducted a diversionary attack off a potential landing beach on the east coast, and dummy parachutists were dropped inland. Supporting the troops as they began the overland assault on Diego Suarez, aircraft from *Illustrious* attacked the base and shipping in harbour while those from *Indomitable* targeted the Antsirane airbase. There were only four French aircraft in the area, the remaining 17 being based at Tananarive, 600 miles south. By the end of the second day, over 13,000 soldiers, 321 vehicles, and 18 guns were ashore.[55] Light resistance was encountered at first but by the end of the day the advance was held up by strong defences, and the British troops, as well as their armour, were in some disarray having encountered an unknown defensive position called the Joffre Line and a large number of particularly aggressive Senegalese troops.[56]

The invaders were opposed by about 4,000 Vichy troops around Diego Suarez, with another 4,000 elsewhere on the island. With the advance stalling, Sturges ordered a night assault and

54 Quoted in Tute, *Reluctant Enemies*, p. 203.

55 Winser, *British Invasion Fleets*, p. 8.

56 The action is compellingly described in Cleve Barkley, 'Mission to Madagascar: British Assault on Diego Suarez Port', 'Warfare History Network', at <http://warfarehistorynetwork.com/daily/wwii/mission-to-madagascar-british-assault-on-diego-suarez-port/>. In terms of the history of amphibious assaults and combined arms landings, this was an historic moment, presaging the much larger beach landings that were to come in North Africa and southern and western Europe later in the war (operations Torch, Husky, Dragoon, and Overlord respectively).

returned to the flagship, *Ramillies*, to consult with Syfret. *Ramillies* was central to the action that followed.

> Facing a strong defensive position that could not easily be out-flanked or by-passed, this was another opportunity to follow the traditional British practice against the French of exploiting mobility provided to land forces by maritime power. Sturges suggested that a party of Royal Marines be landed at Antsirane from an 'expendable destroyer', as a diversion.[57]

The plan was to take Antsirane by a *coup de main*, and so *Ramillies*'s Royal Marines prepared themselves for a daring operation. 'The weapons, so lovingly cleaned', wrote Thomas Russell, 'were to be put to good use. Fifty Marines under Captain Price were to go aboard HMS *Anthony*, a destroyer, which took the Marines from a small landing craft'.[58]

'At last we are to do something in this rotten war', wrote William Smith aboard *Anthony* on 6 May.

> After a quiet day we are now on the way to the harbour of Diego Suarez with fifty marines to take positions in the rear of the town. We have to run the gauntlet of some eighteen guns on shore and a mine field. When we left the Flag Ship made 'Good bye and good luck' quite a Nelson touch. If I am able to continue this story after 10pm I will consider myself very lucky.[59]

Syfret gave the marines a 50 per cent chance of success (his advisers 15 per cent) and he 'did not expect a score to survive the night'.[60] At 8pm the destroyer began to run the gauntlet of the French batteries protecting the entrance to the harbour, responding with its own main armament with supporting fire from the cruisers. Basil Mitchell, serving aboard the Eastern Fleet corvette *Genista*, witnessed the action:

> HMS *Anthony* had been despatched with a party of Royal Marines to create a diversion. After dark she proceeded against heavy seas on a northerly course which brought her before dawn off the heavily defended harbour entrance. At full speed she raced through the narrow gap and was in the harbour itself before those manning the guns were aware of what had happened.[61]

The marines leapt from *Anthony* at Antsirane quay, right opposite Diego Suarez, and their presence created such confusion that resistance crumbled. They 'effected a disturbance out of all

57 Buckley, *Five Ventures*.
58 BBC 'World War Two People's War' oral history archive, Thomas Russell.
59 Ibid., William Smith, 'Serving on HMS *Anthony* during Operation Ironclad', A8187762.
60 Syfret, 'The Capture of Diego Suarez', p. 1592.
61 Basil Mitchell, 'The War Years', private memoir. Derived also from meetings with the late Professor Mitchell (1917-2011) in Woodstock, 2008 and 2009, and his subsequent autobiography, *Looking Back: On Faith, Philosophy, and Friends in Oxford* (Durham: The Memoir Club, 2009).

proportion to their actual numbers', and Syfret subsequently said that the action 'was the principal and direct cause of the enemy's collapse'.[62]

On 7 May *Devonshire*, *Hermione*, and *Ramillies* bombarded Diego Suarez before *Hermione*, *Ramillies*, and the destroyers *Paladin* and *Panther* entered the harbour. Within 60 hours, what had been stiff resistance had been overcome and Diego Suarez captured. But not the rest of the vast island; there was not enough time, and the troops were needed elsewhere. As Churchill told Syfret on 15 May, in one of those perspicuous communications from his position 'on high', suffused with his trademark confidence and a canny measure of the Japanese threat:

> I want you to see clearly our picture of the Madagascar operation. It must be a help not a hindrance. It must be a security and not a burden. We cannot lock up active field army troops there for any length of time. The 13th and 17th Brigades must go to India almost immediately. If you could take Tamatave and Majunga in the next few days they could help you in this, but they have got to go on anyhow.
>
> Since 'Ironclad' was conceived and executed the Indian Ocean situation has changed to our advantage. Time has passed. The Japanese have not yet pressed their attack upon Ceylon or India. On the contrary, these dangers look less near and likely than before ... One can hardly imagine the Japanese trying to take Diego Suarez with less than 10,000 men in transports, with battleships and carrier escort, involving a very large part of their limited fleet. They have to count every ship even more carefully than we do. Therefore your problem is holding the place with the least subtraction from our limited resources.[63]

This prescient summary was evidence of strategic sound sense on the part of the British government and its principal minister.

Two French submarines were sunk by joint sea and air attacks on 7-8 May. One of them, *Le Monge*, recalled from Réunion, arrived off Orangea Point, unsuccessfully attacked *Indomitable*, and was sunk with all hands by the carrier's escorting destroyers. The sloop *D'Entrecasteaux* was crippled by aircraft from *Illustrious* and subsequently beached. The submarine *Bévéziers* was alongside in the harbour and was sunk by the Fleet Air Arm. The submarine *Héros* was recalled from escorting a merchantman sailing to the beleaguered Vichy garrison in Djibouti by Captain Maerten, commanding the naval establishment at Diego Suarez. Reaching Courrier Bay after racing south, she was promptly sunk by a Swordfish from *Illustrious*. On the British side, the corvette *Aricula* had her back broken by a mine on the first day and sank.

A Japanese counterattack

Despite manifold calls on resources and the scale of the threat in the Indian Ocean region, the Eastern Fleet was always at risk of being plundered for operations in other theatres. On 18 May Somerville wrote with relief that 'the rather wet project I was asked to remark on and which was obviously a pet of WC's [to sail the Eastern Fleet through Suez and a fight convoy to Malta and

62 Syfret, 'The Capture of Diego Suarez'.
63 Churchill, *The Second World War*, volume 4, p. 208.

entice the Italian fleet into a major action] is now off'.[64] This was just as well, because the admiral had his hands full. Despite Churchill's justifiable confidence, Japanese forces were nevertheless active in this distant region. Demonstrating the far-reaching range of Japanese forces, an audacious and opportunistic attack was in the offing as the British settled into possession of Diego Suarez. With the port secure and 'the garrison having been reinforced, the ships of the convoy disappeared leaving only the *Ramillies* and two corvettes in occupation of the harbour', wrote Mitchell. The job of the corvettes

> was to maintain anti-submarine watch at the harbour entrance ... One evening [the night of 30-31 May] *Genista* was off duty, moored off the small port at the inner end of the harbour. We were in the wardroom having a drink before dinner, when there was a muffled sound which led the Captain to say, 'Sounds as if Eccles (the Steward) has dropped his false teeth'. A moment later the Bosun's Mate appeared to say that there had been an explosion in the harbour.[65]

There had indeed. From nine miles outside the harbour, the Japanese submarine *I-20* had launched a midget submarine commanded by Lieutenant Saburo Akieda. It was joined by *I-16*'s midget submarine, piloted by Sub-Lieutenant Maoji Iwase, and both vessels headed for Diego Suarez.

> Inside the harbour the old battleship *Ramillies*, having been steaming in monotonous circles all day after the air alert the previous evening, dropped anchor near to the position she had originally occupied. Close by was a destroyer and HMS *Karanja*, an assault landing ship. Nearer the harbour entrance was the tanker *British Loyalty*, while at the quay was another ships, laden with ammunition. Suddenly, at about 8.15pm, the quiet of the evening in the great harbour was shattered when the battleship was hit on the port side by a single torpedo from Lieutenant Akieda's midget. About an hour later the *British Loyalty* was also hit.[66]

Scrambled to action, *Genista* and *Thyme* depth charged the submarines, but both managed to beach. The Japanese sailors fled inland only to be killed in a firefight with the Royal Marines three days later after refusing to surrender. While it might not have prevented the attack, there should have been a force of destroyers stationed there along with the corvettes. But as Somerville reported, *Laforey*, *Lightning*, and *Lookout* had had to leave in order to rendezvous with Force A

64 Simpson (ed.), *The Somerville Papers*, to wife, 18/5/42, p. 420. Somerville benefited from mature top cover from his superiors back in London, who deflected some of Churchill's schemes to employ his assets elsewhere. In July, when Churchill wanted to use most of the Eastern Fleet to reassert British naval power in eastern Mediterranean, Pound and the Naval Staff poured cold water on the idea, the prime minister accepting their advice. 'Although the Eastern Fleet is at present on the defensive', Alexander told him, 'it does not follow that it is not performing an important role'. (Simpson (ed.), *The Somerville Papers*, Alexander to Churchill, 14/7/42, p. 432.) Churchill would have snorted at this, while senior naval officers would have rolled their eyes heavenward. Pound to Cunningham: 'Only politicians would suppose ships doing nothing unless always "rushing about"'. (Roskill, *Churchill and the Admirals*, p. 207.)

65 Mitchell, *Looking Back*, p. 91.

66 Wilson, *A Submariners' War in the Indian Ocean*, p. 86.

north of the Seychelles on 1 June. Without them, Force A would have had to have proceeded to Colombo unscreened because the destroyers *Active* and *Duncan* where at that moment unfit to undertake the passage, and this was a risk to the battlefleet that could not be run.[67]

This action was significant because it was a worrying example of Japan's ability to deploy forces as far away from their new naval bases in Malaya and Singapore as the east coast of Africa, and of their capacity to target important British assets. The midget submarines were part of Rear Admiral Nobura Ishizaki's 8th Submarine Flotilla's 1st Division based on Penang and at the time operating in the Mozambique Channel. *Ramillies* was badly damaged and the oiler *British Loyalty* sunk. A second hit may well have done the same for *Ramillies*. As it was, the damage was severe enough to put her out of action for a year, thus further reducing Britain's battleship strength and weakening the Eastern Fleet's convoy escort capacity, representing an excellent return for the attackers.

The submarine force was operating in conjunction with the armed merchant cruisers and supply ships *Aikoko Maru* and *Hokoku Maru*. Designed as passenger-cargo vessels for the Ossaka Shipping Line and originally destined for the Japan-South America route, the ships had been requisitioned during construction to become armed merchant cruisers, the Japanese equivalent of Germans vessels such as *Atlantis* and *Pinguin*. Weighing over 10,000 tons, they carried a main armament of eight 5.5-inch guns, two three-inch guns, and two fighter-bomber floatplanes. This heavy armament would enable them to overpower any merchant ship, armed or not, and to stand a good chance against enemy warships up to cruiser class. A top speed of 21 knots, along with the carriage of floatplanes, meant they could search far and wide for the enemy.

They had entered service along with the *Kiyozumi Maru* as the 24th Special Cruiser Squadron under Rear Admiral Moriyoshi Takeda and were now supporting Japan's westernmost military operations, working in conjunction with Ishazaki's submarine force.[68] Ishazaki himself was present in submarine *I-10*, specially built to embark a flotilla commander and his staff. His other ships were *I-16*, *I-18*, *I-20*, and *I-30*. These large Japanese submarines used their unique, manned aircraft to reconnoitre Aden, Dar-es-Salaam, Diego Suarez, Djibouti, Durban, and Zanzibar. Flying over Diego Suarez, one of them had spotted a battleship, a cruiser, and other ships at anchor, and it was this report that led to the attack on *Ramillies*. Ishizaki had ordered three of his ships to close the entrance of the harbour and deployed his midget submarines.

By the end of May the situation in the Indian Ocean, despite the tonic provided by the success of Operation Ironclad, had darkened further with the complete loss of Burma. Most indigenous units of the Burma Army had ceased to exist. The 17th Indian Division and 2nd Burma Division, composed largely of British and Indian units, 'with battalions in many cases reduced almost to cadres and lacking all vehicles and 90 per cent of their equipment had crossed into Assam, where they were being collected under the cover of the 23rd Indian Division holding an outpost on the Assam-Burma frontier'.[69] But reinforcements and vital new equipment continued to arrive, rushed east at the Empire's moment of peril. The 5th British Division finally arrived towards the end of May; reinforcements of field artillery and anti-aircraft guns were also landed, and some of India's divisions were brought up to strength. The Eastern Army now

67 'Admiralty War Diaries of World War II', reports of proceedings, 10 May to 5 June 1942.

68 See Bill Stone, 'Japanese Submarines at Madagascar and the Mozambique Channel', at http://books.stonebooks.com/history/mozam.shtml

69 Wavell, 'Operations in Eastern Theatre'.

comprised the 14th, 23rd, and 26th divisions, the Southern Army the 19th and 20th divisions. Ceylon was also reinforced, particularly its anti-aircraft defences. It was now protected by the 34th Indian Division, the 16th Infantry Brigade from the 70th British Division, the 21st East African Brigade, and the the 20th Indian Division, brought into replace the Australian brigades.

June to September 1942

Continuing its perigrinations, Force A arrived at Colombo on 5 June. A conference the following day, attended by Somerville, Layton, Arbuthnot, Rear Admiral A. D. Read (Flag Officer Ceylon designate), the Chief of Staff India Command, and Air Officer Commanding in Chief Ceylon, reviewed Ceylon's defences. In an organizational reshuffle, the historic position of Commander-in-Chief East Indies was to lapse, to be replaced by a Flag Officer Ceylon.[70] An MNBDO Pioneer Section was about to leave Colombo for the Seychelles to relocate the six-inch guns to better counter bombardment sites and to mount two four-inch close range defence guns. Somerville then departed for Addu, 'which is now to be given first priority'. Elsewhere in this vast and busy theatre, the troopship *Queen Mary* was about to leave leave Simon's Town bound for Suez with 9,000 troops aboard, and Somerville told Edwards at Kilindini and the Commander-in-Chief South Atlantic that she should be routed eastward of Madagascar and escorted by a modern cruiser until north of the raider danger area.[71]

Regarding the Persian Gulf, in June the outgoing Commander-in-Chief East Indies, Vice Admiral Arbuthnot, wrote:

> I remained very conscious of the weaknesses in the defences of this vital area, but I was forced to agree that in the circumstances obtaining a marked increase in the numbers of aircraft could hardly be hoped for. However, steps have been taken to prepare landing grounds so that aircraft may operate without delay when the time comes. I have obtained a promise from the Commander in Chief, Middle East to station a battalion at Bahrain, for

70 Rear Admiral Read became Flag Officer Ceylon on 18 June 1942,when Vice Admiral Arbuthnot struck his flag as C-in-C East Indies at sunset and departed for Britain. ('Admiralty War Diaries of World War II', reports of proceedings, 5 June to 1 July 1942). Arbuthnot explained the logic behind the change:

> The organisation then envisaged was, that the ships of the East Indies Squadron (except for those employed on escort duties and as local defence craft) would be absorbed into the Eastern Fleet; the Commander in Chief, Eastern Fleet, would be afloat, with headquarters at Colombo, and I, while retaining command of the Station – that is, the shore bases and their Naval defences – and controlling shipping on the station, would also act as Deputy Commander in Chief, Eastern Fleet, at Colombo. However, after the events of early April that are dealt with below, Admiral Somerville considered it necessary to move his headquarters from Colombo to Kilindini; and as this made it impossible to me to continue as Deputy Commander in Chief and as the diminished East Indies Command no longer justified the appointment of a Commander in Chief Admiral Somerville and I joined in proposing to Their Lordships the termination of my appointment. This was approved in Admiralty message 2028 of the 6th May. The position was replaced by a Flag Officer Ceylon. ('Admiralty War Diaries of World War II', War Despatch, Arbuthnot, 18/6/42).

71 'Admiralty War Diaries of World War II', reports of proceedings, 5 June to 1 July 1942.

> the protection of the refinery there from airborne or submarine borne commando raids. The Naval forces in the Gulf were strengthened by the dispatch there of H.M.S. DANAE (later relived by H.M.S. CERES) and I also sent the Senior Naval Officer H.N.M.S. SOEMBA and H.M.S. PANGKOR, an asdic fitted auxiliary. I had intended sending a second auxiliary warship, H.M.S. KEDAH, but she has been delayed by defects.[72]

A Hormuz patrol scheme was established, and Bandar Abbas in Iran was now employed as a convoy assembly port. The Eastern Fleet's Persian Gulf Division at that moment consisted of nine escort vessels from the Ceylon Escort Group and Aden force augmented by two Hunt class destroyers transferred from the Mediterranean Fleet.[73]

The Japanese continued their operations in the Indian Ocean into the summer months, and Somerville's fleet remained stretched as other enemy vessels arrived. After his squadron's success at Diego Suarez, Admiral Ishizaki sent two submarines to each end of the Mozambique Channel and detached a fifth boat for operations around the Cape. The Japanese surface raiders fuelled the submarines, and continued their own offensive with the sinking of the 6,757 ton British cargo-passenger liner *Elysia* at dawn on 5 June, 350 miles east-north-east of Durban. An ageing vessel of the Anchor Line of Glasgow, *Elysia* had left the Firth of Clyde bound for India, carrying in her holds the vehicles of a motorized battalion of the King's Royal Rifle Corps and crated RAF fighters on her deck. Sailing unescorted from Cape Town for Bombay, Chief Officer Colqhuon, nearing the end of his watch and contemplating bacon and eggs, sighted two ships bearing down on the *Elysia*. Captain Morrison came on deck to examine them, noting their high midships superstructure and a distinctive 'Eastern' look. Morrison turned his ship about and ordered the 4.7-inch gun to be manned.

A Battle of the Atlantic veteran who had distinguished himself in the famous *Jervis Bay* action, Morrison determined to make a fight of it. The faster Japanese ships, steaming in line astern, overhauled him, and 'soon bright stabs of flame reached out from their forecastles … and the shells began to burst around the fleeing *Elysia*'.[74] Morrison ordered that the 'RRR' raider warning signal be transmitted, and his gun crew opened fire. Broadsides were soon bursting either side of the liner, however, and Morrison began an evasive zig-zag and made smoke. For over an hour, under this cover, she weaved. But eventually the ship had to be abandoned to save her crew from being pounded to death, as the Japanese raiders continued to shell the *Elysia*. *Hokoku Maru* also launched her seaplane in order to bomb the target, before torpedoes were fired to try and get her to sink. To their great relief, the crew were not subjected to the atrocities that were to become associated with Japanese vessels in the Indian Ocean, and they were later picked up by a British cruiser. *Elysia* remained afloat, it was reported, for another four days.

Responding to the threat posed by this enemy concentration, Somerville instructed his deputy commander-in-chief ashore, Danckwerts, responsible for Eastern Fleet operations from Kilindini, to do what was needed, even if this meant sending *Indomitable* to the area.[75] Danckwerts had already established a cruiser patrol at the northern end of the Mozambique

72 Ibid., War despatch.
73 Ibid., war diary, war diary, October 1942.
74 Bernard Edwards, *Blood and Bushido* (New York: Brick Tower Press, 1991), p. 28.
75 Danckwerts was his Chief of Staff (Shore) from March 1942, soon created Deputy Commander-in-Chief Eastern Fleet based at HMS *Tana* at Kilindini. He was transferred to Kilindini with the fleet's

Channel where the flotilla of enemy submarines was at large. Vital though it was for the protection of convoys sailing from the Cape, this work inevitably depleted the force available for the other convoys that came within Danckwerts's purview. 'Between 5 June and 9 July when Ishizaki ordered his boats back to Penang, the *I-10* sank eight merchant ships while the *I-18*, which also operated in the southern part of the Channel, sank three ships. At the same time the *I-16* and *I-20*, in the northern part of the Channel, sank three and seven ships respectively'.[76]

On 11 July 1942 the First Sea Lord, Admiral Sir Dudley Pound, informed Churchill of the 'Dispositions of Admiral Somerville's Fleet'. At that moment it comprised three battleships with a fourth, *Valiant*, at Durban readying for service, two fleet carriers (*Formidable* and *Illustrious*) ten cruisers, nine destroyers, and a host of smaller warships and support vessels. The battleships *Nelson* and *Rodney*, and the fleet carrier *Indomitable*, had been detached for special operations, and the battleships *Queen Elizabeth* was at Port Sudan destined for a refit in America.

Throughout 1942 Eastern Fleet battleships and other vessels remained stationed on Mombasa for convoy escort duties and to counter the threat from German and Japanese forces. It was a frustrating way to spend the war. Alec Dennis, first lieutenant of the destroyer *Griffin*, recalls being 'more or less penned up in Mombasa' in 1942. 'It was a "keep out of trouble, strike when you can policy" which got on the nerves and threatened the morale of everyone involved'.[77] While convoy work was essential, it wasn't the same as engaging the enemy directly. '[Y]ou can imagine how I itch to get one back on those bastards', Somerville wrote to North shortly after the Madagascar operation.[78] He aptly summarized the impatience felt throughout the entire fleet at this time when he told his wife that 'What would do us all more good than anything else at the moment is to have some sort of crack at those ruddy Japs and do a bit of shooting at something. Fellows get stale and lose their edge if you don't have a mix-up at reasonably frequent intervals'.[79] Soon after, he wrote to Admiral Pound that

> The outstanding need at the moment is for action of some sort. A few ships had a mild blooding at Diego Suarez but apart from that we suffer badly from not being able to loose off our guns at something. I have considered a carrier attack on Port Blair and Sabang but to be quite honest I do not believe that any results we are likely to achieve would justify risking sending the carriers in except on the grounds that it would certainly be a good tonic to the fleet.[80]

Although attacks on Japanese-held territory were a long way off, there was a modicum of action for British forces in the Indian Ocean during the summer months of 1942. The Comoros Islands were occupied, as was the rest of Madagascar, and the island of Réunion was gently persuaded from the Vichy to the Free French cause (see chapter 4). To take the little-known example of the Comoros, in June it was decided that the islands of Mayotte and Pamanzi should be acquired.

staff and the East Indies Station's operational staff and the warship and merchant plots after the raids. He was responsible for local organization and convoys.

76 Wilson, *A Submariner's War*, p. 87.

77 Christopher Somerville, *Our War: The British Commonwealth and the Second World War* (London: Weidenfeld and Nicolson, 1998), p. 171.

78 Simpson (ed.), *The Somerville Papers*, letter to North, 27/5/42, p. 421.

79 Ibid., p. 425.

80 Ibid., signal to Pound, 29/6/42, p. 428.

The airfields at Mayotte were considered a threat to Allied shipping in the Mozambique Channel, and, conversely, would make a useful addition to the growing network of British flying-boat bases if captured. The Catalinas of 209 Squadron had arrived in East Africa that month, based at Kipevu in Mombasa and tasked with making anti-submarine sweeps.[81] In need of a stepping stone between Mombasa and Madagascar, Pamanzi was considered ideal. Plans to wrest these outposts of the French Empire from Vichy control were given further impetus by Smuts, who thought Pamanzi would make a useful anti-submarine base and staging post for fighters travelling from Tanganyika to Madagascar.

So the die was cast, and an expedition was planned involving the light cruiser *Dauntless* and the destroyer *Active* from the Eastern Fleet, dispatched from Mombasa together with Royal Marines and men of the King's African Rifles (KAR). Hubert Moyse-Bartlett, official historian of the KAR, recounts the raid. Mayotte was the

> residence of the Governor of the Comoros Group, who lived on Dzaudi, an islet joined by a causeway to Pamanzi, where there was an anchorage, a wireless station, and a landing-ground. Use of these facilities would be of considerable benefit to the naval and air forces operating at the northern end of the Mozambique Channel, and it was intended to capture the landing-ground and installations intact. The French Administrator and his chief staff officer were strongly pro-Vichy and ready to sabotage everything, but most of the other Europeans on the islands, who were believed to number 15 all told, were pro-British. The defence forces consisted of about 40 armed police.
>
> Operation 'Throat', as the expedition was called, was a combined operation under the command of Captain J. G. Hewitt, RN. Two warships, HMS *Dauntless* and HMS *Active*, participated. The military force under Lieutenant-Colonel P. A. Morcambe consisted of 30 British Commandos from 101 Force and 'C' Company, 5 KAR, with detachments of mortars, signals and intelligence.
>
> The troops embarked in the warships on 30th June. After a difficult approach by night through the coral reefs to Choa Bay, the landing of the first flight (British commandos and one platoon 5 KAR) began at 3am on 2nd July, in small craft towed by the destroyer *Active*. The second flight, comprising the rest of the KAR and attached troops, was ashore by 4.45am. The first flight took the wireless station; the second surrounded the barracks, and without any alarm being given or opposition offered, captured the police in bed with their wives. On the completion of these two phases, the landing-ground at Pamanzi was occupied by the Royal Marines. At 12.30pm the ceremony of saluting the French flag and hoisting the Union Jack took place with a gust of honour from all detachments. Though the Governor refused to cooperate, most of the French and many natives attended to hear a proclamation drawn up by the Fortress Commander Diego Suarez, and read by the political officer accompanying the expedition. 'C' Company remained to garrison Dzaudi Island, with platoons on Mayotte and Pamanzi.[82]

81 209 Squadron became one of the major ASW [anti-submarine warfare] assets in the area and for the next three years flew patrols over the Indian Ocean using bases in South Africa, Oman and the Seychelles to extend its cover.

82 Hubert Moyse-Bartlett, *The King's African Rifles: A Study in the Military History of East and Central Africa, 1890–1945* (Aldershot: Gale and Polden, 1956), p. 580.

Squadron Leader David Fitzpatrick was involved in the capture of Pamanzi, going

> ashore in an R boat (landing craft) with twelve strapping black soldiers of the King's African Rifles. They were led by a gallant Scots Guards officer who had left his right arm in the desert, Colonel David Kemble. In the middle of the night they captured the Governor in his bed. The latter pleaded for "un quart d'heure" in which to replace the other youthful occupant of the great double bed with his elderly wife. He then surrendered with full dignity, nightcaps, Napoleonic bedheads, mosquitoes and all.[83]

Also in June, it was agreed that plans would be drawn up to capture the rest of Madagascar before the year was out. Despite continuing enemy activity, there was no doubt that the capture of Diego Suarez had eased the situation in the western Indian Ocean for Britain and the Allies and that, conversely, the Axis had missed an opportunity. Japanese chances of a decisive attack in the Indian Ocean were diminishing as British air, sea, and land forces arrived to reinforce India Command and the Eastern Fleet. But what relieved the pressure enormously, not just here but all around the world, was the massive American victory at the Battle of Midway, which led to the destruction of a significant portion of Japan's carrier fleet, a blow from which it never recovered. As Roskill writes of Somerville's position at the time: 'It was lucky for him that the Japanese did not press their advantage but withdrew from the Indian Ocean to strike against the US navy once again. The outcome was the decisive battle of Midway, fought on 4 June [to 7 June], which put an abrupt end to the Japanese period of maritime dominance'.[84] Lucky, perhaps, but Roskill might have allotted a sliver of credit to the British for the reinforcement programme that they were in the process of enacting in the wake of the April raids and their elastic-like resilience. Nevertheless, there is clearly no doubt that Japanese losses at Midway – four carriers sunk – transformed the strategic picture. Three of those carriers had taken part in the raids on Colombo and Trincomalee in April (Nagumo's flagship *Akagi*, *Hiryu*, and *Soryu*), a point at which the Japanese had looked almost invincible. Churchill knew the significance of this battle at once. The 'loss of these four aircraft carriers sensibly improves our position in the Indian Ocean and Bay of Bengal'.[85] Midway, he wrote, 'was of cardinal importance … The moral effect was tremendous and instantaneous. At one stroke the dominant position of Japan in the Pacific was reversed. The glaring ascendancy of the enemy, which had frustrated our combined endeavours throughout the Far East for six months, was gone for ever'.[86] Things were looking up on land as well as Wavell's forces in India continued to grow, another British division, the 2nd, arriving in June, and by that date Wavell's command had 25 operational RAF squadrons on the strength. By the following month, when the monsoon broke, he believed that 'the critical period for India had passed'.[87] At this point, June 1942, the Eastern Fleet was at its greatest strength, not to be matched until mid-1944. Because the moment of crisis passed, so did the urgent need to reinforce, and the Eastern Fleet now began to lose ships to other theatres as the ebb and flow

83 Banks, *Wings of the Dawning*, p. 74.
84 Roskill, *Churchill and the Admirals*, p. 205.
85 Simpson (ed.), *The Somerville Papers*, Churchill to Pound 10/6/42, p. 424.
86 Churchill, *The Second World War*, volume 4, p. 226.
87 Wavell, 'Operations in Eastern Theatre', p. 4665.

of a global conflict altered, and the British found the wherewithal to respond, thanks to their own devices and the actions and resources of their principal allies.

Though the full permutations of battles elsewhere were not immediately apparent to commanders on the ground or, indeed, strategic planners in Allied and Axis capitals, developments in the Middle East and the Pacific intertwined and had some interesting knock-on effects in the Indian Ocean. In July a Japanese force comprising three cruisers and 18 destroyers based in Malaya 'had begun preparations for operations against British communications in the Indian Ocean, but the American landings on Guadalcanal on 6 August 1942 ended these plans'.[88] But the Germans and Italians, at this moment, were doing very well in the Western Desert, and because the Japanese were understandably cagey with their allies regarding the magnitude of the Midway disaster, there were grounds for optimism in Berlin and Rome when viewing the Indian Ocean theatre. With Rommel's forces penetrating deep into Egypt, Italian strategists requested plans for future joint operations with the Japanese in the Indian Ocean. But such initiatives, now, were far from Japanese minds.

In these summer months of 1942, Somerville faced problems that were to become very familiar over the next two years, particularly the need to focus his resources on sea lane protection while attempting also to retain Force A as a credible deterrent at sea. From now on, the moment of high danger having passed, this balancing act was made difficult because the needs of other theatres saw resources either denied to the Eastern Fleet, or removed from it. As he wrote on the first count on 12 June, referring to his inability to strike at Japanese targets, 'At the moment when so much depends upon our holding our position in Egypt I feel it's essential to protect the Middle East communications ... I don't feel it's right for me to gamble at the moment – much as I'd love to'.[89] And as he wrote regarding the removal of resources, either for service in other theatres or for different tasks in the Indian Ocean: 'All these side shows keep taking my ships away or else employing them so I never get my proper Force A together'.[90] *Formidable* had gone to the Mediterranean to take part in the Pedestal convoy to Malta, and he now received a signal from the Admiralty 'to say ... I must lend another carrier for TORCH [the Anglo-American invasion of French North Africa]!'.[91] This was soon followed by a signal from Pound 'to ask me to release 6 destroyers for TORCH! Told him I could let 4 but STREAMLINE [part of the proposed occupation of the rest of Madagascar] would be pretty thin'.[92] Nevertheless, despite Somerville's perfectly understandable frustration, the bigger picture was one in which the men in London responsible for Britain's global war effort knew that they could switch resources between theatres – realizing, crucially, that if Somerville encountered a major Japanese incursion into the Indian Ocean, he could be reinforced in sufficient time and numbers to have a good chance of seeing off such an attack.

This was all in August, and there were other operations afoot, too. In the Bay of Bengal the Eastern Fleet was called upon to conduct a diversionary manoeuvre involving both fleet carriers as well as a strong force of battleships and cruisers. This was Operation Stab, a decoy invasion of the Andaman Islands intended to distract the Japanese as the Americans were invading

88 De Ninno, 'The Italian Navy and Japan', p. 16 proof.
89 Simpson (ed.), *The Somerville Papers*, to Joan Bright Astley 12/7/42, p.433.
90 Ibid., to Joan Bright Astley, 11/8/42, p. 437.
91 Ibid., diary, 5/8/42, p.438.
92 Ibid., diary, 31/8/42, p.438.

Guadalcanal. Dummy convoys comprising merchant vessels and Royal Fleet Auxiliaries protected by the warships sailed from Madras, Trincomalee, and Vizagapatam. Japanese reconnaissance was allowed to spot the invasion fleet, and an aircraft from *Indomitable* accounted for a Japanese flying-boat. Even mounting this diversionary operation illustrated the continued need for Somerville to juggle resources and commitments. He had recently been told of the withdrawal of *Indomitable* and the 19th Destroyer Flotilla. This, and the heavy escort commitments on the Middle East and Indian Ocean sea lanes, together with the general shortage of destroyers, led him to inform the Admiralty of his fleet's weak state. But Operation Stab, though hardly of the highest order of strategic importance, mattered to the lords of the Admiralty. They wanted the whole of Force A to sail east for the operation, along with Force B. The reason for their enthusiasm was that they did not want to show reluctance to the Americans; a new alliance was developing and, apart from anything else, the British would not be shy about asking for American assistance should the situation worsen in the Indian Ocean.

But this requirement made it difficult for Somerville to deal with the Japanese submarine threat in the Mozambique Channel. In order to manage things here given other requirements, he therefore decided to base destroyers and Catalinas on Mayotte in the Comoros. The seaplane tender *Albatross* was sailed to act as parent ship for four flying-boats with *Griffin* and *Foxhound* sent as the striking force.[93] Some requests for assistance just had to be refused, such as Wavell's enquiry as to whether Force A could be stationed at Colombo during a period in August when the Indian National Congress was meeting in Bombay, sparking fears that the Japanese might stage offensive operations to attempt to influence its leaders.

Also in August, a large naval exercise was conducted to test the defences of East Africa, known as Exercise Touchstone. As well as validating the defences against the possibility of a Japanese seaborne invasion by the landing of Royal Marines and naval parties from a naval force off Tanga, Dar-es-Salaam, and Zanzibar, Touchstone was designed to provide both training and cover for the forthcoming Streamline Jane operations in Madagascar aimed at taking the rest of the island. By virtue of the exercise, the 29th Brigade, still at Diego Suarez, was able to refresh its combined operations landing training. Vice Admiral Willis wrote to the governor of Tanganyika regarding the 'attack' on Dar-es-Salaam: 'Don't be alarmed at the scale. Unlikely Japanese could use more than a single cruiser or armed merchant cruiser – not battleships'.[94] He did, however, note that the scale of Japanese attack might increase should they capture Ceylon or one of the Indian Ocean's western islands. Operating from Kilindini, the ships involved were *Warspite*, *Resolution* and *Valiant*, the cruisers *Enterprise*, *Gambia* and Free Dutch *Jacob van Heemskerck*, and the destroyers *Decoy*, *Fortune*, *Foxhound*, *Griffin*, *Inconstant*, *Napier*, *Nepal*, *Tjerk Hiddes*, and *Van Galen*.[95]

The Streamline Jane – or, more correctly, Stream Line Jane – operations the following month were supported by units of the Eastern Fleet.[96] Following the capture of Diego Suarez, the Vichy administration had refused to capitulate. From May to September imperial forces on the

93 'Admiralty War Diaries of World War II', reports of proceedings, 1 July to 18 August 1942.

94 CAC, Willis Papers, 5/5, letter, 29/8/42.

95 Macoun recalls a party of Royal Marines 'capturing' and terrifying a train of Polish refugees who had been released from Soviet labour camps and found shelter in this corner of the British Empire.

96 'Stream' and 'Line' were the landings at Majunga and Tamatave, and 'Jane' was the advance towards the capital Tannanarive.

ground conducted informal discussions with Governor Annet while also preparing to march south from Diego Suarez. This was because other ports, especially Majunga and Tamatave, might still be used by enemy submarines. A conference in Pretoria in June had come to the decision to attack them and then move inland against Tananarive once the rainy season lifted in the autumn. Somerville had pushed hard for these operations, which were to involve a heavy Eastern Fleet contribution. As he explained to his wife, 'I've never liked the idea of leaving the rest of Madagascar open to a Jap assault and I also want the aerodromes and harbours on the W[estern] side to assist in dealing with U-boats in the Mozambique Channel'.[97] Smuts had also continued to express his concerns. Most of the island, after a period under British military administration, was handed over to a Free French administration early the following year, though Britain retained control of 'Fortress Diego' in the north. Madagascar soon began to contribute to the Allied cause through the export of strategic raw materials, which meant the continuation of forced labour exactions for the Malagasy, and the requisitioning of foodstuffs, fuelling the growth of nationalism. The French governor and his garrison finally surrendered in November 1942.[98]

October to the end of the year

Eastern Fleet escort vessels, essential enablers of all kinds of operations, remained in critically short supply, worrying because a new German submarine offensive was in the offing. When the Admiralty asked Somerville if he could send some destroyers to the Cape, he replied that he could do so only by totally immobilizing Force A, the Eastern Fleet's spearhead.[99] He put things more bluntly in a letter to his wife the same day: 'The blasted U-boats have appeared *en masse* off the Cape and TL's [Their Lordships] are shouting at me to send little boats down there'.[100] The request was made at a time when at least 11 ships had been torpedoed off the Cape. The situation was so serious that on 13 October Somerville received a reply from the Admiralty 'saying that Cabinet approve of Force A being immobilised to release destroyers for the Cape'. This was at the time of the battle of Alamein, and protecting troop convoys bound for Egypt was naturally deemed a more important duty for the Eastern Fleet than attacking Japanese targets further east.[101]

One of the ships sunk in the new enemy submarine offensive was the Peninsular & Oriental liner *Orcades*. Built in Barrow in Furness in 1937, she had taken part in the evacuation of Allied forces from the Dutch East Indies earlier in the year. Transiting between Suez and Cape Town on 10 October with 1,065 passengers destined for Britain, she was torpedoed by *U172*. Displacing 23,456 tons, she was one of the largest merchant ships to be sunk during the war. *Orcades*'s master, Captain Fox, knew that U-boats had been reported in the area, and was awakened from

97 Simpson (ed.), *The Somerville Papers*, to wife 10/9/42, p. 441.

98 Somerville wrote that the resistance in Madagascar was inspired by the desire to ensure pensions were intact. 'Admiralty War Diaries of World War II', reports of proceedings, 10 October to 6 November 1942.

99 Simpson (ed.), *The Somerville Papers*, diary, 11/10/42, p. 443.

100 Ibid., to wife, 11/10/42, p. 443.

101 Ibid., diary, 13/10/42, p. 443.

a snooze in his cabin by a loud explosion, 'the sound I had been dreading throughout the war'.[102] Two more explosions followed. The U-boat commander, Carl Emmermann, had seen the huge outline of a liner emerge from a rain squall, framed by a rainbow. The stricken ship was quickly abandoned and 48 people lost their lives. The survivors were picked up by the Polish merchant vessel *Narwik* and landed at Cape Town on 12 October. Emmermann made off quickly after the attack, fearing British reprisals, as *U-179* had been sunk by the destroyer *Active* only two days before as she rounded the Cape en route to Penang.[103] With the Lockheed Ventura's of the South African Air Force's 23 and 25 squadrons nearby, the four submarines of the Polar Bear group, of which *U179* was a part, had scattered and moved away from their Cape hunting ground. The ports of South Africa having proved disappointingly empty, the submarines now embarked on individual operations and by 1 November had destroyed 22 vessels, including three large troop transports. The Polar Bear groups eventual total was 28 ships destroyed, making it one of the most successful single U-boat offensives of the war.[104] The Drumroll group took over from the Polar Bear group operating off the Cape.[105]

The sustained U-boat campaign in this area led to other measures to protect the vital sea lanes around the Cape. In Mauritius, Wing Commander John Barraclough, commanding 209 Squadron, received a signal via the Governor telling him that he should report to Mombasa at full speed. There he was apprised of an urgent mission requiring him to to fly to Saldanha Bay, 100 miles north-west of Cape Town to open a new base and extend the patrol range to a greater distance than the South African Air Force could manage alone. The British also enjoyed some successes in this period, on 11 November destroying one of the Japanese surface raiders that had made such a nuisance of themselves in and around the Mozambique Channel back in May. *Hokoku Maru*, on a new Indian Ocean raiding mission, encountered the Royal Dutch Shell tanker *Ondina* and the Royal Indian Navy minesweeper *Bengal* south of the Cocos-Keeling Islands. With *Aikoku Maru* closing in too, it should have been a one-sided affair. But a shot from *Bengal* hit *Hokoku Maru*'s starboard torpedo tube, causing an explosion and a serious fire that got out of control and reached the main magazine, sinking the ship. *Bengal* survived though damaged, and *Ondina* was left by the remaining Japanese ship in the belief that she was sinking, but managed to make it to Fremantle.[106]

Deception played a part in influencing the enemy, and several schemes were launched to try and make the Japanese think that the British were stronger in the Indian Ocean than in fact they were. In the latter half of 1942, the British government assessed the risk of a Japanese incursion into the western Indian Ocean to have significantly diminished, and so withdrew

102 Banks, *Wings of the Dawning*, p. 22.

103 *Active* had been part of the Madagascar invasion force, and had sunk the French submarine *Monge* on 8 May. On 8 October *U-179* sunk the unescorted British merchantman *City of Athens* sixty miles off Cape Town as she made her way to Alexandria via Freetown, the Cape, and the Mozambique Channel. Subsequent to the attack and on the same day, *Active* illuminated the surfaced submarine with searchlights and star shell, and sunk her with depth charges. See the uboat.net entry at https://uboat.net/allies/merchants/ships/2247.html

104 Paterson, *Hitler's Grey Wolves*, p. 53.

105 Its biggest success occurred when it decimated convoy DN 21 south of Durban. Of the eight merchantmen escorted by *Nigella* and three Royal Navy trawlers, *U-160* sank three and the trawlers lost the convoy. See Paterson, *Hitler's Grey Wolves*, p. 54.

106 See 'The MS *Ondina* Story', at http://www.ssmaritime.com/Ondina.htm

major units – primarily aircraft carriers – from the theatre for employment elsewhere. In late 1942 the demands of the Battle of the Atlantic, the northern convoys, and the landings in French North Africa 'were imposing on the Royal Navy the greatest strain of the entire war'. Somerville had only one carrier, *Illustrious*, on the strength, and she was about to be recalled. There were no other carriers available – but *Indefatigable* was under construction. Cue a classic deception scheme:

> By a combination of radio traffic and agents' reports the story was put over that the *Indefatigable* had been commissioned and was sailing in company with two other vessels to reinforce the *Illustrious* with modern aircraft. The voyage of the *Indefatigable* was projected to the enemy entirely by radio traffic put out by the appropriate commands *en route* until she notionally reached Simonstown, where she came under Somerville's command. Throughout 1943 her existence was sustained through all channels of Deception until December, when she returned to the Clyde, notionally for a refit, in practise to merge her identity with the real *Indefatigable* which was now ready for commissioning. Both German and Japanese intelligence believed there to be two British carriers in the Indian Ocean throughout the period, when in fact there were none.[107]

Though the increment was not great, writes Michael Howard, 'given the narrow margins on which the Royal Navy had to work in the middle years of the war it was significant, and above all credible'.[108]

By December 1942 India and Ceylon boasted two British divisions and six Indian divisions ready for active service, in addition to forces on the North-West Frontier and internal security and training units. It was expected that four more Indian divisions would be ready within three months, and two Indian armoured divisions and two tank brigades by mid-1943. Military infrastructure was being developed at a prodigious pace, having a considerable and deleterious effect on civil projects. As the Secretary of State for India reported to the War Cabinet in London, the construction of 200 aerodromes 'has strained to the utmost India's exiguous engineering resources, and has incidentally delayed considerably the construction of other essentials', such as new roads, factories, and ammunition storage facilities.[109]

India's land forces had also been bolstered by the arrival of a brigade of Valentine tanks for the Eastern Army, which was now mobile. But, like Somerville, Wavell was subject to the demands of other theatres, and soon some of his hard-won new formations were on their way to the Iran-Iraq theatre, another example of the management of stretched resources and British strategic flexibility and calculated risk-taking. The transfer of these troops occurred at a crucial moment in the war in the Soviet Union, when a German assault on the vital oilfields and oil infrastructure of Iran and Iraq was assessed as likely. Since becoming Commander-in-Chief India, Wavell had had an acute interest in the Iran-Iraq region, given its general importance for the imperial war effort and its historic position as an outworking of India's defence. 'A danger more nearly affecting India', he wrote

107 Howard, *Strategic Deception*, p. 225.
108 Ibid.
109 TNA, CAB 66/34/39, 'India's War Effort', War Cabinet, 1/3/43, memorandum by the Secretary of State for India, 1/3/43.

> arose from the German advance towards the Caucasus, which threatened Persia and Iraq and the Persian Gulf. A large proportion of the garrison had been moved across to Egypt to meet the threat to the Delta, and it seemed to me that the only way to reinforce Persia in time to halt a German advance through the Caucasus, should the Russians fail to hold the Caucasus – as at one time seemed possible – would be to send troops from India, weak though her defences were. I therefore offered to make available one or both of the two newly arrived British divisions (2nd and 5th) and an armoured brigade. Eventually the 7th Armoured Brigade and the 5th Division were dispatched to Iraq. They left India in September.[110]

The RAF strength east of Suez continued to build and, with the 10th US Army Air Force, was now able to commence offensive operations in Burma. Setbacks in the Western Desert in June (such as the surrender of Tobruk) had had a knock on effect and meant that the scale of aircraft available was not where it was hoped it would be.[111] Other essential supplies had also arrived, including 320,000 steel helmets and 410,000 stirrup pumps for air raid precaution work, a reflection of the continuing concern about potential Japanese attacks on the Indian mainland.

The growth of local forces contributed to the build up, as the Allies were afforded the time they needed to grow their resources. From the outbreak of war to December 1942 the Royal Indian Navy increased its personnel more than eightfold. It now stood at 12,000 officers and ratings manning 76 vessels. A further 314 vessels were under construction, including sloops, trawlers, motor launches, motor torpedo boats, and landing craft. India's shipbuilding and ship repair capacity had increased enormously. There was new capacity in ports such as Bombay, Cochin, Karachi, and Vizagapatam. In 1942 alone labour in India's west coast ports had increased by 33 per cent.[112] The Royal Indian Navy Dockyard had carried out major repairs to three British and one American cruiser, two destroyers, a depot ship, and 72 other British warships, with a further 34 vessels attended to outside the dockyard. It also repaired, from May to December 1942, 98 tankers and 1,294 merchantmen.[113] The sums were beginning to stack up as the Allies gained in terms of war-making potential around the world, while the Axis powers fell back.

110 Wavell, 'Operations in Eastern Theatre', p. 4667.

111 TNA, CAB 66/34/39, 'India's War Effort'.

112 On 14 April 1944 the British Lend-Lease freighter SS *Fort Stikine* exploded at Victoria Docks Bombay, causing the loss of thirteen other ships and over 700 deaths. See John Ennis, *The Great Bombay Explosion* (New York: Duell, Sloan, and Pearce, 1959) and Michael Mahoney, 'Anatomy of a Disaster: The Bombay Docks Explosion', at http://blog.nationalarchives.gov.uk/blog/anatomy-disaster/. For a Universal News newsreel showing dramatic footage of the explosion and its devastating aftermath, see 'Bombay Docks Explosion 1944', at https://www.youtube.com/watch?v=GuD3esOUlvc

113 TNA, CAB 66/34/39, 'India's War Effort', War Cabinet memorandum by the Secretary of State for India, 1/3/43. The role of Bombay for naval operations in the Indian Ocean region was very important, along with other well-equipped ports such as Colombo and Durban. For an example of an Indian Ocean port's significant contribution to the war, see Ashley Jackson, 'Refitting the Fleet in Ceylon: The War Record of Walker Sons and Company', *Journal of Indian Ocean Studies*, 10, 3 (2002). For a guide prepared for British service personnel visiting wartime Bombay, see *Welcome to Bombay*, a publication prepared by the Hospitality Committee, c. 1942-43, at http://www.cbi-theater.com/bombay/bombay.html

There were other calls on India's resources too; in July there was an expedition against the Fakir of Ipi, and Somerville's Indian Ocean bases at Addu Atoll, Diego Garcia, the Seychelles, and Mauritius, as well as the Cocos-Keeling Islands and Rodrigues, required Indian garrisons.[114] Meanwhile, its air assets were in demand across the Indian Ocean region; 212 Squadron, for example, commenced reconnaissance and anti-submarine patrols in December 1942 in the Persian Gulf and Arabian Sea, mainly from Masirah Island. The squadron, which had its home base in India, 'operated almost continually from dispersed bases, rarely coming together in any one place'.[115]

As 1942 drew to a close, Admiral Somerville returned to Britain for consultations with the Admiralty. He had reason to be pleased; though frustrated by his inability to strike at the Japanese, he had weathered the storm. The Eastern Fleet remained unmolested, and Britain and its allies' continued to be able to use the vital sea lanes of the Indian Ocean. In London he had an audience with the King on 3 December, and a meeting with the Minister of War Transport, Lord Leathers, to discuss the issue of shipping in the Indian Ocean.[116] The demands of other theatres continued to sap his resources. Though there were lots of ships under his command – 'I find that with Fleet auxiliaries and all I have nearly 300 ships under my orders' – there were never enough of the major classes of warships. As he wrote to North, 'My chief preoccupation has been to try and keep my small ration of butter evenly spread over the very large hunk of bread which is my portion'.[117] This, so far, he had managed to achieve, because the Japanese had let him off the hook in spring 1942 and, thereafter, sound British and Allied strategy had reinforced him and taken prudent steps to shore up the position across the Indian Ocean theatre.

What had occurred in the aftermath of the Japanese raids, as Boyd demonstrates, was a rather impressive essay in strategic reinforcement, allied cooperation, and risk management. The British asked the Americans if they could help, as in Churchill's letter to Roosevelt of 15 April. They were not seeking an open-ended commitment, but support for a two-and-a-half month period while they gathered sufficient resources for the Eastern Fleet. *Valiant* was under repair at Durban, *Nelson* and *Rodney* working up after refit, the carriers *Eagle* and *Furious* in refit, and the new battleships *Anson* and *Howe* were expected to be ready in August and October respectively.[118] While the Americans could not at that moment send anything, Admiral King reassured Pound in April that if absolutely necessary, they could do so. The British government knew that, at the latest by September, an enhanced Eastern Fleet with six modern or modernized battleships and four fleet carriers, as well as the three 'R' class battleships then available, could be deployed. Also, that by June, if the Japanese chose to raid Ceylon again, they would face three squadrons of Hurricanes with 50 per cent reserves and three strike squadrons, also with 50 per cent reserves.[119]

114 Wavell, 'Operations in Eastern Theatre'. Wavell wrote that after the occupation of Madagascar, 'I suggested that Mauritius, Rodriguez, and Seychelles could be better garrisoned from East Africa. This was accepted and on 1 September these places passed to the East Africa Command', p. 4668.

115 Dancey, *South East Asia Command*, p. 23.

116 Leathers was also a director of the Pacific and Oriental Line.

117 Simpson (ed.), *The Somerville Papers*, to North, 27/9/43, p. 442.

118 Boyd, *The Royal Navy in Eastern Waters*, p. 386.

119 Ibid., p. 392.

Meanwhile, reinforcements arrived. *Illustrious* joined Somerville's fleet when she entered the Indian Ocean for the Madagascar operation, as did the modern cruiser *Devonshire*, one of the replacements for her two County class sister ships sunk on 5 April, and three more modern cruisers would arrive in the next two months. The Eastern Fleet peaked in July, comprising at its core two modern or modernized battleships (*Warspite* and *Valiant*), two 'R's', two fleet carriers (*Indomitable* having departed for the Pedestal convoy to Malta), a heavy cruiser, three modern six-inch cruisers, six older cruisers, and nine destroyers. By this point the Eastern Fleet was stronger than any force deployed by the Royal Navy to date, and comparable with US Pacific Fleet at that time.[120] The War Cabinet was absolutely clear, in the period January to June, that the Indian Ocean took priority over the Mediterranean.[121] But it still needed to sustain Malta, hence the proposals to sail the Eastern Fleet into the Mediterranean in April, though this was put on hold when it was assessed that Malta could hold until August.

But by autumn, the Eastern Fleet was down to one modern battleship and one fleet carrier. Strategically, this was the result of good things, not bad things. It was a dividend of American victory at Midway, and Churchill's correct belief that the Japanese were spent in this theatre, for the time being at least. It was also down to the government's deft management of risk, as the Mediterranean now, in turn, took priority: in order to generate the massive naval resources needed for Operation Torch, the Eastern Fleet had to be tapped. But as Churchill emphasized to Attlee, this was not a permanent withdrawal from the Indian Ocean, nor a sign that it was unimportant. It was a sign instead that the British, once again, had the luxury of choice, and, given that the Torch landings were discretionary, it was a redeployment that could be cancelled if necessary. If the Japanese had returned, it was the ships now allocated to Torch that would have remained with or, if they had departed, been sent back, to the Indian Ocean.[122] With the travails of 1942 behind them, the British in the Indian Ocean were now to enter a new phase of the war. Unable to take the offensive against Japanese forces occupying the Indian Ocean's eastern rim, they nevertheless continued to guard the sea lanes and began to prepare for the more ambitious operations that were eventually to come.

120 Ibid., p. 399.

121 There was even a brief renaissance in Japanese interest – from the army as well as the navy – in the Indian Ocean in June, driven by German success in the Western Desert and the revival of thoughts about linking hands across the ocean.

122 Boyd, *The Royal Navy in Eastern Waters.*

11

A fleet becalmed: 1943

Though 1943 saw the situation in the Indian Ocean stabilize as the Japanese threat diminished almost to the point of inconsequence, it proved to be a frustrating year for the Eastern Fleet as it remained incapable of striking decisively at Japanese forces occupying the ocean's eastern rim, limited instead to convoy protection. One overstretched imperial power sat on one side of the Indian Ocean, glowering east across the water at a newer, but also overstretched, imperial power on the other. Neither moved very much in the course of 1943, though it was the power on the western side of the water that, for a range of reasons, was gaining in strength.

Though in many ways the Eastern Fleet was becalmed, fundamental progress was being made in terms of the overall war situation impacting the Indian Ocean. This included the growth of Allied air power and the build up of submarine capabilities, meaning that the Allies were now able to contest the sea lanes off Burma and Malaya while remaining firmly in control of those in the western Indian Ocean. More generally, the year witnessed the creation of a new Allied supreme command structure for the region which, in turn, resulted in high level wrangles about what grand strategy should look like in this predominantly British theatre of war, and what operations should be sanctioned in its pursuit.

Five factors accounted for the changing fortunes in the Indian Ocean. Firstly, the naval situation improved elsewhere, and this had a knock-on effect east of Suez. The Battle of the Atlantic, though still deadly, moved inexorably in favour of the Allies. Secondly, the enemy was finally expelled from the African continent as the Anglo-American campaign in North Africa culminated in victory. This had a formidable impact from May on the availability of resources for deployment east and meant that, with the Mediterranean open to Allied shipping once again, there was no longer the need to plough around the Cape when journeying to the Middle East, Asia, and the Far East.

The third factor was the final defeat of Italy. Though much of the country remained stoutly garrisoned by German troops, here, as elsewhere, the boot was now on the Allied foot; Axis power was no longer expanding, indeed it was palpably contracting. Fourthly, Soviet successes culminating in victory at Stalingrad, along with British defensive preparations, meant that Iran and Iraq were now secure. Persia and Iraq Command ceased planning to fight a major campaign against the Wehrmacht and began concentrating exclusively on the delivery of Anglo-American aid to the Soviet Union via the Indian Ocean, its combat forces transferring to North Africa and southern Europe.

The fifth and final factor was that in the Pacific, the Japanese tide was finally stemmed. Though it was yet to be turned back, America's massive and rapidly evolving mobilization made it highly unlikely that Japan would ever have the resources for meaningful operations in the Indian Ocean again. After mid-1943, secure Allied command of the sea, together with the mammoth output of American factories and shipyards, enabled the Allies 'to take full advantage of the mobility of sea communications, making them a source of strength rather than weakness'. Coakley and Leighton write that by 1943, in conjunction with its British allies, the US Army:

> was involved in a vast program of logistical undertakings reaching half-way around the globe. Army ships and cargoes plied around the Cape of Good Hope to the Red Sea, the Persian Gulf, and beyond; Army service troops were scattered along supply routes across Africa and operating supply bases in the Near and Middle East, India, and China. Two foci of this network – the growing service establishments in the Persian Corridor and in the China-Burma-India theatre – had the primary mission of forwarding munitions by rail, truck, and transport aircraft to the Soviet Union and China.[1]

Taken all together, these factors eased the situation east of Suez. Nevertheless, the enemy remained entrenched and aggressive, and the war was far from over. No one on the Allied side had any convincing idea as to how to clear the enemy out of the occupied territories, and even the most perspicacious commanders did not enjoy the luxury of foresight as to how they were going to reverse the battlefield decisions of 1941-42. And for the men and women executing the military plans that presidents, prime ministers, and supreme commanders devised, as well as the civilians caught up in it all, war-related hardships and the threat of injury or death remained paramount factors in their lives.

Yet there was no denying that things were looking up. The shift in fortunes in the war at sea was indicated by the fact that the destruction of eight ships in the Indian Ocean in August 1943 made it the most dangerous place for Allied shipping in the world, as the returns for enemy submarines diminished. But while the Indian Ocean had been a priority for defensive forces in 1942, it was not a priority for offensive forces as the Allies gained the ascendancy. The fact was that the region remained low on the pecking order because the Americans gravitated naturally towards the Pacific, and both Anglo-American powers were determined to prioritize the build up of resources for the long-awaited invasion of Western Europe. John Kennedy wrote that when the General Staff finished 'exhaustive staff studies' regarding Indian Ocean scenarios in October 1943, the 'big over-riding fact' was that 'nothing considerable can be done till the German war is over'.[2] The fact was that the strategic priority in the Indian Ocean was to 'hold', not to 'advance' and, with the Japanese threat diminishing, it was unlikely that it was going to be pumped full of new resources.

Though the wheels turned slowly, moves were afoot at the highest levels of war direction – namely, Churchill, Roosevelt, and the Combined Chiefs of Staff – to plan Allied strategy here in order to effect the reconquest of occupied territory. Among other things, this resulted in the creation of South East Asia Command to supervise and coordinate Allied activity, effectively a

1 Coakley and Leighton, *Global Logistics*, p. 16.
2 Kennedy, *The Business of War*, p. 307.

split of India Command to allow for a dedicated new organization to focus solely on fighting the Japanese while an older organization continued to look to India's security and the management of its military resources.[3] Churchill presented a series of related proposals to the War Cabinet in June, as British strategic planning turned its attention towards the 'reconquest' phase of the war.

> The vigorous and effective prosecution of large-scale operations in South-East Asia and the rapid development of the air route through Burma to China necessitate the reorganization of the High Command in the Indian theatre … The functions of Supreme Operational Command, combined with those of War Member of the Government of India and Commander-in-Chief, India; responsible for all military administration, training and internal security, are more than one man can discharge. It has therefore been decided that the statutory command in India shall be divided from the Operational Command in South-East Asia.[4]

The new command's headquarters were opened in New Delhi in August 1943 but moved to Kandy in the Central Highlands of Ceylon the following April. SEAC's formation was a symbol of British intent, and of its imperial ambitions. As the new Supreme Allied Commander South East Asia, Admiral Lord Louis Mountbatten, wrote in his diary on the day he landed in Karachi to assume his new role: 'I could not help getting a certain thrill at the moment when we crossed the coast of India, to feel that it had fallen to me to be the outward and visible symbol of the British Empire's intention to return to the attack in Asia and regain our lost Empire'.[5]

Improving fortunes were visibly symbolized by the return of the Eastern Fleet's headquarters to Ceylon in September following its enforced exile in Kenya. Although still denied sufficient resources to pursue an offensive strategy, the threat of annihilation so keenly felt the previous year had been lifted. Nevertheless, there were still occasions when it looked as if major Japanese fleet units might return to plunder the Indian Ocean. Only a month before the Eastern Fleet's base returned to Ceylon, Somerville informed London that in his view an attack on Ceylon by Japanese carriers was 'more than a "remote possibility"', and that the potential scale of air attack had been underestimated. The Chiefs of Staff were 'inclined to agree' and emphasized

> the importance of Ceylon for future operations in South East Asia. So long as there is a threat from Japanese carrier-borne aircraft and aircraft based in the Andamans and Northern Sumatra, we consider that not only can no major reductions in the defences be recommended, but they should be maintained in excess of that required to meet the scale of air and sea attack at present assessed.[6]

3 Its neighbouring command to the east was the American South West Pacific Area.
4 TNA, CAB 66/44/14, 'The Reorganization of Command in India and South East Asia', paper by Winston Churchill, 21/9/43.
5 Ziegler (ed.), *The Personal Diary of Admiral the Lord Louis Mountbatten*, p. 6.
6 K. M. De Silva (ed.), *Sri Lanka*, part 1, *The Second World War and the Soulbury Commission, 1939–1945*, British Documents on the End of Empire, series B, volume 2 (London: The Stationery Office, 1997), 'Report by the Defence of Bases Committee for the COS Committee on the Importance of Ceylon for Future Operations in South-East Asia', 6/9/43, WO 203/5174, p. 273.

Ceylon was in the process of being transformed into an offensive, as opposed to a defensive redoubt, but its security needs remained the same.

With large scale offensive operations against the Japanese beyond its reach, the Eastern Fleet had to content itself with its unglamorous but essential convoy escort and policing role struggling, sometimes, even to manage that. The resources vital for offensive, amphibious operations, such as landing craft, aircraft carriers, and the destroyers that escorted them, were usually allocated to the Mediterranean or to Britain in anticipation of the D-Day landings. America was in the driving seat when it came to the allocation of amphibious resources such as landing craft, and the British-dominated Indian Ocean theatre was never going to be at the head of the queue. In fact, as Lieutenant General Pownall wryly observed, South East Asia Command was 'at the bottom of the priority list when it came to equipment and aircraft; all their landing craft were removed for European operations; and a whole series of plans were thrown up, discussed, and regretfully abandoned as utterly impracticable'.[7] The Eastern Fleet continued to be stripped to support other theatres, Somerville ruefully describing it as a 'floating reserve for operations elsewhere'.[8] Trade defence 'became his main preoccupation – and headache – during his stay in East Africa'. Beyond that, he could only conduct feints and deceptions, and keep out of the way of Japanese shore-based defences.[9] Compounding his annoyance, some of the major assets that *were* sent to the Indian Ocean were actually intended for the Pacific, as the Eastern Fleet became the incubator of a new British Pacific Fleet that would eventually operate from Australian and Pacific bases and join the American assault on the Japanese home islands in the final months of the war.

Though the prime minister had other focuses, the situation frustrated him, too. He was far more interested in the Mediterranean theatre – particularly in this period as his cherished Italian campaign got under way – but had his own reasons for retaining a marked interest in the Indian Ocean. It was an inevitably schizophrenic interest, because he was responsible for *all* of the theatres in which British imperial forces fought and British imperial interests were at stake. Indicating his enthusiasm for the Mediterranean, at one point in 1943 he was unpleasantly surprised to learn that resources from that theatre were scheduled to be sent to the Indian Ocean. Returning to a familiar theme, when in summer 1943 U-boats reappeared in the Indian Ocean and began sinking Allied ships in the Mozambique Channel, he complained: 'I am shocked at this new disaster. Where are the destroyers that belong to the Eastern Fleet? Are they all sharing the idleness of that Fleet?'.[10]

When his attention did come to rest on the Indian Ocean, the prime minister focused on the reconquest of Britain's lost colonies, the wellspring of his interest east of Suez. He regretted the fact that the focus for British forces seemed to be supporting American initiatives – such as succouring China, a cause for which Churchill had little time but little choice but to support

7 Bond (ed.), *Chief of Staff*, p. xvi.
8 Simpson (ed.), *The Somerville Papers*, p. 364.
9 Ibid.
10 Roskill, *The War at Sea*, p. 209. Roskill claims that this suggests that 'Churchill never really understood that no nation with world-wide trade to defend can possibly be strong everywhere and all the time'. But one wonders if at least some of his notorious bulling of regional commanders for their alleged inaction, and his propensity to ask for resources from 'X' to be transferred to support 'Y', had more to it than that.

– rather than pursuing avowedly British ends. Such, as he gloomily acknowledged, were the emerging realities of the Anglo-American strategic relationship. But while Churchill favoured the Indian Ocean, his military advisers tended to support a Pacific strategy. The navy was totally against building up all of Britain's strength on Ceylon, Cunningham arguing that 'surely our main purpose should be to defeat Japan'.[11] While the British General Staff also urged plans to join forces with the Americans in the Pacific and leave the Indian Ocean, including the Burma front, in limbo, the prime minister had other ideas.

Churchill was determined, come what may, that British forces would take the surrender of the territories of the lost eastern Empire, from Burma to Hong Kong and, in particular, at Singapore. The British Empire in the east needed to be regained by British arms, not American largesse. At least that way some of the stain could be removed from the imperial escutcheon. He was also keen to pursue an imperial strategy here as it was the only major theatre where Britain had a chance of predominating, and the only one in which the Allied supreme commander was a Briton. While acknowledging the political value of a British presence in the Pacific, his ardent desire to see British arms restore the situation in the Indian Ocean outweighed this consideration. The trajectory of Churchill's thinking can be gauged in a memorandum he wrote for Roosevelt on 9 September 1943 during his fourth visit to the White House. He said that when the Allies gained the Italian fleet, they would also 'gain' the British fleet that had been containing it. This should be used as soon as possible to intensify the war against Japan. A 'strong Eastern Fleet based on Colombo' was needed for forthcoming amphibious operations, and Churchill proposed that it spend four months in the Pacific under American command as it prepared for its Indian Ocean role.[12] If he had been able to determine British policy alone, it is likely that the considerable British commitment to the Pacific theatre – both that planned and that actually in place by the time the atomic bombs were dropped – would have been less significant.

Throughout 1943 and 1944 numerous schemes for major operations in the South East Asia Command area foundered due to the disagreements of British strategic planners, the disagreements of American and British strategic planners, and lack of adequate resources. The period spawned an alphabet soup of operational codenames and Allied powwows; Eureka, Octagon, Quadrant, Sextant, and Trident conferences considered operations such as Anakim, Buccaneer, Bullfrog, Culverin, Dracula, Pigstick, Sceptre, Tarzan, Vanguard, and Zipper, variously involving attacks in Upper Burma, the Andamans, Akyab Island, northern Sumatra, Malaya, Rangoon, the Arakan, and the Kra isthmus.[13]

11 Roskill, *Churchill and the Admirals*, p. 262.

12 Churchill, *The Second World War*, volume 5, *Closing the Ring* (London: Cassell, 1952), p. 119.

13 These are all documented in Willmott's landmark work *Grave of a Dozen Schemes*, which is also an important contribution to the nature and force structure of the Eastern Fleet as well as the British Pacific Fleet. The book chronicles in detail the genesis and fate of these various plans, and has a helpful explanation of the 'British Defense Planning Organization' in 1943. It contains important appendices: Appendix 1, 'The Eastern and East Indies Fleets, 1 January 1944-15 August 1945'; Appendix B, 'Operational Chronologies'; and Appendix C, 'Orders of Battle' (including East Indies Fleet order of battle on 15 August 1945 and that of the British Pacific Fleet on the same date, 324 and 370 vessels respectively); Appendix D, 'Operation Zipper and the British Pacific Fleet'. What is interesting, given that it became the one part of the British war against Japan that impacted subsequent popular memory – in the shape of the oxymoronically well-remembered 'forgotten war' –

The situation persisted even in to 1944, Willmott claiming that on 21 February the Chiefs of Staff determined to resign if Churchill pushed for a commitment to South-east Asia for political (as opposed to military) reasons.[14] On 24 March, Kennedy wrote that

> The strategy against Japan remains in a state of deadlock. The PM issued a directive to the Chiefs of Staff in favour of the Indian Ocean. The Chiefs of Staff have asked him to reconsider ... They have pointed out ... that the Pacific strategy, should it prove to be militarily practicable and politically acceptable, would lead to a substantial shortening of the war against Japan; it would enable us to use the forces and resources of the Empire in a more closely related and concentrated effort than would the Indian Ocean strategy; and, further, it would not delay the recapture, by our own forces, of our own territories in Malaya and the East Indies.[15]

'The PM, up till now', Kennedy continued, 'has been obsessed with the Indian Ocean strategy and he believes that, politically, it is inevitable for us. The Americans have been lukewarm, to say the least of it, in asking our help in the Pacific'.[16] The matter remained under intense discussion. Returning to the subject on 14 July, he wrote: 'Indications are that Winston is going to overrule the COS [Chiefs of Staff] on the Japan strategy and insist on our effort being across the Bay of Bengal toward Malaya etc, instead of from Australia in conjunction with the Americans'.[17] The numerous abortive plans and disagreements between Churchill and the Chiefs of Staff in 1943-44 reflected the British government's search for a strategy.

> [T]he British planning effort for the war against Japan was plagued by distractions, confusion, and fundamental policy differences. Indeed, in this year it proved impossible for the British high command to settle national policy ... The fact that Churchill and the Chiefs of Staff could not decide between the conflicting claims of the Indian Ocean and the Pacific theaters lay at the heart of British difficulties.[18]

Nevertheless, while planners planned and strategists strategized, on the ground there was a war going on. In the Indian Ocean it might lack the proximity (to British audiences) of the Italian campaign, the drama of events in the Pacific, or the anticipation of the Normandy landings, but it was war nonetheless.

is that in all this Burma was viewed negatively by Churchill and other senior British figures. It was of no great value, other than in the need to regain it and Washington's desire to use it as a route to give succour to China. Willmott writes that:

> For the British and the Japanese alike the Chindwin and the Bay of Bengal were a line of mutual exhaustion, convenient to both. Neither had the means to undertake major offensive operations in these theaters, and both ... would have preferred, if left to their own devices, to have accepted a standoff here in order to devote their resources and attentions to other, more important theaters. (Ibid., p. 7).

14 Willmott, *Grave of a Dozen Schemes*, p. 13.
15 Kennedy, *The Business of War*, p. 322.
16 Ibid., p. 323.
17 Ibid., p. 336.
18 Willmott, *Grave of a Dozen Schemes*, p. 18.

Escorts, the air picture, and the submarine threat

The air situation improved throughout 1943. The RAF in the Indian Ocean was organized in groups which controlled squadrons and squadron detachments parcelled out across the vast expanse of water between Africa and South-east Asia. RAF Group headquarters were to be found in Aden, Ceylon, East Africa, and India. There were bases at places such as Karachi and RAF Khormaksar and RAF Sheikh Othman in Aden, and there was an Imperial Airways and RAF staging post at Sharjah in the Trucial Oman, particularly useful for aircraft being flown from Europe to South-east Asia and Australia by way of the Middle East and India. As has been seen, as well as established facilities in places such as Ceylon, India, and South Africa, numerous islands had sprouted air strips and flying-boat anchorages, and new ones were still being created in places such as the Cocos-Keeling Islands as the war moved on and recrudescent Allied air power helped take the war to the Japanese. Reinforcements continued to arrive piecemeal: on 16 February 1943, for instance, 259 Squadron RAF reformed at Kipevu in Kenya with Catalinas, and was deployed on anti-submarine patrols over the Indian Ocean. In March, a detachment was sent to Congella in Natal and in June another went to Langebaan in Cape Province until 262 Squadron was able to take over the area. This meant that the bulk of 259 Squadron now moved to Congella, the whole squadron coming together again in September as a result of a further move, this time to Dar-es-Salaam, where a flying boat base was established at Kurasini Creek. Its flying-boats flew from Masirah and Aden to increase patrol range, while Tuléar in southern Madagascar was also used as British aircraft continued to patrol the sea lanes and help in the hunt for U-boats and their supply ships.[19]

Improvements were made in controlling aircraft operating from scattered bases, especially important as the British submarine offensive now gathered pace, supported from the air, along with other tasks such as anti-shipping patrols and minelaying. In July 1943 the Air Officer Commanding 222 Group Ceylon, Air Vice-Marshal Alan Lees, was given operational control of all general reconnaissance aircraft in the Indian Ocean theatre (excluding Bengal), his forces spread from East Africa and Aden to Ceylon and the Cocos-Keeling Islands. In August Indian Ocean flying-boats were distributed thus: 26 in the Eastern Area, 18 in the Northern Area, 24 in the Western Area, and 23 in the Southern Area.[20]

At sea, during the course of 1943 no less than 48 ships were transferred from the Eastern Fleet to the Mediterranean, reflecting the Indian Ocean's relative security as well as the scale and tempo of operations as the Allies invaded Italy and Sicily and continued the campaign in North Africa. In January *Illustrious* had sailed for Birkenhead for a refit, leaving Somerville without a carrier.[21] Their Lordships also required the return of *Warspite*, his flagship for the past two years, in order to prepare for a role in Operation Husky, the invasion of Sicily. 'I shall have no fleet left before long', he grumbled.[22] A particular concern was the impact these reductions had on the Eastern Fleet's capacity to provide convoy escort – still a problem. In January 1943, for example, the Australian 9th Division massed in the Gulf of Suez awaiting transit home.

19 RAF Historical Section. On 9 March 1945, the first Sunderland arrived to convert the squadron to this type but a month later these were taken away and 259 Squadron disbanded on 30 April 1945.
20 NHB, Eastern Fleet war diary, volume 12.
21 Simpson (ed.), *The Somerville Papers*, pp. 448-9.
22 Ibid., diary entry, 5/3/43, p. 453.

The 'Monsters', the world's largest ocean liners converted for service as troopships, undertook this mission. Docking at Suez to collect their quota of soldiers, they were accompanied by the Armed Merchant Cruiser *Queen of Bermuda*. They were escorted clear of the Gulf of Aden by Mediterranean Fleet destroyers, and then handed over to a solitary Eastern Fleet cruiser, *Devonshire*, which escorted them across the Indian Ocean. As Somerville wrote to North, 'I'd been robbed of my last aerodrome [carrier] & then had to cover the passage of the Diggers from Alex's place [the Mediterranean] to their native shores. Not at all nice & all had to be done on the bluff'.[23]

Willmott writes that in this period:

> In terms of numbers of escorts that might be 'working' at any one time in the Indian Ocean theater it would be lucky to muster thirty, realistically twenty, and quality left much to be desired. For example, the twenty merchantmen of Convoy BA62 were afforded a single sloop as escort for the voyage from Bombay to Aden, while in February 1944 two tankers were sunk and another seriously damaged from a convoy (PA69) that had two escorts, one without a working radar and the other without a working asdic and no radar. Too often escorts had to be provided from what little was available and there was little or no opportunity for units to train together and to absorb the lessons that had been so painfully learned in the North Atlantic.[24]

Britain and its allies continued, however, to move very large numbers of servicemen and women by sea with remarkably low losses. Addressing the Commons on 11 February 1943, Churchill said:

> We have had hardly any losses at sea in our heavily-escorted troop convoys. Out of about 3,000,000 soldiers who have been moved under the protection of the British Navy about the world, to and fro across the seas and oceans, about 1,348 have been killed or drowned, including missing. It is about 2,200 to one against your being drowned if you travel in a British troop convoy in the present war.[25]

Nevertheless, the Eastern Fleet was so reduced over the course of the year that it was only with difficulty that it could perform its core trade protection role. It consisted of the 'R' class battleship *Ramillies* – returned after over a year under repair following her Madagascan misadventure – the escort carrier *Battler*, seven cruisers, 11 destroyers, the 4th Submarine Flotilla, two armed merchant cruisers, 13 escort vessels, and some landing craft. Lack of sufficient destroyers remained a serious problem. Removing destroyers for convoy duties immobilized the big ships, yet without sufficient of them convoys could not be protected. By the end of the year, there were only five available for fleet training, a vital precursor to the attacks on Japanese-occupied territories for which Somerville yearned. With available destroyers engaged on escort duties,

23 Ibid., to North, 22/2/43.
24 Willmott, *Grave of a Dozen Schemes*, p. 153.
25 See http://www.churchillarchiveforschools.com/themes/the-themes/key-events-and-developments-in-world-history/was-churchill-really-worried-about-the-battle-of-the-atlantic-and-if-so-why/the-sources/source-1

submarines were the only force that could be employed offensively, operating against Japanese targets in the waters off Burma and Malaya.

The enemy continued to acknowledge the value of disrupting Indian Ocean sea lanes, of course, and to deploy forces to try and effect this, even though both Germany and Japan were more intensely focused elsewhere and increasingly bereft of sufficient resources themselves. Despite this, the Indian Ocean remained a theatre in which they needed to take an interest, now for defensive as opposed to offensive reasons as the pendulum of war swung against them. For it was here that the Allied forces required to eject the Japanese from South-east Asia and the East Indies were being built up, and they were dependent on safe passage across the Indian Ocean, as was the ever-growing number of merchantmen taking Lend-Lease aid to the Soviet Union. In 1943 the Japanese high command requested that German U-boats operating off southern Africa be transferred to the Arabian Sea. This was because following Allied victory in the Mediterranean, ships taking part in the reinforcement of British forces in Burma and India could now sail via the Suez Canal and the Red Sea and across the Arabian Sea, rather than going around the Cape.

Admiral Dönitz decided to wait until after the next monsoon, when he judged that the arrival of a new force of U-boats in the northern Indian Ocean would have a telling effect. Having withdrawn from the Atlantic in May, deploying U-boats to the Indian Ocean was a sensible alternative, made more attractive by the Japanese finally having agreed, the previous December, to allow German vessels to use its Indian Ocean bases.[26] U-boats deployed to the Indian Ocean would also be supported by special tankers such as *Brake* and *Charlotte Schliemann*.

But only five of the ten Monsoon group U-boats dispatched from Europe reached their destination, the remainder destroyed en route by the Royal Navy and the US Navy. The Monsoon group was led by *U200*, which sailed for the Indian Ocean in June. One of its missions was to deploy a small Brandenburger Regiment contingent to sabotage Durban's dry dock, supported by the Ossewabrandwag. But the submarine was sunk by a Coastal Command Liberator en route, an inauspicious start for the new offensive.[27] Some of the boats did get through, and Eastern Fleet headquarters was aware that four or five submarines were moving north from Madagascar, and recent Japanese sinkings in the Arabian Sea meant that there was little chance of the Germans scoring a surprise blow.[28] On 22 June the tanker *Charlotte Schliemann*, ordered from Japan, refuelled six rust-streaked U-boats 700 miles south of Mauritius, and unsuccessful attempts were made by the British to find her.[29] But pickings were thin for the Monsoon group, which was down to four operational boats by October. To meet the challenge Britain reinforced naval and air units. 621 Squadron, flying Wellington bombers, and 259 and 265 squadrons Catalinas, were moved from East Africa to bases covering the Gulf of Aden.[30] From November 1943 it was decided that Aden's operational area would be extended to cover the Persian Gulf,

26 See Paterson, *Hitler's Grey Wolves*, chapter 5, 'German in Asia', which documents the experience of German forces based in Penang and Singapore and their relations with the Japanese.

27 Paterson, *Hitler's Grey Wolves*.

28 The American tanker *Yamhill*'s battle with a Japanese submarine in the region in April 1944 is recounted in Bill Jopes, *A Voyage to Abadan* (Bloomington, IN: Xlibris Corporation, 1999), chapter 18, 'A Day-Long Battle with a Japanese Submarine'.

29 Paterson, *Hitler's Grey Wolves*, p. 90. On 11 September, five U-boats refuelled from the tanker *Brake*.

30 RAF Historical Section.

and that forces there would work closely with 222 Group based in Ceylon. This brought a unification of operational command which was vital if effective protection was to be provided for shipping dispersed over such a wide area. Mauritius and Tuléar were reinforced with flying-boats as well, as the British continued to shuffle the pack and distribute resources as threats arose.

Another response to the submarine threat in the northern Indian Ocean was to put as much shipping as possible into convoys. Ships that still had to proceed independently were aided by the establishment of approach positions outside the focal areas of enemy attacks, air patrols being provided to cover the routes between these approved positions and the ports of destination. Regular convoys were instituted between Durban and Kilindini, Aden to Bombay, and Colombo to Bombay, along with the provision of anti-submarine escorts. It was also necessary to allow for an increase of escorts for convoys to and from the Persian Gulf. To help out, the Commander-in-Chief Atlantic loaned Somerville eight escort vessels for work on the Aden-Bombay route, and eight corvettes and sloops were transferred from the Mediterranean. The Aden Escort Force numbered ten vessels, the Kilindini Escort Force for the Kilindini-Aden route another ten. There was also an Aden-Bombay-Colombo Escort Force, and reinforcements were also sent to the Persian Gulf.

The challenge, as always, remained to protect convoys while also being ready to meet a Japanese raid in strength into the Indian Ocean. Somerville wrote in October 1943 that

> The present naval forces we had available were barely sufficient to afford normal trade protection and were quite inadequate in numbers and composition to meet any Japanese force of, say, 1 battleship, 5 heavy and light cruisers, 2 carriers and an appropriate destroyer screen. I saw no reason why the Japanese should not be prepared to detach such a force for operations in the Bay of Bengal unless they had good reason to think that a heavy American attack directed against, say, their main base at Truk, was imminent.[31]

As well as establishing convoys and convoy protection forces, another way of addressing the submarine problem was to attempt to degrade Axis intelligence regarding British and Allied shipping so as to lessen the chances of successful submarine sorties. In March 1943, for example, a superannuated group of British reservists attacked German merchantmen in the port of Marmagoa after sailing around the cone of India from Calcutta. Colin Mackenzie, the Force 136 commander based in Meerut who sanctioned what was known as Operation Creek, wrote that Axis submarines were

> seriously affecting the supply of war materials to India, and despite the knowledge that the devastating monthly loss of ships and cargoes continued undiminished due to accurate information transmitted by the powerful secret radio equipment on *Ehrenfels*, one of the four Axis ships interned in the Portuguese Colony of Goa, HMG had for reasons of overall political strategy refused to authorise any violations of Portuguese neutrality … In view of the gravity of the situation, Force 136, a Mission of SOE in South East Asia, decided to take unilateral action in Goa by a sea-borne assault.

31 Simpson (ed.), *The Somerville Papers*, desk diary, 29/10/43, p. 481.

> The assault lasting 47 minutes, by a small force provided by 14 members of the Calcutta Light Horse, A. F. (I) [Auxiliary Forces India], 4 from the Calcutta Scottish, A. F. (I), (both of which were the equivalent of Territorial units in the UK), and 6 from Force 136, was launched at 0130 hours on the morning of 10th March, 1943. The assault was successful despite numerical odds of over 120 to 1. *Ehrenfels* and her secret radio were completely destroyed and the three other ships, which it was known were also prepared for demolition, sank themselves in accordance with their agreed plan. The cessation of information caused the withdrawal of Axis submarines; losses of Allied shipping ceased almost immediately.[32]

The wireless set was kept aboard *Ehrenfels* in a small compartment with a sign on the door saying 'Danger of death! High voltage!'.[33]

Axis exchanges and other activity in the Indian Ocean

As the war developed, the Axis alliance took on greater substance in the Indian Ocean. The relationship between Germany and Japan had, in practical terms, been a slow starter, hampered by distance as well as mutual reservations. But the characterization of the Axis alliance as entirely deficient, Rotem Kowner argues, can overlook regional nuances and significant areas of cooperation – such as the submarine trade and combat cooperation that developed in the Indian Ocean.[34] This 'sometimes intensive and unique collaboration' centred around Malaya and the Java Sea, and blossomed in the last two years of the war. It involved the exchange of strategic raw materials (especially bauxite, rubber, tungsten, and tin) and cutting-edge technology via submarines, and an ideological affinity that resulted in effective German pressure on the Japanese to implement harsher racial policies towards Jewish communities across the Indian Ocean region. 'Crucially, the Axis cooperation in the Indian Ocean culminated in a fully fledged combat collaboration focused on the establishment of German submarine bases in a number of Southeast Asian ports occupied by Japan'.[35]

Blockade runners between 1941 and 1944 delivered 44,983 tons of natural rubber to German and Italian industry from conquered Indian Ocean territories. They also carried 68,117 tons of

32 Dodds-Parker Papers, Magdalen College, Oxford. MC P2/9/IC/3, Colin Mackenzie to Margaret Thatcher, 'Operation Creek Awards', not dated. Also includes the humble petition to the Queen, dated18/10/80. This excerpt is from the citation written by Mackenzie in the 1980s as he attempted to get gallantry awards for the participants, writing to Prime Minister Margaret Thatcher seeking approval for awards to be made by the Queen. Thanks to Andrew Stewart for copies of these documents. For an overview of the operation, see Robert Barr Smith, 'The Daring Calcutta Light Horse', *World War II History* (2015), at http://warfarehistorynetwork.com/daily/wwii/the-daring-calcutta-light-horse-raid/. See also James Leasor's book *Boarding Party: The Last Action of the Calcutta Light Horse* (London: Heinemann, 1978) and the film based upon the action, *The Sea Wolves* (1980), starring Roger Moore, David Niven, and Gregory Peck.

33 Paterson, *Hitler's Grey Wolves*, p. 50-55.

34 Kowner, 'When Economics, Strategy'. See also the fascinating and imaginatively titled book by Horst Geerken, *Hitler's Asian Adventures: The Third Reich and the Dutch East Indies, the Creation of German Naval Bases, the Beginning of the End for Colonial Rule, German Aid for Soekarno's Freedom Fighters and India's Subhas Chandra Bose* (Bonn: BukitCinta, 2015).

35 Kowner, 'When Economics, Strategy', p. 229.

other essential materials, mostly from South-east Asia, such as tungsten, tin, and quinine.[36] But this was a drop in the ocean, and the great irony for the Axis was that although they now in theory had unrestricted access to vital raw materials, transporting them from source to industrial sites was exceedingly difficult. With the Allies exerting an increasing command of the sea and decimating enemy merchant shipping, from 1943 moving raw materials by submarine became the only viable option. Specifically for this trade, the Germans laid down 30 large cargo-carrying U-boats.

Defeat in East Africa had not ended the deployment of Italian submarines to the region and five specially modified Italian submarines were sent out from Europe, three of them equipped to carry 150 ton cargoes to trade with Japan, where they arrived in spring 1943. The submarine *Leonardo da Vinci* made a 120-day cruise in the Indian Ocean in April, sinking a freighter in the South Atlantic on the way out and then four ships in the Indian Ocean. But bound for Bordeaux on the homeward journey, on 24 May she was depth charged and destroyed near the Azores by the British destroyer *Active* and frigate *Ness*, which were escorting a Winston Special convoy when the enemy was detected. Another Italian boat, the *Cagni*, made a record-breaking 137-day cruise and was 90 days into her second Indian Ocean tour when the Italian surrender occurred, whereupon she surprised the port of Durban by surfacing unannounced and the captain turning his boat over to the British authorities on 21 September 1943. *Cappellini*, *Giuliani*, and *Torricelli* reached the Dutch East Indies between July and August.

The pioneering submarine run between Japanese-occupied South-east Asia and Europe occurred shortly after the raid on Ceylon when, on 22 April 1942, *I-30*, a large 3,717 ton type B-1 cruiser submarine, departed its base in Penang with a cargo bound for Germany. Part of Admiral Ishizaki's force that had deployed to the Mozambique Channel, she arrived at Lorient on 5 August and delivered 1,500 kilograms of mica and 660 kilograms of shellac for use in electrical capacitator devices and military pyrotechnics respectively.[37] On its return journey, *I-30* was loaded with advanced German weapons systems, including guns, bombs, torpedoes, radar, and Enigma machines.[38] She reached Penang on 8 October to refuel but five days later hit a British mine three miles off Singapore's Keppel Harbour, and began to sink rapidly. Some of the crew survived and some of the equipment was salvaged. On 20 January 1943 the long-awaited 'Agreement on economic cooperation' between Germany and Japan was signed and exchanges of material and military technology became relatively straightforward, stymied only by mounting losses at sea.

In terms of Axis combat cooperation in the Indian Ocean, submarines featured prominently. The Germans were particularly keen on Japanese operations in the Indian Ocean, increasingly out of desparation. Joachim von Ribbentrop, Hitler's foreign minister, said on the Fuhrer's behalf that this was 'more crucial than a Japanese attack on the far eastern Soviet border'.[39] A new departure occurred when Penang became the operational base for Germany's Monsoon group and its reinforcements, South-east Asia and the waters of the Indian Ocean becoming the only place in the world where the forces of all three Axis powers operated together, though not to very great effect. It was too little, too late.

36 Ibid., p. 233.
37 Ibid., p. 234.
38 Paterson, *Hitler's Grey Wolves*, p. 33.
39 Kowner, 'When Economics, Strategy', p. 240.

In April 1943 the Indian nationalist leader Subhas Chandra Bose, along with a cargo of military material, was exchanged in the middle of the Indian Ocean. His journey east had begun at Kiel harbour on 8 February aboard Captain Werner Musenburg's *U-180*. On 18 April *U-180* sunk the British tanker *Corbis* 500 miles east south-east of Port Elizabeth.[40] Three days later she met the Japanese *I-29* off the coast of Mozambique, where the exchange took place. The Japanese vessel reached Sabang in Sumatra on 6 May, and Bose began the work of reaching out to Indian expatriates across Japanese-occupied territory, as well as establishing a new 'independent' government in the Andaman and Nicobar Islands. Also exchanged were German blueprints for jet engines and V-2 rockets, and Imperial Japanese Navy personnel going to Germany to study submarine construction.

On 6 July 1943 Captain Shinji Uchino's *I-8* sailed for France, carrying a crew that was to take over one of two U-boats that Hitler had given to the Japanese as examples of German construction. On her return, *I-8* carried technical torpedo and gunnery machinery, and reached Singapore and Japan safely despite British knowledge of her passage around the Cape. That November *I-29* sailed from Penang en route for Europe on another 'Yanagi mission', as the Japanese termed these east-west runs.[41] ULTRA intelligence alerted the British to her passage, though there was no suitable cover to allow her to be intercepted; as in other theatres, the chance of attacking the enemy (or saving friendly forces from attack) sometimes had to be passed up in order to preserve ULTRA's integrity. *I-29* carried scientists and specialists who were deposited at Lorient in occupied France, along with a cargo of raw materials. She then took on board German 'scientific equipment and blueprints of new and secret weapons, including the latest Messerschmitt fighter aircraft, the Me163 and Me262'.[42]

Another participant in this Axis trade was *I-34*, which attempted (also in November) the journey to Europe loaded with rubber, tin, tungsten, quinine, and sample weapons. Calling at Singapore to collect cargo, on 11 November she headed for Penang to collect passengers. But British intelligence was tracking her movements, and Lieutenant Commander Mervyn Wingfield's *Taurus*, on patrol 1,300 miles from her base in Ceylon, was instructed to search for her.[43] Lieutenant John Gibson, a member of the British submarine's crew, writes that on the morning of 14 November:

> The sea was like the surface of a mirror in a moonlit room. Rain squalls came down from the north, passing across the sea in noisy gusts, soaking the men on the bridge and chilling them. Visibility was poor. The *Taurus* came on slow towards the dark shape of the island [Penang]. The enemy blackout was complete. The scene was dead. We did not know that to the south of us a Japanese U-boat was coming up the Straits. She was coming up from Singapore to join the enemy flotilla at Penang. As we cruised slowly in the shallows this

40 *Corbis*, bound from Abadan for Cape Town, was carrying 13,100 tons of diesel oil and 50 tonnes of aviation spirit. Fifty of her complement of 60 died in the attack, the survivors drifting in an open boat before being rescued by a South African Air Force launch and landed at Port Elizabeth.

41 See Bob Hackett, 'World War II: Yanagi Missions – Japan's Underwater Convoys', *World War II Magazine* (October 2005), reproduced at http://www.historynet.com/world-war-ii-yanagi-missions-japans-underwater-convoys.htm

42 Wilson, *A Submariners' War*, p. 90.

43 Ibid., p. 115.

other boat was getting closer. Unseen, unheard, she was creaming confidently through the pale waters.[44]

Two miles off the entrance the *Taurus* dived. The early light was dangerous. It was at this time that the enemy might send out air patrols and they would see us, a dark blob on the flatness. They would see our wake in the brilliant green phosphorescence … In these waters there was an uncertainty; the war was waiting to blow up, and each side was on guard. There was a pulsating stillness and for months there had been complete quiet. Submarines had not been operating here for some time. The Japanese were waiting, tense, motionless. They hung on to their steaming jungles and listened for the first light footfall that would mean that the Allies were about to strike. In that nervous and apprehensive state they were liable to be very dangerous. We went carefully.

But the U-boat coming from the south was without care. She came chugging along and her crew would be shaving and getting ready to go ashore. They would be looking forward to a hot breakfast. How well we knew that tendency to relax during the last few miles when home is in sight! That relaxation cost that crew their lives.

We were heading north, parallel to the coast, waiting for the sun to rise. Through the periscope the view was dim and rain squalls limited vision. The reflection of small black clouds swept across the moonlit surface. In the warm, well-lit messes we were having breakfast. The Officer of the Watch plotted our course on the chart and had another look at the long black island that lay against the sunrise. With routine thoroughness he swung round to look out to sea, his head covered in a black hood that hid the instruments lights from his eyes. He was able to adapt his sight to the deep blue of morning seen through a periscope.

At 5.30 the enemy must have been about four miles away. He was eventually sighted at a range of two thousand yards. By this time the sky was very much lighter, but the sun had not yet risen. It was an indistinct shape that was first seen, a black blob that came on through the rain squalls until it was suddenly in a clear patch. Then it was obvious – a U-boat! The most satisfactory of all targets. The news was through the boat in a flash. Perhaps it was the *I-8* – a Japanese U-boat that had sunk a British vessel some months earlier and then massacred the crew. Wingfield, by now at the periscope, was tense. We swung to port, and for an eternity the target was lost in a squall. Then Wingfield gave the order to fire; it was a snap attack, no deliberating, no calculation. The whole thing was over in three minutes and the torpedoes were on their way. By now the enemy diesels were clearly heard on the hydrophones, dim and feeble behind the strident noise of six torpedo engines. Two thousand yards at forty-five knots. The single explosion was dead on time. It was a deep and thunderous roar and for a moment the whole boat shook. The Captain raised the periscope and had a look. Nothing in sight. Not a thing. The noise of diesels had ceased. Three minutes after the explosion, six after the first sighting, we were back in our messes finishing our breakfasts.[45]

44 John Gibson, *Dark Seas Above* (London: William Blackwood, 1974).
45 Ibid.

I-34 was sunk in the Malacca Strait just 30 nautical miles off Penang. Of the 94 people on board, 80 lost their lives.[46]

The Eastern Fleet's Cinderella status throughout 1943 was a sign of Allied strategic success. While frustrating for Somerville, it was due to the lack of a credible Japanese threat, and because of the priorities of the Mediterranean as the Allies went on the offensive. And as the next chapter explains, British submarines were about to gain prominence as the Eastern Fleet itself took to the offensive; 1944 was going to be a busy year.

46 See Vernon Miller, *Analysis of Japanese Submarine Losses to Allied Submarines in World War Two* (Hoosick Falls, NY: Merriam Press, 2013).

12

On the offensive: 1944

In 1944 the Eastern Fleet grew in strength and firepower, enabling it to undertake offensive operations while sustaining its essential defensive tasks. Mounting Japanese weakness in the Pacific worked in the Allies favour in the Indian Ocean. As well as supporting land operations in Burma, Allied naval and air forces began to attack Japanese bases, to harry shipping attempting to supply the Imperial Japanese Army in the Andamans, Burma, and Malaya, and to mine the approaches to Japanese-occupied harbours such as Penang and important seaways like the Malacca Strait.[1] Now, conducting carrier and battleship attacks on Japanese positions, the fleet was able to synchronize offensive action in order to assist American naval forces fighting in the south-west Pacific, mounting diversionary attacks with the aim of drawing off Japanese forces. Ceylon's role had turned from defensive stronghold to offensive launch-pad from which the war could be taken to the enemy, a giant aircraft carrier and fleet base.

In early 1944 the British began to look in earnest at the size of the forces they would commit to the war against Japan, including a new British Pacific Fleet. At this stage, British staff were planning to send six army division, 140 RAF squadrons, and a fleet built around 15 carriers and eight battleships, some 675,000 military personnel in total.[2] On 4 January Somerville was informed by the Admiralty that

> *Renown*, *Illustrious*, *Victorious*, 4 cruisers, 12 fleets [destroyers], 10 frigates, *Woolwich*, *Unicorn*, and *Resource* are to form a British Naval Pacific Force and that it would leave for the Pacific towards the end of March. Any other reinforcements to the Eastern Fleet will also go to the Pacific. This information suggests almost conclusively that no major amphibious operations are to be staged in this Theatre and that our role will be to contain the Japanese forces and act as a stepping stone for reinforcements for the Pacific area.[3]

Despite growing strength, the exhaustively-discussed amphibious assaults on Japanese-held territory remained on the planning-room table, and the British continued to proceed with

1 The maritime assets of other commands contributed to these activities in the Indian Ocean region, minelaying missions to Surabaya in Java, for example, being undertaken by Catalinas operating out of Darwin. See Brett Hilder, *Navigator in the South Seas* (Adelaide: Seal Books, 1978).

2 Willmott, *Grave of a Dozen Schemes*, p. 11.

3 Simpson (ed.), *The Somerville Papers*, desk diary, 4/1/44, p. 501.

caution. As early as April 1943 Smuts and Somerville had 'agreed that the possibility of Japanese attack directed against India or Ceylon was now remote unless the US suffered a major naval reversal'.[4] Yet although Japan was an increasingly 'fireless dragon' in the Indian Ocean, the British did not want their reach to exceed their grasp. This was because there was no urgent drive for action here as there was in other theatres; the fact was that the war would not be won or lost in the Indian Ocean region, and while ridding occupied territories of the enemy and killing Japanese personnel was of course highly desirable, doing so here would not materially affect the war's outcome.[5] Continuing to protect the sea lanes, on the other hand, remained a matter of vital strategic importance.

Given that Mountbatten believed that an amphibious offensive would be the centrepiece of Britain's war against Japan, the dearth of adequate landing craft was a problem, as was the continued wrangling over Indian Ocean versus Pacific strategy. At one point the assets that he had managed to scrape together were summarily taken away as the Allied high command prioritized the Normandy landings. Nevertheless, improvements elsewhere meant that more ships could be spared for operations in the Indian Ocean, and the Eastern Fleet became better able to raid Japanese-occupied territory, and nurtured a new fleet that would be sent to join the Americans in the Pacific before the year was out.

The enemy in the Indian Ocean was increasingly inoffensive, though, like a porcupine, was dangerous if prodded. The Germans and Japanese also continued to deploy submarines here, and at the start of 1944 the Germans had five U-boats at Penang and the Japanese eight.

> [B]ut despite the dispatch of twenty-three U-boats from European waters for the Far East during 1944, circumstances conspired to ensure that the number on station could not be maintained, still less increased. No fewer than fourteen of the U-boats were lost on passage and four of the boats that were on station in January 1944 or arrived in the Far East during 1944 succumbed in the course of a year that saw the logic of the Pacific priority exert itself to ever greater effect in terms of the number of Japanese submarines that could be spared for service in the Indian Ocean.[6]

Allied strength meant that Penang become untenable as an operational base and further diminishing their potency, the fact that Axis submarines were increasingly devoted to blockade-running meant there were never more than three at sea at any one time after December 1943 in an anti-shipping role (other than in February-March and December 1944).

Still, they presented a threat. Though the British were both skilled and lucky when it came to protecting troop-carrying ships, occasional disasters were inevitable. In February 1944 *Khedive Ismail* sailed from Mombasa as part of the five-ship troop convoy KR8, destined for Colombo. The ship's 1,511 passengers included the 996 officers and men of the 301st Field Regiment East African Artillery on their way to join the 11th East African Division in Ceylon ahead of deployment to Burma. There were also 271 Royal Navy personnel, 178 crew members, 53 nurses, and

4 Ibid., summary of conversation with Smuts, 7/4/43, p. 456.
5 Ibid., p. 379.
6 Willmott, *Grave of a Dozen Schemes*, p. 152. The boats on station also suffered from torpedo and battery maintenance problems.

nine members of the Women's Transport Service on board.[7] She was sunk by *I-27*, commanded by Lieutenant Commander Toshiaki Fukumura. The Japanese boat had already sunk a number of American and British freighters and passenger ships in the Indian Ocean, including the *Alcoa Protector*, *Fort Mumford*, *Montanan*, and *Sambridge*. The sinking of *Khedive Ismail* cost the lives of 1,134 people, most of them belonging to 301st Field Regiment and some killed by the British depth charges.

Following the sinking, *I-27* was attacked by the destroyers *Petard* and *Paladin*, which formed the convoy escort along with *Hawkins*. Initially, the submarine attempted to hide under *Khedive Ismail*'s survivors, though this did not cause the British attack to abate, it being grim policy to prosecute attacks at the expense of survivors given the destruction that such a vessel would continue to inflict if it got away. After ramming *I-27* and sustaining damage, *Paladin* made for Port T, within sight of which the *Khedive Ismail* had been sunk as she passed through the One and a Half Degree Channel. There *Paladin* was patched up by the repair ship *Lucia*, the Royal Fleet Auxiliary repair ship *Salviking* having been sunk en route by *U-168*. Meanwhile, *I-27* was sent to the bottom with a combination of shelling, depth charges, and torpedoes, 99 of her 100-strong compliment losing their lives. Seaworthy once again, *Paladin* returned to the site of the *Khedive Ismail* sinking to join the search for survivors, as did a salvage ship.

The incident dismayed Churchill, who wrote to the First Lord of the Admiralty and the First Sea Lord: 'This is a serious disaster. Who were the 1,055 drowned? Were they troops outward or homeward bound? British or American? How is it that in a convoy of this kind more could not be rescued?'.[8] It would be interesting to know what the prime minister's thoughts were when he learned that they were predominantly Africans. An investigation into the sinking, ordered by Somerville, blamed the lack of adequate escorts for the tragedy (the Eastern Fleet had only 20 destroyers at the time). While the *Khedive Ismail* was at sea, Eastern Fleet escort forces and RAF aircraft from Ceylon were busy covering the passage across the Indian Ocean of a giant floating dock that was to be installed at Trincomalee. Furthermore, operations in support of the army in Burma were scheduled to take place, which required destroyer cover too. Also inhibiting the Eastern Fleet's ability to protect convoys at this particular juncture, major warships in Ceylon, including *Illustrious* and *Renown*, were due to form the British Pacific Fleet in the near future, and therefore needed their destroyer escorts to hand.[9] 'In view of the *Khedive Ismail* sinking', wrote Somerville, 'I informed the Admiralty I felt we were no longer justified in accepting, as we have had to hitherto, such light escorts for troop convoys, and that until troops movements at present envisaged were completed I must take destroyers from the Fleet for the purpose'.[10]

7 See Brian Crabb, *Passage to Destiny: The Sinking of the SS* Khedive Ismail *in the Sea War against Japan* (Stamford, Lincolnshire: Paul Watkins, 1997). Covering the operations against the German tankers and the *Khedive Ismail* sinking, see also Crabb, *In Harm's Way: The Story of HMS* Kenya, *a Second World War Cruiser* (Stamford, Lincolnshire: Paul Watkins, 1998).

8 Churchill, *The Second World War*, volume 5, *Closing the Ring*, p. 615.

9 They were scheduled to form part of the new British Pacific Fleet, that was to begin forming in March 1944. In the end, this did not take place until later in the year.

10 Simpson (ed.), *The Somerville Papers*, diary, 13/2/44, p. 515. There were numerous 'near misses' too. In November 1942 the passenger line *Tilawa* was torpedoed and sunk. *Birmingham*, on passage from Bombay to Kilindini, was diverted to search for survivors and managed to rescue 670 people and return them to Bombay. *Carthage* was ordered to the position to search for the 280 still unaccounted

The sad tale of the *Khedive Ismail* reminds us that though the war might have been unlosable by 1944, it was not won. Willmott offers an instructive perspective on shipping and ship sinkings in the Indian Ocean at this time:

> The defeat of the enemy attack on shipping was all but fact as 1943 gave way to 1944, though this was not readily apparent at the time. Between March 1943 and March 1944 shipping losses in the Indian Ocean were greater than those incurred in all other theaters with the exception of the North Atlantic, and indeed the losses incurred in the Indian Ocean were greater even than those of the North Atlantic if the returns of spring 1943 are deleted from consideration.

Total losses in that year were 99 ships of 604,104 tons. Willmott notes that

> in the context of this theater any loss was very difficult to absorb. The ships that were lost in the Indian Ocean tended to be larger – and, in the case of tanker traffic working the Gulf, more valuable – than those lost in the North Atlantic and, even more important, their loss could involve as long as an eighteen-month lead time in terms of cargo.[11]

One way of addressing the submarine problem was to destroy the supply tankers on which the U-boats depended when operating far from their European or South-east Asian bases. Early in 1944 Somerville received intelligence telling him that a German tanker might proceed from the Sunda Strait to the southern Indian Ocean to refuel submarines. In the last ten days of January, six independently routed British ships had been sunk in the Indian Ocean by four U-boats working in the Gulf of Aden and north of the Maldives. Somerville's plan to intercept the tanker, which turned out to be the *Charlotte Schliemann*, was to concentrate warships on Mauritius as an operational base in order to search an area 900 miles south-east of the island. The cruisers *Suffolk* and *Sussex* were the only ships available with sufficient endurance to achieve an interception, and the Admiralty told Somerville that it was very important to try and effect this. 'I ordered *Newcastle* and *Kenya* from Madras and *Suffolk* from Trincomalee to proceed to Colombo', Somerville wrote, 'and told the *Battler*, at present with an Aden-Bombay convoy, to proceed to the Seychelles with one frigate, refuel, and then go to Mauritius. *Canton* and *Nepal* from Durban were also ordered to Mauritius'.[12]

The escort carrier *Battler* carried 834 Squadron FAA and was accompanied by the frigate *Bann*. Seven Catalinas were ordered from East Africa to Mauritius to screen the task force, and fuel oil was prepositioned by the Royal Fleet Auxiliary *Olynthus*. Because of cyclone condition, however, only three of the Catalinas had arrived by the time the operation commenced. Several fruitless searches were made before bad weather forced the termination of the operation. A second operation was mounted in early February. This time, the British had better

for, but only managed to find four. 'Admiralty War Diaries of World War II', Eastern Fleet War Diary, November 1942.

11 Willmott, *Grave of a Dozen Schemes*, pp. 151-52.

12 Simpson (ed.), *The Somerville Papers*, 12/1/44, p. 502. For *Kenya* in the Indian Ocean, see Brian Crabb, *In Harms Way: The Story of HMS* Kenya *a Second World War Cruiser* (Stamford: Paul Watkins, 1998), chapter 12, 'Eastern Fleet Duties'.

luck. A Mauritius-based Catalina spotted the German tanker, and *Relentless* was zoned in to destroy her. This she did with the 'rather extravagant expenditure of eight torpedoes' and she also opened up with her 4.7-inch armament.[13] The destroyer then rescued 41 of the 88 crewmen. Although two lifeboats with 20 men aboard were never seen again, two others, containing 21 men, managed through an incredible feat of navigation to make it to Madagascar, about 1,600 nautical miles away from where the ship sank, after 26-30 days at sea.

Attention now turned to the other known German 'milch cow', *Brake*. The operation to track her down was based on another one of Somerville's hunches as well as ULTRA intelligence. With *Charlotte Schliemann* gone, he assumed that *Brake* or some other vessel would be sent from Singapore to succour the U-boats and he duly laid plans to intercept.[14] Operation Sleuth, he wrote to Mountbatten, 'which is now being laid on is at present a shot in the dark, but I feel in my bones the Germans must do something about the water-hogs who have lost their sow'.[15] *Illustrious*, now restored to the fleet, was already out searching for her, and intelligence intercepts informed Somerville that German submarines hunting British vessels in the Arabian Sea would soon need refuelling. When *Brake* duly rendezvoused with *U-188*, *U-532*, and *U-168*, Eastern Fleet headquarters learned of this assemblage. Mauritius was again used as an operational base, demonstrating the enduring utility of colonies and the infrastructure that they offered in a global war.

A force codenamed CS4 gathered in the island's ports, consisting of *Battler*, *Bann*, the cruisers *Newcastle* and *Suffolk*, the destroyers *Quadrant* and *Roebuck*, and seven Catalina flying-boats from 259 and 265 squadrons. The ships sailed from Mauritius on 6 March, *Battler*'s aircraft making long reconnaissance sweeps ahead of the task force in spite of appalling weather. On 12 March one of her Swordfish spotted a tanker – which was identified as *Brake* – with two submarines alongside. One of the submarines, *U-188*, had just finished refuelling, having recently sunk the *Fort Buckingham* and *Fort La Maune* in the Arabian Sea. *Roebuck* was homed in on the covey of German vessels by *Battler*'s Swordfish, which dropped messages onto the destroyer's deck giving range and bearing as she sped towards the tanker's position. *Roebuck* established visual contact at 13 miles and opened fire, the crew deciding to scuttle. The two U-boats were attacked with rockets from *Battler*'s Seafires, one being severely damaged and *U-188* escaping unscathed.

To remain for a moment with *Battler*, having contributed to these victories, the carrier proceeded to Durban for a refit and her complement of Seafires and Swordfish flew off to the Royal Naval Air Station at Stamford Hill. *Battler* was an example of the reinforcements now arriving in the Indian Ocean, and the benefits bestowed by Lend-Lease. Escort carriers were smaller than fleet carriers, weighing around 11,000 tons and built from converted merchant hulls. They joined the Royal Navy in large numbers, extending its capacity by augmenting the number of ships available to ferry aircraft around and able to provide air cover at sea to convoys. Laid down as a freighter in April 1941, the hull that would become *Battler* was originally requisitioned by the US Navy in the rush to rearm in the weeks following Pearl Harbor. She was

13 See 'Operation Canned: 8-13 February 1944', at http://www.hmsrelentless.co.uk/opcanned.pdf. The document includes the report on the operation written by Read Admiral Read, commanding 4th Cruiser Squadron, 18/2/44. It also contains a memorable account written by one of the German survivors, radio operator Alfred Moer.

14 Simpson (ed.), *The Somerville Papers*, desk diary, 21/2/44, p. 518.

15 Ibid., signal to Mountbatten, 23/2/44, p. 521.

named USS *Altamaha*, though the following March was loaned to the Royal Navy under the Lend-Lease scheme.[16] She commenced service with the Eastern Fleet by escorting convoys from Aden to Bombay in company with her escorts, the destroyers *Quality*, *Quiberon*, and *Rotherham*.

The vigil against Axis submarines continued. In May 1944 *U-852* was attacked by half a dozen 621 Squadron Wellingtons flying from Aden. The U-boat grounded on the coast of British Somaliland, and the survivors were captured by the Somaliland Camel Corps while a Royal Navy landing party took the beached submarine.[17] More escort carriers and other resources were arriving. In the period May to August 1944 the U-boats found the Indian Ocean become even more unattractive as a hunting ground as the Eastern Fleet became better equipped as well as better trained. Shipping zones were constantly patrolled by aircraft, Diego Garcia and Addu Atoll played their part as mid-ocean air bases, and a hunter-killer group was formed by the Eastern Fleet consisting of nine frigates and sloops and two more recently-arrived escort carriers, *Begum* and *Shah*.

As 1944 wore on, the Eastern Fleet was reinforced to a level not attained since summer 1942. More battleships arrived along with more destroyers and, as they slipped out of American shipyards, more escort carriers. In February 1944 *Queen Elizabeth*, *Renown*, and *Valiant* arrived in the Indian Ocean, and in a move symbolizing the eastward swing of British naval power, the Admiralty chose to designate this the 1st Battle Squadron, a title that had for years been held by the main Royal Navy force in the Mediterranean. Vice Admiral Arthur Power had hoisted his flag aboard *Renown* as commander of the squadron and second in command of the Eastern Fleet at Rosyth the previous December as the ship prepared for foreign service. Collecting *Queen Elizabeth* and *Valiant* at Scapa Flow, the battleships had progressed to the Indian Ocean via the Suez Canal, entering Trincomalee harbour on 2 February along with the carriers *Illustrious* and the repair carrier *Unicorn*.[18] On 10 February Somerville called a conference ashore to discuss a request from the army to bombard Ramree Island in support of Fourteenth Army operations, and that evening *Renown*, *Illustrious*, *Emerald*, *Tromp*, and seven destroyers were heading across the Bay of Bengal. By March there were also 12 modern cruisers, three flotillas of destroyers, 70 anti-submarine ships on station, and a rising number of submarines.

Submarine service

Submarines now became one of the fleet's main offensive arms. Submarines infiltrated, exfiltrated, and supplied behind-enemy-lines forces in Malaya, Sumatra and Thailand, mined sea lanes used by the enemy, and hunted its supply vessels and warships. Cumulatively, these activities obliged the Japanese to expend vast efforts in an area previously considered safe. *Adamant* had arrived as depot ship for the 4th Submarine Flotilla in 1942, and in March 1944 *Maidstone* arrived as depot ship for a second flotilla, the 8th.[19] A third flotilla, the 2nd, was formed when the depot ship *Wolfe* arrived in August.

16 See http://www.royalnavyresearcharchive.org.uk/ESCORT/BATTLER.htm#.Wg_7EhPtmko
17 Paterson, *Hitler's Grey Wolves*, p. 174.
18 'Admiralty War Diaries of World War II', Office of Vice Admiral Eastern Fleet, War Diary, 9/2/44.
19 With the arrival of the depot ship *Wolfe* in August 1944, *Maidstone* sailed with her flotilla of ten submarines for Fremantle, Australia, to operate under the Americans in the South China Sea.

The submarine offensive was in many ways the star turn of the British assault on Japanese forces in the region, and the extensive service of *Tally-Ho* illustrates the utility of submarines at this stage of the war. She variously sank Japanese merchant vessels and warships, and inserted Free Thai and US Office of Strategic Services agents into occupied territory.[20] On 9 January 1944 she sighted the light cruiser *Kuma* and her destroyer escort exercising outside the north entrance of Penang harbour.

> To the chagrin of the entire crew, the cruiser zigzagged away before [Lieutenant Commander] Bennington could make an attack. It was therefore all the more gratifying when the same ship was sighted again two days later. A bow salvo of seven torpedoes was fired at a range of just under one mile ... Two large explosions were heard in rapid succession, and these hits were sufficient to sink the cruiser. The escorting Japanese destroyer reacted quickly and the *Tally-Ho* was subjected to a number of counter-attacks. Eighteen depth charges were dropped ... The submarine crept away from the scene, heading inshore where she was least expected to go. Before the patrol was over another attack was made, which resulted in the sinking of a merchant ship, the *Ryuko Maru*, off the Nicobar Islands on 14 January.[21]

On 3 February *Tally-Ho* left Trincomalee on her fourth patrol. Bennington planned to work his way south from the One Fathom Bank in the Malacca Strait, hoping to find plenty of Japanese traffic. Enemy patrols made this difficult, however, so he abandoned the idea as he had a special mission to carry out later which could not be compromised by detection at this stage. This was Operation Gustavus VI, requiring the submarine to deposit ten Force 136 operatives and their stores in Malaya.

At 5:15am on 15 February, 'while proceeding on the surface, the Officer of the Watch sighted what he thought was a surfaced U-boat. Bennington was already on the bridge at the time of the sighting and immediately took over'. Certain that this was an enemy vessel as there were no British or Dutch boats in the area, he altered course into an attacking position. Just as *Tally-Ho* was steadying on a firing course, the report 'Second U-boat broad on the port bow' was heard.

> Bennington acknowledged the report and gave the order to fire at the first target before issuing the instruction to dive. As Bennington went below it was reported that the second submarine was in fact only a junk. As the *Tally-Ho* went down to eighty feet the crew waited anxiously for some evidence of their success. At the expected time they were rewarded with the sound of a hit and the noise of the target's diesel engines ceased immediately.[22]

Bennington thought that the submarine was Japanese but it was in fact the German *UIT-23*, originally the Italian *Reginaldo Giuliani*, on her way from Singapore to Penang and thence to France with a cargo of tin destined for the Fatherland.

20 See Bruce Reynolds, *Thailand's Secret War: OSS, SOE, and the Free Thai Underground during World War Two* (Cambridge: Cambridge University Press, 2010).

21 Wilson, *A Submariners' War*, p. 120. For the unexpurgated account, and details of *Tally-Ho*'s remarkable career with the Eastern Fleet, see Ian Trenowden, *The Hunting Submarine: The Fighting Life of HMS* Tally-Ho (London: William Kimber, 1974), pp. 83-90.

22 Wilson, *A Submariners' War*, p. 121.

Tally-Ho's success continued. On 24 February she

> was patrolling off the Sembilan Islands, where two days previously a Japanese merchant ship had been sunk by a single hit from their salvo of five torpedoes ... Towards midnight one of the lookouts sighted two wakes ahead, but it was too dark for the silhouette of a ship to be seen. To Bennington ... the bow wake had the appearance of an approaching surfaced submarine and he was uncertain if it was enemy or friendly. He had to be sure, as both the *Truculent* and the *Tactician* were known to be in adjacent areas. The immediate need was to avoid a collision and Bennington altered course sharply to port.
>
> A signalled challenge from the *Tally-Ho* brought no reply. Instead the other vessel bore down on the submarine at full speed, dropping depth charges. Only rapid alterations of course by Bennington avoided violent impact. The enemy ship was faster and better armed than the submarine, and if the *Tally-Ho* dived she would present a perfect target for ramming, gunfire and depth charges while she was seeking safety in the depths. Bennington knew that his only chance was to keep end on to the enemy, altering course as late as possible when necessary to avoid ramming.
>
> During one such manoeuvre the Japanese ship came in again, attempting to ram. Her funnel was clearly visible, belching smoke and sparks as her engine room crew gave full power, her bow wave creaming and foaming. At the last Bennington ordered, 'Hard a starboard'. It seemed at first that the submarine would surely be struck, but then she slowly began to turn and the vessels passed close to one another on opposing parallel courses. The submarine's Oerlikon gun had jammed, rendering the gunner unable to rake the enemy's bridge. 'The Japanese guns could not depress enough to hit the submarine. The submariners' nostrils were assailed by the acrid stench of funnel gases and scorched paintwork as the other ship rushed by ... The Japanese ship was so close that the propeller on the starboard side tore at the *Tally-Ho*. The rapidly revolving screw, made of phosphor bronze, bit into the mild steel of the port ballast tanks, ripping out chunks in a regular patter as the ship passed down the submarine's side.[23]

As Somerville wrote after visiting *Tally-Ho*, the damage 'is most spectacular and shows that the propellers of the torpedo boat ripped open practically the whole of her port tanks by means of a series of vertical gashes'.[24]

Tally-Ho was one of a number of British submarines operating in the eastern Indian Ocean during this phase of the war. Another was Lieutenant Dennis Beckley's *Templar*. On 28 January the Japanese cruiser *Kitakami* was approaching the Malacca Strait following a convoy escort run to the Andaman and Nicobar Islands when she was struck by two torpedoes fired at long range. The damage took six months to repair at Singapore, and the cruiser was never the same again. On 7 August Somerville visited the crew of Lieutenant Commander Edward Young's *Storm* at Trincomalee. She had just returned, he wrote, from 'a very successful patrol in which she had entered the harbour [probably Tavoy Island off Burma] in broad daylight on the surface and sunk two A/S [anti-submarine] vessels by gunfire; subsequently she attacked and sunk four

23 Ibid., pp. 121-124.
24 Simpson (ed.), *The Somerville Papers*, desk diary, 8/3/44, p. 527.

small MV's [merchant vessels] including one laden with ammunition for Rangoon'.[25] These successes were tempered by the loss of *Stonehenge*, which left Trincomalee the following month on 25 February to patrol off the coast of Sumatra – or possibly on a secret mission – and was never heard of again, lost with all hands. On 21 November, *Stratagem* was spotted by a Japanese aircraft in the shallows of the Malacca Strait and depth-charged by a destroyer. Only eight crewmen survived, and only two of them survived subsequent Japanese incarceration.

A significant feature of the work of Eastern Fleet submarines was the transit, supply, and recovery of special forces operating behind enemy lines. Reflecting 'regular' service prejudices and reservations regarding the effectiveness of 'irregular' units, Somerville disapproved of this method of employing his resources, contending that SOE-style missions took up patrol time and 'are there to give these "types" something to do'.[26] Layton, Commander-in-Chief Ceylon, harboured similar misgivings, making 'no secret of his dislike of irregular army units'.[27] Nevertheless, he had to tolerate them, especially given the Supreme Allied Commander's enthusiasm for their activities. SOE, which became known as Force 136 in this region from April 1944, had commenced operations from Ceylon in January 1943, targeted predominantly at the Andaman Islands and Malaya. It was responsible for organizing the transport and planning all operations from Ceylon as well as providing the men, while the Inter-Service Liaison Department gathered intelligence for its missions. Commanded in Ceylon by Colonel C. J. P. Hudson, there was a Malaya Country Section and an Anglo-Dutch Country Section which focused on the East Indies. Hudson in turn reported to Colin Mackenzie at headquarters in Meerut until he moved his headquarters to Ceylon too in the wake of Mountbatten's relocation there. Throughout its existence, Force 136 operations depended on the Royal Navy, the Royal Netherlands Navy, and the RAF for their transport.

The Force 136 series of missions undertaken as part of operations Baldhead and Bunkum supported activities in the Andaman Islands. These operations relied on the knowledge of Major Denis McCarthy, who had been stationed there before the war as Commandant of the Military Police Battalion and District Superintendent of Police, escaping when the islands were invaded. On 14 January 1943 the Dutch submarine *O 24* left Colombo bound for the Andamans, travelling submerged by day and on the surface at night (most special operations in 1943 used Dutch submarines under British command). Lieutenant Commander W. J. de Vries identified the landing beach on the west coast of Middle Andaman Island, and a Force 136 party was put ashore at night. Returning two months later, *O 24* carried out a patrol of the route used by Japanese traffic between Rangoon and Singapore during which she attacked a 4,000 ton ship with her gun. The party had been in the Andamans for 65 days when, on 21 March, *O 24* returned, de Vries cautiously approaching the pre-arranged rendezvous point and observing two canvas squares placed on the beach as a signal.[28] The submarine also landed and hid three tons of stores at a new base camp on South Andaman Island, ripping off her Asdic dome on a coral reef during the manoeuvre. The Gustavus operations, which commenced in May 1943, were targeted at Malaya. Of course, the Force 136 operations in the region, at the end of the day,

25 Ibid., desk diary, 7/8/44, p. 581. *Storm*'s career with the Eastern Fleet is well covered in Young's *One of Our Submarines*.
26 Simpson (ed.), *The Somerville Papers*, p. 503.
27 Trenowden, *Operations Most Secret*, p. 75.
28 Ibid., p. 69.

had little operational effect: like behind-enemy-lines forces in occupied France, their overriding purpose was to prepare the ground for Allied invasion, but Japanese forces throughout the region were to surrender before this took place. Nevertheless, they contributed to the Allies' intelligence picture of the situation in the occupied territories territories, and those brave souls involved in these extensive operations did so in the belief that they were helping defeat the enemy and preparing for the moment when liberation, of a kind, would come.

By September 1944 there were 26 submarines based on Ceylon. As well as supporting covert operations and attacking enemy vessels, mining sea lanes frequented by Japanese shipping was another key task. Eastern Fleet submarines laid 490 mines off enemy-held coast in an extensive campaign from that spring, concentrating on the Malacca Strait and the coastal waters of Burma and Thailand. The aim was to force Japanese shipping away from the coast into deeper water, where it could be attacked by the Eastern Fleet's surface ships and the RAF. Submarine patrols from Trincomalee were extended to the western coast of Burma and both coasts of Sumatra as the Japanese visibly wilted in the Indian Ocean.

In this period the Eastern Fleet continued to conduct operations intended to divert forces in conjunction with American offensives. At the end of August, for example, Operation Boomerang saw the fleet provide air-sea rescue cover for a 20th US Bomber Command attack on Sumatra, and it conducted its own operation, a carrier strike on Padang (Operation Banquet), intended to coincide with American moves against Hollandia. The Eastern Fleet also continued to develop in terms of modern carrier aircraft.

Japanese surface ships

The Imperial Japanese Navy had not followed up its devastating though mercifully brief April 1942 raids in the Indian Ocean. But the British could not entirely discount the possibility of a repeat performance, and American activities in the Pacific were yet to render the Japanese incapable of such offensives. Indeed, early in 1944 pulses quickened at Naval Headquarters Colombo when it was discovered that a powerful Japanese force was assembling at Singapore. Pownall, now Mountbatten's Chief of Staff, wrote from Ceylon on 25 February:

> some interesting news comes in from special sources. The Japs are in the process of concentrating their main fleet at Singapore. Some seven Battleships, two Fleet carriers, five or six heavy cruisers, [twenty-four destroyers] etc. No doubt their primary reason for this is that the waters south and south-east of Japan are likely to get a bit too hot for them and there is no likelihood, at present, of an attack on Japan or Formosa except by carrier task forces which can best be dealt with by shore-based aircraft ... It's improbable that having got there they will hang around and do nothing at all ... So we can expect them to emerge and do something; the question is, what? They have a nice 'covered approach' to the western shores of Australia, or Darwin. They can get out into the Indian Ocean and disturb our sea communications there. Or they can enter the Bay of Bengal and not only play up the shipping but possibly shoot up, by air or gun or both, Ceylon and the east coast of India.[29]

29 Bond (ed.), *Chief of Staff*, p. 145.

This was indeed an interesting development on a number of levels, and revealed Britain's continued vulnerability in terms of fleet capabilities. It also reaffirmed the ongoing differences between Churchill and the Chiefs of Staff regarding British strategy east of Suez. In terms of available airpower, on Ceylon at that moment there were three squadrons of Hurricane day-fighters, one squadron of Beaufort night-fighters, two of Beauforts on antisubmarine patrols, one of Liberator bombers, and four of Catalinas. *Illustrious*, Somerville's sole fleet carrier, was at that moment engaged on Operation Sleuth, a sweep to the south of the Cocos-Keeling Islands as part of her working up programme. The admiral was told that two extra escort carriers and additional FAA squadrons were being dispatched to reinforce him. (In April the escort carriers *Atheling* and *Begum* arrived brim-full of aircraft for FAA squadrons, some offloaded at Madras, others at Trincomalee, before both ships joined the Eastern Fleet. *Begum* brought 24 Barracudas, 20 Hellcats, and 4 Wildcats for Ceylon. The aircraft transport ships *Athene* and *Engadine* also delivered new carrier aircraft). While the Chiefs of Staff did not seem too fazed by the Japanese concentration at Singapore, Churchill seized upon it, entering a meeting in a towering rage on discovering that he had not been immediately informed of this development. Its possible implications then became entangled in arguments about whether British strategy against Japan should be focused on an Indian Ocean or a Pacific strategy. The prime minister 'insisted that the enemy move to Singapore was proof of the need to concentrate in rather than abandon the Indian Ocean', and grumbled that the Chiefs were ganging up on him in order to stymie his plans for an attack on Sumatra, Operation Culverin.[30] This 'unexpected event', as Churchill termed it, exercised him so because it put a stop 'for the time being to "Culverin" or other amphibious adventures in Indian waters'. This was because, with the main strength of the Imperial Japanese Navy peering into the Indian Ocean from Singapore, 'We no longer had even local naval superiority. I immediately recognised this unpleasant fact'.[31]

The episode hastened reinforcements to Somerville's aid, and formed part of the background to the loan of the American carrier *Saratoga*. Washington agreed to transfer a Liberator squadron from West Africa and another of Beaufighters from the Mediterranean, and a detachment of Wellingtons and a squadron of Sunderlands was also made available. Of course, these forces would take time to arrive. With the threat of a raid in the Bay of Bengal, Somerville 'decided that the fleet would go west of Maldives if Japanese moved towards BB [Bay of Bengal] rather than remain at Trincomalee as a target'.[32] But the Admiralty considered that such a tactical withdrawal would be bad for morale. Somerville vented his frustration to Mountbatten:

> It is maddening to me that I should find myself in the same position now as I was two years ago, i.e. with a quite inadequate force which would be a gift for the Japanese if they came out in full strength. With another two fleet carriers out here I feel sure the Japanese would not show their noses outside the Malayan Barrier.[33]

But while Somerville's ire was understandable, the situation, in reality, was quite different. Though the British remained prudently cautious, the threat of a calamitous Japanese foray into

30 Willmott, *Grave of a Dozen Schemes*, p. 61.
31 Churchill, *The Second World War*, volume 5, p. 508.
32 Simpson (ed.), *The Somerville Papers*, desk diary, 23/2/44, p. 519.
33 Ibid., 23/2/44, p. 520.

the Indian Ocean had evaporated. There was no real danger, and the arrival of the main enemy fleet at Singapore was a measure of weakness, not strength. The large force that mustered there did so in order to undertake a docking programme now that their main base at Truk in the Pacific was within range of American bombers.

The only Indian Ocean activity from Japanese surface ships that did occur in this period involved the heavy cruisers *Aoba*, *Chikuma*, and *Tone*, forming the 16th Squadron of the Imperial Japanese Navy's South West Area Fleet under Vice Admiral Naomasa Sakonju. Veterans of Pearl Harbor, the Java Sea, and Midway, the three ships were sent to attack shipping on the main Aden to Fremantle sea lane, entering the Indian Ocean through the Sunda Strait on 1 March, they steamed towards Ceylon supported by submarines and aircraft from Java and Sumatra. Aware that something was going on, Somerville ordered shipping to be diverted from these trade routes. The Japanese squadron began patrolling south of the Cocos-Keeling Islands in line abreast, intent on falling in with Allied merchant traffic. Running short of merchant ships themselves, the Japanese were looking to replenish their stock by capturing enemy or neutral vessels. As the cruisers entered the Indian Ocean, the British passenger-cargo ship *Behar*, built on the Clyde the previous year, was leaving Melbourne on her maiden voyage, loaded with zinc bound for Britain and sailing towards Mauritius.[34] Unusual for a merchant ship, she carried Asdic and depth charges, a powerful deck armament of one four-inch and one three-inch gun, a multiple rocket launcher, 20mm Oerlikons and .5-inch Browning machine guns. She was crewed by British officers, Defensively-Equipped Merchant Ship (DEMS) gunners, Asdic operators, and Indian ratings under the command of Captain Maurice Symonds. Unfortunately, even such impressive armament was of little avail against a bevvy of cruisers.

On the morning of 9 March *Behar* encountered *Tone*, the cruiser's turrets trained on her, and was ordered to heave-to. *Behar*'s wireless room began transmitting the 'RRR' 'warship raider' warning signal. The Japanese heard this, and immediately *Tone* hoisted her colours and opened fire. The shelling was so intense that *Behar* was unable to man her guns, and soon the order to abandon ship was given. Only three of the 111-strong crew were missing as the lifeboats filled. The men were ordered to board the Japanese cruiser, where their hands were tied behind their backs and ropes looped about their necks. After hours on deck, they were taken below and beaten with bamboo batons. Mistreatment continued for some days while a dispute raged between *Tone*'s commander, Captain Mayazumi, and Vice Admiral Sakonju, the latter furious not only that *Behar* had been sunk rather than captured, but that *Tone* had taken prisoners. Sakonju ordered Mayazumi to 'dispose' of them. Thirty-six of the prisoners were transferred to *Aoba*, but the remaining 72 survivors were massacred on *Tone*'s deck. 'At the subsequent war crimes trial it was revealed that all seventy-two were butchered like animals in a slaughterhouse, each man being felled with a blow to the stomach before being beheaded. The scuppers of the

34 See David Sibley, *The Behar Massacre: The Execution of 69 Survivors from the British Merchant Ship* Behar *in 1944 by the Imperial Japanese Navy* (Stockport: A. Lane Publishers, 1997). On this subject generally see Raymond Lamont-Brown, *Ships from Hell: Japanese War Crimes on the High Seas* (Stroud, Gloucestershire: The History Press, 2002); Bernard Edwards, *Blood and Bushido: Japanese Atrocities at Sea, 1941-1945* (Upton-Upon-Severn: The Self-Publishing Press, 1991); and Lord Russell of Liverpool, *The Knights of Bushido: A History of Japanese War Crimes during World War Two* (London: Frontline Books, 2013).

Japanese cruiser ran red with the blood of those innocent souls on that tranquil night in the Java Sea'.[35]

There were other atrocities, too. In January the *Daisy Moller* had been torpedoed north of Madras, the lifeboats subsequently rammed and machine-gunned.[36] Also in March, the *I-8* sunk the merchantman *Tjisalak* en route from Australia to Colombo, survivors again being massacred.[37] On 2 July, the American *Jean Nicolet* was torpedoed by *I-8*. The blazing Liberty ship was abandoned, and the Japanese submarine picked up approximately 100 men from the sea. A few were taken below, while the rest were subjected to shootings, beatings, and stabbings. Many were forced to run a gauntlet of Japanese crewmen armed with pipes and knives. The ordeal only stopped when the *I-8* detected an aircraft, submerging with 30 men still bound, helpless, on deck. Amazingly, some of them managed to swim back to the still burning *Jean Nicolet* and launch life-rafts. It is quite possible that the aircraft in question was a Catalina flying-boat from Diego Garcia.[38]

Eastern Fleet carrier strikes

As a result of the attack on *Behar*, the Eastern Fleet made a sweep along the Australia-India trade route. It did this in conjunction with a pre-planned operation, Operation Diplomat, intended as a training run to practice the operational procedures that would be used by ships currently serving with the Eastern Fleet but earmarked for the British Pacific Fleet when it formed. Part of the Eastern Fleet left Trincomalee and Colombo on 21 March and arrived at a point some 850 miles south of Ceylon. The force comprised the battleships *Queen Elizabeth*, *Renown*, and *Valiant*, the carrier *Illustrious*, the cruisers *Ceylon*, *Cumberland*, *Gambia*, and *London*, and ten destroyers. They rendezvoused three days later with three tankers escorted by the Dutch cruiser *Tromp* and practised refuelling at sea for the next two days. Then, on 27 March, they met up with US Task Group 58.5 which comprised the carrier *Saratoga* and her destroyer escorts *Cummings*, *Dunlap*, and *Fanning*. The combined fleet returned to Trincomalee, and FAA aircrew spent two days learning procedures from their American counterparts and generally benefiting from their experience. This period of intensive training was in anticipation of a major raid against Sabang, as the main strength of the Eastern Fleet – finally – switched to the offensive.[39]

35 Edwards, *Blood and Bushido*, p. 149. Sakonju was tried and executed by the British in Hong Kong in 1947, while Mayazumi was sentenced to seven years imprisonment.

36 Simpson (ed.), *The Somerville Papers*, p. 501. She carried a year's supply (22) of steamrollers for the army.

37 Ibid., p. 535.

38 Naval Historical Center, 'Naval Armed Guard Service: Japanese Atrocities Against', http://www.history.navy.mil/faqs/faq104-5.htm

39 For the carrier strikes see for example 'The Carrier-Borne Aircraft Attacks on Oil Refineries in the Palembang (Sumatra) Area in January, 1945', *Supplement to the London Gazette*, 39191 (London: HMSO, 1951). See also the brilliant website armouredcarriers.com at http://www.armouredcarriers.com/. Subtitled 'The Untold Story of the Royal Navy's Struggle to Invent Carrier Warfare', this gorgeously-presented and expert web resource has a section dedicated to Indian Ocean operations, including original documents. See also David Hobbs, *The British Pacific Fleet: They Royal Navy's Most Powerful Strike Force* (Barnsley: Seaforth, 2011), chapter 3, 'Evolution and Expansion' and chapter 4, 'Strikes Against the Sumatran Oil Refineries'.

Saratoga had travelled from Pearl Harbor to support the drive in the Marshall Islands before leaving the Pacific to aid Britain's offensive in the Indian Ocean. Somerville was thrilled to have its carrier group attached to his fleet, describing it as 'a vast accession of strength'.[40] Just before her arrival, he told Mountbatten of his plan to make a raid when the American and British ships rendezvoused. 'I believe very strongly that providing we can make a show of force in the area between Ceylon and Australia the Japanese are unlikely to attempt to raid'. It was very strange, he continued, 'that [they] should show so little initiative and that they have failed to seize the golden chance of scoring a few points by attacking us before we were ready'.[41] The Anglo-American fleet left Trincomalee on 16 April, and three days later Operation Cockpit saw aircraft from *Illustrious* and *Saratoga* strike oil and harbour installations at the port of Sabang on the northwest coast of Sumatra. The raid was mounted in conjunction with American forces in the Pacific which had requested an operation in order to draw as many Japanese vessels as possible away from the theatre while General MacArthur attacked Hollandia. Somerville had selected Sabang because it commanded the entrance to the Malacca Strait and contained valuable Japanese installations, including a radar station, dockyard, and airfield.

Covered by RAF reconnaissance flights, the operation involved 27 warships from six nations, 'perhaps the most cosmopolitan naval operation of the war'.[42] Among their number was the Free French battleship *Richelieu*, which had joined the Eastern Fleet days before the task force set out. The attack was witnessed by Lieutenant-General Adrian Carton De Wiart, VC, Churchill's representative to the Chinese leader Chiang Kai-shek and Mountbatten's liaison officer in Chungking. He wrote:

> On one of my trips to Kandy I had the luck to meet Admiral Sir James Somerville, Commander-in-Chief of the East Indies Fleet, and he kindly offered to take me for a sea journey as he was about to bombard Sabang. The Admiral flew his flag in the *Queen Elizabeth* and I was delighted to accept his invitation. The greatest secrecy was to be observed over this operation, for the success of it depended on our arriving off Sabang in the very early morning unsuspected. I sat comfortably on the bridge of the *Queen Elizabeth* in a deck-chair and prepared to watch the proceedings.
>
> The destroyers tore into Sabang Harbour and in my land-trained mind I compared their attack with a cavalry charge. The noise was hell let loose, and as I had never been in a ship firing anything heavier than ack-ack guns the difference was somewhat marked. I had been expecting a good deal of noise and vibration, for everything had been removed from the walls of the ship, but it was nothing to what I heard and felt.
>
> Aeroplanes from the aircraft carrier were taking an active part in the bombardment, and without doubt, they were the masters of the Jap planes and shot down a number of them. We lost only one plane, and the pilot baled out into the sea and was safely picked up by us. The Jap reply to our shelling was very feeble, and although I believe they did put two shells through one of our destroyers, neither of them exploded. Our casualties numbered two, both war correspondents.

40 Simpson (ed.), *The Somerville Papers*, p. 379.
41 Ibid., signal to Mountbatten, 11/3/44, p. 529.
42 Willmott, *Grave of a Dozen Schemes*, p. 64.

> The bombardment over, we started back and late in the afternoon some Jap fighters came after us. Up went our planes from the carrier and drove the Japs off quickly and decisively, with enough time to spare to enable them to land on the carrier before dark. When they landed safely in the nick of time, I could sense the relief of Admiral Somerville, and I marvelled at the enthusiasm of the pilots for their very dangerous game.[43]

Somerville, in characteristic fashion, reported that he had caught the Japanese commander 'with his kimono up'. On numerous occasions since the outbreak of war with Japan, the British had been caught with their trousers down, so this was a moment to savour.

The Eastern Fleet developed a taste for this kind of action, and the attack on Sabang was followed up with a much heavier blow against the port and oil refineries of Surabaya, the main Japanese base in Java. On 6 May two task forces left Ceylon for Operation Transom. Because of the distances involved the joint force replenished from the Royal Navy's Task Force 67 at Exmouth Bay in Australia, which consisted of six fleet tankers and a water tanker escorted by the cruisers *London* and *Suffolk*. Early on 17 May, from a position south of Java, 45 Avengers and Dauntless dive bombers, escorted by 40 Hellcat and Corsair fighters, took off from *Illustrious* and *Saratoga* to attack the harbour and oil refineries. The bombing of the dry dock severely hampered the Japanese ship repair programme, 35,000 tons of shipping was sunk, 12 aircraft destroyed, and the destruction of oil installations curtailed the supplies available to the Japanese army in Burma and other occupied territories. With their merchant marine decimated by American submarines in the Pacific and their coastal freighters attacked in the Indian Ocean by British and Dutch submarines and aircraft, the Japanese were finding it increasingly difficult to supply isolated armies and garrisons. The operation successfully concluded, on 18 May the *Saratoga* task force returned to the Pacific. 'As the American ships formed in column, so, one by one, on her port side steamed the entire array of Eastern Fleet ships, and with each ship's company manning the side, the air echoed to the sound of cheering as they bade their farewell'.[44] Somerville wrote:

> Our US friends left us today and we gave them a great send-off – the whole fleet in single line and as they passed down the line on opposite course they were cheered by all ships. It's interesting to note how formal the Yanks always are. Their men were all fallen in meticulously and dressed in white whereas ours were all massed on the foc'sles in shorts and no shirts.[45]

43 Adrian Carton De Wiart, *Happy Odyssey: The Memoirs of Lieutenant-General Sir Adrian Carton De Wiart* (London: Jonathan Cape, 1950), pp. 261-2.

44 This moment was captured on film. For ten glorious minutes one can view footage of the American ships processing past the British ships (shot by the British in black and white) and of the British ships passing the American ships (shot by the Americans in colour). See 'Eastern Fleet: USS Saratoga Salute' at https://www.youtube.com/watch?v=g74ma4vxYDA. As well as the American carrier and her destroyer escort, ships include County class heavy cruisers, Town or Colony class cruisers, *Renown*, *Illustrious*, *Queen Elizabeth*, the Free French battleship *Richelieu* and several destroyers which parade past *Saratoga*.

45 Simpson (ed.), *The Somerville Papers*, to wife, 18/5/44, p. 557.

There was plenty more to come as the British worked up their carrier strike capability and did the training 'on the job' in anticipation of deployments to the Pacific. Attacks on the Andaman and Nicobar Islands and the Dutch East Indies became a main feature of the Eastern Fleet's work for the remainder of the war, so routine as to earn the sobriquet 'club runs'. On 19 June Operation Pedal, a carrier attack on Port Blair in the Andaman Islands, commenced. The Eastern Fleet's Force 60 was a powerful collection of vessels, comprising *Renown* and *Richelieu*, *Illustrious*, the cruisers *Ceylon*, *Kenya*, *Nigeria*, and *Phoebe*, and eight destroyers. Fifty-seven aircraft were embarked on *Illustrious*, and at one time she had 51 in the air simultaneously, a major achievement for British maritime air power. A power house, a motor transport yard, a seaplane base, barracks, and radar stations were all bombed and strafed by Barracudas and Corsairs. The carrier *Victorious* arrived at Trincomalee on 5 July. On 22 July she sailed in company with *Illustrious* for Operation Crimson, another attack on Sabang. While the two carriers launched their squadrons against the Japanese base, the battleships and cruisers bombarded targets ashore, firing 294 fifteen-inch shells, 134 eight-inch shells, 324 six-inch shells, 500 five-inch shells, and 123 four-inch shells. As Admiral Somerville recorded, Sabang was hit by 'an air strike and heavy bombardment from four capital ships and several cruisers, while a daring inshore squadron shot up port installations at virtually point blank range'.

It is worth pausing to reflect from the vantage point of summer 1944, as the Eastern Fleet ramped up its support of operations in Burma and began striking at Japanese positions in the East Indies and the Andaman and Nicobar Islands. The latest Sabang raid was Captain Charles Lambe's first taste of action with the Eastern Fleet, having just arrived to take command of *Illustrious*. He had left Britain aboard *Indomitable* on 12 June, just days after the Normandy landings, which must have been a peculiar time to be sailing away for the distant war in the east. Arriving at Colombo on 7 July he was welcomed by his old friend and new boss Somerville, who immediately dispatched him to Kandy, to see another of Lambe's old friends, Mountbatten – Somerville's boss – in an attempt to use him to iron out differences between the two men regarding control of the Eastern Fleet.[46] As Lambe's biographer writes:

> The position in the Indian Ocean theatre when Charles Lambe joined the Fleet was that, as the Japanese threat to India on the Manipur front had failed, the 14th Army was presented with a chance, which it took, to throw the enemy aross the Chindwin river. This put Mandalay within range. Mountbatten decided that its capture should be attempted without delay, and an advance continued south to Rangoon. At this point the Eastern Fleet's offensive task became apparent. Poor roads and an insufficient railway system made air supply of the Army essential if it was to keep up momentum, and for this an air supply base in the Arakan Peninsula was necessary. This in turn called for the capture of the Arakan airfields, which involved an amphibious assault, combined with an offensive thrust on land. To ensure success, it was necessary to have complete maritime control not only

46 The creation of SEAC caused classic command tensions; Somerville insisted that the Eastern Fleet was not wholly subordinate to Mountbatten's command as it had duties to perform that were not SEAC's business. Mountbatten, meanwhile, wanted the Eastern Fleet under his command. On the disagreements between Mountbatten and Somerville, see Roskill, *Churchill and the Admirals*, chapter 14, 'The Indian Ocean and the Far East 1944'. Simpson's *The Somerville Papers* also contains extensive coverage, pp. 366-76.

> over the Bay of Bengal but over the sea area bounded by the Andaman and Nicobar Islands, the Tenasserin and Kra coasts, and the northern end of Sumatra, including the island of Sabang.[47]

Supporting operations in Burma, continuing its work of sea lane defence, regaining control of eastern Indian Ocean waters, and preparing the way for the reinvasion of Malaya and Dutch East Indies, the Eastern Fleet was now engaged on large scale operations involving multiple battleships, battlecruisers, carriers, and cruisers covering a considerable area.

The carrier strength grew further with the return of *Indomitable* to eastern waters in July. *Howe* arrived at Colombo on 3 August before sailing into Trincomalee harbour on 9 August, the first modern battleship in eastern waters since the loss of *Prince of Wales*. Unfortunately, the day before, *Valiant* had been seriously damaged when the floating dock she was berthed in collapsed, so the fleet's battleship strength remained the same.[48] Also in August, a battleship and carrier attack was made on Padang on the west coast of Sumatra where a cement works supplying pillboxes and tank traps to the Japanese army was targeted. It had last been visited by Allied warships when civilians were being evacuated in February 1942. Now more than two years later, the offensive operations, for which Somerville had yearned through the long, long months since the initial Japanese onslaught, were well under way. Yet the admiral's time in eastern waters was drawing to a close. In August he relinquished command of the Eastern Fleet and was replaced by Admiral Sir Bruce Fraser. He was sad to be leaving just as the fleet had entered this new, offensive phase of operations. 'I've been concerned with bluffing the little yellow gents since 1937', he wrote, 'and I'd have enjoyed playing a hand agin them which had a few aces in its constituency!'.[49]

Somerville had successfully achieved the objectives he had been set when appointed in the dark days following the loss of *Prince of Wales* and *Repulse*. He had kept his forces intact, developed it as a credible deterrent to the Japanese, and kept the sea lanes of the Indian Ocean secure, while adding steel and resolve to a command that could easily have been destabilized by low morale. He had worked hard to turn his composite fleet into a well trained force used to operating as one, and had had the pleasure of commanding the largest British fleet at sea as it commenced heavy and sustained attacks on enemy targets.

47 Warner, *Admiral of the Fleet*, pp. 121-22.

48 *Valiant* sailed for Alexandria where there were suitable docking facilities to conduct the required major repairs, making only eight knots and unable to steer a straight course. But she grounded on entering the Suez Canal, so had to go back to Devonport, sailing around the Cape. She arrived home and was promptly paid off. The damage required nearly two years of repairs and when complete the battleship was renamed and became a harbour training ship. See her details of war service at http://www.naval-history.net/xGM-Chrono-01BB-Valiant.htm. The dock remained on the bottom for another 25 years. The First Sea Lord, Admiral Sir Andrew Cunningham, was so angry that he ensured that uncompromising disciplinary measures were taken.

49 CAC, Edwards Papers, REDW 2/17, Somerville, 7/8/44.

The air picture

As was the case at sea, British air power gained in strength during 1944, and land forces also grew in size and capability. The situation was similar to that pertaining in Europe, where for many months before D-Day, Anglo-American forces foregathered. Along with the considerable resources of the US Army Air Force stationed in India, the British wrested control of the air from the Japanese. Now dominant in Burmese skies and conducting land operations that utilized control of the air, Allied aircraft ventured further afield than ever before, appearing over the occupied East Indies, Malaya, Singapore, and Thailand. From July 1942 until the end of the war the RAF allocated more and more squadrons to India Command and Air Command South East Asia. In July 1942 there had been 21 squadrons in the Indian Ocean region, a figure that rose to 34 in July 1943, 56 in July 1944, and 71 by March 1945, as British air power swung eastwards.

As well as supporting land offensives, securing sea lanes remained a primary task, now for the purposes of offence rather than survival; operating at the end of a long supply route, safe shipping lanes were essential as SEAC forces, especially the Fourteenth Army, were built up and sustained. Aiding the Eastern Fleet in securing the sea lanes, between January and July 1944 RAF general reconnaissance squadrons flew 3,696 sorties over the Indian Ocean. Typical of these units was 31 Squadron, which had been associated with India and its environs since its formation in the First World War. Flying Vickers Valentias and Vincents as a bomber-transport unit of Indian Bomber Transport Flight, 31 Squadron had moved from the Middle East to India in summer 1939. In April 1941 it flew troops and supplies to Iraq ahead of the Anglo-Iraq war and during the Japanese invasion of Burma evacuated casualties and flew supply drops to army units retreating to India. Upgrading to Douglas aircraft and then Dakotas, the squadron now operated from India in support of the Fourteenth Army in Burma, before moving to Singapore and then Java.[50]

Significant air raids against Japanese targets now became frequent, such as that conducted on 27 October when Liberators of South East Asia Command's Strategic Air Force attacked and mined the approaches to Penang, the main enemy submarine base in the region, used by both German and Japanese vessels. The Japanese had no means of clearing the mines, and the Germans stopped using the harbour and moved to Batavia. Mine-laying became a 159 Squadron speciality, along with attacks on the Burma-Thailand railway. Between November 1943 and October 1944 the RAF laid over 1,100 mines in the region.[51] Aerial mining rendered the ports of Rangoon and Bangkok inoperative too, and Japanese shipping was driven from the Bay of Bengal. As well as mining, photo reconnaissance also became an important air force task ahead of the anticipated amphibious assaults on occupied territory and during the Allied advance in Burma.

A significant improvement in terms of central control and coordination occurred in May 1944 when new staff joined RAF 222 Group Headquarters Ceylon to supervise reconnaissance operations. This led to the creation of Indian Ocean General Reconnaissance Operations under the aegis of 222 Group, a unified control centre for all RAF reconnaissance units in the Indian Ocean that applied knowledge and skills gained in the Battle of the Atlantic. This helped the RAF and navy coordinate their actions as they hunted enemy submarines and supply vessels. The threat from Axis submarines, which had for long been 222 Group's primary concern, had

50 Dancey, *South East Asia Command*, p. 5.
51 Ibid., pp. 15-16.

passed by the end of 1944. Nevertheless, its Catalinas and Liberators kept patrolling Indian Ocean sea lanes in an anti-shipping role. The liabilities brought by far-flung conquest could not be met by the Japanese merchant marine after the Imperial Japanese Navy's loss of control of the sea, yet it still needed to maintain communications and send supplies to the tens of thousands of troops in the Indian Ocean region. The enemy now depended on coaster-size ships to supply their forces in Burma, given the disruption to communications inland wrought by the Fourteenth Army and the air formations supporting it.

Given this, a great deal of effort was invested by the navy and the RAF in intercepting the wooden coastal vessels – ferries, coasters, junks and sampans – that the Japanese had taken to using for supply and communication purposes as their ocean-going vessels were destroyed and not replaced. Some of these vessels crept along the Chinese coast and entered the Indian Ocean through the Malacca Strait, where British submarines waited for them. Japanese vessels further north were prey to British flying-boats and Liberators in the Bay of Bengal, as well as the fighter aircraft which scoured the coasts and the creeks. Light coastal forces of the Royal Navy and Royal Indian Navy also stalked them, and in an attempt to degrade the construction of wooden coasters, the Eastern Fleet attacked the sawmills on the Andaman Islands that produced them.

Flying-boats and land-based reconnaissance aircraft in the Indian Ocean were dedicated to sea lane protection, particularly in areas such as the Persian Gulf, the Gulf of Aden, and the approaches to Bombay and Ceylon. One of the squadron's involved in this work was 191 Squadron, a Catalina unit based at Korangi Creek near Karachi (a photograph of which appears on the cover of this book). Until the end of 1943, it patrolled the Arabian Sea and the Persian Gulf, sending detachments to bases in Bahrein and elsewhere to extend its cover. In 1944 the squadron's activities were concentrated off the east coast of India and its machines were based in Addu Atoll, southern India and Ceylon. From 1943 these aircraft were also used to mount a regular air service between Ceylon and Australia as part of the British Overseas Airways Corporation-Qantas Australia-Britain route, a non-stop flight of 2,650 miles.[52]

American B-29 Superfortresses struck far and wide, India now a major centre of American air power. 20th US Bomber Command, for instance, was based around Calcutta, with its headquarters at Kharagpur from March. The command's aircraft had arrived via Marrakech, Cairo, Karachi, and Calcutta as part of Operation Matterhorn, the B-29 offensive against Japan, and by May there were 230 of these devastating aircraft in India. The first B-29 raid on 5 June 1944 saw 98 aircraft attack targets in Thailand. The Americans used advanced bases in Ceylon – particularly the China Bay aerodrome – to extend their raids to Sumatra. In August, for example, 45 B-29s of the 30th US Army Air Corps, operating from China Bay, bombed oil installations at Palembang. This was a 4,030 mile, 19 hour mission, the longest American air raid of the war. Allied air power was now inflicting severe punishment on Japanese positions, even far behind the front line. They were even able to strike the Japanese home islands, conducting the first air attacks since the Doolittle Raid.

One of the most important roles performed by Allied aircraft and warships was survivor rescue, and the knowledge that the air force and the navy routinely searched for survivors was an inestimable comfort to those who faced the prospect of enemy attacks at sea. They had not only to

52 See Barry Pattison and Geoffrey Goodall, *Qantas Empire Airways (Western Operations Division) Indian Ocean Service, 1943-1946* (Footscray, Victoria: Aviation Historical Society of Australia, 1979).

deal with the possibility of death through drowning, shark attacks, or starvation, but the knowledge that both German and Japanese ships were liable to perpetrate atrocities, even beyond the machine-gunning of survivors in the water. Thousands of people were rescued by the efforts of the RAF and Royal Navy, 222 Group aircraft alone rescuing over 1,000 survivors from sunken vessels.[53] There were many ambitious survivor rescue missions. In February 1944, for example, 205 and 413 squadrons based at RAF Koggala in Ceylon flew 800 miles to search for survivors from the *Fort Buckingham*, sunk close to the Laccadive Islands by *U-188*. When the British liner *Nellore* and the American Liberty ship *Jean Nicolet* were sunk within days of each other in June-July, a rescue mission was organized and in an operation lasting 14 days, 34 sorties were flown by RAF Catalinas based on Diego Garcia and RAF Liberators and Sunderlands from Addu Atoll. As a result, 234 of *Nellore*'s compliment of 341 were rescued (as well as those from *Jean Nicolet* who had not been bayoneted or shot by the Japanese).[54] The Eastern and Australian Steamship Navigation Company ship *Nellore*, en route from Bombay to Sydney, had been hit by *I-8* on 29 June, 800 miles south of Ceylon. A remarkable result of this sinking was the epic open boat journey of a party of survivors. At sea for 28 days, 44 men including 28 Goanese stewards, a Javanese woman, and two babies, floated in an undecked boat, eventually reaching Madagascar. Ten survived the journey.[55]

Despite rescue operations, hundreds of people continued to lose their lives in the treacherous waters of the Indian Ocean. When the *El Madina* was torpedoed by the Japanese on its way from Calcutta to Chittagong on 16 March, 500 perished, most of them soldiers. In September Lieutenant Commander Lynch Maydon's submarine *Tradewind*, on patrol from its base at Trincomalee, landed two agents on the Sumatran coast and later sighted an escorted enemy merchant ship, the *Junyo Maru*. She was sunk with two torpedoes, and it was later discovered that the vessel had in fact been carrying a human cargo, one of the Japanese 'hell ships' used for transporting slave labourers. On board were 1,377 Dutch prisoners, 64 from Australia and Britain, eight Americans, and 4,200 Javanese slaves. They were being moved from Batavia to Padang to help build the infamous Sumatran railway. Only 723 people survived the attack. In contravention of international law, these Japanese ships did not display the Red Cross, and so Maydon had no idea as to the ship's cargo. Because of this, 5,620 people died in one of the worst maritime disasters of the war.[56]

John Winton writes that the Eastern Fleet operations of 1944 were 'a kind of muted accompaniment in a minor key to the great themes of the Pacific'.[57] But they were the operations to hand, and served to ensure that as the war enter its final months, the Allies dominated the Indian Ocean. It was of course ironic that the Eastern Fleet and air commanders gained the resources necessary to take the war to the Japanese at the moment when the enemy was visibly wilting as an offensive force. As Willmott writes, by the last stages of the war Japan's strategic mobility had been destroyed, and the vast majority of sinkings (of Japanese vessels) occurred in Japanese home waters.

53 An Officer of the RAF, 'A Resume of the Activities of 222 Group RAF', prepared for a radio broadcast in 1945, transcribed from TNA, AIR 23/4802, and available at http://www.rquirk.com/speech222gp.html

54 See Patrick Bollen, 'The Sinking of SS *Nellore* by the Japanese in 1944', *United Service*, 63, 1 (2012).

55 Macdonnell, *Valiant Occasions*, chapter 14, 'Lifeboat', featuring the daily log of *Nellore*'s bosun, J. Sheather.

56 See '*Junyo Maru: Torpedoed by HMS* Tradewind', at http://www.historynet.com/juno-mayru-torpedoed-by-british-submarine-hms-tradewind.htm

57 Winton, *Sink the* Haguro!, p. 15.

13

Victory Japan

By late 1944 the Eastern Fleet had grown to become once again the most powerful British force afloat, a predominantly British fleet including ships and crews from India and the dominions and still containing a significant Dutch component and a more recently-arrived Free French one. It had successfully made the transition from a fleet anxious to avoid the enemy's main strength while concentrating on sea lane protection, to one ready and able to seek out its opponent and strike targets all along the enemy-held rim of the Indian Ocean. The same held true on land and in the air, as with the help of its allies, Britain reasserted itself in a region that before 1942 it had dominated virtually unchallenged for generations. Increasingly, its Japanese foe was forced to skulk around as it strove to maintain contact with garrisons, its maritime and air power faltering and its sea lanes besieged. Attacking Japanese positions in the East Indies, sweeping sea lanes clear of enemy vessels and treacherous minefields, and supporting land advances in Burma were the features of the final year of the war here. So, too, were large scale preparations for the invasion of Malaya and Singapore, the ultimate goal towards which Mountbatten's South East Asia Command was driving. What ailed the enemy of course was the crushing weight being brought to bear by the Allied powers in Europe and the Pacific, meaning that the Indian Ocean, by this stage of the war, had become a sea too far. Japanese achievements in 1941-42 were proving to have been chimerical. The Indian Ocean raids had been symptomatic of this, achieving nothing of strategic value yet augmenting a sense of overconfidence that had led slap-bang into the disastrous battle of Midway. On land, Burma turned out to have been only a partial victory: 'Though the Japanese conquest was impressive … securing Burma led them nowhere. Burma was a cul-de-sac in which they were ultimately trapped and crushed. In this Burma reflected the overall Japanese effort during the war, for their initial victories had bought the Japanese a defensive perimeter that they could not maintain'.[1]

The reason for the Eastern Fleet's strength in the latter half of 1944 was twofold: on the one hand, victory in the Mediterranean allowed Britain to shift resources east, and on the other, it was in fact two fleets within the bosom of one. For much of 1944 it had incubated the new fleet that would spearhead Britain's contribution to the war in the Pacific. Heralding Britain's reappearance east of Singapore, and symbolizing its determination to take part in the march on the Japanese home islands, on 22 November 1944 the British Pacific Fleet duly hatched

1 Willmott, *Empires in the Balance*, p. 432.

from the Eastern Fleet in Trincomalee harbour. Destined for bases in Australia, the new fleet's advance guard left Ceylon on 2 December led by its commander, Admiral Sir Bruce Fraser, aboard his flagship *Howe*.[2] Fraser was replaced as Commander-in-Chief East Indies by Admiral Sir Arthur Power. Continuing the sequence of carrier and battleship strikes, Palembang was attacked by East Indies Station and British Pacific Fleet vessels as the latter made its way to its new Pacific base.[3]

When the split occurred, the ships that remained in Ceylon – the weaker portion – assumed the name East Indies Fleet, returning, almost, to the nomenclature employed before the Eastern Fleet's creation in late 1941. Its role remained the same: to secure the sea lanes of the Indian Ocean and to work with the land and air forces of South East Asia Command as they strove to expel the Japanese from Burma, Malaya, the Dutch East Indies, and French Indo-China. This meant denying the enemy the use of the Indian Ocean; cutting seaborne supply lines to the Japanese armies in Burma; giving close support to the flank of the Fourteenth Army's 15th Indian Corps in the new Burma offensive that opened in December; and attacking Japanese shipping, oil, and harbour installations. But despite the continued importance of its role, the sailors of the East Indies Station could be forgiven for feeling that they were missing out on the action. 'In the first months of 1945', writes John Winton, 'the East Indies Fleet's sense that they were in an operational backwater increased. In Ceylon the fleet was in the war, but not of it'.[4]

The East Indies Fleet continued to strike Japanese targets. In Operation Lentil on 4 January 1945, for example, the carriers *Indefatigable*, *Indomitable*, and *Victorious*, the cruisers *Argonaut*, *Black Prince*, *Ceylon*, and *Suffolk*, and 14 destroyers attacked the oil refineries at Pangkalan Brandan in Sumatra. As well as its inherent military logic, the operation was intended to offer

2 The British Pacific Fleet was created to achieve two things: to visibly demonstrate both the return of British seapower to the waters east of the Malacca Strait and Britain's commitment to the final defeat of Japan alongside America. Though the war in Europe was winding down, there was reason to expect that the fight against Japan had years left to run. London's intention therefore was that this powerful naval force would be joined by a Commonwealth Corps of three to five divisions for the invasion of Japan (Operation Downfall), and Tiger Force, a tactical air force comprising very long range heavy bombers to be based on Okinawa. At the second Quebec conference in September 1944, Churchill had pledged 500 to 1,000 bombers once Germany had been defeated, though American misgivings gradually whittled this down to a figure of between ten and fifteen squadrons.

3 As it was again when Vice Admiral Philip Vian departed Trincomalee with the rest of the British Pacific Fleet the following month. For the British Pacific Fleet see Jon Robb-Webb, *The British Pacific Fleet: Experience and Legacy, 1944-1950* (Fanham: Ashgate, 2013); Peter Smith, *Task Force 57: The British Pacific Fleet, 1944-1945* (London: Kimber, 1969); Nicholas Sarantakes, *Allies Against the Rising Sun: The United States, the British Nations, and the Defeat of Imperial Japan* (Lawrence, KS: University of Kansas Press, 2009); Sarantakes, 'One Last Crusade: The US-British Alliance and the End of the War in the Pacific', *The Royal United Services Institute Journal*, 149, 4 (2004); 'One Last Crusade: The British Pacific Fleet and its Impact on Anglo-American Relations', *English Historical Review*, 121, 491 (2006); Sarantakes, 'The Royal Air Force on Okinawa: The Diplomacy of a Coalition on the Verge of Victory', *Diplomatic History*, 27, 4 (2003); John Winton, *Forgotten Fleet*, and David Hobbs, *The British Pacific Fleet: The Royal Navy's Most Powerful Strike Force* (Barnsley: Seaforth Books, 2012). For the fleet's aircraft, see Will Iredale, *The Kamikaze Hunters: Fighting for the Pacific, 1945* (London: Pan, 2015). Forgotten admirals, forgotten armies, and forgotten fleets; see also Henry Probert, *The Forgotten Air Force: The RAF in the War Against Japan, 1941-1945* (London: Brassey's, 1995).

4 Winton, *Sink the* Haguro!, p. 22.

the ships of the East Indies Fleet – and the portion of the British Pacific Fleet yet to depart – the chance to further hone their skills.[5] The attack severely damaged the oil refinery and over 30 Japanese aircraft were shot down or destroyed on the ground. The force returned to Trincomalee, from where, later in the month, Rear Admiral Philip Vian, who had been in charge of aircraft for the Eastern Fleet and would now command the air component of the British Pacific Fleet, led the remaining ships of the British Pacific Fleet away from Ceylon for the last time, off to join Fraser in the Pacific. En route, more strikes were conducted in the Dutch East Indies: Operation Meridian One was an air strike on oil refineries at Pladjoe and Soengei Gerong near Palembang, the first of the two largest strikes undertaken by the Fleet Air Arm to date. The attack went in with 43 Avenger bombers, 12 Firefly fighter-bombers with rockets, and 50 Hellcat, Corsair, and Seafire fighters. Operation Meridian Two, which again targeted oil refineries, took place in the dying days of January. Thirty Japanese aircraft were shot down in air engagements and 38 destroyed on the ground, for the loss of 16 British aircraft.[6]

Supporting the fighting in Burma and Andaman attacks

By the beginning of 1945, the Fourteenth Army – previously part of India Command's Eastern Army – numbered a million men.[7] In supporting its offensive, particularly the operations of 15th Indian Corps in the Arakan, the East Indies Fleet demonstrated the range of capabilities brought by maritime forces in support of land forces, as it had done earlier in the war during the campaigns in East Africa, Iran, Iraq, and Madagascar. The combined forces attack on Ramree Island in January-February affords an example of this cooperation. Admiral Power instructed his Chief Staff Officer, Captain E. W. Bush, to offer all support to Major-General C. E. N. Lomax, commander of the 26th Indian Infantry Division, which had been tasked with clearing the enemy from Ramree and capturing the strategic port of Kyaukpyu and the nearby airfield. This was

> part of the strategic advance of the 15th Indian Corps down the Arakan coast with a view to securing airfields on Ramree Island from which the Fourteenth Army could be supplied on their advance to Rangoon, and operations could be mounted for the capture of that port by sea should it become necessary, and which in fact did prove the case.[8]

In what was very much a joint operation (Matador), the East Indies Fleet contributed a range of ships, including the battleship *Queen Elizabeth*, the cruiser *Phoebe*, two destroyers, a British

5 Operations in this period included Aintree (escort of Duke of Gloucester, on passage to become Governor-General of Australia), Balsam, Collie, Gable, Irregular, Livery, Passbook, Penzance, Pharos, Onboard, Sankey, and Transport.

6 Power, 'The Carrier-Borne Aircraft Attacks'. See also Warner, *Admiral of the Fleet*, pp. 125-27 for an account of *Illustrious*'s role in these strikes.

7 In the reorganization, Eastern Army was split, a new Eastern Command taking over administrative and rear echelon tasks, Fourteenth Army taking on the actual fighting against the Japanese in Burma.

8 Arthur Power, 'Naval Operations in Ramree Island Area 19 January to 22 February 1945', *Supplement to the London Gazette*, 38269 (London: HMSO, 1948). See also Peter Haining, *The Banzai Hunters: The Forgotten Armada of Little Ships that Defeated the Japanese, 1944-1945* (London: Robson Books, 2006), Chapter 9, 'Invasion of Crocodile Island'.

sloop and a Royal Indian Navy sloop, and the aircraft of the escort carriers *Ameer* and *Raider*, along with marine contingents. The operation was covered in the air by Thunderbolts, Mitchells, and 85 Liberators from 224 Group RAF.

The initial attacks took place on 21 January and five days later two brigades were landed on Ramree, joined later by a third, all under the watchful eyes of the RAF, the FAA, and the guns of the fleet. The navy established a headquarters ashore and began to develop the strategic port of Kyaukpyu as an anchorage, which entailed clearing mines, an undertaking supervised by Commander E. J. C. Evans, Commander Minesweepers Bay of Bengal. The army had to eject the Japanese from well-defended positions around Ramree Town and the beaches near Thames Point which entailed fighting inland, where naval gunfire support was difficult to provide. One of the Indian brigades began a rapid advance southward, supported by destroyers and sloops. Meanwhile Force Wellington, consisting of Royal Marines from the East Indies Fleet with naval support, secured Cheduba Island. Experiencing difficulties crossing the Yan Bauk Chaung on Ramree after the joint force commanders had told Lieutenant General Sir Philip Christison, commander of 15th Indian Corps, that all of the island, rather than only the parts needed for airfields, would have to be captured, one of the brigades and elements of another were committed to investing Ramree Town. Surveys of the Kaleingdaung River had already been conducted, and this enabled two destroyers, preceded by minesweepers, to penetrate inland and assume bombarding positions.

Soon the Japanese troops had been defeated by the combined attack, with those remaining alive attempting to escape by sea. This possibility had been considered by the combined staffs, and it was concluded that by using the motor launches of the Arakan Coastal Force, Landing Craft Support vessels, Landing Craft Assault vessels, and minesweepers, the two possible escape routes to the open sea could be blocked.[9] Operation Block duly began on 8 February. The RAF strafed boat concentrations and along with the army drove the Japanese off the island into the mangrove swamps 'where they were successfully dealt with by the navy', camouflaged vessels ambushing the Japanese soldiers. 'Disadvantages to the Japanese lay in the indescribable horrors of the mangrove swamps. Dark during the day as well as during the night, acres of thick impenetrable forest; miles of deep black mud, mosquitoes, scorpions, flies, and weird insects by the

9 The Arakan Coastal Forces were developed by Major T. L. F. Firbank, starting with remnants of the old Burmese Inland Water Transport services to develop a small armada. It was based at Teknaf, on a narrow peninsula 50-odd miles from Cox's Bazaar. In February 1942 the company's fleet had comprised over 650 vessels of all types, steamers, paddle boats, ferries, tugs. General evacuation order to 'proceed upcountry and scuttle all units at different places'. (P. Haining, *The Banzai Hunters*, p. 8) Within days, much of the fleet was lying on river beds or sunk in the *chaungs* – in the market town of Katha, 75 ships were sunk in as many hours. A number steamed off to Indian ports, some to Cox's Bazaar and Teknaf. Arakan Coastal Forces manned by Royal Indian Navy personnel, South African and Burma motor launch flotillas. The Force played a part in securing the seaward flank of the 5th Division's operations on land, 'bringing in supplies, landing agents and reconnaissance parties, and carrying out the occasional bombardment'. (Ibid., p. 18). See also O. A. Goulden, *From Trombay to Changi's a Helluva a Way: The Story of the Arakan Coastal Forces* (London: The Chameleon Press, 1987) and Tony Mackenzie, *44 (RM) Commando: Achnacarry to the Arakan: A Diary of the Commando at War, August 1943 to March 1947* (Brighton: Tom Donovan, 1996). Another local force was the Tenasserim Coast Patrol maintained by Royal Indian Navy sloops between latitudes 10 degree north and 14-30 degrees north until the end of July 1945.

billion and – worst of all – crocodiles. No food, no drinking water to be obtained anywhere'.[10] Of the 1,200 to 1,500 Japanese originally on the island, few survived, 'the remainder either killed in battle or drowned in the mangrove swamps'.[11] Supporting the army in the Arakan, between 14 December 1944 and 1 March 1945 East Indies Station ships fired 23,000 rounds of four- to fourteen-inch ammunition.[12]

Elsewhere, Ceylon-bases photo reconnaissance aircraft had surveyed the Andaman and Nicobar Islands and Allied bombers and fighters periodically attacked them. In concert with submarines, surface vessels had joined the work of interdicting enemy lines of communication and ensuring that Japanese forces were effectively besieged, unable to evacuate and receiving limited supplies. East Indies Fleet destroyers began a series of anti-shipping sweeps (like the battleship and carrier strikes, also known as 'club runs') in the Andaman Sea to look for whatever targets intelligence suggested or chance might afford. In February, the first reconnaissances of the Kra Isthmus, Phuket, and northern Sumatra were made by Hellcats from the escort carrier *Ameer* as Allied assets continued to roam further afield with ever-growing confidence.

In March Force 70, comprising the East Indies Fleet destroyers *Rapid*, *Saumarez* and *Volage*, was sent to attack targets in the Andaman and Nicobar Islands. C. S. V. Solent served aboard *Volage*, which on 19 March arrived off the Andamans with the intention of shooting up whatever it could find in Port Blair harbour after a leisurely day steaming up and down examining the bays of Great Nicobar and searching for targets. Finding nothing, *Saumarez* entered Stewart Sound cautiously:

> *Volage* was involved in an engagement at the Andamans with a Japanese shore gun battery of three six-inch guns at Stewart Sound along with the destroyers *Saumarez* and *Rapid*. *Rapid* had been hit by two shells and was still in the water. *Saumarez* closed alongside *Rapid* to tow her to safety. *Volage* charged past the other destroyers to engage the gun batteries, coming under fire, and laying a smokescreen around the other two destroyers to enable them to escape to sea. *Volage*, hit and steering out of control and heading for enemy shore, used her secondary steering and escaped by entering her own smokescreen. *Rapid* had seventeen killed and twenty wounded, *Volage* three killed. Under air cover the following morning they retreated to Akyab Island off the Burmese coast, recently taken by imperial forces.[13]

This action was an example of how the Japanese, though now beaten, still offered pockets of resistance and would always fight back. Part of the character of the war in the region, famously documented in the case of the Burma campaign, was the need to kill or capture Japanese forces; they were never going to lay down their weapons and surrender. The battered Force 70 reached Akyab on 20 March. *Rapid* soon sailing to Simon's Town for repairs while *Volage* was patched up alongside the cruiser *Cumberland*, involving, among other things, the installation of a complete

10 Power, 'Naval Operations in Ramree Island'.
11 Ibid.
12 'Admiralty War Diaries of World War II', Eastern Fleet War Diary, March 1945.
13 BBC 'World War Two People's War' oral history archive, C. S. V. Solent, 'HMS *Volage*, Part Two: The Reluctant Survivors'. A5845403. This particularly vicious action is described at length in Winton, *Sink the* Haguro!, pp. 30-36.

plywood starboard side for the wardroom, which had been hit during the action, destroying its wine store and bottled ale supplies. *Saumarez* and *Volage* were now joined from Trincomalee by the destroyers *Vigilant* and *Virago*. On 25 March they set out on an anti-shipping sweep between Malaya and the Andamans, spread out in line abreast formation hoping for radar contact with the enemy. 'So once again we were at sea, seeking out Jap convoys bringing supplies to their army', wrote Solent.

> All ships were at defence stations, four hours on, four hours off for the ships' company, day followed night, a contact was made next morning and sighted. A small Jap convoy had been sighted. Action Station ordered on British ships. Enemy consisted of five ships, largest being a troopship of 5,000 tons, a small coaster, and three small submarine chasers. The greater superiority lay with the British ships, and the Jap sub chasers took off in different directions. Captain 'D' [Destroyers] Manley Power ordered his ship *Saumarez* plus *Vigilant* and *Virago* to engage other ships. Captain 'D's orders were to engage at a distance as British ships could outgun with larger calibre 4.7-inch guns ... to save British casualties. In the ensuing battle the three sub chasers, highly manoeuverable, took some time to sink.[14]

During the action Solent worked as part of *Volage*'s 'A' gun crew to the repeated order 'load, load, load!'. The transports were sunk by the fire of the destroyers and patrolling Liberators of 222 Group RAF with which *Saumarez* had made contact. They made their attacks almost at sea level, one of them dipping its wing and cartwheeling into the sea. In an 'exasperatingly unsatisfactory action', the four destroyers had expended 18 torpedoes, 3,160 rounds of 4.7-inch ammunition, and a considerable amount of Bofors ammunition before all the enemy ships were sunk.[15] The convoy had been carrying 'entertainment' women to the Andamans garrison as well as desperately needed rations. The food situation on the islands was now so serious that atrocities were being perpetrated on the civilian population, 'useless mouths' killed by firing parties or left to die on remote islands.

After this action, the destroyer flotilla returned to Ceylon on 28 March, *Volage* carrying Japanese prisoners. Most of the Japanese survivors had swum away from rescue; some had cut their own throats, and one attacked a destroyer's side with a shell case as he gripped the rescue net. Of the prisoners they did manage to get on board alive, one managed to use a loincloth to hang himself by jumping off a toilet seat in the chief and petty officers' bathroom.

> As we closed to Trincomalee for entering harbour, HMS *Saumarez* leading the other ships line astern. Procedure as always for entering harbour was that ship's company line the side, standing to attention, captain saluting if possible, to ship whose captain is senior to us. To our surprise as we passed down the line of battleships, aircraft carriers, cruisers etc, all the ships companies lined the ships sides cheering us in turns, having such a reception we could not believe. Without permission we cheered back. Our reception, new to us younger ones, seemed unbelievable.[16]

14 BBC 'World War Two People's War' oral history archive, C. S. V. Solent, 'HMS *Volage*, Part Two.
15 Winton, *Sink the* Haguro*!*, p. 38.
16 BBC 'World War Two People's War' oral history archive, C. S. V. Solent, 'HMS *Volage*, Part Two.

Solent and his crewmates were told by the old hands that it was a procedure to welcome Royal Navy ships that had achieved a victory, a naval tradition. A variety of operations continued: On 8 April Vice Admiral Harold 'Hook' Walker left Trincomalee with a powerful East Indies Station collection, Force 63, for a mixed programme of air strikes, anti-shipping sweeps, bombardments, and photo-reconnaissance flights over Port Swettenham and Port Dickson (Operation Sunfish). Nicknamed 'Hooky' because he wore a hook in place of a hand lost in the First World War, Walker had arrived in Ceylon in December 1944 as Power's second in command and flag officer commanding the 3rd Battle Squadron.

By 1945 the air situation had been transformed in the Indian Ocean region, as India and Ceylon became home to about 3,000 British and American aircraft, most under the auspices of South East Asia Command, some under separate American command and dedicated to supplying China over 'the Hump'. There were now 120,000 RAF personnel in the Burma-Ceylon-India region. Bombers, reconnaissance aircraft, and fighters enjoyed almost total air superiority as Japanese aircraft numbers plummeted. Many bombing sorties were flown over Malaya from bases in Ceylon, supplemented by RAF Liberators from the Cocos-Keeling Islands. Air and sea supremacy in the Bay of Bengal meant that ships could now sail without escort, except for troopships. Signs of success abounded; escort forces were being disbanded, black out restrictions lifted, routine anti-submarine and minesweeping patrols discontinued, rear bases reduced, and shore defences stood down. Across the theatre, it was a now rush to the attack. From February 1945 222 Group mounted attacks off the Arakan coast using units such as 203 Squadron, its Liberators operating from Kankesanterai in northern Ceylon. Mining remained a major occupation, 160 Squadron based at Minneriya in Ceylon undertaking 'some of the longest sorties on record to lay nearly a thousand mines in enemy waters off the Malay peninsula, the Kra isthmus, and South East Indies'.[17] On 26 March eight of this squadron's Liberators made the 3,460 mile round trip from Ceylon to Singapore to mine the harbour. Stripped of armaments, armour plating, and even chemical toilets to lighten the airframes, they were the first RAF aircraft to fly over the island stronghold since its capitulation in February 1942. The RAF also continued to participate in the attacks in the Andaman Sea, and in a four month period Liberators operating from Ceylon and India destroyed or damaged 50 Japanese vessels.

On 27 April two naval forces left Trincomalee to protect convoys as Operation Dracula, the long-awaited airborne and amphibious attack on Rangoon, got under way. The Rangoon landings were given fighter cover from the 21st Aircraft Carrier Squadron led by Commodore Oliver flying his pennant from *Royalist*, a light cruiser specially furnished as an air group command centre, with the carriers *Emperor*, *Hunter*, *Khedive*, and *Stalker*. The entire East Indies Fleet was involved in Dracula and the covering operation, Bishop, which was intended to confuse the Japanese and prevent any possible interference with the landings. British submarines patrolled in the southern Malacca Strait, the eastern Bay of Bengal and off the Tenasserim coast while RAF Liberators and Sunderlands patrolled from the Arakan. It was not known at the time that the success of the Fourteenth Army's advance meant that the Japanese were already evacuating the great port city.

Task Force 63, allotted to Operation Bishop, comprised the battleships *Queen Elizabeth* and *Richelieu*, the escort carriers *Empress* and *Shah*, the cruisers *Ceylon*, *Cumberland*, *Suffolk*,

17 Ibid.

and *Tromp*, and escorting destroyers. A dawn bombardment of the Nicobar Islands took place on 30 April, and Port Blair was attacked that evening. For a number of days while events were unfolding in and around Rangoon, Force 63 shuttled between targets in the Andaman and Nicobar Islands and Malacca, and mounted an armed reconnaissance patrol of the shipping lanes between the Mergui archipelago and Victoria Point. In one of the many actions, the Japanese gun positions at Stewart Sound in the Andamans, which had given the British destroyer force such a hard time back in March, was 'cleaned out' by 'four crisp 15-inch shells' from *Queen Elizabeth*.[18] The pressure on the enemy was remorseless, the cruisers *Ceylon* and *Phoebe*, for instance, in company with six Royal Indian Navy frigates, taking turns to patrol between the Mergui archipelago and Port Blair in order to prevent the evacuation and resupply of Japanese troops. While such deployments have meant little to the historical record – even in this theatre, with its narrative dominated by Burma and plans for the invasion of Malaya – they were meaningful actions aimed at exerting British authority and choking off a stubborn enemy in order to regain lost imperial territory and hasten the end of the war.

Surveying the situation in early May, the fleet war diary recorded that 'the picture now represented by the naval situation following the unopposed entry into Rangoon, is of the western area of the Station virtually free from threat of any kind and of little surface opposition elsewhere, while all available strength is being prepared for the first important strikes in the next, post Burma, phase'.[19] This meant that now, with the enemy virtually eradicated from the seas west of Malaya, the navy and the RAF began to look further east, hunting further and further afield. As an RAF officer at 222 Group headquarters wrote:

> Crossing the Kra Isthmus, [our] Sunderlands, now operating from Rangoon, began to reconnoitre the Gulf of Siam. They found a multitude of small vessels, coasters, frigates, and so on – and immediately began working destruction among them … Every cargo that went to the bottom of the Gulf of Siam was an irreplaceable loss to men still holding out in Burma or attempting to force a way over the mountains and into Siam and Indo-China.[20]

VE Day and the sinking of *Ashigara* and *Haguro*

Following operations Bishop and Dracula, the ships involved in the Rangoon operations returned home to Trincomalee. Midshipman John Robathan of *Venus* wrote that

> By the afternoon of the 9th the whole fleet – two battleships, six escort carriers, five cruisers and thirteen destroyers – was back in harbour and began to refuel and rearm. Everybody was tired out by DRACULA and BISHOP. Apart from the depressing effect of the gloomy weather, anti-climax in war was often as exhausting as action. The ships had spent days altering course to fly off and land on aircraft, changing screen formations by day and night, exercising gun drills and routine action stations, waiting for attacks which never came.

18 Winton, *Sink the* Haguro*!*, p. 54.
19 'Admiralty War Diaries of World War II', Eastern Fleet War Diary, review of period 22 November 1944-3 May 1945.
20 An Officer of the RAF, 'A Resumé of the Activities of 222 Group'.

> Nobody would have believed that a city of the stature of Rangoon could be taken without a savage reception from the Japanese.[21]

People across the Indian Ocean region marked victory in Europe. The ships of Force 63 spliced the mainbrace as they returned to Ceylon following their attack on the Andaman and Nicobar Islands. VE Day found Cyril Battell at HMS *Bambara*, the Royal Naval Air Station at China Bay:

> The navy have spliced the main brace [sic] and most people seemed to be quite drunk. Celebrations go on until midnight when we are turned out of our hut and paraded at the navy Reg office and threatened with a mutiny charge. Celebrations continue next day with a combined church parade held in the bombed out hangars down on the airfield. Lunch is also special with turkey on the menu and the whole camp again spliced the main brace.[22]

'The men of the East Indies Fleet listened to Winston Churchill broadcasting to the nation and then later, during the Middle Watch by Ceylon time on the 9th, to HM the King. As Robathan wrote, still tired from days at sea, 'all we could do was think of home and wish we were there to join in the celebrations and hear the church bells'.[23]

> At Trincomalee there were few facilities for celebrations but the men of the destroyer flotillas, spurred on by an extra tot to splice the mainbrace and an extra pint of Australian beer to mark VE Day, did their best. When the radio in the Fleet Canteen announced that celebratory bonfires were being lit at home, some men of the 26th Destroyer Flotilla shouted, 'There's a bonfire here!' and burned down part of the canteen and nearby *basha* huts.
>
> Meanwhile the 11th Flotilla had an unarmed combat with ratings from *Richelieu*. In *Cumberland* the celebrations included the throwing overboard of a mounted fragment of a French shell which had inflicted damage on the ship at Dakar in 1940. But for many of the fleet, it was a quiet evening on board, with a film on the fo'c'sle, reminiscences on the messdecks and in the wardroom. It was still a long war in the east, but just for this evening, there seemed to be time for a smoke and reflection.[24]

'VE Day celebrations passed off quietly in Kandy', wrote Mountbatten. Not that he was there to witness them, as he was visiting the Burma front line, Lieutenant General Frederick 'Boy' Browning, his Chief of Staff, deputizing at a big inter-Allied parade in Colombo.[25] Alan

21 Winton, *Sink the* Haguro*!*, p. 55.
22 BBC 'World War Two People's War' oral history archive, Cyril Battell, 'VE Day Ceylon', A4034314. *Bambara* was commissioned on New Year's Day 1944 and was new collective appellation for Royal Naval Air Station China Bay, the navy's Aircraft Maintenance Yard at Clappenburg Bay, and the Naval Accommodation Camp Nachchikunda. From 'Naval Air Stations', Fleet Air Arm Officers Association, at https://www.fleetairarmoa.org/fleet-air-arm-naval-air-stations
23 Winton, *Sink the* Haguro*!*, p. 55.
24 Ibid., p. 55-6.
25 Ziegler, *Personal Diary of Admiral the Lord Louis Mountbatten*, p. 206. Browning had arrived in theatre at the end of 1944, just in time to witness the unique investiture in which Field Marshal

Brundrett, a young sailor working in the Naval Secretariat, remembered the 'great excitement'. 'Flags and coloured lights were everywhere on buildings. Crowds of people were talking in the street. There was plenty of celebrating going on in the bar of our hotel'. Cinemas were open to men and women in the armed forces for free. The Governor's House was

> bathed in floodlighting of pale rose and turquoise. Over the arch at the entrance were the letters 'GR' [George Regina] and the crown, formed by light bulbs ... Many of the public buildings and the Galle Face Hotel displayed an illuminated 'V' sign. Crowds gathered here to watch a fireworks display. Bonfires were lit. Dancing, eating and drinking were going on everywhere. Even the snake-charmers were out in force. An altogether memorable sight; one we shall have etched in our minds for a long time.[26]

On 13 May Brundrett attended the Victory Parade on Galle Face Green. Service personnel marched past a saluting base where the governor, Sir Henry Monck-Mason Moore, and the Commander-in-Chief Ceylon, Admiral Layton, took the salute, while 'ships of the Royal Navy steamed by close in shore, and planes flew over in formation'.[27] The destroyer *Rotherham* was returning from a strike against Japanese forces in the Nicobar Islands when there was received a 'signal from the King: "To all ships and establishments: Splice the mainbrace"'. Celebrations followed when she reached Trincomalee the following day. But VE Day meant little, from a working point of view, for the personnel of the East Indies Fleet and the airmen, soldiers, and sailors engaged in the ongoing war against Japan. They had a job to do, and still faced the prospect of potentially fatal encounters with the enemy. Indeed, even at this significant moment, celebrations were cut short when it was learned that the heavy cruiser *Haguro* was loose in the Indian Ocean. 'At 10pm that evening a general alarm was flashed around Trincomalee, ordering almost every ship there to raise steam and prepare to leave harbour at 6am the next morning'.[28]

Haguro was one of the very few big Japanese warships still in the region by this stage of the war. The South-West Pacific Fleet was restricted to operations around the Philippines and a new fleet, the 10th Area Fleet, had been created for the rest of the South-West Pacific including the Indian Ocean, commanded by Vice Admiral Shigeru Fukudome.[29] The nascent Japanese Empire was crumbling at the edges and units were being withdrawn from outer areas to reinforce core areas. In February the 10th Area Fleet had been placed under Field Marshal Count Terauchi, Commander-in-Chief Southern Army Area, headquartered at Saigon, and he planned four major withdraws to concentrate his forces in Malaya and Indo-China. Troops were to be evacuated from the Andaman and Nicobar Islands to Singapore; from Singapore to Indo-China; from Timor to Singapore; and from Borneo to Surabaya. *Haguro* and her sister

Wavell, Viceroy of India, knighted generals Slim and his three corps commanders, Philip Christison, Geoffrey Scoones, and Monty Stopford on the field of battle. See *General Boy: The Life of Lieutenant General Sir Frederick Browning* (Barnsley: Pen and Sword, 2010), Chapter 23 'Kandy (December 1944-May 1945')'.

26 Alan Brundrett, *Two Years in Ceylon: The Diary of a Navy Secretariat Member, 1944-1946* (Lewes, Sussex: Book Guild, 1996), p. 204-205.

27 Ibid., p. 211.

28 Winton, *Sink the* Haguro*!*, p. 55-56.

29 Winton details the strength of this force, ibid., pp. 26-27.

ship, *Ashigara*, along with the destroyer *Kamikaze*, were the only sizeable warships operational in the 10th Area Fleet capable of protecting these troops movements.[30]

Haguro had been operating as a supply ship for Japanese forces in the Andaman and Nicobar islands, Burma, and the East Indies. Now, news of her presence was revealed by intelligence intercepts from the broken Japanese naval code JN 25, provided by Far East Combined Bureau in Colombo. These reports were confirmed visually by British submarines patrolling in the Malacca Strait, alerting the British to Japanese plans to withdraw from the Andaman and Nicobar Islands and fall back on Singapore. A task force of 16 ships left Ceylon on 8 May to intercept the convoy – indicative of the sledgehammer to crack a walnut situation pertaining in the region, where the Allies were now remarkably strong, and the Japanese correspondingly weak. The British force comprised the battleships *Queen Elizabeth* and *Richelieu*, the cruisers *Cumberland*, *Royalist* and *Tromp*, the escort carriers *Emperor*, *Hunter*, *Khedive* and *Shah*, and eight destroyers. In an action resembling a fox hunt, the riders going pell-mell after their quarry, soon the ships remaining in Trincomalee, including the cruiser *Nigeria* and three destroyers, joined the chase. *Haguro* was found and engaged on the night of 16/17 May by the five ships of the 26th Destroyer Flotilla, following earlier attacks from the escort carrier *Emperor*. A total of 900 men perished when she was sunk in what came to be known as the Battle of the Malacca Strait.[31] On 8 June further intelligence intercepts helped locate *Ashigara*, and she was subsequently torpedoed by the submarine *Trenchant* in the Bangka Strait south of Singapore. She was approaching from Batavia carrying 1,600 troops when she was trapped by *Trenchant* along with *Stygian* and the American submarine *Blueback*. The escorting *Kamikaze* attacked *Trenchant* unsuccessfully, and *Ashigara* was unable to avoid the submarine's spread of torpedoes. Over 1,200 soldiers and 100 crewmen lost their lives. The operations mounted against these last Japanese warships reflected growing Allied naval power as the Pacific war took its toll on the Japanese. After the sinking of these two cruisers, the 10th Area Fleet based at Singapore was left with only one significant warship, the appropriately-named *Kamikaze*.[32] As Japanese air and maritime capabilities declined precipitously, British strength continued to grow, in June the 11th Aircraft Carrier Squadron – *Colossus*, *Vengeance*, and *Venerable* – arriving in Ceylon en route to join the British Pacific Fleet.

In contrast to the dark days of 1942, overconfidence was now a pitfall for British air and naval forces in the Indian Ocean region, such was the extent to which the tide had turned. But though the Royal Navy was in the ascendant, the enemy still had teeth, and its work remained perilous. In January the minelaying submarine *Porpoise* was attacked and sunk by a Japanese submarine chaser and aircraft after a mining mission in the Malacca Strait, the seventy-fifth and final British submarine to be sunk during the war.[33] In July the 7th Minesweeping Flotilla lost the Algerine class minesweepers *Squirrel* and *Vestal* within the space of two days. Operating off Thailand, *Squirrel* struck a mine and had to be abandoned, subsequently dispatched by gunfire from Force 63 ships. At the same time, the escort carrier *Ameer* was subjected to kamikaze attacks and *Vestal* was wrecked by a kamikaze bomber and had to be scuttled. This was the last British warship sunk during the war, lost off Phuket two days after *Squirrel*'s demise. These

30 Ibid., pp. 28.
31 Ibid. This was Operation Dukedom.
32 Ibid., p. 154.
33 Ibid., p. 20.

vessels were taking part in what remained a crucial East Indies Fleet task, minesweeping ahead of the planned amphibious attacks on Japanese-held territory, and at that moment the fleet had over 30 minesweepers on the strength.

All thoughts were now on preparations for the big 'final push', the invasion of Malaya. Assault forces massed, the approaches were swept clear and air supremacy had been achieved. Ceylon-based aircraft supported Force 136 operations in occupied Malaya, 160 Squadron, for example, being converted from minelaying to become a Special Duties Squadron. By August Force 136 had infiltrated 371 personnel including 120 British officers into Malaya and around 5,000 guerrillas had been armed and trained to help lead the resistance when the liberators arrived.[34] But then, all of a sudden, the war ended when the atomic bombs fell on Hiroshima and Nagasaki. Though British imperial forces were to storm ashore in Malaya as planned, they did so after hostilities had ceased.

Victory Japan

On 14 August, wrote Alan Brundrett, 'news came through that Japan accepted unconditional surrender ... Everyone here went wild. Although we had expected it any time, its impact nevertheless hits us'.[35] Corporal L. V. Wills celebrated Victory Japan at 145 Repair and Salvage Unit Ratmalana, Ceylon, by drinking beer with his pet monkey Jenny.[36] Ken Waterson, meanwhile, was on the middle watch aboard *Relentless* in Trincomalee harbour when the news came through:

> That night Trincomalee had its celebrations. There were rocket (distress flares) displays, jumping jacks and concerts. The weather was cooler, the oppressive heat had subsided. VJ evening started just before sunset. Ships were dressed, every colour of flag was flown. There were lots of nationalities. The alphabet went down the USA (America) and USSR (Russia), the latter flew the hammer and sickle. All the flags were hauled down at sunset but were then immediately re-hoisted. The dark night showed up illuminated Vs made up of coloured light bulbs. Some of these were in many colours.
>
> When the last shadows had gone, the ship next to us let loose with her siren. It was a horrible noise, worse than a air-raid siren. After an interval of about 15 minutes every ship in the harbour was blowing off a different note. The result was an awful din. In time various Vs could be distinguished on different sirens. Some put in a J after the V making VJ in Morse code; Rockets (distress flares) and Vary lights (bright light flares) were being fired freely by now all over the harbour. Green, red, yellow and white ones. These offset the regular starboard and port navigation lights, green and red. Green and red lights shooting up into the sky and then down into the sea. Rustic VJs on hooters and much cheering completed an unreal atmosphere. Blackout was abandoned.
>
> By 09:00pm the fun increased in tempo. Many were drunk now, where they got spirits and beer from is a mystery. We had none. Early an attempt had been made to mount a

34 Trenowden, *Operations Most Secret*, pp. 209-10.
35 Brundrett, *Two Years in Ceylon*, p. 255.
36 *RAF News*, 26/9/08.

> concert but the hooters drowned out any attempt to sing. Shooting pretty lights into the air became tame after a while. Ships started firing rockets at each other. Then they all started firing at the aircraft lined up on the upper deck of the aircraft carrier. An urgent signal was sent round the harbour to stop firing rockets. Various petty officers went round their ships to put a stop to the practice. It says something for discipline that the rocket shooting stopped. How it started I know not as I thought all rockets were kept under lock and key.
>
> Instead jumping jacks were fired from rocket launchers. These were fearsome projectiles. They came in various colours and shot from left to right, from front to rear. Shooting down between deck awnings they scattered all and sundry. They were powerful, much stronger than bonfire night jumping jacks. They possibly were Chinese ones but who got them and from where is not known. The awnings were burnt in various place and a fire arose on one of the gun covers.
>
> This led to hoses being turned on to put out all the small fires that had started. Generously ships put out each other's fires by hose. After that the hoses were turned on the other ship's crews. Everybody was wet through. Chaps coming back on board from shore leave were caught in this deluge.
>
> After that things died down; various concert parties were got up impromptu. We were tied up alongside the Woolwich, the destroyer parent ship. We got up a singing party and wheeled our piano out onto the quarter deck so that others could see and hear us. The quarter deck was beautifully decorated with bunting. Out came our players in their costumes and started to sing. The stokers on the Woolwich did not seem to appreciate our singing, they turned a hose pipe on us. The drums were soaked as was the piano, the bunting all bedraggled. They did have the foresight to close the bulkhead that gave us access to their ship. Had we made contact, World War III would have broken out between us. By now a lot of people were drunk, where they got their booze from is not known we had none.
>
> After all this excitement things quietened down, just Vary lights now and then. A 'feel good factor' abounded. The only alcohol we had was from the splicing of the main brace (an extra tot of rum).[37]

On 16 August there was a Victory March, wrote Brundrett, from 'village hall to Camp restaurant in which we all have to take part'. On 25 August he was back in Colombo for the big Victory Parade on Galle Face Green, a stretch of open space on the sea front, flanked by the Galle Face Hotel and important government buildings. Mountbatten took the salute, and there were 'formations of Flying Fortresses, Sunderlands, Hellcats, and Barracudas. Meanwhile ships of the East Indies Fleet steamed up and down the coast'.[38] Mountbatten wrote proudly in his diary that 'the great Victory Parade was held in Colombo, at which some 3,500 representatives of all the services marched past in 35 minutes. At this rate, the 1,380,000 men in SEAC would take nearly 9 days and 9 nights to march past!'.[39] Considering the size of his command, he continued:

37 BBC 'World War Two People's War' oral history archive, Ken Waterson, 'HMS *Relentless*: The End of the Japanese War, 1945', A2237591.

38 Brundrett, *Two Years in Ceylon*, p. 262.

39 Ziegler, *Personal Diary of Admiral the Lord Louis Mountbatten*, p. 238.

> Incidentally, few people realize the immense scale of the enlarged South East Asia Command, which includes a million and a half square miles of territory, has a population of 128 millions, nearly half a million Japs and over 200,000 prisoners of war and internees to be repatriated. From the northwest corner of SEAC, which starts a few hundred miles west of Karachi, down to the easternmost limits, halfway through New Guinea, is a distance of 6,050 statute miles. This is 150 miles more than the distance from the northwest corner of SEAC to St Johns, Newfoundland![40]

Elsewhere in South East Asia Command territory, thousands of miles across the ocean in the Cocos-Keeling Islands, 99 Squadron was about to mount a strike on Japanese shipping in and around Singapore. But hearing news of the surrender the commander of 231 Heavy Bomber Group, Major General Jimmy Durrant, chalked 'cancelled' on the operations board. 'That night was a riotous one on the Cocos, everyone celebrating VJ'.[41] Yet even though victory had been won, there was to be no end to the labours of South East Asia Command for some time to come. In the first place, the surrender had to be taken the length and breadth of the Indian Ocean's eastern rim, and civil order maintained. On 27 August an East Indies Fleet force, Task Force 11, sailed under Vice Admiral Walker. He led the battleship *Nelson*, the cruiser *Ceylon*, the escort carriers *Attacker* and *Hunter*, three destroyers and two Landing Ships Infantry to Penang, where men of 3 Commando Royal Marines went ashore. This became the first Malay state to be liberated, and on 3 September the surrender ceremony took place aboard the battleship.[42] Then, on 9 September, the long-anticipated invasion of Malaya took place. Over 100,000 troops were landed, escorted by a fleet from Trincomalee including *Nelson* and *Richelieu*, *Ceylon*, *Cleopatra*, *Nigeria*, and *Royalist*, the escort carriers *Archer*, *Emperor*, *Hunter*, *Khedive*, *Pursuer*, *Stalker*, and *Trumpeter*, and 15 destroyers. On 12 September, and with much ceremony, Mountbatten took the Japanese surrender at the Municipal Buildings in Singapore.

As the guns fell silent, as the last bomber missions were flown over Malaya and Sumatra, and as the last Japanese coaster was torpedoed, Allied forces throughout the region began a new and urgent mission: rescuing prisoners of war and civilian internees and delivering aid to liberated territories. Flying from Ceylon, 222 Group Liberators were quickly turned into 'mercy' aircraft, stripped of armaments and turned into flying hospitals. 'Within three weeks they had dropped over 280,000 lbs of Red Cross parcels and medical supplies to Allied prisoners of war in Malaya, Singapore, and the Dutch East Indies'.[43] 99 Squadron in the Cocos-Keeling Islands turned its attention to dropping food and medical supplies in the Dutch East Indies, losing an aircraft near Palembang on 1 September in the process. Elsewhere, the mercy ship *Bandra* was dispatched from Calcutta with emergency supplies for 143 Allied prisoners who had been kept on a starvation diet in the Andaman and Nicobar Islands.

40 Ibid.

41 Fail, 'Forward Strategic Airbase'. The Cocos detachment had lost its last aircraft the day before, shot down by the Japanese near Rakata Island in the Sunda Strait, leading to some crew deaths and 356 Squadron's last operation of the war searching for survivors.

42 An event captured on film. See Imperial War Museum, ABY 163.

43 An Officer of the RAF, 'A Resumé of the Activities of 222 Group'.

Reflection

In the first half of the Second World War the British had successfully managed the challenges presented by the Germans and Italians in the Indian Ocean region. They had done so by virtue of their established presence and concomitant base infrastructure, their preponderance of military (particularly sea) power, and their operational nous. Japan presented a much sterner challenge and a genuine crisis of empire. Nevertheless, the British were able to survive the Japanese onslaught because of their strategic depth in the Indian Ocean, which allowed them to fall back while continuing to protect their most vital concerns, which lay west of India, not east. Rather than being solely a product of British capacity – though this capacity simply cannot not be dismissed – it was a result of its opponents over-extension and the rise of American power. From the Battle of Midway in June 1942, Japan was on the back foot in this region, though this is easy to see with hindsight – and one looks askance at some accounts of the war that almost scorn the British war effort in the Indian Ocean because there were not more enemy targets to destroy and no strategically vital battles to win.[44] One historian in particular seems anxious to deny that *any* effort on behalf of the British, and specifically the Eastern Fleet, contributed to Axis incapacity and ineffectiveness here. This 'take' on the efforts of the Royal Navy in the Indian Ocean is not new. In February 1945 A. W. MacWhinnie, writing in the *Illustrated*, said that 'British naval strikes against the Japanese were of the tip and run variety, and that certain individual efforts amounted to little more than banging on the back door of the Japs and running away before the door was opened'.[45] Another variation of this dismissiveness arises from what might be termed a 'body count' mentality – the idea that places aren't really worthy of notice unless the casualty rates are high, the numbers of units engaged large, the bombing epic. In total, 50 German U-boats had operated in the Indian Ocean by the conclusion of hostilities, according to Paterson's figures, and 31 Japanese submarines. Willmott claims that 385 British, Allied, and neutral vessels were sunk in the region (a figure that does not include Allied and Axis warships and submarines destroyed). Of this number, 250 were sunk by submarines.[46] If nothing else, as Kowner writes, 'the limited results of the inter-Axis cooperation in the Indian Ocean tell us a great deal about the horrendous potential it could have had, had Japan and Germany overcome their mutual suspicions and coordinated their efforts two or three years earlier'.[47]

44 The implicit, perhaps unintended, diminution of the war effort in this region that one sometimes encounters is astonishing. Historians focused on the 'big' battles, the killer strategic blows, the hunt for the 'turning point' moments, sometimes appear almost to mock the war effort in this region because of the fact that the war was not won here, and that by the time Britain and its allies were in great strength in the Indian Ocean, there weren't really any significant enemy forces to defeat. This is potty – and frankly disrespectful to the memory of hundreds of thousands of servicemen and women, and just goes to show that if you focus on the big things, the 'small' things can get forgotten. I was staggered once to receive a comment that work on the Indian Ocean theatre wasn't really that important because 'only 8 per cent' of Allied and neutral shipping losses occurred there. Never mind the condescension of posterity, this is the condescension of history and its beguiling, though distorting, outrider, hindsight.

45 Winton, *Sink the* Haguro*!*, p. 21.

46 Willmott, *Grave of a Dozen Schemes*, p. 157. Jurgen Rohwer claims that German U-boats destroyed 133 ships in the Indian Ocean. Paterson, *Hitler's Grey Wolves*, p. 265.

47 Kowner, 'When Economics, Strategy', p. 250.

The first reason for the diminution of the enemy threat in the Indian Ocean region was because the Japanese military decided not to press the advantage they possessed following their conquests of December 1941 to May 1942. Now fighting at the end of their logistical tether, they had achieved more than they expected when they first went to war. Meanwhile, the British and their allies had successfully built up forces in the Indian Ocean that the enemy could not defeat, or circumvent, and even had capacity to spare. The second reason was that American operations against Japanese forces across the Pacific and towards the home islands themselves became more and more intense from mid-1942. But though the Americans predominated, it was not just their show; China's refusal to capitulate meant Japan had to fight a two-front war, tying down substantial forces which could have gone to fighting fronts in Burma and India, or to the Pacific. 'Ironically', writes Christopher O'Sullivan, 'Chinese resistance made it possible for the British colonial empire to live another day, particularly in India'.[48] In entertaining this point, however, it is important not to lose sight of the fact that British imperial forces played a major part in this too, and that India was never undefended.[49]

Following Japan's entry into the war, British and Allied forces in the Indian Ocean needed a chance to get their breath back, to regroup, and to reinforce. In doing this the British and their allies rode their luck on two counts. They were lucky that the Indian Ocean theatre was only ever peripheral to overall Japanese war strategy. They were fortunate on a second count in that the Axis alliance, and its strategic comprehension and direction, was rudimental and ineffective, certainly when compared to the Allied equivalent. While the requisite knowledge, in the hands of vociferous advocates of an Indian Ocean strategy, existed in both German and Japanese political and military circles, too few influential decision-makers were aware of the chance that they had to deal the British Empire a potentially mortal blow in the Indian Ocean. Both German and Japanese political-military structures, from the highest level down, were afflicted by internal power struggles that led to incoherent alignment between strategic objectives and operational endeavours. Basically, the Axis powers were bad at working together, and snatching opportunities presented to them. 'Our opponents remained indifferent to each other's possibilities, ambitions and requirements and pursued their own aims without reference to their partners. For the Japanese the Indian Ocean was good teasing ground but strategically beyond their capacity to conquer and dominate except close to the shores they had already'.[50]

The Indian Ocean was one of the great might-have-beens for the Axis. The window that opened here for the Japanese in late 1941 remained wide open for the first half of the following year. If the Germans had taken the Levant more seriously, writes N. A. M. Rodger, and the Japanese the Indian Ocean, Britain 'might have lost the whole (and not just the fringes) of its eastern empire, and the course of the war would have been very different'.[51] As Michael Simpson puts it, 'If the British fought a five-ocean war with a two-ocean navy, the Japanese fought a

48 Christopher O'Sullivan, 'Colonialism in Asia' in Thomas Zeiler (ed.), *A Companion to World War Two*, volume 1 (Chichester, West Sussex: Wiley-Blackwell, 2013), p. 64.

49 There is a persistent tendency, in correctly – sometimes correctively – seeking to ascribe key aspects of Allied victory over the Axis to the war efforts of the Americans, the Chinese, and the Soviets, to almost wilfully diminish, sometimes to the point of inconsequence, the role of British imperial forces and, behind them, the war effort of the people of the British Empire, gladly offered or not.

50 Simpson (ed.), *The Somerville Papers*, p. 363.

51 Personal communication, Rodger to Jackson, January 2000.

two-ocean war with a one-ocean navy. Thus the British, bereft of the means to resist further encroachments, were let off the hook'.[52] This is true, but only up to a point. Because it is legitimate to ask, even given Britain's difficulties in facing the Japanese in the Indian Ocean region in 1942, 'What could the Japanese realistically have achieved?'. Could they have gained and maintained the bases required to then sustain a concerted and decisive war on the sea lanes? Could they have overcome the reinforcements Britain and its allies sent, and could send, to defend their vital Indian Ocean interests? In particular, even if they had lodged themselves in Ceylon – perhaps, even, parts of India (for they could surely never have taken it all) – would they then have been able to impact the British Empire's strategic bottom line and destroy its ability to use the sea lanes of the western Indian Ocean to funnel men and material to the Middle East by way of the Red Sea, to extract oil from the Persian Gulf, and send thousands and thousands of military vehicles and aircraft to the Soviet Union? Even if, somehow, the British had been knocked out, or their war effort severely diminished, would the Americans and Soviets have looked on with indifference? The answer is 'no', for the bridge between them, across the Indian Ocean, was of fundamental importance, and they would have done what was necessary to maintain it. The ideologues of the Greater East Asian Co-Prosperity Sphere initially envisaged the Malay Barrier and the East Indies as its western borderlands, though a future war, it was hoped, would bring much wider Asian conquests. But delusional dreams of global empire were a million miles away from Japan's actual capacity for sustained conquest in the early 1940s.

The situation that pertained in the Indian Ocean was, at the end of the day, a simple matter of geography; the region represented, respectively, the easternmost and westernmost extremity of German and Japanese activity. As the war progressed, their attention became focused ever closer to home as the ring closed in upon their heartlands and the chances of regional, never mind global, dominance receded as the Hydra's heads were lopped off one by one in other theatres as Allied strength waxed. For Britain, on the other hand, the Indian Ocean was central because its sea lanes were fundamental to sustaining the war effort in the Middle East and for accessing the British Empire's main sources of oil. As has been shown, they were of fundamental importance to the war aims of America and the Soviet Union too.

Simpson articulates the defensive, as opposed to offensive, significance of the Indian Ocean well:

> The underlying if harsh fact was that the Indian Ocean was not a crucial theatre in the offensive sense. It was essential that the Allies maintained their sea and air communications across the Indian Ocean; that they held on to their main bases in India and Ceylon; that they prevented a conjunction of the three Axis powers; and that they continued to derive vital resources – especially oil and metals – from the region.[53]

'But all this', continued Simpson, 'implied a defensive strategy'; the ultimate defeat of the enemy could only occur via offensive thrusts towards its metropolitan heartlands.[54]

Several points follow from this analysis. The first is that while all of this is discernable with hindsight, it was not known to those living life forwards and trying to do the best they could

52 Ibid.
53 Simpson (ed.), *The Somerville Papers*, p. 373.
54 Ibid.

to defend vital interests and face enemy threats at the time. Furthermore, while it might be said that the Indian Ocean region was saved from the worst by events elsewhere, it does not follow that history should ignore, or worse, belittle, the extremely significant deployments and reinforcements made by Britain and its allies to defend the region. American arms fighting the Japanese in the Pacific were only ever part of the story.

Furthermore, seemingly disparate activities need to be construed as part of a coherent strategic whole, rather than ignoring certain elements, or focusing too narrowly on others, such as the Burma campaign. Taken all together, efforts in the Indian Ocean, like those in the Iran-Iraq region that are similarly overlooked, were undertaken to secure a region of primary strategic importance for both the British Empire and all of its major allies – a vital theatre supporting other theatres where fighting was more pronounced. It is also important not to overplay Japanese achievements, remarkable though they were. For sure, in the early stages of Japan's eruption across the Pacific and Indian oceans Britain and its allies suffered defeat after defeat leading to retreat after retreat. But there is an enormous difference between winning regional battles and conquering territory, and winning a war and claiming an empire.

The British Empire's war against Japan continued, every single day and every single week, even after the loss of *Prince of Wales* and *Repulse*, the fall of Singapore, and the dissolution of ABDA Command – and not just in Burma. Too often, these defeats appear as strategic full stops in the narrative of the British war against Japan, which doesn't really get going again until the abortive Arakan offensive of 1943 gives way to the sustained operations in Burma from late 1944. Lamenting a similar tendency in the historiography of the Pacific war, Kehn writes that '[m]ost histories of the Pacific War – *even now* – leapfrog from the attacks on Pearl Harbor in December 1941 to the Doolittle Raid of April 1942 or the Battle of the Coral Sea that May, with no mention of the fight for the East Indies or the wasting of the Asiatic Fleet'.[55] As this book has shown, even after the calamitous fall of Singapore the British war against Japan never ended. It continued not only in Burma but in Malaya and the coastal waters of South-east Asia and the Dutch East Indies, in the skies above Ceylon, and beneath the waves in the Bay of Bengal and as far west as the Mozambique Channel. Though a Cinderella theatre at times starved of resources, British Empire troops, ships, aircraft, and infrastructure enabled the Allies to retain control of the Indian Ocean, and Mountbatten's South East Asia Command succeeded in building up to such a pitch that from 1944 it was able to take the war to the Japanese across the region.

Far from the loss of *Prince of Wales* and *Repulse* and the fall of Singapore being the end of Britain's struggle against Japan, they represented the beginning of a tenacious essay in imperial defence and reconquest, underpinned by American power in the Pacific. The standard view of the eastern war has dwelt far too much upon British weakness without a wider understanding of British strength and the continuous nature of the Empire's war against Japan. Even with the loss of the two capital ships and the Singapore base, British strength in the East enabled it to hold on and to avoid defeat and to continue to support the war theatres of the Middle East and South Asia and control the supply lines of the Persian Gulf. This capacity to carry on was founded upon Britain's grip on infrastructure across the ocean and its enormous naval resources that – even when facing great danger in other theatres – enabled it to find the wherewithal to protect

55 Kehn, *In the Highest Degree Tragic*, p. xi.

convoys, defend ports, and keep imperial trade flowing. Britain retained the ability, against the odds, to move military resources around the world, the most telling benefit of the seapower it had maintained for hundreds of years and that none of its foes ever managed to overcome.

This brings us full circle to one of the main purposes of this book. The British had to protect sea lanes using warships and aircraft that required bases, because of the enormous distances involved in policing the Indian Ocean and the Atlantic, and their lack of the kind of fleet train support that the Americans were so effectively to pioneer. Ports all around the African coast and across the Indian Ocean were essential for Allied military operations – for inserting ground forces, patrolling sea lanes, moving men, and attacking enemy-held ports which threatened those sea lanes and that might enable the enemy to sustain campaigns on land. And also, of course, in order simply to handle the vast quantities of troops, supplies, and equipment that waging war across great distances entailed. Islands, ports, and sea lanes in this region were vital during the Second World War for three key reasons: because powerful nations required the export of African, Asian, and Middle Eastern resources for their economies and war-related utility, and needed to deny the same to the enemy; because sea lanes around the continent and across the Indian Ocean needed to be defended using ports and island bases; and because fighting took place on air, land, and sea in and around Africa and the Indian Ocean, which meant that ports and islands were therefore contested for both operational and strategic reasons.

To avoid the impression that African and Indian Ocean ports were only valued for reasons related specifically to the war, it is necessary to emphasize their continued importance in terms of resource extraction and global trade too. The history of Western engagement with territories in Africa and the Indian Ocean region had been dominated by the harvesting of resources and their transport to the coast for shipment overseas. This was augmented by war: now, not only did the colonial powers need to sustain their export of valuable commodities, wartime damage to the system of international trade, and the Allies' loss of key strategic resources to Japanese occupation further east, meant that African and Indian Ocean resources became even more important. For example, Allied losses in South-east Asia and the East Indies meant that demand for colonial products including foodstuffs, oil, rubber, pyrethrum, sisal, and tin rocketed, just as the widening conflict required the unforeseen recruitment of hundreds of thousands of colonial subjects from across Africa and the islands and territories of the Indian Ocean rim as soldiers and labourers. All across the Indian Ocean region, people's lives were affected by the consequences of global war and their colonized status, and it behoves us not to neglect this in our core memories and histories of the conflict.

As well as luck and the resources of powerful allies and a vast empire, British capacity in the region was predicated on the imperial strategic vision that centuries of empire-building had bequeathed the British state. Even when faced with the prospect of Japanese ascendancy in the Indian Ocean and possible defeat in the Middle East, the British succeeded in acting and thinking imperially, sending scarce resources, often in minute quantities, to protect tiny islands or to at least give the semblance of doing so. Luck, skill, and hard-won victories here and in other regions meant that at the end of the war the Indian Ocean was still a 'British lake', and its sea lanes had played a crucial role in Allied victory.

By August 1945 the men and women of the East Indies Station/Eastern Fleet/East Indies Fleet had achieved a significant victory against Japan, made up of the operations of submarines and motor launches, naval duels at sea, shore attacks from battleships and carriers, and a range of other activities that meant that, at the end of the war, the Royal Navy was the proverbial last man standing, more important in this theatre, though less famed, than the imperial army in Burma. It should not be denied its laurels. It had been tireless in its efforts to take the war to the Japanese and to defend the vital sea lanes connecting Europe, the Middle East, Asia, and Australasia. It was also responsible for nurturing and training the force that was sent to the Pacific in early 1945 to join the American navy for the final assault on the Japanese home islands. As Willmott writes:

> [t]he issue of defeat and victory was resolved elsewhere and by other means and was never dependent upon events in the Indian Ocean ... Nonetheless, military forces can only defeat what they face, and most certainly the victory that was won in the Indian Ocean was comprehensive. The victory may have been the product and not the cause of supremacy, and certainly victory was the product of American supremacy in the Pacific, but both victory and supremacy in the Indian Ocean in 1945 were nevertheless very real.[56]

In his brilliant account, Boyd writes, that in the final analysis the Royal Navy 'just had enough latent strength in modern ships, modern technology, fighting effectiveness, and global support and experience' to meet its 'inescapable commitment' in the Indian Ocean, providing it had enough time to redeploy the necessary forces.[57] 'The standard portrayal of a Royal Navy reduced to tokenism in the East, the inevitable consequence of a flawed interwar Singapore strategy, is misplaced. In the ultimate crisis, the British war leadership was prepared to withdraw all major units from the Mediterranean and run significant risks with the Home Fleet in order to secure the East'.[58]

* * *

Today the Second World War has a vestigial presence in the region, for those who care to look.[59] There are manicured war cemeteries, airports that began life as RAF aerodromes, and jetties, wharves, and accommodation buildings constructed as the Allies expanded port facilities across the region. Rodrigues has its Winston Churchill Bridge in Port Mathurin, built in 1947 and reconstructed in 2009, and the six-inch naval guns still keep their vigil at Port Victoria in the Seychelles. Mauritius boasts the 'Spitfire Boulangerie' in Beau Bassin and an ex-servicemen's league. The wreck of the *Umbria* still lies on the seabed at a depth of 35 metres off Port Sudan, together with the original cargo of now increasingly dangerous ordnance.[60] The wreck of *British Loyalty* remains where she was scuttled in the Maldives, and *Hermes* lies a few miles off the coast

56 Willmott, *Grave of a Dozen Schemes*, pp. 155-56.
57 Boyd, *The Royal Navy in Eastern Waters*, p. 398.
58 Ibid., p. 399.
59 Souvenirs, trophies, and other reminders are of course to be found in Britain too. The Allied flags that fluttered from the bonnet of Mountbatten's staff car are preserved in a Higher Command and Staff Course syndicate room at the Joint Services Command and Staff College, and the last 99 Squadron Liberator to leave the Cocos-Keeling Islands is now in the RAF Museum at Cosford. See the aircraft's history at https://www.rafmuseum.org.uk/documents/collections/74-AF-790-Consolidated-Liberator.pdf
60 The wreck of the *Umbria* is one of the numerous vessels sunk in the Indian Ocean during the war that is regularly visited by divers. See http://cassiopeiasafari.com/umbria/ and for photos see http://

of Sri Lanka. The wreck of *Haguro* was discovered by divers lying in 68 metres of water 55 miles off Penang, though has subsequently been severely degraded by illegal salvagers. The wrecks of the Australian cruiser *Sydney*, lost with all hands, and the German raider *Kormoran*, which had fought each other to the death in November 1941, were discovered off Western Australia in 2008, reigniting the controversy and mystery surrounding their final moments.[61] In 2018 the wreck of the *Sagaing*, sunk during the Japanese raid on Trincomalee, was raised from the harbour bed by the Sri Lankan navy.[62]

There are other wrecks, too. The shattered frame of 259 Squadron's Catalina 'E', which crashed while landing on 7 June 1943 killing all but one crew member, is occasionally visible on Lake St Lucia's mudflats near Mitchell Island in South Africa. 240 Squadron's Catalina 'Katie' still sits on its idyllic palm-fringed beach in Diego Garcia, gradually sinking into the sand and visited by American service personnel stationed on what is now part of the colony of British Indian Ocean Territory. The war also left its physical mark in the form of buildings and other structures all around the Indian Ocean. Mauritius's Sir Seewoosagur Ramgoolam International Airport is the former RAF Plaisance airbase, opened in 1942. The aerdrome built by the Royal Navy on Gan in Addu Atoll is now Gan International Airport. In Kenya, meanwhile, Moi International Airport at Mombasa began life during the war when South African sappers built a base at Port Reitz for the aircraft of the Eastern Fleet, RAF flying-boats patrolling off the East African coast, and the South African Air Force.[63] Naturally, places which suffered sustained military action tend to be more obviously marked, no place more so than Singapore, a country whose history is intimately entwined with its harrowing experiences of occupation. In Mumbai, 14 April is still marked as Fire Service Day, commemorating the 1944 dock explosion in the course of which 66 members of the Bombay Fire Brigade, along with hundreds of others, lost their lives following the explosion of the ammunition aboard the merchant ship *Fort Stikine*.

There are war memorials and graves, too, from the enormous and oft-visited, such as Singapore's Kranji War Cemetery with its 4,400-plus Second World War graves and its striking architecture, to the small and seldom seen, such as Diego Garcia's Point Marianne Cemetery. Here lie the remains of Private G. D. Appado, Corporal A. H. M. Atchia, Private L. P. Hardy, Gunner F. Montocchio, and Private I. Pierre-Louis, all of the Mauritius Regiment. Also, the remains of Gunner Buta Khan, Gunner Mehdi Kan, Gunner Muhammad Latif Sha, and Cook Samundar Kham, all of the Royal Indian Artillery.[64] Testament all to the efforts and sacrifices of thousands of servicemen and women, of long-departed fleets, garrisons, and squadrons.

Despite these visible remains, the enormous impact of the war upon people in Africa and the territories of the Indian Ocean region, and the importance of their resources and locations to the major belligerent powers, remains underappreciated. There are numerous reasons for this, including a dominant Western narrative of the war that focuses on battles, strategies, and high

www.bbc.co.uk/oceans/locations/redsea/umbria.shtml, the website of the BBC series *Oceans*. For a wreck dive video, see https://www.youtube.com/watch?v=oUEnWX2I95Q.

61 M. McCarthy (ed.), *From Great Depths: The Wrecks of* HMAS Sydney *II and HSK* Kormoran (Crawley, Perth: UWA Publishing, 2016).

62 Only to be removed from the harbour and sunk again. Reported by the BBC, see http://www.bbc.co.uk/news/world-asia-43607838

63 *Final Report, Mombasa Port Master Plan including Dongo Kundu* (Japan International Cooperation Agency, 2015), p. 2-57.

64 Forsberg, *Islands at the Edge of Everywhere*.

politics, not the experiences of colonized peoples or the crucial role of non-Western resources, both human and material, in winning the war. It is also because regional historians seldom focus on military and strategic matters, especially at a pan-continental and oceanic level, and because the war has been peripheral to African and Indian Ocean national histories, or viewed severally rather than continentally or oceanically. What little we do know is often locked away in single-country histories and micro histories known only to specialists, or simply unknown in the published realm and confined to often oblique references in the archives.[65] As Kwei Quartey argues in an article demonstrating how academic research can help shape popular understanding, the war's historiography needs to be widened to give Africans and other people around the world their due.[66] To achieve this, Africa and the Indian Ocean region need to be viewed holistically and assessed in terms of its strategic significance for the Allied war effort.

Though the early years of the war witnessed significant operations against German, Italian, and Vichy forces, it was the struggle against Japan in the eastern Indian Ocean that defined Britain's war east of Suez, bringing as it did the calamitous loss of Burma, Malaya, and Singapore, doomed rear-guard operations in defence of the Dutch East Indies, and attacks on Ceylon and India. The cost of the war in this vast region, particularly the strain placed upon Indian society and the ramifications of embarrassing British defeats, were to prove disastrous for the Empire, and victory, when it came, was a pyrrhic one, heavily underwritten by the waxing might of America. But, it must not be forgotten, it was victory nonetheless.

65 Consider this excerpt from a document prepared for the War Cabinet towards the end of the conflict:

> On Masirah Island a considerable amount of trouble was encountered with the local inhabitants in connection with the unloading of stores for HM [His Majesty's] Forces stationed there. As a result, most of the people fled from the Island and only a few have since returned. There are, however, now several hundred Muscati and a few Aden labourers who have been brought to the Island for the work required by the British and US Forces there. TNA, CAB 66/66/3, Arabia – acquisition of Masirah Island as a permanent RAF base, memorandum by the secretaries of state for Air and India, 29/5/45.

66 Kwei Quartey, 'How West Africa Helped Win World War Two', *Foreign Policy in Focus*, 6 June 2012. Quartey's article draws on the theme of non-European participation in the war, and detail of West Africa's involvement, developed in the current author's work.

Bibliography

Archival sources

Papers have been consulted in, or from, (in London) The National Archives, the Imperial War Museum, the National Army Museum, the Naval Historical Branch (since moved to Portsmouth), and the British Library. Don Kimble has done a great service by making available online the text of Admiralty war diaries. In Cambridge, the Churchill Archives Centre at Churchill College. Overseas, there are echoes here of researches in the national archives and other institutions in Mauritius, Sri Lanka, and the United States' National Archives and Records Administration. The BBC 'World War 2 People's War' oral history archive has been a great help, as have materials from several different archives generously shown to me by colleagues, chief among them Professor Andrew Stewart.

Printed and secondary sources

'Actions against Raiders', *Supplement to the London Gazette*, 38459 (London: HMSO, 1948).

Africa and the Second World War: Reports and Papers of the Symposium Organized by UNESCO at Benghazi, Libyan Arab Jamahiriya, from 10 to 13 November 1980 (Paris: UNESCO, 1985).

Augustus Agar, *Footprints in the Sea* (London: Evans Brothers, 1961).

Yomi Akenyeye, 'The Air Factor in West Africa's Colonial Defence, 1920-1945: A Neglected Theme', *Itinerario: International Journal on the History of European Expansion and Global Interaction* 25, 1 (2001).

Harrison Akingbade, 'US-Liberian Relations during World War II', *Phylon*, 46, 1 (1985).

John Alden, *Salvage Man* (Annapolis, MD: Naval Institute Press, 1997).

Richard Aldrich, *The Faraway War: Personal Diaries of the Second World War in Asia and the Pacific* (London: Corgi, 2006).

Louis Allday, 'German Propaganda in Sharjah', at http://blogs.bl.uk/untoldlives/2013/07/german-propaganda-in-sharjah.html.

Edward Alpers, *The Indian Ocean in World History* (Oxford: Oxford University Press, 2013).

——, 'On Becoming a "British Lake": Piracy, Slaving, and British Imperialism in the Indian Ocean during the First Half of the Nineteenth Century', in Robert Harms, Bernard Freamon, and David Blight (eds), *Indian Ocean Slavery in the Age of Abolition* (New Haven: Yale University Press, 2013).

'Armoured Carriers' at http://www.armouredcarriers.com/.

Desmond Ball, *Signals Intelligence (Sigint) in South Asia: India, Pakistan, Sri Lanka (Ceylon)* (Canberra: Strategic and Defence Studies Centre, 1996).
Ian Ballantyne, Warspite, *From Jutland Hero to Cold War Warrior* (Barnsley: Pen and Sword, 2001).
Arthur Banks, *Wings of the Dawning: The Battle for the Indian Ocean, 1939-1945* (Malvern: Images, 1996).
Rene Barendse, *The Arabian Seas: The Indian Ocean World of the Seventeenth Century* (London: Routledge: 2001).
'Battle of the Java Sea, 27 February 1942', *Supplement to the London Gazette*, 38346 (London: HMSO, 1948).
Christopher Bayly and Tim Harper, *Forgotten Armies: Britain's Asian Empire and the War with Japan* (London: Allen Lane, 2004).
Cecil Beaton, *Near East* (London: Batsford, 1943).
C. B. A. Behrens, *Merchant Shipping and the Demands of War* (London: HMSO, 1955).
Tim Benbow, 'The British Invasion of Madagascar: Operation Ironclad, May 1942', in T. A. Lovering (ed.), *Amphibious Assault: Manoeuvre from the Sea – Amphibious Operations from the Last Century* (London: Ministry of Defence, 2005).
——, '"Menace" to "Ironclad": The British Operations against Dakar (1940) and Madagascar (1942), *Journal of Military History* 75, 3 (2011).
David Bercuson and Holger Herwig, *One Christmas in Washington: Churchill and Roosevelt Forge the Grand Alliance* (London: Weidenfeld and Nicolson, 2005).
Patrick Bernhard, 'Hitler's Africa in the East: Italian Colonialism as a Model for German Planning in Eastern Europe', *Journal of Contemporary History*, 5, 1 (2016).
Marcus Binney, *Secret War Heroes: The Men of Special Operations Executive* (London: Hodder and Stoughton, 2005).
Kevin Blackburn and Karl Hack, *Did Singapore Have to Fall? Churchill and the Impregnable Fortress* (London: Routledge, 2003).
Robert Blyth, *Empire of the Raj: India, Eastern Africa, and the Middle East, 1858-1947* (Basingstoke: Palgrave Macmillan, 2003).
Peter Boer, *The Loss of Java: The Final Battles for the Possession of Java Fought by Allied Air, Naval and Land Forces in the Period of 18 February to 7 March 1942* (Singapore: National University of Singapore Press, 2011).
See Patrick Bollen, 'The Sinking of SS *Nellore* by the Japanese in 1944', *United Service*, 63, 1 (2012).
Brian Bond (ed.), *Chief of Staff: The Diaries of Lieutenant-General Sir Henry Pownall*, volume 2, *1940-1944* (London: Leo Cooper, 1974).
Horst Boog et al (eds), *Germany and the Second World War*, volume 6, *The Global War* (Oxford: Clarendon Press, 2001).
Sugata Bose, *A Hundred Horizons: The Indian Ocean in the Age of Global Empire* (Cambridge, MA: Harvard University Press, 2006).
Andrew Boyd, *The Royal Navy in Eastern Waters: Linchpin of Victory, 1935-1942* (Barnsley: Seaforth, 2017).
Carl Boyd, *Hitler's Japanese Confidante: General Oshima Hiroshi and Magic Intelligence, 1941-1945* (Lawrence, KS: University Press of Kansas, 1993).

John Bradley and Jack Dice, *The Second World War: Asia and the Pacific* (New York: Square One Publishers/Department of History, U. S. Military Academy West Point, 2002).
H. J. Brennecke, *Ghost Cruiser HK33* (London: Futura, 1974).
Maurizio Brescia, *Mussolini's Navy: A Reference Guide to the Regia Marina, 1940-1945* (Barnsley: Seaforth, 2012).
Siegfried Breyer, *Pocket Battleship* Admiral Graf Spee (West Chester, PA: Schiffer, 1989).
Martin Brice, *The Royal Navy and the Sino-Japanese Incident, 1937-1941* (London: Ian Allan, 1973).
John Bright-Holmes (ed.), *Like it Was: The Diaries of Malcolm Muggeridge* (London: HarperCollins, 1981).
Angus Britts, 'Neglected Skies: The Far East Demise of British Naval Superiority, 1922-42', M. Phil. Thesis (University of Sydney, 2015).
——, *Neglected Skies: The Demise of British Naval Power in the Far East, 1922-42* (Annapolis, M. D.: Naval Institute Press, 2017).
Cecil Brown, *Suez to Singapore* (New York: Random House, 1942).
Alan Brundrett, *Two Years in Ceylon: The Diary of a Navy Secretariat Member, 1944-1946* (Lewes, Sussex: Book Guild, 1996).
Andrew Buchanan, *World at War: A Global History of World War Two, 1931-1953* (Chichester, West Sussex: Wiley-Blackwell, 2019).
Christopher Buckley, *Five Ventures: Iraq-Syria-Persia-Madagascar-Dodecanese* (London: HMSO, 1977).
Judith Byfield, Carolyn Brown, Timothy Parsons, and Ahmad Sikaingi (eds), *Africa and World War Two* (Cambridge: Cambridge University Press, 2015).
Lee Cable, 'Empire, Modernity and Design: Visual Culture and Cable & Wireless Corporate Identities, 1924-1955', Ph. D. Thesis (University of Exeter, 2014).
T. J. Cain, *HMS* Electra (London: Futura, 1976).
Ralph Callebert, *On Durban's Docks: Zulu Workers, Rural Households, Global Labor* (Rochester, NY: University of Rochester Press, 2017).
John Chapman (ed.), *The Price of Admiralty: The War Diary of the German Naval Attaché in Japan, 1939-1943*, 4 volumes (Ripe, East Sussex: Saltire Press, 1989).
A. J. Christopher, *The British Empire at its Zenith* (London: Croom Helm, 1988).
Winston Churchill, *The Second World War*, volume 3, *The Grand Alliance* (London: Cassell, 1950).
——, *The Second World War*, volume 4, *The Hinge of Fate* (London: Cassell, 1951).
——, *The Second World War*, volume 5, *Closing the Ring* (London: Cassell, 1952).
Anthony Clayton, '"Deceptive Might": Imperial Defence and Security, 1900-1968', in William Roger Louis and Judith Brown (eds), *The Oxford History of the British Empire*, volume 4, *The Twentieth Century* (Oxford: Oxford University Press, 1999).
J. A. Clayton, 'The South African Air Force in the Madagascar Campaign 1942', *Military History Journal*, 9, 2 (1992).
D. H. Cole, *Imperial Military Geography: General Characteristics of the Empire in Relation to Defence* (London: Sifton Praed, 1933).
D. Collins, *The Royal Indian Navy, 1939-1945*, part of the *Official History of the Indian Armed Forces in the Second World War* (Bombay: Orient Longmans/Combined Inter Service Historical Section India and Pakistan, 1964).

'Convoy Web: The Website for Merchant Ships during World War Two', at http://www.convoyweb.org.uk/ws/index.html?ws10.php?convoy=10_1~wsmain

Valentine Cornish, *A Geography of Imperial Defence* (London: Sifton Praed, 1922).

Noel Coward, *Middle East Diary* (London: William Heinemann, 1944).

Brian Crabb, *Passage to Destiny: The Sinking of the SS* Khedive Ismail *in the Sea War against Japan* (Stamford, Lincolnshire: Paul Watkins, 1997).

——, *In Harm's Way: The Story of HMS* Kenya, *a Second World War Cruiser* (Stamford, Lincolnshire: Paul Watkins, 1998).

Noel Crusz, *The Cocos Islands Mutiny* (Freemantle: Freemantle Arts Centre Press, 2000).

Thomas Culbert, 'South Atlantic/Trans-Africa Air Route', in Walter Boyne (ed.), *Air Warfare: An International Encyclopaedia* (Santa Barbara: ABC-CLIO, 2002).

Eve Curie, *Journey Among Warriors* (New York: Doubleday, Doran, and Co., 1943).

Peter Dancey, *South East Asia Command* (Bromley: Galago Books, 2004).

Alex Danchev and Daniel Todman (eds), *War Diaries, 1939-1945: Field Marshal Lord Alanbrooke* (London: Weidenfeld and Nicolson, 2001).

Raymond Dannreuther, *Somerville's Force H: The Royal Navy's Gibraltar-Based Fleet, June 1940-March 1942* (London: Aurum Press, 2005).

Lance Davis and Robert Huttenback, *Mammon and the Pursuit of Empire: The Political Economy of British Imperialism, 1860-1912* (Cambridge: Cambridge University Press, 1986).

Hugh Denham, 'Bedford-Bletchley-Kilindini-Colombo' in F. H. Hinsley and Alan Stripp (eds), *Codebreakers: The Inside Story of Bletchley Park* (Oxford: Oxford University Press, 1993).

Fabio De Ninno, *I Sommergibili del Fascismo: Politica Navale, Strategia e Uomini tra le Due Guerre Mondiali* (Milan: Unicopli, 2014).

——, 'I Piani della Regia Marina per l'Oceano Indiano, 1922-1934', in Virgilio Ilari and Mariano Gabriele (eds), *Naval History: The SISM (Società Italiana di Storia Militare/Italian Society for Military History) Remembers Alberto Santoni* (1936-2016) (Rome: SISM, 2014).

——, 'The Italian Navy and Japan: The Indian Ocean, Failed Cooperation, and Tripartite Relations (1935-1943), *War in History* (2018).

Adrian Carton De Wiart, *Happy Odyssey: The Memoirs of Lieutenant-General Sir Adrian Carton De Wiart* (London: Jonathan Cape, 1950).

Peter Dennis, *Troubled Days of Peace: Mountbatten and South East Asia Command, 1945-46* (Manchester: Manchester University Press, 1987).

Ken Dimbleby, *Turns of Fate: The Drama of HMS* Cornwall (London: William Kimber, 1984).

Klaus Dodds, *Pink Ice: Britain and the South Atlantic Empire* (London: I. B. Tauris, 2002).

Peter Doling, *From Port T to RAF Gan: An Illustrated History of the British Military Bases at Addu Atoll in the Maldive Islands, 1941-1976* (Bognor Regis, West Sussex: Woodfield Publishing, 2003).

Athalie Ducrotoy, *Air Raid Sirens and Fire Buckets: Wartime Seychelles, 1939-1945* (Kent: Rawlings Publications, 1997).

Paul Dull, *A Battle History of the Imperial Japanese Navy, 1941-1943* (Annapolis, MD: Naval Institute Press, 1978).

James Duffy, *Hitler's Secret Pirate Fleet: The Deadliest Ships of World War Two* (Westport, CT: Praeger, 2001).

Charles Eade (ed.), *Secret Session Speeches by the Right Honourable Winston S. Churchill* (London: Cassell, 1946).

Bernard Edwards, *Blood and Bushido: Japanese Atrocities at Sea, 1941-1945* (Upton-Upon-Severn: The Self-Publishing Press, 1991).

——, *Beware Raiders! German Surface Raiders in the Second World War* (Barnsley: Leo Cooper, 2001).

Edward Ellsberg, *Under the Red Sea Sun* (New York: Dodd, Mead, and Company, 1946).

Dave Engstrom, 'Kagnew Station: The Earliest Days' (2012).

John Ennis, *Bombay Explosion* (London: Cassell, 1950).

J. E. H. Fail, 'Forward Strategic Air Base Cocos Island', at http://www.rquirk.com/cocos/coco-sart.htm

D. A. Farnie, *East and West of Suez: The Suez Canal in History, 1854-1956* (Oxford: Clarendon Press, 1956).

Brian Farrell, *The Defence and Fall of Singapore, 1940-1942* (Stroud, Gloucestershire: Tempus, 2005).

—— (ed.), *Churchill and the Lion City: Shaping Modern Singapore* (Singapore: National University of Singapore Press, 2013).

Mike Felton, *Yanagi: The Secret Undercover Trade between Germany and Japan, 1942-1945* (Barnsley: Pen and Sword, 2003).

James Fenton, *The Forgotten Army: A Burma Soldier's Story in Letters, Photographs, and Sketches* (Stroud: Fonthill Media, 2012).

Valdo Ferretti, *Il Giappone el la Politica Estera Italiana,* (Japan and Italian foreign policy) *1935-1941* (Milan: Giuffrè, 1995).

Andrew Field, *Royal Navy Strategy in the Far East, 1919-1939: Preparing for the War Against Japan* (London: Frank Cass, 2004).

T. J. Finlayson, *The Fortress Came First: The Story of the Civilian Population of Gibraltar during the Second World War* (Gibraltar: Gibraltar Books, 1991).

Jack Ford, 'The Forlorn Ally: The Netherlands East Indies in 1942', *War and Society*, 11, 1 (1993).

Steven Forsberg, 'Island at the Edge of Everywhere: A History of Diego Garcia', M. A. Thesis, Sam Houston State University (2005).

Adrian Fort, *Archibald Wavell: The Life and Times of an Imperial Servant* (London: Jonathan Cape, 2009).

Horst Geerken, *Hitler's Asian Adventures: The Third Reich and the Dutch East Indies, the Creation of German Naval Bases, the Beginning of the End for Colonial Rule, German Aid for Soekarno's Freedom Fighters and India's Subhas Chandra Bose* (Bonn: BukitCinta, 2015).

Charles Gibson, *Death of a Phantom Raider: The Gamble that Triumphed and Failed, Atlantic, 1942-43* (London: Robert Hale, 1987).

Erik Gilbert, *Dhows and the Colonial Economy of Zanzibar, 1860-1970* (Oxford: James Currey, 2004).

Martin Gilbert, *Finest Hour: Winston S. Churchill, 1939-1941* (London: Heinemann, 1984).

Giorgio Giorgerini, *Da Matapan al Golfo Persico: La Marina Militaire Italiano dal Fascismo alla Repubblica* (Milan: Mondadori, 1989).

John Gooch, *Mussolini and His Generals: The Armed Forces and Fascist Foreign Policy, 1922-1940* (Cambridge: Cambridge University Press, 2007).

H. R. Gordon-Cumming, *Official History of the South African Naval Forces during the Second World War, 1939-1945* (Simon's Town: Naval Heritage Trust South Africa, 2008).

O. A. Goulden, *From Trombay to Changi's a Helluva a Way: The Story of the Arakan Coastal Forces* (London: The Chameleon Press, 1987).
Gerald Graham, *The Politics of Naval Supremacy: Studies in British Maritime Ascendancy* (Cambridge: Cambridge University Press, 1965).
——, *Great Britain in the Indian Ocean: A Study in Maritime Enterprise, 1810-1857* (Oxford: Clarendon Press, 1967).
Edwyn Gray, *Operation Pacific: The Royal Navy's War against Japan, 1941-1945* (London: Leo Cooper, 1990).
Graham Greene, *The Heart of the Matter* (London: William Heinemann, 1948).
Arthur Grimble, *A Pattern of Islands* (London: John Murray, 1952).
Diya Gupta, 'Propaganda Wars: India as a Contested Site between Rival Imperialist Powers', at https://www.iwm.org.uk/sites/default/files/bbc_monitoring_paper_for_website.pdf; and
Bob Hackett, 'World War II: Yanagi Missions – Japan's Underwater Convoys', *World War II Magazine* (October 2005).
Stephen Haddelsey, *Operation Tabarin: Britain's Secret Wartime Mission to Antarctica, 1944-1946* (Stroud, Gloucestershire: The History Press, 2014).
Albrecht Hagemann, 'Very Special Relations: The "Third Reich" and the Union of South Africa, 1933-1939', *South African Historical Journal*, 27 (1992).
Peter Haining, *The Banzai Hunters: The Forgotten Armada of Little Ships that Defeated the Japanese, 1944-1945* (London: Robson Books, 2006).
Richard Hall, *Empires of the Monsoon: A History of the Indian Ocean and its Invaders* (London: HarperCollins, 1996).
James Hamilton-Paterson, *Empire of the Clouds: When Britain's Aircraft Ruled the World* (London: Faber and Faber, 2011).
F. Kenneth Hare, 'The Takoradi-Khartoum Air Route', *Climatic Change* 1, 2 (1977).
Stephen Harp, *A World History of Rubber: Empire, Industry, and the Everyday* (Chichester, West Sussex: Wiley-Blackwell, 2016).
John Harris, *A Funny Place to Hold a War* (London: Hutchinson, 1984).
Christina Phelps Harris, 'The Persian Gulf Submarine Telegraph of 1864', *Geographical Journal*, 135, 2 (1969).
E. D. R. Harrison, 'British Subversion in French East Africa: SOE's Todd Mission, 1941-1942, *English Historical Review*, 114, 456 (1999).
——, 'On Secret Service for the Duce: Umberto Campini in Portuguese East Africa, 1941-43', *English Historical Review*, 122, 499 (2007).
John Hawkins and Ward Hawkins, *History of the 835th Signal Service Battalion, 1942-1946* (World War Two Operational Documents, 1946).
Jonathan Helmreich, *United States Relations with Belgium and the Congo, 1940-1960* (Newark: University of Delaware Press, 1998).
Jeffrey Herf, *Nazi Propaganda for the Arab World* (New Haven: Yale University Press, 2010).
Norman Herz, *Operation Alacrity: The Azores and the War in the Atlantic* (Annapolis, MD: Naval Institute Press, 2004).
Brett Hilder, *Navigator in the South Seas* (Adelaide: Seal Books, 1978).
'His Majesty's Ships – HMS *Moonstone*', *The War Illustrated*, 10, 241 (1946).
David Hobbs, *The British Pacific Fleet: The Royal Navy's Most Powerful Strike Force* (Barnsley: Seaforth, 2011).

Richard Hough, *The Hunting of Force Z: The Sinking of the* Prince of Wales *and the* Repulse (London: Phoenix, 1999).

Erik Benson, 'Suspicious Allies: Wartime Aviation Developments and the Anglo-American International Airline Rivalry, 1939-1945', *History and Technology: An International Journal* 17, 1 (2000).

Michael Howard, *Strategic Deception in the Second World War: British Intelligence Operations Against the German High Command* (London: Norton, 1995).

Stephen Howarth, *Morning Glory: A History of the Imperial Japanese Navy* (London: Arrow Books, 1985).

Kenneth Inglis, 'The Imperial Connection: Telegraphic Communications between England and Australia, 1872-1902', in Frederick Madden and Wyndraeth Morris-Jones (eds), *Australia and Britain: Studies in a Changing Relationship* (London: Frank Cass, 1990).

Richard Ingrams, *Malcolm Muggeridge: The Biography* (London: HarperCollins, 1996).

Will Iredale, *The Kamikaze Hunters: Fighting for the Pacific, 1945* (London: Pan, 2015).

Ashley Jackson, *Botswana 1939-1945: An African Country at War* (Oxford: Clarendon Press, 1999).

——, *War and Empire in Mauritius and the Indian Ocean* (Basingstoke: Macmillan, 2001).

——, 'Supplying War: The High Commission Territories' Military Logistical Contribution in the Second World War', *Journal of Military History*, 66 (2002).

——, 'The Mutiny of the 1st Battalion The Mauritius Regiment, Madagascar, 1943', *Journey of the Society for Army Historical Research*, 80 (2002).

——, 'The British Empire in the Indian Ocean', in Sanjay Chaturvedi and Dennis Rumley (eds), *Geopolitical Orientations in the Indian Ocean* (New Delhi: South Asian Publishers, 2002).

——, 'Refitting the Fleet in Ceylon: The War Record of Walker Sons and Company', *Journal of Indian Ocean Studies*, 10, 3 (2002).

——, *The British Empire and the Second World War* (London: Continuum, 2006).

——, 'The Colonial Empire and Imperial Defence', in Greg Kennedy (ed.), *Old World Order: Imperial Defence, 1856-1956* (London: Routledge, 2007).

——, *Mad Dogs and Englishmen: A Grand Tour of the British Empire at its Height* (London: Quercus, 2009).

——, '"Defend Lanka Your Home": War on the Home Front in Ceylon, 1939-1945', *War in History*, 16, 2 (2009).

——, *Distant Drums: The Role of Colonies in British Imperial Warfare* (Brighton: Sussex Academic Press, 2010).

——, 'Britain in the Indian Ocean Region', *Journal of the Indian Ocean Region*, 7, 2 (2011).

——, 'Military Migrants: British Service Personnel in Ceylon during the Second World War', *Britain and the World*, 6, 1 (2013).

——, 'Empires and the Second World War', in John MacKenzie (ed.), *The Encyclopaedia of Empire* (Chichester, West Sussex: Wiley-Blackwell, 2016).

——, 'Axis Broadcasts Relating to India, Australia, Iran, and Iraq', at https://www.iwm.org.uk/sites/default/files/images/gallery/Axis%20Broadcasts%20relating%20to%20Australia%2C%20India%2C%20Iran%20and%20Iraq%20-%20Ashley%20Jackson%20.pdf.

——, 'Ceylon's Home Front during the Second World War', in Mark Crowley and Sandra Trudgen Dawson (eds), *Home Fronts: Britain and the Empire at War, 1939-1945* (Martlesham, Suffolk: Boydell and Brewer, 2017).
——, *Persian Gulf Command: A History of the Second World War in Iran and Iraq* (London: Yale University Press, 2018).
——, *Ceylon at War, 1939-1945* (Solihull: Helion, 2018).
——, 'The Commonwealth as a Strategic Alliance', in Alex May (ed.), *The Oxford History of the British Empire*, companion series, *The Commonwealth* (Oxford: Oxford University Press, forthcoming).
—— and David Tomkins, *Illustrating Empire: A Visual History of British Imperialism* (Oxford: Bodleian Library Publishing, 2011).
Bill Jopes, *A Voyage to Abadan* (Bloomington, IN: Xlibris Corporation, 1999)
'*Junyo Maru:* Torpedoed by HMS *Tradewind*', at http://www.historynet.com/juno-mayru-torpedoed-by-british-submarine-hms-tradewind.htm
Robert Kaplan, *Monsoon: The Indian Ocean and the Failure of American Power* (London: Random House, 2010).
Milo Kearney, *The Indian Ocean in World History* (London: Routledge, 2004).
Donald Kehn, *In the Highest Degree Tragic: The Sacrifice of the US Asiatic Fleet in the East Indies during World War II* (Lincoln, NE: Potomac Books, 2017).
Greg Kennedy (ed.), *British Naval Strategy East of Suez, 1900-2000: Influences and Actions* (London: Routledge, 2004).
——, *Imperial Defence: The Old World Order, 1856-1956* (London: Routledge, 2008).
—— and Keith Neilson (eds), *Far Flung Lines: Essays in Imperial Defence in Honour of Donald Schurman* (London: Frank Cass, 1996).
John Kennedy, *The Business of War: The War Narrative of Major-General Sir John Kennedy, GCMG, KCVO,KBE, CB, MC* (London: Hutchinson, 1957).
Paul Kennedy, 'Imperial Cable Communications and Strategy, 1870-1914', *Historical Review*, 86, 341 (1971).
David Killingray, 'Imperial Defence', in Robin Winks (ed.), *The Oxford History of the British Empire*, volume 5, *Historiography* (Oxford: Oxford University Press, 1999).
David Killingray and Richard Rathbone (eds), *Africa and the Second World War* (Basingstoke: Macmillan, 1986).
George Kirk, *The Middle East at War, 1939-1945* (London: Oxford University Press).
Rotem Kowner, 'When Economics, Strategy, and Racial Ideology Meet: : Inter-Axis Connections in the Wartime Indian Ocean', *Journal of Global History*, 12 (2017).
Theodore Krancke, *Pocket Battleship: The Story of the* Admiral Scheer (London: Norton, 1958).
A. Kroese, *The Dutch Navy at War* (London: Allen and Unwin, 1945).
Raymond Lamont-Brown, *Ships from Hell: Japanese War Crimes on the High Seas* (Stroud, Gloucestershire: The History Press, 2002).
Gordon Landsborough, *The Battle of the River Plate: The First Naval Battle of the Second World War* (Barnsley: Frontline Books, 2016).
Nancy Lawler, *Soldiers, Airmen, Whisperers, and Spies: The Gold Coast in World War II* (Athens, OH: Ohio University Press, 2002).
Brian Lavery, *Churchill's Navy: The Ships, Men, and Organization, 1939-1945* (London: Conway, 2006).

James Leasor, *Boarding Party: The Last Action of the Calcutta Light Horse* (London: Heinemann, 1978).

J. M. Lee and Martin Petter, *Colonial Office, War, and Development Policy: Organization and the Planning of a Metropolitan Initiative, 1939-1945* (London: Maurice Temple Smith/The Institute of Commonwealth Studies, 1982).

Richard Leighton and Robert Coakley, *Global Logistics and Strategy, 1940-43*, US Army in World War Two series (Washington, DC: The War Department, Center of Military History, US Army, 1995, first published 1955).

Brian Lett, *Ian Fleming and SOE's Operation Postmaster: The Untold Top Secret Story* (Barnsley: Pen and Sword, 2012).

Michael Lewis, Abdul Azeez Yousuf, Kriangkrai Lerdthusnee, Ahmed Razee, Kirkvitch Chandranoi, and James Jones, 'Scrub Typhus Reemergence in the Maldives', *Emerging Infectious Diseases*, 9, 12 (2003).

P. F. Lupinacci, *Le Operazioni in Africa Orientale*, volume 10, *La Marina Italiana nella Seconda Guerra Mondiale* (Rome: Ufficio Storico della Marina Militaire (the Italian navy's historical department), 1961).

Robert Lyman, *The Longest Siege: Tobruk – The Battle that Saved North Africa* (London: Macmillan, 2009).

J. E. Macdonnell, *Valiant Occasions* (London: Constable, 1962).

Donald Macintyre, *Fighting Admiral: The Life and Battles of Admiral of the Fleet Sir James Somerville, GCB, GBE, DSO* (London: Evans, 1961).

John MacKenzie, *Imperialism and Popular Culture* (Manchester: Manchester University Press, 1986).

Compton Mackenzie, *All Over the Place: Fifty Thousand Miles by Sea, Air, Road and Rail* (London: Chatto and Windus, 1948).

Tony Mackenzie, *44 (RM) Commando: Achnacarry to the Arakan: A Diary of the Commando at War, August 1943 to March 1947* (Brighton: Tom Donovan, 1996).

Michael Macoun, *Wrong Place, Right Time: Policing the End of Empire* (London: Radcliffe Press, 1996).

Robert Mallett, *The Italian Navy and Fascist Expansionism, 1935-1940* (London: Frank Cass, 1988).

Arthur Marder, *Operation Menace: The Dakar Expedition and the Dudley North Affair* (Oxford: Oxford University Press, 1976).

Arthur Marder, *Old Friends, New Enemies: The Royal Navy and the Imperial Japanese Navy*, 2 volumes (Oxford: Oxford University Press, 1981 and 1990).

Christoph Marx, *Oxwagon Sentinel: Radical Afrikaner Nationalism and the History of the Ossewabrandwag* (London: Lit Verlag, 2011).

——, 'The Ossewabrandwag as a Mass Movement, 1939-1941', *Journal of Southern African Studies*, 20, 2 (1994).

John Masters, *The Road Past Mandalay* (London: Michael Joseph, 1961).

John McAleer, *Britain's Maritime Empire: Southern Africa, the South Atlantic, and the Indian Ocean, 1763-1820* (Cambridge: Cambridge University Press, 2016).

M. McCarthy (ed.), *From Great Depths: The Wrecks of* HMAS Sydney *II and HSK* Kormoran (Crawley, Perth: UWA Publishing, 2016).

Neil McCort, *HMS* Hermes *1923 and 1959* (Cheltenham, Gloucestershire: Fan Publications, 2001).

W. David McIntyre, *The Rise and Fall of the Singapore Naval Base, 1919-1942* (London: Macmillan, 1979).

Richard McMillan, *The British Occupation of Indonesia, 1945-46: Britain, The Netherlands, and the Reoccupation of Indonesia* (London: Routledge, 2005).

Richard Mead, *General Boy: The Life of Lieutenant General Sir Frederick Browning* (Barnsley: Pen and Sword, 2010).

Vernon Miller, *Analysis of Japanese Submarine Losses to Allied Submarines in World War Two* (Hoosick Falls, NY: Merriam Press, 2013).

Basil Mitchell, 'The War Years', private memoir (undated).

——, *Looking Back: On Faith, Philosophy, and Friends in Oxford* (Durham: The Memoir Club, 2009).

Alan Moorehead, *A Year of Battle* (London: Hamish Hamilton, 1943).

Daniel Moran and James Russell (eds), *Maritime Strategy and Global Order: Markets, Resources, Security* (Washington, DC: Georgetown University Press, 2016).

Edgar Ansel Mowrer and Marthe Rajchman, *Global War: An Atlas of World Strategy* (London: Faber and Faber, 1942).

Hubert Moyse-Bartlett, *The King's African Rifles: A Study in the Military History of East and Central Africa, 1890-1945* (Aldershot: Gale and Polden, 1956).

August Karl Muggenthaler, *German Raiders of World War Two* (Englewood Cliffs, NJ : Prentice Hall Inc., 1977).

Malcolm Muggeridge, *Chronicles of Wasted Time: The Infernal Grove* (London: Morrow, 1974).

Archie Munro, *The Winston Specials: Troopships via the Cape, 1940-1943* (Liskeard: Maritime Books, 2005).

Benjamin Oldcorn, 'On the Wire: The Strategic and Tactical Role of Cable and Wireless during the Second World War', Ph. D. Thesis (University of Exeter, 2013).

Richard Osborne, *World War Two in Colonial Africa* (Indianapolis: Riebel-Roque, 2001).

Christopher O'Sullivan, 'Colonialism in Asia' in Thomas Zeiler (ed.), *A Companion to World War Two*, volume 1 (Chichester, West Sussex: Wiley-Blackwell, 2013).

James Owen, *Commando: Winning World War II Behind Enemy Lines* (London: Abacus, 2013).

Jonathan Parkinson, *The China Station, Royal Navy: As Seen Through the Careers of the Commanders-in-Chief, 1864-1941* (Kibworth Beauchamp, Leicestershire: Matador, 2018).

J. H. Parry, *The Discovery of the Sea* (New York: Weidenfeld and Nicolson, 1974).

Lawrence Paterson, *Hitler's Grey Wolves: U-Boats in the Indian Ocean* (Barnsley: Pen and Sword, 2016).

Barry Pattison and Geoffrey Goodall, *Qantas Empire Airways (Western Operations Division) Indian Ocean Service, 1943-1946* (Footscray, Victoria: Aviation Historical Society of Australia, 1979).

D. J. Payton-Smith, *Oil: A Study of Wartime Policy and Administration* (London: HMSO, 1971).

Michael Pearson, *The Indian Ocean* (London: Routledge, 2003).

Gordon Pirie, *Air Empire: British Imperial Civil Aviation, 1919-1939* (Manchester: Manchester University Press, 2009).

——, *Cultures and Caricatures of British Imperial Aviation: Passengers, Pilots, Publicity* (Manchester: Manchester University Press, 2012).

Les Pivnic, 'Durban Harbour, 1942-1945: The War-Time Memories of a Schoolboy during the Second World War', *Military History Journal*, 16, 3 (2014).
William Platt, General Officer Commanding in Chief, East Afria, 'Operations of East Africa Command 12 July 1941 to 8 January 1943', *Supplement to The London Gazette*, 37655 (London: HMSO, 1946).
Kenneth Poolman, *Escort Carriers of World War Two* (London: Weidenfeld, 1989).
Dudley Pope, *The Battle of the River Plate* (London: The Ramage Company, 1974).
Peter Post (ed.), *The Encyclopaedia of Indonesia in the Pacific War* (Leiden: Brill, 2009).
Arthur Power, 'Naval Operations in Ramree Island Area 19 January to 22 February 1945', *Supplement to the London Gazette*, 38269 (London: HMSO, 1948).
——, 'The Carrier-Borne Aircraft Attacks on Oil Refineries in the Palembang (Sumatra) Area in January, 1945', *Supplement to the London Gazette*, 39191 (London: HMSO, 1951).
Henry Probert, *The Forgotten Air Force: The Royal Air Force in the War against Japan, 1941-45* (London: Brassey's, 1995).
Kwei Quartey, 'How West Africa Helped Win World War Two', *Foreign Policy in Focus*, 6 (2012).
Nicholas Rankin, *Defending the Rock: How Gibraltar Defeated Hitler* (London: Faber and Faber, 2017).
Patrizio Rapalino and Giuseppe Schivardi, *Odissea di un Sommergibilista: Dal Mar Rosso al Mediterraneo, 1940-1943* (Milan: Mursia, 2008).
John Rasmuson, *A History of Kagnew Station and American Forces in Eritrea* (US Army Garrison Kagnew Station, 1973).
Deborah Wing Ray, 'The Takoradi Route: Roosevelt's Prewar Venture beyond the Western Hemisphere', *Journal of American History* 62, 2 (1975).
Bruce Reynolds, *Thailand's Secret War: OSS, SOE, and the Free Thai Underground during World War Two* (Cambridge: Cambridge University Press, 2010).
Jon Robb-Webb, *The British Pacific Fleet: Experience and Legacy, 1944-1950* (Farnham: Ashgate, 2013).
Stephen Robinson, *False Flags: Disguised German Raiders of World War Two* (Wolombi, NSW: Exisle, 2016).
William Roger Louis, *Imperialism at Bay: The United States and the Decolonization of the British Empire, 1941-1945* (New York: Oxford University Press, 1978).
Stephen Roskill, *The War at Sea, 1939-1945*, 3 volumes (London: HMSO, 1954-61).
——, *Churchill and the Admirals* (Barnsley: Pen and Sword, 2004).
V. H. Rothwell, *War Aims in the Second World War: The War Aims of the Key Belligerents, 1939-1945* (Edinburgh: Edinburgh University Press, 2005).
Gerry Rubin, *Durban 1942: A British Troopship Revolt* (London: Hambledon, 1992).
Lord Russell of Liverpool, *The Knights of Bushido: A History of Japanese War Crimes during World War Two* (London: Frontline Books, 2013).
James Sadkovich, *The Italian Navy in World War Two* (Westport, CT: Greenwood Press, 1994).
Nicholas Sarantakes, *Allies against the Rising Sun: The United States, the British Nations, and the Defeat of Imperial Japan* (Lawrence, KS: University Press of Kansas, 2009).
——, 'The Royal Air Force on Okinawa: The Diplomacy of a Coalition on the Verge of Victory', *Diplomatic History*, 27, 4 (2003).
——, 'One Last Crusade: The US-British Alliance and the End of the War in the Pacific', *The Royal United Services Institute Journal*, 149, 4 (2004).

——, 'One Last Crusade: The British Pacific Fleet and its Impact on Anglo-American Relations', *English Historical Review*, 121, 491 (2006).

Joseph Scalia, *Germany's Last Mission to Japan: The Failed Voyage of* U-234 (Annapolis, MD: Naval Institute Press, 2000).

Eiji Seki, *Mrs Ferguson's Tea-Set, Japan, and the Second World War: The Global Consequences Following Germany's Sinking of the SS* Automedon *in 1940* (Folkestone, Kent: Global Oriental, 2007).

Abdul Sheriff, *Dhow Cultures of the Indian Ocean: Cosmopolitanism, Commerce, and Islam* (London: Hurst, 2010).

Christopher Shores, *Dust Clouds in the Middle East: The Air War for East Africa, Iraq, Syria, Iran, and Madagascar, 1940-1942* (London: Grub Street, 1996).

Christopher Shores and Brian Cull with Yasuho Izawa, *Bloody Shambles: The First Comprehensive Account of Air Operations Over South-East Asia, December 1941-April 1942* (London: Grub Street, 1992).

David Sibley, *The Behar Massacre: The Execution of 69 Survivors from the British Merchant Ship* Behar *in 1944 by the Imperial Japanese Navy* (Stockport: A. Lane Publishers, 1997).

Daniel Silverfarb, 'The British Government and the Question of Umm Qasr, 1938–1945', *Asian and African Studies*, 16, 2 (1982).

Michael Simpson (ed.), *The Somerville Papers: Selections from the Private and Official Correspondence of Admiral of the Fleet Sir James Somerville, GCB, GBE, DSO* (Aldershot: Scolar Press for the Navy Records Society, 1995).

Colin Smith, *Singapore Burning* (London: Penguin, 2006).

Michael Smith, *The Emperor's Codes: Bletchley Park and the Breaking of Japan's Secret Ciphers* (London: Bantam, 2000).

Peter Smith, *Task Force 57: The British Pacific Fleet, 1944-1945* (London: Kimber, 1969).

——, *Fist from the Sky: The Story of Captain Takashige Egusa, The Imperial Japanese Navy's Most Illustrious Dive-Bomber Pilot* (London: Crecy, 2006).

David Smurthwaite (ed.), *The Forgotten War: The British Army in the Far East, 1941-1945* (London: National Army Museum, 1992).

Christopher Somerville, *Our War: The British Commonwealth and the Second World War* (London: Weidenfeld and Nicolson, 1998).

Daniel Owen Spence, *Colonial Naval Culture and British Imperialism, 1922-1967* (Manchester: Manchester University Press, 2015)

——, *A History of the Royal Navy: Empire and Imperialism* (London: I. B. Tauris, 2016).

William Stanley, 'The Trans-South Atlantic Air Link in World War Two', *GeoJournal* 33, 4 (1994).

Freya Stark, *Dust in the Lion's Paw: Autobiography, 1939-1946* (London: John Murray, 1961).

Donald Stevens, 'Franklin D. Roosevelt and the Azores Dilemma, 1941', *Historian*, 54, 4 (1992).

Andrew Stewart, '"This Temporary Strategic Withdrawal": The Eastern Fleet's Wartime African Sojourn', in Craig C. Felker and Marcus O. Jones (eds), *New Interpretations in Naval History: Selected Papers for the Sixteenth Naval History Symposium Held at the United States Naval Academy, 10-11 September 2009* (Newport: Naval War College Press, 2012).

——, 'Malaria: Sierra Leone's Other War', Defence-in-Depth, at https://defenceindepth.co/2015/04/27/malaria-sierra-leones-other-war/

——, 'The Second World and the "Quiet Colony" of Sierra Leone', in Ashley Jackson, Yasmin Khan, and Gajendra Singh (eds), *An Imperial World at War: Aspects of the British Empire's War Experience, 1939-1945* (London: Routledge, 2016).

——, *The First Victory: The Second World War and the East Africa Campaign* (London: Yale University Press, 2016).

Helmut Stoecker, *German Imperialism in Africa: From the Beginnings Until the Second World War* (London: Hurst, 1986).

Rob Stuart, 'Leonard Birchall and the Japanese Raid on Colombo', *Canadian Military Journal* (Winter 2006-2007).

E. N. Syfret, Flag Officer Commanding Force 'F', 'The Capture of Diego Suarez', *Supplement to the London Gazette*, 38225 (London: HMSO, 1948).

Alfred Tembo, 'The Impact of the Second World War on Northern Rhodesia (Zambia), 1939-1953, Ph. D. Thesis (University of the Free State, 2015).

David Thomas, *Battle of the Java Sea* (London: André Deutsch, 1968)

Martin Thomas, 'Imperial Backwater or Strategic Outpost? The British Takeover of Vichy Madagascar, 1942', *Historical Journal* 39 (1996).

——, *The French Empire at War, 1940-1945* (Manchester: Manchester University Press, 1998).

Peter Thompson, *The Battle for Singapore: The True Story of the Greatest Catastrophe of World War II* (London: Portrait, 2006).

Christopher Thorne, *Allies of a Kind: The United States, Britain, and the War against Japan, 1941-1945* (London: Hamish Hamilton, 1978).

Ian Trenowden, *The Hunting Submarine: The Fighting Life of HMS* Tally-Ho (London: William Kimber, 1974).

——, *Operations Most Secret: SOE, the Malayan Theatre* (London: William Kimber, 1978).

Peter Tsouras, 'Operation Orient: Joint Axis Strategy', in Kenneth Macksey (ed.), *The Hitler Options: Alternative Decisions of World War Two* (Mechanicsburg, PA: Greenhill, 1995).

Warren Tute, *The Deadly Stroke* (New York: Coward, McGann, and Geoghegan, 1973).

——, *The Reluctant Enemies: The Story of the Last War between Britain and France, 1940-1942* (London: William Collins, 1989).

'The British Pacific and East Indies Fleets', 'The Forgotten Fleets of World War Two', compiled by the Royal Navy Research Archive, at http://www.royalnavyresearcharchive.org.uk/BPF-EIF/EIF_Ships.htm#.WxSyYhNViko

J. Alan Thompson, *Military Honours* (London: Fortune Books, 1946).

——, *In the East My Pleasure* (London: Andrew Dakers, 1949).

——, *Only the Sun Remembers* (London: Andrew Dakers, 1950).

L. C. F. Turner, H. R. Gordon-Cumming, and J. E. Betlzer, *War in the Southern Oceans, 1939-1945* (Cape Town: Oxford University Press, 1961).

Christopher Vasey, *Nazi Intelligence Operations in Non-Occupied Territories: Espionage Efforts in the United States, South America, and Southern Africa* (Jefferson, NC: McFarland, 2016).

Richard Walding, 'Mombasa Forts: Kilindini and Mombasa Harbours in World War Two', at http://indicatorloops.com/mombasa_forts.htm

——, 'Indicator Loops: Royal Navy Harbour Defences, Kilindini Island, Mombasa', at http://indicatorloops.com/mombasa.htm.

Ben Warlow, *Shore Establishments of the Royal Navy Being a List of the Static Ships and Establishments of the Royal Navy* (Liskeard: Maritime Books, 1992).

Oliver Warner, *Admiral of the Fleet: The Life of Sir Charles Lambe* (London: Sidgwick and Jackson, 1969).

Alan Warren, *Burma 1942:The Road from Rangoon to Mandalay* (London: Continuum, 2011)

Elizabeth Watkins, *Cypher Officer* (Brighton: Pen Press, 2008)

Graham Watson, 'Organization of the Royal Navy, 1939-1945', at http://www.naval-history.net/xGW-RNOrganisation1939-45.htm.

Evelyn Waugh, *Men at Arms* (London: Chapman and Hall, 1952).

Archibald Wavell, 'Operations in East Africa, November 1940-July 1941', *Supplement to the London Gazette*, 37645 (London: HMSO, 1946).

——, 'Operations in Eastern Theatre, Based on India, from March 1942 to December 31, 1942', *Supplement to the London Gazette*, 37728 (London: HMSO, 1946).

Nigel Wenban-Smith and Marina Carter, *Chagos, A History: Exploration, Exploitation, Expulsion* (Chagos Conservation Trust, 2016).

Andre Wessels, 'South Africa and the War against Japan, 1941-1945', *Military History Journal*, 10, 3 (1996).

Susan Williams, *Spies in the Congo: The Race for the Ore that Built the Atomic Bomb* (London: Hurst, 2016).

H. P. Willmott, *Empires in the Balance: Japanese and Allied Pacific Strategies to April 1942* (Annapolis, MD: Naval Institute Press, 1982).

——, *The Barrier and the Javelin: Japanese and Allied Pacific Strategies, February to June 1942* (Maryland, MD: Naval Institute Press, 1983).

——, *Grave of a Dozen Schemes: British Naval Planning and the War Against Japan, 1943-1945* (Shrewsbury: Airlife, 1996).

——, *The War with Japan: The Period of Balance, May 1942-October 1943* (Willmington, DE: Scholarly Resources, 2002).

Brian Wilson, *A Submariners' War in the Indian Ocean, 1939-1945* (Stroud, Gloucestershire: Tempus, 2000).

John Winser, *British Invasion Fleets: The Mediterranean and Beyond, 1942-1945* (Gravesend: The World Ship Society, 2002).

John Winton, *Sink the* Haguro*! The Last Destroyer Action of the Second World War* (London: Seeley, Service, & Co., 1979).

John Winton, *The Forgotten Fleet: The Story of the British Pacific Fleet, 1944-1945* (London: Michael Joseph, 1969).

Suke Wolton, *Lord Hailey, the Colonial Office and the Politics of Race and Empire in the Second World War: The Loss of White Prestige* (London: Macmillan, 2000).

Richard Woodman, *The Battle of the River Plate: A Grand Delusion* (Pen and Sword, 2008).

David Wragg, *Fighting Admirals of World War Two* (Barnsley: Pen and Sword, 2009).

The Escort Carrier of the Second World War: Combustible, Vulnerable, Expendable (Barnsley: Pen and Sword, 2015).

Donald Wright, 'That Hell-Hole of Yours', *American Heritage*, 46, 6 (1995).

Bob Wurth, *1942: Australia's Greatest Peril* (Sydney: Pan, 2010).

Edward Young, *One of Our Submarines* (London: Rupert Hart-Davis, 1952).

Benjamin Zachariah, 'Nazi Hunting and Intelligence Gathering in India on the Eve of the Second World War', in Jackson, Khan, and Singh (eds), *An Imperial World at War.*

Philip Ziegler (ed.), *Personal Diary of Admiral the Lord Louis Mountbatten Supreme Allied Commander, South East Asia, 1943-1946* (London: Collins, 1988).

Index

Index of People

Index of Places

Index of Military Formations & Units

Index of Ships

Index of Operations